YOSEMITE

CLIMBS

GEORGE MEYERS & DON REID

CHOCKSTONE PRESS
1987

ISBN 0-934641-05-6

Published and distributed by
CHOCKSTONE PRESS, INC.
526 Franklin Street
Denver, Colorado 80218
(303) 377-1970

TABLE OF CONTENTS

WARNING

This is only a guide book. It is merely a composite of opinions from many sources on the whereabouts and difficulties of various routes. It is not an instructional book on mountaineering technique or a substitute for the user's judgement. Rock climbing is a high risk sport and the user of this book assumes full responsibility for his or her safety.

PREFACE

The eleven years since the first edition of this guide has seen fervent activity by those seemingly intent on making the job of guidebook writers an endless one. Fortunately, the addition of Don Reid has improved the accuracy of the guide immeasurably. As in the previous books, a number of Yosemite's climbs have been excluded, mostly pre-1970 in origin and of dubious interest to contemporary climbers. The 1971 *Climber's Guide to Yosemite Valley,* written by Steve Roper and published by the Sierra Club, is a valuable archive of information for these routes.

The introduction material has been greatly expanded in this edition. John Dill provided a valuable and illuminating analysis of the serious climbing accidents that have occurred in the park since 1970. In addition, an account of Yosemite's climbing history was constructed from several sources. The early history was reprinted from a 1954 writing, and the period covering the fifties and sixties was reprinted from Steve Roper's 1971 guide (with his kind permission). The incredibly complex activity that evolved over the last 15 years was compiled with the help of many of the major participants of that time. The authors are grateful for their help. John Bachar was instrumental in outlining the traditions of Yosemite free-climbing ethics.

While all uncredited photos are taken by George Meyers, the authors wish to thank the National Park Service, and particularly John Dill, for the use of their photos, some taken from perspectives impossible to duplicate without a helicopter. In addition, the authors want to thank Henry Barber, Phil Bard, Jim Bridwell, David Brower, Mark Chapman, Tom Frost, Allen Steck, and Kevin Worrall for the action climbing photos.

The topos are the result of compiling route information from many sources. Those climbers who provided information for previous editions of this guide are to be thanked again; they helped build the framework for this book. Once again, many people were generous with their time by providing detailed lists of corrections to the previous work, and many others unselfishly shared with the authors information about their new routes. This guide is clearly the result of a group effort. Of particular note are the following people, who devoted an extraordinary amount of time and effort to ensure that this guide be as accurate as possible: John Bachar, John Barbella, Alan Bartlett, Dimitri Barton, Scott Burke, Jim Campbell, Mark Chapman, Mike Corbett, Scott Cosgrove, Clint Cummins, Michael Forkash, John Middendorf, Walt Shipley, Rob Slater, Tucker Tech, John Tuttle and Jonny Woodward.

The authors wish to acknowledge and thank the United States Geological Survey for the "Map of Yosemite Valley – 1:24 000 scale" that has been reproduced at the back of the book.

There will be errors in this book. It is requested that corrections, as well as new route information, be sent to the authors care of Chockstone Press, 526 Franklin Street, Denver CO 80218.

N.P.S.

INTRODUCTION

Hundreds of rock climbing areas have been developed around the world in the last 100 years, yet none have so fired the imagination of climbers, or meant so much to the high standards of contemporary mountaineering, as Yosemite Valley. As a result, the Valley has taken on an increasingly international flavor, as thousands of climbers from around the world have traveled here to climb. Fun-in-the-sun rock climbing is what Yosemite is all about, but it is more than just a crag area: it is a complicated valley, with the many cliff formations placed in such ways as to require of the climber some greater mountaineering skills.

Located 150 miles east of San Francisco, Yosemite Valley is the dramatic centerpoint of Yosemite National Park. Although only seven square miles in size, it contains some of North America's most exquisite scenery and is popular with tourists; millions of people visit the Park each year, though primarily in summer. While the Valley remains the traffic center for this 1,200- square-mile park for both tourist and climber alike, the intricate terrain provides adequate cover for the rock climber wishing to lose sight of the tourists and gain some sense of a wilderness experience. Not all climbers adopt this option, of course, and in full season roadside crags are often crowded.

Direct flights can be taken to Los Angeles or San Francisco from most major cities of the world. Buses travel regularly to the nearby cities of Fresno and Merced, and on to Yosemite, albeit somewhat inconveniently. Hitchhiking is commonly successful in California, especially for those prepared with destination signs and interesting-looking climbing paraphernalia.

WHEN TO COME

The best time to climb in Yosemite is during the months of April and May, and September and October. Pleasant temperatures, lack of summertime tourist crowds, and the fact that the waterfalls are in their full glory make the spring the most popular time for climbers; April can be pretty rainy, however. Autumn is usually quieter and normally has great climbing weather, but the days are short and it can storm just about anytime. Summer sees most of the local climbers heading to Yosemite's high country domes at Tuolumne Meadows to escape the heat. In spite of occasional 100°F temperatures in summer, climbing can still be comfortable on the shady south side of the Valley. The first snowfall of the season usually comes to Yosemite Valley sometime after November 15th; the last snows fall sometime before April 15. Only during the dead of winter will the snow remain unmelted in the shade. Winter climbing activity is usually slow, although there can be long periods of clear, dry, and mild weather.

The main information office for Yosemite National Park can be reached at P.O. Box 577, Yosemite CA 95389, or by calling (209) 372-0264 for a recording, or (209) 372-0265 during business hours. A road, weather, and camping recording is available at (209) 372-4605.

STAYING IN THE PARK

Upon entering the Park, the visitor is charged $5 per car. It is a one-time fee for most climbers, who usually never leave the Park during the course of their stay. For those who do, a $15 Yosemite Pass allows yearly access to this park only. A $25 Golden Eagle Pass may instead be purchased; this allows annual passage into parks and monuments nationwide. Yosemite Village has a bank, post office, medical clinic, grocery store, video rental, delicatessen, crafts store, gift shops, auto repair shop, and hair salon, to provide the anxious climber with day-to-day needs. Climbers on a low budget, however, may desire to save considerably by purchasing food in one of the bigger towns prior to entering the Park.

The Yosemite Park and Curry Company is the main concessionaire for Yosemite National Park and provides more than just expensive store goods. Yosemite Lodge sits across the road from the climbers' main campground and in addition to many varied housing options contains gift shops, the Mountain Room Bar, two restaurants (the Four Seasons and Mountain Room Broiler), and cafeteria. For those climbers on the dole or in need of other than camp cooking, the cafeteria offers the most calories for the money. At the other end of the Valley is Curry Village, with more gift shops, accomodations, cafeteria, and showers that may be rented (the $1 fee includes soap and towel). Also at Curry is the Yosemite Mountaineering School and Mountain Shop, that may be relied upon to provide basic rock climbing equipment, clothing, and camping supplies. For more specialized climbing equipment the mail order Mountain Tools (P.O. Box 22788, Carmel CA 93922; (408) 625-6222) can provide 3-day mail service to Yosemite. Laundry facilities are available at Curry Housekeeping from spring through the fall. Tucked away somewhat from the masses visiting the Park is the Ahwahnee Hotel, a splendid place with a wonderful restaurant, lounge and bar, and a perfect retreat for the natty climber who wants to stay with style, or to seek temporary relief from the filth and degredation of climbing partners.

A free shuttle bus system runs between the Lodge, Village, Ahwahnee, and Curry, providing easy access to climbs within the east end of the Valley. Bicycles work well in the main Valley, but for climbers without cars, hitchhiking may be required to get to cliffs in the lower canyon.

Most climbers will want to stay amid the boulders of Sunnyside Campground (formerly known as Camp Four), the sole "walk-in," no-cars-allowed, campground in the Valley. Sunnyside does tend to get the sun a tad sooner than most spots in the Valley, has boulders located within the campground itself, is the cheapest official site in the confines of Yosemite, is located just across from the Yosemite Lodge, with its spontaneously unchanging and dull nightlife, and is the traditional choice of climbers. Camp Four has nothing to recommend itself to those hoping for a wilderness camping experience. It is a place to sleep, cook, meet climbers, and feel a little bedraggled. Currently campsites are rented for $2 per person per night with six persons allowed to share a site. While the campground is officially full as early as mid-April, in reality, many sites are not at capacity, and a few inquiries may find additional space. During the summer season, from June 1 to September 15, there is a seven-day camping limit in the Valley; the rest of the year the limit is 30 days. Climbers wishing to stay longer are encouraged to maintain a sufficiently low profile such that the issue never arises.

The conventional car campgrounds will be more spacious and clean, but also more expensive and full of large and noisy recreational vehicles. Advance reservations for car camping are also necessary from the spring to early fall, particularly on the weekends. These may be made up to, but no more than, eight weeks in advance of your visit, at any Ticketron outlet, by mail through Ticketron's mail order department (Ticketron, Dept R, 401 Hackensack Ave. Hackensack NJ 07601), or in person at the NPS campground reservation office in the Curry Village parking lot. There is a Ticketron processing fee in addition to campground fees. Pets are permitted in designated campgrounds only and must be leashed at all times. Pets are not allowed on any park trails.

Good bouldering extends from the woods west of Sunnyside all the way to Swan Slab. Other good areas include Curry Village west to the LeConte Memorial, the area behind the Ahwahnee Hotel, as well as in the woods below Sentinel and Lost Brother. Most of the problems are strenuous face and mantle problems, though a few thin crack problems show up here and there. For a rest day, it is recommended that an onslaught on the various top rope problems that are listed in this book would serve the climber with techniques more applicable to the Valley's routes.

Poison oak is found throughout the Valley, although it grows most abundantly west of the Pohono Bridge throughout the Lower Merced Canyon. Rattlesnakes can be encountered in warm weather months basking in the sun along the base of cliffs. Rarely do they provide more than just a notable nuisance on an approach to a climb.

Yosemite Valley is no wilderness, and the climber must share the relatively small space with thousands of other visitors. It is still possible for the imaginative climber to find a quiet day, alone with the cliffs and the swallows. While the crowded camping experience may leave some climbers cold, those who complain of the crowded climbing experience are simply unimaginative in their route-finding abilities. Nighttime is a different story; Yosemite after dark is known among the regulars for its boring nights as much as its exciting days. The options are limited: the Lodge- wandering circuit, with bar or restaurant, or back to camp. Books help, but it's difficult to find a place to read. Solution? – there is no solution, but you will have lots of company.

Yosemite Valley has all the ingredients of a small town, and does not revolve around the world of the climber. About 1,200 people live or work throughout the year in the park, mostly in Yosemite Valley; the number rises to perhaps 2,200 during the height of the tourist season. These residents all fall into various social groups but, except for a minute percentage, share a total lack of interest in climbing or climbers. Curry employees, both career professionals and the incredibly temporary juveniles, form the bulk of the work force. Then there is the Park Service employee, from the dedicated naturalist to the Law Enforcement Officer. It is the latter group that spells trouble for anyone who loves to climb a lot in Yosemite and also needs to be loud about it. Keeping in mind that to most of the residents of Yosemite, climbers are merely tourists who spend little, can be disorderly, and try to stay as long as possible, it is not difficult to understand why some Law Enforcement rangers see their job as challenged by those who bend the rules. There are rangers who climb very actively, however, and keeping in mind that the mandate of the Park Sevice is to protect the natural resource, most rangers will be found to be very helpful.

Interaction between the Park Service and the climbing community is bridged in one other way; with a couple of sites in Camp Four reserved for the free use of the most experienced Yosemite climbers, the Park has a competent and obligated source for paid help on technical searches and rescues. The experience of the Yosemite Search and Rescue Team is invaluable to all climbers by providing feedback on the prevention of major accidents.

STAYING ALIVE

Most climbers do a good job of coping with the hazards of their sport, yet more than 100 climbing accidents occur in the park every year. What factors contribute to them? What, if anything, can climbers do about them? And just how dangerous is climbing, anyway? With these questions in mind, the National Park Service (NPS) recently examined most of the serious accidents that occurred in the park during the 17 years from 1970 through 1986. The conclusions, compiled by John Dill, are illuminating for those wishing to stay alive.

Forty-three climbers died from traumatic injuries in that period, and a dozen more, critically hurt, would have died without rapid transport and medical treatment. In addition, there were many serious but survivable injuries, from fractured skulls to broken legs (at least 50 fractures per year), and a much larger number of "minor" cuts, bruises, and sprains. Not surprisingly, most injuries occurred during leader falls and involved feet, ankles, or lower legs; for many, these are the accepted risks of climbing. However, leader falls accounted for only 25% of the fatal and near-fatal traumatic injuries. Of the rest, roughly 7% were from rockfall, 28% from being unroped, and 40% from simple mistakes with gear. Many cases are not clear cut, of course. Several factors may share the credit, and it's sometimes hard to quantify the weird adventures climbers have.

Not to be overlooked in the "body count" are environmental injuries. Inadequately equipped for the weather, four climbers died of hypothermia and perhaps 40 more would have died of the cold or the heat if not rescued.

Fifteen to 25 parties require an NPS rescue each year. Sixty more people stagger into Yosemite's medical clinic on their own, and an unknown number escape statistical immortality by seeking treatment outside the park (or at the Mountain Room Bar).

Most Yosemite victims are experienced climbers: 60% have been climbing for three years or more, lead 5.10, are in good condition, and climb frequently. Short climbs and big walls, easy routes and desperate ones – all get their share of the accidents.

The NPS keeps no statistics on how many climbers use the park, but 25,000 to 50,000 climber-days-on-the-rock annually is a fair estimate. With this in mind, 2.5 deaths and a few serious injuries per year may seem a pretty low rate. It's much too high, however, for the guy whose climbing career is cut short by a broken hip. It's also too high when you consider that at least 80% of the climbing fatalities, and many injuries, were easily preventable. In case after case, ignorance, a casual attitude, and/or some form of distraction proved to be the most dangerous aspects of the sport.

Obviously, climbers are independent minded and will do whatever they want; this essay simply addresses the areas where climbers have had problems in the past. As the saying goes, "good judgement comes from bad experience." In the pages that follow are condensed 17 years of "bad experience" – the situations

Yosemite climbers faced, the mistakes they made, and some recommendations for avoiding "bad experiences" of your own. This information comes in many cases from the victims' own analyses or those of their peers.

ENVIRONMENTAL DANGERS

In mid-October, 1983, a climber on El Cap collapsed from heat exhaustion. On the same date in 1984, a party on Washington Column was immobilized by hypothermia. You can expect this range of weather year-round.

Heat No Yosemite climber has died from the heat, but a half-dozen parties have come close. Too exhausted to move, they only survived because death by "drying-up" is a relatively slow process, allowing rescuers time to get there.

Temperatures on the sunny walls often exceed 100°F. Even in cool weather, climbing all day requires lots of water. The generally accepted minimum, two quarts per person per day, may not replace what you use, so don't let the desire for a light haulbag be your overriding concern. Do not put all your water in a single container, and watch out for leaks!

Climbers often underestimate the time and water they'll need to do a route. If you find yourself rationing water, remember that dehydration will seriously sap your strength, slowing you even further. It's not uncommon to go from mere thirst to a complete standstill in a single day. Continuing up may be the right choice but several climbers have said, "I should have gone down while I could."

Storms We still hear that "it never rains in Yosemite." In fact, there are serious storms year-round. Four climbers have died of hypothermia and almost 40 have been rescued, most of whom would not have survived otherwise. Several were very experienced, with winter alpine routes, Yosemite walls, and stormy bivouacs to their credit – experts, by most measures. In many cases they took sub-standard gear, added another mistake or two, and couldn't deal with the water.

Mountain thunderstorms are common in spring, summer, and fall. They may appear suddenly out of a clear blue sky and rapidly shift position, their approach concealed by the route you are on. A few minutes warning may be all that you get. Thunderstorms may last only a couple of hours, but they are very intense, with huge amounts of near-freezing water often mixed with hail, strong winds, and lightning. The runoff can be a foot deep and fast enough to cause rockfall. A common scenario involves a panicky retreat, a jammed rope, and cries for help. (The standard joke is that someone will drown on a Tuolumne climb one of these days – it's actually possible.) No climber has died in such a storm yet because rescuers were able to respond. No climbers have died from lightning either, but there have been several near misses, and hikers on Half Dome and elsewhere have been killed. Get out of the way of a thunderstorm as fast as you can, and avoid summits and projections.

The big Pacific storm systems have been the most dangerous. They sweep through the Sierra at any time of year, most frequently from September through May. They are unpredictable, often appearing back-to-back after several weeks of gorgeous, mind-numbing weather. It may rain on Half Dome in January and snow there in July. These storms are dangerous because they are usually warm enough to be wet, even in winter, yet always cold enough to kill an unprotected climber. They last from one to several days, offering little respite if you're in trouble.

With no soil to absorb it, rain on the walls quickly collects into streams and waterfalls, pouring off overhangs and perhaps down the corner you're trying to climb up or sleep in. Wind blows the water in all directions, including straight up. It may rip apart a plastic tube tent or blow a portaledge up and down until the tubing breaks or the fly rips. Overhanging faces and other "sheltered" spots are not always immune – rain or waterfalls several yards away may be blown directly onto your bivvy, and runoff will wick down your anchor rope. Even a slow but steady leak into your shelter can defeat you. Temperatures may drop, icing over the next pitch and freezing your wet sleeping bag.

Once cold and wet, you are in serious trouble and your options run out. If you leave your shelter to climb or rappel, you deteriorate more rapidly from the wind and water. (Even with good gear, water runs down your sleeve every time you reach up.) As your body temperature drops, you begin making dumb mistakes, such as clipping in wrong or dropping your rack. This is the onset of hypothermia. Eventually you will just hang there, no longer caring. It happens very quickly. In two separate incidents, three climbers on the last pitch of the Nose left what protection they had to make a run for the top. They all died on that pitch.

Staying put may be no better. If you need help, no one may see you or hear you, and reaching you may take days longer than in good weather. Survivors say they had no idea how helpless they'd be until it happened to them. To find out for yourself, stand in the spray of a garden hose on a cold, windy night. How long will you last?

Big Wall Bivouacs Despite this grim scenario, reasonable precautions will turn stormy big-wall bivouacs into mere annoyances:

- Check the forecast just before you start up but don't rely on it. For several parties it provided no warning whatsoever.
- Always assume you'll be hit, and that you'll not have a choice of bivvies.
- Ask friends to check on you if the weather or the forecast turns bad, and/or take advantage of the NPS voluntary registration system.
- Evaluate, ahead of time, the problems of retreat from any point on the route. Did you bring a bolt kit? For reversing overhanging pitches, consider taking a "cheater stick" for clipping into bolts and stuffing Friends into cracks.
- If it's starting to rain, be careful about climbing "just one more" pitch – once wet you won't dry out. It's generally better to set up your bivvy while you're still dry.
- Plan on being wet from your own condensation but insulated enough to stay warm. Your goal is to keep the wind and outside water away.
- Stick with high quality gear that is in good condition, and don't leave important items behind to make the hauling easier. Don't go up with a poorly equipped partner – it will be your neck as well.

Never rely on cotton or down (even if covered with one of the waterproof/breathable fabrics). Wool and/or the modern synthetic insulators stay warm when wet. Take long underwear, pants, sweater, jacket, balaclava/hat, gloves, sleeping bag, insulating pad, extra socks (or booties), and plenty of food and water (hypothermia victims are often dehydrated).

For the rain, take coated nylon, sailors' oilskins, or the waterproof/breathable fabrics (but see below!): rain pants and jacket, overmitts, bivvy bag, and hammock or portaledge with waterproof fly. Be sure all seams are properly sealed. For sleeping on ledges, take a big tent fly or a piece of heavy-duty, reinforced plastic and the means to pitch it. Then hope that your ledge doesn't turn into a lake. Do you know how to run your anchor through a fly without making a hole that water will leak through? Do you spend more for lycra than rainwear?

A Warning: several climbers have blamed the waterproof/breathable fabrics for their rescues or close calls. They claim that no version of it can take the punishment of a storm on the walls. Whether true or not, you must be the judge; test this type of gear ahead of time under miserable conditions, but where your exit is an easy one.

Unplanned Bivouacs Most unplanned bivouacs are the result of long day routes. Such nights spent out accounted for one of the four hypothermia deaths and several close calls. Getting caught by dark is easy: you may climb slowly, lose the route (climb or descent), jam a rope, or sprain an ankle. It happens almost routinely on longer day climbs and descent routes, e.g., **Royal Arches** and the Cathedral Rocks. It's usually nothing to get upset about, but if a storm (even a mild one) or simply a cold wind catches you unprepared, the situation becomes serious. To avoid becoming a statistic:

- Consider the following gear for each person's day pack: long underwear, gloves, balaclava (all can be lightweight polypro, in warmer weather), rain jacket and pants (doubles as wind protection). If that's too heavy for you, at least take one of those disposable plastic rainsuits or tube tents that take up virtually no space. A headlamp with spare bulb and new batteries is very important for finding safe anchors, signaling for help, or avoiding that bivvy altogether. Matches and heat-tabs are needed to light wet wood. Food and water always is welcome. Take more warm clothes in colder weather. Keep your survival gear with you whenever practical, not with the other guy – climbers get separated from their gear (and each other) in imaginative ways, sometimes with serious consequences.
- Standing in slings on poor anchors is not the way to spend a night. If a bivvy is inevitable, don't rush until the last moment; find a safe and comfortable spot while you've got enough light.

Descents Be wary of advice that "the way down is obvious." Consult the guidebook and your friends, but also look the route over ahead of time. If you carry a topo of the route up, consider one for the way home, or perhaps a photograph. Your ultimate protection is routefinding ability, and that takes experience. Some trouble spots to watch out for: North Dome Gully, the Kat Walk, Michael's Ledge, the El Cap East Ledges.

- Many rappel epics are born when an easy descent (often a walk- off) is missed. Search for it thoroughly before you commit to a big drop.
- Footprints and rappel anchors often lead nowhere, so be willing and able to retrace your steps. Remember that the trickiest part may not be at the top. If you're still intent on descending in this "blind" manner, consider first rappelling a single line as far as possible (160 feet if you have one rope, 320 feet if two.) to evaluate the rest of the "route" before committing yourself. Do this anytime you can't find an anchor where there ought to be one. Learn to be comfortable on the rope and be willing to swing around a corner to look for the next anchor. Carry enough gear to go back up your rope – and know how to use it.
- Any time you can't see anchors all the way to the ground, don't commit

without the gear to set your own and the means to get back up. That goes for established routes, as well, since ice and rockfall can destroy anchors. It sometimes means carrying a bolt kit.

- Consider taking a second (7-9mm) rope, even when there's a walk-off. You descend faster, depend on fewer anchors, leave less gear, and can more easily reverse the climbing route in an emergency – an advantage of leading on double ropes. (Don't forget that thinner ropes are more vulnerable to sharp edges.)
- Friction from wet or twisted ropes, slings, ledges, cracks and flakes may jam your rope. Plan ahead when you rig the anchor and be willing to leave gear behind to avoid friction. (You can retrieve the gear tomorrow.)
- Rappelling through trees? Consider short rappels from tree to tree. It's slow but avoids irretreivable snarls.
- You can always go back up and rerig, as long as you keep both ends of the rope until you're sure it will pull. Don't forget to untie the knots in the ends before you pull.
- DON'T DROP ANYTHING!

Loose Rock There's plenty of it in Yosemite. Eight percent of all injuries are associated with rockfall, including four deaths and one permanent disability. In several other deaths, loose rock was implicated but not confirmed (probable broken handholds, for example). Spontaneous rockfall is not the problem – all the fatal and serious accidents were triggered by the victim, the rope, or by climbers above.

Rocks lying on ledges and in gullies are obviously dangerous. Not so obvious is that "old reliable" mantle block, "wedged" in place, five times your weight and worn smooth by previous climbers. With distressing regularity, bombproof blocks, flakes, even ledges collapse under body weight, spit out Friends, or fracture from the pressure of a piton. This is true even of the steepest and most "solid" parts of El Cap. The forces placed on anchors and protection even from rappelling may be far higher than you generate in a "test." Handholds may pass your scrutiny, then fail in mid-move. The rock you pull off can break your leg after falling only a couple of feet. Finally, watch out for rotten rock, responsible for two of these fatalities. It's common on the last couple of pitches of climbs that go to the rim, YPB and Washington Column, for example.

Some of these accidents may not be preventable, short of staying home, but being aware of the hazard and following a few guidelines will cut the injury rate:

- Back up everything except rotten rock – it's too unreliable to use in the first place. A sling around a rotten horn may give you a quick ride to the Valley floor.
- Adopt the habit of throwing in an occasional piece on long, easy runouts "just for the hell of it." Loose or rotten rock can send you on a long fall.
- Ropes "cause" almost as much rockfall as climbers do. Watch where you run your lead rope. Use directionals to keep it away from loose (and sharp) stuff, and check it frequently. Keep in mind that your bag or pack, when hauled, may dislodge everything in its path. When you pull your rappel ropes, stand to one side, look upward, and watch out for delayed rockfall.
- You have no control over what a party above you does, but by being below you accept the risk. If you are catching up, don't crowd them – ask for permission

to pass. You can probably work it out with relative safety, but remember that climbers have been killed or hurt by rocks dislodged by parties above, including those they allowed to pass. The party you want to pass may have gotten an early start to avoid that risk. They have no obligation to let you by. When you are above someone else (including your partner) put yourself in their shoes. Slow down, watch your feet and the rope.

CLIMBING UNROPED

Everybody does it, to some extent. There's no reason to stop, but good reason to be cautious: Fourteen climbers were killed while unroped, at least six of whom climbed 5.10 or better. Most, if not all, of those accidents were avoidable. Climbers may find themselves unroped and climbing in several situations, on third-class terrain, while free-soloing a route, and as spur- of-the-moment fifth-class.

Sometimes you lose the way on the approach or unrope at what you thought was the top of the climb only to find "just a few feet" of "easy" fifth class blocking your way. At least it looks easy (and it doesn't look loose). Your rope is tucked away in your pack, and you're in a hurry. Before you start out, remember that you didn't plan to free-solo an unknown quantity today. Four have died this way, falling from fifth-class terrain climbed on the spur of the moment.

Six of the 14 killed while unroped were previously rappelling or were otherwise tied in. They unroped, for various reasons of convenience, without clipping into a nearby anchor. Three (good climbers among them) slipped off their stances, a ledge collapsed under another, and two tried to climb their rappel ropes hand-over-hand to attend to some problem. Like the previous group, they had all gone unroped onto fifth class terrain on the spur of the moment. In addition, they all had a belay immediately available. Did its nearness give them a false sense of security?

Third-class terrain may be easy, but add a bit of sand, loose or wet rock and/or darkness, plus a moment of distraction, and the rating becomes meaningless. Four climbers have died this way, typically on approach/descent routes such as North Dome Gully, all in spots that did not demand a rope.

No free-soloer has been killed. It will happen eventually, most likely the result of a loose hold. Is the free-soloer more alert to the task, having planned it in advance, than those above who unroped on the spur of the moment? Were the unlucky fourteen still relaxed in their minds and not quite attuned yet to their new situation? We can only speculate.

Keep these cases and the hidden hazards in mind as you travel through any steep terrain. Be aware of what is under foot at each moment. Be patient enough to retrace your steps to find the easy way, and if there's a belay hanging in front of you, think twice before rejecting it. Remember, finally, that your climbing ability has probably been measured on clean, rated routes, not unpredictable sand and wet moss. Being a 5.11 climber does not mean you can fly.

LEADING

Eight climbers died and six were critically injured in leader- fall accidents. Most fell simply because the moves were hard, and they were all injured because they hit something before their protection stopped them. Either they did not place enough protection (1/3 of the cases) or what they placed pulled under the force of the fall (the remaining 2/3). Their injuries were so serious because, in all cases, they fell on their sides or headfirst (head, neck, and trunk damage). Half fell 50 feet or less, the climber falling the shortest distance (25 feet) dying, and the longest (270 feet!) surviving.

Were these catastrophes avoidable? It's sometimes hard to tell, but the answer is often yes. The art of leading safely is beyond the scope of this essay, but here are a few lessons frequently learned the hard way.

- First, how's your belay? Is your tie-in snug and in-line with the fall force? Have you practiced with that belay device and set it up correctly? Did you clip through a bombproof directional as you started out? All are common problems in the park – no deaths yet, but serious injuries to climbers of all abilities.
- Don't cheat on your ground fall calculations (a good belayer will keep you honest). With rope stretch and slack in the system, you may fall twice as far below your last protection as you are above it – if it holds.
- A tug on a marginal nut is worthless as a test. Tiny nubbins may hold the nut "firmly" under those conditions but give way in a fall. Be especially cautious about placements you can't see. Back them up.
- Nuts want to fall out. One nut that falls out below you can turn a comfortable lead into a ground-fall situation. The upper nut may hold long enough in a fall to yank the lower ones out sideways, then fail, itself.
- Friends and other hi-tech gadgets "fail" regularly, but it's seldom the fault of the device. It's more likely due to haste, coupled with blind faith in technology.
- Fixed pitons loosen from freeze-thaw cycles and repeated use. They may not have been installed well to begin with. A hammer is the only reliable way to test and reset them, but you don't see many hammers on free routes these days. You don't see them on rappel routes, either, but you may find yourself hanging from anchors that belong in a museum. If you don't test pitons properly, do not depend on them – routinely back them up.
- There is no reliable way to test bolts but plenty of reasons to want to. For example, the common ¼" split-shaft type was not designed or intended for life support, especially for rock climbing. Their quality varies: several have broken under body weight, and others like them are still out there. Reliability also depends on the quality of the rock and the skill of the bolter. Add years of weathering and mistreatment by climbers and the result is many bolts that are easily pulled out by fingers or a sharp yank with a sling. Several bolt hangers have cracked as well, with one fatal accident so far.
- Never test a bolt with a hammer. Instead, examine the surrounding rock, the bolt, and the hanger for cracks (but they may be too small to see). Is the bolt tight and fully seated in the hole? Is the nut snug? Good luck.
- Never trust a single bolt or piton for an anchor, and always equalize the load among the pieces. Back up untested fixed protection with something else.
- Okay. So you know this stuff. You're a little shaky on the lead right now and you've had some trouble getting your pro to stick, but the book said this was 5.10a, and besides, two teenage girls just walked up this pitch. It's only 20 feet more and one of those pieces is bound to hold. Think for a minute. Are you willing to free-solo this pitch? Keep your answer in mind as you climb, because poorly placed protection amounts to just that.

About Falling There's an art to falling safely – like a cat. Bouldering helps to give the alertness required. Controlling your fall may not be possible on those 200-foot screamers but will go a long way toward preventing injury from "routine" falls.

• A chest harness will keep you upright once you stop, but it may not keep you upright as you fall. It may be life-saving to the injured climber, however.
• The wall may look vertical below you, but even glancing off of a steep slab can be fatal. Three climbers died this way.
• Pendulum falls are particularly dangerous. Swinging into a corner from 20 feet to the side is equivalent to falling straight down 20 feet to a ledge and landing on your side. Two climbers died of head and neck injuries in pendulum falls that might otherwise have been survivable. Others suffered fractured skulls (a 20-foot sideways slide, on the Apron!), pelvises and ribs. It doesn't take a very big projection of rock to crack something. Don't forget to protect your second from this fate when you lead a hard traverse.

Learning to Lead Four of the 14 killed or critically injured while leading were very good climbers on well- defined routes, but the majority were "intermediates," often off route. There may be a couple of lessons in that.
• Don't get cocky because you just led your first 5.8 or your protection held on your first fall. Experienced climbers have died from errors "only a beginner would make," so you have plenty of time left in your career to screw up.
• Climbing and protecting are separate skills but both keep you alive; don't challenge yourself in both at the same time. You may not have the skill and presence of mind to get out of a tight spot. If you're out to push your climbing ability, pick a route that's well defined and easy to protect, and be willing and equipped to back off.
• Routefinding is another survival skill. A mistake here can quickly put you over your head in climbing, protecting, or both. Learn to look ahead and recognize what you want to avoid, before you get there.
• Some "easy" terrain in the valley is actually pretty dangerous; low-angle gullies are often full of loose blocks cemented together with moss. Such places present other problems of climbing, protecting, and routefinding that can defeat the inexperienced climber. These problem areas are not usually "cataloged" routes. Three or four climbers have been killed, or nearly so, on such terrain while looking for easy routes to climb.
• A Leading Problem: The last pitch of the **Nutcracker**, with tricky protection and tricky moves over a low-angle slab, provides a subtle challenge for the fledging 5.8 leader. It may not seem so if you cruise through it, but some fail to recognize the trap until too late; this pitch has scored several broken ankles, and a more serious injury is possible. The problem is not necessarily the mantle. There are many such situations throughout the valley; again, experience is the key to recognizing problem areas before you are committed.

THE BELAY CHAIN

Whether you are climbing, rappelling, or just hanging out, the belay chain is what connects you to the rock. There are many links, and various mistakes have killed 18 climbers, 40% of all Yosemite climbing fatalities. In every case the cause was human error. In every case the injury was completely preventable, not by the subtle skills of placing protection on the lead, but by some simple precaution to keep the belay chain intact. Experienced climbers outnumbered inexperienced in this category two to one.

Mistakes with the belay chain can occur at any time. Make one and you'll fall to the end of the rope . . . or farther. Minor injuries are rare. Here are some key points to remember.

• Before you commit yourself (or someone else) to a system, always apply a few pounds of tension in the directions in which it will be loaded, analyzing it like an engineer – what if this happens . . . or that? Check every link. You would be amazed at the inadequate systems often built by "experts." (It takes a real expert only a few seconds to run a proper check.)

• Talk the system through with your partner. He could lose his life as well. Seven climbers have died in multi-victim accidents.

• Even if your system passed the test initially, check it periodically while you're using it. Directions of force often change after you set up the system (two died when their anchors failed for this reason), ropes and slings can wear through (one death and serious injuries) and gear can come undone (two climbers died when a wiggling bolt hanger unscrewed its nut – they were relying on a single bolt).

• Are you about to rappel? Stay clipped to the anchor for a few seconds. Check both the anchor and your brake system, as above. If one anchor point fails, will you remain attached to the other? Are the knots in your rappel slings secure? Skipping this process cost eight deaths plus serious injuries, from poorly tied slings, partially dismantled anchors (a simple misunderstanding), relying on single carabiners, and other reasons. The next time it will be something new, but preventable by double-checking.

• Two climbers died by rappelling off the ends of their ropes. However, both had tied knots in the ends as a safety measure! In one case the knots pulled through the brake. In the second, the victim forgot to double-check the ropes after a knot had been untied to deal with a problem. Knots are still a recommended safety procedure, but do not take anything for granted. Tie both strands into one knot or knot each separately – there are pros, cons, and tricks to each method.

• When rappelling in unpredictable circumstances – when it's dark or windy, when communications are poor between you and your partner, with unknown anchors below – consider a prusik (or similar) knot or a mechanical ascender as a safety. A prusik won't stop you if you fall; unless it's been pre-tightened it may slip and melt through. It is primarily for quickly but deliberately stopping yourself to deal with other emergencies. Both of those who rappelled off their ropes would have survived with prusik safeties.

• In separate incidents, four climbers somehow became detached from their ropes while climbing with mechanical ascenders – not the fault of the devices. Only two of the climbers were tied to the rope at all (at the lower end). All four died because they had not tied in "short." To tie in short, tie a loop in the rope just below your ascenders and clip it to your harness. As you climb, repeat the process often enough to limit your fall should you come off your rope. At the very least, do this when you must pass one ascender around protection, make traverses, or change to another rope. (Is that other rope anchored well? Ask your partner first. One climber died partly because his wasn't.) In addition, always be tied into both of your ascenders.

• Self-belayers should also tie in short: One died when his prusik belay melted during a fall, and at least two were treated to close calls when other types of self-belay systems jammed open.

• Clip into a new belay point before unclipping from the old one. During those few, vulnerable seconds pitons have pulled, hero loops have broken, rocks have struck, and feet have slipped.

• Two climbers were killed and one critically injured by "failures" of single-carabiner tie-ins and rappel anchors. Be careful of relying on a single non-locking carabiner for any link in the chain. The rope or sling may flip over the gate and unclip itself, especially if it is slack or shock-loaded. Even if you watch it carefully and/or it is "safely" under tension, you may become distracted (a common occurrence). Use either two non-locking carabiners with gates opposed and reversed or a locking carabiner. Don't forget to lock it! For most applications the two-carabiner method is safer and faster to operate.

• Ropes have been cut in three fatal accidents. They did not break, but were stressed over sharp edges, a condition never intended by the manufacturer. Two of these accidents were avoidable: one climber should have tied in short (to prevent a 100 foot fall that cut the rope); the other climber should have protected a fixed rope from a well-defined sharp edge. Ascending a rope produces a weighted, see-sawing action that can destroy it, even over a rounded but rough edge.

• Like ropes, most gear failure falls into the "misuse" category. Failure from a design or manufacturing flaw is rare. It was the initiating factor in one fatal accident, in which three climbers died when a bolt hanger broke at a two-bolt rappel anchor. The tragic outcome would have been avoided, however, had the climbers noticed they were not properly backed up to the second bolt.

These cases illustrate one of the rules most commonly overlooked: BACK YOURSELF UP. No matter what initially pulled, broke, slipped, jammed, or cut, the incident became an accident because the climber did not carefully ask himself, "What if . . . ?" By leaving yourself open, you play the game of roulette against a variety of unpredictable events. You don't lose very often, but when you do, you may lose very big.

Beginners! You have the right, from your first day, to inspect any system you're committing your life to, and to ask questions about it. It's a good habit to get into and a good way to learn. If your "expert" partner or instructor is offended, find someone else to climb with. Never change the system or the plan, however, without your partner's knowledge.

HELMETS

About eight percent of all Yosemite climbing injuries involve the head. Helmets would have significantly increased the survival chances for three to five of the 43 trauma fatalities, slightly increased it for three or four more, and lessened or eliminated the damage in six of those critically injured. Furthermore, helmets offer excellent protection against "less serious" skull fractures, concussions, and scalp lacerations.

Most deaths involved impacts of overwelming force and/or mortal wounds other than to the head – beyond the protection offered by a helmet. This is not an argument against helmets. The point is, a helmet doesn't make you invincible. What goes on inside your head is more important than what you wear on it.

When to wear a helmet is a personal choice, but it is strongly recommended for: roped solo climbing, any route exposed to ice fall (brick-sized chunks bombard several El Cap routes in winter and spring), and all approaches, descents, and climbing routes that are crowded and/or particularly loose. The **East Buttress** of Middle Cathedral Rock, for example, is a well-known "bowling alley" – the site of many rockfall injuries. The Northwest Face of Half Dome is another, with the added excitement of tourist "firing squads" on the summit, dropping rocks on unwary climbers below.

STATES OF MIND

This is the key to safety. It's impossible to know how many climbers were killed by, say, haste or overconfidence. Many accident survivors will tell you that, somehow, they lost their good judgement long enough to get hurt. It's a murky subject and sometimes a touchy one. Nevertheless, here are some comments on three states of mind: ignorance, casualness, and distraction.

Ignorance Even the most conscientious climber can get into trouble if he's unaware of the danger ("I thought it never rained . . . "). The most important message in this essay may be that there is always something more to learn, and certainly a simple outline like this one can't say it all. There are two steps to fighting ignorance.

- Continue to read, and listen to climbers who have survived. Back issues of all the climbing magazines are full of pertinent articles. Case histories in the American Alpine Club's *Accidents in North American Mountaineering*, a yearly compilation of accident reports, will show you how subtle factors may combine to catch you unaware. Such accounts are the next best (or worst?) thing to being there.
- Practice. Reading may make you aware but not competent. In fact, you can be dangerously misled by what you read. Important details are often left out, the advice may be incorrect, and in the long run you must think and act for yourself. Several climbers, for example, have waited to learn how to prusik until it was dark, raining, overhanging and they were actually in trouble. They had read about it, but they had to be rescued despite having the gear to improvise their own solutions. Book- learning alone gave them a complacency that could have proved fatal.

Casualness "I just didn't take it seriously." It's a common lament. It's often correct, but it's more a symptom than a disease – there may be deeper reasons for underestimating your risk. Ignorance is one, and here are some more.

- Habit reinforcement occurs when nothing goes wrong. The more often you get away with risky business the more entrenched your lazier habits become. Have you unconsciously dropped items from your safety checklists since you were a chicken-hearted (or hare- brained) beginner?
- Your attitudes and habits can be reinforced by the experiences (and states of mind) of others. The sense of awe and commitment of the 1960's is gone from the big-wall "trade routes," and young aspirants with no Grade VI's (or even V's) to their credit speak casually about them. Yet most of the accidents on El Cap occur on "easy" pitches.

Memory Decay "I'm not going up again without raingear – I thought I would die!" A week later this climber had forgotten how scared he had been in that thunderstorm. Raingear was now too heavy and besides, he'd rap off the next time. Many of us tend to forget the bad parts. We have to be hit again.

Civilization With fixed anchors marking the way and ghetto blasters echoing behind, it may be hard to realize that the potential for trouble is as high in Yosemite as anywhere. Some say the possibility of fast rescue added to their casualness. Maybe, but who wants a broken leg, or worse, in the first place?

Overconfidence "It'll never happen to me. I'm a safe, cautious climber." Many of those killed were described by friends as very cautious.

Distraction It is caused by whatever takes your mind off your work: fear, thirst, sore feet, skinny-dippers below – the list is endless. Being in a hurry is one of the most common causes. Here are two ways it has happened:

• Experienced climbers have often been hurt after making "beginner errors" (their words) to get somewhere quickly. There was no emergency or panic, but their minds were elsewhere – on a cold beer, a good bivvy, or just sick of being on that route for a week. (It's often called "summit fever.") Their mistakes were usually short cuts in protecting easy pitches, on both walls and day climbs. As one put it, "We were climbing as though we were on top."

• Darkness had caught two day climbers for the first time. Unprepared, upset, and off route, they rushed to get down, arguing with each other about what to do. After several errors, which they knew to avoid, one climber was killed rappelling off the end of his rope.

• Learn to recognize when you or your partner are becoming distracted. Stop, get your act together, then go.

RESCUES

• Despite the best of preparations, an accident can happen to anyone. Self-rescue is often the fastest and safest way out, but whether it's the wise course of action depends on the injury and how well prepared you are. Combining with a nearby party will often give you the margin of safety you need, but do not risk aggravating an injury or getting yourselves into a more serious predicament – ask for help if you need it. (Sometimes a bit of advice, delivered by loudspeaker, is all that's required.)

• If you don't have formal first aid training (which is strongly recommended), at least know how to keep an unconscious patient's airway open, how to protect a possible broken neck or back, and how to recognize and deal with flail chest, external bleeding, and serious blood loss (shock). These procedures are life-saving, do not require fancy gear, and are easy to learn.

• Head injury victims are apt to be irrational and very strong. Even if he's unconscious, if you have to leave one alone, make it impossible for him to untie himself.

• If ropes are lowered to you from a helicopter for any purpose, do not attach them to your anchors unless you are specifically instructed to do so – if the helicopter has to leave suddenly it could pull you off the wall. If you are told to anchor a rope, rescuers will be using a system that does not expose you to that risk; anchor that rope securely – it may be a rescuer's lifeline. Follow instructions exactly.

Who pays for rescues? The taxpayer does – the NPS does not charge for the cost of rescues. This is true even if you do not use the Voluntary Registration System (despite rumors to the contrary), and even if you are fined by the courts for negligence (a separate charge altogether – see below). But rescues can be expensive and what the future holds is anybody's guess. The NPS is examining the possibility of charging all victims for the full cost of their rescues, and partial costs are charged in some parks now. This issue is complex, but it is clear that responsible behavior by those who use the park will minimize the threat.

RISK, RESPONSIBILITY, AND THE LIMITS TO CLIMBING

The NPS has no regulations specifying how you must climb. There is one regulation, however, requiring all park users to act responsibly. This applies to climbers, in that rescuers and other climbers are always at risk (one rescuer has been killed in the park). Thus, if your own negligence got you into trouble, you may be charged with "creating a hazardous condition" for others. As an example, a climber was fined because he became stranded by a hailstorm while attempting to free-solo the **Steck-Salathé** on Sentinel Rock. Storms had been predicted, and his rescue should not have been necessary.

Even avoidable accidents are understandable; thus legal charges are not frequently filed. Of all park users, however, climbers should be a particularly well-educated group: they know that their sport is dangerous, that safety lies in education and training, and that there is an information network available.

Therefore, take what you'll need with you on the climb, or have competent friends ready to back you up. The climber stranded on Sentinel, for example, could have been rescued by friends without NPS participation or knowledge – the way it must often be done on expeditions. "Freedom of expression" and self- responsibility need not be incompatible.

Climbing will always be risky. It should be clear, however, that a reduced accident rate is possible without seriously restricting the sport. The party in its fifth day on the Nose and the party passing them in its fifth hour may each be climbing safely, or they may be blindly out of control. You have a right to choose your own climbing style and level of risk, but you owe it to yourself and everyone else to make that choice with your eyes wide open.

OTHER NOTES

Voluntary Registration System: If you wish, register at the Valley Visitor Center before your climb. If you don't return by the date you specify, the NPS will look for you. Please check back in, or much time and money will be spent unnecessarily to make sure you're OK. The NPS does not monitor your progress during your climb, so your best insurance is a friend who checks on you frequently.

To Report An Emergency: By public phone, dial 911. No money is needed to make the call. Stay at the phone until a ranger arrives or unless you are specifically told to return to the victim.

Accident/Hazard Reporting: If you have had an accident or a close call that might be instructive, or know of dangerous route conditions such as loose rock or bad anchors (that you couldn't repair yourself), please tell a ranger. This is strictly voluntary, but your information will help other climbers. Hazard information is posted at the Camp Four kiosk and at the Mountain Shop in Curry Village.

WARNING: The NPS does not inspect or maintain climbing or descent routes, including fixed anchors, loose rock or any other feature. You are strictly on your own.

Tossing Haulbags: Do not throw your haul bag off a wall. You cannot always be sure the coast is clear, and the bag may drift in the wind. No one has been hurt yet, but it will happen – there have been a few close calls. Bag-tossing also creates a carnival atmosphere, a big mess (of your gear), and lots of false alarms for rescuers. (Tourists usually think it's a body.)

Sources of Information: Try the local climbers, found in the parking lot at Camp Four (irreverently called Sunnyside Campground by the NPS), the bulletin board at the Camp Four kiosk, the Mountain Shop, the Visitor Center at Yosemite Village, any ranger, or the NPS library (next to the Visitor Center). The library is the home of the American Alpine Club's Sierra Nevada Branch Library. It carries magazines, journals, and books on all aspects of climbing, mountaineering, and natural history and is a great place to spend a rainy day.

CLIMBING HISTORY

The following history section, covering the years from 1870 to World War II, was written by Richard Leonard, David Brower and William Dunmire and appeared in Steve Roper's guide book *A Climber's Guide to Yosemite Valley*, published by the Sierra Club in 1971.

. . . Even in those prehistoric days before the discovery of the incomparable Valley, there were legendary rock climbing exploits. Such was the first descent to the base of the Lost Arrow. The Indian maiden Tee-hee-neh rappelled on lodgepole saplings joined together with deer thongs to recover the lifeless body of her lover, Kos-soo-kah. By means of thongs and the strong arms of the other members of the tribe, they were brought back to the rim of the Valley, where Tee-hee-neh perished in grief. This legend is reported in many different sources; Hutchings, in 1886, stated the height of the rappel to be 203 feet, a truly remarkable rock climbing achievement.

It was not until 1833 that the white man is known to have seen Yosemite Valley. From reports published long before the later and widely publicized discovery of the Valley, we learn that Joseph Reddeford Walker and party came from the vicinity of Bridgeport, perhaps over Virginia Pass and along the divide between the Tuolumne and the Merced rivers, to the Valley rim. There they marveled at waterfalls over "lofty precipices . . . more than a mile high." The first rock climbing attempt by white man was soon stopped by difficulty, for "on making several attempts we found it utterly impossible for a man to descend."

In 1851, however, Yosemite Valley was really made known to the world, when the Mariposa Battalion, organized by harassed settlers of the foothills, trailed Indians to their stronghold in Ahwahnee – "deep grassy valley."

Yosemite soon became a source of attracton for tourists from all over the world. One of the earliest to arrive was James M. Hutchings, who first came to the Valley in 1855. Throughout the early history of the Valley he was interested in attempting to climb every point around the Valley.

John Muir first came to the Sierra in 1868. Through him more than any other man has the beauty of the region been made known to the entire world. His climbs in Yosemite Valley and the High Sierra, many of them the earliest of which we have knowledge, place him among the pioneers of California mountaineering. His Sunnyside Bench, east of the lip of Lower Yosemite Fall is still one of the untrammeled beauty spots of the Valley. His early exploration of the Tenaya Canyon led to route finding in the Grand Canyon of the Tuolumne. He made the first ascents of Cathedral Peak and Mount Ritter, and was the first to traverse under the Lost Arrow along Fern Ledge, beneath the crashing power of the Upper Yosemite Fall.

In early October of 1864 Clarence King, assisted by Richard Cotter, fresh from a victory over Mount Tyndall, made the first serious topographical and geological reconnaissance of the Yosemite Valley. On this survey they climbed practically every summit on a circuit of the rim of the Valley. This circuit included only the easier points, such as El Capitan, Eagle Peak, Yosemite Point, North Dome, Basket Dome, Mount Watkins, Sentinel Dome, and the Cathedral Rocks. Any summits which were much beyond this standard of difficulty seemed to them completely beyond the range of human ability. In 1865 the California Geological Survey wrote concerning Half Dome, Mount Starr King and Mount Broderick, "Their summits are absolutely inaccessible."

Spurred by this challenge James M. Hutchings and two others made the first recorded attempt on Half Dome in 1869, but were stopped at a saddle east of the Dome. After at least two intervening attempts the Scotch carpenter and trail-builder, George G. Anderson, finally engineered his way to the top on October 12, 1875.

Inspired by the success on Half Dome, adventurous climbers turned their attention to Mount Starr King, the "extremely steep, bare, inaccessible cone of granite" referred to by Whitney in the *Yosemite Guide Book*. George B. Bayley and E. S. Schuyler made the ascent in August 1876, somewhat to the dismay of Anderson, Hutchings and J. B. Lembert, who, using a different route, a year later found the summit monuments built by the first party. Bayley was one of the most remarkable climbers of the time. In 1876 Muir recorded that "Mount Shasta, Whitney, Lyell, Dana, and the Obelisk (Mount Clark) already have felt his foot, and years ago he made desperate efforts to ascend the South Dome (Half Dome), eager for the first honors." Later he was distinguished by an early ascent of Cathedral Peak, and an ascent of Mount Rainier during which he was seriously injured by a fall into a crevasse, recovering only to be killed in a city elevator.

After the great ascents of the "inaccessible" summits of Yosemite, there was a period of quiet in the climbing history, for everything seemed to have been done. Hutchings had claimed the ascent of all Yosemite points, except Grizzly Peak and the Cathedral Spires, and a climber of another generation came forward in 1885 to make the ascent of Grizzly Peak. He was Charles A. Bailey, who later became an enthusiastic member of the Sierra Club, locating, climbing, and naming Sierra Point for the Club.

Since it now appeared that all the major summits in the Yosemite region had been climbed, there was a long gap in the climbing history, broken only by the exploratory routes of a few outstanding climbers of the period. Those whose climbs are best known are S. L. Foster, Joseph N. LeConte, Charles and Enid Michael, William Kat, and Ralph S. Griswold. Foster was best known for his canyoneering in the Merced and Tenaya canyons beginning in 1909. LeConte has been remembered through the description of his ascent of the gully on Grizzly Peak, which permits a route to the Diving Board on Half Dome. He also wrote of several other "scrambles about Yosemite" of nearly three decades ago. It has been said of the Michaels that they climbed everything that did not require pitons. The same description might apply to Kat and Griswold. All have been so modest that it is possible we may never know the true history of the interesting routes which they have pioneered.

Again it seemed that nothing more could be done. However, in the early thirties, a new phase of rock climbing was growing, based on the development of modern technique in Europe. In the summer of 1931, Robert L. M. Underhill, the leading American exponent of the use and management of the rope in rock work, interested Californians in this phase of climbing. It has been mentioned that some very remarkable climbing was done without the knowledge of this safety technique; but the early climbers who have discussed the matter agree that their climbing frequently involved unjustifiable hazard. Moreover, it was clear to them that they could not attempt routes of very high angle and small holds. Thus the introduction of a new type of climbing, combined with the protection of pitoncraft, again opened a new field.

It was not until September 2, 1933 that the first rock climbing section of the

Sierra Club felt competent to make organized attempts upon the spectacular unclimbed faces and spires of Yosemite. Although as long ago as 1886 Hutchings, in reporting the relatively easy ascent of Grizzly Peak, claimed that the last "unclimbed summit" of Yosemite had been ascended, nevertheless the Cathedral Spires, the Church Tower, the Arrowhead, Split Pinnacle, Pulpit Rock, Watkins Pinnacles, and the Lost Arrow still stood forth without even an attempt ever having been recorded against them. In addition to these summits there was a field, practically unexplored, of route finding on faces, arêtes, gullies, and chimneys. Among these may be mentioned Washington Column. **Royal Arches** Panorama Cliff, Glacier Point, Yosemite Point Couloir, **Cathedral Chimney**, and the arête of the Lower Brother. Ropes, pitons, and trained experience in their use were the keys to these ascents, which were later to become so popular. Climbers, profiting by the achievements of their predecessors, added still more ascents to the growing list of Yosemite routes . . .

The following section, covering the years from 1941 to Chuck Pratt's climb of the **Crack of Doom** in 1961, was written by Steve Roper and and appeared in his 1971 book. The remainder of the history section, covering the years from 1962 to the present, was compiled by George Meyers.

During the eight years between the 1933 trip and the entry of this country in World War II, about forty first ascents were made. The most active climbers of this period were Kenneth Adam, David Brower, Jules Eichorn, Morgan Harris, Richard Leonard, L. Bruce Meyer, and Hervey Voge. Brower made eighteen first ascents, twelve of them with Harris. Perhaps the most continually popular routes of this era were the regular routes on both the Cathedral Spires, and the **Royal Arches Route**.

During World War II there was a climbing hiatus, but when the war ended a new generation of climbers quickly appeared. Few of the climbers active in the 1930's were to establish new routes in the post-war era. In 1945, a Swiss blacksmith named John Salathé came to Yosemite to hike, climb, and live with nature. He became a vegetarian as a result of a fleeting conversation with "angels" – these same apparitions later pointed out to him three great Valley routes: the Lost Arrow, the southwest face of Half Dome and the north face of Sentinel Rock. All had been attempted in the 1930's and all were considered great prizes. Two factors allowed Salathé to become a legendary climber: his determination and his development of the world's finest pitons. It had long been known and accepted that traditional soft iron pitons couldn't be forced into bad cracks; they would buckle and bend. Employing the skills of his life work, Salathé was able to fashion extremely stiff and durable pitons from Model A Ford axles. Using such iron, he was able to climb, with Anton Nelson, the southwest face of Half Dome without bolts. It is safe to guess that many bolts would have been necessary had conventional pitons been used. Thus, it can be seen that the invention of hardened steel alloy pitons opened up an almost limitless number of first ascent possibilities. Other climbers were not quick to accept the new pitons and the corresponding new standards; Salathé was the great pioneer of the late 1940's. His solo escapades on the Lost Arrow will be remembered far longer than the first "ascent," members of which threw ropes over the summit and prusiked. His notable five-day ascent of the **Lost Arrow Chimney**, also climbed with Nelson, was the first Grade V climb done in the country.

Although Salathé was the finest aid man of his day, he was not known as a good free climber. He often remarked, "Enough of this *hiking*, let us get on to the *climbing*," the hiking referring to free climbing. And yet, at times, he was bold on free climbing; a climb called the Hand, in Pinnacles National Monument, was led by Salathé, using four pitons for protection. Although only 5.6 in difficulty, the Hand is fearsomely exposed and the route is devious. Bolts have now replaced his pitons and it is impossible to see how he managed to place them. One assumes that they were used to reassure the belayer, who was out of sight around a corner.

John Salathé, 1950.
Allen Steck

After climbing Sentinel in 1950, Salathé began to fade from the scene; he had done his three climbs, there were marital problems and he was over fifty years old. He soon left for his native land. Returning to America in 1962, he occasionally visited the Valley, where he would be surrounded by idolators. Surreptitious tape recordings and photographs were made as John Salathé sat oblivious, cooking the grasses from a nearby meadow. A healthy glow was ever-present in his blue eyes: he could chastise Allen Steck, his climbing partner on Sentinel: "You see, Al, if only you had eaten as I did you would have felt better on the wall." Then Allen would say, "You know, John, they have done our route in three hours now." And the serene reply, "But not the same route, Al – they could not do our route that fast. Oh, now that the bolts are in, perhaps...three days?" Then he would shake his head.

Steck was the leader of the post-Salathé generation; in a period of three years he climbed not only Sentinel's north face, but also two of the classic buttress routes in the Valley: **Yosemite Point Buttress** and the **East Buttress** of El Capitan.

Most of the noteworthy climbers in Yosemite from 1933 to 1955 came from the San Francisco area. Los Angeles, the other great population center of California, developed good climbers during that period, but their efforts were largely confined to a local cliff, Tahquitz Rock. An exception was the venerable Chuck Wilts, who had vied with Salathé for the prize of the **Lost Arrow Chimney**. Wilts and his wife, Ellen, made the first ascent of Rixon's Pinnacle, at that time one of the hardest short routes.

In 1954 a pudgy beginner named Mark Powell was taken up the Lower Cathedral Spire, and of the resulting fiasco his partner could only say, "That fellow Powell just doesn't have it." But he did, and the mid-1950's can only be thought of as the Powell Era. With climbing partners of the caliber of Wally Reed, Bill Feuerer and Warren Harding, Powell established nineteen new routes. In one active ten-month period, he put up ten routes, including such classics as the **Arrowhead Arête**, the **South Face of North Dome**, and the **Powell-Reed Route** on Middle Cathedral Rock. A serious ankle injury in September 1957 put an abrupt end to his productive efforts. Of Powell's three main climbing partners, all went on to achieve various degrees of notoriety. Reed was without question the most unheralded climber ever to come out of the Valley; few knew of his amazing control on 5.9 routes. In the early 60's, before he "retired" to go back to school, he made many first free ascents. Feuerer became known as the "Dolt" for some of his infamous blunders, and in the 60's he began making beautiful and ultra-expensive climbing equipment. While Reed and Dolt went on to other activites, Harding was just beginning to make a name for himself.

He started climbing in 1952 and was a weak member of a Grand Teton ascent, causing someone to remark on his lack of endurance. This could well be an apocryphal story, for Harding became known as the iron man of Yosemite climbing, the man who could drill bolt holes all night. His perseverance on the **Nose** of El Capitan is well-known by now; the first El Cap route is a testimonial to his drive and vision. Pleased by this success, he turned to other intimidating walls, overcoming with bolts and siege tactics cliffs which no one had yet dreamed possible. It has been suggested that Harding was ahead of his time, that his 110-bolt ascent of the Leaning Tower would certainly be done someday, so why not in 1961. However, at the time, Harding was criticized for an apparent prediliction for security. (Perhaps the question is reopened by the 1986 27-bolt ascent of a line that parallels the Harding route.) His 1970 ascent of the **Wall of the Early Morning Light** strained most climbers' perception of the justifiable use of bolts, and in the years that followed, Harding only occasionally climbed in the Valley, establishing a few routes up obscure and somewhat ugly walls.

Before Powell and Harding even began climbing, Royal Robbins was putting up America's first 5.9 climbs on Tahquitz Rock. During the 1950's he made few trips to the Valley, but among his early accomplishments were the second and third ascents of the north face of Sentinel and the fourth ascent of the Arrow Chimney. Of his three first ascents in the fifties, the major one was the first Grade VI in the country: the great face of Half Dome, climbed in 1957 with Jerry Gallwas and Mike Sherrick. Five days were spent on the wall. During his 1958-59 incarceration in the Army, Robbins heard stories of what was going on in the Valley: Powell had just put up his great routes and a young Bay Area upstart, Chuck Pratt, was responsible for some of the best climbs of 1958 and 1959.

Pratt had immediately shown a great interest in free climbing and seemed to possess a supernatural ability. An early free lead on Phantom Pinnacle and a great crack lead midway up the north face of Middle Cathedral Rock were among his first climbs. As the productive decade of the 60's dawned, Pratt and Robbins, totally committed to climbing, were the dominant figures. These two, accompanied by Tom Frost and Joe Fitschen, made the second ascent of the Nose in six and a half days. This convinced them that even the greatest Valley walls were possible without fixing ropes from bottom to top. Robbins made first ascents of seven Grade VI's in a three-year period. Pratt, meanwhile, was quietly climbing big walls and leading the most difficult crack climbs yet established; his **Crack of Doom**, climbed in 1961, was for many years the hardest crack climb in the Valley. Later, his strenuous and difficult-to-protect **Twilight Zone** left a route still well respected.

In this same period, attention turned to the monolithic El Capitan. The year 1961 saw Robbins, Pratt, and Frost put together a circuitous route up the broad southwest face of El Capitan that required only 13 bolts and had much free climbing. The **Salathé Wall** was as much an effort to reduce the number of bolts needed to climb El Cap (the **Nose** had required 125) as it was a progression toward less reliance on fixed ropes. With El Cap's first route behind them, Robbins and company started to look at the style in which the next routes would be established.

The next major route on El Cap, the 1962 ascent of the **Dihedral Wall**, by Ed Cooper, Jim Baldwin and Glen Denny, was novel in two ways: it involved individuals from the periphery of the regular Yosemite community; it also seemed somewhat retrograde of the stylistic standards that Robbins had adopted on the **Salathé**. Fixed ropes were used to 1,900 feet and about 100 bolts were placed. Other walls were climbed on El Cap and elsewhere in the Valley over the next few years. The development of aid climbing during the early 60's was in large part due to the efforts and energies of Robbins, who climbed most of the major rock formations. His 1963 solo ascent of the Harding route on the Leaning Tower was the first solo ascent of a major Yosemite Wall. The culmination of the aid techniques of this period was the 1964 ascent of the **North America Wall**, the first route to venture onto the compact, steep, and "unretreatable" southeast face of El Cap. Four of the strongest climbers Yosemite had trained, Robbins, Frost, Pratt, and Yvon Chouinard, teamed up to create what was clearly the hardest wall climb ever done anywhere. From sieged, fixed rope routes, on to semi-fixed, to reconnoitered (as was the **NA Wall**, climbed previously by Frost and Robbins to half height), the natural progression of wall development was for a two-man team to manage a big new route on their own. Chouinard and TM Herbert accomplished this in 1965. Robbins culminated his Yosemite career three years later by making the second ascent of the **Muir Wall**, the first time El Cap was soloed.

The 60's saw the first of the climbing bums, when the hard-core activists had left the lifestyles of the "outer world" largely behind them for a total commitment to the pursuit of climbing cliffs. Perhaps ten to twenty climbers were in full-season residence during the early 60's. This number was to double by the middle of the decade, and by 1970 perhaps double again.

The walls were not the sole magnet for young climbers of the 60's. Soon after

Tom Frost, Royal Robbins, and Yvon Chouinard, **North America Wall**, 1964.
Chuck Pratt

Chuck Pratt plied the shorter cracks in search of difficult testpieces, Frank Sacherer arrived on the scene and used a driven approach in his free climbing to consolidate the standards that Pratt had earlier established. In a period of two years, 1964-65, he put up many free climbs and succeeded in eliminating the aid from many of the older aid routes. These included such fifties classics as the **East Buttresses of El Cap and Middle Cathedral Rock**, the **Lost Arrow Chimney**, and the **Direct North Buttress** of Middle. His remarkable shorter efforts included dispensing with aid on the **Dihardral, Bridalveil East**, and the right side of the **Hourglass**. These latter routes pushed the free climbing standards up a notch to around 5.10c. Other climbers were also active during this period: Ken Boche, Yvon Chouinard, Glen Denny, TM Herbert, Bob Kamps, Layton Kor, Jim Madsen, Steve Roper, Galen Rowell, and Kim Schmitz. Sacherer left the Valley scene in 1966 to pursue a physics career (though he died in the Alps in the late-70's) and it was left to Pratt, Chris Fredericks, and particularly to newcomer Jim Bridwell to lead the way to higher free standards.

Bridwell first climbed in the Valley in 1962, and after some tutelage under the likes of Pratt, Layton Kor, and Sacherer, he started to repeat many of the harder wall climbs of the Robbins era, including (sometimes last known) ascents of walls such as **Arches Direct, East Face of Higher Cathedral Rock** and the **Direct Northwest Face** of Half Dome. Bridwell, together with Kim Schmitz and Jim Madsen, among others, represented the new generation of wall climbers. These wall climbers of the late 60's, while somewhat slow to establish new wall routes, made quick ascents of the existing ones.

Since the thirties, when the routes followed major chimney and crack systems, new routes had followed progressively thinner crack systems. In the 70's, this trend saw routes that included long successive pitches of knifeblades and rurps, and the free climbing of finger cracks, something almost unheard of in the 60's.

While A5 was introduced by Robbins in the 60's, using pitons and rurps, oftentimes in piton stacks (perhaps most notoriously on the 10-hour, A5 pitch on **Arches Direct**), the years following the consolidation of the late 60's saw A5 expressed by more and more technical means. Routes impossible using 60's technology were later climbed using mashable copperheads (and tiny alumiheads) and an impressive array of skyhooks. The technology of the 60's aid climbers was also used more often and in a more sustained fashion. The use of rurps saw new light with Charlie Porter's ascent of the **Shield** in 1972, where he placed 35 in a row. Porter, a former auto mechanic and metallurgist, was the most notable of a new imaginative generation of aid climbers. In addition to his many major El Cap routes, Porter produced slider nuts (refined from Bridwell's designs of 1965) and camming nuts that foresaw the future in free climbing protection. After the introduction of Friends, in 1978, the previously scary nemesis of the wall climber, expanding flakes, became slightly less scary, and some routes, on Half Dome in particular, saw ascents that had intimidated earlier generations of climbers.

The huge area of El Cap to the right of the **North America Wall**, referred to by Robbins at one point as "rotten," was opened up in the early 70's. This was done first, ironically, by Robbins himself, in an unsucessful bid for the first solo first ascent of an El Cap route, and most significantly, by Charlie Porter. In quick succession Porter climbed the **Zodiac** and **Tangerine Trip**, now seen as some of the best aid climbing on the cliff, and certainly among the steepest.

While Porter opened many eyes to the possibilities of expanded hard aid, connecting the thinnest of flake systems to create routes up inobvious walls, it was Jim Bridwell who leaped upon the idea with characteristic energy. First he pushed a major new route up the wall to the left of the **North America Wall**, the **Pacific Ocean Wall**, with Coloradan Billy Westbay in 1975, and then over the years progressively harder and more tenuous lines: **Sea of Dreams, Bushido,** and **Zenyatta Mondatta.** One technique that was first seen with the Bridwell routes was the use of a chisel to clean loose rock from small slots in which to mash copperheads. (Later climbers have expanded this chisel use to the plain manufacture of copperhead slots in blank corners.) Also, Bridwell borrowed from Kim Schmitz and Jim Madsen the timesaving use of dowels, and from Harding, drilled hook placements.

Jim Bridwell, **Pacific Ocean**, 1975.
Billy Westbay

Much of the relatively slow pace at which El Cap routes were being established was due to the plainly formidable appearance of such a huge cliff. But the aura of intimidation that surrounded the big aid routes was shaken when outsiders Chuck Kroger and Scott Davis drove into the Valley and up to El Cap in 1970, and without fanfare, established the **Heart Route** in impeccable style. El Cap's image suffered considerably further when Steve Sutton and Hugh Burton, teenagers from Squamish Chief, came to the Valley in 1972 and climbed a good new route on the cliff, capping their accomplishment with a bit of irreverence by naming it the **Magic Mushroom**, as much a defiance of the self-serious attitudes of the Robbins era as it was a celebration of the drugs they quaffed enroute.

Others were active in establishing big aid routes. During the 70's **Nose** veteran and crag rat Warren Harding was occasionally active on the walls, climbing big, steep, obscure and often blank routes that have not seen second ascents and that are now largely ignored. Most notable was his ascent of the **Wall of the Early Morning Light** with Dean Caldwell in 1970, a route that stirred such controversy (because of the 300 holes drilled) that Robbins felt compelled to chop the route. Impressed with the standard of the climbing, he abandoned his bolt removal efforts about halfway up the route. Rick Sylvester, most known for his ski/parachute leaps off El Cap, was one of the first of the 70's Yosemite residents to establish a new route up El Cap – **The Heart Woute** – and he furthered his reputation for weird boldness by establishing a route up the path of Upper Yosemite Fall, climbing with Bugs McKeith during a period when the fall had temporarily dried up. In the decade of the 70's the number of El Cap routes alone rose from ten to 38, primarily due to the efforts of Dale Bard, Hugh Burton, Mark Chapman, Bruce Hawkins, Ron Kauk, Bill Price, Steve Sutton, and others, who, partnered with Porter, Bridwell, or among themselves, established numerous routes on El Cap and Half Dome. The El Cap route tally now stands at 60; the first six years of the 80's has seen activity by John Barbella, Charles Cole, Jay Smith, Mike Corbett, Steve Grossman, Steve Schneider, and others, including old hand Jim Bridwell. Corbett, incidentally, notably holds a record 36 trips up El Cap, via 24 different routes. Unfortunately, the Harding Dawn Wall debate over justifiable bolting reemerged with the ascent of **Wings of Steel**, where close to 145 drilled holes were placed over 1,200 feet. In the 70's, foreign ascents of classic El Cap routes became commonplace, even exceptional (the second ascent of the difficult **Pacific Ocean Wall** was done by Australians). By the 80's four new routes were established on El Cap by foreigners, two by the Spanish Gallegos brothers, and two that included Australian Greg Child.

Since Royal Robbins first soloed El Cap in 1968, perhaps half the El Cap routes have seen solo ascents. Jim Dunn was the first to solo a new route, **Cosmos**, in 1972. Later that year, Charlie Porter soled two new routes. In the last ten years another four solo routes have been established.

While the walls were being assailed and as the available store of big, blank rock in need of a route was running out, free climbing underwent the same development of standards seen elsewhere in the country during the period. With the move toward thinner crack systems that accompanied the search for virgin territory, standards were forced to rise. The tentative acceptance of gym chalk, tincture of benzoin, and protection nuts helped crystalize the common perception that rock climbing was not as much in search of a summit as it was a gymnastic activity. In the early 70's, in the "granite gymnasium," this attitude presented hundreds of opportunities. Supple, smooth-soled shoes allowed better use of thin cracks, and their superior smearing capabilities were a boon to the developing face climbs. But development of nut protection probably did more for the rise in free-climbing standards than any other technological advance. With nuts, and particularly nuts that would work in Yosemite's parallel-sided cracks, protection could be placed quickly, non- violently, and with one hand. At first, the use of nuts and the climbing of First All-Nut Ascents, was an event in itself, with a "Nutbook" recording all these events; practically all the classic walls of the 60's received first (and sometimes last) all nut ascents. The climbs on the Nuts Only Wall date from this period. The development of more sophisticated crack protection has paralleled the increasing standards of the sport. Ray Jardine's Friends, introduced in 1978, were matched perhaps in their impact on the climbing scene only by the Chouinard stoppers of 1972 and Polycentrics a couple years later. The 1980's see many alternative devices for use in the parallel-sided cracks of Yosemite.

Coincidental to the late 60's and early 70's development of the 5.10 standard was the change from the clunky kletterschuhe to the supple E.B. For the next dozen years this shoe was standard footwear for all Yosmite free climbing. The development in the last five years of newer "sticky rubber" climbing shoes has had perhaps the biggest effect on the Valley's face climbs. Some Apron routes are significantly easier with the new shoes, perhaps an improvement equal to the break made in about 1970 from edging the Apron climbs to frictioning them.

Jim Bridwell was by 1970 the moving force on the free-climbing scene. While he had always demonstrated an extraordinary ability during his apprenticeship under Pratt and Sacherer in the 60's, by 1970 he had moved out on his own, cleaning massive amounts of dirt and vegetation from routes that have since become classic, including **Gripper, New Dimensions, Butterfingers** and **Outer Limits.** Other climbers got into the act and pushed the standards, most notably Barry Bates on **Lunatic Fringe, Center of Independence, Vanishing Point,** and **Five and Dime,** and Rik Rieder on **Paradise Lost, Chain Reaction,** and **A Mother's Lament.** Bridwell's partner on many of his early 70's free climbs was Mark Klemens, whose talent for off-width cracks led to **Steppin' Out, Cream,** and ultimately **Basket Case.** Peter Haan combined technical difficulty with bold climbing when he free climbed the **Left Side of the Hourglass,** a route well respected even today. Under the wing of Bridwell, younger aspiring climbers were encouraged to push themselves up harder and harder routes. One of the earliest and most talented partners Bridwell brought out was Mark Chapman, who lead his way up some of the hardest climbs of the early 70's, including **Hotline,** the coveted first ascent of the **Nabisco Wall,** and the freeing of **La Escuela,** the first Yosemite climb with two 5.11 pitches. Bridwell's "Brave New World," as he titled a 1973 article, involved climbers beyond just the resident Yosemite community. Easterner Steve Wunsch was active over many years, on routes such as **Orangutan Arch,** and with Barry Bates, on **New Dimensions.** The visit by Henry Barber in 1973 shook up the somewhat tightknit Yosemite community with his firey ascent of **Butterballs** (creating Yosemite's hardest testpiece), an unroped and rapid climb of the **Steck-Salathé,** and his energetic stacking of such classics as **New Dimensions, Nabisco Wall,** and **Midterm** into a single day. Jim Donini pushed standards to a new high in 1974 with his multi-fall effort on **Overhang Overpass,** a route made all the more remarkable considering the parallel-sided crack and the crude nuts of the day. Barber returned in 1975 to produce a new standard with the **Fish Crack,** a route difficult to protect even today, and still well respected at 5.12b. More frequently, visitors to the Valley were climbing well enough to contribute routes of a good standard. England's Pete Livesey was particularly active, with first free ascents of **Crack-a-Go-Go,** in 1974, and **Moratorium,** in 1975.

By 1974 Bridwell presided loosely over a spontaneous group of young California climbers. Known as the Stonemasters, this group was the mainspring behind much of the incredible new route activity that followed over the next five years. Amid the talents of John Bachar, Dale Bard, Mark Chapman, Mike Graham, Ron Kauk, John Long, Tobin Sorenson, Kevin Worrall, John Yablonski, and others, Bridwell was no longer the top dog; he went from the sharp end of the rope to a role of director, but as such was instrumental in the establishment of some of the best routes of the time: **Hot Line,** the right side of the **Folly, Geek Towers,** and **Crucifix.** Even Bridwell's ten- year experience with the changing scene did not prepare him for the speed with which new routes were evolving. After the first ascent of **Hot Line** in 1973, Bridwell predicted with some force that the 15 feet of aid would last at least ten years; two years later Ron Kauk and John Bachar climbed the route totally free as one of the first 5.12 routes. The Stonemasters did much throughout the mid 1970's to solidify the 5.11 grade and to develop what are now hailed as classic routes. Ron Kauk emerged as perhaps the dominant figure on the free-climbing scene for the next ten years; his flash ascent of **Butterballs** and climbs like **Blind Faith** and

Kauk-ulator solidified hard climbing in an uncomplicated style. While not climbing at the extreme level of Kauk or Bachar, Chapman and Kevin Worrall unearthed a host of obscure yet classic routes, including **Windfall** and **Beggar's Buttress.** Many others were also active up through the mid-70's: Vern Clevenger, Chris Falkenstein, Ed Barry, Werner Braun and Rick Sylvester.

In 1976 and 1977 Ray Jardine made quite an impact on the free- climbing scene, though with controversial methods. Unlike the style that had evolved with most other climbers in Yosemite, where the failing leader would lower (yo-yo) to the last no-hands rest between attempts, Jardine would openly rest on protection to work out the moves. He distinguished between a "flash" ascent (climbing on sight from bottom to top without resort to any form of aid – either resting or falling on protection) and a "free" ascent (where the climb was lead from the bottom to top – albeit after much rehearsal – without falls or resting on protection). He searched out extreme problems to work on, and over the course of many days he would get in shape, rest on protection, and get a little bit higher each time. Eventually, he would be able to lead the climb from bottom to top without resorting to a rest – his "free" ascent. Throughout this time Jardine was fortunate to have many Friends along – the world supply of these protection devices was solely and secretly his – and they were of immeasureable help on his characteristically long endurance problems. In fact, on **Elephant's Eliminate**, the flared crack was unprotectable without the devices. Jardine's most difficult routes, **Hangdog Flyer, Crimson Cringe, Rostrum Roof, Elephant's Eliminate**, and **Phoenix** were among the hardest routes done at the time. **Phoenix**, climbed in 1977 at 5.13, remains one of the hardest Yosemite testpieces. As belayer for many of Jardine's efforts, John Lakey got in a good bit of climbing on these extreme routes himself, and in a curious twist of fate, was the first to manage the 5.12 **Owl Roof** when the team gave that longstanding problem a try in 1977. Jardine's style of climbing on these routes was perhaps not as close to his "flash" ideal as other leading climbers might have done (John Bachar flashed the second ascent of the **Cringe**, without Friends, soon after the first ascent), but it can be said that he simply altered in degree the means by which many of the most difficult ascents of the last 15 years were done; the main difference was his wiring of the moves by continuing to climb after resting on protection, in preparation for a final "free" ascent. It should be noted that during the period of these difficult ascents Jardine was prolifically making excellent new routes of a lower standard – "flashed", or at least climbed with only minimal compromising of that standard – throughout the Valley, from the base of Washington Column, the Ribbon Falls amphitheatre, to Elephant Rock. After the remarkable free ascent with Bill Price up the **West Face of El Cap** in 1979, he turned his attention to free climbing the **Nose**, and through misguided and inexcusable action chiseled face holds in several spots to enable him to climb to Camp Four. It was later apparent that some "hold hacking" had been done on some of his earlier routes.

Other climbers were active at pushing the 5.12 standard with more conventional tactics. As mentioned elsewhere, Henry Barber was the first to introduce 5.12 to the Valley, in 1975. Ron Kauk climbed the intimidating **Tales of Power** in 1977, the dramatic **Separate Reality** in 1978, as well as more recent contributions, such as **Back to the Future**, in 1986. Many other climbers were active at the top levels, including John Bachar, Dale Bard, Bill Price and Tony Yaniro. By 1980 Price had established a solid 5.13 with **Cosmic Debris.** During the last five years many of the world's best climbers have come through Yosemite, but most active establishing high- standard routes have been Dimitri Barton, Werner Braun, Rick Cashner, Scott Cosgrove, Peter Croft, Ron Kauk, Steve Schneider, and Jonny Woodward. Unquestionably it has been left to local John Bachar to push the standards on the free climbing scene. Bachar has sought to counter the extreme hangdogging that has characterized much of the hardest climbing elsewhere (styles further removed from Jardine's old "flash" ascents than Jardine's himself!) by establishing difficult routes in unpreviewed fashion and doing bold routes that do not allow compromises of style. **The Believer**, at 5.12, steep and runout, is characteristic of his best routes. The 5.13 **Phantom**, climbed in 1986, is as much a testpiece because of its move difficulty as the traditional style in which it was first ascended.

Many others have been prolifically establishing quality routes over the last five years, including Ken Ariza, Scott Burke, Dave Hatchett, Grant Hiskes, Bruce Morris, Don Reid, Walt Shipley, Dave Schultz, Kurt Smith.

Third classing of difficult routes is a theme that has accompanied the history of Yosemite climbing. Since the late 60's, when Royal Robbins showcased his boldness with solo ascents of contemporary testpieces such as **Reed's Direct**, various climbers have occasionally sought out difficult routes to free solo. Mark

John Bachar,
New Dimensions, 1982.
Phil Bard

Klemens first soloed the **Left Side of Reed's**; Peter Haan followed with **Crack of Despair.** Henry Barber's on-sight solo of the **Steck-Salathé** in 1973 clearly set a new standard in unroped climbing. This was followed by Earl Wiggins up the two pitches of **Outer Limits** in 1974, and probably the boldest solo of the 1970's: Charlie Fowler, in a remarkable on-sight solo of a circuitous route, the **Direct North Buttress** of Middle Cathedral Rock in 1974. John Bachar climbed the familiar but 5.11 **New Dimensions** in 1976, and later that year cruised up more familiar territory on the **Nabisco Wall** via **Butterballs.** In 1980, Bachar made the hardest climb in Yosemite yet soloed on sight, the 5.11b **Moratorium.** Peter Croft has been active, soloing many of the 60's classics in remarkable bursts of energy; on a more ambitious day he soloed the **North Buttress of Middle Cathedral Rock**, the **Northeast Buttress of Higher Cathedral Rock, Steck- Salathé, Royal Arches, North Dome**, and **Arrowhead Arête**. In 1986, German Wolfgang Gullich free soloed **Separate Reality**. In the 80's, many of the classic 5.10 testpieces of 15 to 20 years ago serve as training ground for Valley regulars, and as medium for gaining a lot of ground fast, as if doing laps in a pool.

Another recurrent theme that has expressed itself sporadically throughout the last 20 years of Yosemite climbing has centered around speed ascents of the big walls. Eric Beck and Frank Sacherer stunned the 1965 Yosemite community with their one-day climb of the **West Face of Sentinel**, the first time a Grade VI had seen a one-day ascent, and this without Jümars. This was followed a year later when Steve Roper and Jeff Foott climbed the **Northwest Face of Half Dome** in a day. Since the late 60's, when Kim Schmitz and Jim Madsen were halving the standard times on the classic 60's walls, climbing the **Nose** in a day had been an unspoken goal; Bridwell teamed up with John Long and Billy Westbay in 1975 to do just that. Since then many of the walls have seen very quick ascents, culminating in an extraordinary day in 1986 when John Bachar and Peter Croft climbed both the **Nose** and the **Northwest Face of Half Dome** in 18 hours and 3 minutes.

The mid-70's saw a concentrated effort to reduce or eliminate aid from the big walls. The super-clean **East Face of Washington Column** was a natural target of free-climbing efforts. While it saw several attempts by 1974, the route went totally free to John Long, Ron Kauk, and John Bachar in 1975. A year later Kauk returned, leading all the pitches in a no-falls ascent, a feat repeated by Bachar a short time later. **Astro Man**, as the line was renamed, provided the most sustained free climb yet produced in Yosemite, and even today remains as one of the very best free climbs in the world. While the beauty of **Astro Man** directed many to the resource of big aid routes that lined the Valley, it was clear that free climbing on the walls demanded an incredible energy; **Astro Man** had produced twice as many hard pitches as any other route at the time.

While free climbers had attacked various parts of the **Nose** of El Cap over the years (Jim Bridwell and Jim Stanton had freed the Stovelegs as early as 1968, leaving a climb popular in itself for a few years), it was ripe in 1975 for a team to climb the route with free climbing as a primary objective. John Bachar, Ron Kauk, and Dale Bard succeeded in freeing all but 400 feet of the 3,000-foot wall. In efforts ranging over a period of several years, Coloradans Jim Erickson and Art Higbee finally free climbed the classic **Northwest Face of Half Dome** in 1976.

By 1979, with free climbing being the preferred mode of ascent throughout the continent (Colorado's walls were falling fast to the free climbers), El Cap finally saw a totally free ascent with Bill Price and Ray Jardine's climb of the **West Face**. This was particularly remarkable in that the free route turned out to be surprisingly moderate compared to the standard of the time.

The **North Face of the Rostrum** saw much development and several free routes. John Long and various partners freed the classic **Chouinard-Herbert** route up Sentinel Rock, and John Bachar and Mike Lechlinski free climbed all but six aid moves of the **West Face**. Max Jones and Mark Hudon were particularly active by the late 70's; the pair completely freed the classic **North Face Route on East Quarter Dome**, at 5.12, producing **Pegasus**, and soon after freed all but seven aid moves on the **South Face of Mt. Watkins**, also at 5.12.

Similar to the **Nose** as an attractive free prospect, much of the remaining aid on the **Salathé Wall** had been eliminated over the years, starting with a free connection from the first pitch of the **Nose** to the **Salathé's** Half Dollar by Kevin Worrall and Mike Graham, during which Graham showed some audacity and created controversy by chopping the original Robbins bolt ladder. Later, John Long freed the third-pitch roof and with a gang Stonemaster effort the route was freed to Mammoth Terraces, creating the **Free Blast**. Five years later Max Jones and Mark Hudon continued the theme higher on the wall and except for the Hollow Flake pendulum, pushed the route free all the way to two pitches above El Cap Spire. The trend to free climb on the walls continued with the 1982 free ascent (aside from a short bolt ladder) of the **Gold Wall** going to Rick Cashner and Werner Braun (the free variation renamed **Silent Line**), and in 1986, the freeing by Braun and Scott Cosgrove of the Ribbon Falls **West Portal** and the **Northeast Corner of Higher Cathedral Rock**.

As the free-climbing revolution developed in the 70's, it became clearer that the potential for difficult new routes was not limited to crack climbs. With some minor exceptions (the **Snake Dike** and **Peanut**, among others), face and slab climbing had traditionally been the domain of Glacier Point Apron, where since the 1960's bolts had been placed to protect the wandering slab climbing. The 70's saw incredible development on the Apron, in large part due to the advent of friction shoes. The main participants in the early 70's included Mike Breidenbach, Vern Clevenger, Tim Harrison, and Rik Reider (who with Rabb Carrington produced in 1972 the most difficult and serious face route for the next seven or eight years – **A Mother's Lament**). By the late 70's, Bruce Morris and Chris Cantwell were attacking the right side of the Apron, producing many short but worthwhile routes. Unfortunately, many of the leading aficionados of Apron climbing have elected a boldless use of the bolt. In search of another route to the top of Glacier Point, in 1980 Cantwell, Morris, Scott Burke, and Dave Austin completed work on a line that accomplished just that. Called the **Hall of Mirrors**, it involved several bolt ladders that have doubtfully been as free as reported. The 1980's have seen further route development, but with the introduction of the new high-friction shoes, any routes of significance in the future must show far greater boldness.

While face climbing has always been a means to reaching otherwise inaccessible crack routes, the early 70's saw a burgeoning interest in face routes, somewhat the result of so many local climbers with active pasts at Tahquitz and Suicide Rocks, in Southern California. Routes up the slabs of the Royal Arches, while tentatively explored as early as 1958, with the freeing of **Arches Terrace**, were climbed seriously in 1973 with **Shakey Flakes**, followed the next year with **Greasy but Groovy**, by Tahquitz veterans John Long, Rick Accomazzo, and Richard Harrison. Other routes have been added subsequently, most notably **Friday the 13th**, a serious route put up in 1985 by Dimitri Barton and Scott Burke. The early 70's face revolution was fueled in large part by the legacy Frank Sacherer left with his 1960's climbs on the incredibly free climbable Cathedral Rocks: **East Buttress, DNB**, and **Sacherer-Fredericks.** Ray Jardine and Rik Reider were among the first to see the possibilities with their 1972 route, **Paradise Lost**. They were followed quickly by a small group that included John Long, George Meyers, and Kevin Worrall, who were primarily responsible for major face routes that often had a seriousness not found on the hard crack

Kevin Worrall, Middle Cathedral Rock, 1975

climbs. **Stoner's Highway**, **Black Primo**, **Quicksilver**, and the freeing of the **Bircheff-Williams** were products of this time. Ron Kauk and Kevin Worrall teamed up in 1977 to create the excellent and serious **Space Babble**. The 18-pitch **Mother Earth**, climbed in 1976, showed the possible quality and length of Middle Rock free climbing, a potential that was realized again in 1984 with the **Smith-Crawford**. In 1976 enthusiasm for the steep face poured over onto Lower Cathedral Rock, where Richard Harrison, Rick Accomazzo, and John Yablonski established serious routes that ten years later have yet to see second ascents.

Face climbing is found throughout the Valley, and the last ten years have seen short testpieces show up on practically every cliff. Scott Burke, Bruce Morris, Steve Schneider, and others have been active in establishing good face routes. North Dome and, particularly, Half Dome have rewarded many face climbers of the last few years with excellent routes that are long, clean, and difficult. Several routes have been done on the face near the classic 1965 **Snake Dike.** Most impressive is the 12- pitch **Autobahn,** done by Charles Cole, Rusty Reno, and John Middendorf in 1985, and next to it, the **Fast Lane.** But the most striking of the 1980's face lines is **Karma,** a 13-pitch route that weaves a difficult course up the broad south face of Half Dome to the right of the Harding/Rowell aid line. First climbed in 1986 by Dave Schultz, Ken Yager, and Jim Campbell, its 74 bolts protect 5.11+ face climbing up a series of steep dikes, connected with only short sections of aid.

As the most difficult new crack lines have gotten thinner, it is perhaps somewhat inevitable that they share many of the characteristics of steep face climbing, but with the more visible line and protection that a crack provides. Since on many of the modern testpieces natural protection is supplemented and sometimes completely replaced with bolts, they require an inordinate amount of energy to establish, and the style in which protection is arranged has become the subject of debate.

With many climbers in year-round residence, climbing activity has occurred year round. In 1974 some of the temporarily frozen waterfalls saw ascents by those too impoverished to travel. The first to receive an ascent was the upper part of **Sentinel Falls,** a four pitch, sometimes vertical, ice route, climbed by Mark Chapman, Kevin Worrall, and Jim Orey in late 1974. With Worrall's first ice experience behind him, and Chapman's inexperience bettered, the following February they launched up the frozen **Widow's Tears,** which luckily remained frozen long enough for the 11-pitch ascent. Other ascents of **Sentinel Falls** have followed off and on over the years, but the Widow's Tears has seen fewer climbers, due as much to the infrequent buildup of ice as to the seriousness of the route. In 1976, ice built up enough to allow Chapman, Worrall, and Pete Minks an ascent of the **Silver Strand,** a smooth sheet of ice that occasionally flows around the wall west of the **Widow's Tears.** Charlie Porter climbed a couple of chutes and gullies in the Valley in 1973, and a few minor routes have been done by others. In 1987 an ascent was made of the lower **Sentinel Falls.** The 80's now see many parties primed to take advantage of the proper conditions of cold and wetness which can produce incredible possibilities.

The lifestyle and state of the committed resident climber of Yosemite is no better exemplified than by Werner Braun. Braun has repeated many of the harder climbs over and over, refining his technique and flow with a driven furvor. By 1987, he had climbed **Astro Man** 27 times, the last nine times in an eight- month period. Short routes like **Outer Limits, Meat Grinder, Lunatic Fringe,** and **Five and Dime** he has climbed 50 times or more, often times third class, clearly demonstrating in near perfect, efficient motion the closest match of rock and the climbing man. Braun also exemplifies a clean style of climbing that is Yosemite's heritage. He disdains hanging on protection, yet is active in the exploration of the hidden gems that seem to be a constant resource of Yosemite. This is a man who simply loves the motion of rock climbing in a beautiful place.

Perhaps no other route demonstrates the progression of Yosemite climbing better than the **Steck-Salathé.** After the frustrations of numerous parties and finally a 5-day ordeal, Allen Steck and John Salathé earned the summit of Sentinel Rock on a July day in 1950; their climb became a classic. Robbins made the second ascent in three days, and during the course of the 60's the route was whittled down to a totally free, three- hour climb. In 1973 Henry Barber stepped into a new realm of commitment by climbing the **Steck-Salathé** on sight and unroped (though with the aid of a 25-foot sling at the crux move). Today, on-sight free-solo ascents of this 5.9 route by committed climbers are not uncommon. Similar episodes echo throughout the Valley on routes like the **Northeast Buttress of Higher Cathedral Rock, Yosemite Point Buttress,** and the **East Buttress of El Cap.** The **North Face of the Rostrum,** first aid climbed over a period of days, next climbed clean, then free climbed at 5.11, was free soloed after rehearsal by Peter Croft in a couple of hours.

Different stages of evolution exist for different routes. There are climbs yet unseen by the climber's eye. Who will free-solo the **East Face of Washington's Column?** Can an all-free way be found up the sweeping South Buttress of El Capitan (**The Nose**) or **Salathé** without rock desecration? The **West Face of Sentinel** was climbed in a day long ago, climbed clean a dozen years ago, yet a segment on the fifth pitch has barred a host of top free climbing talent from an all-free ascent. Aside from simply technical prowess, the best of Yosemite climbing has always involved some degree of audacity and daring: the early explorations of Anderson and Bayley, the 1934 ascents of the Cathedral Spires, Salathé on the **Lost Arrow** and Sentinel, Harding's vision on the **Nose,** the adventurous first ascent of the **Salathé Wall,** and the bold efforts of Pratt and Sacherer. These events were followed by Jim Dunn on **Cosmos,** Barber alone on the **Steck-Salathé,** the winter climb of the **Widow's Tears,** the audacious routefinding of **Karma** and the remarkable free solos of John Bachar. Will the future development of climbing standards depend on these traditions of stylistic boldness?

Climbers have always accompanied their outreach to higher standards and newer climbs with a bending of the commonly accepted rules of the game. Even as early as the ascent of the Nose, older climbers had disdain for the number of bolts that were used in that ascent. In 1961 Robbins (who had always preached that bolts would or could destroy climbing by overuse or thoughtless use) used 13 bolts on the **Salathé Wall.** By 1969 he had put up a route two-thirds the size (**Tis- sa-ack**) with 110 bolts. He justified it by saying that it was a "route worth bolting for" – and one that would eventually be climbed. (If Robbins had been told in 1961 that he would someday do a 20-pitch route with 110 bolts he would surely have denied any such thing.) In the 70's Bridwell and others innovated aid climbing with the use of the chisel and copperhead. Robbins never would have considered this, having once said that he felt that 20 routes on El Cap would be about right. Now, thanks to new, non-"traditonal" techniques, there are three times that number. Jardine used extreme hangdogging so he could climb above his ability and accomplish his climbing goals. Bachar began using aid to place bolts on free climbs (in Tuolumne), an unheard-of tactic that Bob Kamps and Tom Higgins (who themselves had bent earlier rules a bit by their use of bolts) never used, but which opened up much otherwise unprotectable rock. (Bachar now eschewed that technique as too compromised.)

Now we are left to wonder just how far the free climbers of tommorrow will bend the rules to accomplish their goals. In most other areas hangdogging is the most popular means to getting up extreme climbs. More and more bolts are being placed on rappel. How will the Yosemite climber deal with these new ethical dilemmas? Is there a chance that the inevitable evolution will result not only in higher standards of technical difficulty, but in higher standards of boldness and imagination as well, a tradition that has its roots with the earliest Yosemite pioneers?

Morgan Harris, Lower Brother, 1937. *David Brower*

FREE CLIMBING STYLES AND ETHICS

Yosemite has a longstanding tradition of bold and innovative climbers; clearly there have been individuals who have stepped outside generally accepted climbing styles. Aside from issues of credibility and personal integrity that surface when a climber misrepresents his particular means of success, the issues of climbing style is nobody's business but the climber's own – until that style affects the ethical traditions that have their roots in the history of Yosemite climbing.

Ethics concern other climbers. Ethical rules protect the best efforts of the climbers who have gone before us, and protect the rock for the climbers who will come after us. What follows is a short account of the ethical traditions of Yosemite.

1. Keep the cliffs clean of trash. Used tape, cans, and old rappel slings have no place littering the base of the rock. The use of the Park is a privilege that is jeopardized in no greater way than by climber litter.

2. Do not chisel new holds on the rock. Chiseling hurts everyone and is a permanent eyesore. Chiseled holds are a record of your unsportsmanship and disrespect for the rock.

3. Do not add bolts to existing routes. If a route does not have enough bolts for your liking, then the route is too hard for you. Protection is a form of difficulty. Existing climbs should never be brought down to the level of the climber; rather the climber should raise himself to the standard of the climb. (Old bolts should be replaced only by drawing the defunct bolt from the hole, deepening and/or widening the hole, and placing a new bolt.)

4. Similarly, do not add or use pitons on a route that has been done "clean" or "hammerless." Someone who does a route without pitons has proven that it is humanly possible to ascend that particular route without permanent damage to the rock. If you can not do the route to the clean standards established, you should retreat and come back another day when you are capable of doing the route clean.

5. Bolts should be placed on first ascents only, on sight and on the lead. Bolts placed on rappel or on the lead after rehearsal or previewing may be unfairly placed for a party to repeat in an on-sight situation, particularly when "runouts" are constructed into the route. Yosemite tradition has always held that the only legitimate ascent is one made from the ground up. Come back another day, week, month, or year when you are a better climber and can ascend the route, instead of descending the route first and lowering the climb to your level, by preplacing bolts or rehearsing in order to be able to lead it.

The personal style that a climber adopts in seeking success on the free routes is ultimately only the concern of the climber. However, in an effort to facilitate communication among climbers, the following list defines some of the means by which the tops of climbs are reached.

Flashing: climbing a route from bottom to top without resorting to physical aid of any sort – no resting on protection; no falls. Also known as redpoint.

On sight: climbing without prior hands-on knowledge of a route.

Alpine style: climbing a route from bottom to top, without previewing, rehearsal, or sieging.

Yo-yo: using the rope by any means to fall, lower to rest, switch leaders.

Previewing: gaining close up knowledge of a route prior to an ascent, usually

by rappel or previous aid ascent.
Rehearsal: having prior experience on the route, through previous attempts or ascents.
Pre-placed protection: protection placed on aid, either by rappel or from an aid ascent.
Sieging: working on a climb over a period of days, leaving equipment fixed overnight.

RATINGS

FREE RATINGS

The Yosemite Decimal System is used throughout this guide. Developed at Tahquitz Rock in the early 1950's and applied to great extent in Yosemite, the decimal ratings found in the Valley represent the standards by which climbs thoughout the country are compared. With the continuing rise of free climbing standards, the Decimal System has ceased to be strictly decimal, and instead reflects the open-ended nature of free climbing possibilities. Today there are routes of 5.10, 5.11, 5.12 and so on, but in the early 70's, the top grade, 5.10, was considered by many to be too broad in scope, describing routes that were as varied in difficulty as 5.7 was from 5.9. Consequently, a "subgrading" system was promoted by Jim Bridwell to further delineate between the "easiest" 5.10 and the "hardest" 5.10. This system was widely accepted and today the upper rock climbing grades will often show an a, b, c, or d suffix that further defines the difficulty. An effort was also made at that time to establish a standard for the various grades. The following list represents routes by which others may be graded. Similar to the first 5.10 in the Valley, **Crack of Doom**, the first 5.11, **New Dimensions**, cannot be downgraded.

5.10a **Sacherer Cracker**
5.10b **Vendetta, Gripper**
5.10c **Meat Grinder, Lunatic Fringe**
5.10d **The Folly, Right Side, Vanishing Point**
5.11a **New Dimensions**
5.11b **Orangutan Arch, Anticipation**
5.11c **Butterballs**
5.11d **Energy Crisis**
5.12a **Hot Line**
5.12b **Fish Crack, Tales of Power**
5.12c **Owl Roof**
5.12d **Elephant's Eliminate**
5.13a **Cosmic Debris**

These represent pitch ratings. Yosemite has usually addressed the difficulty of its continuously strenuous cracks as a pitch-by-pitch problem, not one of move-by-move. Thus an incredibly sustained route like **Meat Grinder**, which holds no single move over 5.9 in difficulty (and few under), is rated 5.10c. Some topo pitches in this book show several ratings; this usually is an effort to more accurately show the continuousness of the (most often, face) climbing. Face and slab climbs have evolved to be rated the difficulty of their hardest move, regardless of how sustained the pitch is. Such are the vagaries of the Yosemite Decimal System. There is, however, some interest among Yosemite-ites in applying two ratings to some pitches, one for the move difficulty, the other for the pitch as a whole. (For example, **Butterballs** would be rated as 5.10c/5.11c. The first rates the hardest move; the second the overall difficulty.) While this could take some time to implement without confusion, the system would certainly define the scope of the climbing.

The Decimal System gives no information on the protection possibilities for a climb. This is left to the leader to ascertain on the lead. As a rule, on the crack climbs you are climbing your source of protection. On the face and slab routes, you must rely more on your ability to judge the terrain ahead of you.

AID RATINGS

The aid ratings of Yosemite are unlike the free grades in that they reflect both technical placement difficulty and how a pitch is protected. It is a closed rating system that reflects difficulty only in terms of security and does not take into account the incredible advances in aid climbing technology. Thus the A5 climber of 1965 could find the A5 climb of today well beyond reach without modern tools. In addition, the advent of better belay technology has given the modern climber a boldness to risk longer and longer falls. A broad selection of hooks, Friends and the like (useful for expanding flakes) supplement the more traditional knifeblades and rurps, and a chisel seems to be a standard tool to prepare slots for tiny malleable copperheads and alumi-heads.

Other than technical changes, A1 placements still hold trucks, A2 is more difficult to place and holds less, and A3 will hold a short fall. A4 holds only body weight and A5 entails enough A4 placements to risk a good 50- or 60-foot fall. The amount of stress that the belay would undergo in the event of a fall affects the aid rating. Any A4 climbing where a fall would endanger the climber is A5. Thus A5 may reflect a single difficult aid move 30 feet above a ledge or a long string of A4 placements. Given all this, there is general disagreement on how different situations are rated, particularly on the harder routes; the ratings in the topos may reflect these variations. Thus, A1 may be a #1 stopper in a good crack or handrail hook placements, and A5 may present a 300 foot fall potential.

Traditionally, a part of the route rating was the so-called overall grade, expressed as a Roman Numeral from I to VI. This was based on factors of commitment, difficulty, ease of escape, and length of the route. It is not widely used these days except to differentiate between a Grade V (a very long day or one overnight) and a Grade VI (hard, long and generally taking three or more days for the average party). In topo form the route descriptions speak for themselves.

CLIMBING THE WALLS

Yosemite is known for cliffs that are clean and beautifully sheer, big and plentiful. El Capitan and Half Dome are familiar to climbers the world over for their sculptured and dramatic rises of 3,000 and 2,000 feet respectively. Throughout the Valley are dozens of sheer faces that rise over 1,200 vertical feet, some in fact still unclimbed. Ascents of these big walls usually involve aid techniques, methods that are neither fast nor uncomplicated. No one appreciates the size of El Cap more than one who has spent days climbing it. The fledgling wall climber may find, however, that technical climbing prowess counts less for success than tenacity.

Aside from the cautions expressed above, the climber unfamiliar with wall-climbing techniques can prepare for an El Cap or Half Dome route in several ways. One-pitch aid climbs are sprinkled throughout the book. Pitches like **Pink Pussycat, Kat Pinnacle, Coffin Nail, Sun Blast,** and **El Cap Tree** allow the beginning aid climber to sort out the basics of artificial climbing. One can work out the needed organization for belay switches, hauling and cleaning on a small route where, with some tenacity, even a slow, fumbling effort can find the top. The more popular examples of this kind of route are **Washington Column's South Face**, or **South Central, Liberty Cap's Southwest Face Route**, and the **West Face of the Leaning Tower**. On routes requiring hanging bivouacs, the comfort of the state-of-the-art folding platform beds (Cliff Dwellings) is blissful.

Pitons are still in common use for the walls, though sophisticated nuts and Friends form the backbone of the aid rack. The newer routes usually require more specialized gear and more extensive piton racks. Walls that have seen much free climbing can usually be protected without resorting to pitons. Routes like the **Nose, Northwest Face of Half Dome**, and **Salathé** should be respected as pitonless climbs. It is wise to carry a few copperheads and certainly a selection of hooks when venturing away from the trade routes. A bolt kit is recommended as a precaution on all walls; self rescue is always the preferred escape, but seek retreat before blasting a way up a route that is too difficult for you. Keyhole bolt hangers, dowel and rivet hangers, and sometimes even a laddered extendable "cheater stick" are essential for using the hangerless bolts, rivets, and dowels of the newer routes. Hardware lists in this book that refer to "all hooks" require large diameter hooks based on the old ring-angle claw, like the currently produced Fish Hook. In an attempt to keep the rock resource alive a little longer, a minimal use of copperhead chiseling is urged.

From the standpoint of fighting litter, it is imperative to carry down what is carried up. Old slings, wads of tape, and assorted wall trash found at the base of obscure and remote cliffs discredit the notion that climbers are actively respectful of the natural environment. Few issues threaten the climbers' freedom as seriously as littering. Officially, Park Service policy says that anything above 4,200 feet is wilderness and everything that is carried in should be packed out. Practically, paper bags are of use to throw excrement off the wall, though the better answer is to seek a toilet spot off route that will let the shit break up before it hits the ground. It pays to be the highest party on a route, but try to balance concern for the party below with the horrendous litter at the base of some routes.

Due to the need to protect the nesting habitat of the peregrine falcon, the routes on El Cap from **Pacific Ocean** inclusive to **Tangerine Trip** are off limits to climbing from January 1 to August 1.

Some Recommended Wall Routes

El Capitan, Lurking Fear
El Capitan, Excalibur
El Capitan, Son of Heart
El Capitan, Shield
El Capitan, Muir Wall
El Capitan, Salathé Wall
El Capitan, Nose
El Capitan, Mescalito
El Capitan, Pacific Ocean Wall

El Capitan, Zodiac
Lost Arrow Direct
Washington Column, The Prow
Mt. Watkins, South Face Route
Mt. Watkins, Bob Locke Memorial Buttress
Quarter Domes, North Face Route
Half Dome, Regular Northwest Face
Half Dome, Direct Northwest Face
Half Dome, Tis-sa-ack
Half Dome, South Face Route
Liberty Cap, Southwest Face Route
Leaning Tower, West Face Route

FREE CLIMBING

Most climbers first come to Yosemite for the big aid routes, but ninety percent of them spend ninety percent of their time free climbing. Within the seven square miles of the Valley are cliffs that provide a wide variety of climbing experiences. Arch Rock, the Cookie, and Reed's Pinnacle area have short steep crack climbing. The cliffs around Cascade Falls abound in knobs ("chickenheads") so big and plentiful that runners are particularly useful for protection. The Royal Arches provide high-angle slab climbing on sharp flakes; North Dome and Half Dome provide high-angle face climbing on crystals and dikes. Glacier Point Apron boasts the world's best low angle – and occasionally not so gentle – friction climbing. Face climbing on steep, beautiful, and compact rock is found in the complicated and pristine setting of the Cathedral Rocks. Elephant Rock is split by long, vertical crack and chimney systems. The big walls provide some of the best free climbing in Yosemite. The **Nose**, **Salathé**, and the **West Face of El Cap** hold some of the steepest and longest free climbs anywhere. **Astro Man**, the **Rostrum**, **Crucifix**, **West Face of El Cap**, and the **ABC Lost Arrow Route** are among the great free-climbing challenges in the world.

Yosemite's free climbs are often characterized by parallel-sided cracks, so Friends, Tri-cams, Quickies, and the like are particularly useful. Most climbers carry as a standard rack a selection of Rocks to ½", some medium to large Hexentrics, and Friends to perhaps a #4. Small wires and RP's are useful on many climbs, particularly the face climbs. Tube chocks and super-sized Friends may be necessary to protect off- width cracks. Only the confidence of familiarity will protect the long moderate chimneys sometimes encountered. Fixed pitons exist on some of the slab routes, but assume that they are worthless, or carry a hammer to test them, since practically no one else does. Rock shoes with some torsional flexibility seem to work best for crack routes, while face routes naturally require more precision. A shoe with a flat toe is nice for thin cracks. Many climbers will gain jamming skills using adhesive tape to protect their hands against rough rock and/or poor technique. Tincture of benzoin helps hold the tape in place. Rolls of cloth tape can be purchased at the Mountain Shop. Chalk is commonly used everywhere in the Valley.

Some Recommended Free Climbs

The following is a list of free-climbing routes that the first-time visitor to Yosemite may find useful. Short and easy climbs are not plentiful in Yosemite, but the Cascades, (pages 64-66), Knob Hill (page 74), and Manure Pile

Buttress (page 175) contain enough to get started. An assertive approach, coupled with frequent conditioning on the boulders and top-rope problems will ensure fast progress to the harder and better- quality routes.

SHORT ROUTES

Anticipation 5.11b
Midterm 5.10b
Gripper 5.10b
New Dimensions 5.11a
Back to the Future 5.12a
Outer Limits 5.10b
Meat Grinder 5.10c
Nabisco Wall 5.11c
Cookie Center 5.9
Vendetta 5.10b
New Diversions 5.9
Separate Reality 5.11d
Phantom 5.13a
Reed's Pinnacle 5.8-5.10a
Lunatic Fringe 5.10c
Catch-U 5.11b
Little Wing Area 5.7-5.11d
Peter Pan/Peter Left 5.9-5.10c
The Slack 5.10a-5.10c
The Mark of Art 5.10d
La Cosita/Little John 5.7-5.9
Moby Dick 5.9-5.10a
The Believer 5.12a
Champagne on Ice 5.11c
After Six 5.6
Nutcracker 5.8
Essence 5.11b
Rixon's Pinnacle, West Face 5.10c
Stay Free 5.11b
Commitment 5.9
Ten Years After 5.10d
Via Aqua 5.7
Firefingers 5.11b
JoJo 5.10b
Synapse Collapse 5.10a
The Grack 5.7-5.9
The Mouth 5.9
Goodrich Pinnacle, Right Side 5.9
Coonyard Pinnacle 5.9
The Token 5.11d
Overhang Overpass 5.11c
The Thief 5.10d
The Sermon 5.10b

MODERATE LENGTH ROUTES

Slab Happy Pinnacle 5.10b-5.11a
Hawkman's Escape 5.8
The Folly, Right Side 5.10d
Arrowhead Arête 5.8
Royal Arches Route 5.7 A1 or 5.9
Half Dome, Snake Dike 5.7
Half Dome, Salathé Route 5.10b
Hoppy's Favorite 5.10b
Angel's Approach 5.9
Phantom Pinnacle, Left Side 5.9
Lower Cathedral Spire, Regular Route, 5.9
Higher Cathedral Spire, Regular Route 5.9
Higher Cathedral Rock, Braille Book 5.8
Middle Cathedral Rock, Bircheff-Williams 5.11c
Middle Cathedral Rock, Central Pillar 5.10a
Middle Cathedral Rock, North Face Apron 5.9-5.11
Lower Cathedral Rock, East Face Routes 5.10
Return to the Stone Age 5.11
Bridalveil East 5.10c
Trundling Juan 5.10b
Hotline 5.12a
Crack of Despair 5.10a

LONGER ROUTES

Silent Line 5.10c A1
El Capitan, West Face 5.11b
El Capitan, East Buttress 5.10b
Lost Arrow Chimney 5.10a
Greasy But Groovy 5.11a
Astro Man 5.11c
Mt Watkins, South Face Route 5.12 A1
Pegasus 5.12
Half Dome, Northwest Face 5.12
Half Dome, Autobahn, 5.11d
Half Dome, Karma 5.11d A0
Sentinel Rock, Chouinard-Herbert 5.11c
Sentinel Rock, Steck-Salathe 5.9
Sentinel Rock, West Face 5.11d A1
Ochre Fields 5.11a
Hall of Mirrors 5.12
Higher Cathedral Rock, Northeast Buttress 5.9
Higher Cathedral Rock, Crucifix 5.12a
Higher Cathedral Rock, Power Point 5.11d
Middle Cathedral Rock, East Buttress 5.10c
Middle Cathedral Rock, Direct North Buttress 5.10b
Middle Cathedral Rock, Mother Earth (lower half) 5.11d
The Rostrum, North Face 5.12a
The Rostrum, Blind Faith 5.11d

ICE CLIMBING IN THE VALLEY

As mentioned in the history section, there is ice in Yosemite, though how much and how long it lasts depends greatly on the weather. Yosemite Valley is simply too low in elevation to maintain good ice conditions with reliability. The possible exception to this is the upper Sentinel Falls, approached with a long slog up the Four Mile Trail, or with a ski-in from the Badger Pass Ski Area. What usually greets climbers is four good pitches of moderately steep and thick ice. The lower Sentinel Falls has been climbed, but it's formation is sporadic at best. The Widow's Tears is the longest ice route in the Valley, although it may not ice up enough for an ascent but every few years. Similar conditions prevail on the Silver Strand, just around the corner to the west. Other climbs have been done. Thin routes on Glacier Point Apron sometimes ice up, and runnels to the west of Cloud's Rest provide long and moderate routes. The main strategy for climbing Yosemite ice is simply to come up to the Valley when the weather has been cold for a while and look around to see what is iced up; a week later may see all the routes melted out.

ARRANGEMENT AND USE OF THE GUIDE

The routes in this book are arranged in geographical order, starting from the west end of the north side of the Valley. The south side follows, from east to west. The maps of the Valley located at the back of the book locate all the cliff formations. To assist in identifying the climbs on the cliffs, the photos identify the major routes. Occasionally, the photo pages may provide the sole description for obscure routes; in this case the caption will include the rating. On the topo page will be the route name, grade, and any unusual protection needs for the climb. This assumes that a selection of nuts from wired stoppers to something for a three and ½ inch crack is usually carried, and that special needs for particular climbs were provided to the guidebook authors. At the back of the book is a partial list of the more difficult free climbs, compared by the predominant or crux climbing type, and a list of first ascent and first free ascent parties, arranged in the same order as the guide. This final list includes climbs not described in this guide for various reasons.

KEY TO THE TOPOS

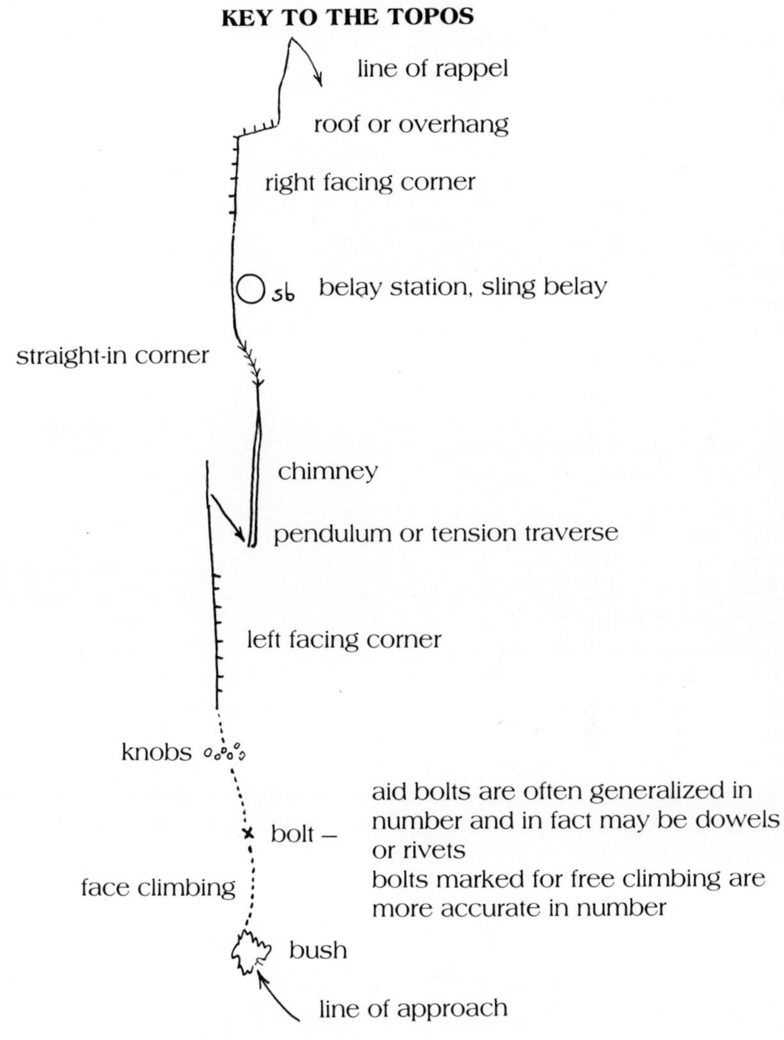

Other Abreviations

lb	lieback	KB	knifeblade
chim	chimney	LA	Lost Arrow pitons
ow	off-width (3½"-8")	pro.	protection needed beyond a standard rack
thin	thin crack (to 1½")		

PARKLINE SLAB

Approach Park at a small (riverside) turnout directly beneath Parkline Pinnacle. A nearby streambed provides brush-free access up to munge covered ledges. Work right, then back left along the base of Parkline Pinnacle.

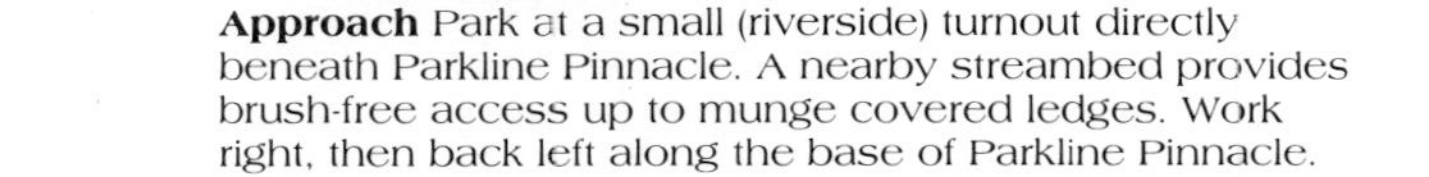

The Cockshead
A Woody Woodpecker 5.9
B Sawyer Crack 5.9
C Color Me Gone 5.9
D The Hawaiian 5.10a

Parkline Pinnacle
E Cool Cliff 170 5.8
F Center Route 5.9
G Right Side 5.7

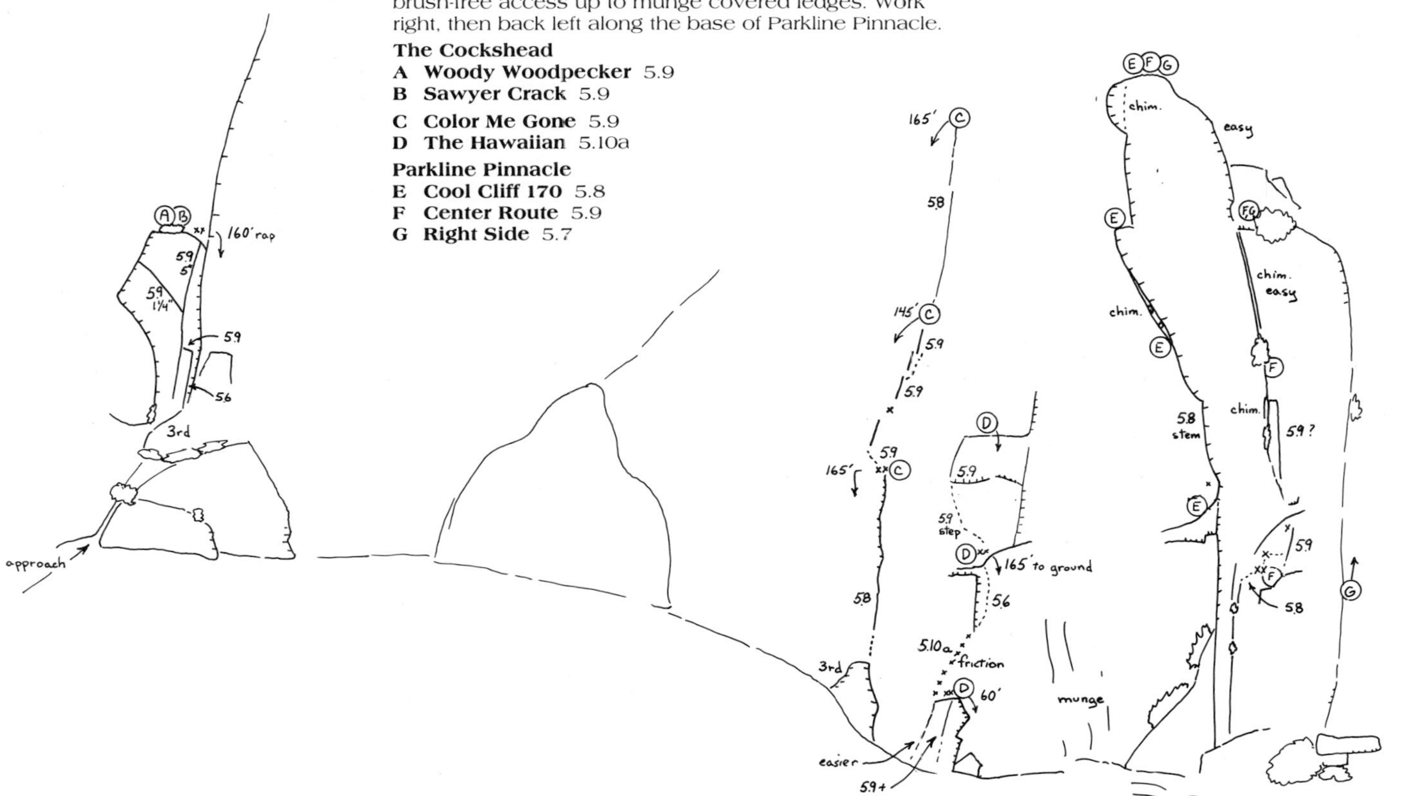

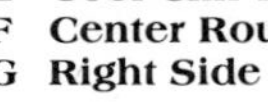
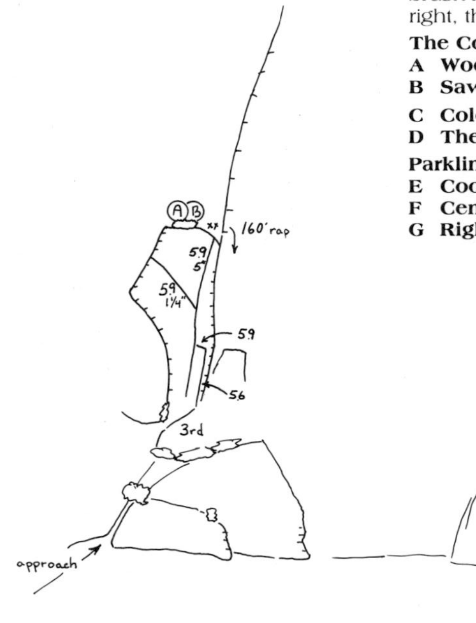

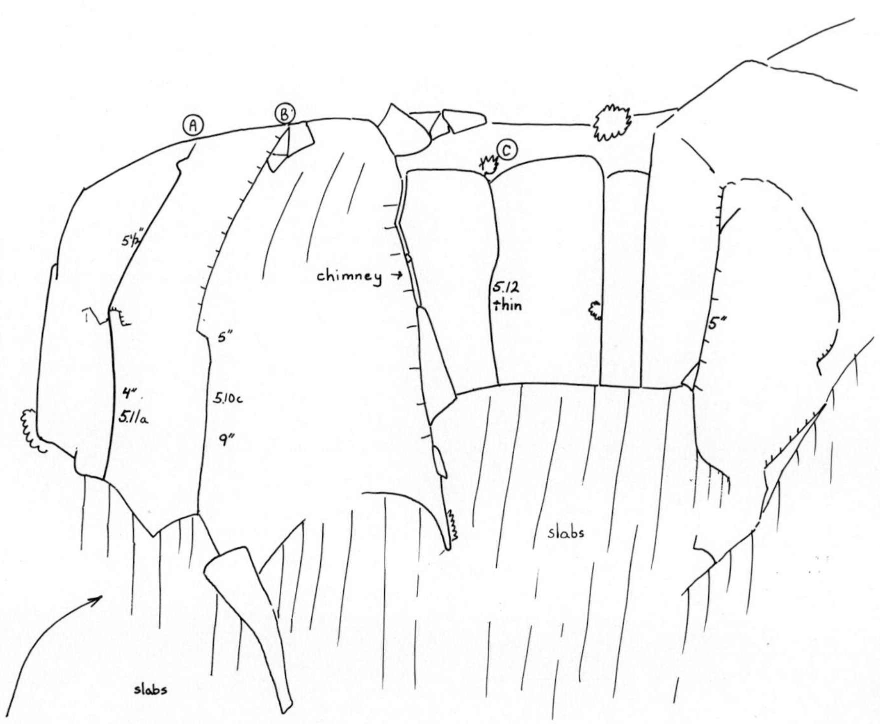

NARROW ESCAPE CLIFF

Approach This little cliff lies outside the Park entrance station at Arch Rock. Perhaps because of the need to re-enter the Park and thus conceivably repay entrance fees, this excellent, non-serious retreat from the upper Valley weather is seldom visited. Approach from directly below, where the cliff can be seen clearly just uphill from a prominent prow of rock that juts out over the road. There are parking turnouts nearby.

A A Desperate Kneed 5.11a
B Narrow Escape 5.10c
C Remember Ribbon Falls 5.12

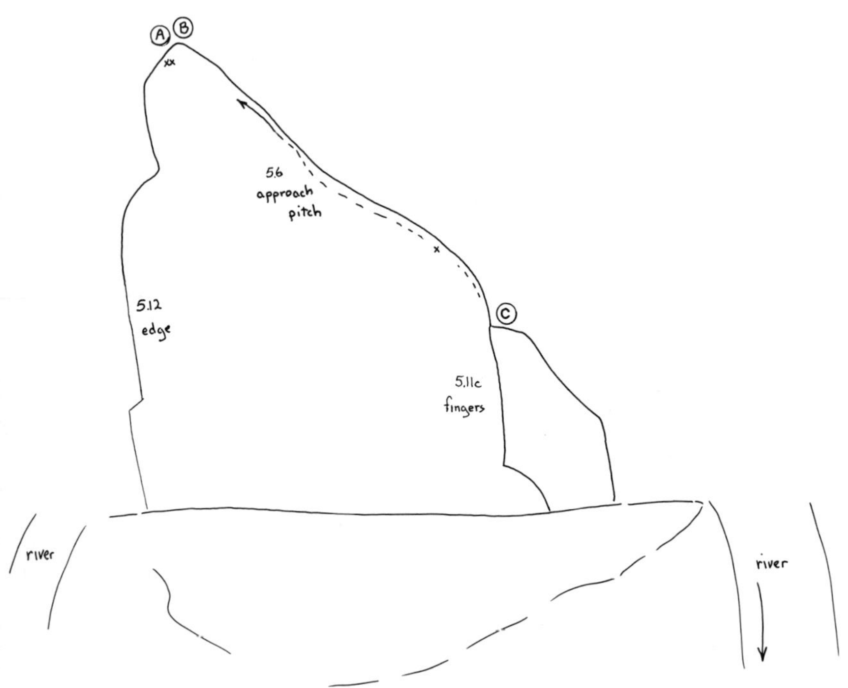

BOULDER CRACKS

Approach This huge split boulder lies on an island 0.1 mile upriver from the Arch Rock parking. The routes face downriver.

A **666** 5.12 tr
B **Round em' up** A3
C **Short Circuit** 5.11c tr

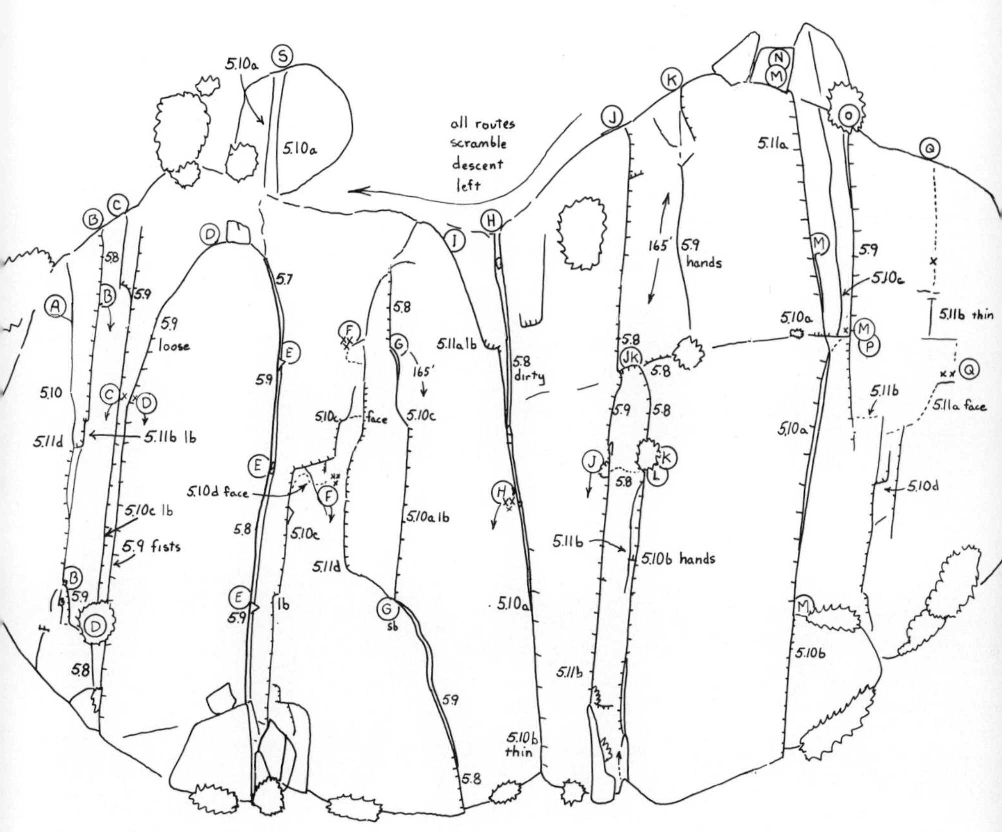

ARCH ROCK

Approach From the parking area at the entrance station, walk up the road to a clearing adjacent to the power lines. Class 2 talus leads directly up to the base of Midterm.

A Constipation 5.11d pro: to 3"
B Anticipation 5.11b pro: to 3", incl. 2ea. 1/8"-3/4"
C Supplication 5.10c pro: to 3", extra 5/8"-1½"
D Application 5.9 pro: many large to 3½"
E Entrance Exam 5.9 pro: to 3"
F Blotto 5.10d pro: to 3", incl. many 3/4"-1¾"
G English Breakfast Crack 5.10c pro: to 2½"
H Midterm 5.10b pro: to 3½"
I Sidetrack 5.11a pro: to 3½"
J Leanie Meanie 5.11b pro: to 3½"
K Gripper 5.10b pro: to 3½"
L Gripped 5.11b
M New Dimensions 5.11a pro: to 3"
N Voyage 5.10c pro: to 3"
O Klemens' Escape 5.9 pro: to 3"
P Inchworm 5.11b
Q Grokin' 5.11b

ARCH ROCK AREA

Approach From the parking area at the Arch Rock entrance station, hike east up the road to the small turnout on the cliff side and move up 2nd class talus to the base of Arch Rock.

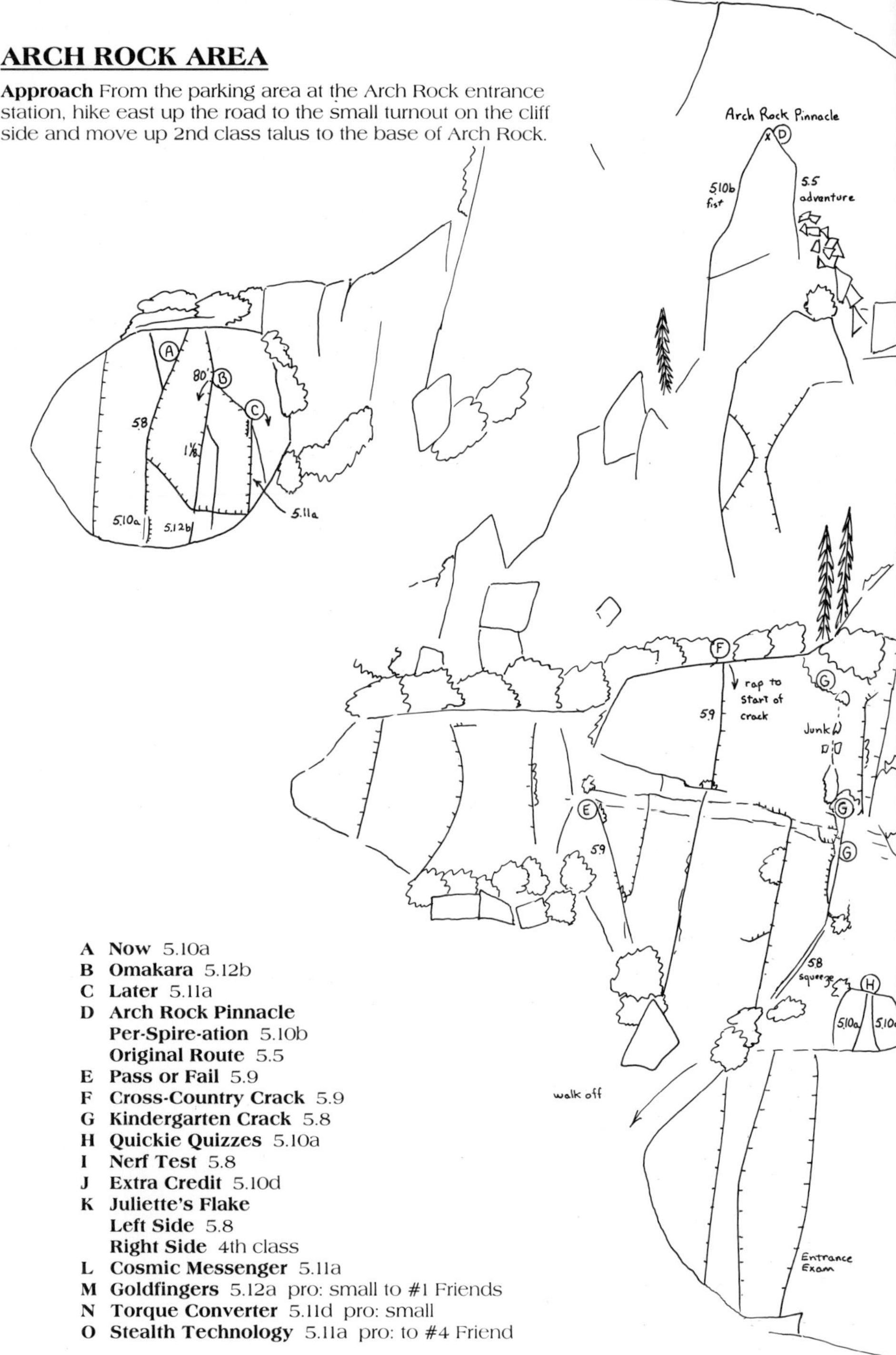

A **Now** 5.10a
B **Omakara** 5.12b
C **Later** 5.11a
D **Arch Rock Pinnacle**
Per-Spire-ation 5.10b
Original Route 5.5
E **Pass or Fail** 5.9
F **Cross-Country Crack** 5.9
G **Kindergarten Crack** 5.8
H **Quickie Quizzes** 5.10a
I **Nerf Test** 5.8
J **Extra Credit** 5.10d
K **Juliette's Flake**
Left Side 5.8
Right Side 4th class
L **Cosmic Messenger** 5.11a
M **Goldfingers** 5.12a pro: small to #1 Friends
N **Torque Converter** 5.11d pro: small
O **Stealth Technology** 5.11a pro: to #4 Friend

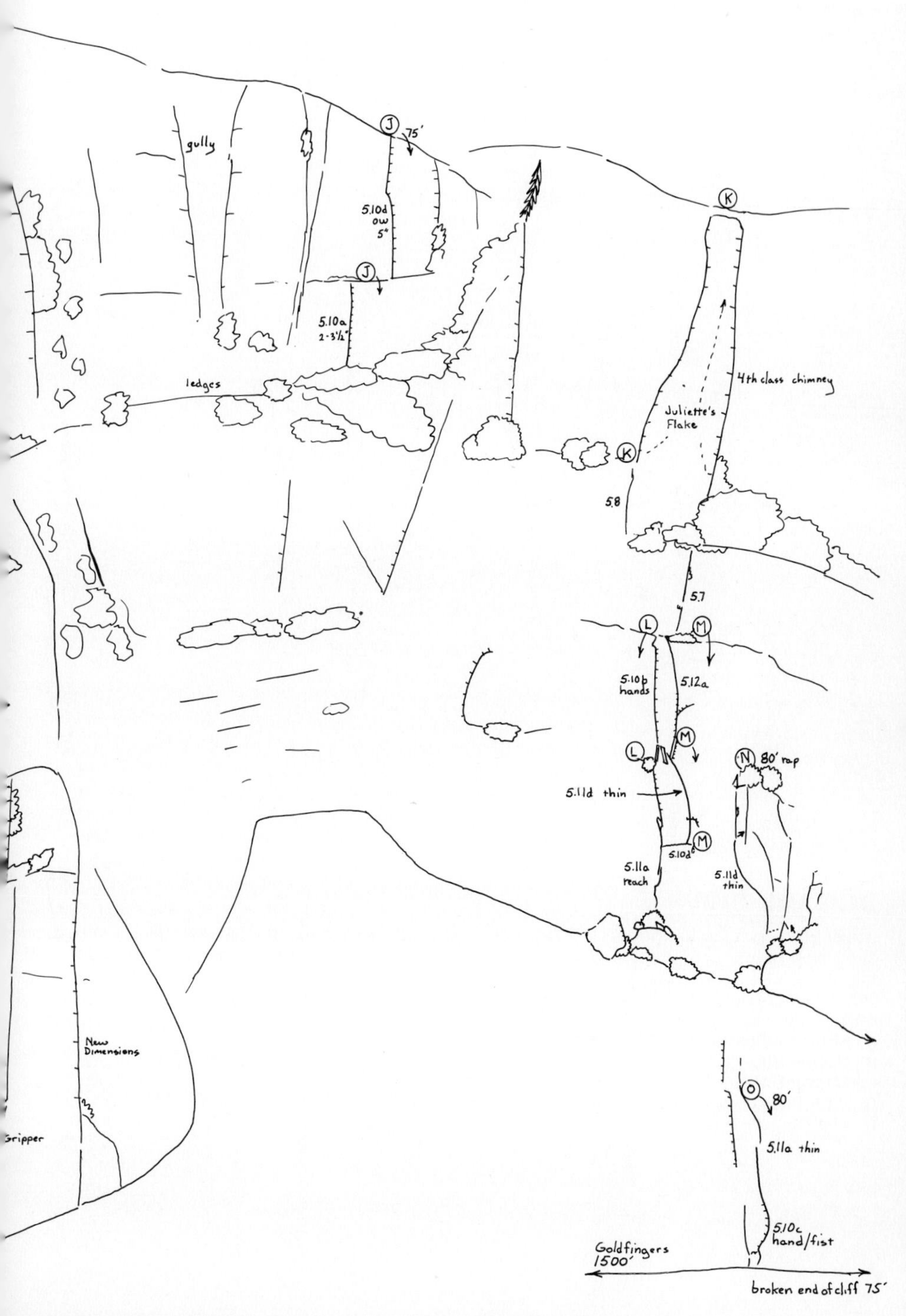
gully
J
75'
5.10d
ow
5"
J
5.10a
2-3½"
ledges
K
4th class chimney
Juliette's
Flake
K
5.8
5.7
L
M
5.10b
hands
5.12a
L
M
N
80' rap
5.11d thin
M
5.10d
5.11a
reach
5.11d
thin
New
Dimensions
Gripper
O
80'
5.11a thin
5.10c
hand/fist
Goldfingers
1500'
broken end of cliff 75'

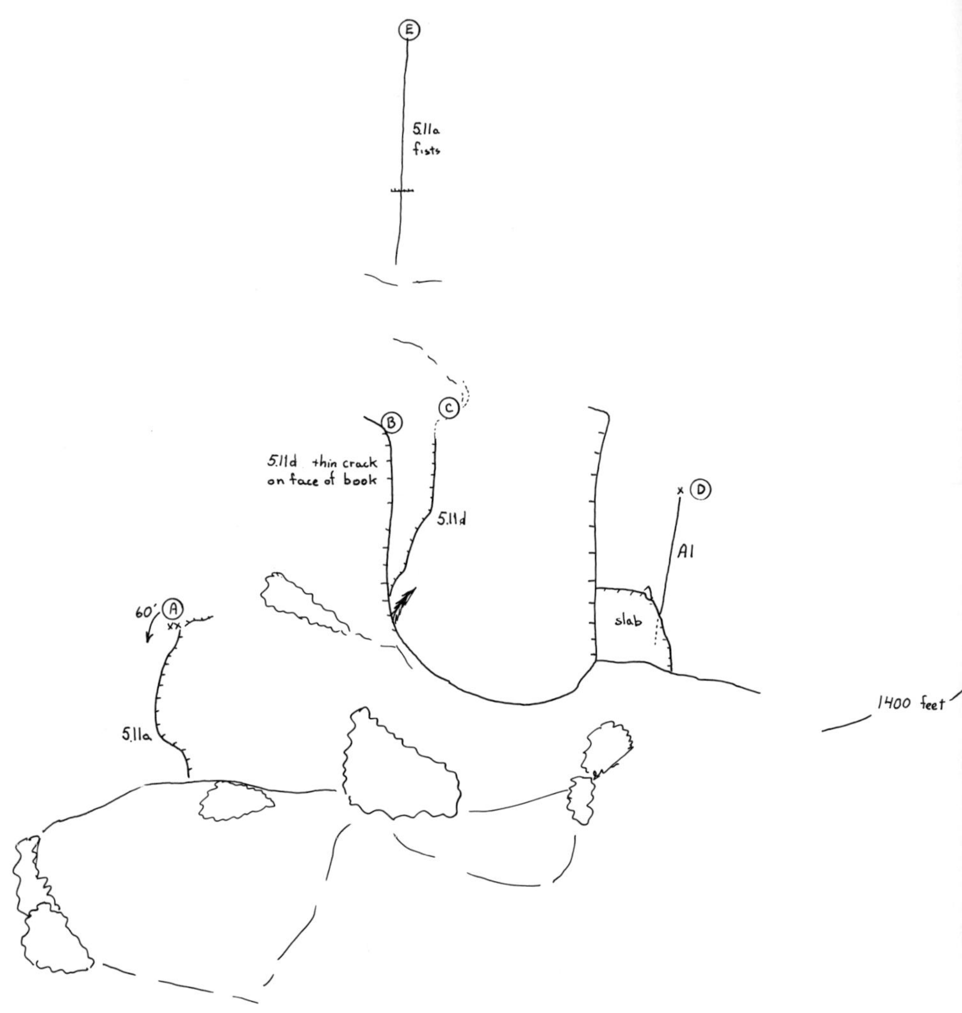

DOG DIK CLIFF

Approach From the turnout 0.8 mile east from the Arch Rock parking walk downriver to brush-free talus. Hike up, skirting the first cliff on its right. For Short but Thick go a bit higher, then follow a 2nd and 3rd class ledge system that diagonals up and left. For Opposition, Happy Days, etc. continue up and right on steep dirt and brush slopes. Fist Puppet is reached from above after circuitous easy 5th class and a rappel.

A Short but Thick 5.11a
B Opposition 5.11d
C Happy Days 5.11d
D Pink Pussycat A1 needs many baby angles
E Fist Puppet 5.11a

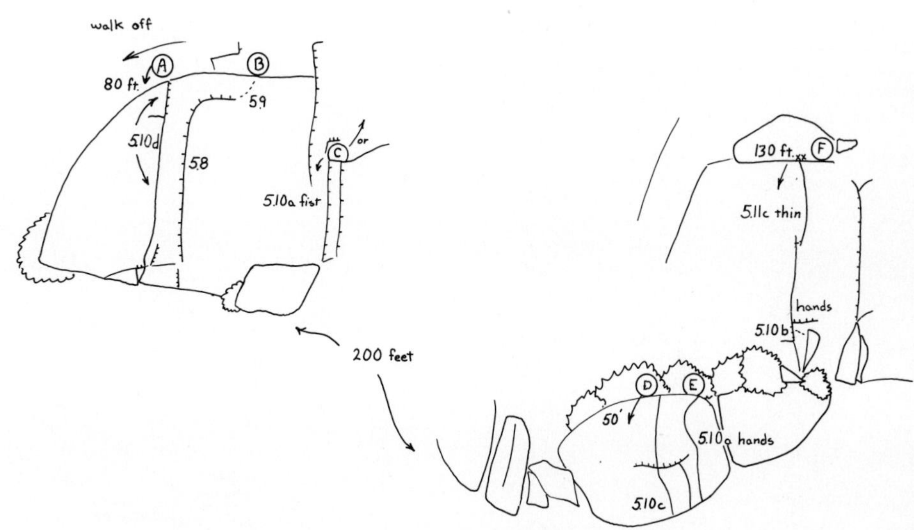

FINGER LICKIN' AREA

Approach From a turnout 1 mile east from the Arch Rock parking, a tricky scramble up a poison oak laced roadcut begins a steep dirt and brush march on a vague trail that leads to Snatch Power. An offshoot just before this leads left and up for Finger Lickin'.

A **Finger Lickin'** 5.10d
B **Fun Flake** 5.9
C **Pandora's Box** 5.10a
D **Snatch Power** 5.10c
E **Jawbone** 5.10a
F **Pinky Paralysis** 5.11c

ROADSIDE ATTRACTION AREA

Approach Parking for the various cliffs of this area is located 3.5 miles west from the Hwy 120/140 junction.

A **River Boulder** 5.11d
B **Outa Hand** 5.11b pro: tiny to 2½", esp. ¾"-1¼"
C **Hand Out** 5.10c
D **Roadside Attraction** 5.12a tr
E **Roadside Infraction** 5.12b tr

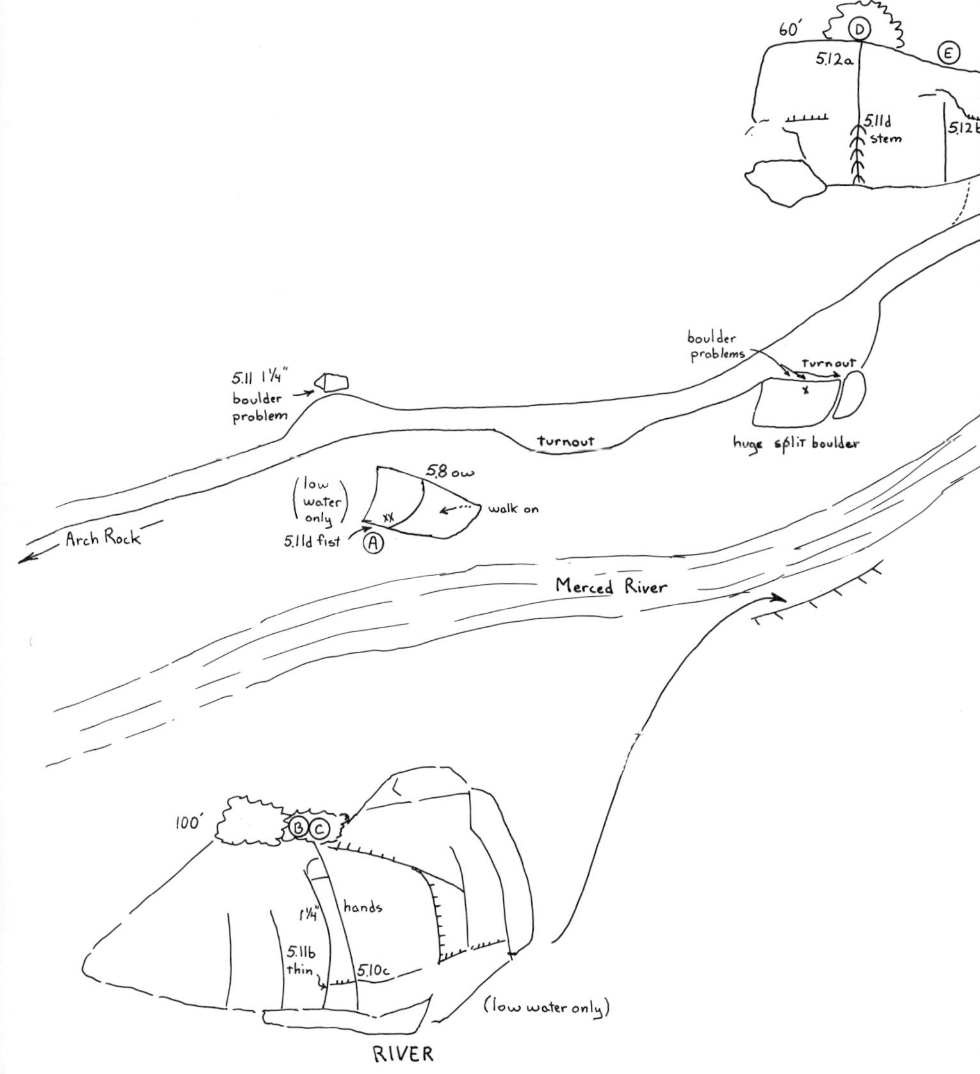

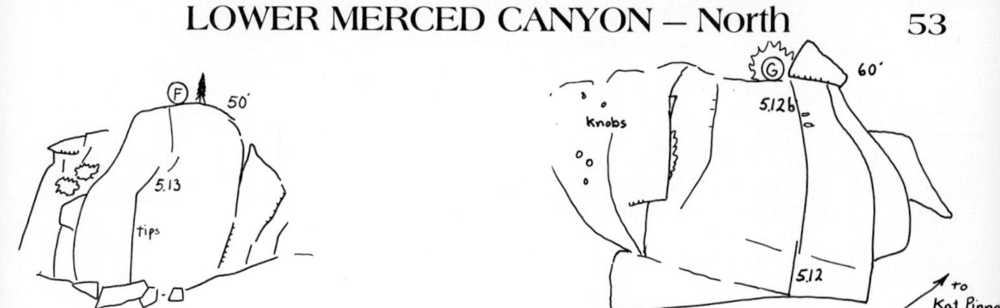

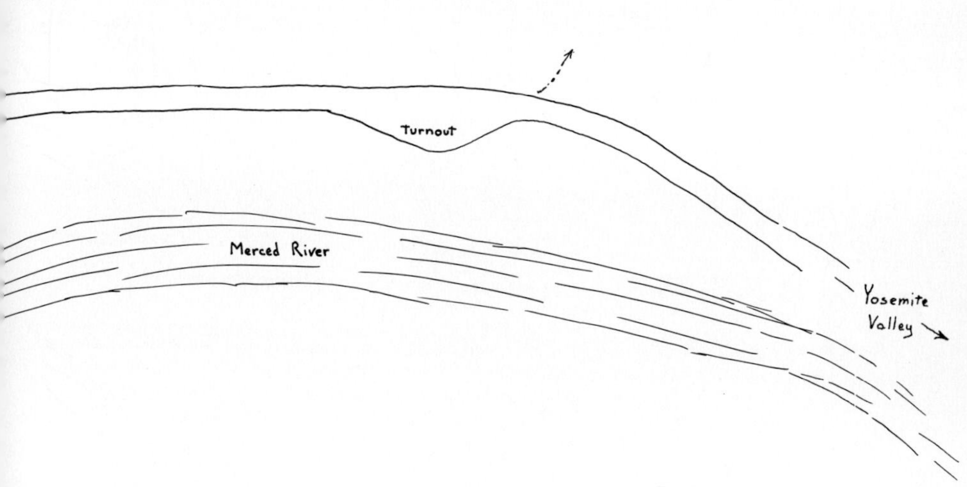

ROADSIDE ATTRACTION AREA

Approach From a dirt (riverside) turnout just upriver from Roadside Attraction, the obvious cliff just above the road is a useful landmark. Dale's Pin Job is at the extreme downriver end of the cliff; Back to the Future is at the extreme upriver end. A pair of leaning cedars mark the start of the rough approach trail (also useful for the tramp up to Kat Pinnacle).

F **Dale's Pin Job** 5.13

G **Back to the Future** 5.12b

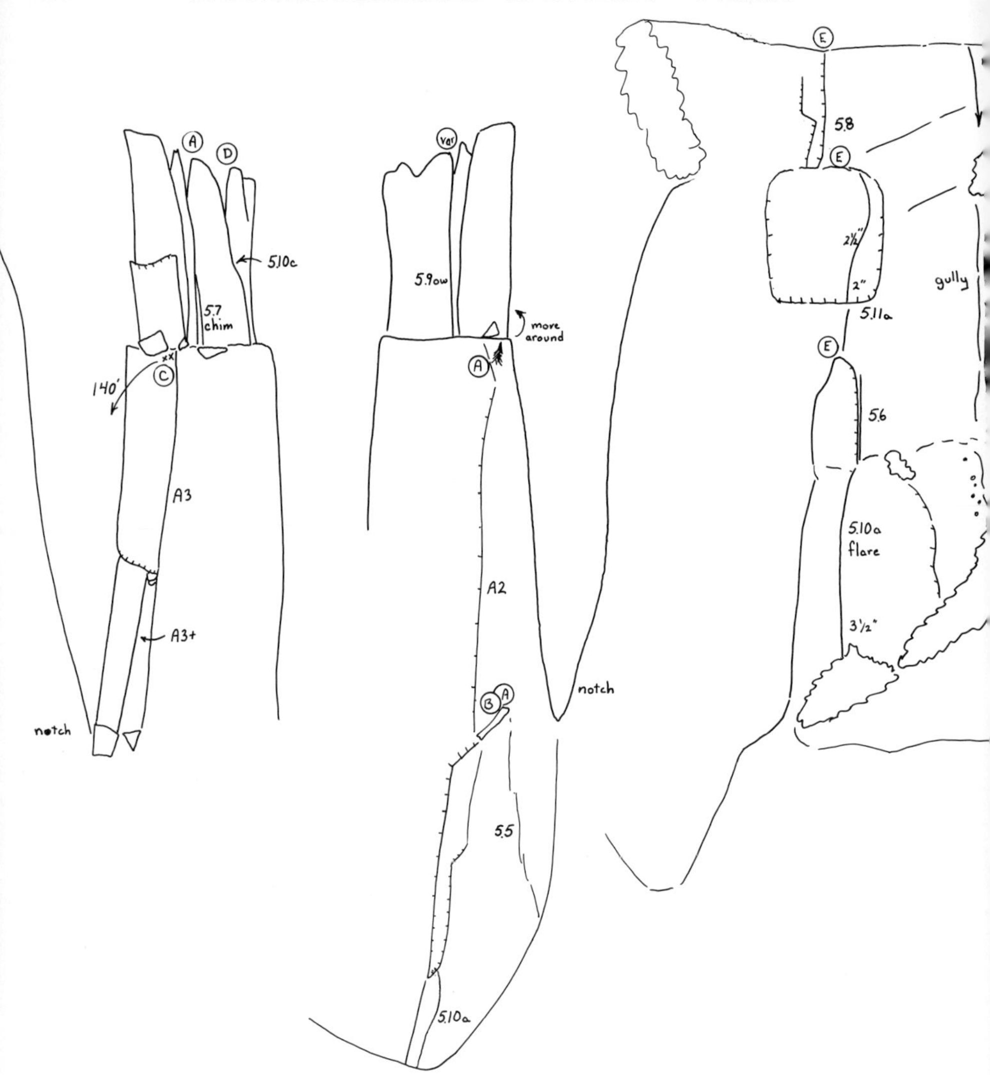

KAT PINNACLE

Approach Walk up the slope from the dirt parking lot described for approach to Back to the Future, previous page. ala Moana is approached from above, from below a broad flat pine tree area (near the Dynamite Crack) about a mile up the Cookie Road.

A Northwest Corner 5.7 A2
B Katchup 5.10a
C Southwest Corner 5.7 A3+
D Compass 5.10c
E ala Moana 5.11a

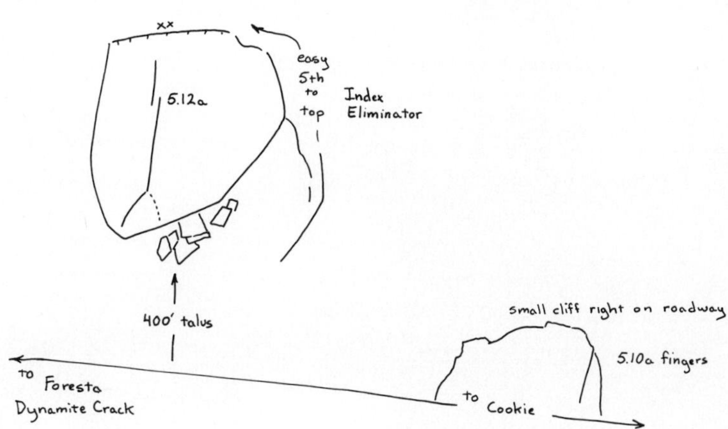

BOULDER CRACKS

Index Eliminator 5.12a
Dynamite Crack 5.10
Approximately one mile further up the Cookie Road, at a level area that is characterized by a large open pine forest, is an explosion-fractured 20' high boulder. A 5.10 finger crack is located on the west side.

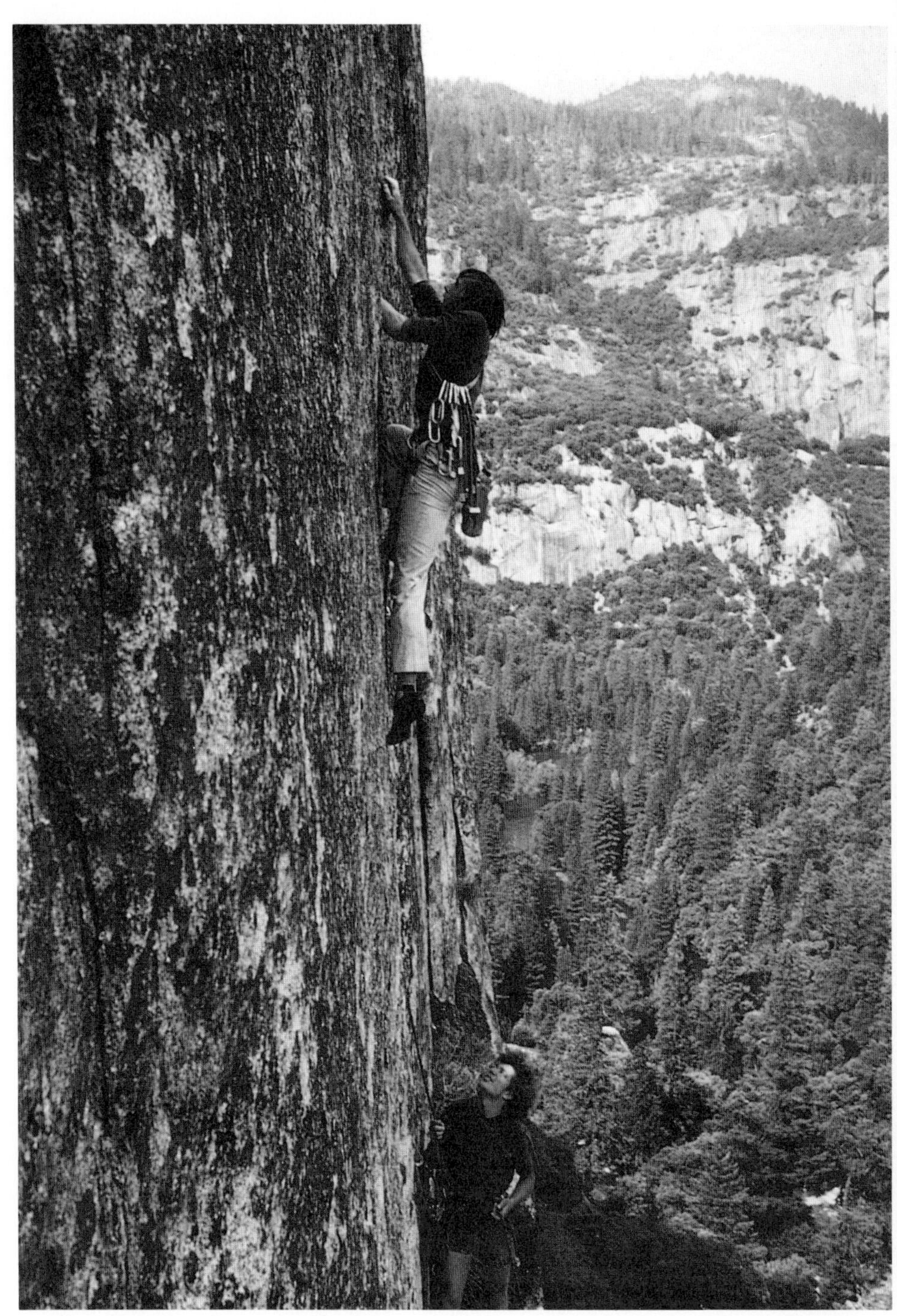

Henry Barber climbs **Butterballs**, 1973. *Jib Knight/Henry Barber collection*

THE COOKIE CLIFF AND ABOVE

1 **Capital Punishment** 5.8
2 **Hobknob** 5.8
3 **Gait of Power**
4 **Separate Reality**

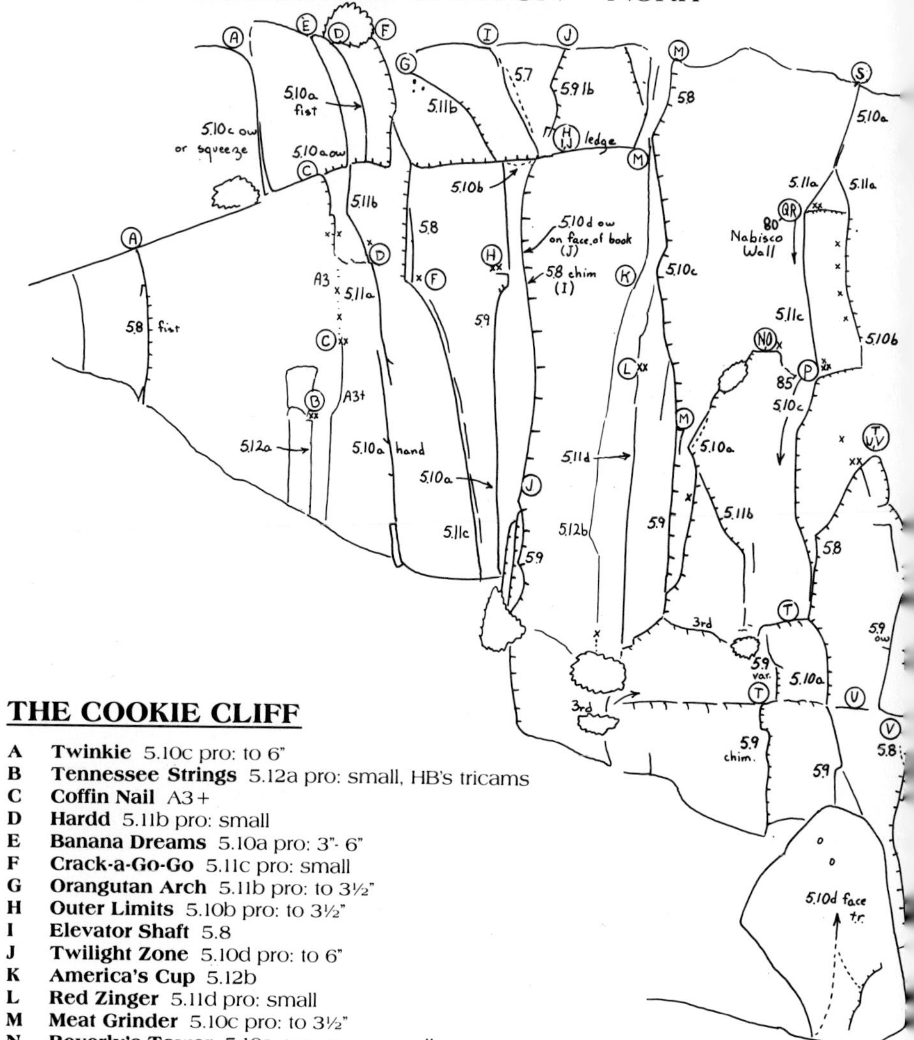

THE COOKIE CLIFF

A **Twinkie** 5.10c pro: to 6"
B **Tennessee Strings** 5.12a pro: small, HB's tricams
C **Coffin Nail** A3+
D **Hardd** 5.11b pro: small
E **Banana Dreams** 5.10a pro: 3"- 6"
F **Crack-a-Go-Go** 5.11c pro: small
G **Orangutan Arch** 5.11b pro: to 3½"
H **Outer Limits** 5.10b pro: to 3½"
I **Elevator Shaft** 5.8
J **Twilight Zone** 5.10d pro: to 6"
K **America's Cup** 5.12b
L **Red Zinger** 5.11d pro: small
M **Meat Grinder** 5.10c pro: to 3½"
N **Beverly's Tower** 5.10a pro: many small
O **Aftershock** 5.11b pro: many small
P **Waverly Wafer** 5.10c pro: to 3"
Q **Butterballs** 5.11c pro: extra ¾"-1¼"
R **Wheat Thin** 5.10b pro: to 3½"
S **Butterfingers** 5.11a
Ladyfingers 5.11a (right side start)

The Cookie

T **Left Side** 5.10a pro: to 3½"
U **Center Route** 5.9 pro: to 2½"
V **Right Side** 5.9 pro: to 2½"

W **Vendetta** 5.10b pro: to 5"
X **Infraction** 5.9
Y **Anathema** 5.10b pro: to 4"
Z **Jardine's Hand** 5.11a
AA **The Cleft** 5.9
BB **Catchy** 5.10d
CC **Catchy Corner** 5.11a pro: to 2½", extra ½"-¾"
DD **Void Continuation** 5.10d
EE **The Void** 5.11b pro: to 3"
FF **The Stigma** 5.13 A3 pro: thin
GG **The Enigma** 5.9
last pitch variations, from left:
Ramp of Deception 5.9
Abstract Corner 5.11d
Escape 5.8
Shortcake 5.11b pro: to 3½"
HH **Enema** 5.11b pro: to 3"
II **Ray's Pin Job** 5.12c
JJ **Something for Nothing** 5.11d
KK **Terminator**
Left 5.11b
Right 5.11a

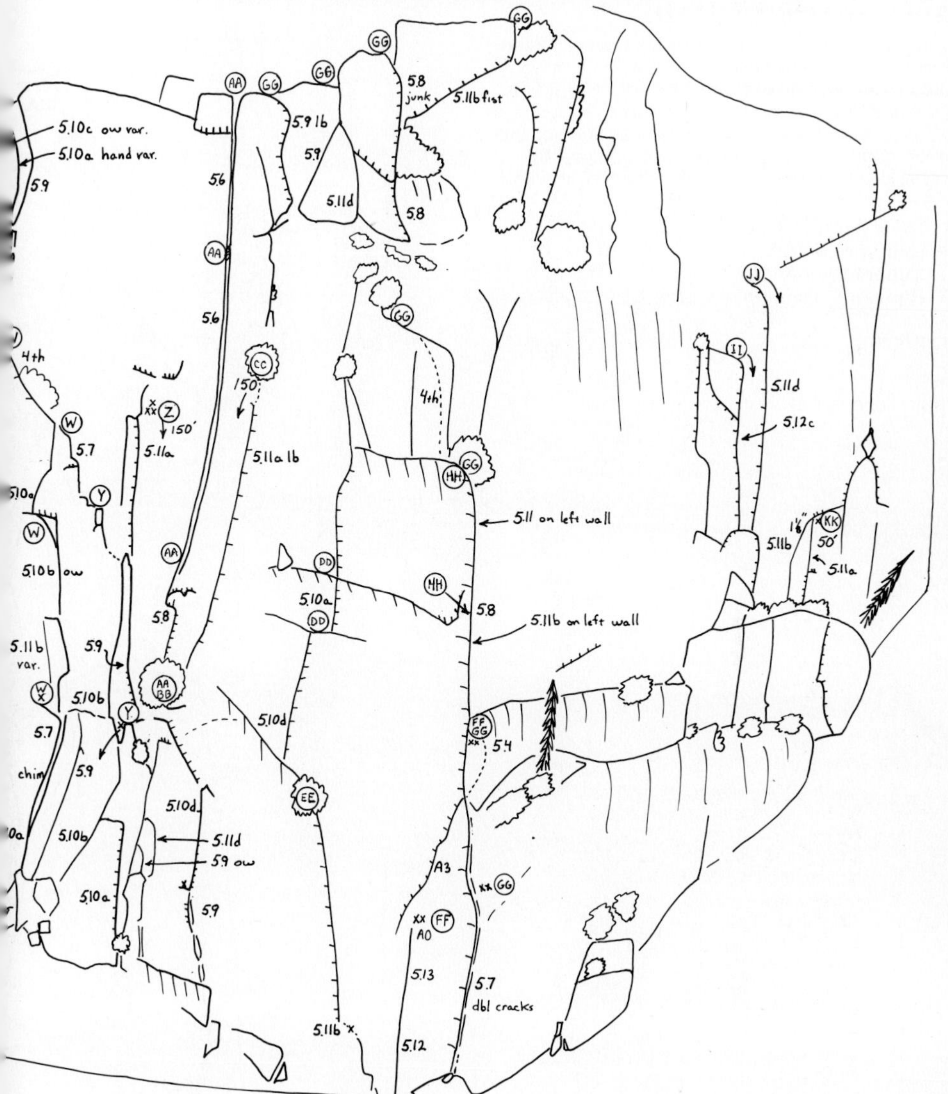

THE COOKIE CLIFF

Approach Park at the turnout adjacent to the river (.5 miles down from the Cascade Falls Bridge) amid giant white talus boulders. Follow a climbers trail somewhat left of the talus field to meet the old road at the base of the cliff.

Descent Contour left (downriver). Near the margin of the cliff angle down steep dirt, skirting short walls. One 3rd class move near the bottom of this section leads to the ground a short distance west of Twinkie.

Photo on page 57.

ABOVE THE COOKIE

Approach For Gait of Power and Tunnel Vision walk out the ventilation side tunnel within the longest tunnel on Hwy 120. One rappel leads to the slabs below. One more diagonal rappel or an easy traverse leads to the start of the climb. The other climbs are approached from below, by working up through woods and talus to the right of the Cookie Cliff.

- **A Joe's Garage** 5.11c
- **B Gait of Power** 5.11d
- **C Tunnel Vision** 5.12d
- **D Romantic Tension** 5.10d pro: to 3", plus a 4" tube
- **E Klingon** 5.11c

Photo on page 57.

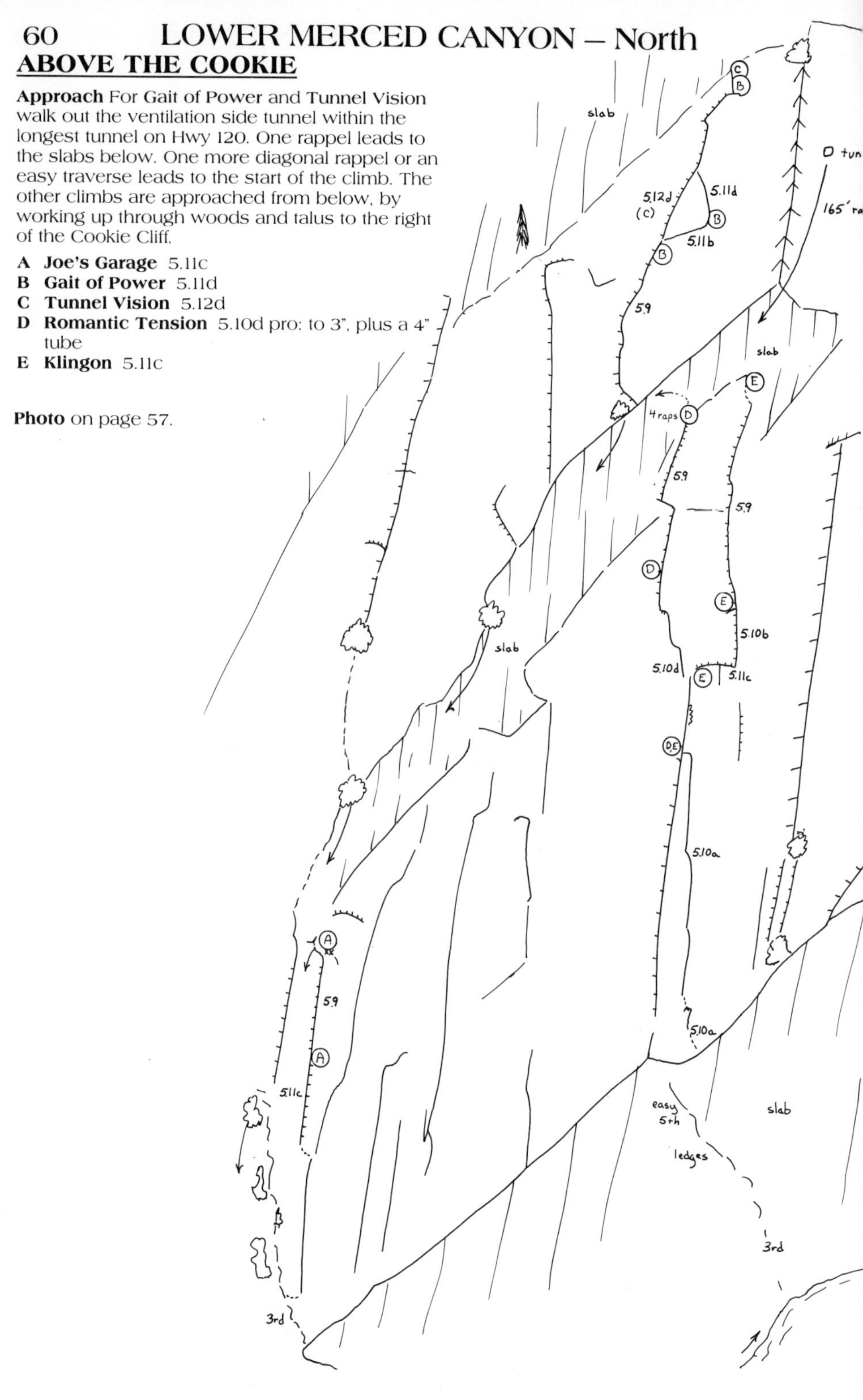

ABOVE THE COOKIE

Approach From the eastern end of the longest tunnel on Hwy 120 scramble down brush and slabs to the edge. Rappel 165' from a cedar between Skunk Crack and Tales of Power.

Photo on page 57.

- **A** **Miramonte** 5.10c
- **B** **Uncertain Ending** 5.10b
- **C** **Obscure Destiny** 5.11a
- **D** **Skunk Crack** 5.11b A1
- **E** **Tales of Power** 5.12b pro: to 3", extra ½"-1¾"
- **F** **Separate Reality** 5.11d

THROUGH BEIN' COOL

Approach Park at a spring beside a long paved turnout just west of the Cascade Creek bridge on Hwy 120. Trace the water course toward the canyon (still somewhat east of Tamarack Creek). Skirt a 50 foot wall near the rim via class 2 chutes to a flat grove beside a minor waterfall. Rappel 80 feet from there.

- **G** **Through Bein' Cool** 5.10c
- **H** **Meatheads** 5.10d tr
- **I** **Prime Time** 5.9

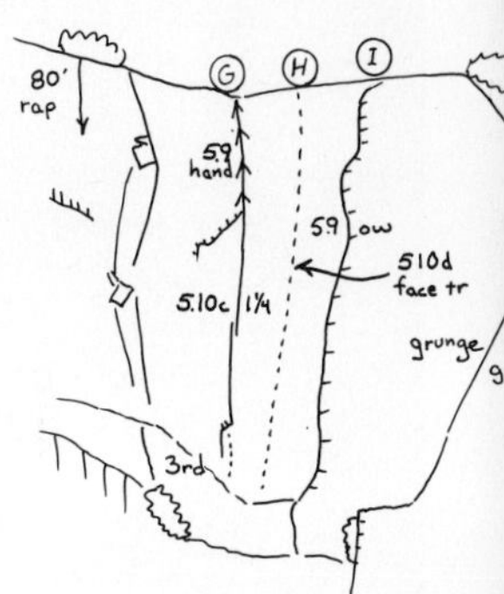

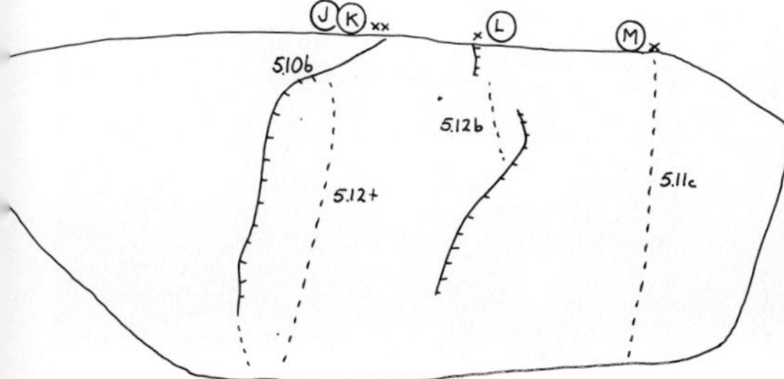

KNOBBY WALL

Approach This small but incredibly steep top rope boulder is located 20 yards to the north of Hwy 140, .3 mile west of the Cascade Creek Bridge, .4 mile east of the Cookie Cliff parking.

- **J** **The Flake** 5.10b tr
- **K** **Meltdown** 5.12+tr
- **L** **Changos Cabrones** 5.12b tr
- **M** **Shaft of the Penetrator** 5.11c tr

Ray Jardine on Phoenix, 1977

CASCADE AREA

1 PAT AND JACK PINNACLE
2 My-Toe-Sis
3 The Wedge
4 The Tube
5 Golden Needles
6 Phoenix

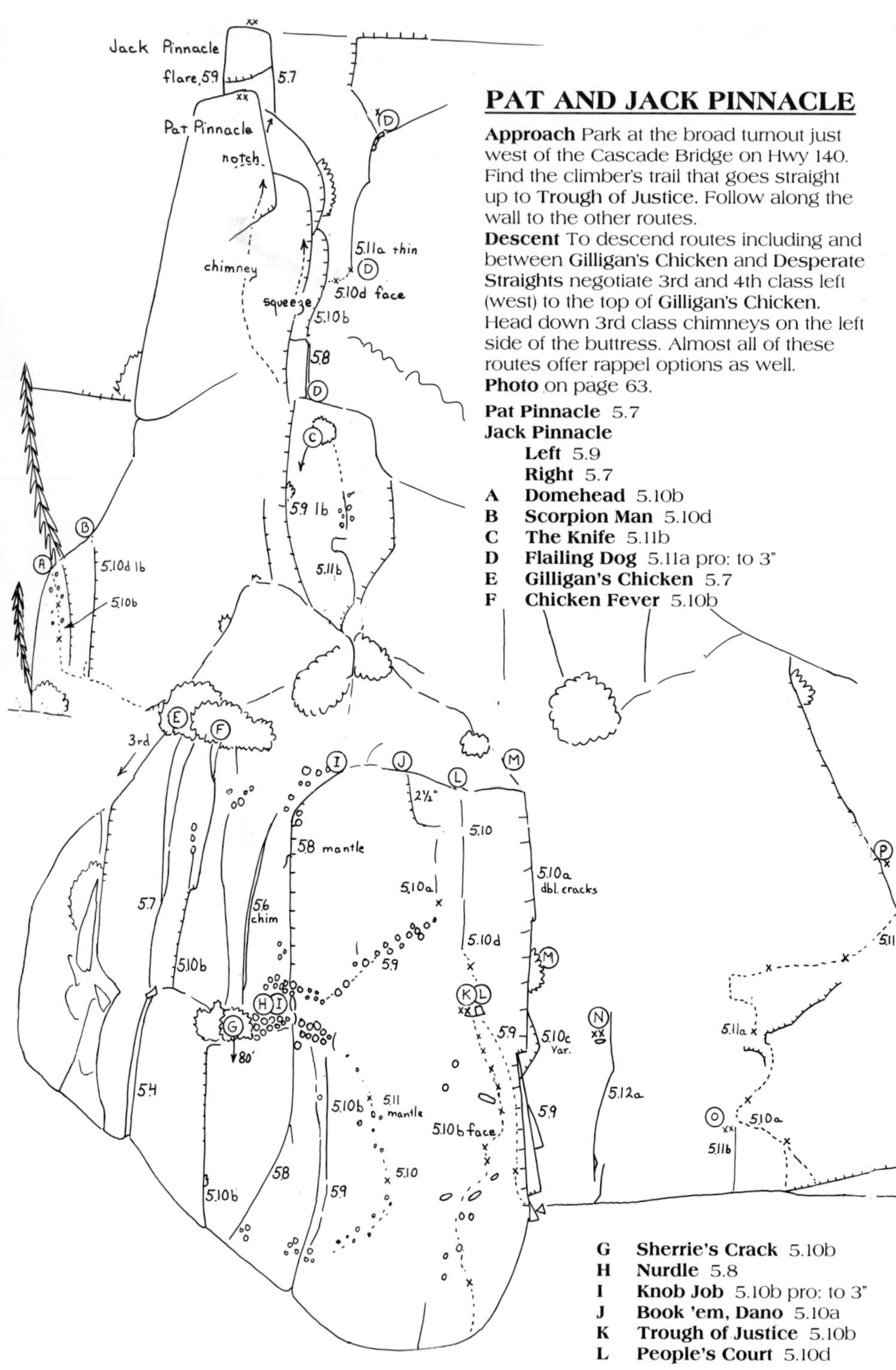

PAT AND JACK PINNACLE

Approach Park at the broad turnout just west of the Cascade Bridge on Hwy 140. Find the climber's trail that goes straight up to **Trough of Justice**. Follow along the wall to the other routes.

Descent To descend routes including and between **Gilligan's Chicken** and **Desperate Straights** negotiate 3rd and 4th class left (west) to the top of **Gilligan's Chicken**. Head down 3rd class chimneys on the left side of the buttress. Almost all of these routes offer rappel options as well.

Photo on page 63.

Pat Pinnacle 5.7
Jack Pinnacle
  Left 5.9
  Right 5.7

A **Domehead** 5.10b
B **Scorpion Man** 5.10d
C **The Knife** 5.11b
D **Flailing Dog** 5.11a pro: to 3"
E **Gilligan's Chicken** 5.7
F **Chicken Fever** 5.10b

G **Sherrie's Crack** 5.10b
H **Nurdle** 5.8
I **Knob Job** 5.10b pro: to 3"
J **Book 'em, Dano** 5.10a
K **Trough of Justice** 5.10b
L **People's Court** 5.10d

M **Desperate Straights** 5.10a pro: to 3"
N **Cat's Squirrel** 5.12a
O **Nine Lives** 5.11b
P **Black Heads** 5.11b
Q **The Tube** 5.11a pro: to 3"
R **Guardian Angel** 5.11b
S **Gay Bob's** 5.10b
T **Tricky Fingers** 5.10c pro: to 3", extra ⅛"-¾"
U **Brainbucket** 5.10d
V **Babble On** 5.10a pro: to 3"
W **Porker Party** 5.11b
X **Wart Hog** 5.8
Y **My-Toe-Sis** 5.11b pro: to 3½"
Z **Eraser Flake** 5.11a pro: incl. 2 #.5 Friends
AA **Sunblast** A3 pro: rurps, KBs, LAs, nuts to 2½"
BB **The Wedge** 5.11b pro: small to an 8" tube

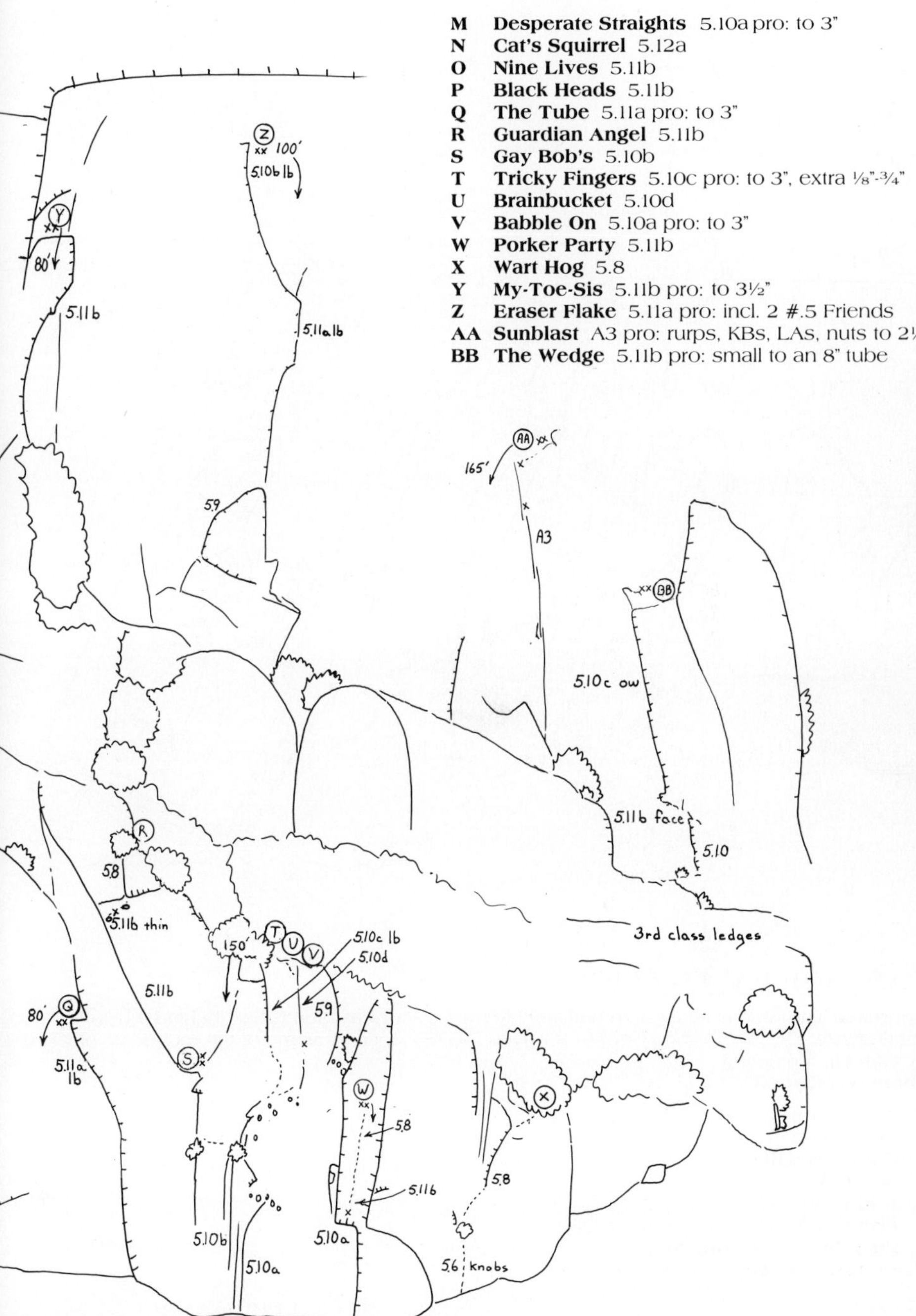

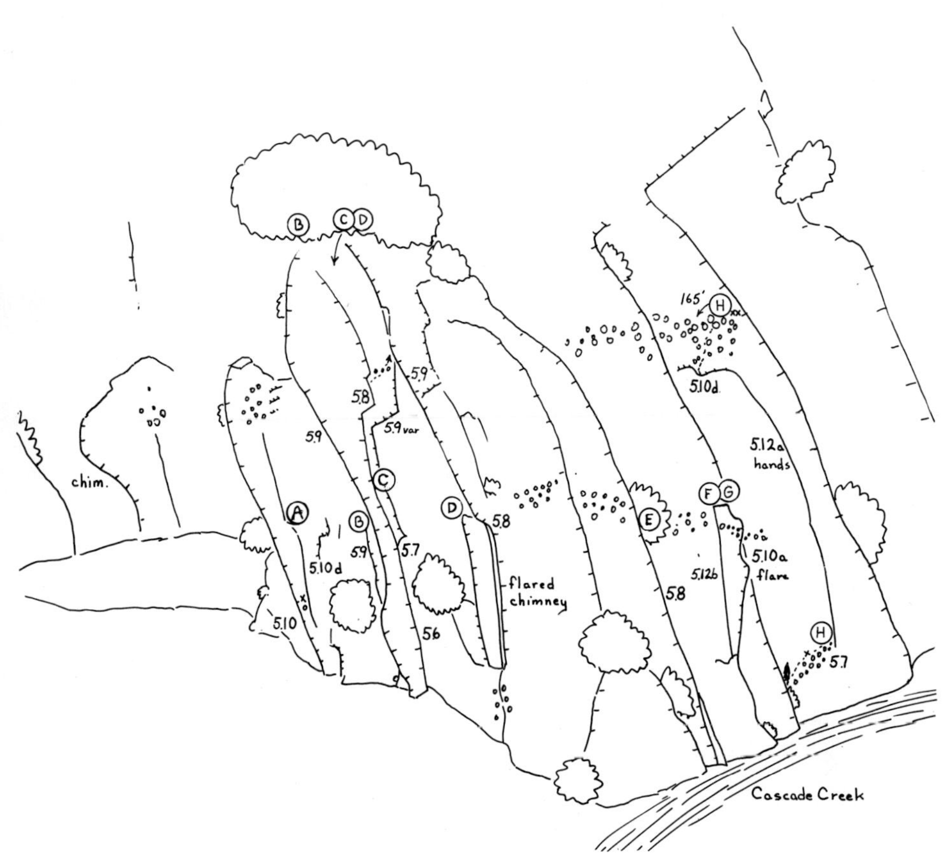

CASCADE FALLS LEFT

Approach This area is located immediately to the west of Cascade Creek, behind the large parking area 1.8 miles down Hwy 140 from the 140/120 junction. Some of the routes are blocked by water in the spring.

Photo on page 63.

A **White Cloud** 5.10d
B **Filthy Rich** 5.9
C **Golden Needles** 5.8
D **Scurv** 5.9
E **Mud Shark** 5.8
F **Fish Crack** 5.12b pro: many small
G **Free Press** 5.10a pro: to 3½"
H **Crimson Cringe** 5.12a pro: to 3", incl. many 1"-1¾"

CASCADE FALLS RIGHT

Approach Phoenix is located on the upper west side of Cascade Falls. It is approached from above via Hwy 120 and two rappels. From the west end of the Tamarack Creek bridge, (2.0 miles west of the Hwy 120/Hwy 140 junction) walk down to an open flat area. Cross the brook and contour to the brink of the cliff. At a faint arête make a short rappel from small trees to a one bolt, two piton station. From here a 140 foot rappel leads to the bottom of the crack. **Verde** is located just above Hwy 140 on the right side of Cascade Creek and is reached with a simple walk from the Cascade Falls parking lot.

Photo on page 63.

A Phoenix 5.13a
B Verde 5.9

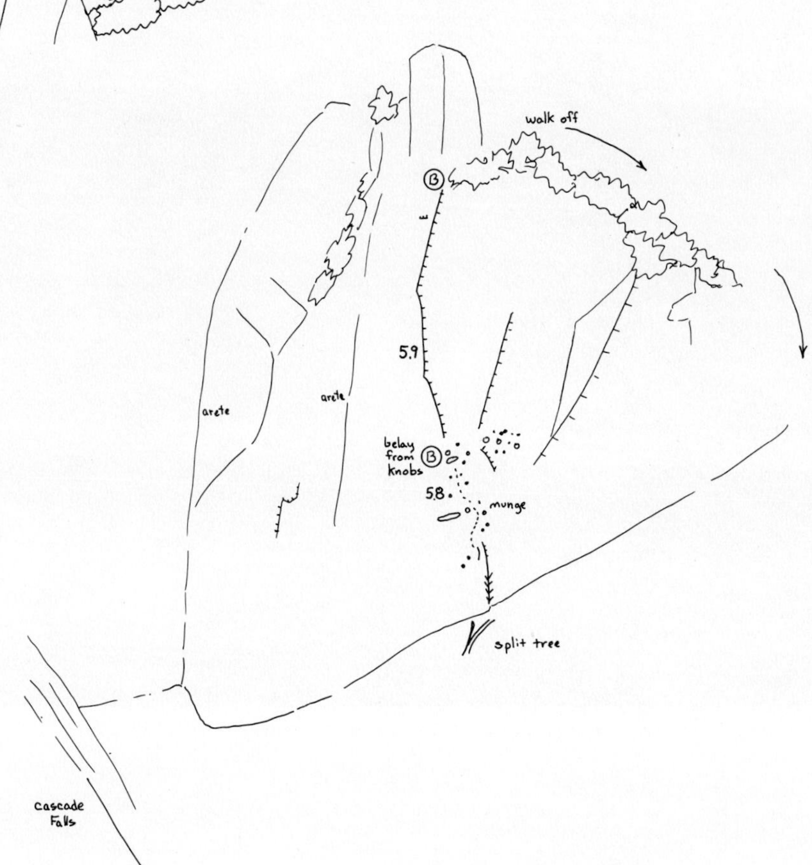

THE OWL
NOB HILL
Hwy 120
THIS AND THAT CLIFF

LOWER MERCED CANYON

1 **The Iota**
2 **REED'S PINNACLE**
3 **INDEPENDENCE PINNACLE**
4 **Fasten Your Seat Belts**

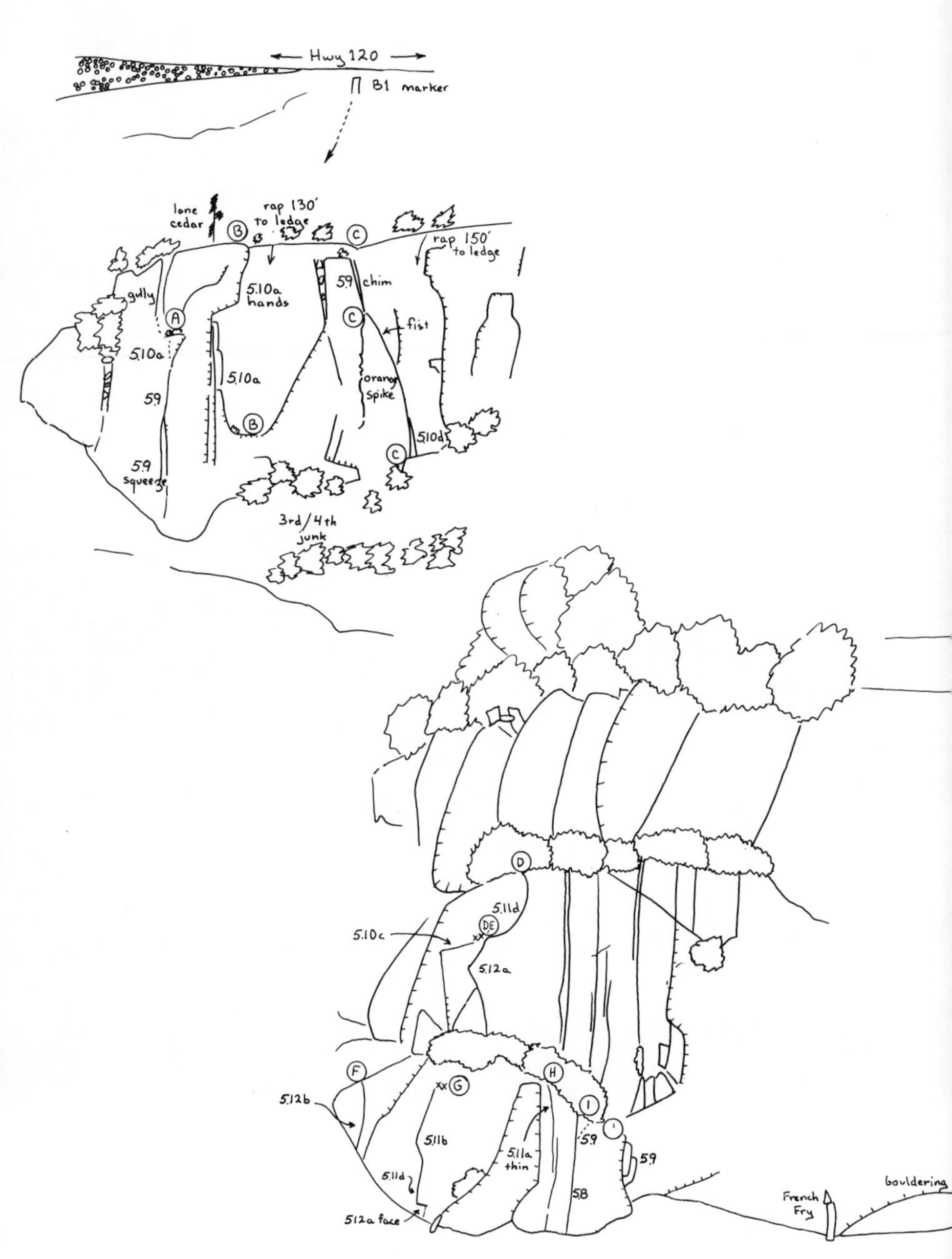
The Owl
Hwy 120
B1 marker
lone cedar
rap 130' to ledge
rap 150' to ledge
gully
A
B
C
5.10a
5.9
5.9 squeeze
5.10a hands
5.10a
5.9 chim
fist
orange spike
5.10d
3rd/4th junk
D
DE
5.11d
5.10c
5.12a
F
G
H
I
5.12b
5.11b
5.11d
5.12a face
5.11a thin
5.9
5.9
5.8
French Fry
bouldering

THIS AND THAT CLIFF

Approach The upper routes (**Weird Scenes . . .** through **Agent Orange**) are approached from above. Park at the Owl Roof turnout on Hwy 120. Locate the B-1 marker beside the road and hike down to the edge of the cliff. Bring one rope for the rappel approach and one rope with which to climb out. The other routes are approached from Hwy 140, starting from a gravel parking area across from some houses, 1.5 miles down west of the Hwy 120/140 junction. Two main climber's trails access the cliff. One goes straight up to **Tips**; the eastern one heads for **Cramming**.
Photo on page 68.

A **Weird Scenes in the Gold Mine** 5.10a
B **King Cobra** 5.10a
C **Agent Orange** 5.10d
D **Gotham City** 5.11d
E **Robin** 5.12a
F **Stubs** 5.12b
G **Tips** 5.12a
H **Back in the Saddle** 5.11a
I **Whim** 5.9
J **Said and Done** 5.9
K **This and That** 5.10a pro: to 4"
L **Humdinger** 5.10d
M **Pink Banana** 5.10d A1
N **Cramming** 5.10d pro: extra ¾"-1½"

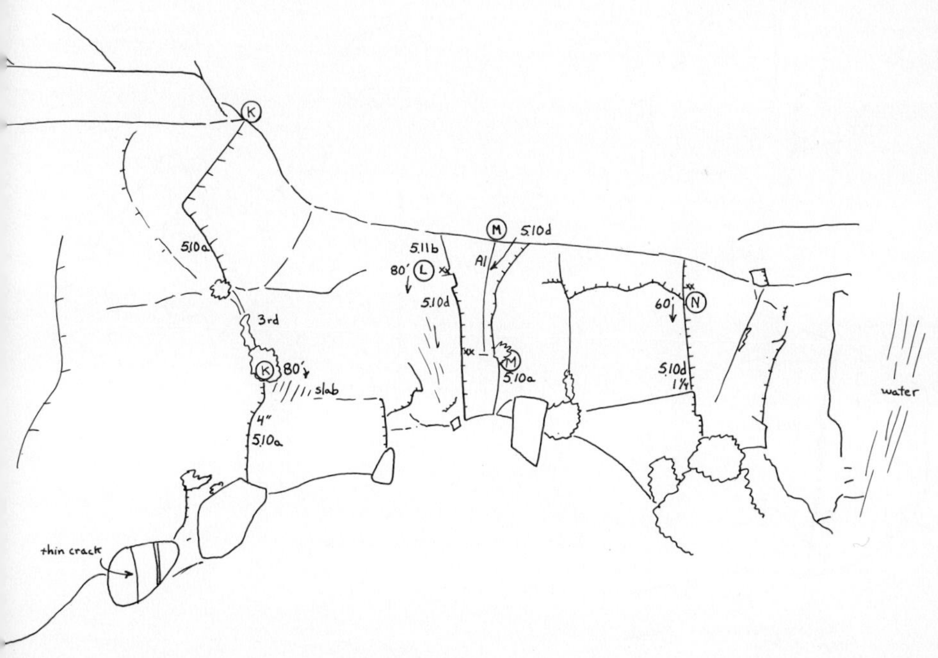

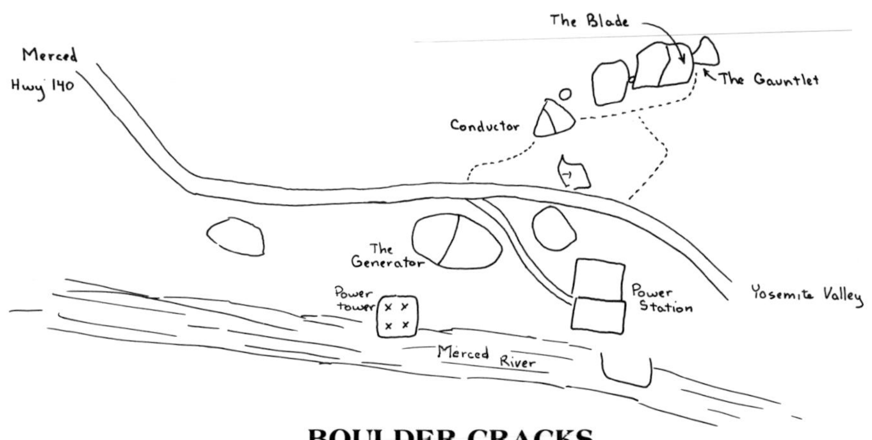

BOULDER CRACKS

Approach These various top rope problems are located near the old generator station off Hwy 140, 1.2 miles west of the 120/140 junction.

- **A Conductor Crack** 5.10d tr
- **B Generator Crack** 5.10c tr
- **C The Blade** 5.12 tr
- **D The Gauntlet** 5.11c tr

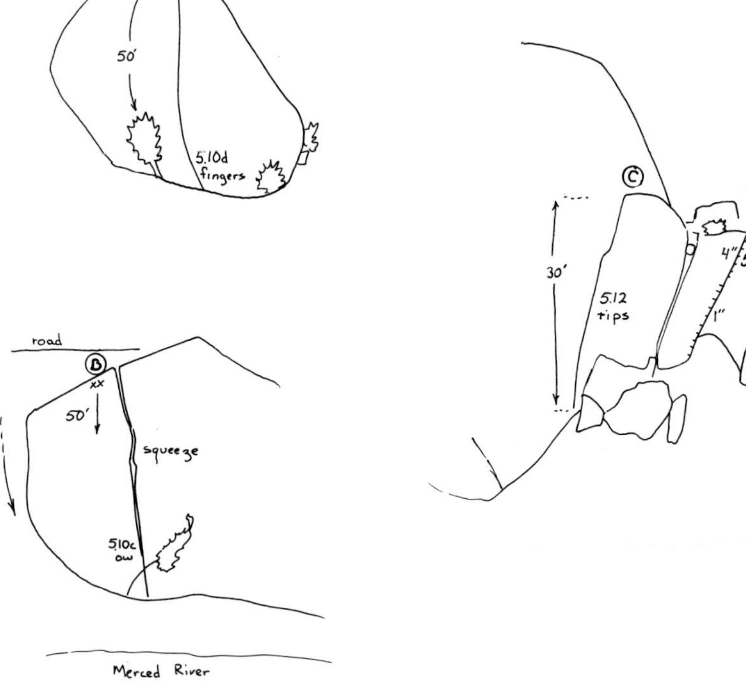

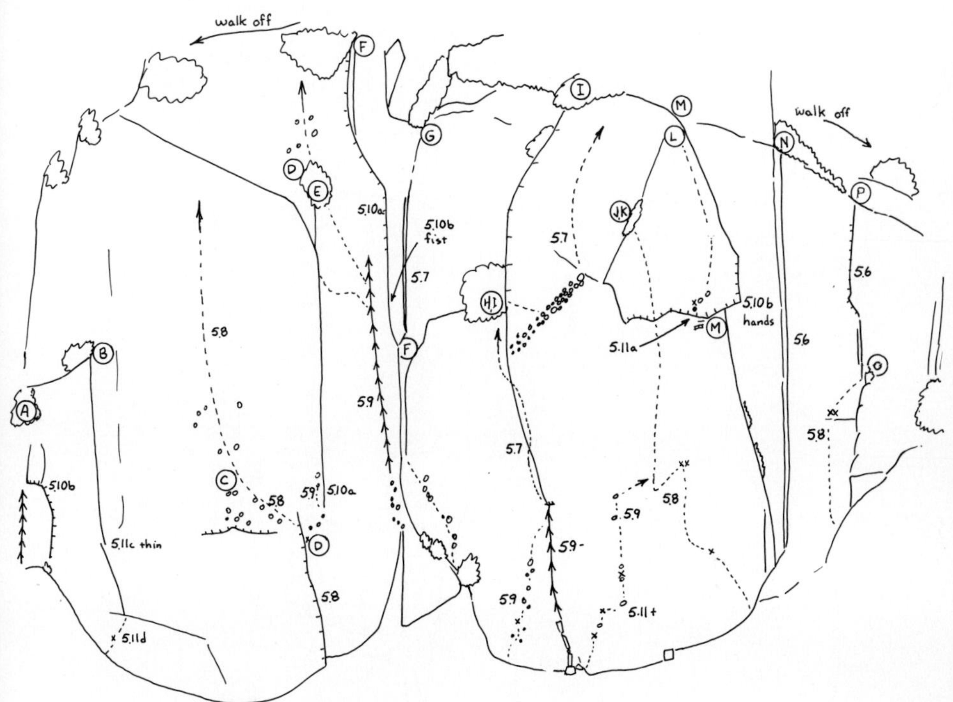

NEW DIVERSIONS CLIFF

Approach From the old generator station off Hwy 140, 1.2 miles west of the 120/140 junction, walk up the hydro-line about 200 feet. The climber's trail begins to the left, and leads up to the base of the wall.

Photo on page 69.

A **Falcon** 5.10b
B **Rocket Man** 5.11d
C **Chicken Pox** 5.8
D **New Diversions** 5.9 pro: to 3"
E **Wasp** 5.9
F **Strangers in the Night** 5.10b
G **Electric Gully** 5.7
H **Radical Chic** 5.9
I **Chicken Pie** 5.9
J **Catch a Wave** 5.11+
K **Jugs** 5.8
L **Spring Chicken** 5.11a
M **Shake, Rattle and Drop** 5.10b
N **Chimney for Two** 5.6
O **Holidays** 5.8
P **Tail End** 5.6

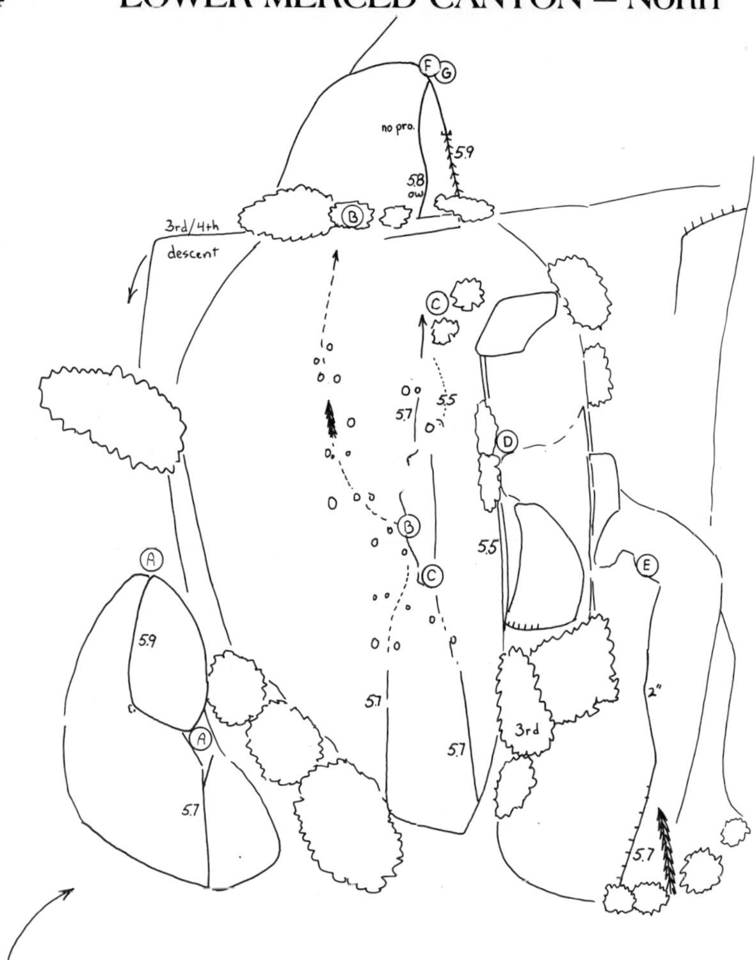

KNOB HILL

Approach This bluff is located above Hwy 120 immediately to the east of Cascade Creek. Park across the road in a paved parking area and scramble steeply up and right to the base of the cliff. **Descent** Scramble off the top of Knob Hill to the west, encountering steep and dirty 3rd class chimneys and gullies. **Photo** on page 68.

A Pot Belly 5.9
B Sloth Wall 5.7
C Anti-Ego Crack 5.7
D Sloppy Seconds 5.5
E Chicken Pie 5.7
F Knob Hill Rapist 5.8
G Deception Gully 5.9

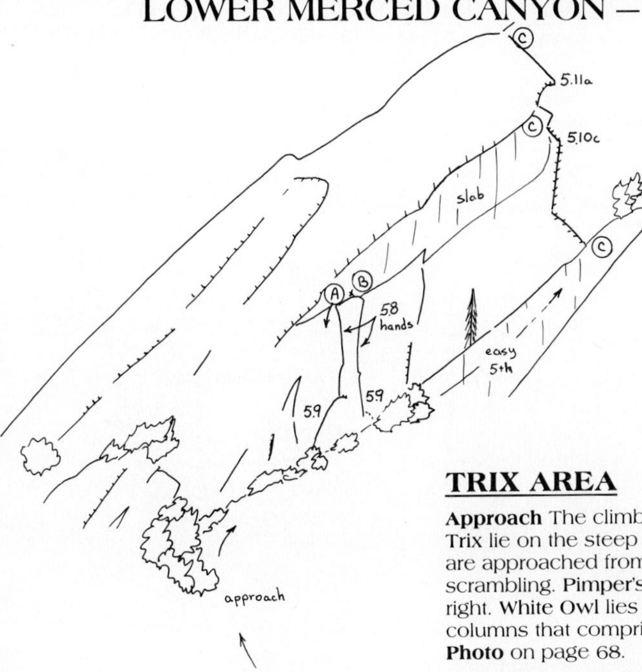

TRIX AREA

Approach The climbs Arlington Heights through Trix lie on the steep east wall of Knob Hill, and are approached from directly below via steep scrambling. Pimper's Paradise lies well to the right. White Owl lies on the farthest left of the columns that comprise the Owl Area.
Photo on page 68.

A **Arlington Heights** 5.9
B **Hampton Estates** 5.9
C **Trix** 5.11a pro: to 6"
D **Pimper's Paradise** 5.11d
E **White Owl** 5.11d

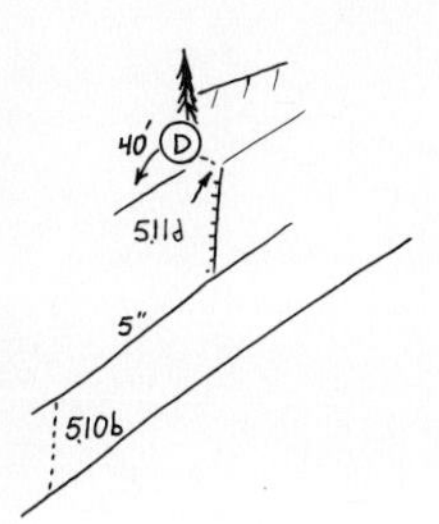

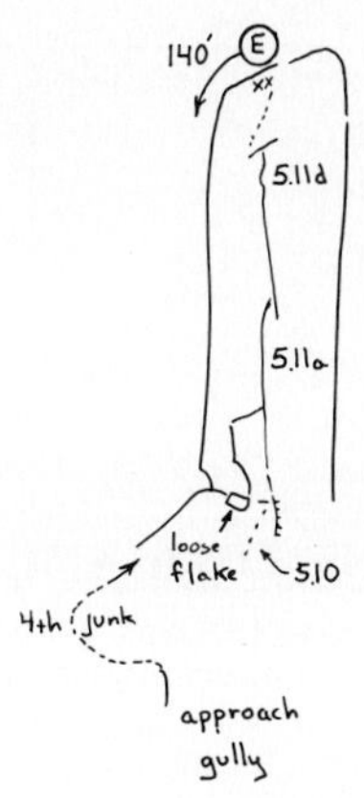

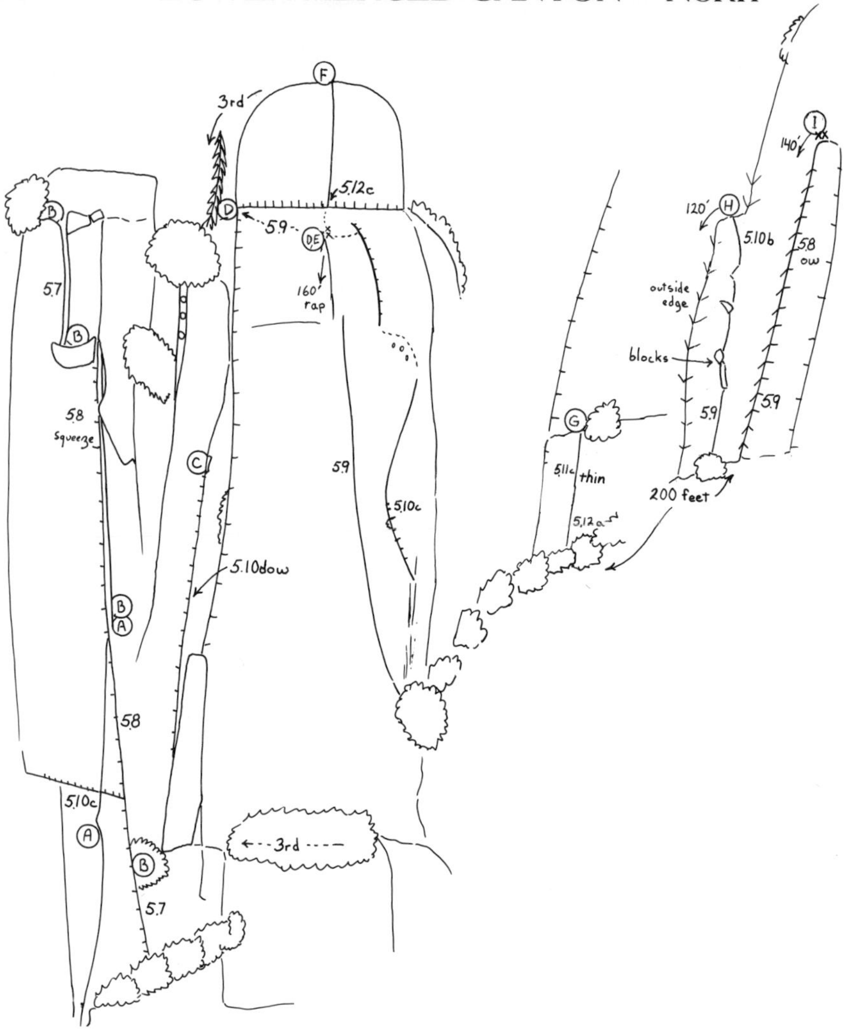

THE OWL AREA

Approach A paved turnout is found directly below the Owl on Hwy 120, a bit west of Reed's Pinnacle Area. Scramble up a short roadcut, then approach the formation somewhat from the right. **Photo** on page 68.

A **Dromedary Direct** 5.10c pro: to 2½", extra ¾"-2"
B **Dromedary** 5.8
C **The Shaft** 5.10d pro: 2½"-6"
D **The Owl Bypass** 5.9
E **Stroke (My Erect Ear Tufts)** 5.10c pro: 2 ea. Friend to #3
F **Owl Roof** 5.12c pro: to 6"
G **Mirage** 5.12a pro: extra ½"-1"
H **Wicked Jones Crusher** 5.10b
I **Walrus** 5.9

GOLDRUSH AREA

Approach Park at Reed's Pinnacle Area (the turnout between the two short tunnels on Hwy 120). **Goldrush** is easily seen as the crack immediately left of the (western) tunnel. From the area atop **Goldrush** drop down to a strange tunnel, through blocks to reach the start of the climb. For the other routes in the area drop steeply down from the road at the western tunnel.
Photo on page 69.

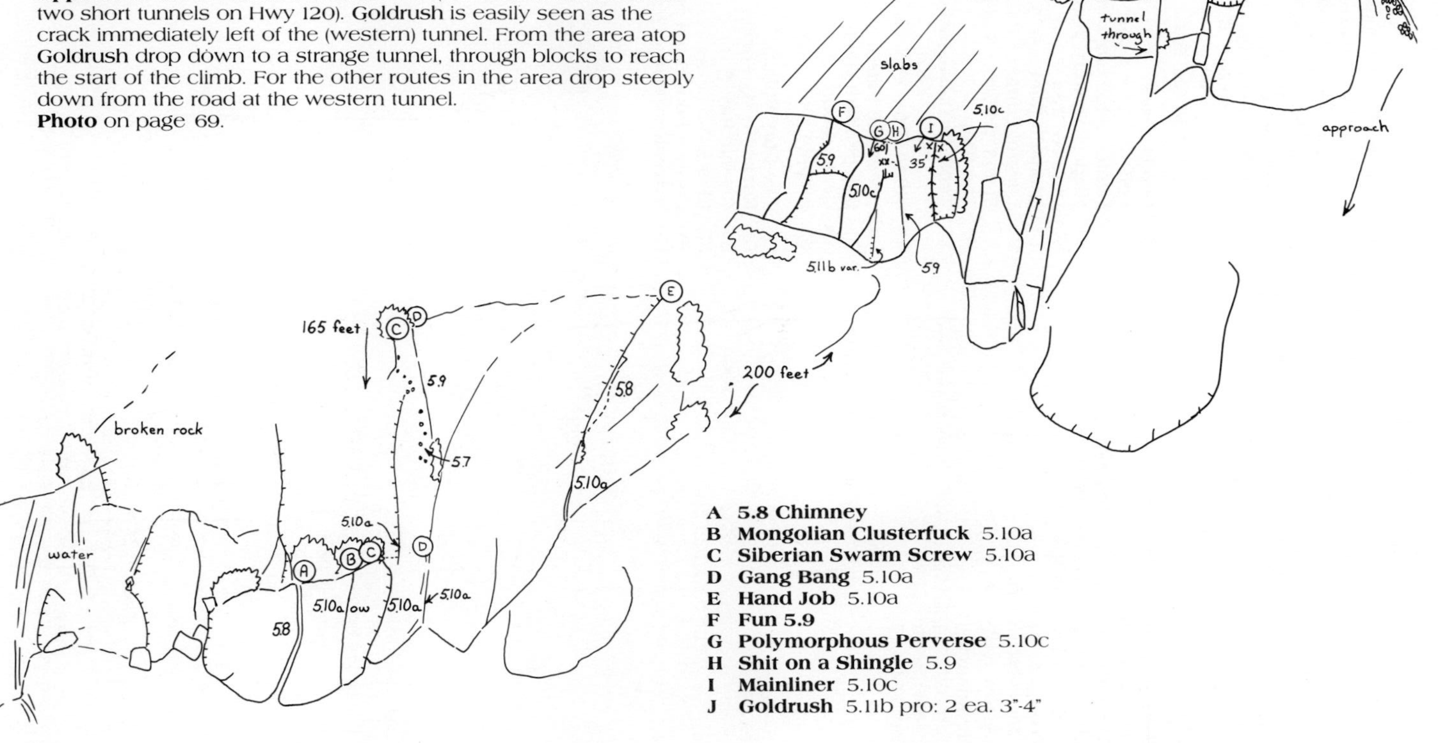

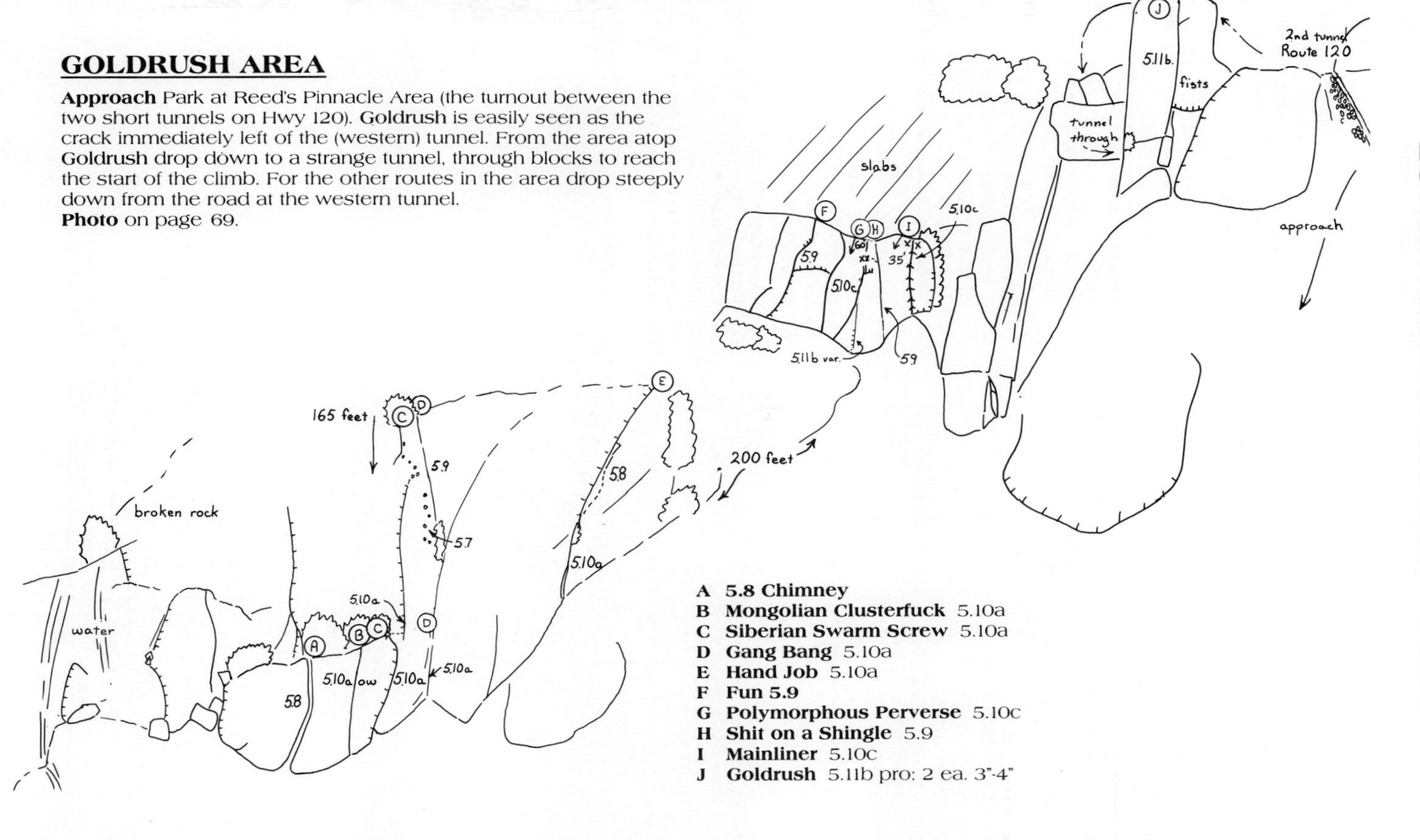

A **5.8 Chimney**
B **Mongolian Clusterfuck** 5.10a
C **Siberian Swarm Screw** 5.10a
D **Gang Bang** 5.10a
E **Hand Job** 5.10a
F **Fun 5.9**
G **Polymorphous Perverse** 5.10c
H **Shit on a Shingle** 5.9
I **Mainliner** 5.10c
J **Goldrush** 5.11b pro: 2 ea. 3"-4"

REED'S PINNACLE AREA

Approach Park between the two short tunnels on Hwy 120 in a paved turnout that overlooks the lower canyon. Access that avoids steep roadcuts is made by walking 100 feet (west) up the road before cutting up to the cliff. For the **Iota** and the routes left of it walk (west) up the road nearly to the mouth of the western tunnel. Follow the class 2 gully above until an inobvious access right leads to the massive chamber of the **Iota**.

Photo on page 69.

- **A** **Danger Will Robinson** 5.10d
- **B** **Anal Tongue Darts** 5.10c
- **C** **Olga's Trick** 5.10d pro: to 3"
- **D** **Crazy Train** 5.10c
- **E** **Isotope** 5.11d
- **F** **Chingando** 5.10a pro: to 5"
  The Iota leads up a 5.4 chimney behind Chingando. It is approached from the ledges below **Olga's Trick**.
- **G** **Phantom** 5.13a
- **H** **The Tooth** 5.10a
- **I** **Micron** 5.11b

The Remnant

- **J** **Left Side** 5.10b pro: to 3½"
- **K** **Center Route** 5.12a
- **L** **Right Side** 5.7

Reed's Pinnacle

- **M** **Left Side** 5.10a pro: to 4"
- **N** **Direct** 5.10a pro: to 3"
- **O** **Blazing Buckets** 5.9+
- **P** **Regular Route** 5.9
- **Q** **Bongs Away**
  Left 5.8
  Center 5.10a pro: extra 2½"-3"
- **R** **Magical Mystery Tour** 5.10a pro: to 3
- **S** **Old Five Ten** 5.10d
- **T** **Midnight Rampest** 5.10d
- **U** **Lunatic Fringe** 5.10c pro: to 3", extra
- **V** **Flatus** 5.9 pro: extra 2½"-3"
- **W** **The Rorp** 5.7
- **X** **Tooth or Consequences** 5.11b pro: to 3½", esp. 1¼"-3½"
- **Y** **Stone Groove** 5.10b

Independence Pinnacle

- **Z** **Independent Route** 5.10b pro: to 4"
- **AA** **Center Route** 5.10d pro: to 3"
- **BB** **Steppin' Out** 5.10d pro: to 6"
- **CC** **The Gray Bullet** 5.8
- **DD** **Rocket in My Pocket** 5.11a
- **EE** **Cosmic Ray** 5.11a
- **FF** **Ejesta** 5.8
- **GG** **Porter's Pout** 5.10a pro: to 3"
- **HH** **Sylvester's Meow** 5.11a

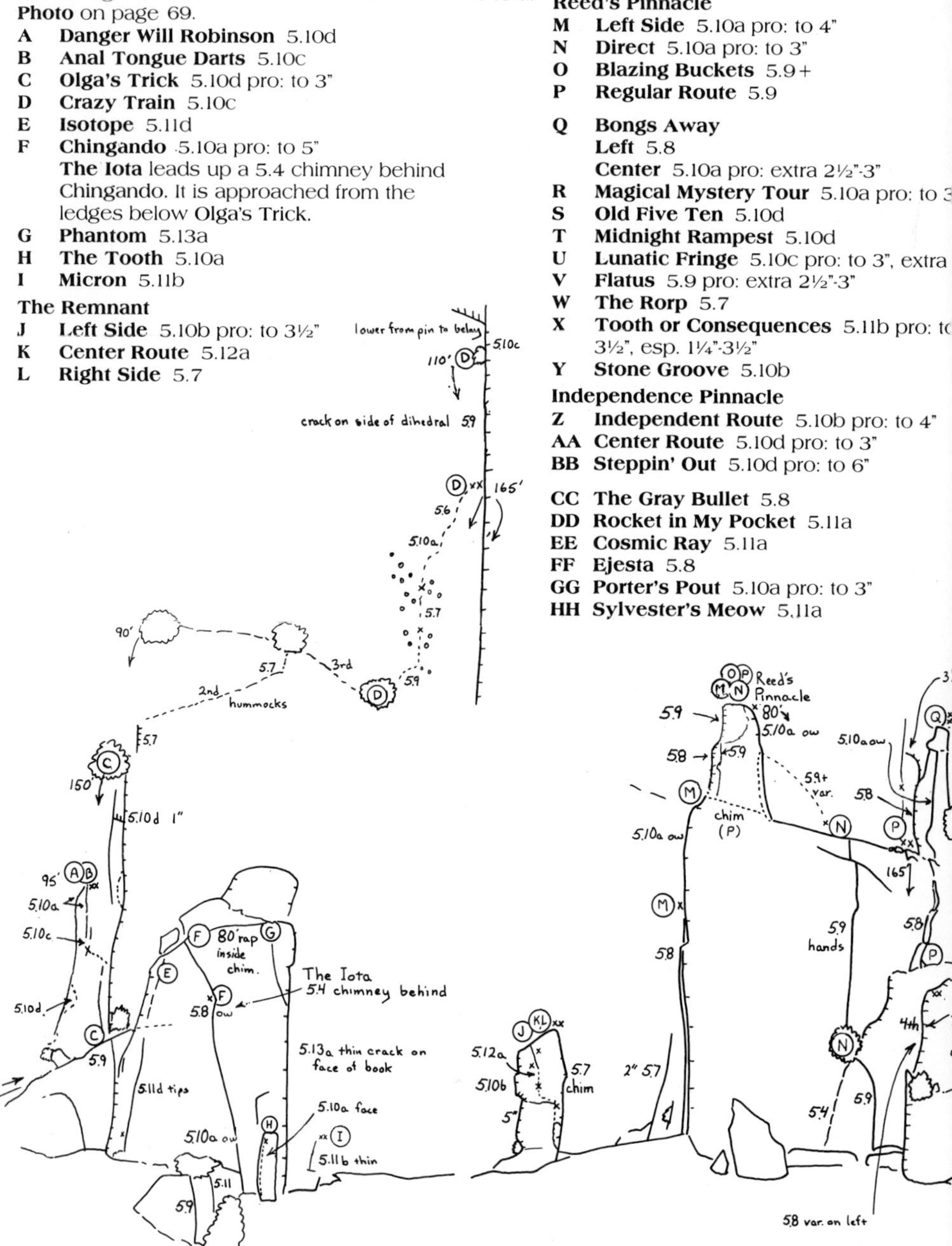

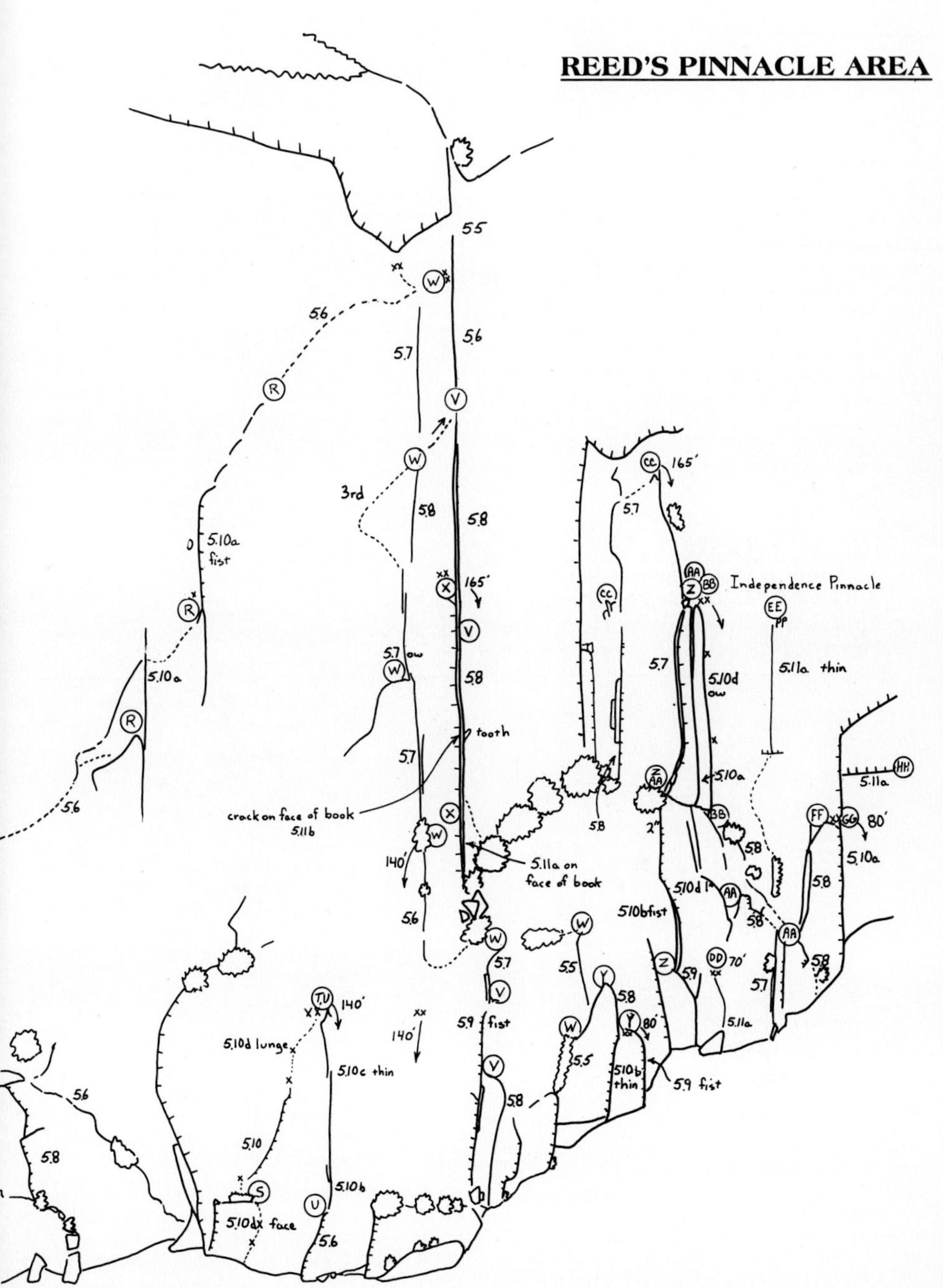
REED'S PINNACLE AREA
Independence Pinnacle
5.5
5.6
5.7
5.8
3rd
165'
5.10a fist
5.10a
5.6
5.7 ow
tooth
crack on face of book 5.11b
5.11a on face of book
140'
5.6
5.7
5.9 fist
5.8
5.10d lunge
5.10c thin
140'
5.10
5.10b
5.10dX face
5.6
5.8
5.5
5.10b thin
80'
5.9 fist
5.10b fist
5.10d
5.10a
2"
5.11a thin
5.11a
80'
5.10a
70'
5.11a
5.10d ow

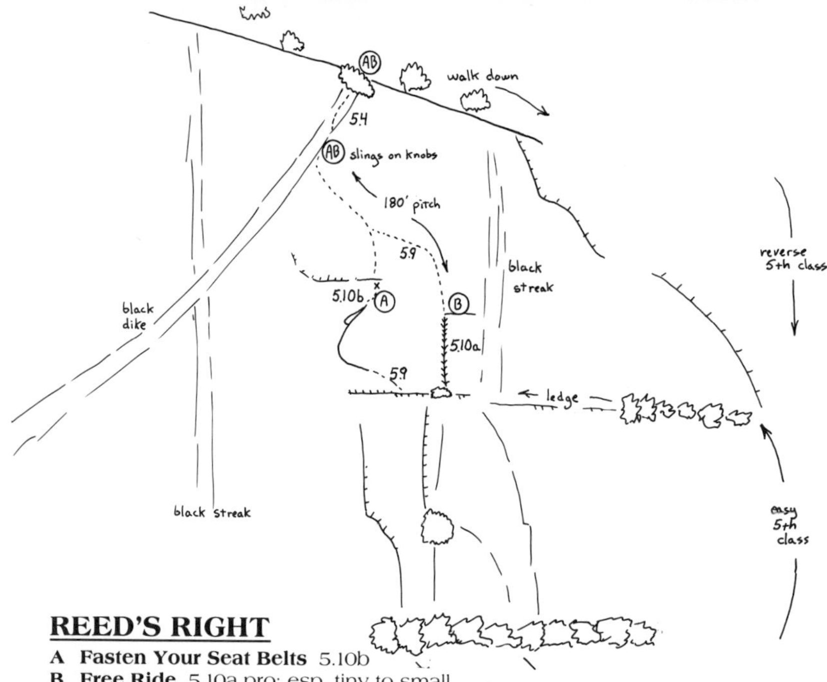

REED'S RIGHT

A Fasten Your Seat Belts 5.10b
B Free Ride 5.10a pro: esp. tiny to small

Approach From Porter's Pout walk up and right; start atop the buttress above the tunnel. **Photo** on page 69.

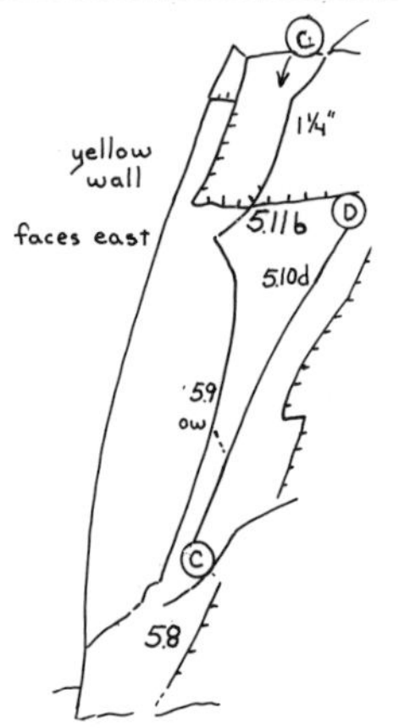

Approach Park at Reeds and walk down Hwy 120, through the tunnel and approximately ¼ mile further. Ten minutes up a steep dirt slope leads to a minor buttress. The climb is on the right (east facing) wall. (The top part of this route can be seen on the drive up to Reed's, as an orange wall split by a crack.)

C Cro Magnon Capers 5.11b
D Nothing Good Ever Lasts 5.10d

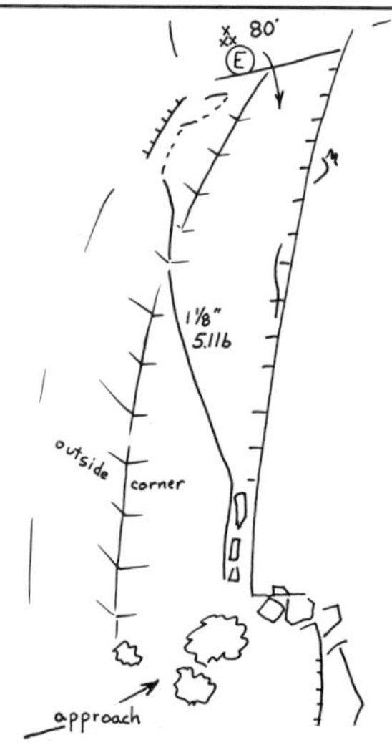

Approach Park in the first paved turnout on the right, west of the 120/140 junction. Walk up the road another .4 mile. The climb can be seen from the road as a left slanting crack that crosses a yellow east facing corner. Hike up the dirt slope (past poison oak), and enter onto the perch from where the climb starts.

E Spring Fever 5.11b pro: small to 2½", esp. ¾"-1"

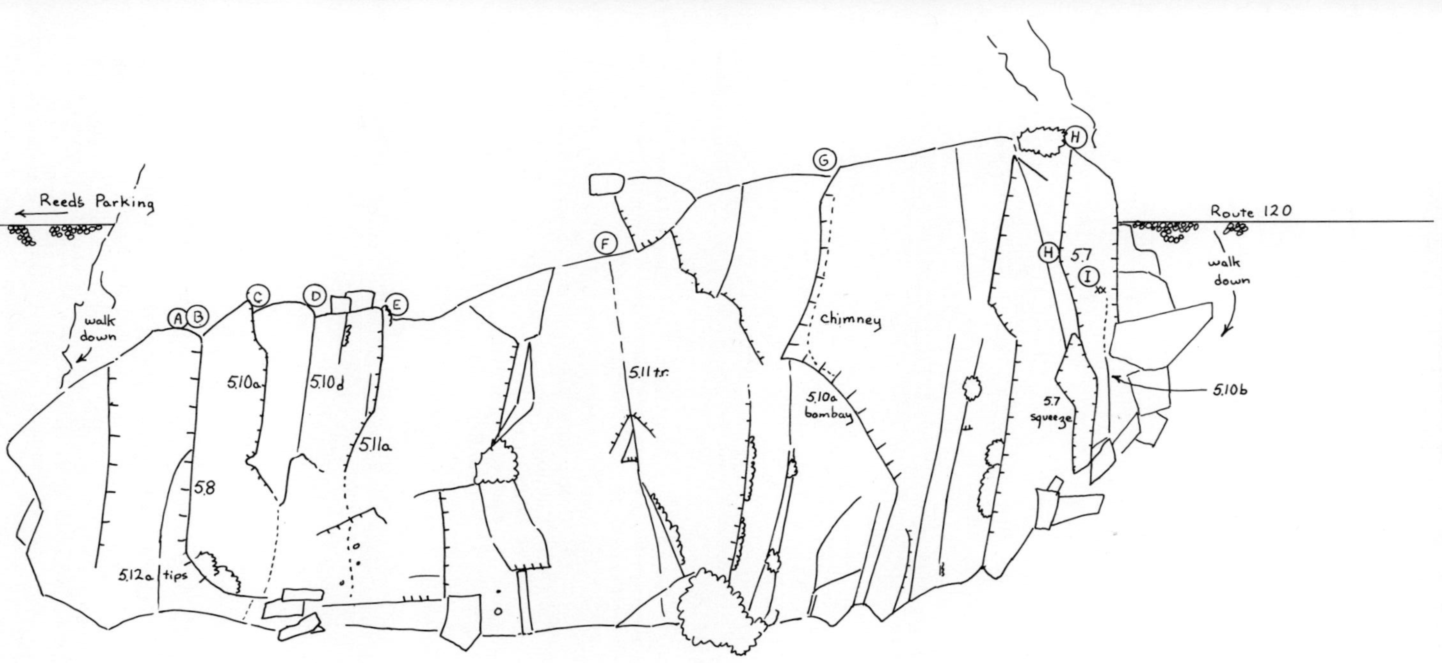

FIVE AND DIME CLIFF

Approach Park at Reed's Pinnacle Area (between the two short tunnels up Hwy 120) and walk to the mouth of the eastern tunnel. A climber's trail leads first to the top of the cliff, then drops down circuitously to the base.

Photo on page 69.

- **A Chump Change** 5.12a
- **B Keystone Corner** 5.8
- **C Copper Penny** 5.10a pro: to 6"
- **D Five and Dime** 5.10d pro: to 2½"
- **E Whack and Dangle** 5.11a pro: to 2½"
- **F Penny Ante** 5.11 tr
- **G The Reception** 5.10a
- **H Inner Reaches** 5.7
- **I Crack n' Face** 5.10b

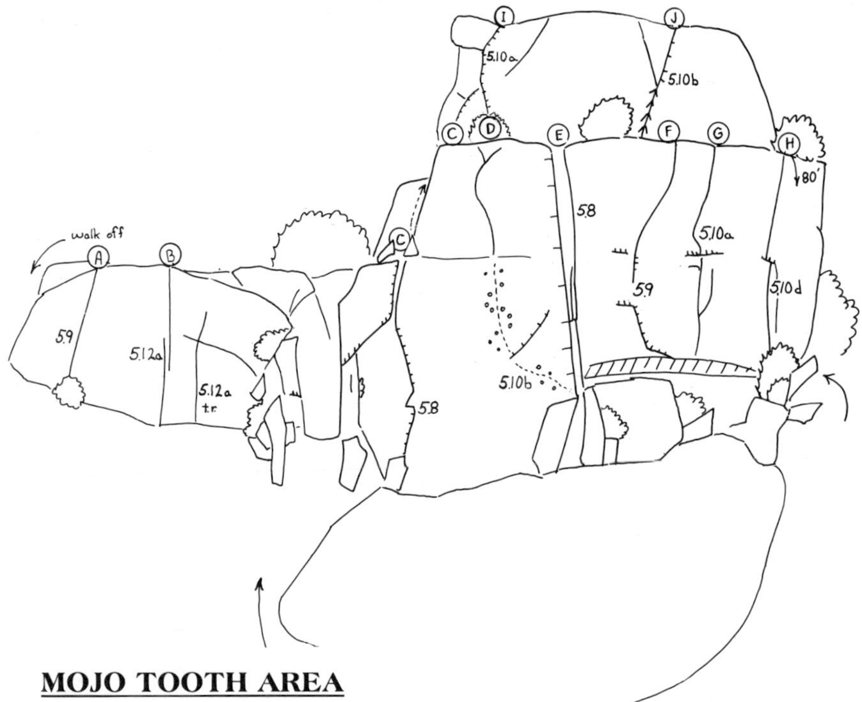

MOJO TOOTH AREA

Approach The parking area at the junction of Hwy 120/140 lies directly below this formation. F the regular Mojo Tooth and routes left, head up steep dirt slopes. For those climbs to the right sloppy dirt and talus leads up and right. Move left where one can contour onto a sloping ledg the starting point for the other routes.

- **A Fluke** 5.9
- **B Tongue and Groove** 5.12a
- **C Mojo Tooth** 5.8
- **D New Traditionalists** 5.10b
- **E Figment** 5.8
- **F Grape Nuts** 5.9
- **G Euellogy** 5.10a
- **H Mighty Crunchy** 5.10d
- **I Bad News Bombers** 5.10a
- **J Natural End** 5.10b

Approach This bluff is unseen from the road. Park at the first turnout east of the Mojo Tooth. A large flat boulder in the Merced River marks the spot. The routes lie a short distance up the hill.

- **K Hey Walt** 5.10b
- **L Highway Star** 5.10a

LAST RESORT CLIFF

1 Plumkin
2 Ready or Not

LAST RESORT CLIFF

Approach Park at the first turnout east of the Hwy 120/140 junction. A large flat boulder in the Merced River marks the spot. Head up and slightly right. About halfway to the cliff house-sized boulders (at the right margin of a talus field) mark a traverse left through the talus and up to the toe of the cliff.
Photo on page 83.

- **A** **Turning Point** 5.10c pro: to 2½"
- **B** **Side Kick** 5.9
- **C** **Tiger's Paw** 5.10a A1
- **D** **Plumkin** 5.10a
- **E** **Moon Age Daydream** 5.11a
- **F** **The Steal** 5.10a
- **G** **Sex, Drugs and Violence** 5.10a
- **H** **P.M.S.** 5.11a
- **I** **B & B** 5.10a

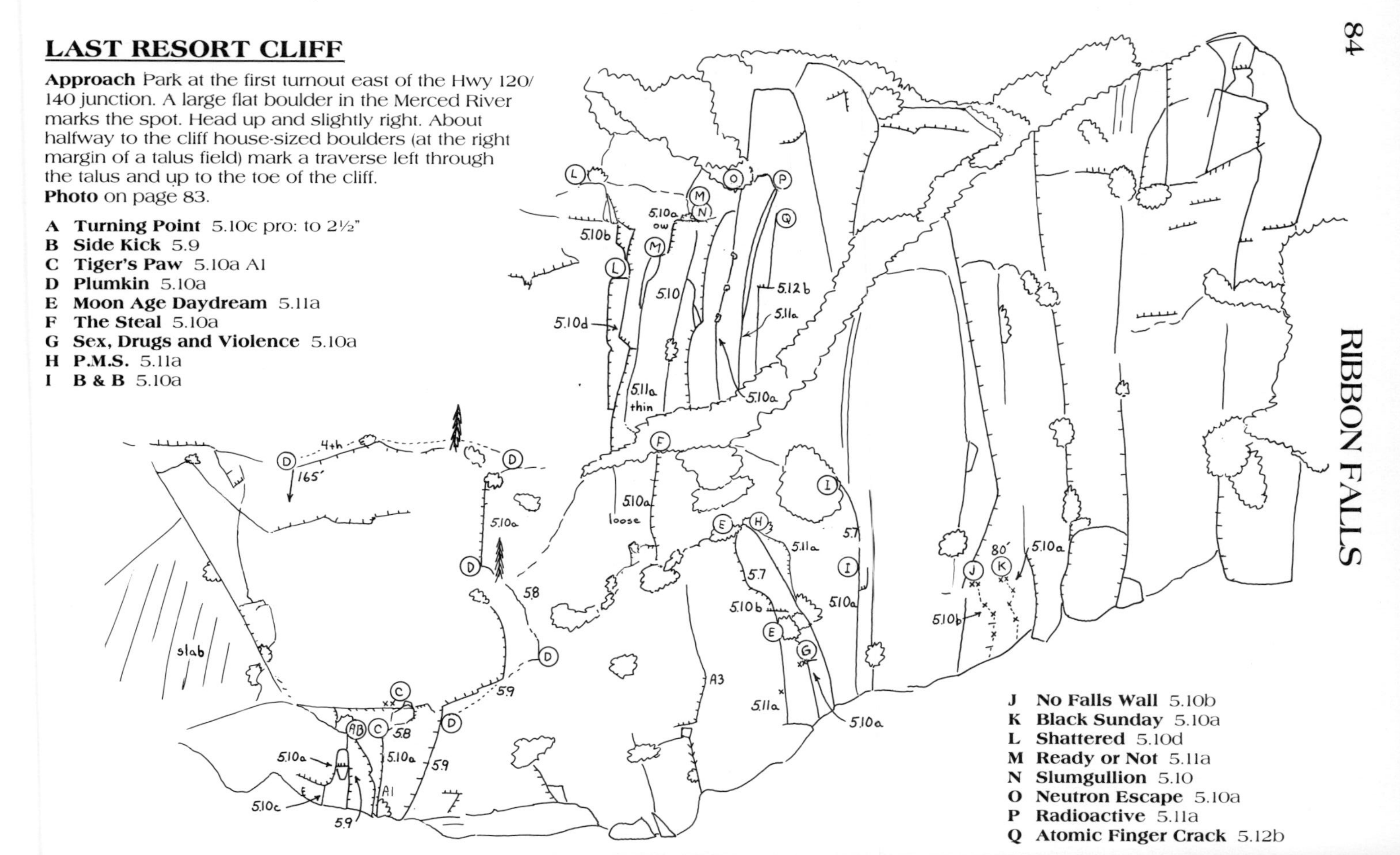

- **J** **No Falls Wall** 5.10b
- **K** **Black Sunday** 5.10a
- **L** **Shattered** 5.10d
- **M** **Ready or Not** 5.11a
- **N** **Slumgullion** 5.10
- **O** **Neutron Escape** 5.10a
- **P** **Radioactive** 5.11a
- **Q** **Atomic Finger Crack** 5.12b

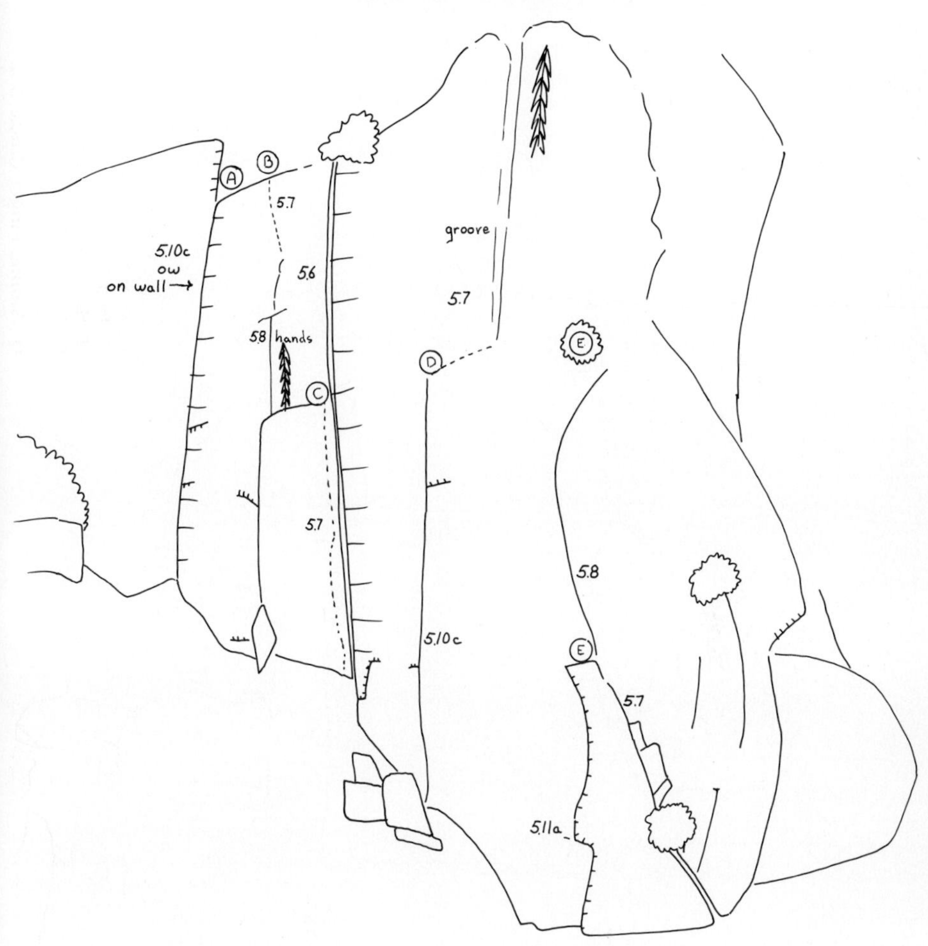

AUDUBON BUTTRESS

Approach This small cliff, as well as the Nuts Only Cliff and Little Wing Area, is made from the Old Big Oak Flat Road, the head of which is located as a service road to a woodyard, .2 mile west of El Cap Meadow. Walk straight north up the hill before finding the main roadbed that angles gently up to the west. Ten or fifteen minutes of hiking, sometimes past rock slides, leads to open talus slopes below the Nuts Only Wall. A few minutes further on leads to the roadside Little Wing Cliff. After 45 minutes of hiking, a railing that overlooks the Last Resort Cliff is reached. To find the Audubon Buttress, hike an additional ten minutes from this point. The cliff lies hidden in the woods directly above. (The hike-up point is a bit before the road curves gently right, then left, moving past a spring area.)

A **Wild Turkey** 5.10c pro: to 6"
B **The Dove** 5.8
C **Birds of a Feather** 5.7
D **Eagle Feather** 5.10c
E **Duncan Imperial** 5.11a

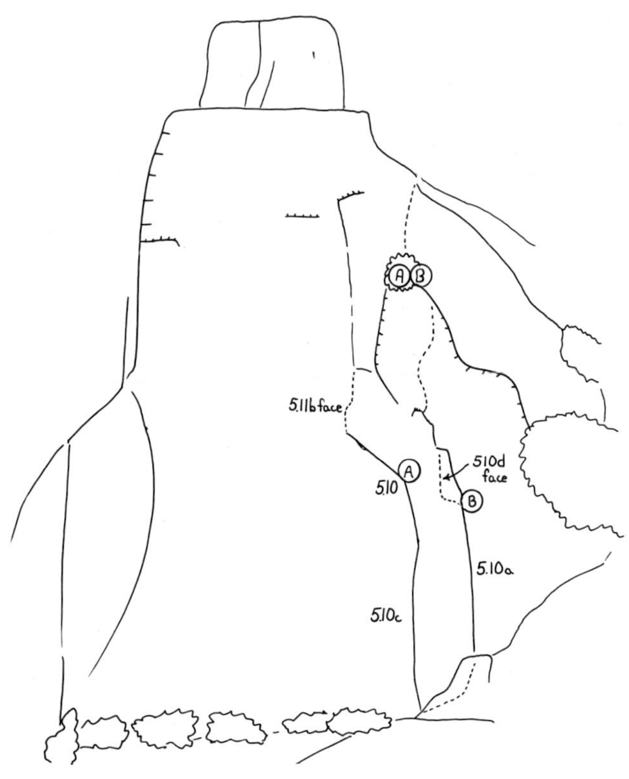

NUTS ONLY CLIFF

Approach Hike to this cliff as described on the previous page.

A **Catch-U** 5.11b pro: double nuts to 3½"
B **W'allnuts** 5.10d pro: to 3", extra 1¼"

LITTLE WING AREA

Approach Hike to this cliff along the Old Big Oak Flat Road, as described on page 85.

A **Scuz Ball** 5.7
B **Squeeze-n-Tease** 5.8
C **L.D. Getaway** 5.8
D **Andy Devine** 5.7
E **He Can't Shout, Don't Hear You** 5.7
F **Gunks Revisited** 5.11c
G **Honor Thy Father** 5.10c pro: to 3"
H **Leisure Time** 5.10b pro: to 3"
I **The Riddler** 5.10a pro: to 3"
J **Little Wing** 5.10d pro: double on small pro.
K **Dolly Dagger** 5.9
L **Building Blocks** 5.8
M **Angelina** 5.8
N **Little Thing** 5.11c/d
O **Red House** 5.10a
P **Too Much Paranoia** 5.10b

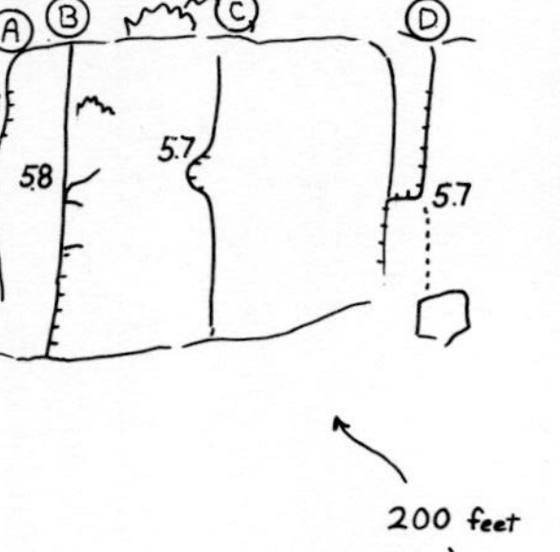

RIBBON FALLS AMPITHEATRE

N.P.S.

1 **West Buttress** 5.8 A3
2 **Golden Bough**
3 **Gold Wall**
4 **Fool's Gold**
5 **Keel Haul**
6 **East Portal**
7 **Gold Ribbon**
8 **Vain Hope** V 5.7 A3
9 **Chockstone Chimney**
10 **The Lionheart**
11 **Nottingham**
12 **THE HOURGLASS**

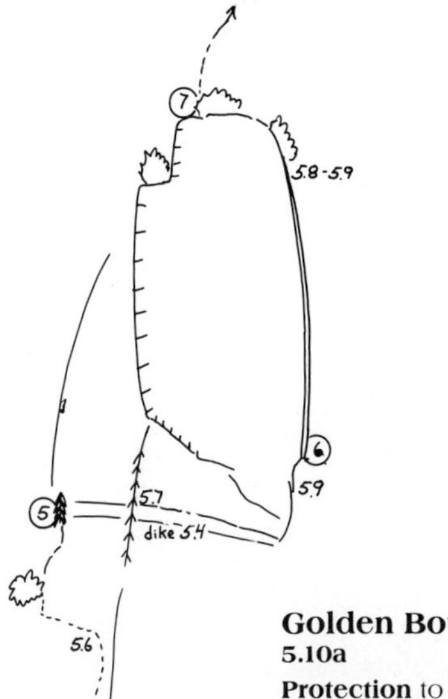

Golden Bough

5.10a

Protection to 3½"

Approach For this and all routes in the Ribbon Falls area, start from the service road and woodyard that is .2 mile west of El Cap Meadow. Walk up forested slopes, staying left of Ribbon Creek, to meet the wall near the start of the **Gold Wall**. During times of high water the creek may be difficult to cross; routes on the east side of the creek are best approached from that side.

Descent Work up and left towards a large straight tree, then drop down and work left, rappelling from tree to tree on steep slabs.

Photo on page 88.

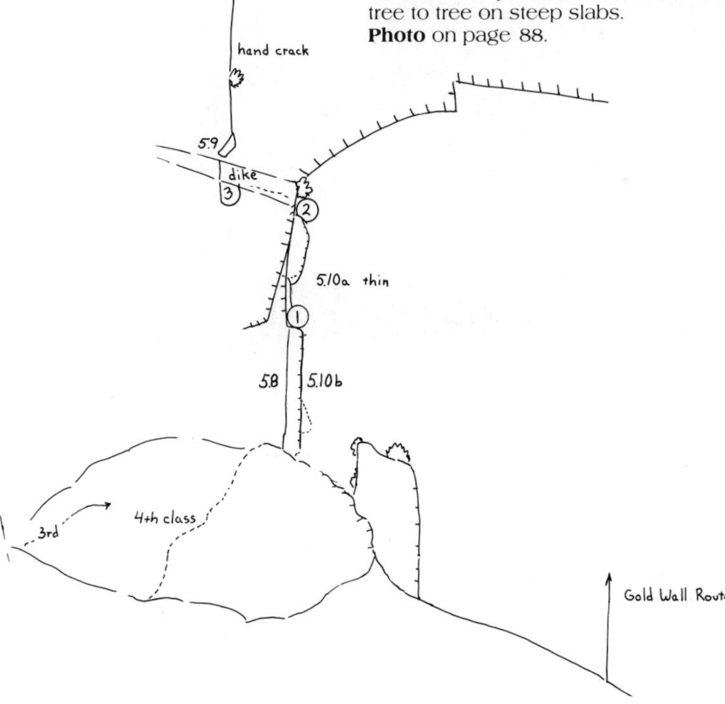

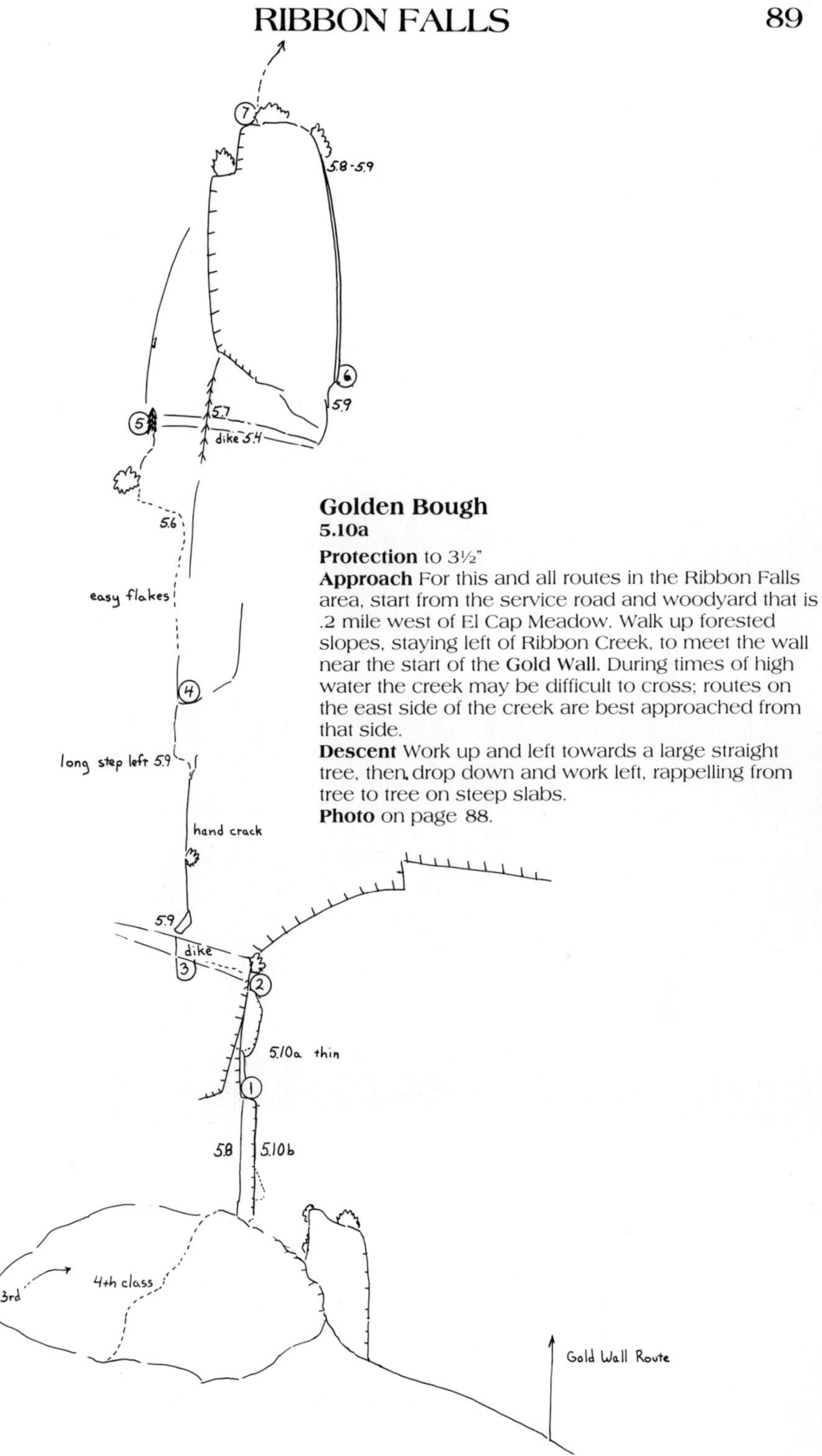

Gold Wall

V 5.10 A3

Approach Walk up as described on page 89.
Descent From the top of the last pitch, walk left on ledges to a gully that leads to the top. Walk up and left to ramps that lead down. Keep to the west until a ledge runs out to two pitons that provide the anchor for the first of three rappels to trees and eventually the final descent ledges.
Photo on page 88.
Hardware

2 KB
2 LA
2 ea. ½"-1¼"
1 ea. 1½"
25 nuts and Friends to 3", incl. many small wires

Silent Line (free variation)

5.10c A1

Protection small nuts
3 ea. Friend to #3, 1 ea. #4

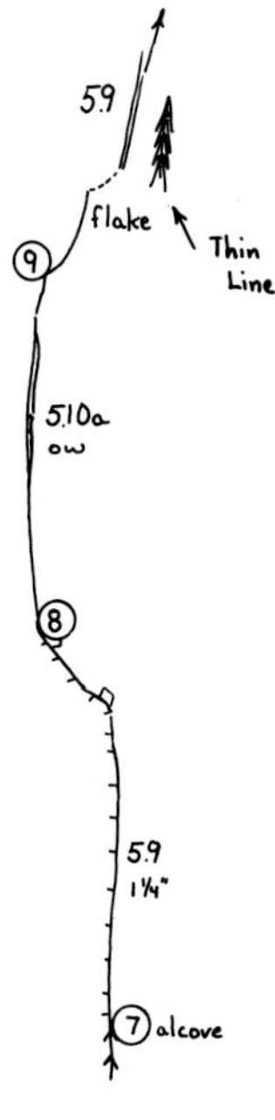

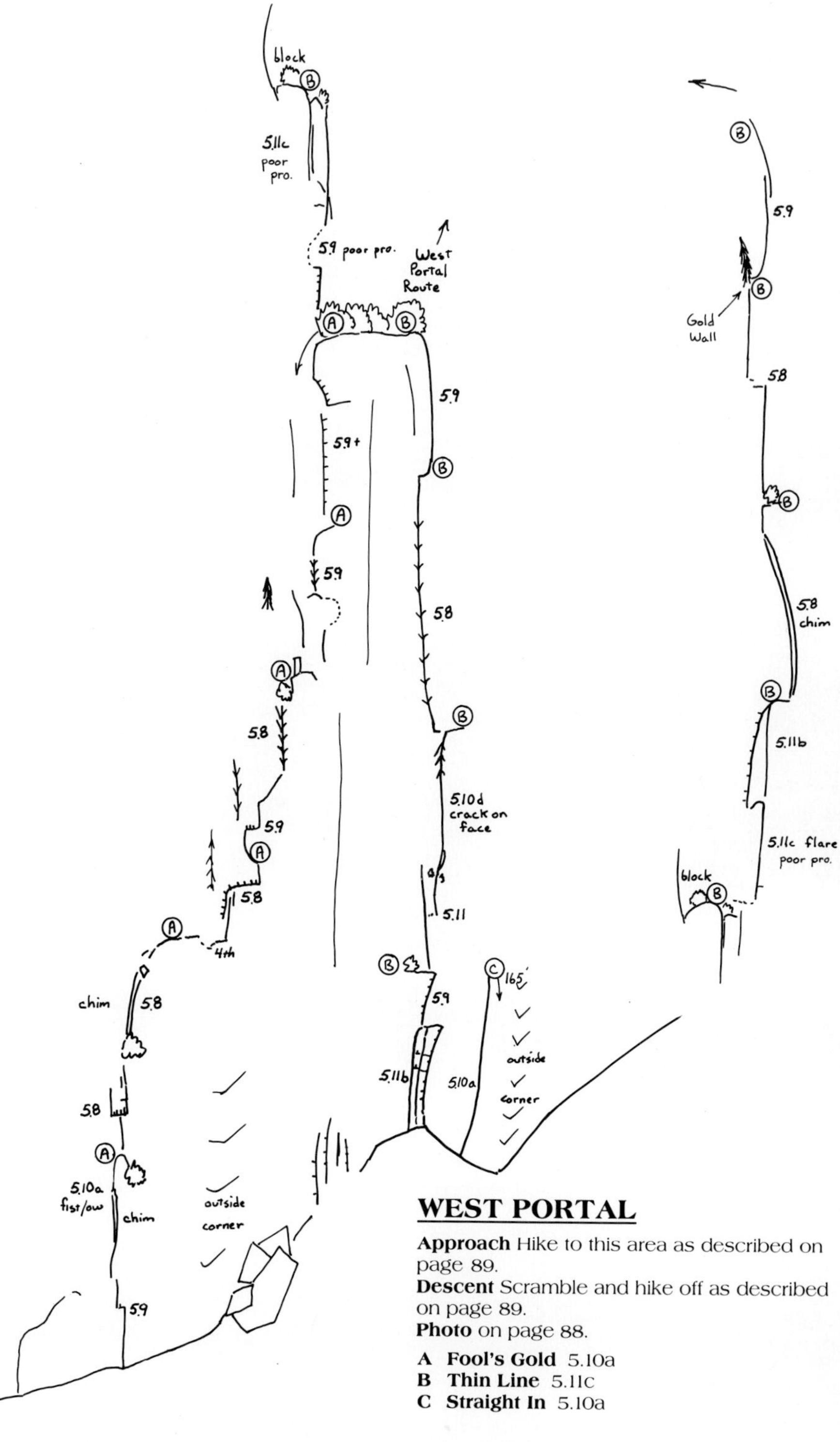

WEST PORTAL

Approach Hike to this area as described on page 89.
Descent Scramble and hike off as described on page 89.
Photo on page 88.

A Fool's Gold 5.10a
B Thin Line 5.11c
C Straight In 5.10a

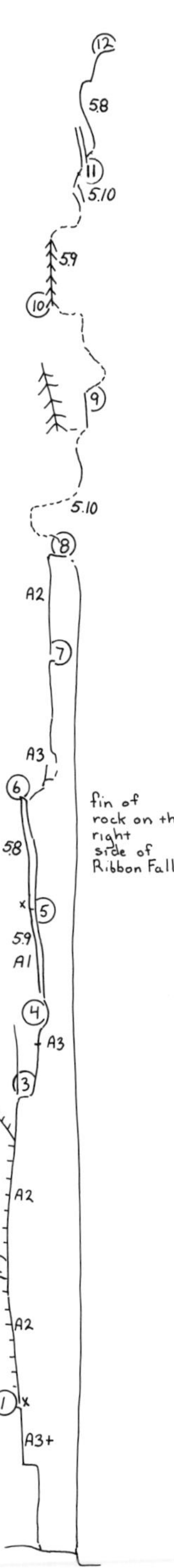

Keel Haul

VI 5.10 A3

Approach Hike up to the Ribbon Falls Ampitheatre as described on page 89. This route starts just left of a major fin of rock on the right side of the falls.
Descent Hike along the rim of the valley to the east, and pick up the trail that leads north off the top of El Capitan toward Tamarack Flat Campground.
Photo on page 88.
Hardware

standard wall rack
1 ea. 3"
3 ea. 2½"
2 ea. 2"

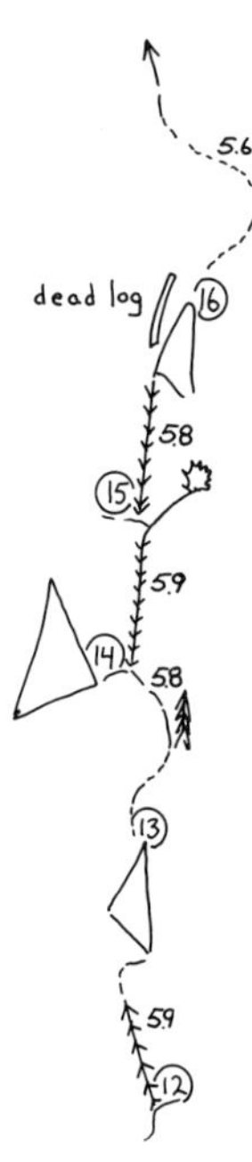

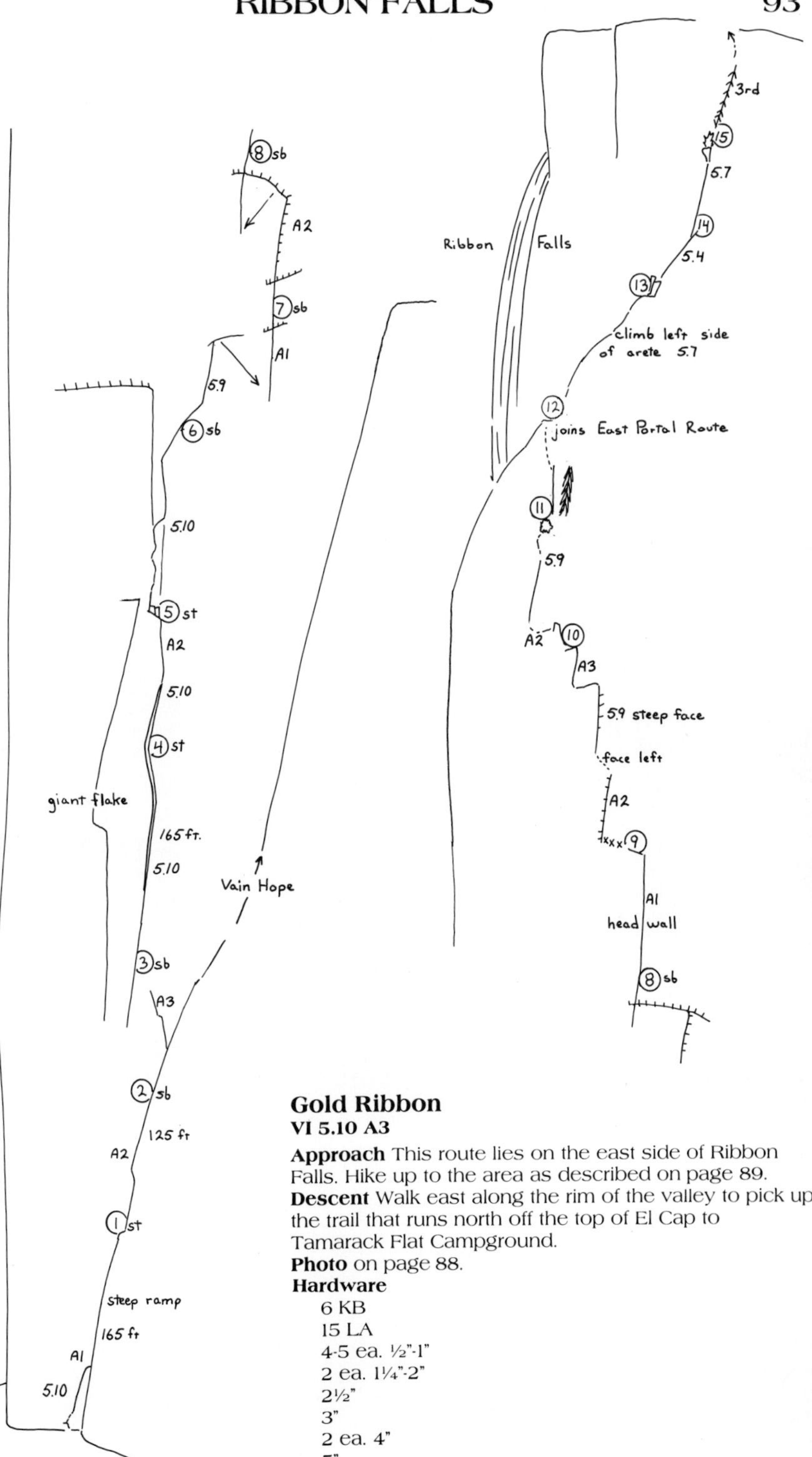

Gold Ribbon

VI 5.10 A3

Approach This route lies on the east side of Ribbon Falls. Hike up to the area as described on page 89.
Descent Walk east along the rim of the valley to pick up the trail that runs north off the top of El Cap to Tamarack Flat Campground.
Photo on page 88.
Hardware

6 KB
15 LA
4-5 ea. ½"-1"
2 ea. 1¼"-2"
2½"
3"
2 ea. 4"
5"
nuts, Friends and tubes to 7"

RIBBON CREEK AREA

Approach Hike up to this area along the right side of Ribbon Creek, as described on page 89.
Photo on page 88.

A Chockstone Chimney 5.9
B The Lionheart 5.10b
C Nottingham 5.10a

The Hourglass
D Left Side 5.10d
E Right Side 5.10a

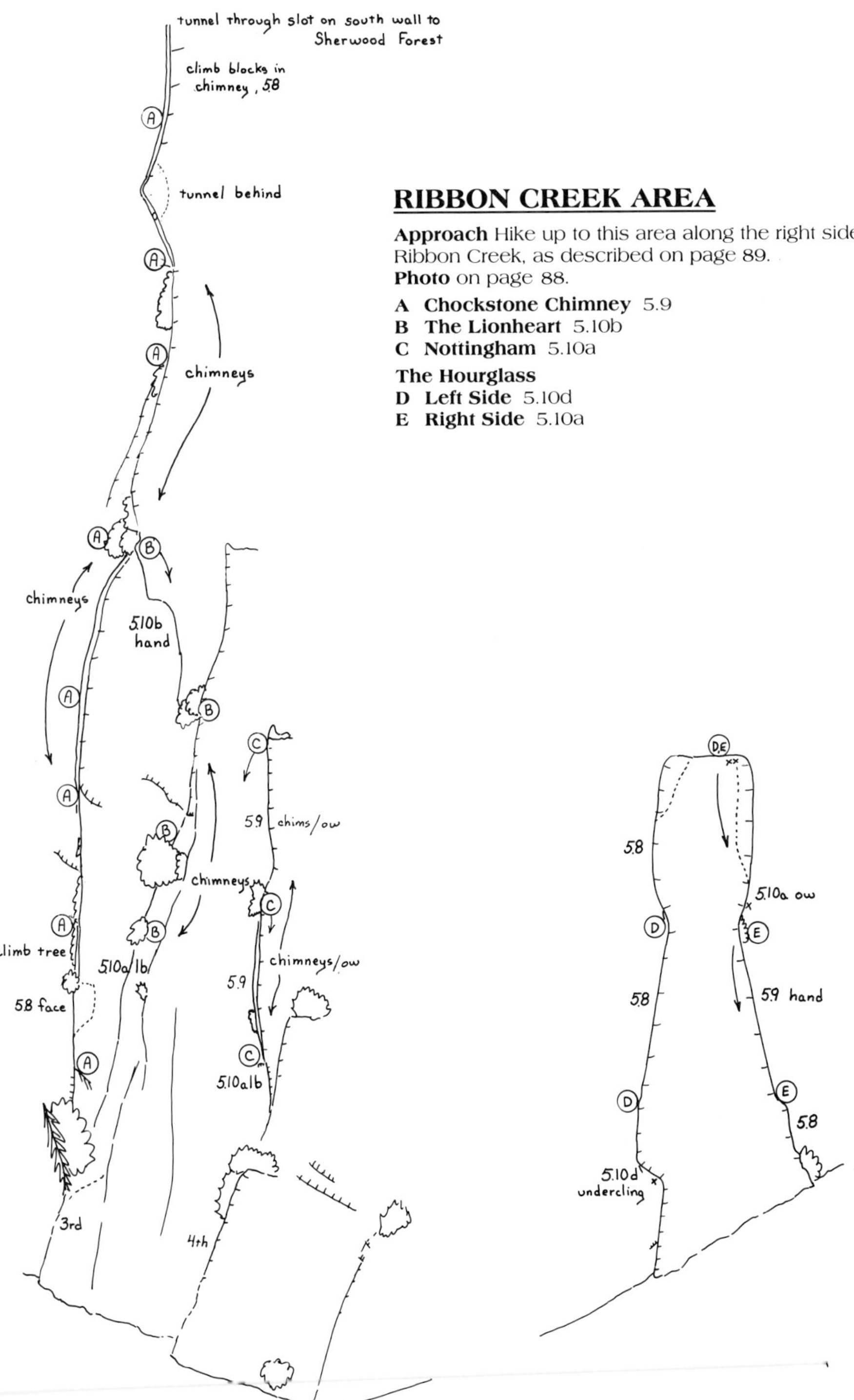

EL CAPITAN

Approach Park 0.1 mile west of the El Cap Bridge. Take the climber's trail that heads back through the woods directly toward the **Nose.** Beneath that route, the trail divides, leading along both sides of the cliff. For routes in the **Zodiac** area, a more direct but strenuous approach ascends talus directly above a picnic pullout 2.1 miles west of the gas station.

For the climbs beyond **Captain Hook** skirt the scruffy gray barrier by dropping down and around the corner to a 3rd class path that leads up. To proceed further up the **West Chimney**, for **Mirage** and the **West Face**, stay left of the main chimney on a 3rd class rib until above the chockstone.

The next ten pages describe short routes that climb to exfoliated "summits" that sit just above the base of El Capitan. The southwest side is described first, from furthest up the hill by the **West Buttress** down along the wall to the **Nose** and then on eastward along the base of the southeast face. As one walks up and left from the **Nose** the major formations are encountered in the following order: Pterodactyl Terrace, Moby Dick, Little John, La Cosita, The Slack, La Escuela, Delectable Pinnacle, Captain Hook and Peter Pan. Walking up and right from the **Nose** is Negative Pinnacle, the slab routes below the obvious ampitheatre, Gollum, The Footstool and finally the orange striped slab located at the far east end of the wall.

West of El Capitan are two prominent gullies separated by a long, brushy serrated ridge. The left gully is **El Capitan Gully.** It is in large part a talus slope, although exposed 3rd class slabs must be negotiated before the rim can be reached. Among the many pinnacles of the ridge to the east one spire stands out most prominently. This is **K-P Pinnacle.** Its summit is easily reached with easy 5th class climbing from the east. The gully/chimney that lies immediately below the West Face of El Cap is the **West Chimney.** Most of the large chockstones that occasionally block the gully can be avoided with circuitous and exposed scrambling. At its top the **West Chimney** ends atop the **K-P Pinnacle** ridge where a short rappel leads west into the **El Capitan Gully.**

Descent Most climbers descend from the top of El Cap to the Valley floor by one of the following ways: **1.** Hike up several hundred yards to the rounded summit knoll and pick up the trail that heads back into the woods. The campground off the Tuolumne road at Tamarack Flat can be reached after about five miles of rolling but gently downhill hiking. Consult a map. **2.** From the woods behind El Cap a trail can be taken east along the rim past Eagle Peak to the Yosemite Falls Trail for a descent directly to Camp Four. The Falls Trail part of this eight mile alternative is grueling in its continuous steepness. **3.** The East Ledges descent requires some 3rd class scrambling and some rappels but does offer the advantages of being snow-free in the early season and being only about 2½ hours to the Valley floor. See pages 168 and 174 for more exact information.

EL CAPITAN

Approach described on page 95.
Photo on page 114.

- **A** **West Buttress variation** 5.9
- **B** **Peter Pan** 5.9+ pro: to 6"
- **C** **Cuthulu** 5.10d pro: extra 1"-2"
- **D** **Indubious Battle** 5.11a
- **E** **Peter Left** 5.10c pro: to 3½"
- **F** **Tinkerbell**
  Left 5.7
  Right 5.9 pro: to 3½"
- **G** **Lost Boys** 5.9
- **H** **Wendy** 5.9
- **I** **Smee's Come-on** 5.11a
- **J** **Captain Hook**
  Left 5.7
  Right 5.9
- **K** **Captain Crunch** 5.11b

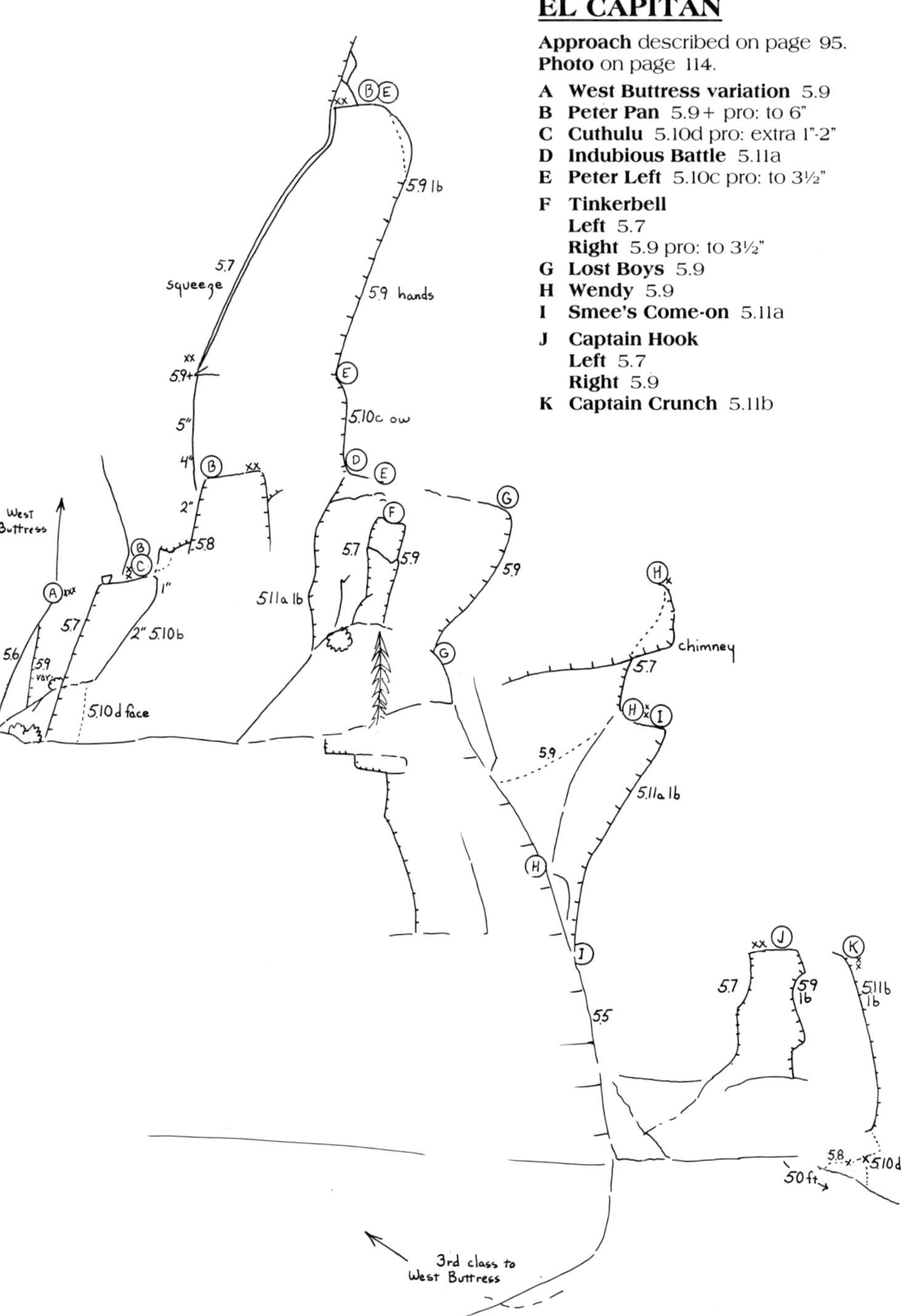

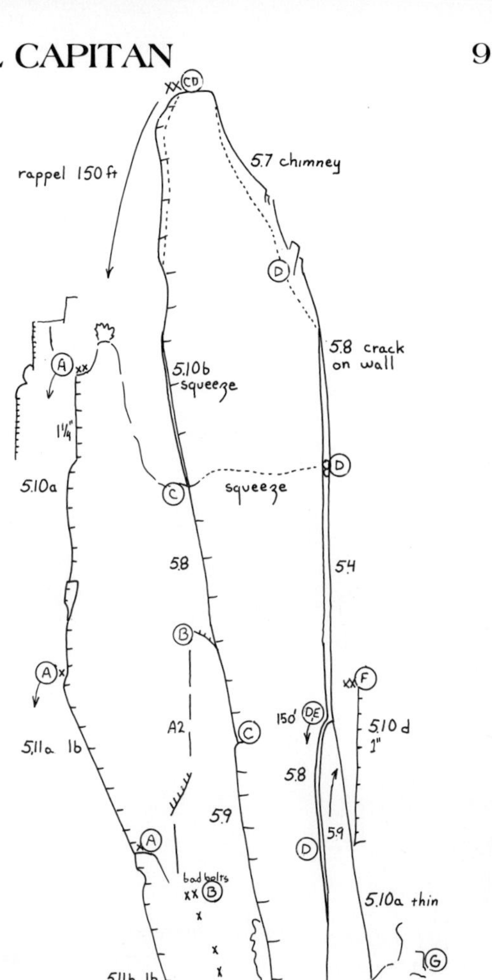

EL CAPITAN

Approach described on page 95.
Photo on page 114.

A La Escuela 5.11b pro: many small
B La Escuela Direct A4

The Slack
C Left Side 5.10b
D Center Route 5.10d pro: to 3½"
E Sacherer Cracker 5.10a pro: to 3½"
F The Mark of Art 5.10d pro: extra ¾"-1½"
G Short but Thin 5.11b

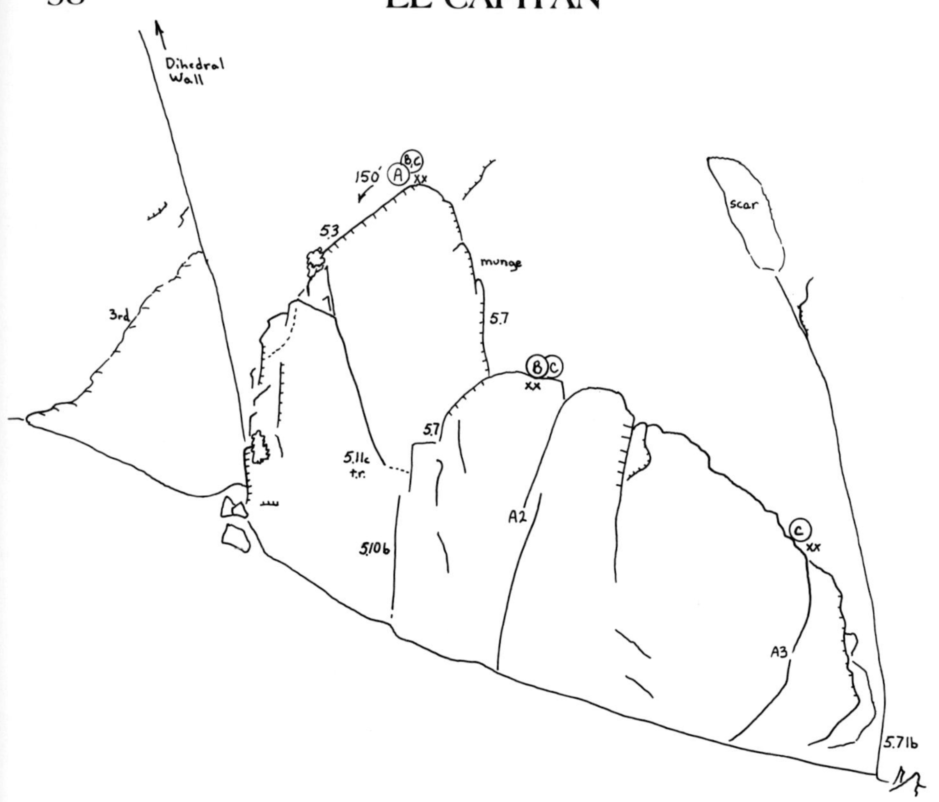

EL CAPITAN

Approach described on page 95.
Photo on page 114.

Delectable Pinnacle
A Left Side 5.3
B Center Route, free variation 5.10b
C Right Side 5.7

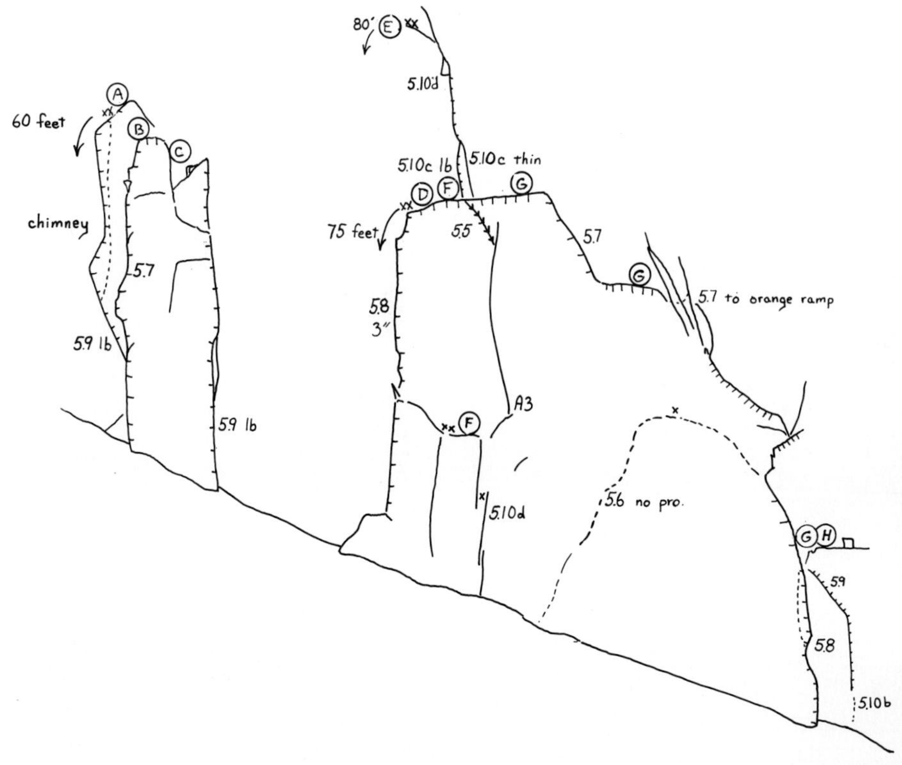

EL CAPITAN

Approach described on page 95.
Photo on page 114.

La Cosita

A Left Variation 5.9 pro: to 2½"
B Left Side 5.7
C Right Side 5.9

Little John

D Left Side 5.8 pro: to 3½"
E Hardly Pinnacle 5.10d
F Center Route 5.10d A3
G Right Side 5.8 pro: to 3"
H Sunday Driver 5.10b

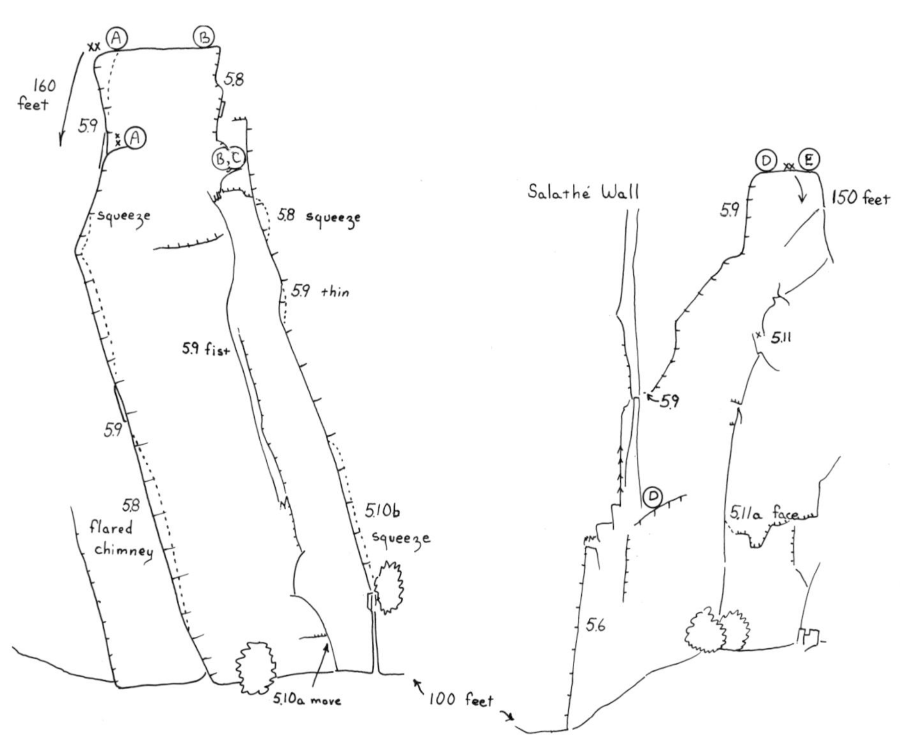

EL CAPITAN

Approach described on page 95.
Photo on page 114.

Moby Dick
A Left Side 5.9 pro: to 3"
B Center Route 5.10a pro: extra to 3½"
C Ahab 5.10b pro: to 3"

Pterodactyl Terrace
D Left Side 5.9
E Right Side 5.11a pro: RP's up

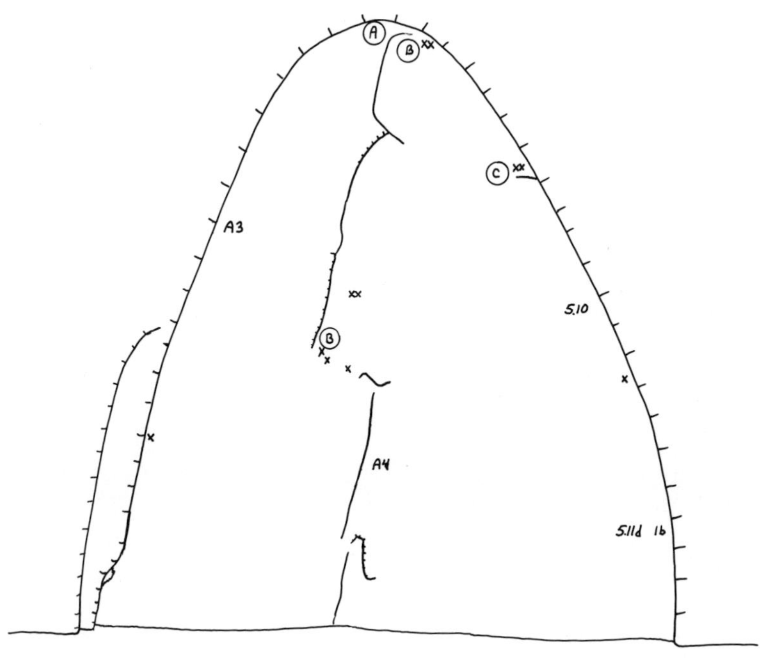

EL CAPITAN

Approach described on page 95.
Photo on page 138.

Negative Pinnacle

A Left Side A3
B Center Route A4
C The High Arc 5.11d

EL CAPITAN

Approach described on page 95.
Photo on page 138.

A **Rock Neurotic** 5.11a
B **Armageddon** 5.10d
C **Say Mama, Say Daddy** 5.10a
D **Simulkrime** 5.9

Gollum

E **Left Side** 5.10a
F **Right Side** 5.8

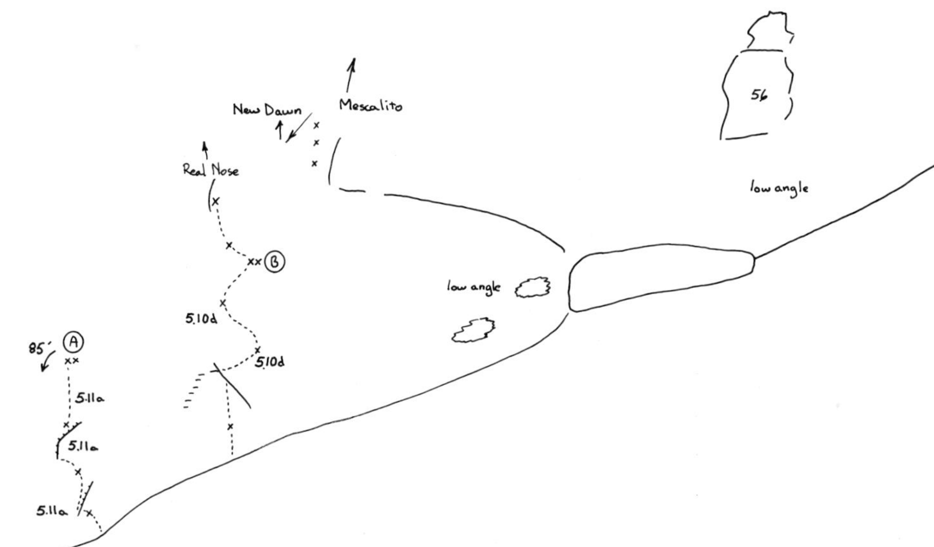

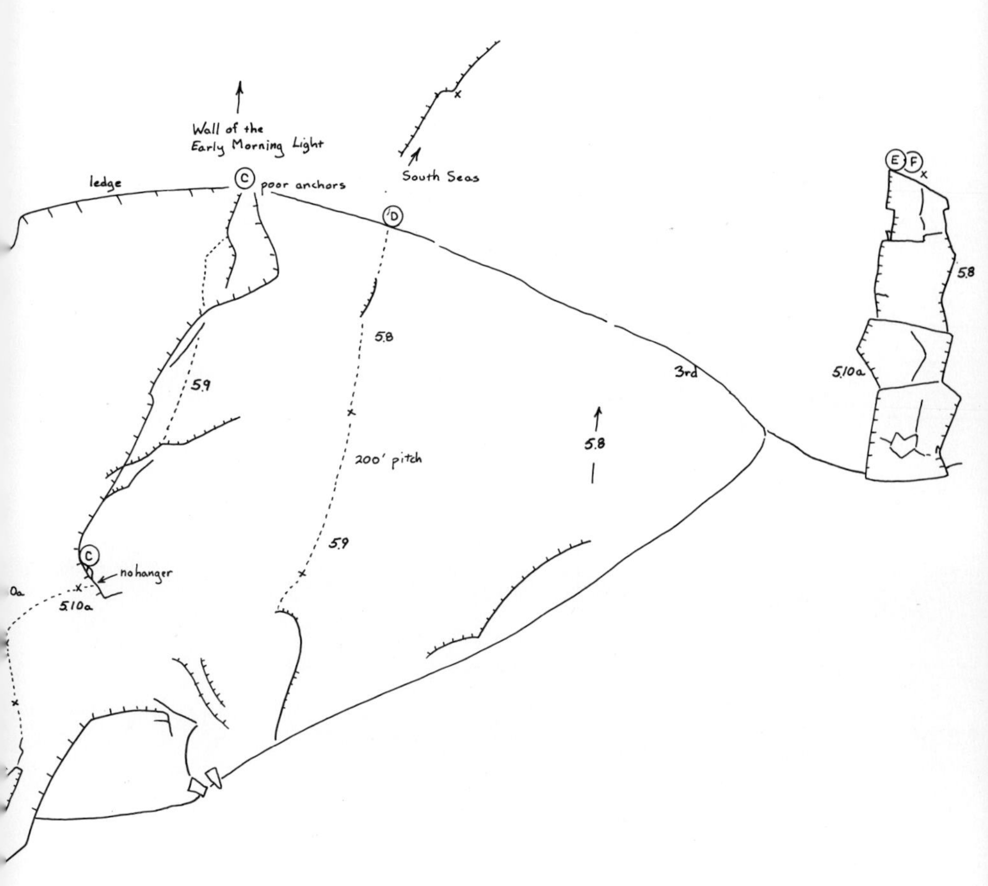
Wall of the
Early Morning Light
South Seas
ledge
C
poor anchors
D
E
F
5.8
5.8
3rd
5.10a
5.9
200' pitch
5.8
5.9
C
no hanger
0a
5.10a

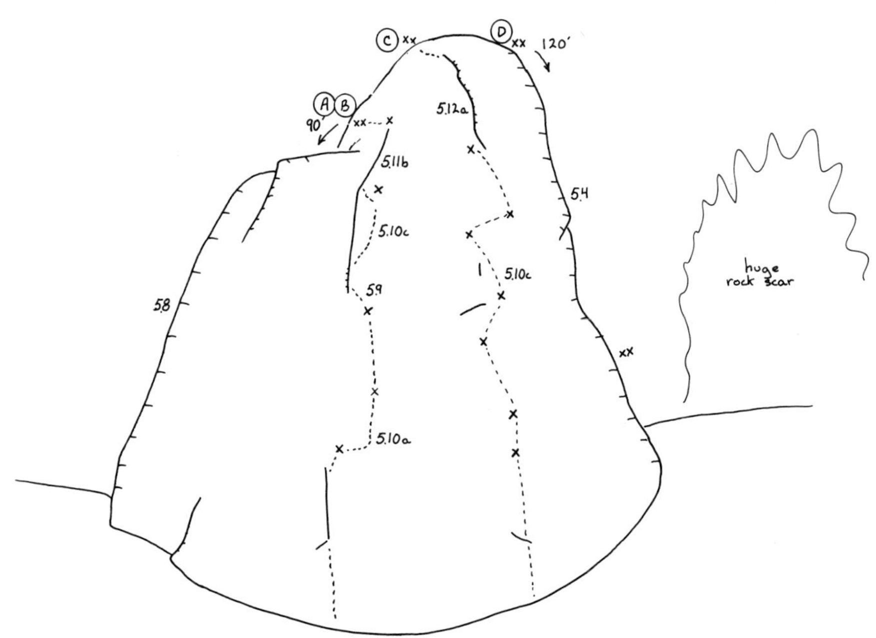

EL CAPITAN

Approach described on page 95.
Photo on page 138.

The Footstool
A Left Side 5.8
B The Promise 5.11b
C The Believer 5.12a
D Right Side 5.4

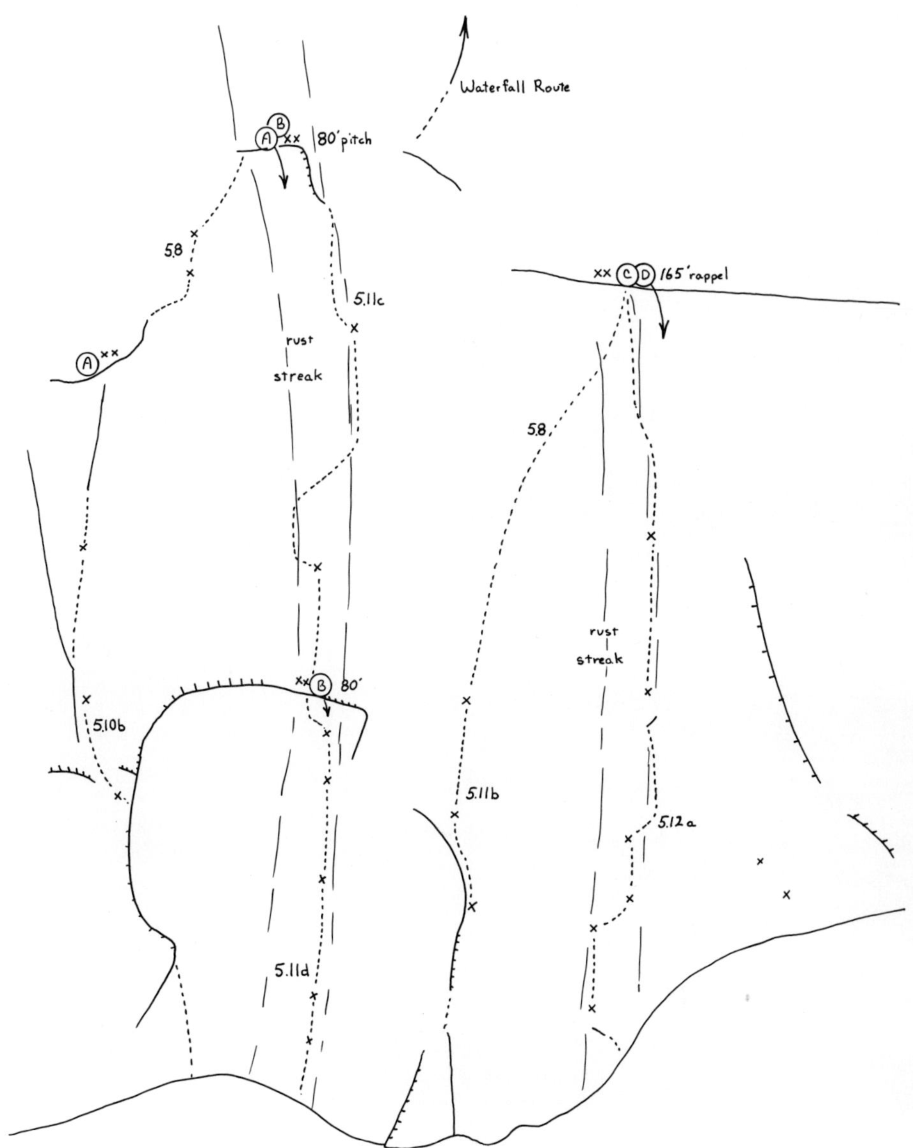

EL CAPITAN

Approach described on page 95.
Photo on page 138.

A Waterfall Route start 5.10b
B Champagne on Ice 5.11d
C Submen 5.11b
D El Matador 5.12a

EL CAPITAN – West Face

1 West Face Route
2 Mr. Midwest
3 Realm of the Flying Monkeys
4 Mirage
5 Lurking Fear

EL CAPITAN

Salami Ledge

5.7 A2

Approach This route starts from a low angle talus area in the West Chimney, just before the final steep part.

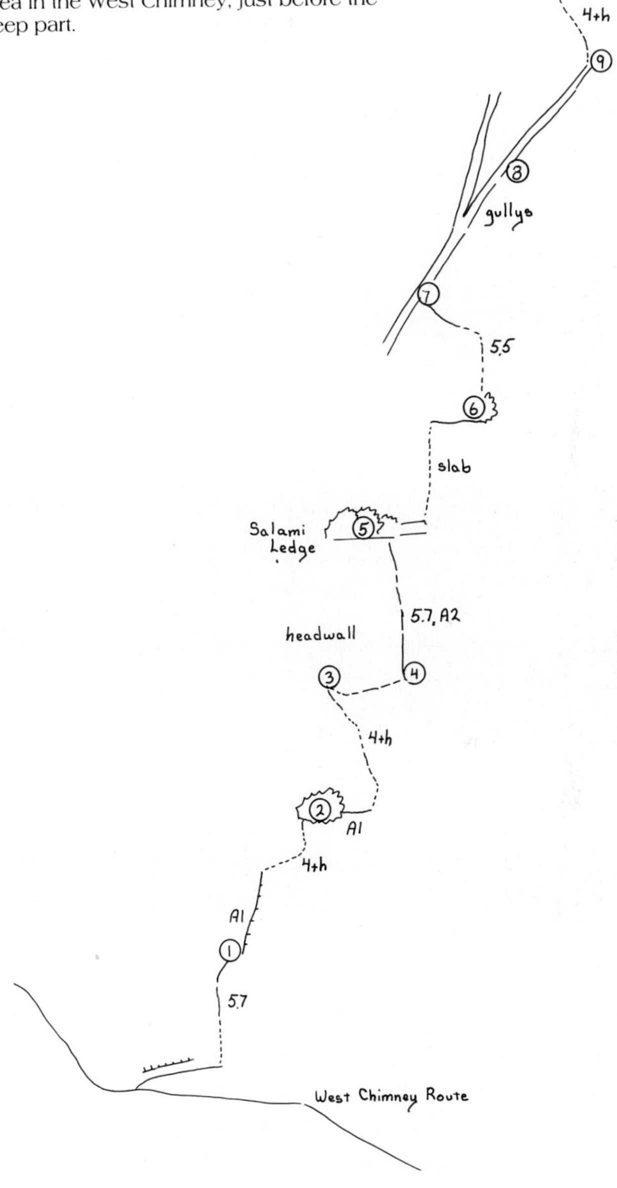

EL CAPITAN

West Face

VI 5.11b

Photo on page 106.

Hardware

RP's
Stoppers
Friends to #4

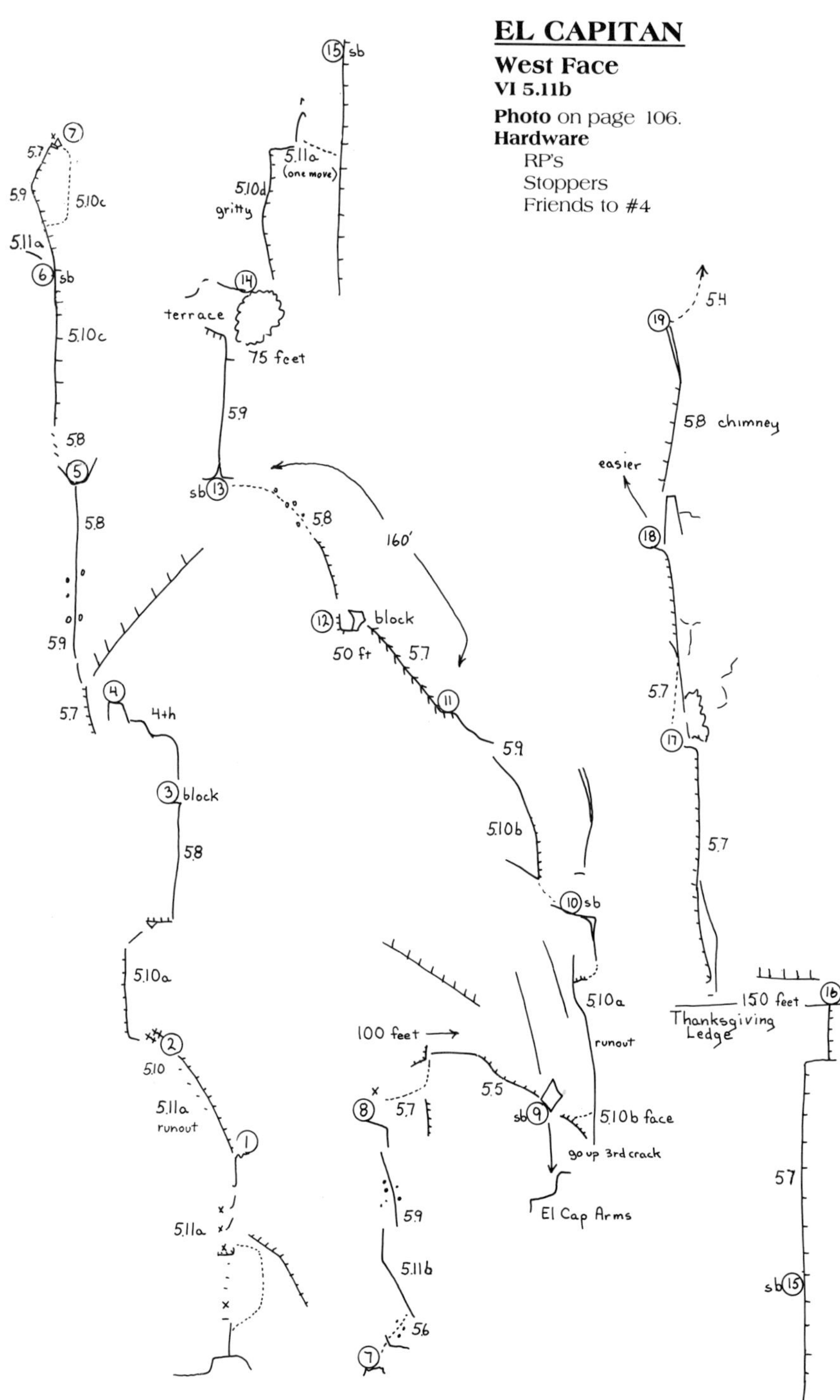

El CAPITAN

Mr. Midwest
VI 5.10 A3+

Photo on page 106.

Hardware
7 KB
10 LA
3 ea. ½"-1"
1 ea. 1¼"-2"
Friends to #5
hooks

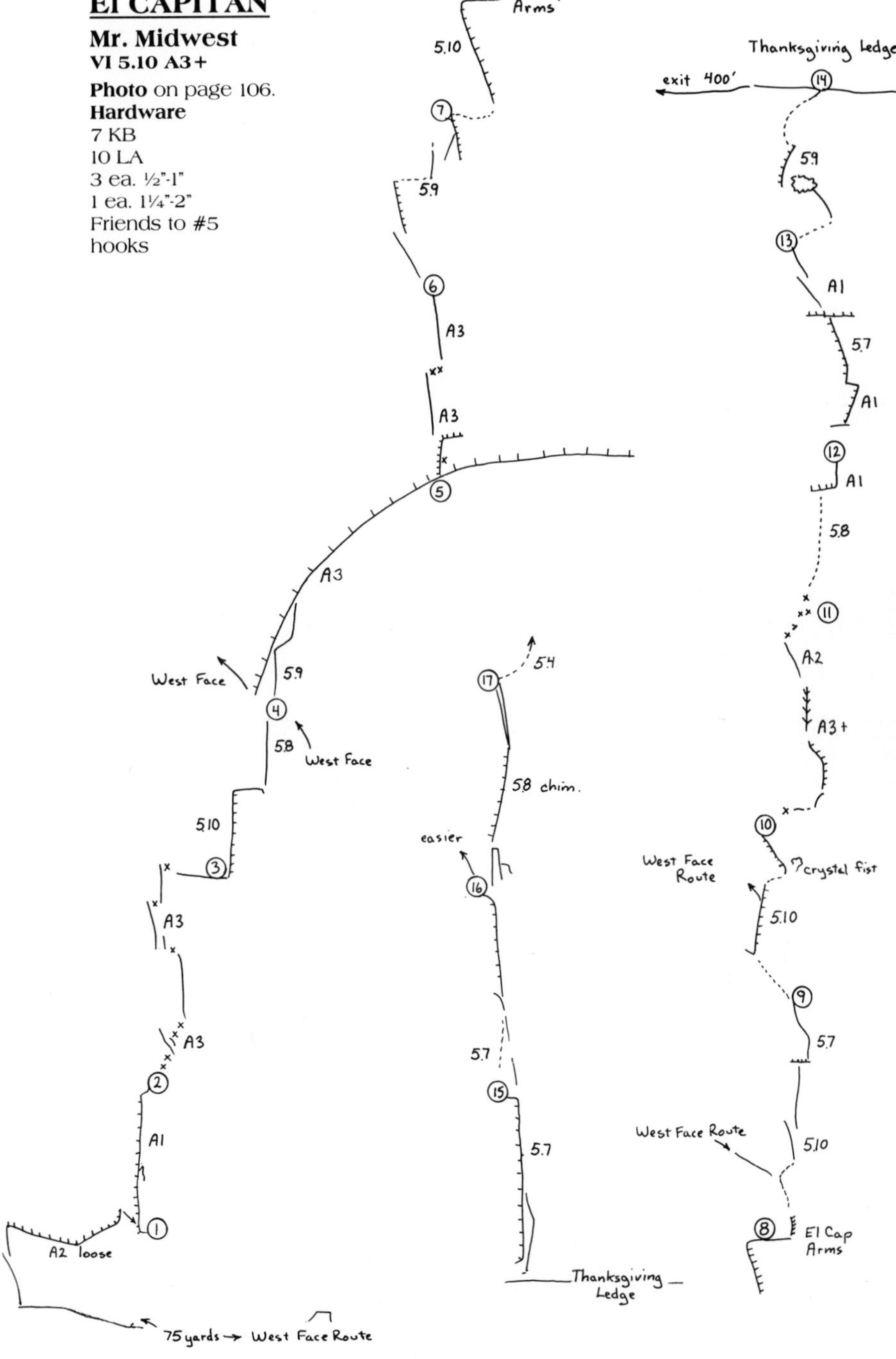

EL CAPITAN

Realm of the Flying Monkeys

VI 5.10a A3

Photo on page 106.

Photo on page 106.

Hardware

Friends
nuts
25 assorted pitons
hooks

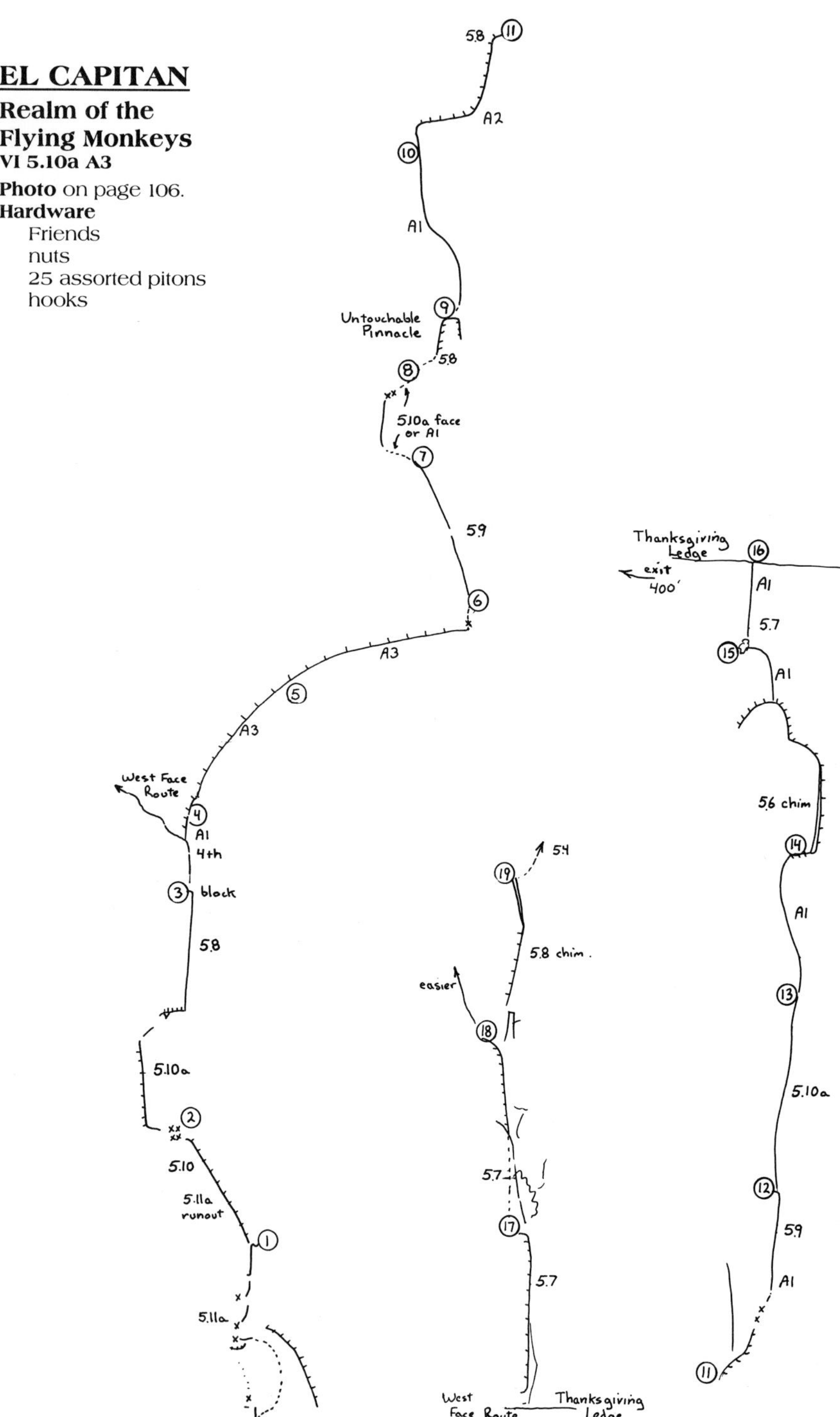

EL CAPITAN

Mirage
VI 5.9 A4

Photo on page 106.

Hardware
- 5 KB
- 12 LA
- 3 ea. ½"-¾"
- 2 ea. 1"
- 1 ea. 1¼"-1½"
- nuts
- Friends
- bolt hangers

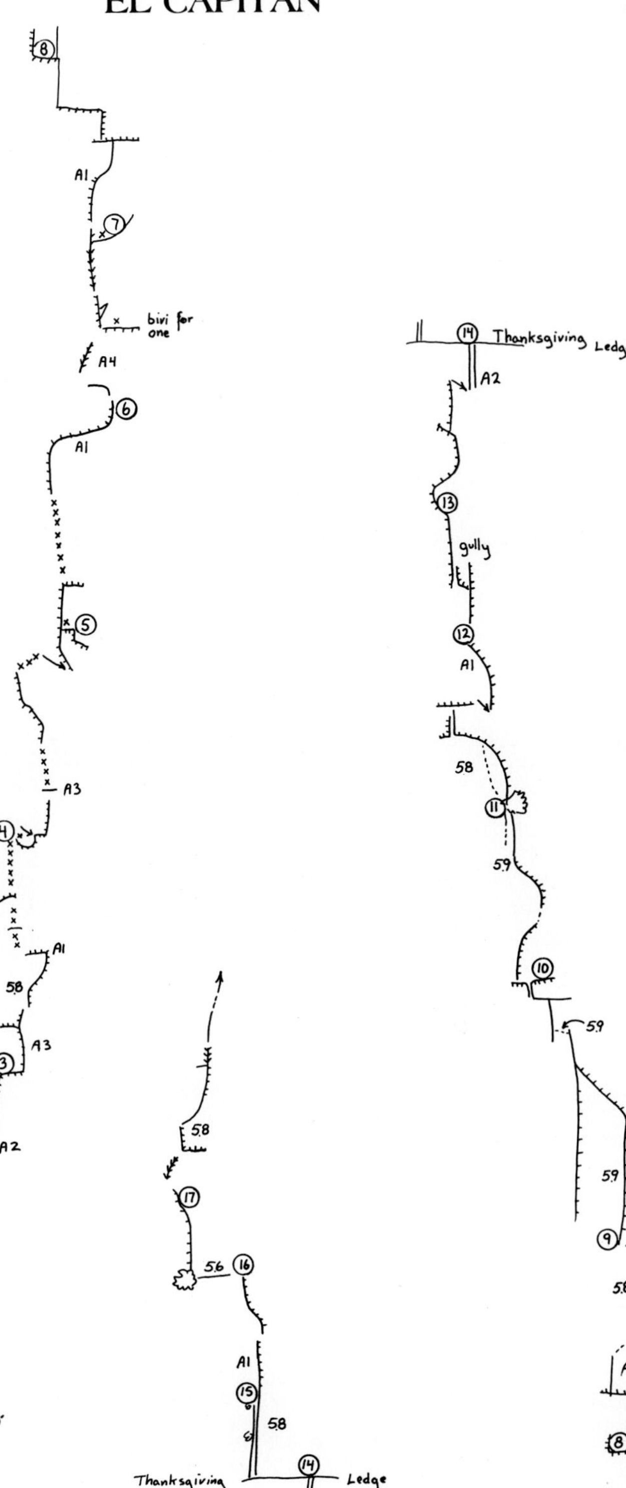

EL CAPITAN

Lurking Fear

VI 5.10 A3

Photo on page 106.

Hardware

2 rurps
6 KB
12 LA
4 ea. ½"-1½"
2 ea. 2"-3"
1 ea. 4"
Friends
nuts

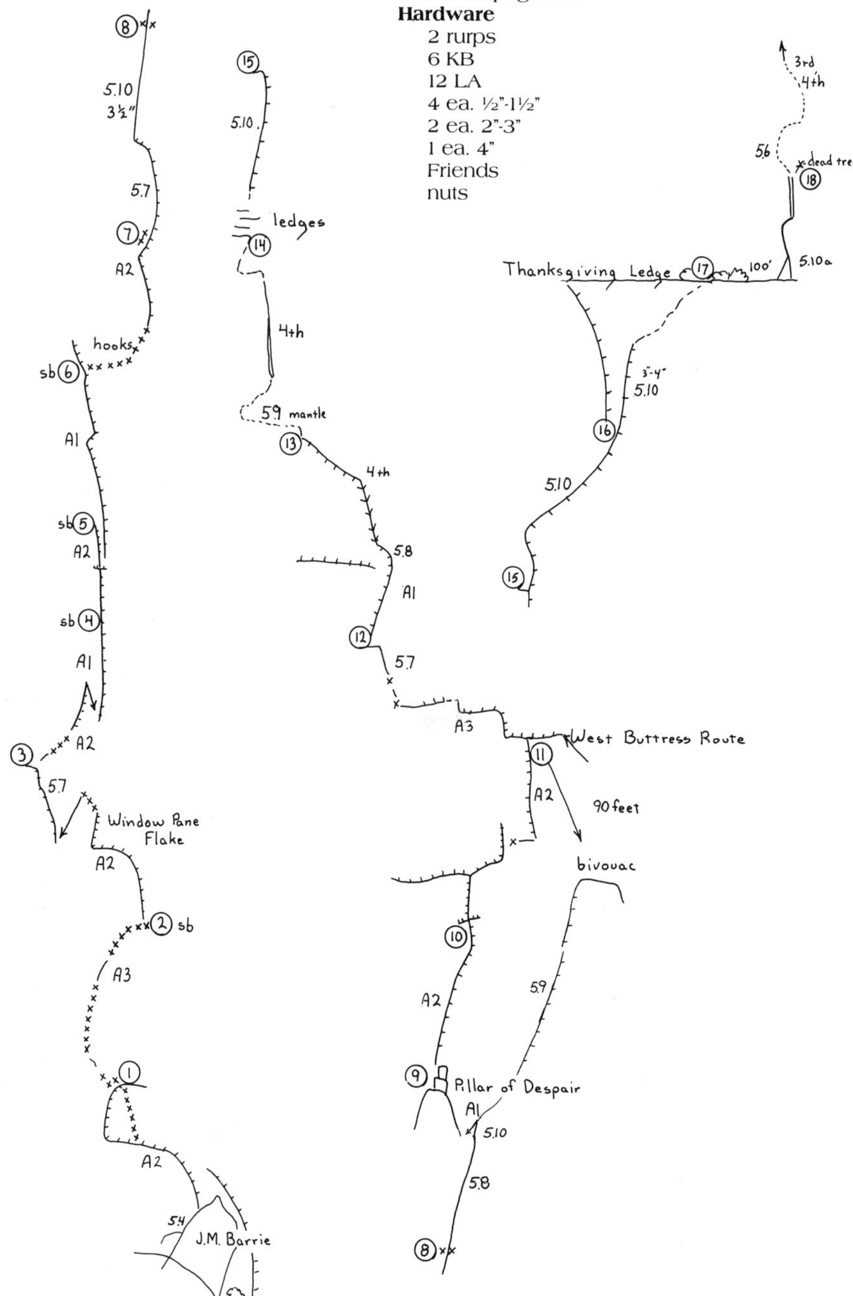

EL CAPITAN

Lost World

VI 5.10 A3+

Photo on page 114.

Hardware
- 4 rurps
- 5 KB
- 12 LA
- 4 ea. ½"-1½"
- 2 ea. 2"-3"
- 1 ea. 4"

Squeeze Play

VI 5.10 A3+

Hardware
- 2 rurps
- 5 KB
- 15 LA
- 3 ea. ½"-1½"
- 1 ea. bong
- nuts to 3½"
- Friends
- hooks

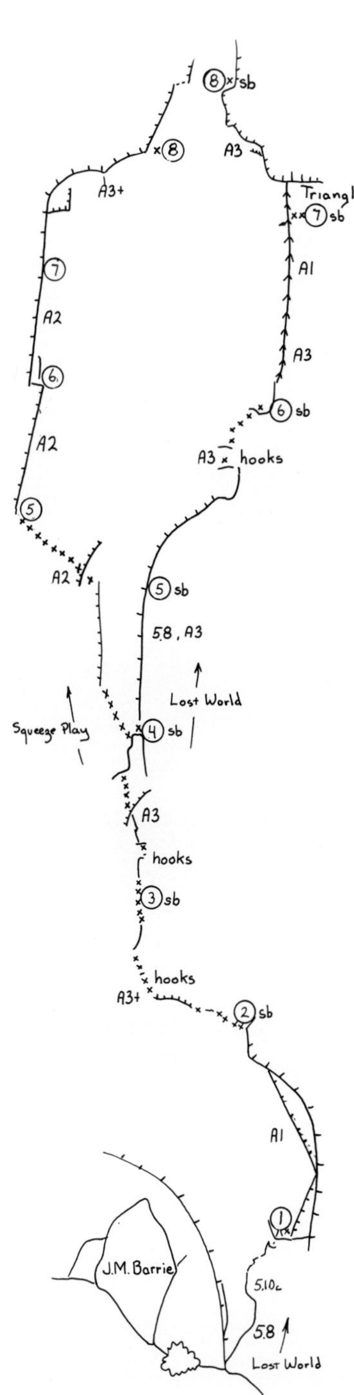

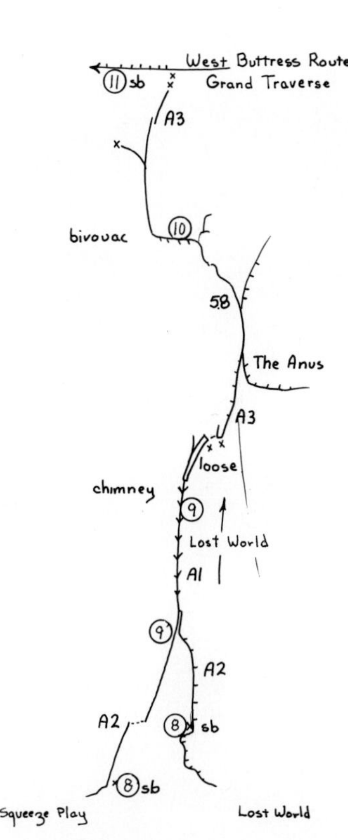

28
24
15
13
25
29
14
18
20
12
22
7
8
23
17
3
4
5
6
19
1
16
26
11
14
15
25
2
24
9
10
27
13
12
20
15
28
19
21
17

EL CAPITAN – Southwest Face

1 Squeeze Play
2 Lost World
3 West Buttress
4 Never Never Land
5 Aquarian Wall
6 Wings of Steel
7 Horse Play
8 Horse Chute
9 Dihedral Wall
10 Cosmos
11 Excalibur
12 Salathé Wall
13 Bermuda Dunes
14 Pacemaker
15 Heart Route
16 Verano Magico
17 Son of Heart
18 Sunkist
19 Jolly Roger
20 Magic Mushroom
21 Dorn Direct
22 Shield
23 False Shield
24 Muir
25 Turning Point
26 Mediterraneo
27 Grape Race
28 Nose
29 Real Nose

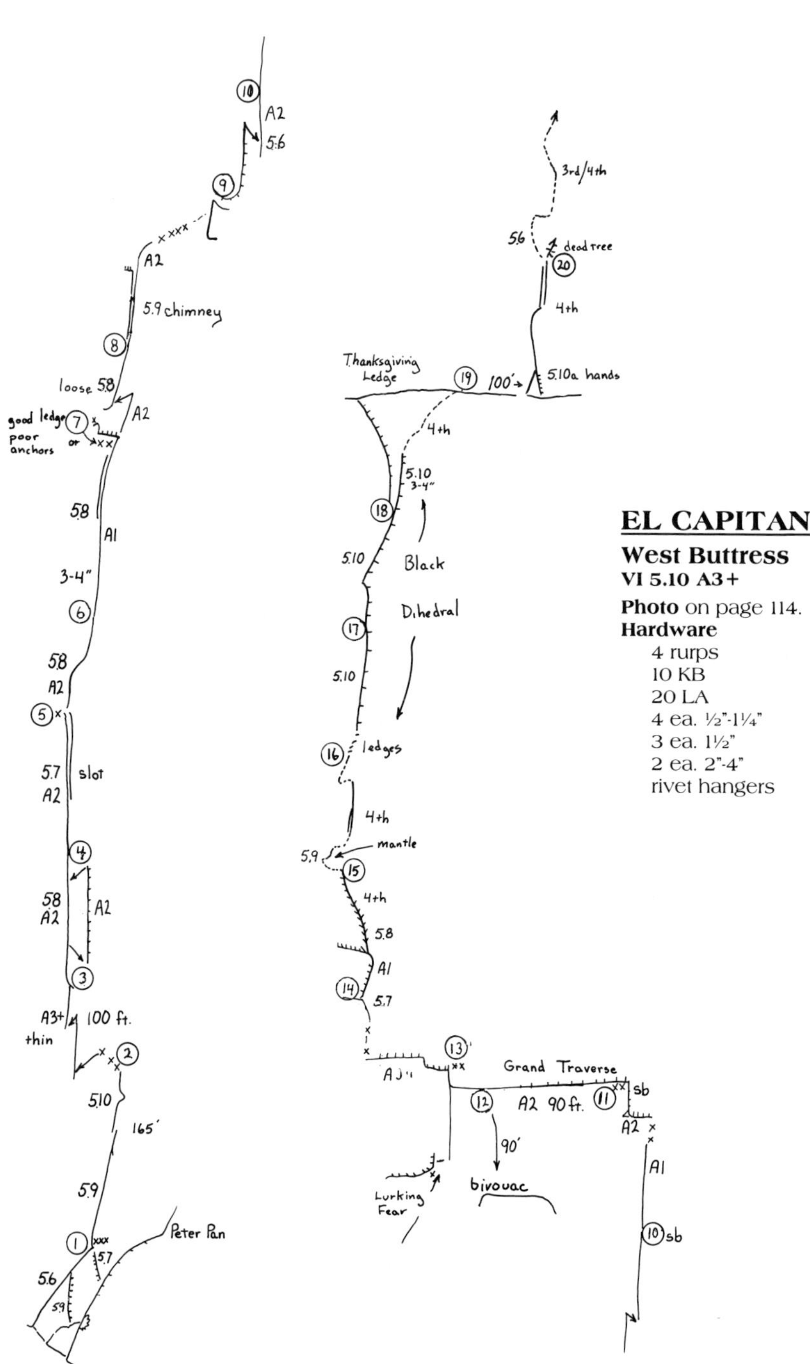

EL CAPITAN

West Buttress
VI 5.10 A3+

Photo on page 114.

Hardware

4 rurps
10 KB
20 LA
4 ea. ½"-1¼"
3 ea. 1½"
2 ea. 2"-4"
rivet hangers

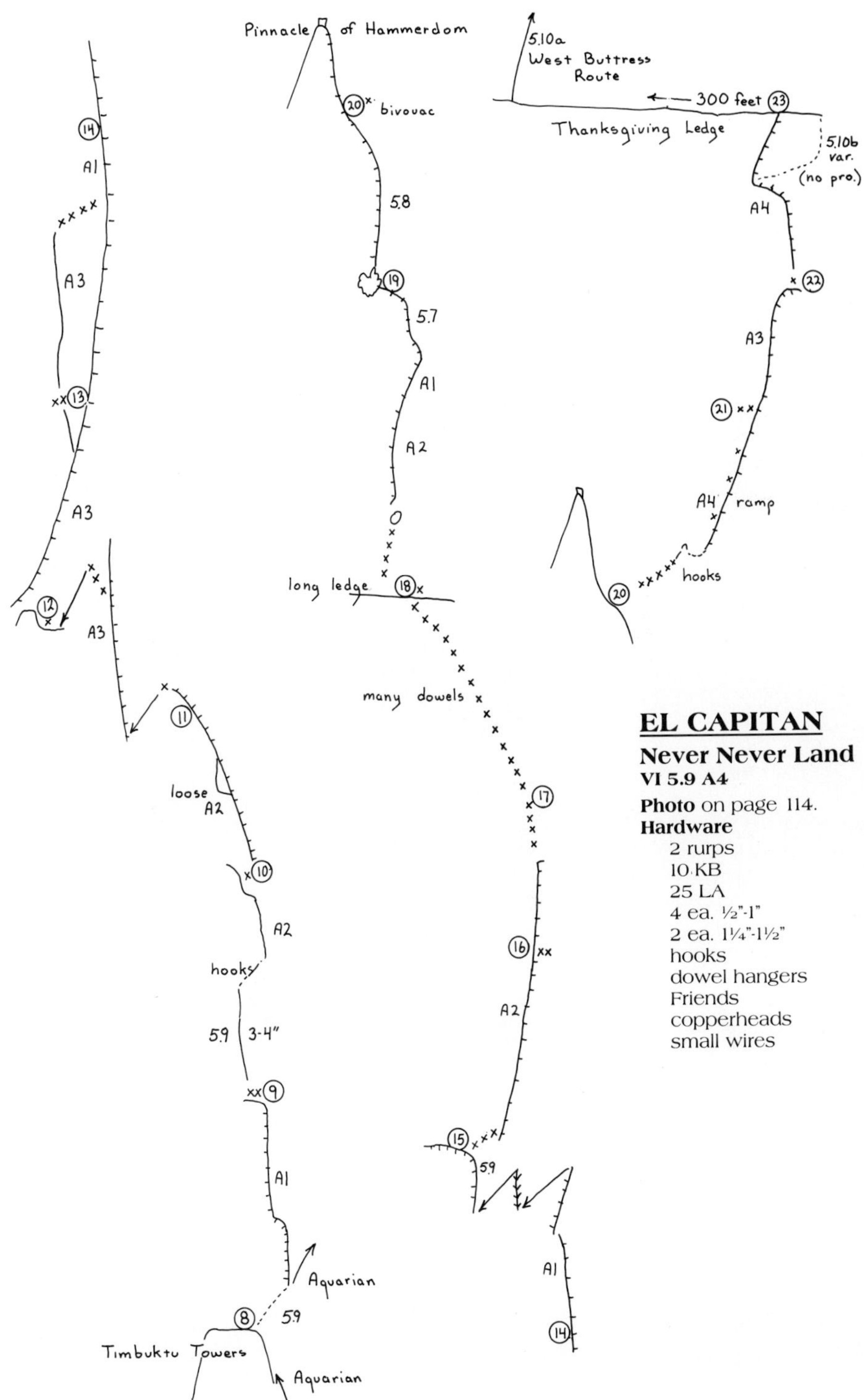

EL CAPITAN

Never Never Land

VI 5.9 A4

Photo on page 114.

Hardware

2 rurps
10 KB
25 LA
4 ea. ½"-1"
2 ea. 1¼"-1½"
hooks
dowel hangers
Friends
copperheads
small wires

EL CAPITAN

Aquarian Wall

VI 5.9 A4

Photo on page 114.

Hardware

1 rurp
4 KB
10 LA
4 ea. ½"-1½"
3 ea. 2"
Friends to #4
nuts
rivet hangers

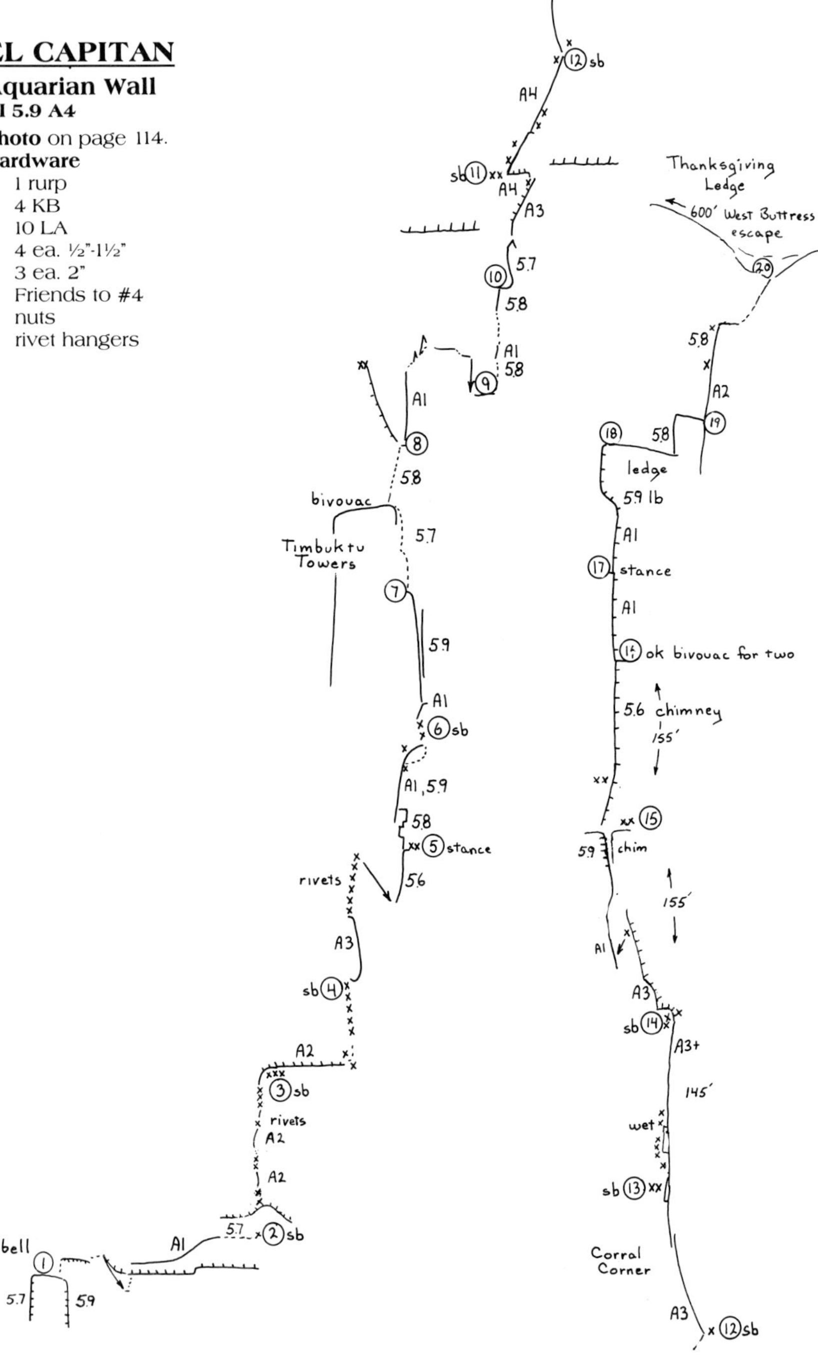

EL CAPITAN

Wings of Steel

VI 5.10+ A4

Photo on page 114.

Hardware

- 5 rurps
- 5 KB
- 5 LA
- 3 ea. ½"-¾"
- 4 ea. 1"
- 8 ea. 1¼"
- 3 ea. 1½"
- 1 ea. 2"-4"
- small wires
- Friends, incl. 2 ea. #3-4
- 40 copperheads
- all hooks
- rivet loops
- Aquarian Wall rack

note: there are many rivets on this route

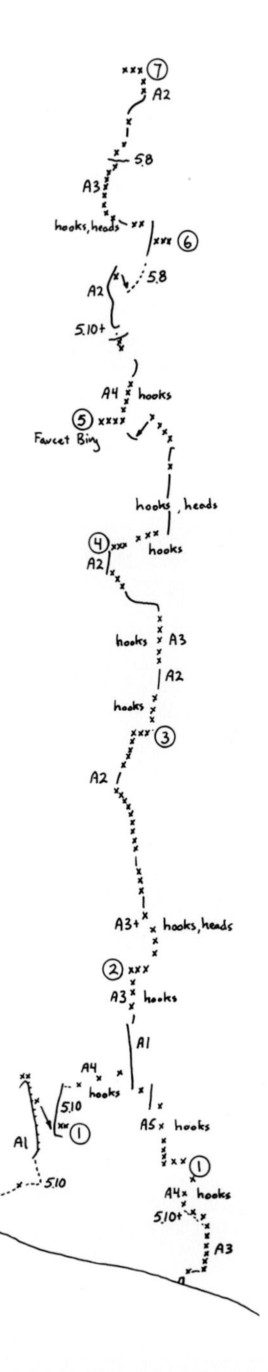

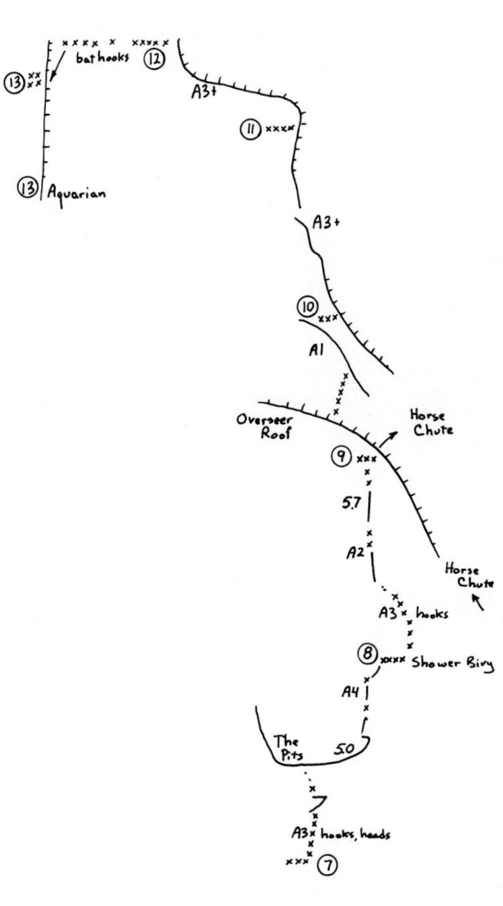

EL CAPITAN

Horse Chute

VI 5.9 A3

Photo on page 114.

Hardware

- 3 rurps
- 2 KB
- 25 LA
- 4 ea. ½"
- 6 ea. ⅝"-1¼"
- 1 ea. 1½"-2½"
- 2 ea. Friends
- wires
- rivet hangers

Horse Play

VI 5.9 A3

Hardware

same rack as Horse Chute plus
10 copperheads, mostly small

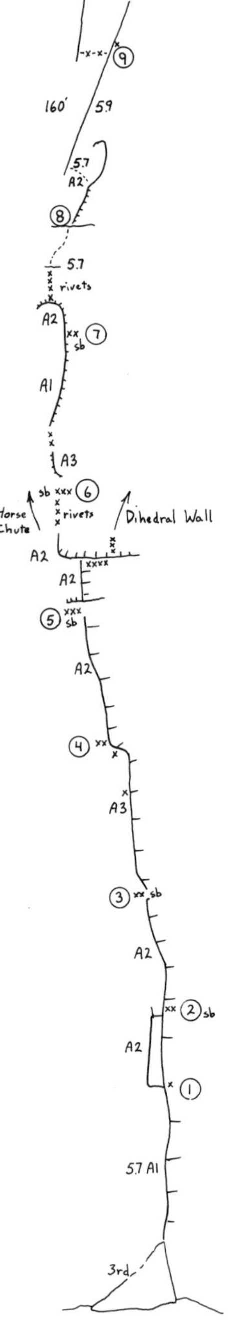

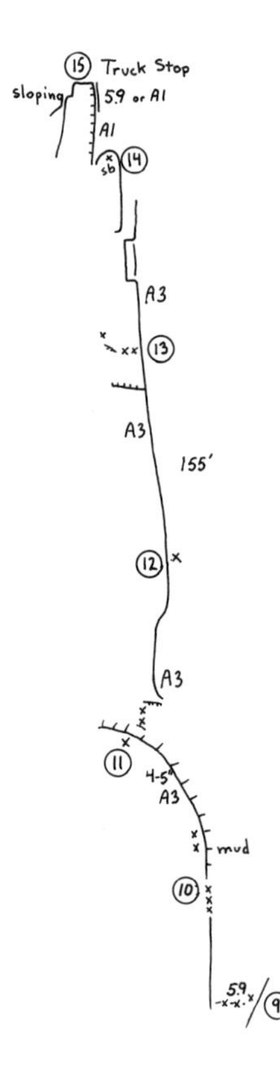

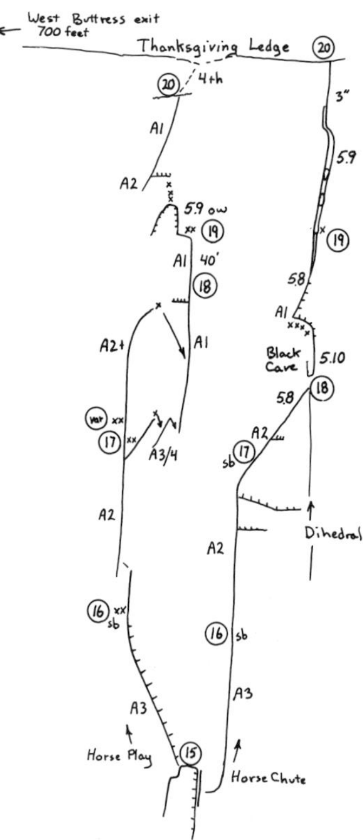

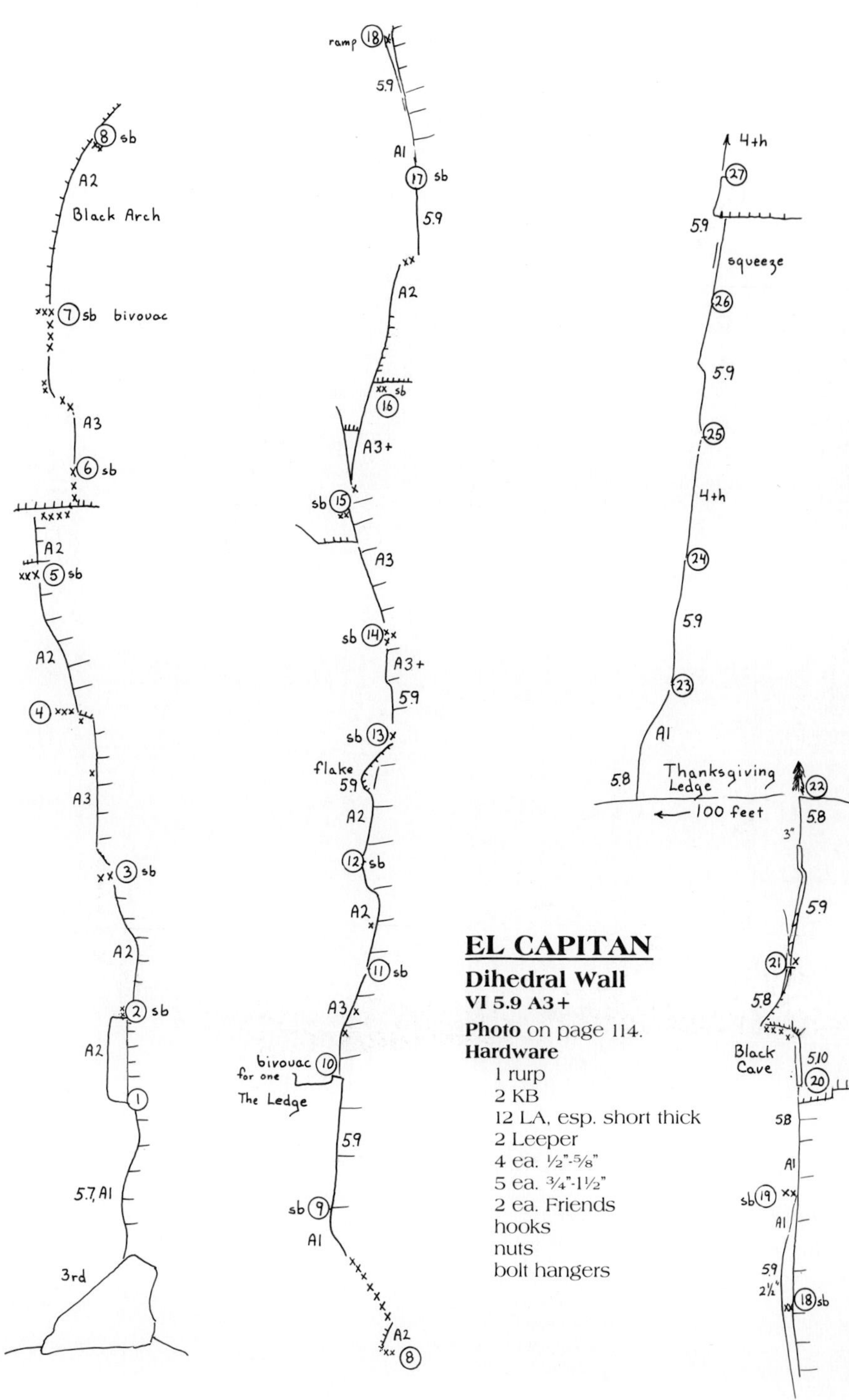

EL CAPITAN

Dihedral Wall
VI 5.9 A3+
Photo on page 114.
Hardware

- 1 rurp
- 2 KB
- 12 LA, esp. short thick
- 2 Leeper
- 4 ea. ½"-⅝"
- 5 ea. ¾"-1½"
- 2 ea. Friends
- hooks
- nuts
- bolt hangers

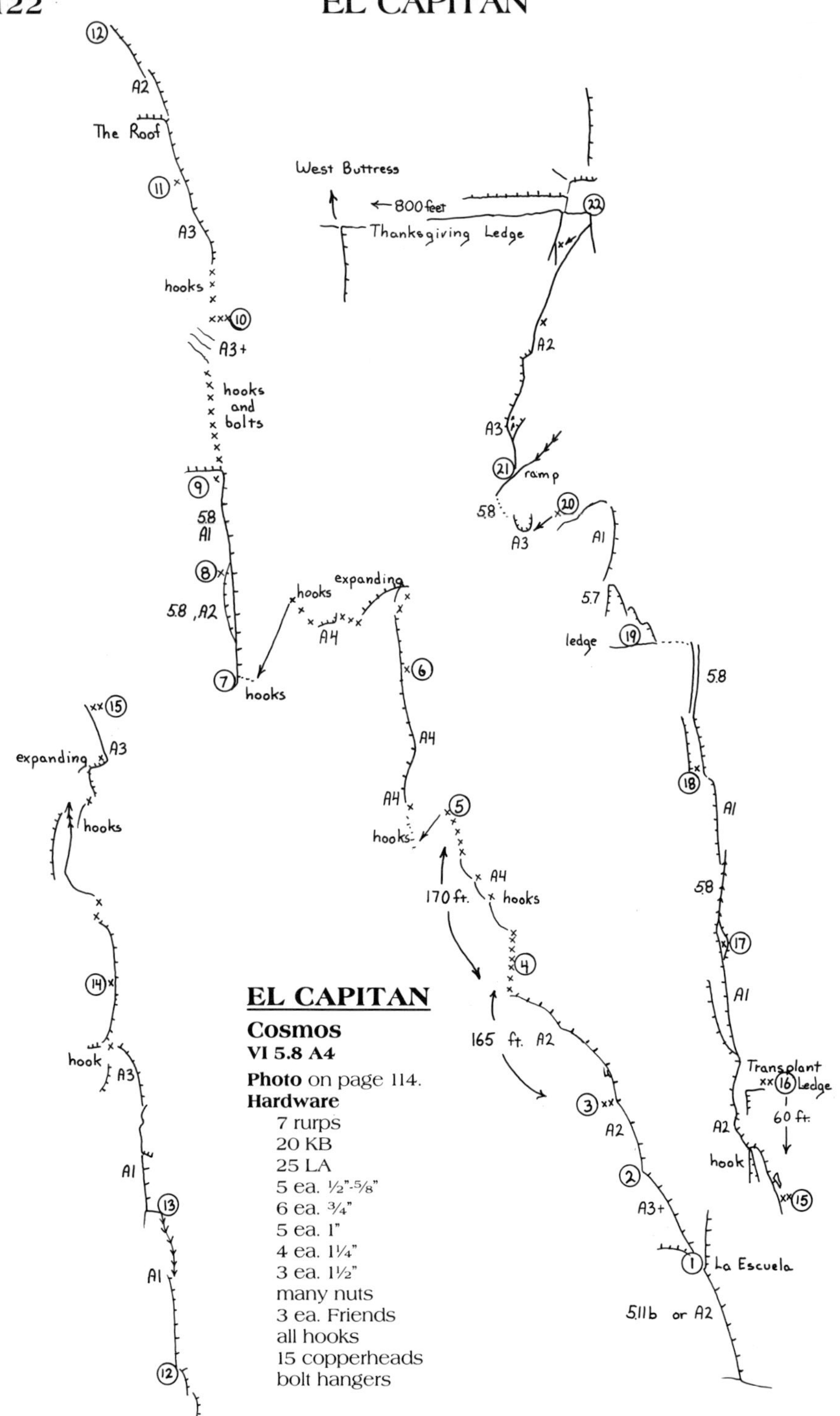

EL CAPITAN

Cosmos

VI 5.8 A4

Photo on page 114.

Hardware

7 rurps
20 KB
25 LA
5 ea. ½"-⅝"
6 ea. ¾"
5 ea. 1"
4 ea. 1¼"
3 ea. 1½"
many nuts
3 ea. Friends
all hooks
15 copperheads
bolt hangers

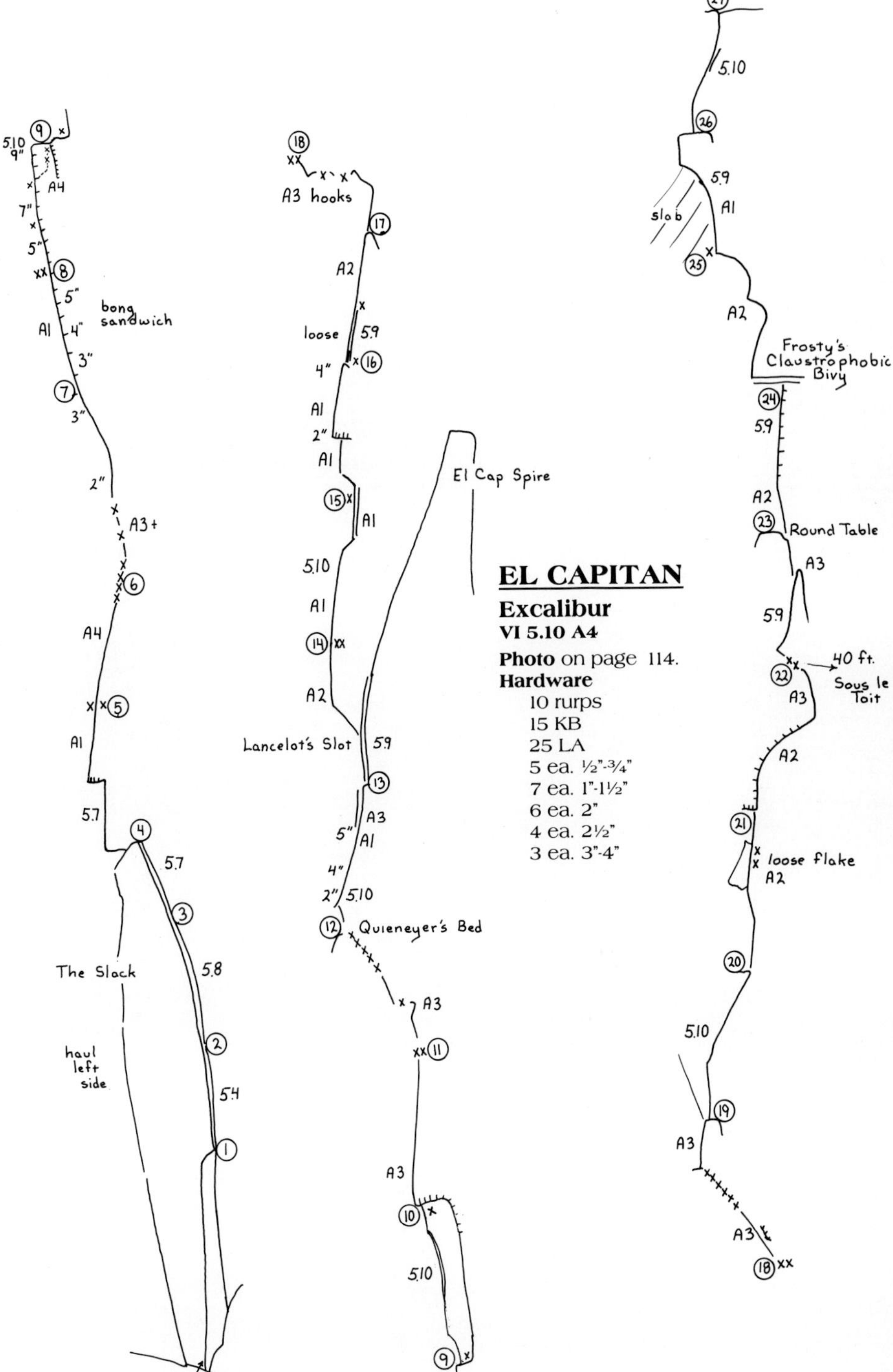

EL CAPITAN

Excalibur

VI 5.10 A4

Photo on page 114.

Hardware

10 rurps
15 KB
25 LA
5 ea. ½"-¾"
7 ea. 1"-1½"
6 ea. 2"
4 ea. 2½"
3 ea. 3"-4"

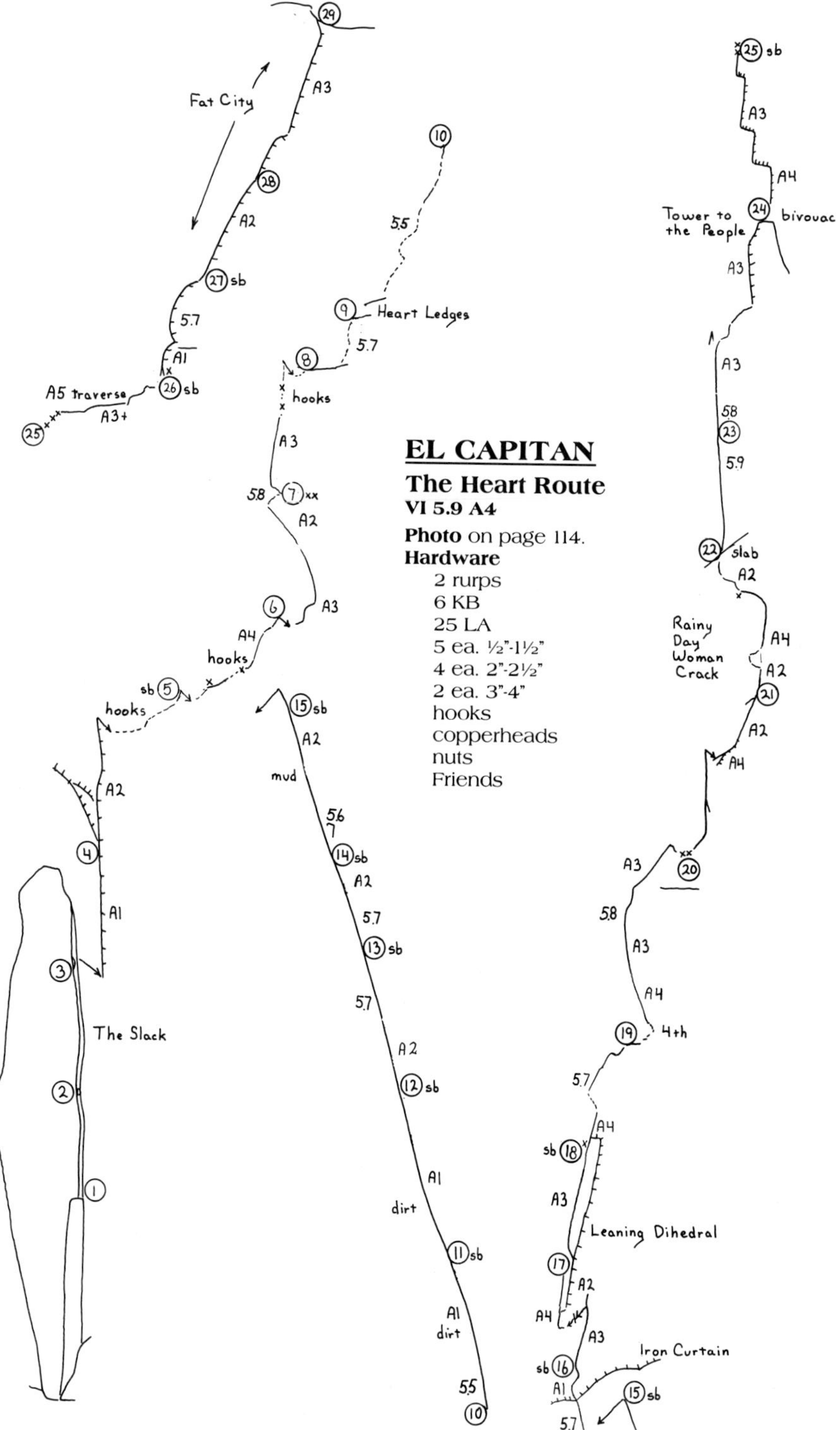

EL CAPITAN

The Heart Route

VI 5.9 A4

Photo on page 114.

Hardware

- 2 rurps
- 6 KB
- 25 LA
- 5 ea. ½"-1½"
- 4 ea. 2"-2½"
- 2 ea. 3"-4"
- hooks
- copperheads
- nuts
- Friends

EL CAPITAN

Bermuda Dunes

VI 5.11c A4+

Photo on page 114.

Hardware

10 rurps
20 KB
20 LA
4 ea. ½"-1"
1 ea. 1¼"-1½"
1 ea. 5"-7" tubes
wires
4 ea. Friends, incl. 1 #5
hooks

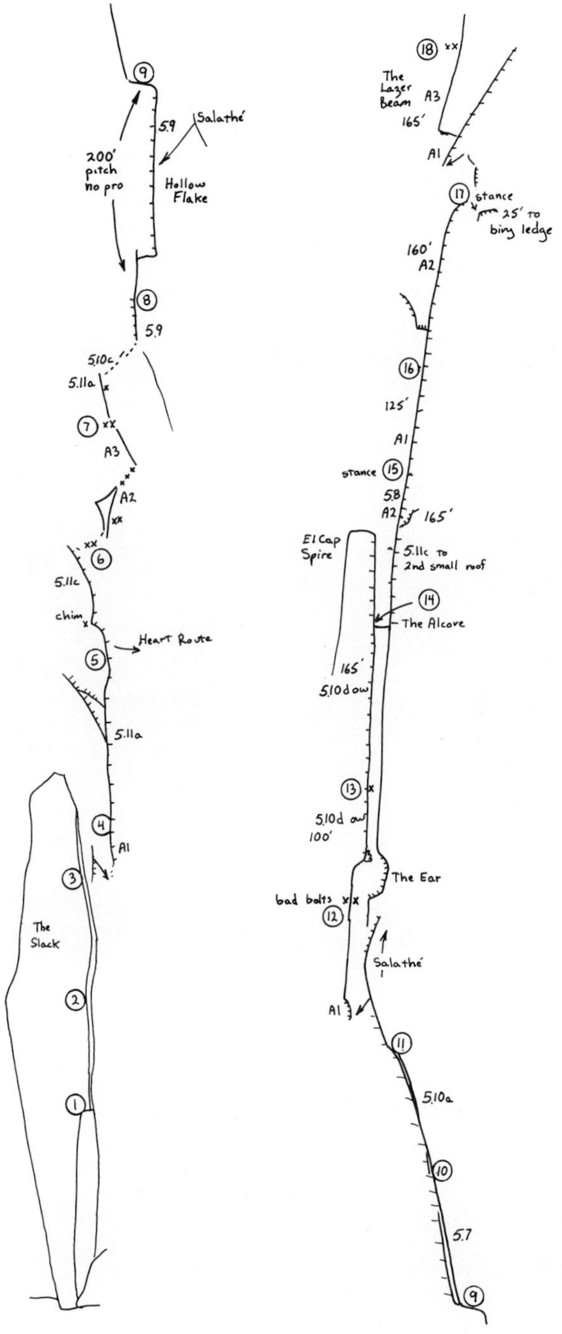

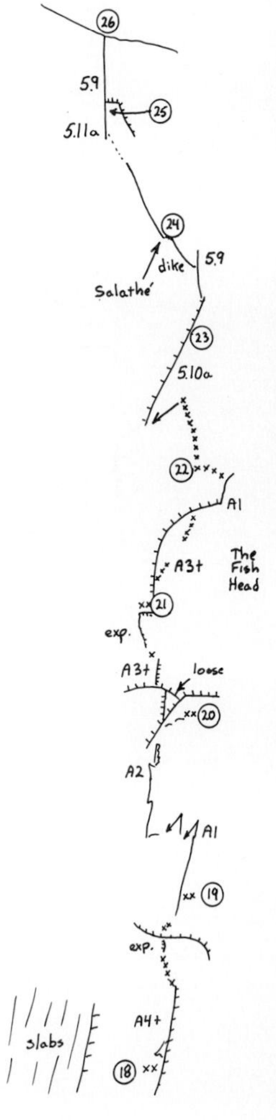

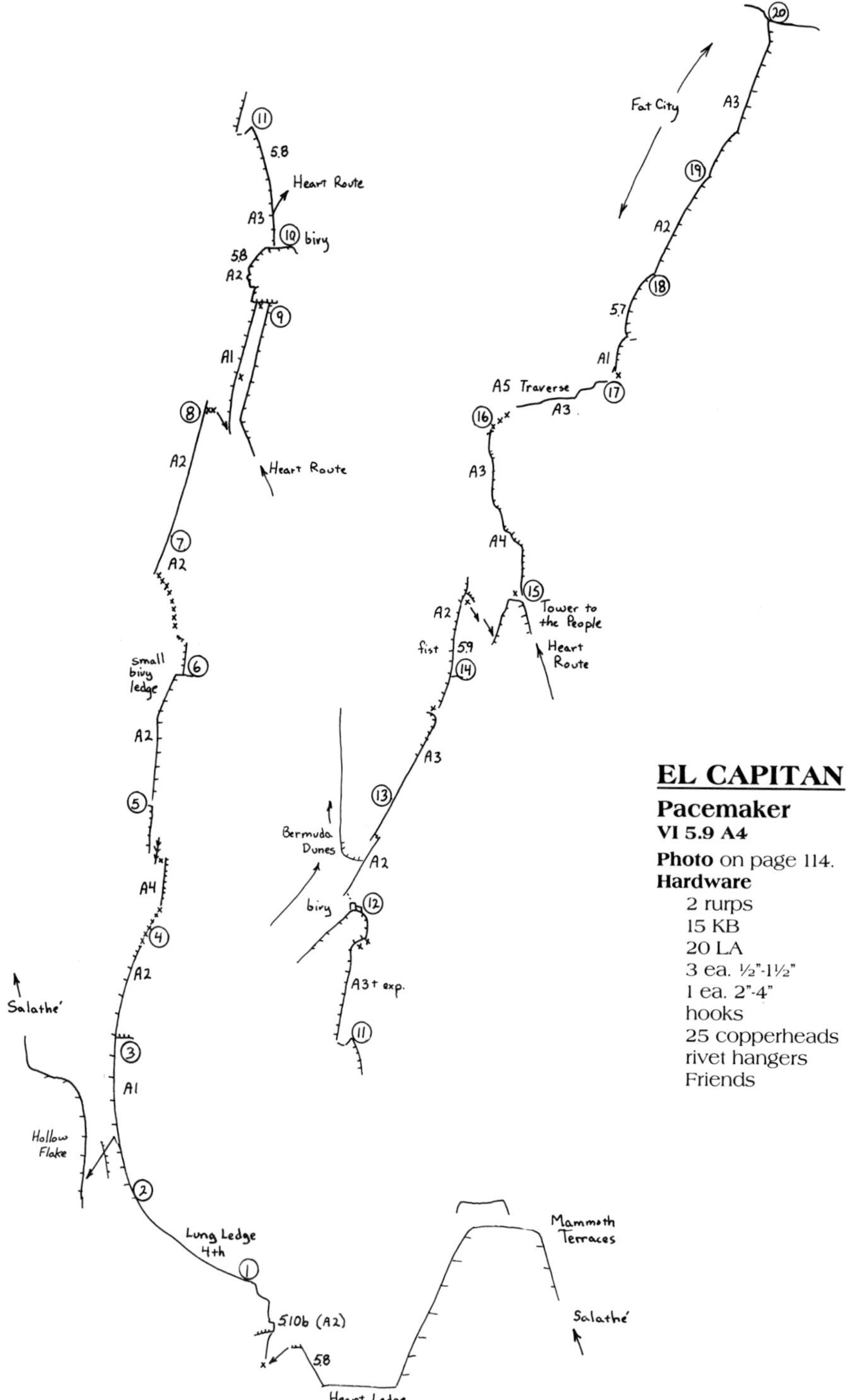

EL CAPITAN

Pacemaker

VI 5.9 A4

Photo on page 114.

Hardware

2 rurps
15 KB
20 LA
3 ea. ½"-1½"
1 ea. 2"-4"
hooks
25 copperheads
rivet hangers
Friends

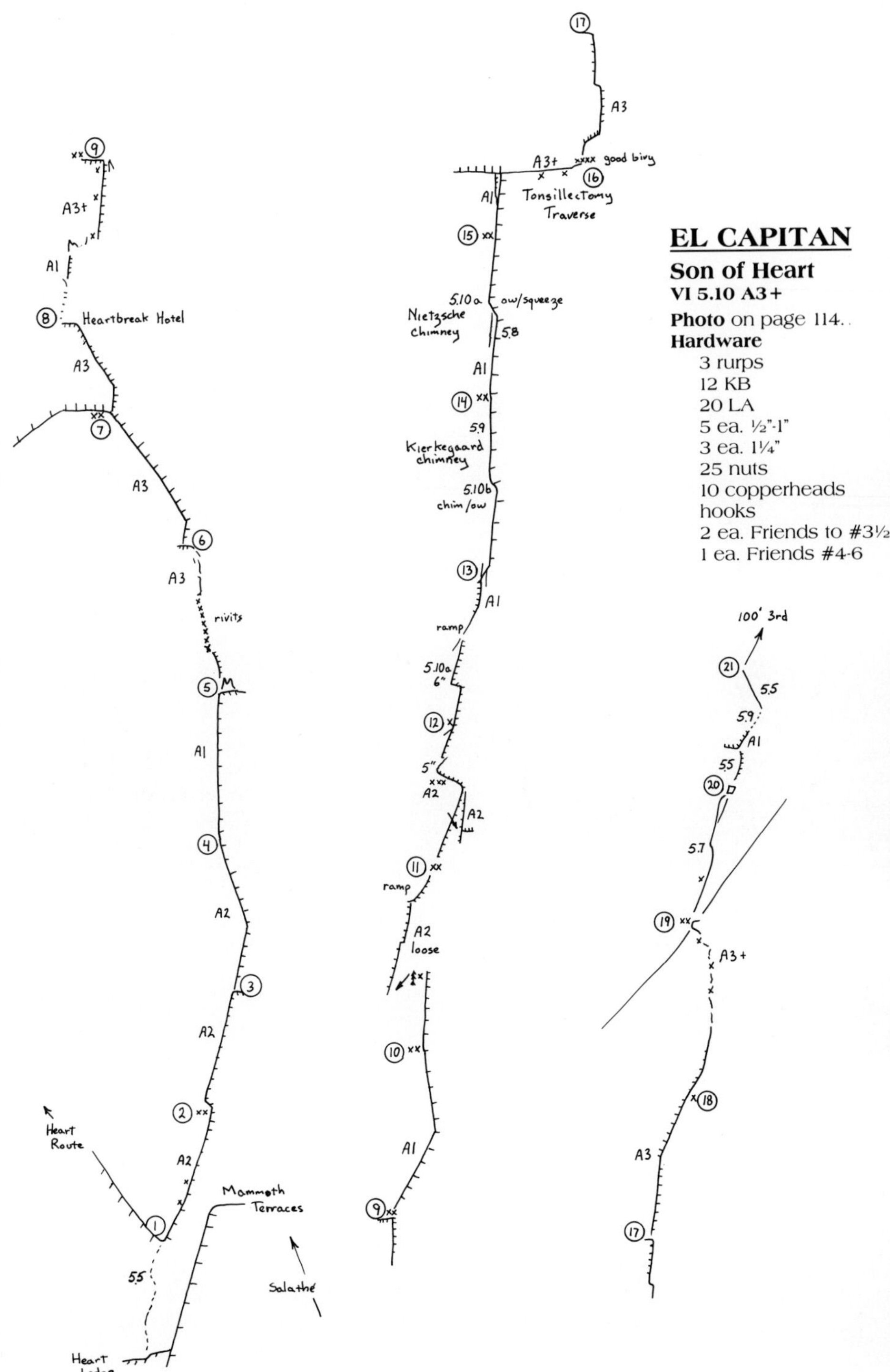

EL CAPITAN

Son of Heart
VI 5.10 A3+

Photo on page 114.

Hardware
- 3 rurps
- 12 KB
- 20 LA
- 5 ea. ½"-1"
- 3 ea. 1¼"
- 25 nuts
- 10 copperheads
- hooks
- 2 ea. Friends to #3½
- 1 ea. Friends #4-6

EL CAPITAN

Sunkist

VI 5.9 A5

Photo on page 114.

Hardware

- 25 rurps
- 25 KB
- 25 LA
- 3 ea. ½"-¾"
- 2 ea. 1"-1½"
- 50 copperheads, incl. circleheads
- all hooks
- wires

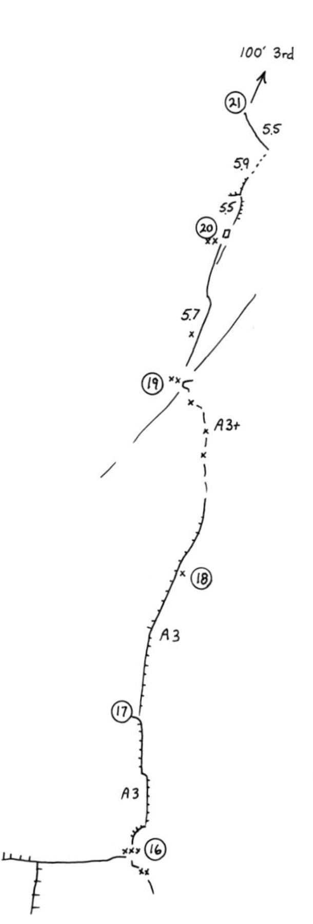

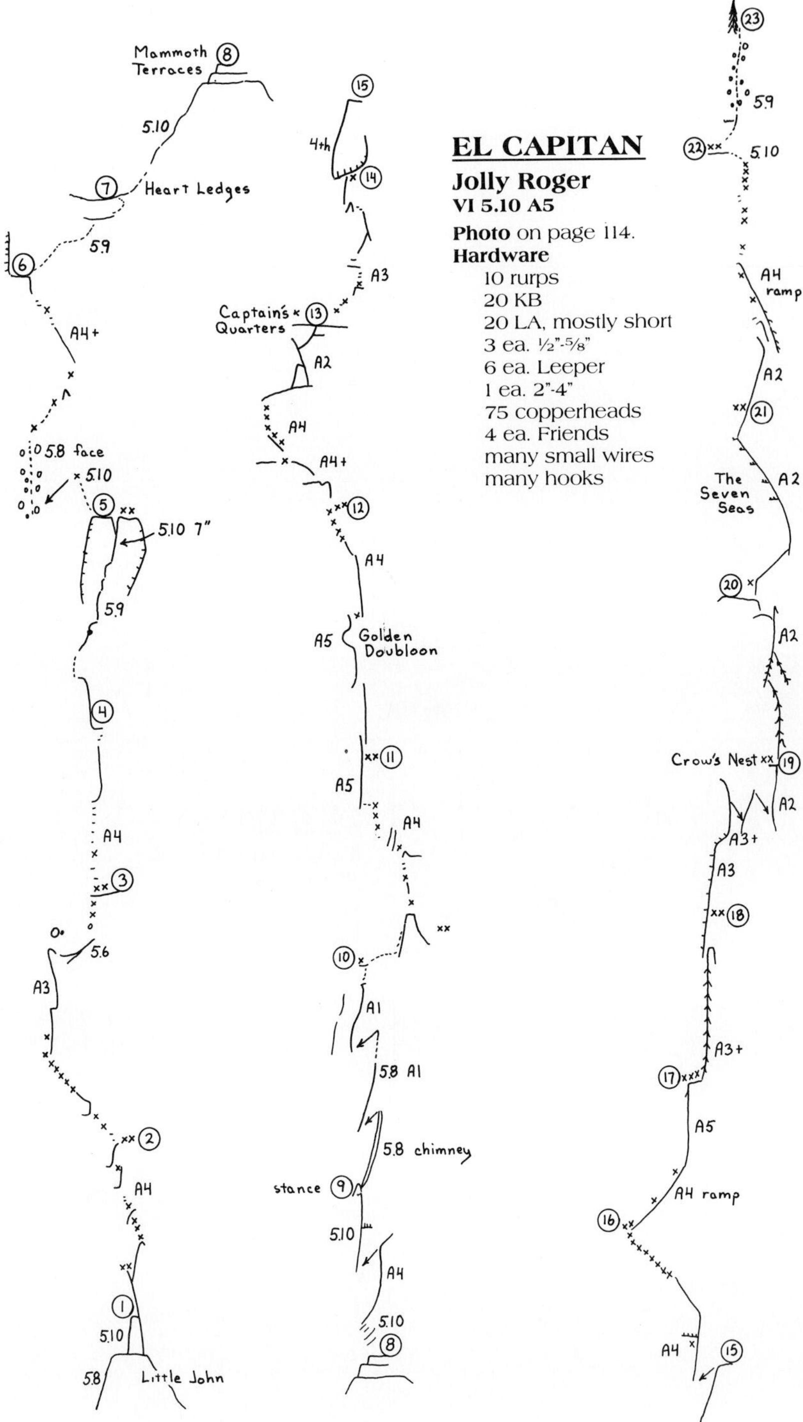

EL CAPITAN

Jolly Roger

VI 5.10 A5

Photo on page 114.

Hardware

10 rurps
20 KB
20 LA, mostly short
3 ea. ½"-⅝"
6 ea. Leeper
1 ea. 2"-4"
75 copperheads
4 ea. Friends
many small wires
many hooks

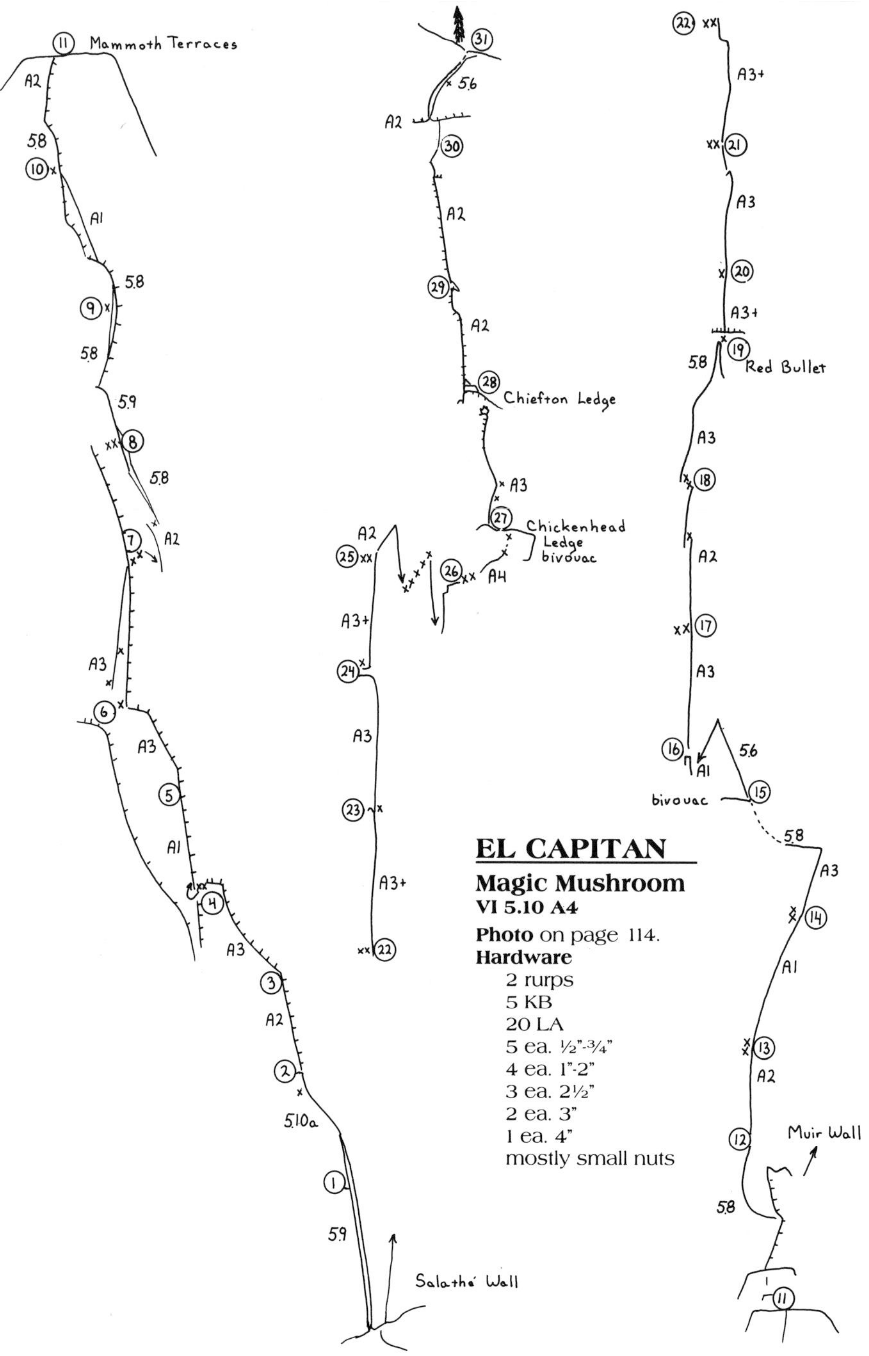

EL CAPITAN

Magic Mushroom

VI 5.10 A4

Photo on page 114.

Hardware

2 rurps
5 KB
20 LA
5 ea. ½"-¾"
4 ea. 1"-2"
3 ea. 2½"
2 ea. 3"
1 ea. 4"
mostly small nuts

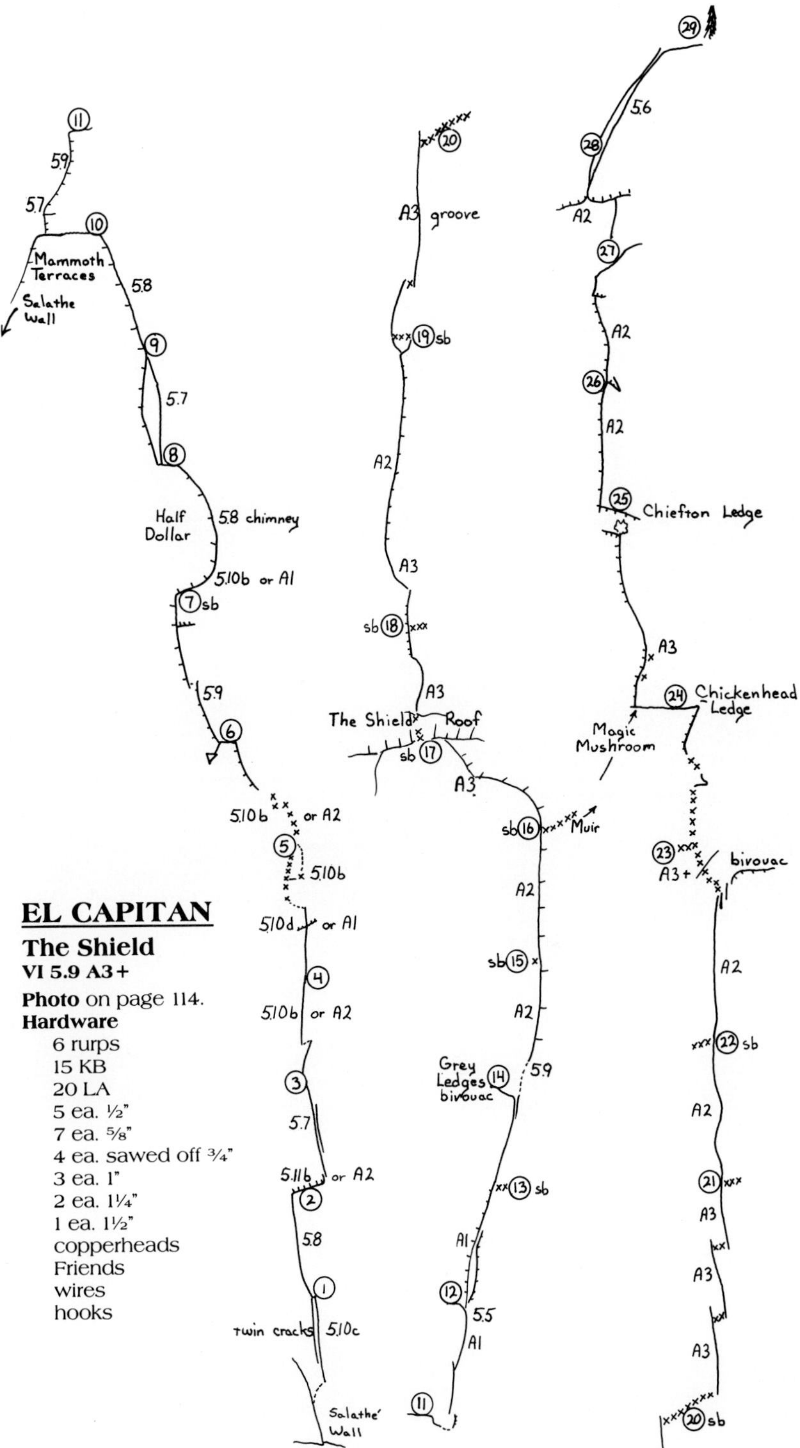

EL CAPITAN

The Shield

VI 5.9 A3+

Photo on page 114.

Hardware

6 rurps
15 KB
20 LA
5 ea. ½"
7 ea. ⅝"
4 ea. sawed off ¾"
3 ea. 1"
2 ea. 1¼"
1 ea. 1½"
copperheads
Friends
wires
hooks

EL CAPITAN

Dorn Direct (to Shield)

VI 5.9 A4

Photo on page 114.

Hardware

- 10 rurps
- 20 KB
- 20 LA
- 4 ea. ½"-1"
- 2 ea. 1¼"-1½"
- hooks
- bolt hangers
- nuts
- Friends
- rivet hangers

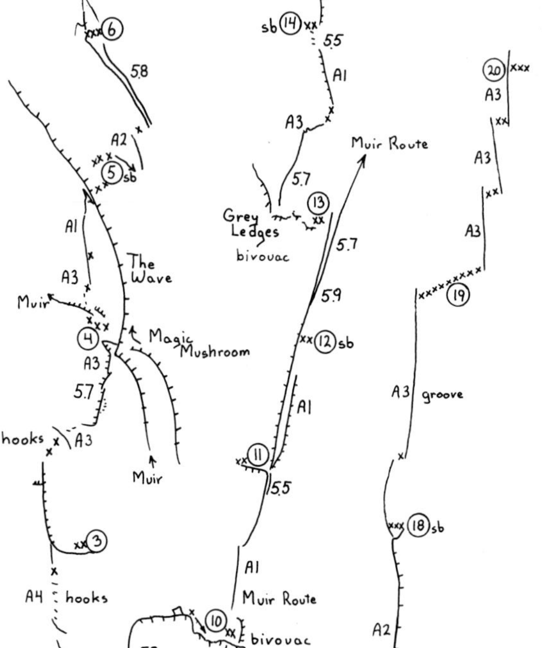

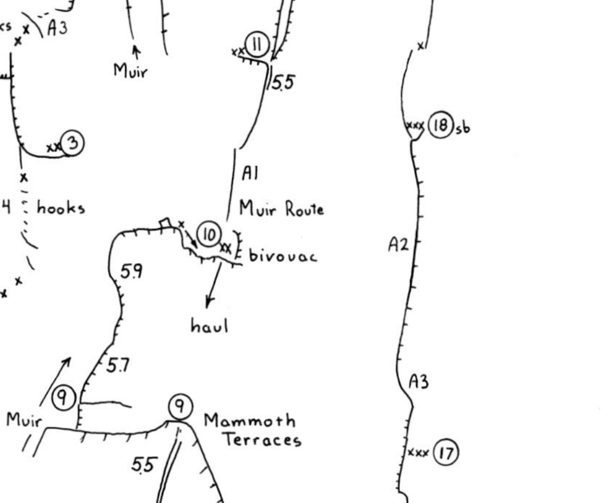

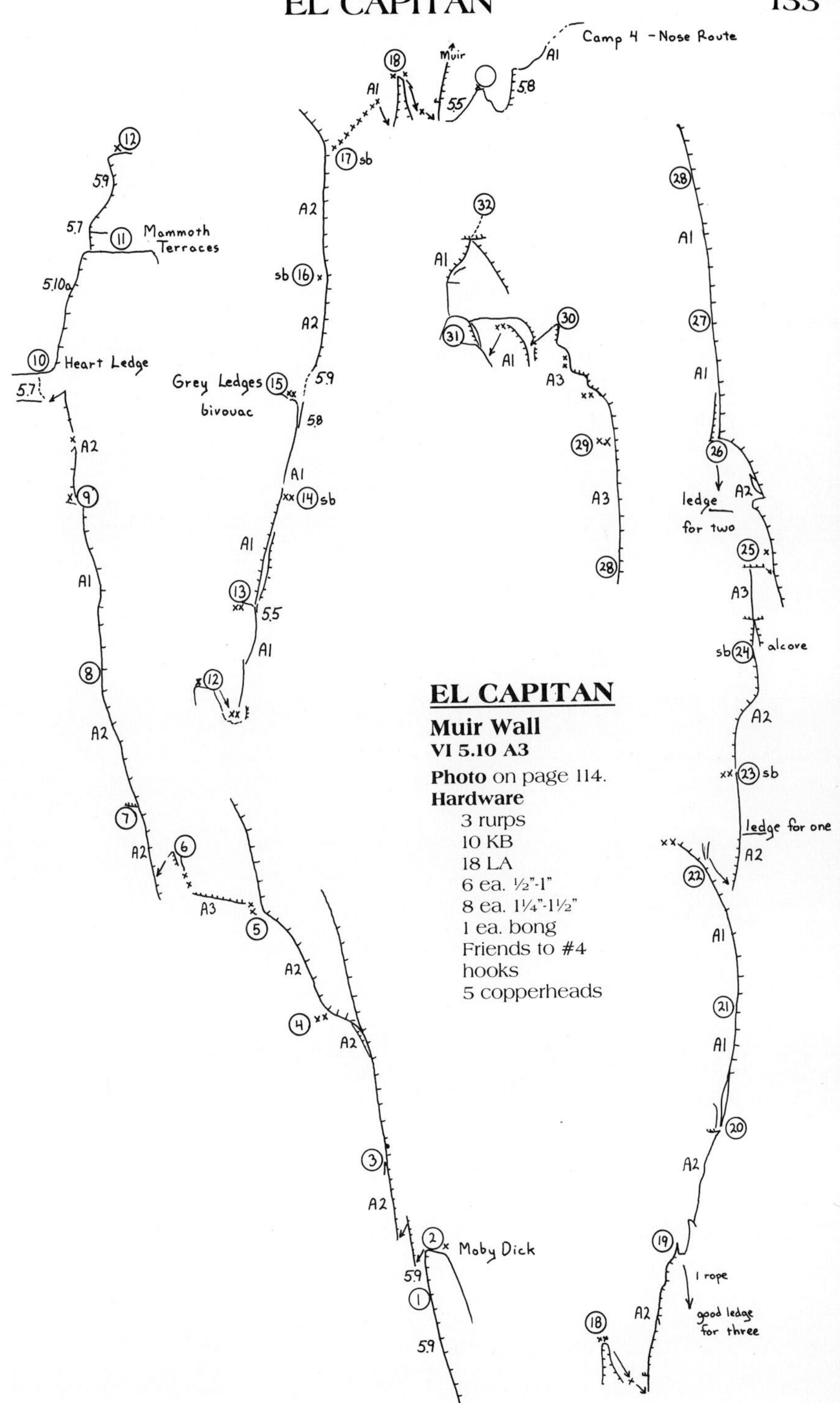
EL CAPITAN
Muir Wall
VI 5.10 A3
Photo on page 114.
Hardware
3 rurps
10 KB
18 LA
6 ea. ½"-1"
8 ea. 1¼"-1½"
1 ea. bong
Friends to #4
hooks
5 copperheads
Camp 4 - Nose Route
Muir
Mammoth Terraces
Heart Ledge
Grey Ledges bivouac
Moby Dick
ledge for two
alcove
ledge for one
1 rope
good ledge for three

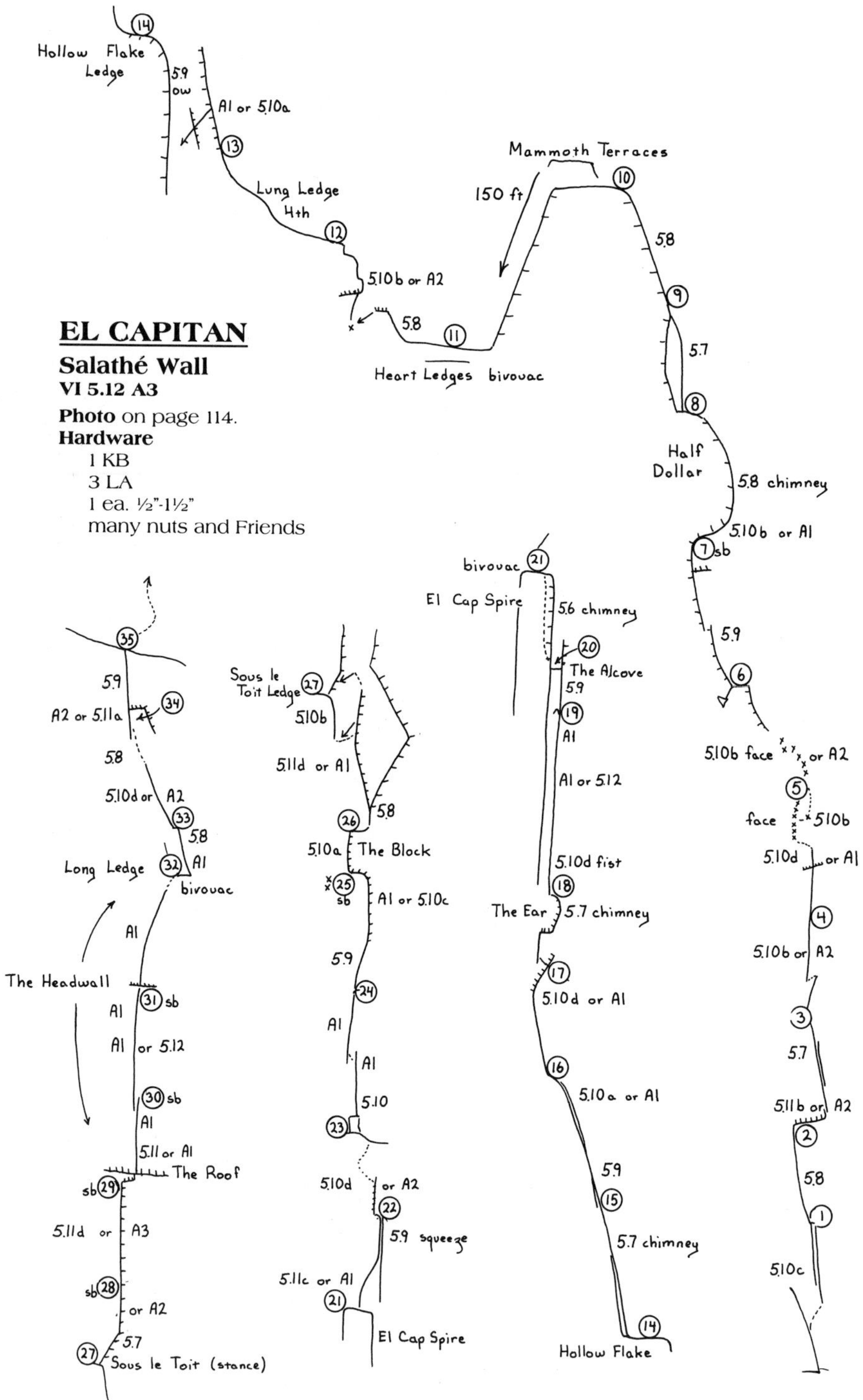

EL CAPITAN

Salathé Wall
VI 5.12 A3

Photo on page 114.

Hardware

1 KB
3 LA
1 ea. ½"-1½"
many nuts and Friends

Royal Robbins, El Cap Spire, Salathé Wall, 1961. *Tom Frost*

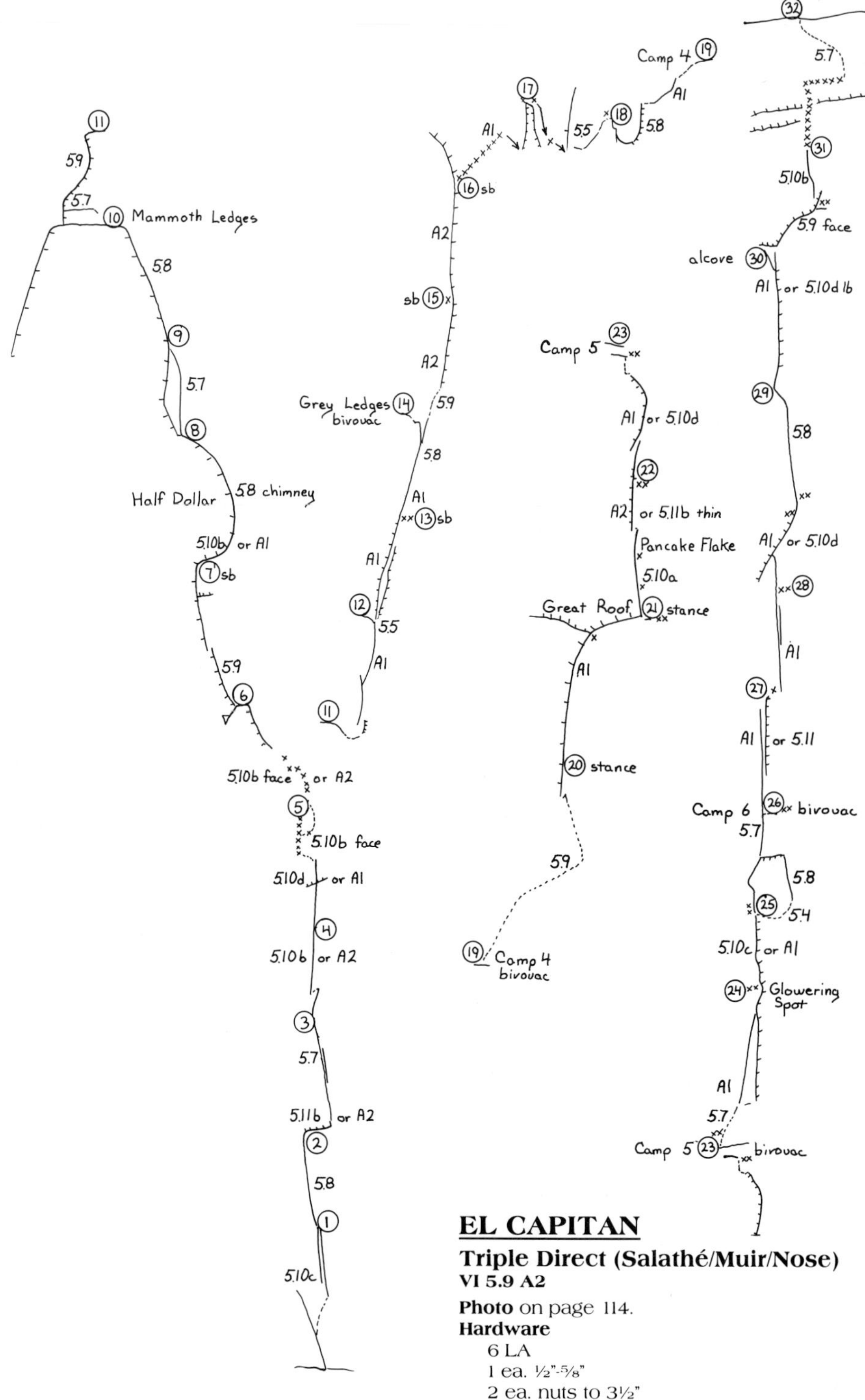

EL CAPITAN

Triple Direct (Salathé/Muir/Nose)
VI 5.9 A2

Photo on page 114.

Hardware

6 LA
1 ea. ½"-⅝"
2 ea. nuts to 3½"
Friends

EL CAPITAN

Grape Race

VI 5.9 A5

Photo on page 114.

Hardware

Many hooks, rurps, copperheads, KBs, in addition to a rack for the Nose.

10
5.9
A1
9
A2
8
A4
7
hooks, bolts and dowels
A4
6
A5
5 ledge
A4+
5.9
4
5.9
Nose Route
5.11 or A3
3
5.10c or A2
2
5.11a or A2
1
5.10d or A2

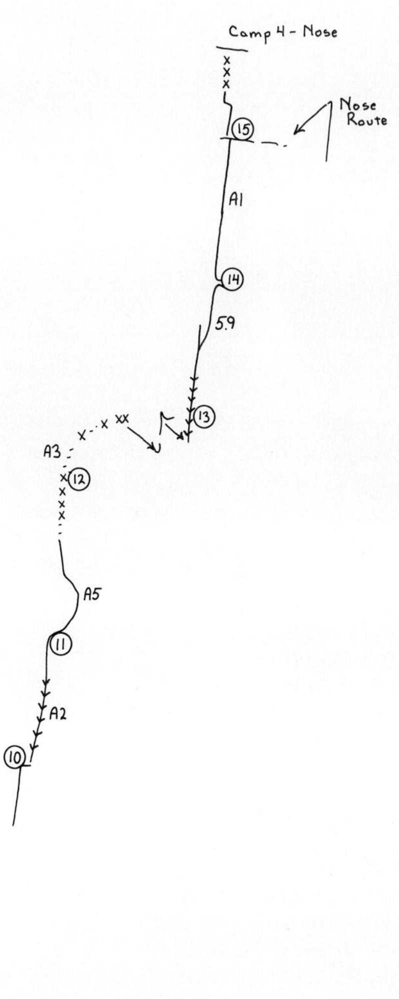

EL CAPITAN – Southeast Face

1 Nose
2 Real Nose
3 New Dawn
4 Tribal Rite
5 Wall of the Early Morning Light
6 Mescalito
7 Hockey Night in Canada
8 Space
9 South Seas
10 Pacific Ocean Wall
11 Sea of Dreams
12 North America Wall
13 Wyoming Sheep Ranch
14 New Jersey Turnpike
15 Atlantic Ocean Wall
16 Iron Hawk
17 Aurora
18 Tangerine Trip
19 Lost in America
20 Zenyatta Mondatta
21 Zodiac
22 Lunar Eclipse
23 Born Under a Bad Sign
24 Eagle's Way
25 Waterfall Route
26 Chinese Water Torture
27 Snake
28 East Buttress
29 Eura Mura

EL CAPITAN

The Nose

VI 5.11 A3

Photo on page 138.

Hardware

wires
2 ea. Friends to #4
2 ea. all nuts to 3½"

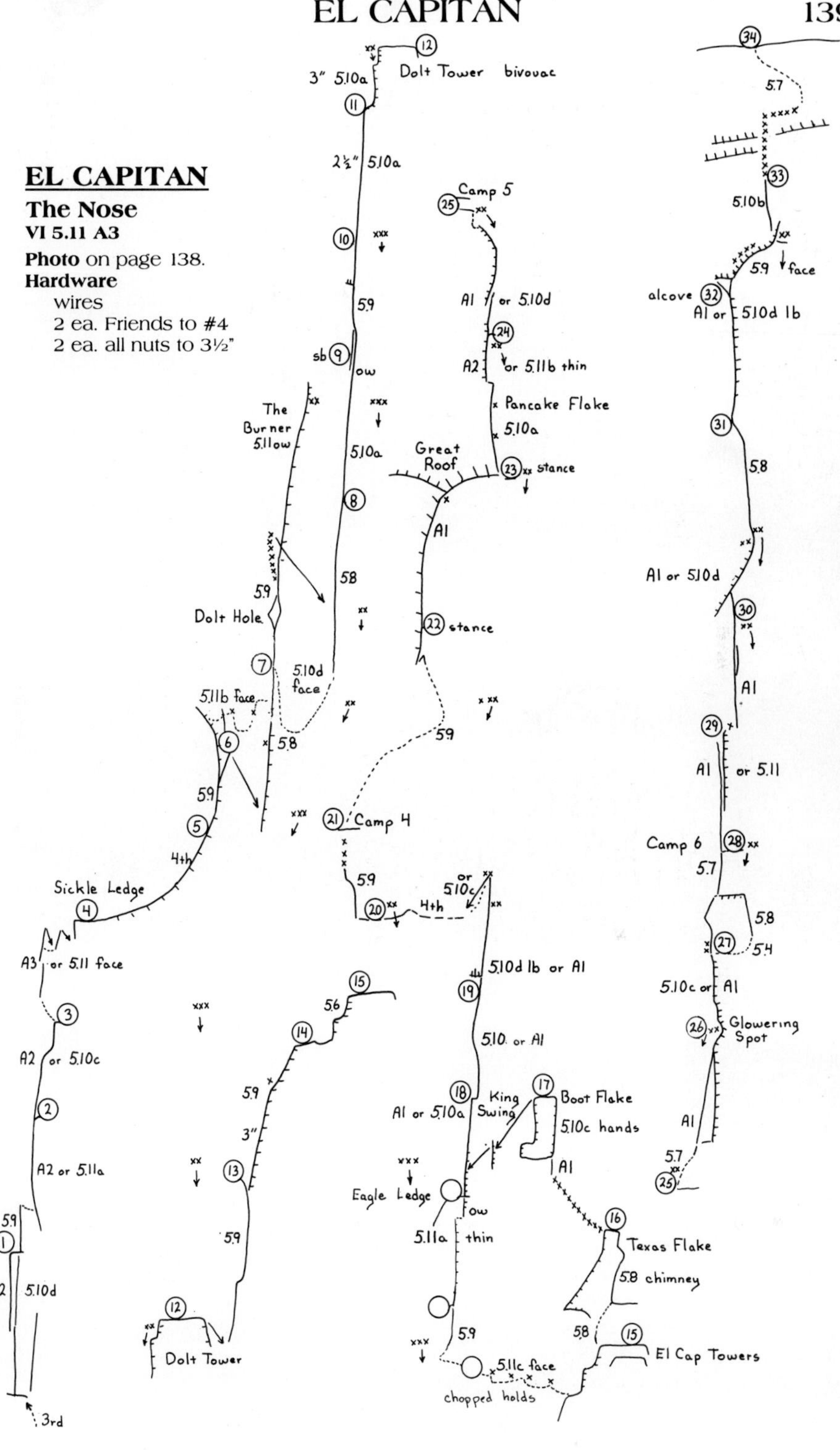

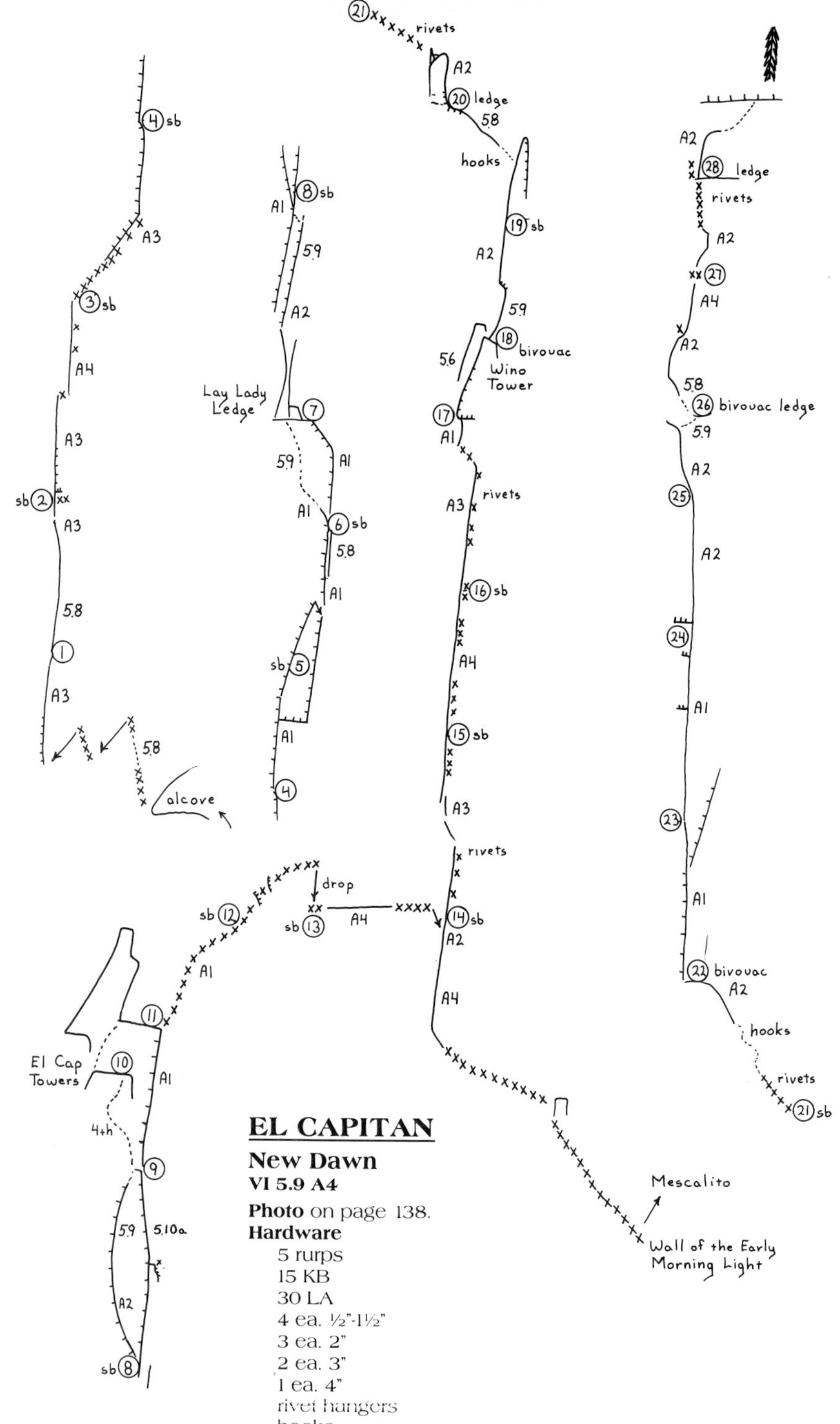

EL CAPITAN

New Dawn

VI 5.9 A4

Photo on page 138.

Hardware

- 5 rurps
- 15 KB
- 30 LA
- 4 ea. ½"-1½"
- 3 ea. 2"
- 2 ea. 3"
- 1 ea. 4"
- rivet hangers
- hooks

EL CAPITAN

Mescalito

VI 5.9 A4

Photo on page 138.

Hardware

- 3 rurps
- 5 KB
- 20 LA
- 4 ea. ½"-¾"
- 3 ea. 1-1½"
- small copperheads
- rivet hangers
- bolt hangers
- all hooks
- 2 ea. Friends

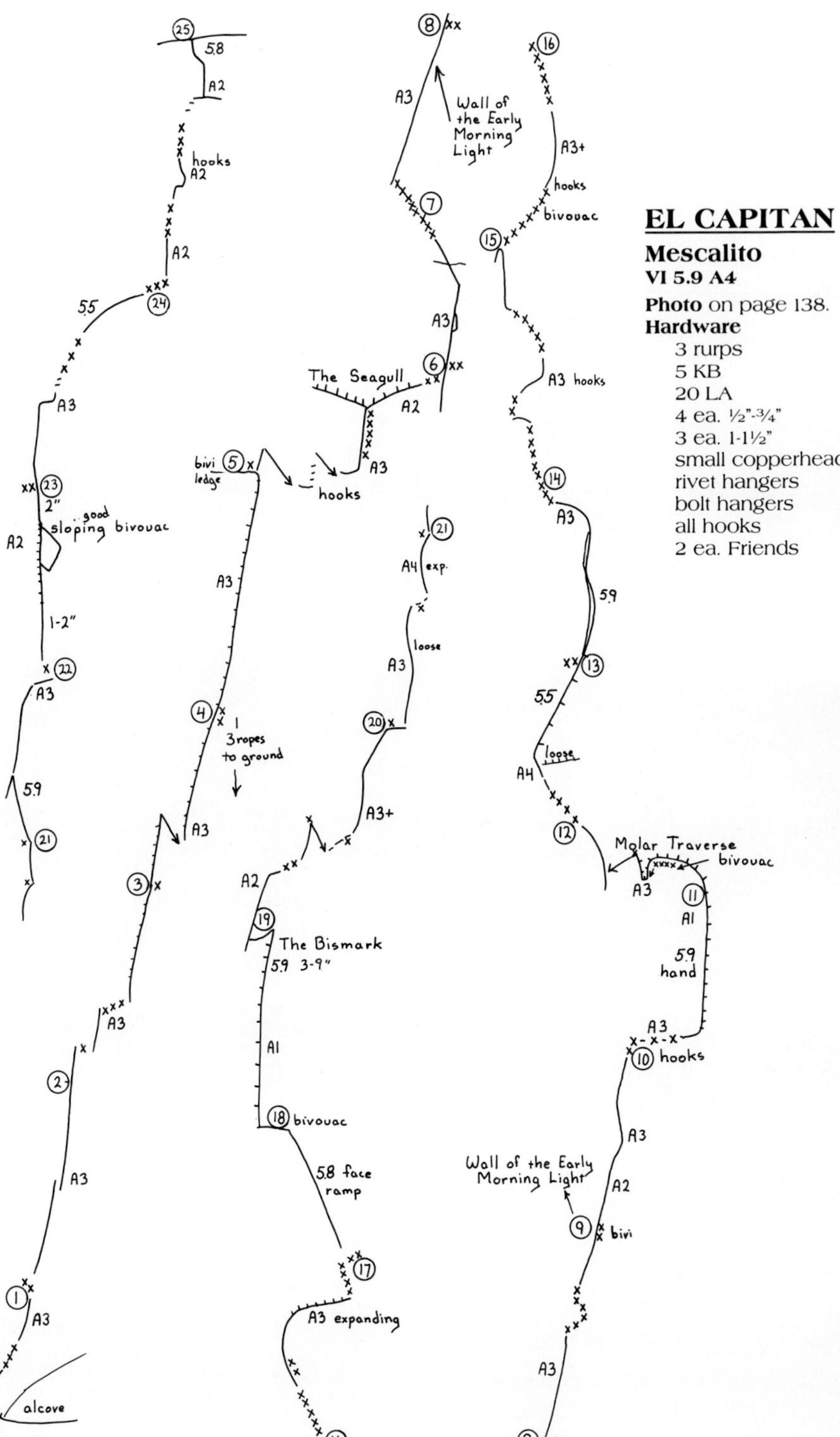

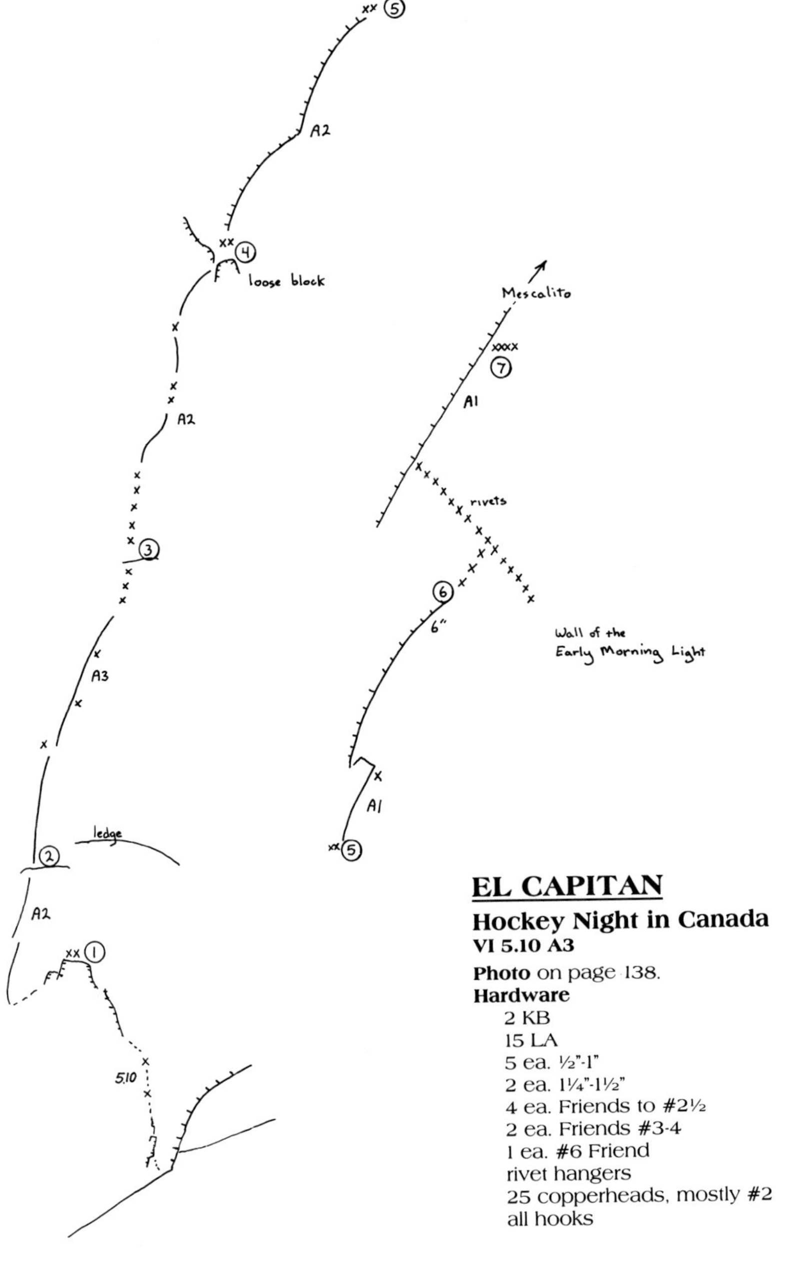

EL CAPITAN

Hockey Night in Canada

VI 5.10 A3

Photo on page 138.

Hardware

- 2 KB
- 15 LA
- 5 ea. ½"-1"
- 2 ea. 1¼"-1½"
- 4 ea. Friends to #2½
- 2 ea. Friends #3-4
- 1 ea. #6 Friend
- rivet hangers
- 25 copperheads, mostly #2
- all hooks

EL CAPITAN

South Seas

VI 5.8 A5

Photo on page 138.

Hardware

- 10 rurps
- 25 KB
- 20 LA
- 4 ea. ½"-1"
- 2 ea. 1¼"-4"
- 45 copperheads, incl. circleheads

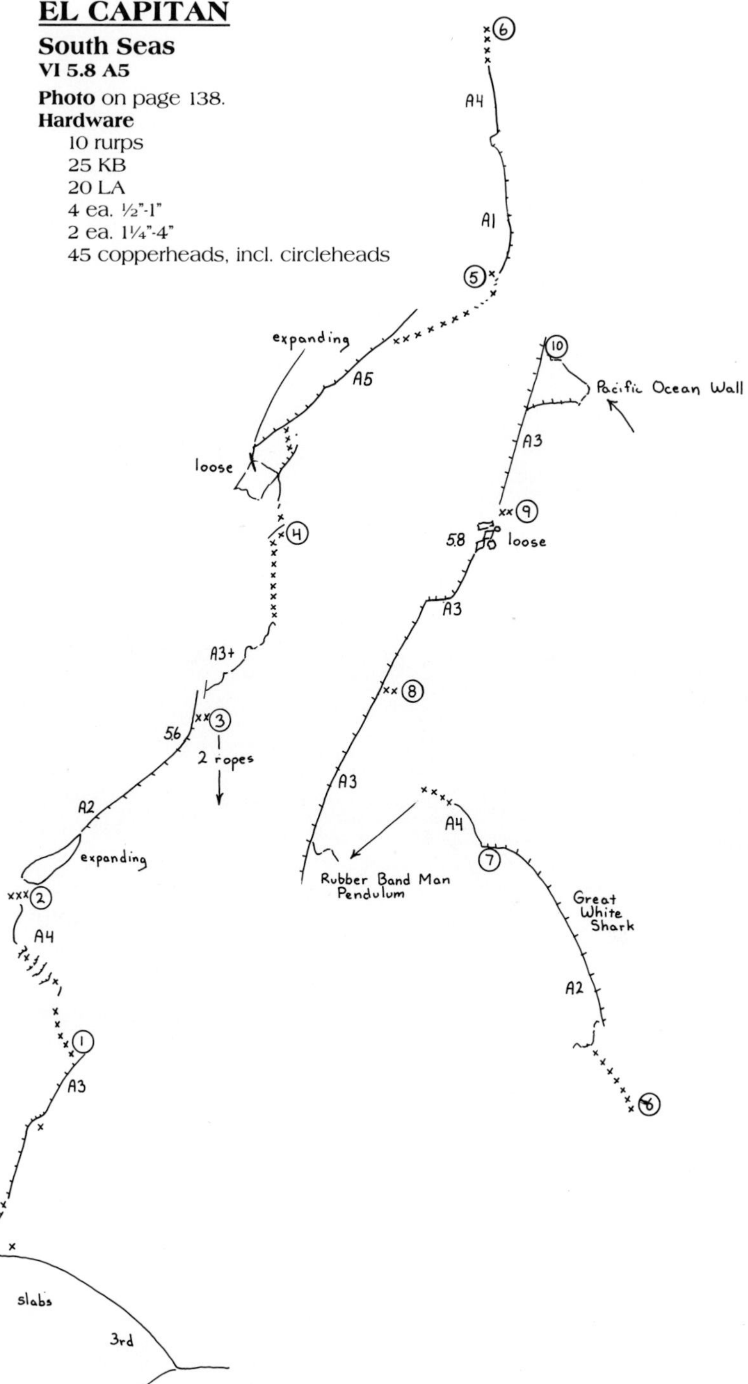

EL CAPITAN

Pacific Ocean Wall

VI 5.9 A4

Photo on page 138.

Hardware

5 rurps
10 KB
18 LA
5 ea. ½"-⅝"
3 ea. ¾"-1"
1 ea. 1¼"-1½"
3 ea. Friends
35 copperheads, mostly small hooks

Note This route is closed to climbing from January 1 to August 1 to protect peregrine falcon nesting sites.

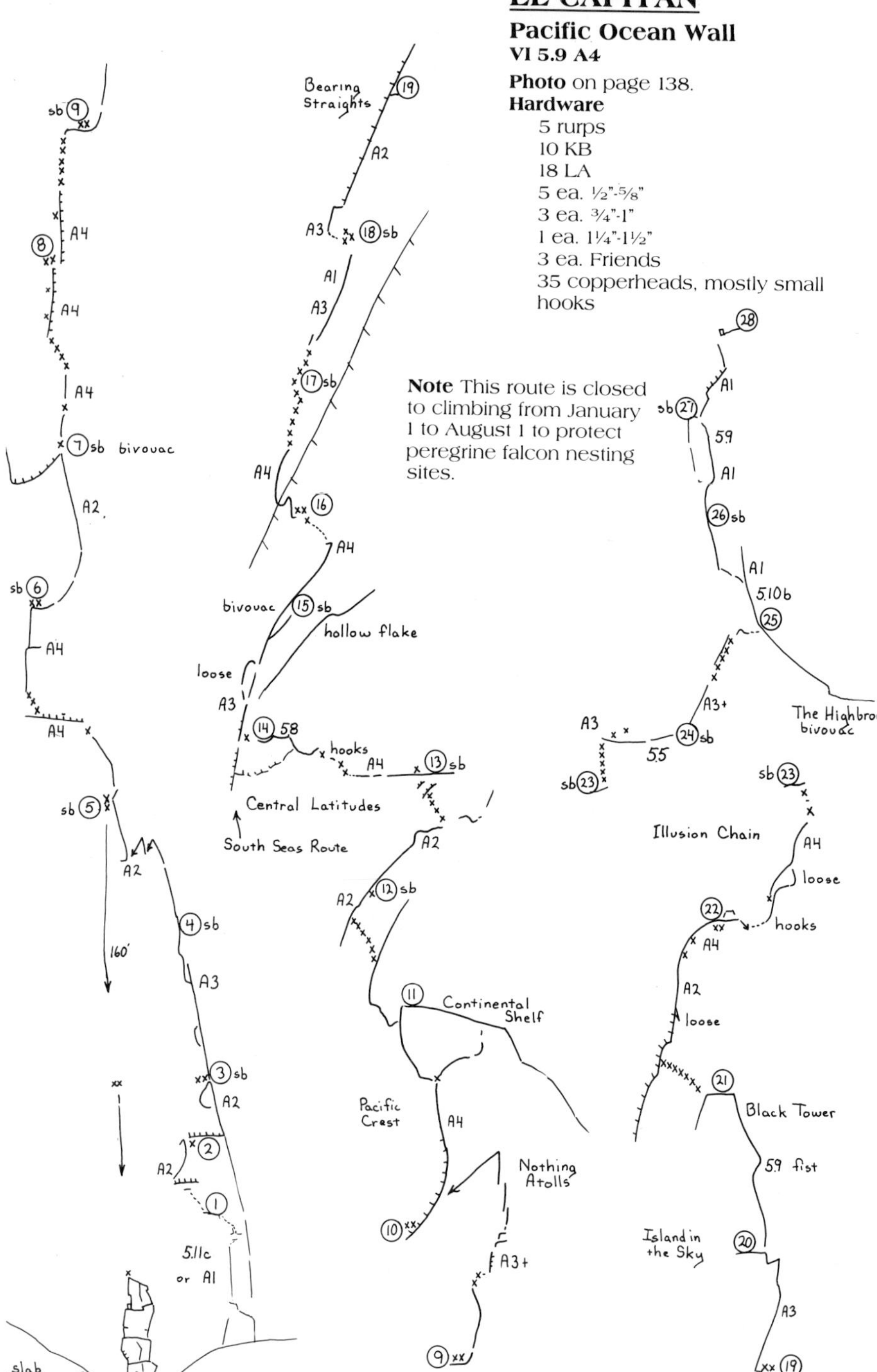

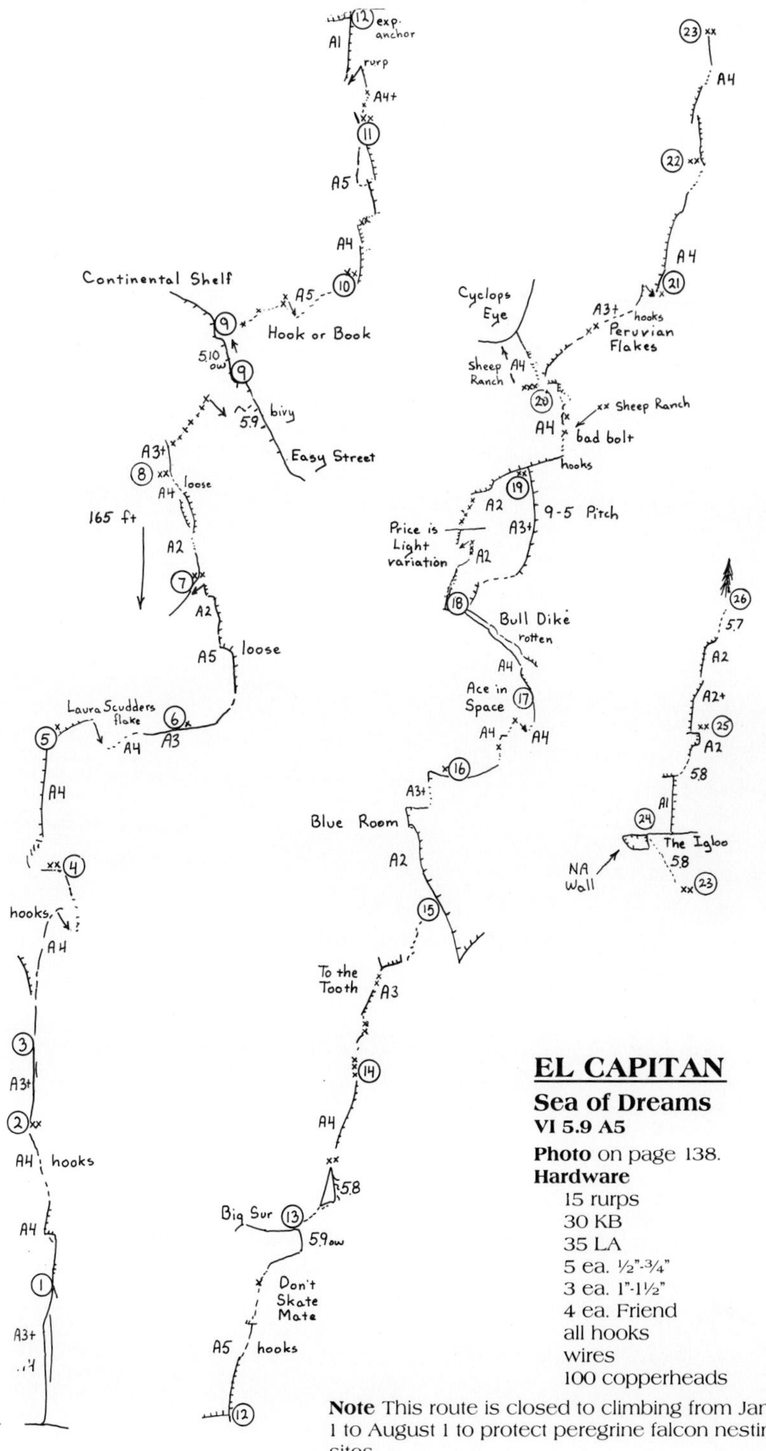

EL CAPITAN

Sea of Dreams

VI 5.9 A5

Photo on page 138.

Hardware

15 rurps
30 KB
35 LA
5 ea. ½"-¾"
3 ea. 1"-1½"
4 ea. Friend
all hooks
wires
100 copperheads

Note This route is closed to climbing from January 1 to August 1 to protect peregrine falcon nesting sites.

EL CAPITAN

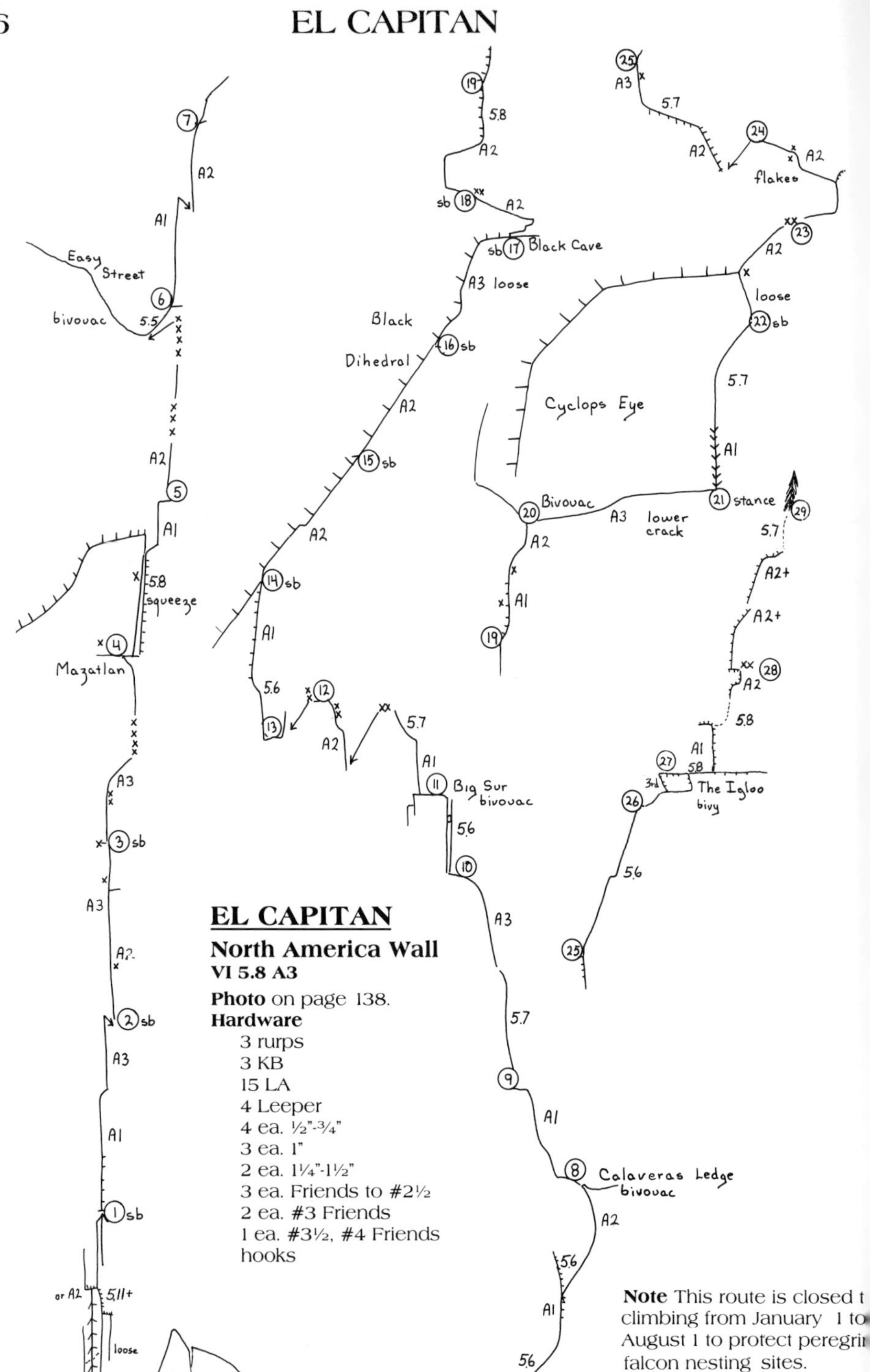

North America Wall
VI 5.8 A3

Photo on page 138.

Hardware
- 3 rurps
- 3 KB
- 15 LA
- 4 Leeper
- 4 ea. ½"-¾"
- 3 ea. 1"
- 2 ea. 1¼"-1½"
- 3 ea. Friends to #2½
- 2 ea. #3 Friends
- 1 ea. #3½, #4 Friends
- hooks

Note This route is closed t climbing from January 1 to August 1 to protect peregri falcon nesting sites.

EL CAPITAN

Wyoming Sheep Ranch

VI A5+

Photo on page 138.

Hardware

- 5 rurps
- 35 KB
- 25 LA
- 5 ea. ½"-1¼"
- 4 ea. Friends
- wires
- 100 copperheads
- all hooks

Note This route is closed to climbing from January 1 to August 1 to protect peregrine falcon nesting sites.

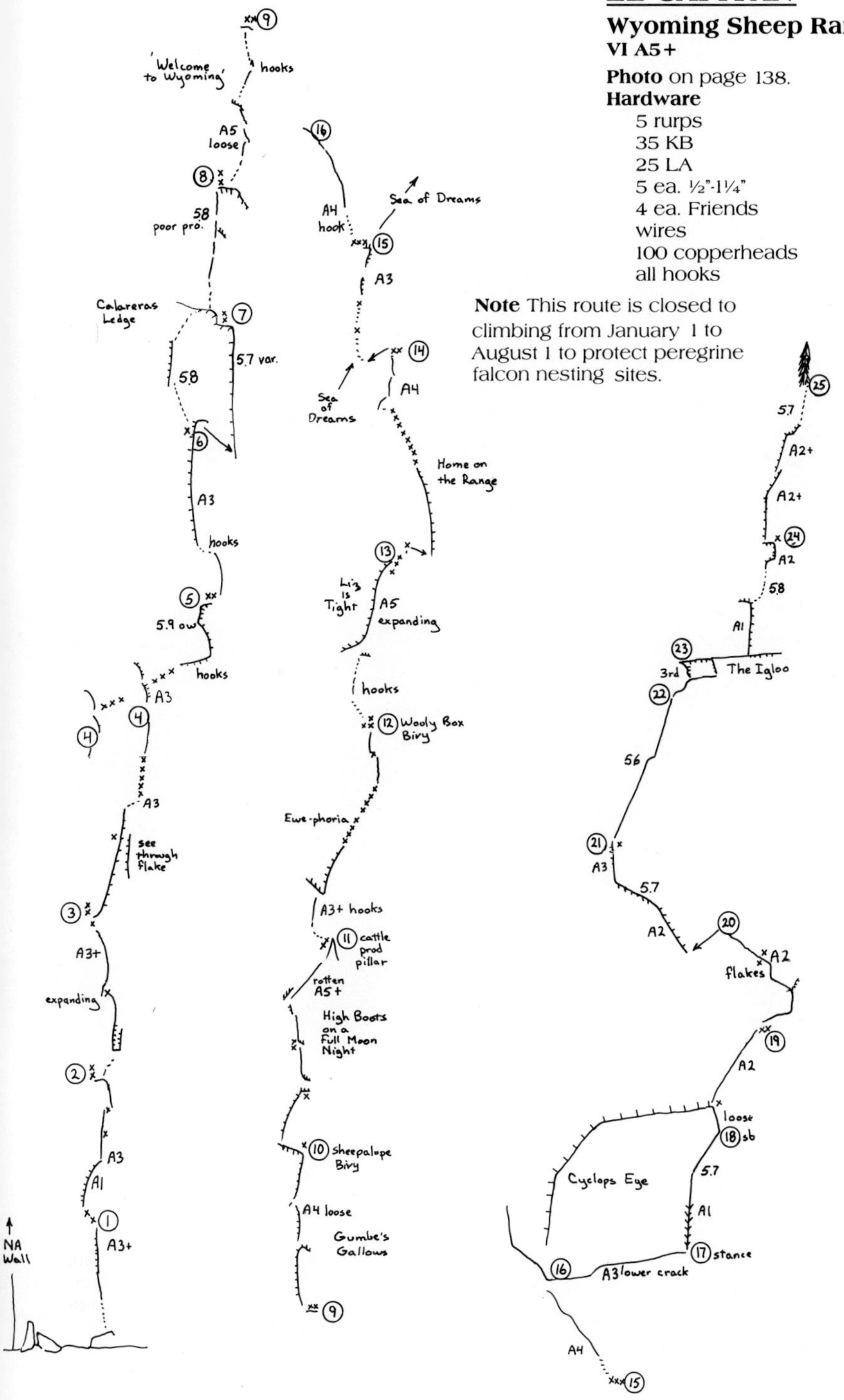

EL CAPITAN

New Jersey Turnpike

VI 5.10 A4+

Photo on page 138.

Hardware

- 5 rurps
- 10 KB
- 25 LA
- 6 ea. ½"-⅝"
- 5 ea. ¾", incl. sawed-off
- 2 ea. 1"
- 1 ea. 1¼"
- all hooks
- 50 copperheads, mostly #1-2

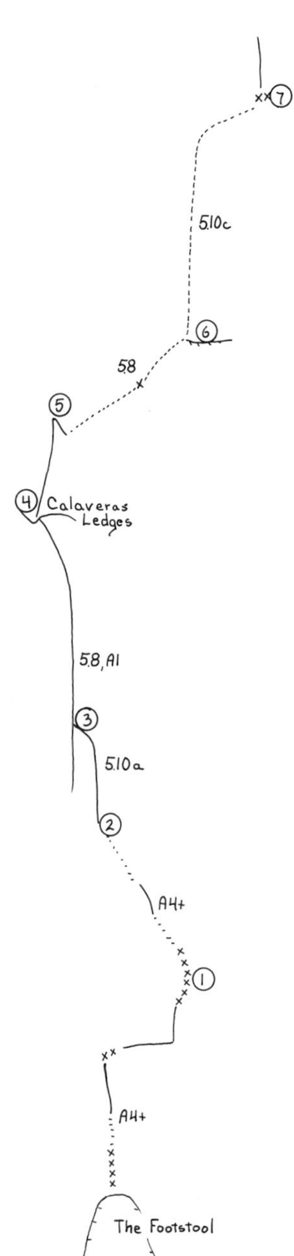

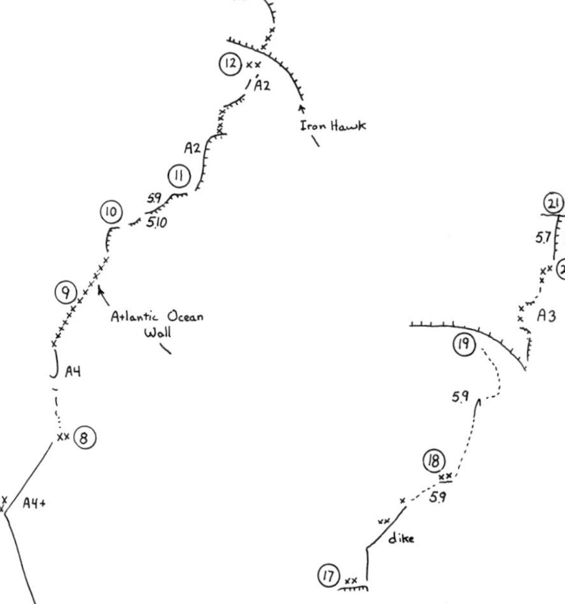

Note This route is closed to climbing from January 1 to August 1 to protect peregrine falcon nesting sites.

EL CAPITAN

Atlantic Ocean Wall

VI 5.10 A5

Photo on page 138.

Hardware

- 3 rurps
- 30 KB
- 25 LA
- 5 ea. ½"-⅝"
- 3 ea. ¾"
- 2 ea. 1"
- 1 ea. 1¼"-1½"
- 60 copperheads
- wires
- all hooks
- Quickies
- keyhole hangers
- 4 ea. Friends #½-#5

Note This route is closed to climbing from January 1 to August 1 to protect peregrine falcon nesting sites.

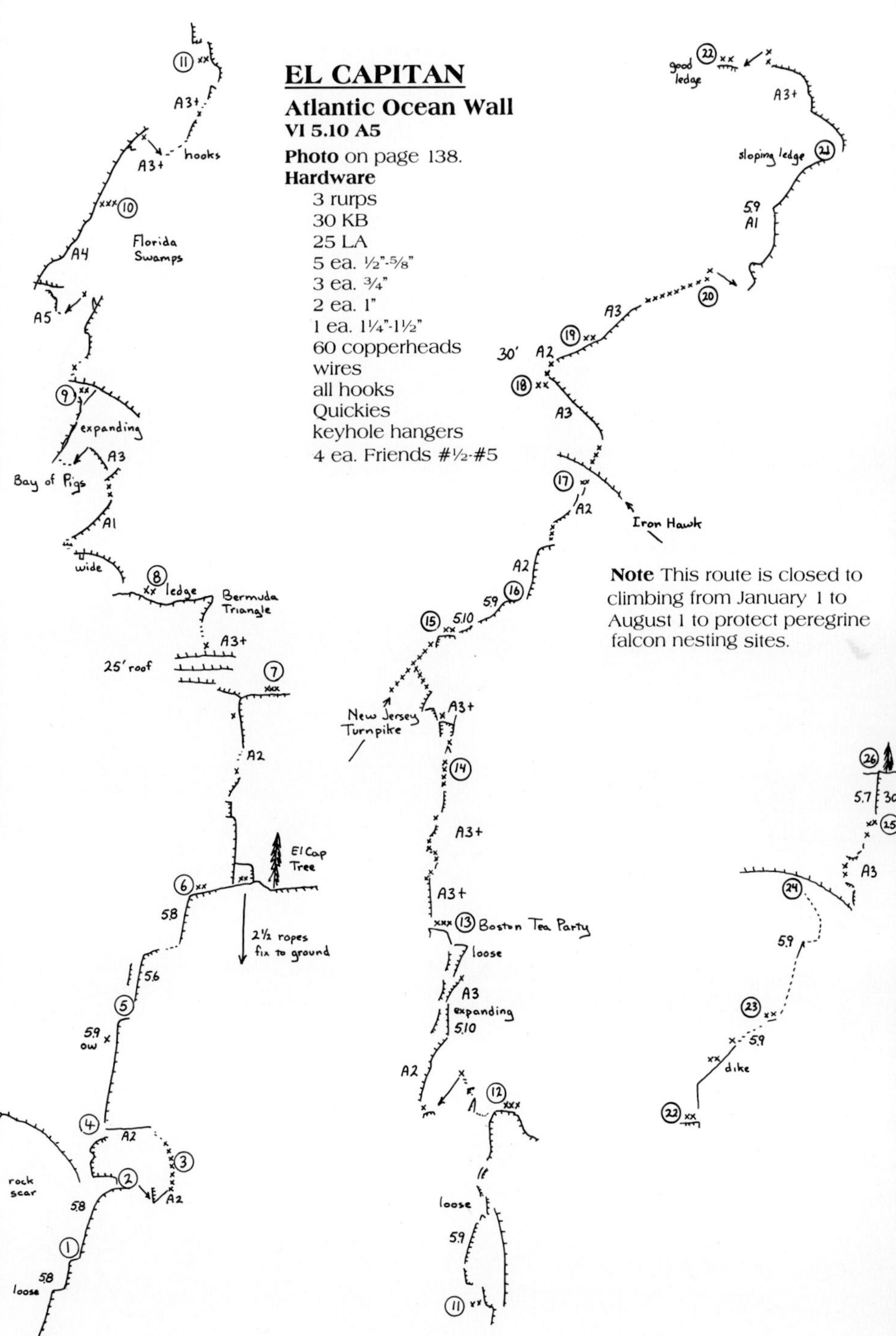

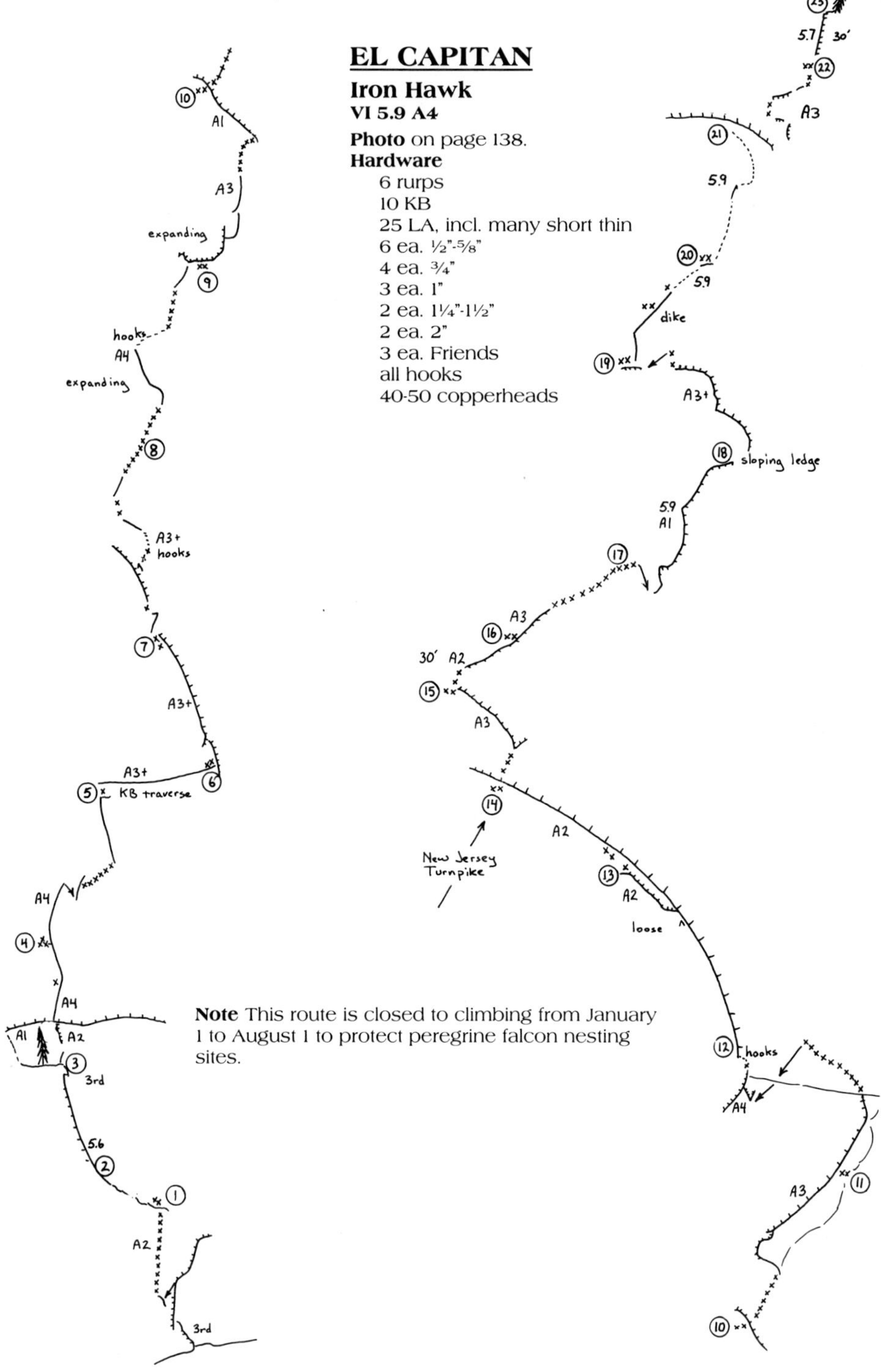

EL CAPITAN

Iron Hawk

VI 5.9 A4

Photo on page 138.

Hardware

6 rurps
10 KB
25 LA, incl. many short thin
6 ea. ½"-⅝"
4 ea. ¾"
3 ea. 1"
2 ea. 1¼"-1½"
2 ea. 2"
3 ea. Friends
all hooks
40-50 copperheads

Note This route is closed to climbing from January 1 to August 1 to protect peregrine falcon nesting sites.

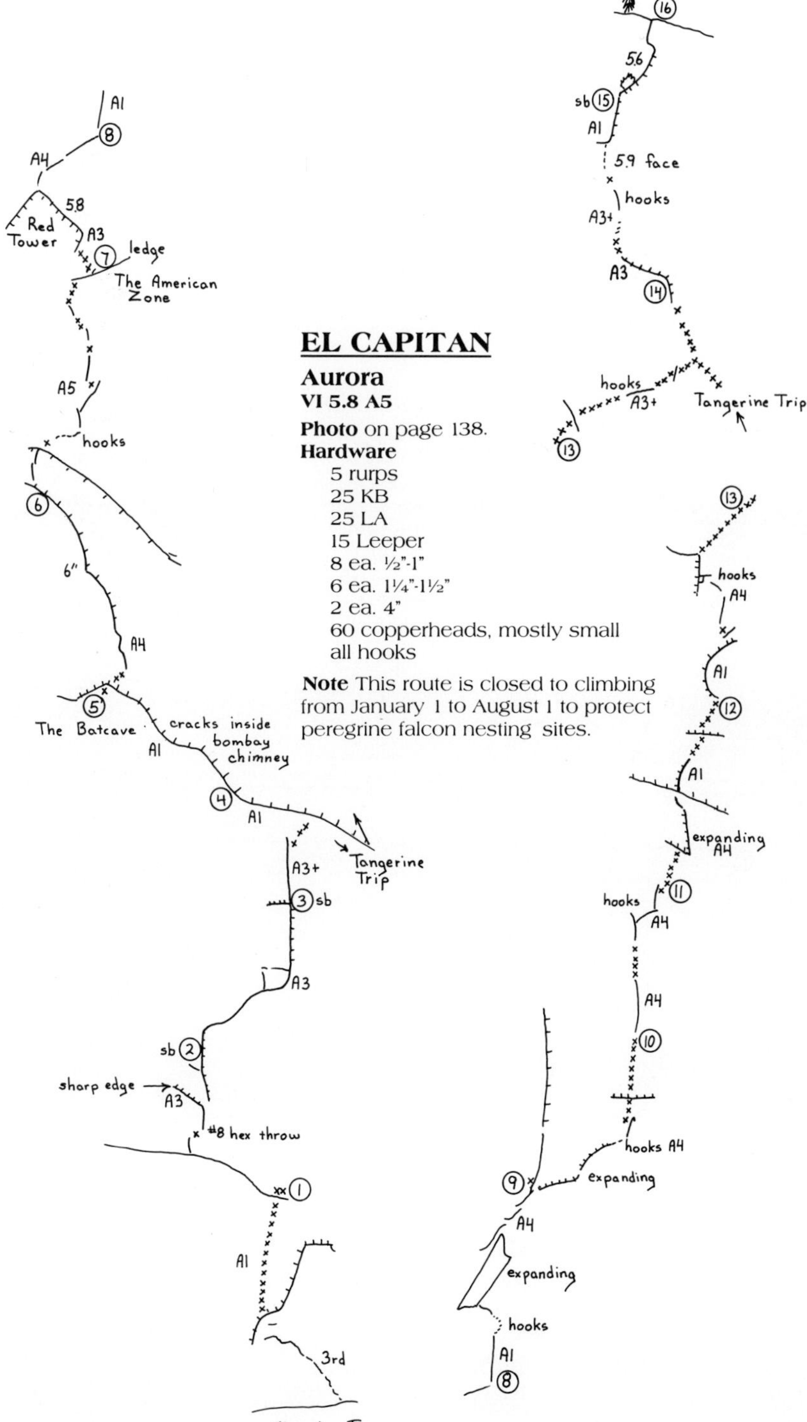

EL CAPITAN

Aurora

VI 5.8 A5

Photo on page 138.

Hardware

- 5 rurps
- 25 KB
- 25 LA
- 15 Leeper
- 8 ea. ½"-1"
- 6 ea. 1¼"-1½"
- 2 ea. 4"
- 60 copperheads, mostly small
- all hooks

Note This route is closed to climbing from January 1 to August 1 to protect peregrine falcon nesting sites.

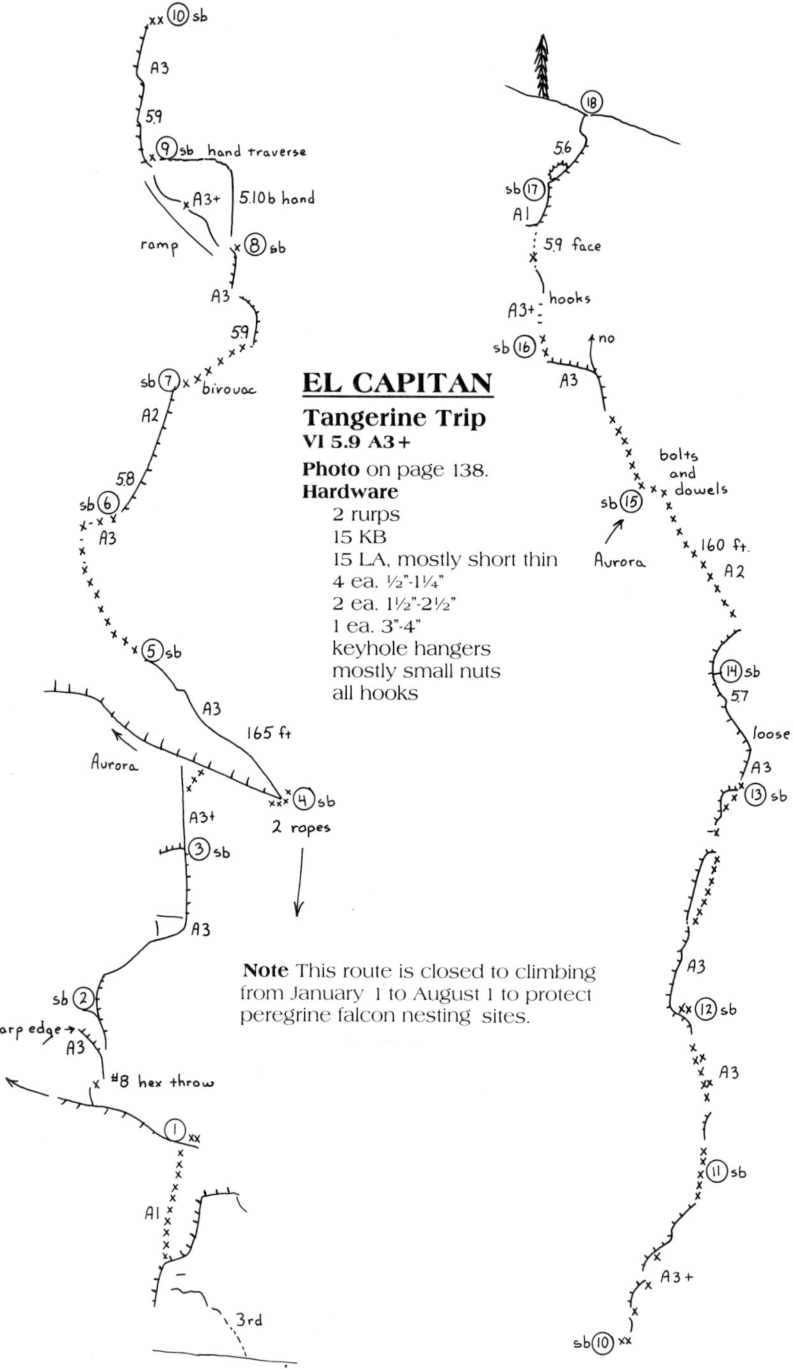

EL CAPITAN

Tangerine Trip
VI 5.9 A3+

Photo on page 138.

Hardware

- 2 rurps
- 15 KB
- 15 LA, mostly short thin
- 4 ea. ½"-1¼"
- 2 ea. 1½"-2½"
- 1 ea. 3"-4"
- keyhole hangers
- mostly small nuts
- all hooks

Note This route is closed to climbing from January 1 to August 1 to protect peregrine falcon nesting sites.

EL CAPITAN

Lost in America

VI 5.9 A5

Photo on page 138.

Hardware

- 3 stars
- 5 rurps
- 50 KB
- 25 LA
- 7 Leeper
- 3 ea. ½"-1"
- 80 copperheads
- 3 ea. Friends to #3
- 2 ea. Friends #3½-#6
- 3 wire nuts
- rivet hangers
- bolt hangers
- keyhole hangers
- hooks
- extender "cheat" stick

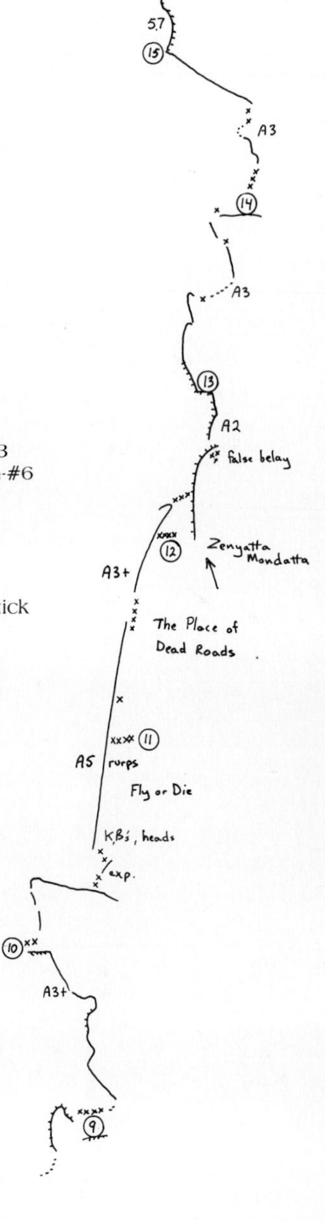

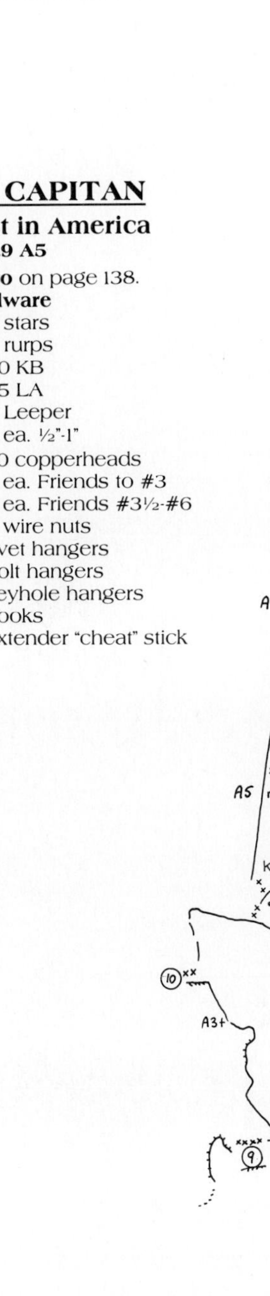

Dale Bard, **Sea of Dreams**, 1978. *Jim Bridwell*

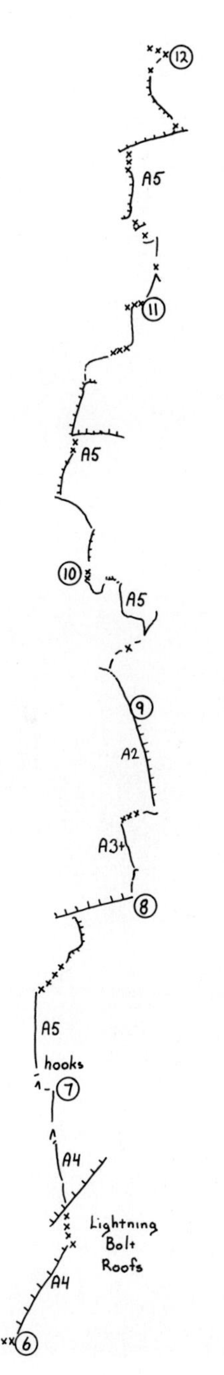

EL CAPITAN

Zenyatta Mondatta

VI 5.7 A5

Photo on page 138.

Hardware

5 rurps
30 KB
25 LA
6 ea. ½"-⅝"
3 ea. ¾"-1"
50 copperheads
all hooks
Friends

A **Blankout** 5.11c
pro: to 4½"

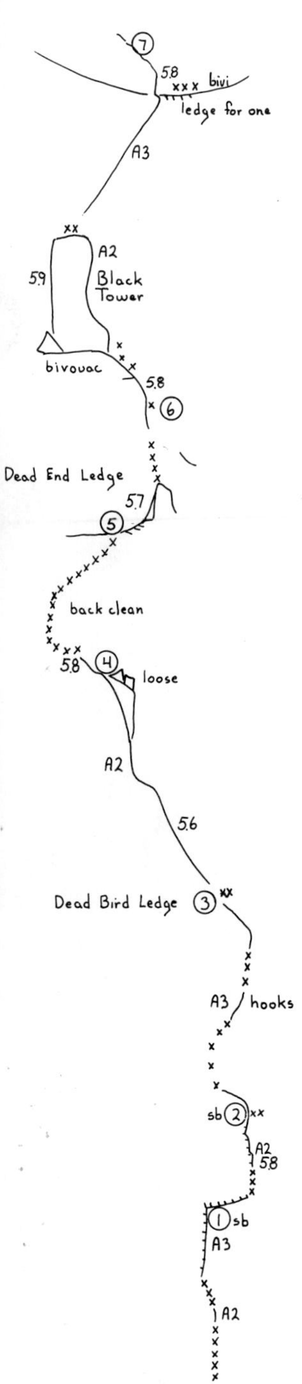

EL CAPITAN

Zodiac

VI 5.11 A3+

Photo on page 138.

Hardware

- 2 rurps
- 2 KB
- 15 LA, mostly short thick
- 3 ea. ½"-1½"
- nuts to 2"
- 2 ea. Friend
- hooks
- 10 bolt hangers

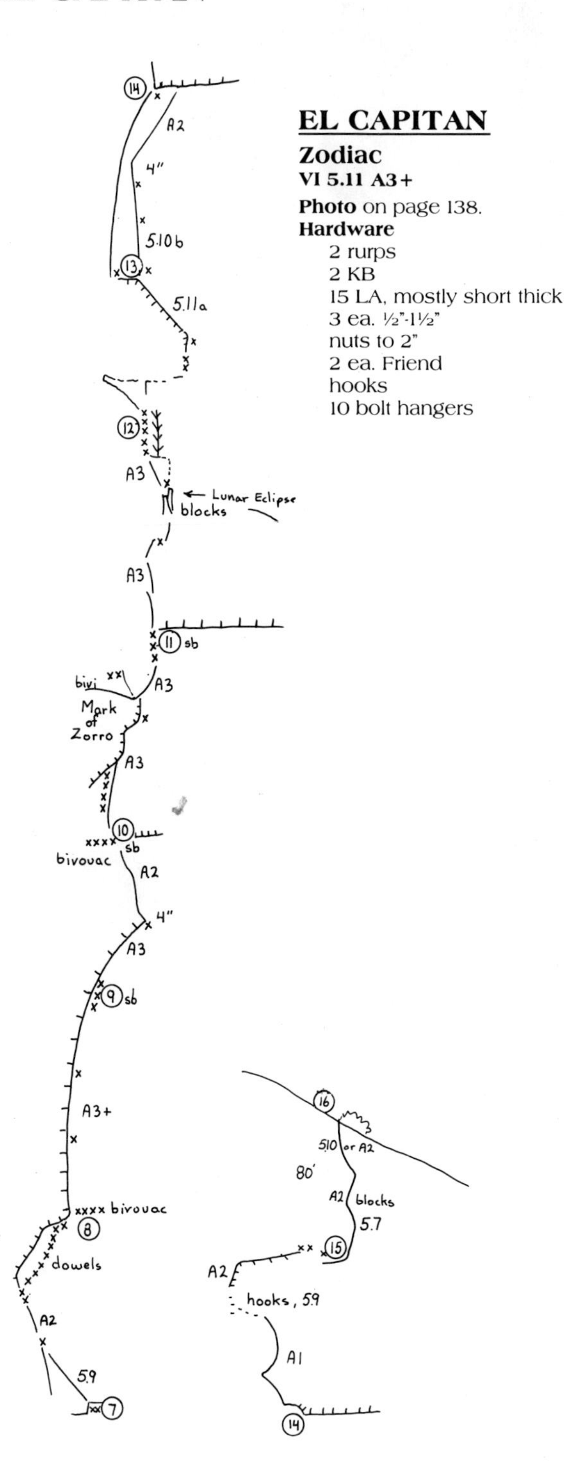

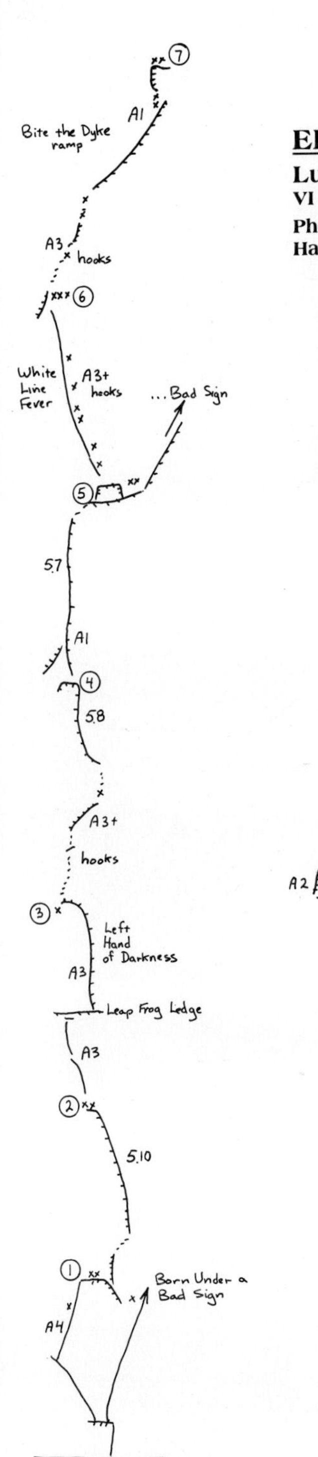

EL CAPITAN

Lunar Eclipse

VI 5.10 A4

Photo on page 138.

Hardware

- 5 rurps
- 20 KB
- 20 LA
- 3 ea. ½"-¾"
- 2 ea. 1"-1½"
- 3 ea. Friends
- 3 ea. RP's
- nuts to 1"
- 20 copperheads
- hooks
- rivet hangers

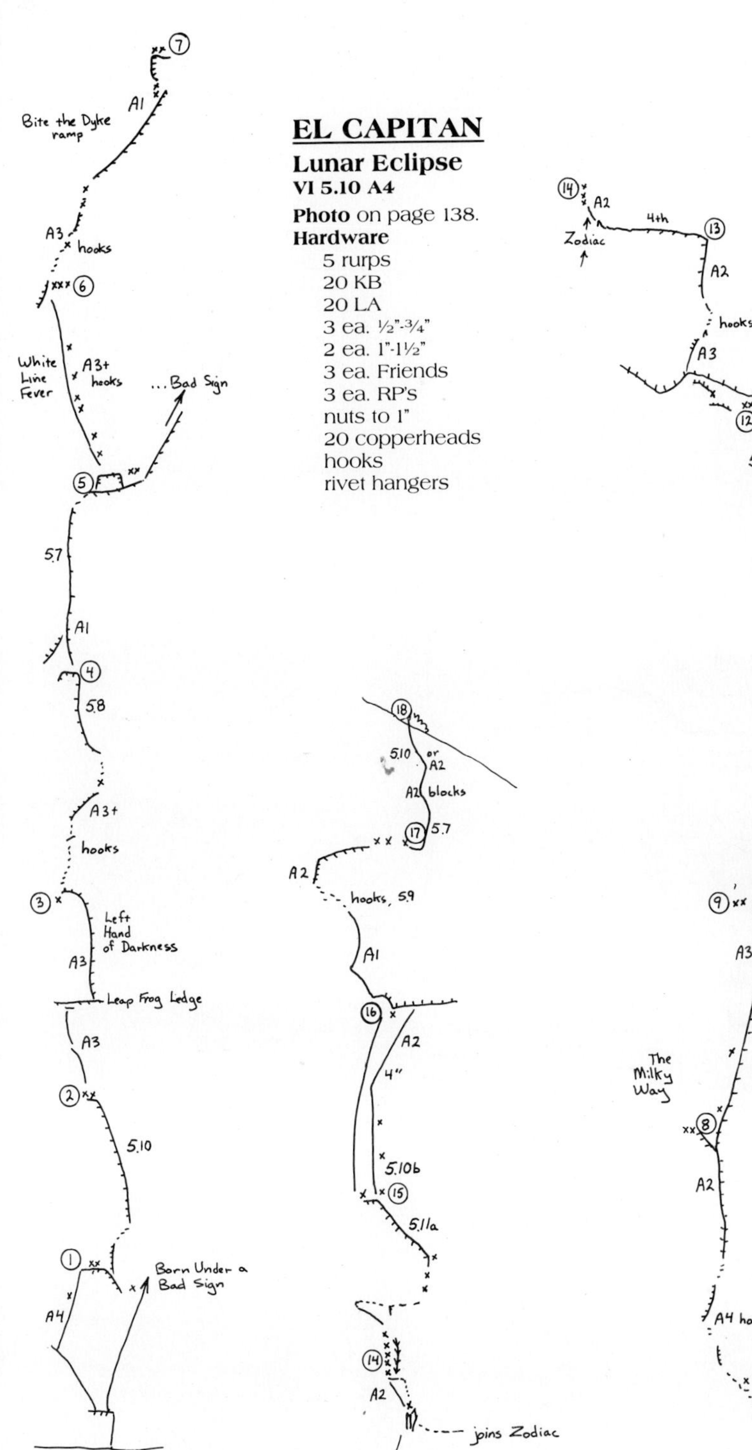

14 A2
Zodiac
4th
13
A2
hooks
A3
Devil's Brow
12
A2
5.10a loose
11
A1
hooks
A3
10
A3
hooks
A2
9
A3
The Milky Way
8
A2
A4 hooks
7

18
5.10 or A2
A2 blocks
17 5.7
A2
hooks, 5.9
A1
16
A2
4"
5.10b
15
5.11a
14
A2
joins Zodiac

EL CAPITAN

Born Under a Bad Sign

VI 5.10 A5

Photo on page 138.

Hardware

20 rurps
20 KB
15 LA
4 ea. ½"-¾"
2 ea. 1"-1½"
nuts to 3½"

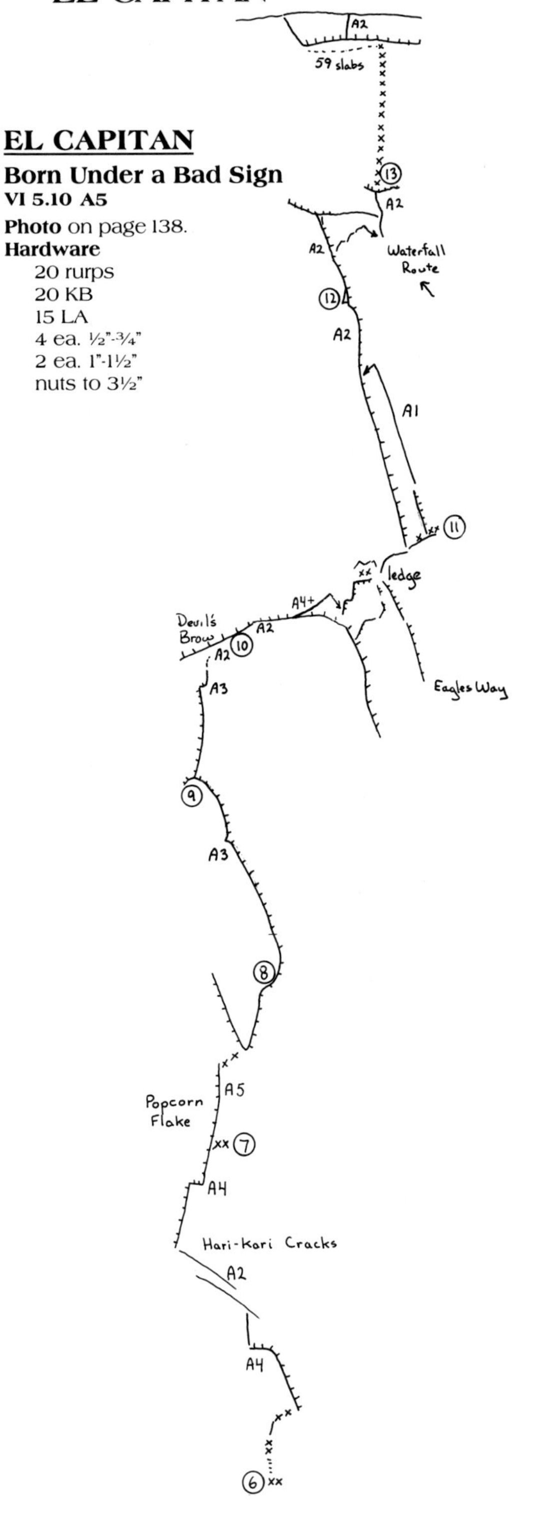

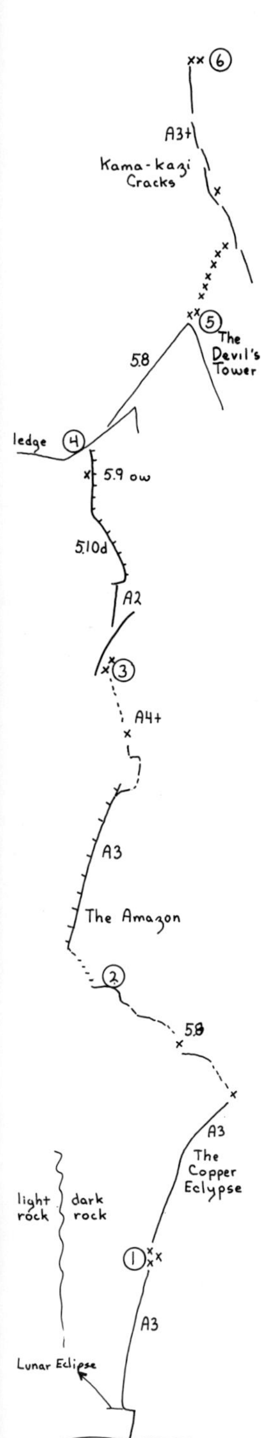

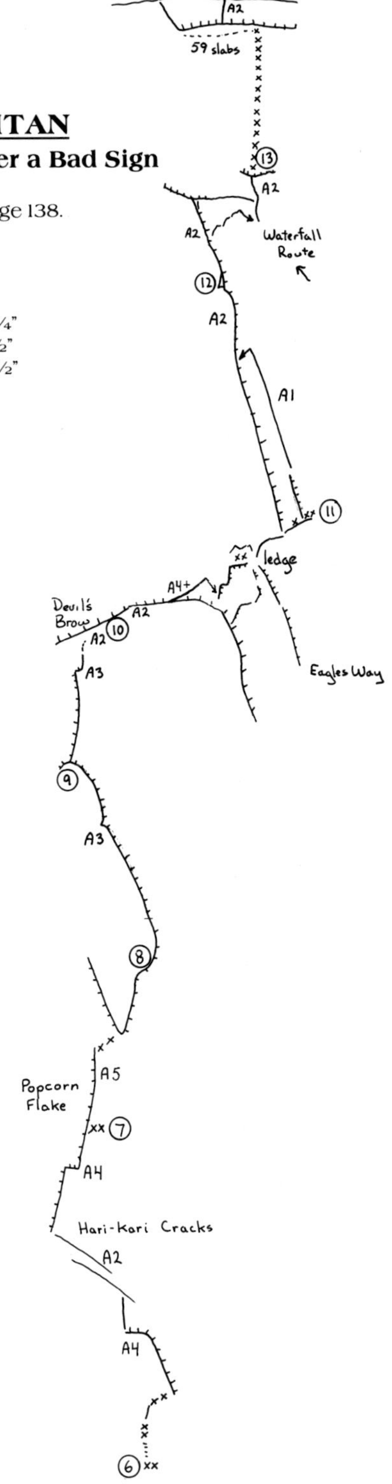

EL CAPITAN

Bad to the Bone

VI 5.9+ A4

Photo on page 138.

Hardware

10 rurps
25 KB
15 LA
3 ea. ½"-1"
1 ea. 1¼"
3 ea. Friends to #3
2 ea. #4 Friends
2 ea. #6 Friends
25 copperheads
many wires
all hooks

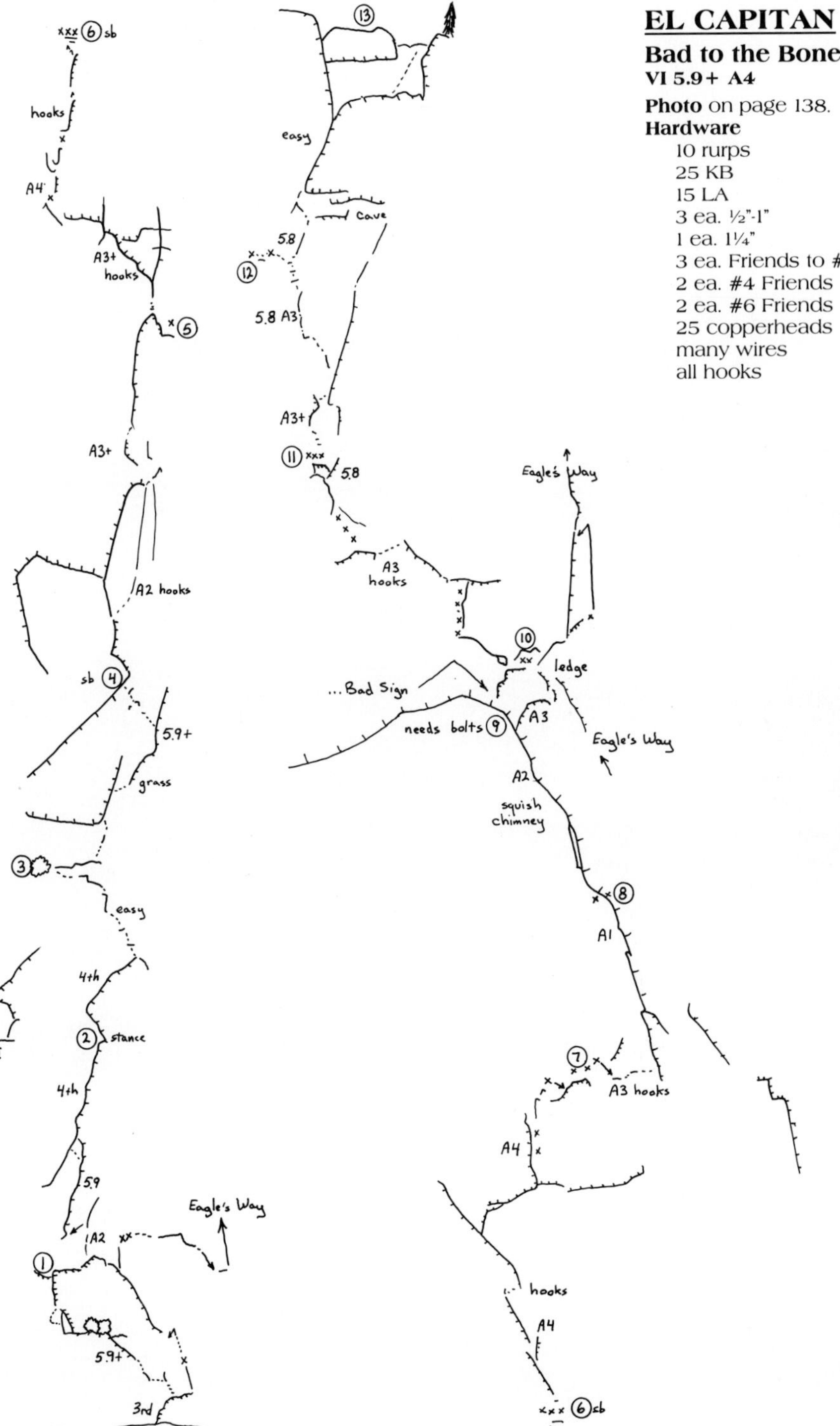

EL CAPITAN

Eagle's Way

VI 5.9 A4

Photo on page 999.

Hardware

10 rurps
15 KB
20 LA
6 ea. ½"-⅝"
5 ea. ¾"-1½"
1 ea. 2"-4"
10 copperheads
bolt hangers

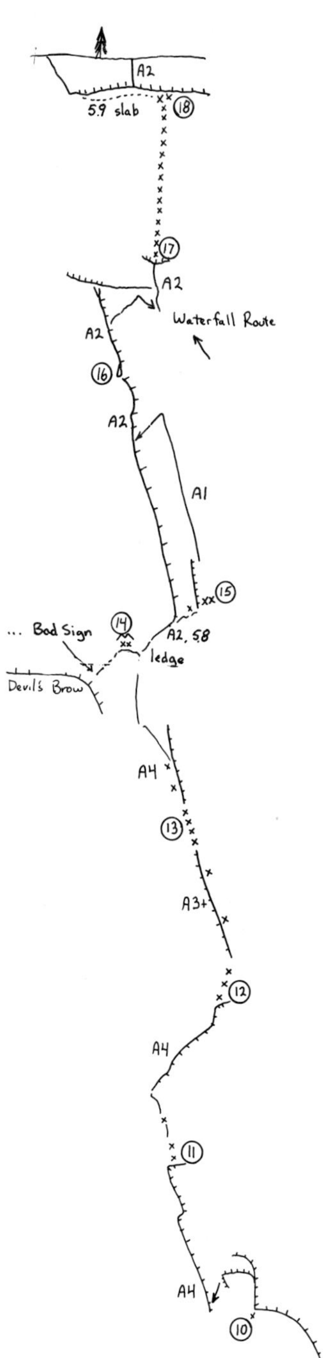

EL CAPITAN

On the Waterfront

VI 5.9 A5

Photo on page 138.

Hardware

5 rurps
12 KB
15 LA
3 ea. ½"-¾"
4 ea. 1"
2 ea. Friends to #4
hooks
rivet hangers
10-15 copperheads

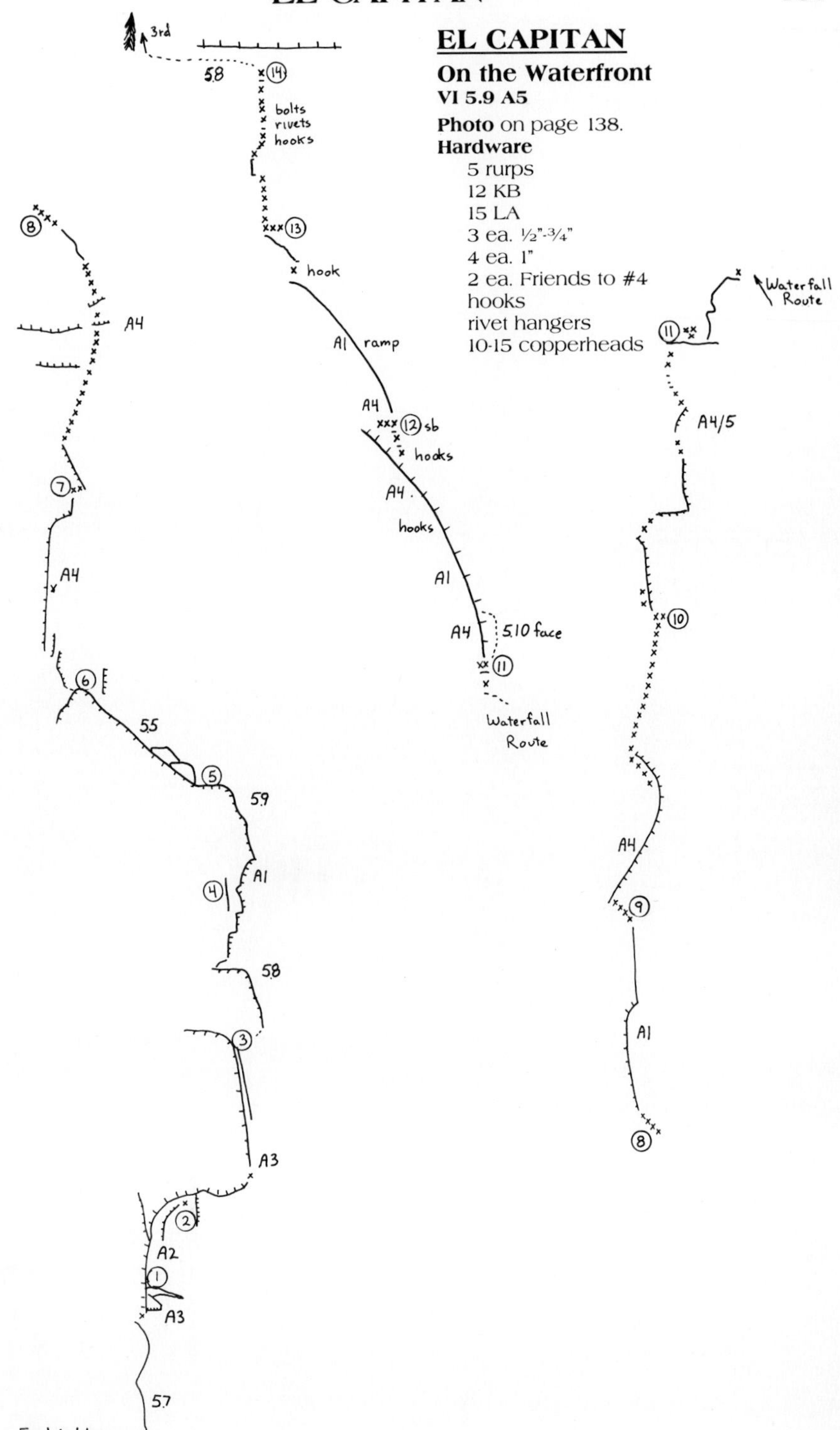

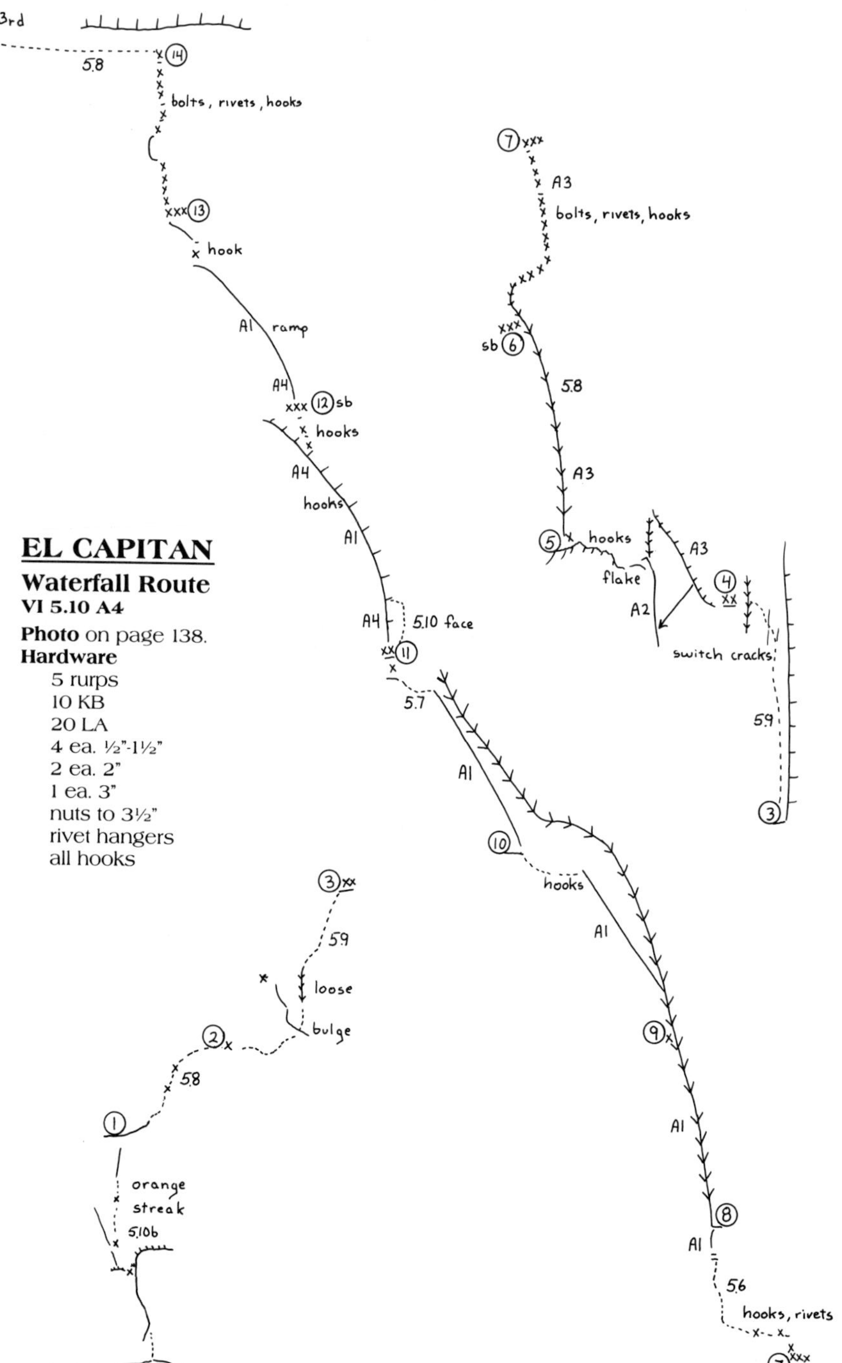

EL CAPITAN

Waterfall Route

VI 5.10 A4

Photo on page 138.

Hardware

5 rurps
10 KB
20 LA
4 ea. ½"-1½"
2 ea. 2"
1 ea. 3"
nuts to 3½"
rivet hangers
all hooks

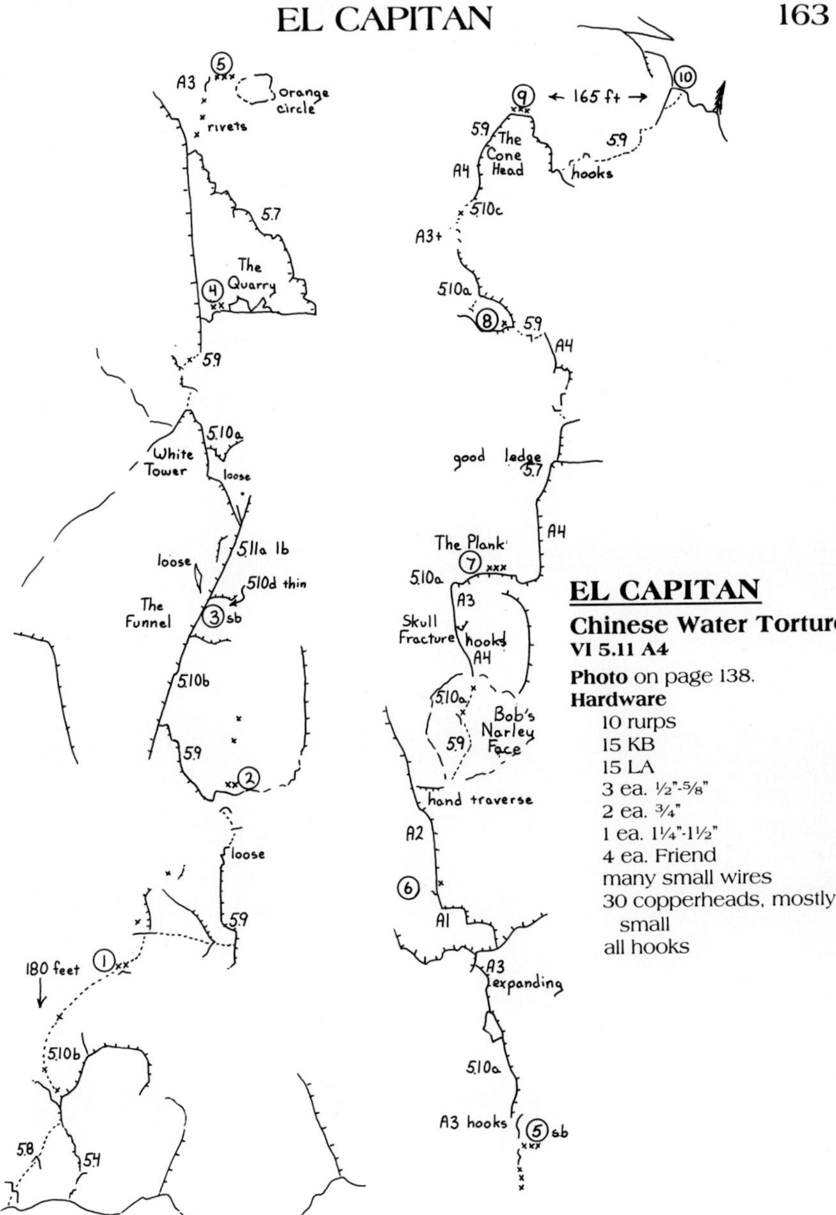

EL CAPITAN

Chinese Water Torture

VI 5.11 A4

Photo on page 138.

Hardware

- 10 rurps
- 15 KB
- 15 LA
- 3 ea. ½"-⅝"
- 2 ea. ¾"
- 1 ea. 1¼"-1½"
- 4 ea. Friend
- many small wires
- 30 copperheads, mostly small
- all hooks

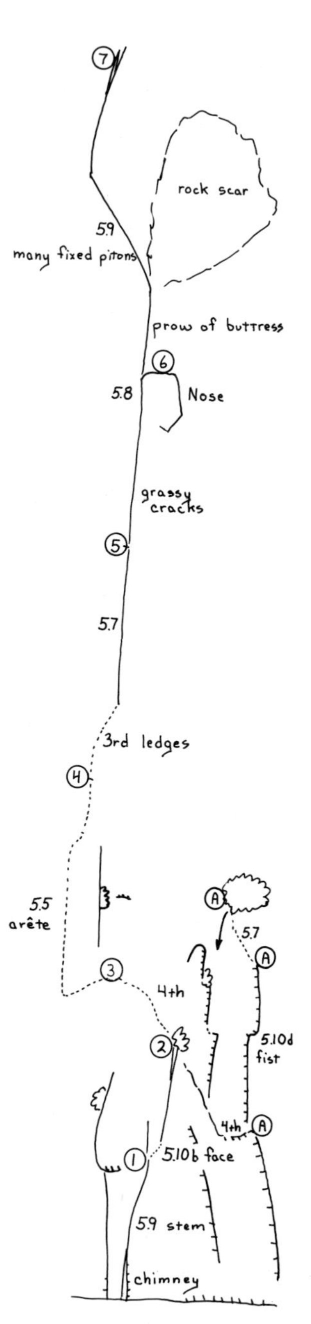

EL CAPITAN

East Buttress
5.10b

Protection to 3"
Photo on page 138.
A End of the World 5.10d

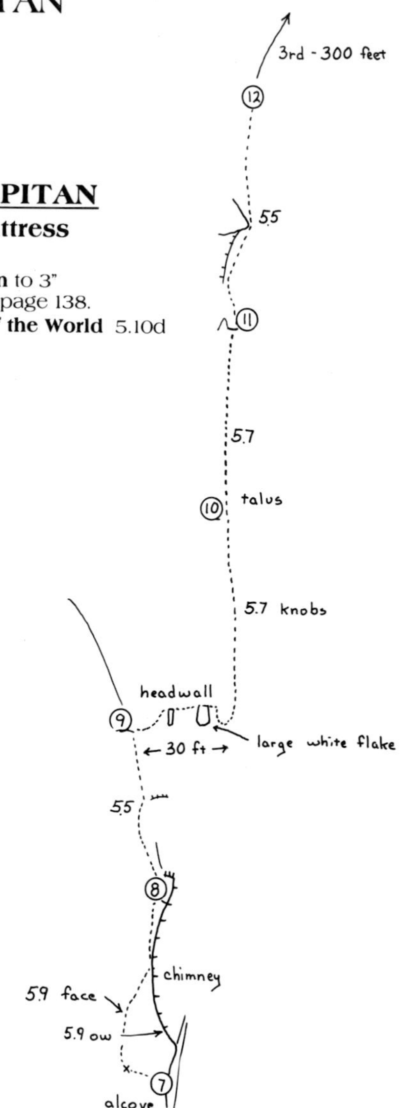

Willi Unsoeld on El Capitan, East Buttress, 1953. *Allen Steck*

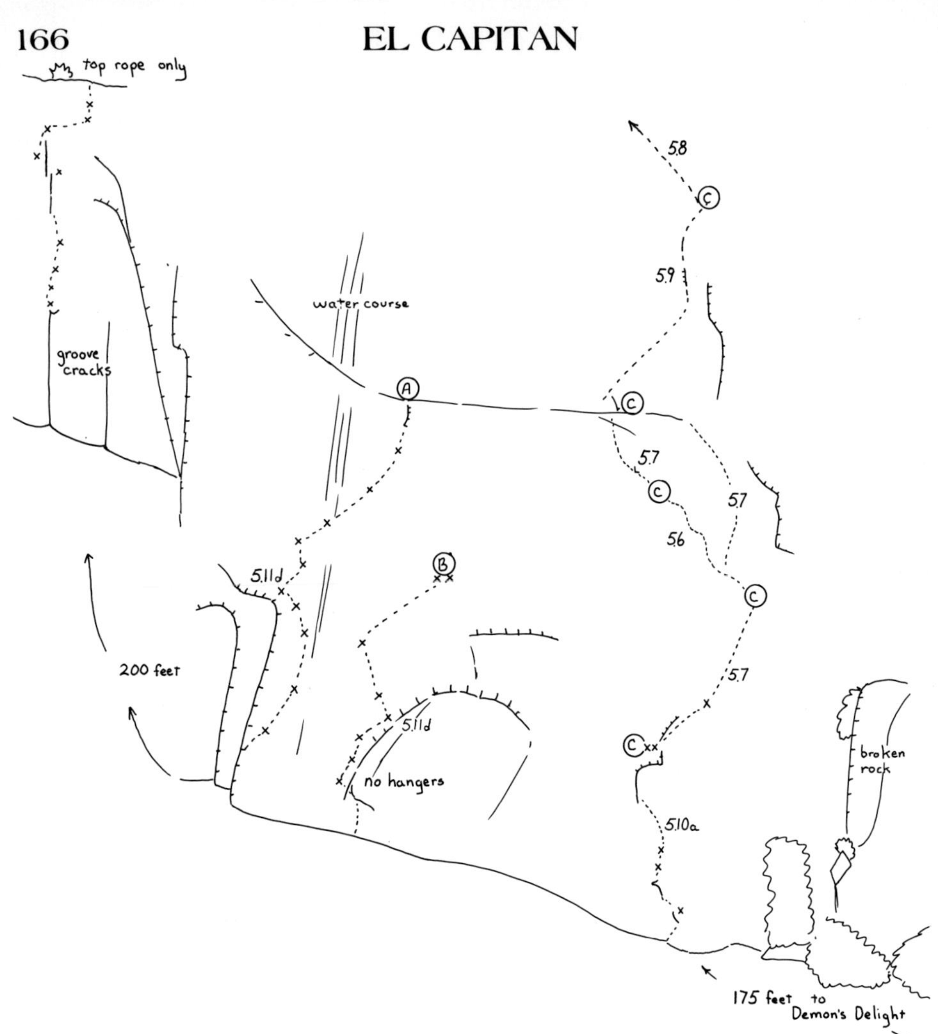
top rope only
5.8
5.9
water course
groove
cracks
5.7
5.7
5.6
5.11d
200 feet
5.7
5.11d
no hangers
broken
rock
5.10a
175 feet to
Demon's Delight

SCHUTZ'S RIDGE – West Side

Approach Park in the dirt turnout just past the "S" curve, 1.9 miles west of the gas station, or in the picnic pullout located 2.1 miles beyond the station. A short walk leads to the routes.
Photo on page 168.

A **The White Zone** 5.11d
B **Annette Funicello** 5.11d
C **Bikini Beach Party** 5.10a
D **Demon's Delight** 5.11a
E **Supertoe** 5.10d
F **Brown Sugar** 5.9
G **Free Bong** 5.11a

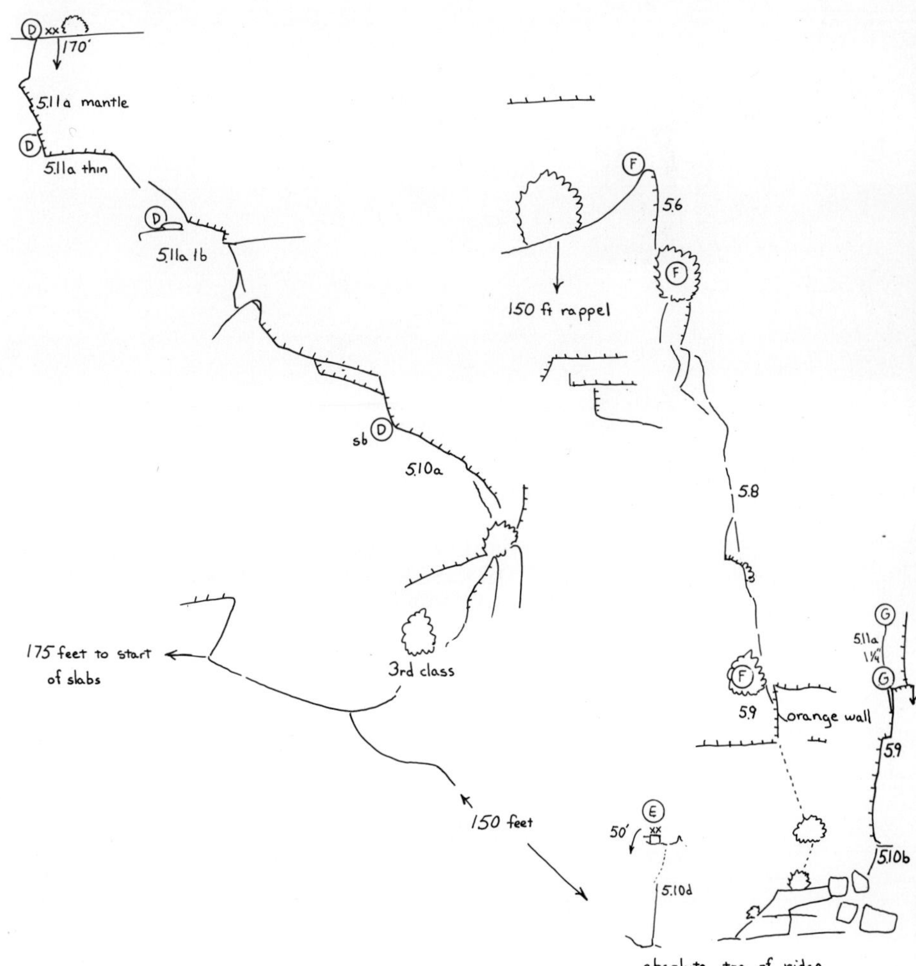

EAGLE CREEK

1 SCHULTZ'S RIDGE
2 LOGGERHEAD BUTTRESS
3 SLAB HAPPY PINNACLE
4 East Ledges Descent
5 COMMISSIONER BUTTRESS
6 SPLIT PINNACLE
7 Essence

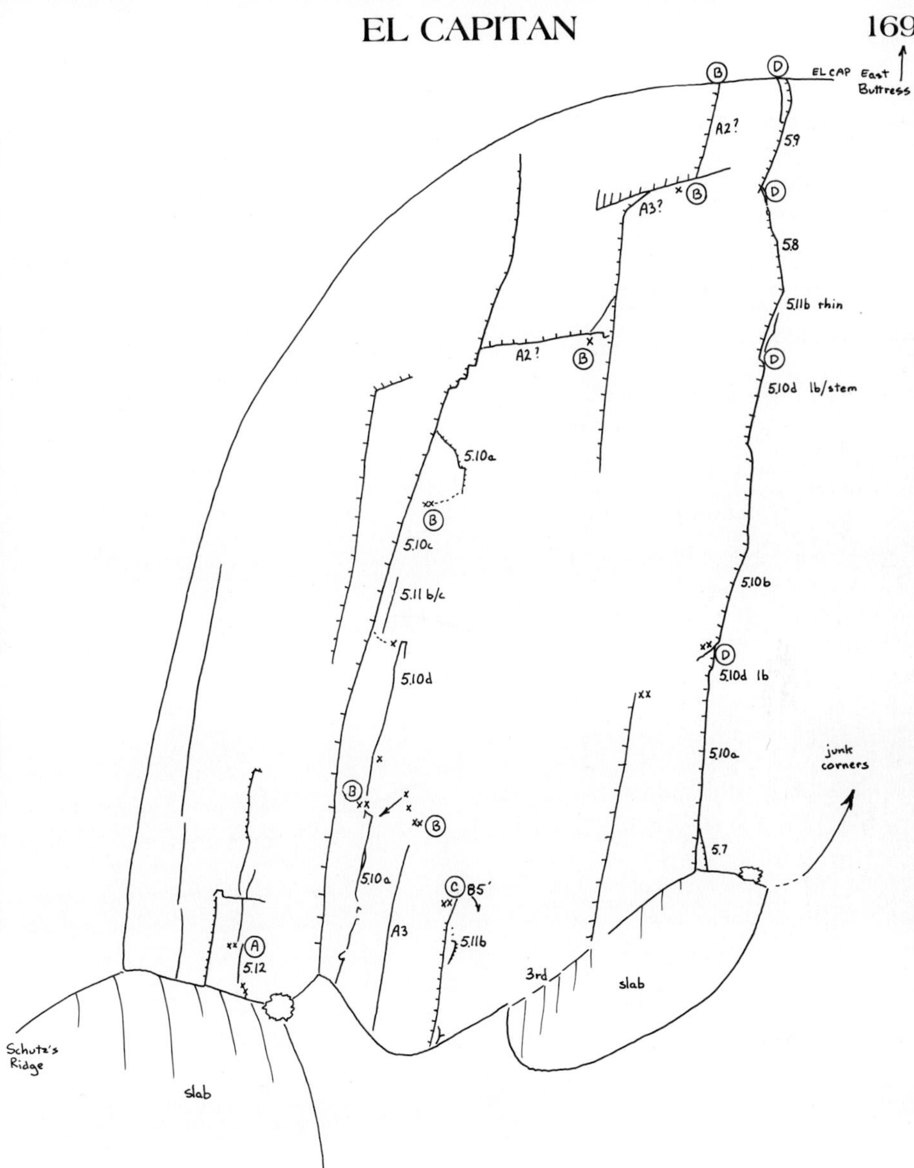

SCHULTZ'S RIDGE – East Side

Approach Park in the dirt turnout just past the "S" curve, 1.9 miles west of the gas station and walk up through the woods to the base of the wall.

Photo on page 168.

A **Ain't That a Bitch** 5.12
B **Abazaba** 5.11b/c A3
C **End Game** 5.11b pro: #1- #3½ Friends
D **Moratorium** 5.11b pro: to 2½"

LOGGERHEAD BUTTRESS

Approach Park in a dirt turnout 1.7 miles west of the gas station and .1 mile past the El Cap Picnic Area. Hike up the hill to the toe of the buttress and trend along its base for the variou routes.

Photo on page 168.

A **Orange Juice Avenue** 5.10a pro: to 5"
B **Lycra Virgin** 5.11d
C **Le Nocturne** 5.10a pro: to 2½"
D **Here on the Outside** 5.11a
E **Chow Chow Chow** 5.10c

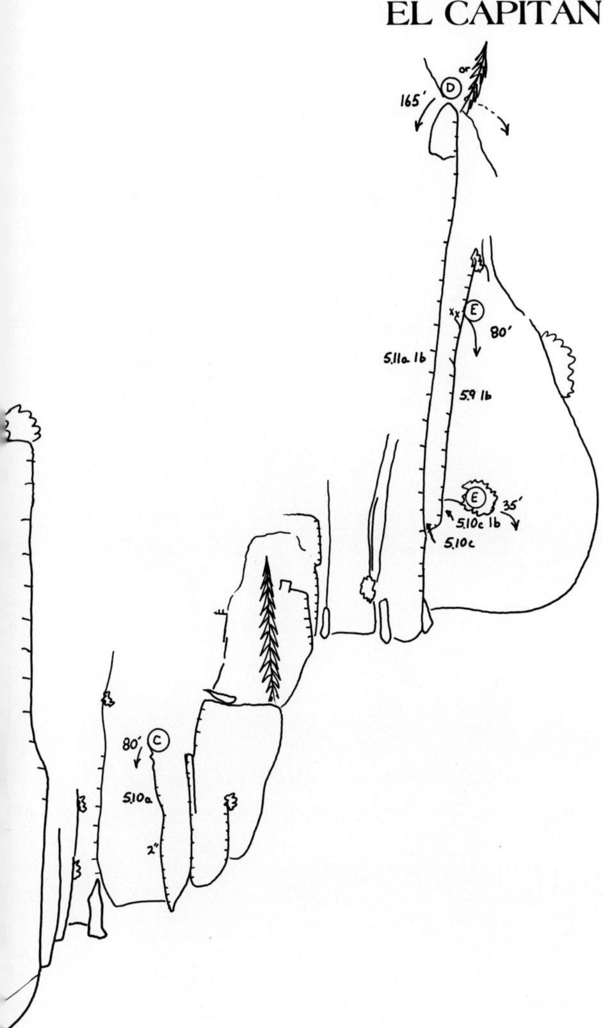
or
D
165'
E
80'
5.11a 1b
5.9 1b
E
35'
5.10c 1b
5.10c
80'
C
5.10a
2"

Ron Kauk on **Lycra Virgin**, 1986. *Kevin Worrall*

SLAB HAPPY PINNACLE

Approach Park in the dirt turnout 1.7 miles west of the gas station and .1 miles past the El Cap Picnic Area. Hike up the hill, skirting the east side of Loggerhead Buttress. Traverse right along a barrier until 3rd class passage can be made to the main wall. Slab Happy is out to the left along a broad ledge system.

Photo on page 168.

A **Left Side Route** 5.11a pro: to 3"
B **Center Route** 5.10b
C **The Dihardral** 5.10c pro: to 3"

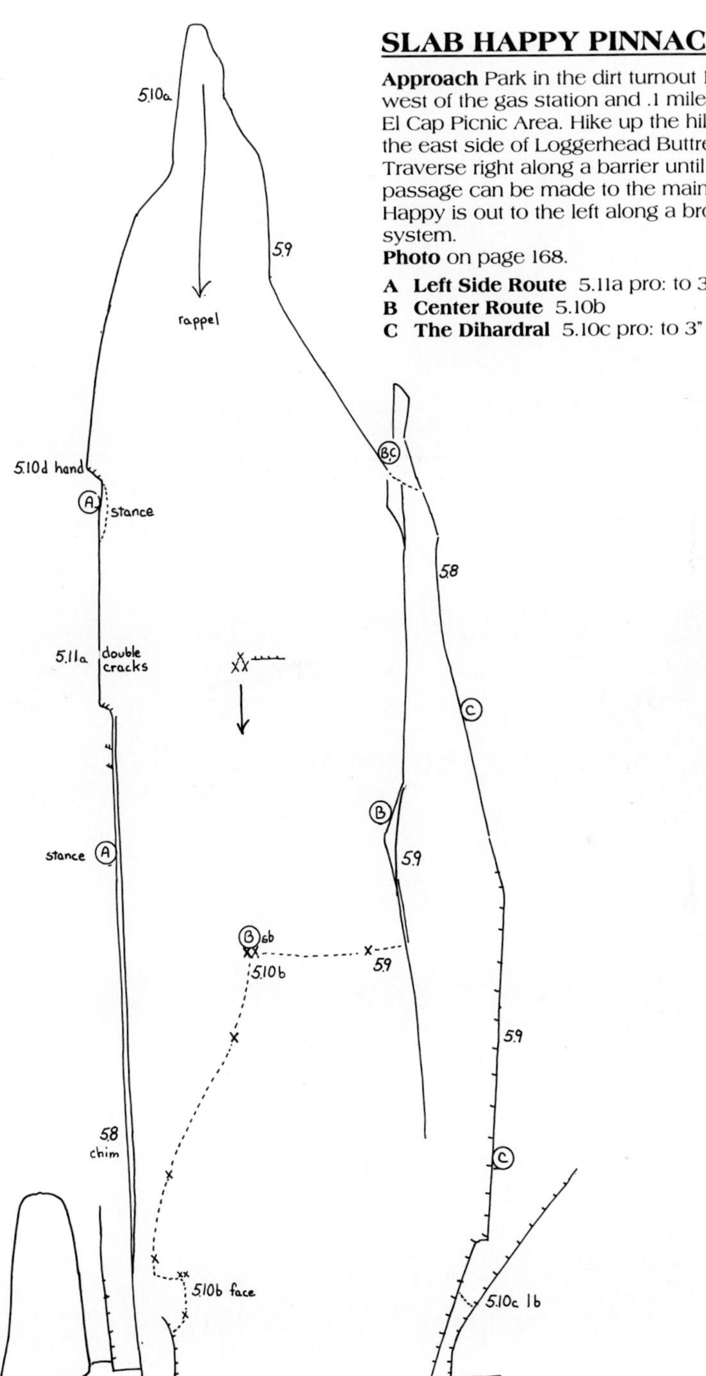

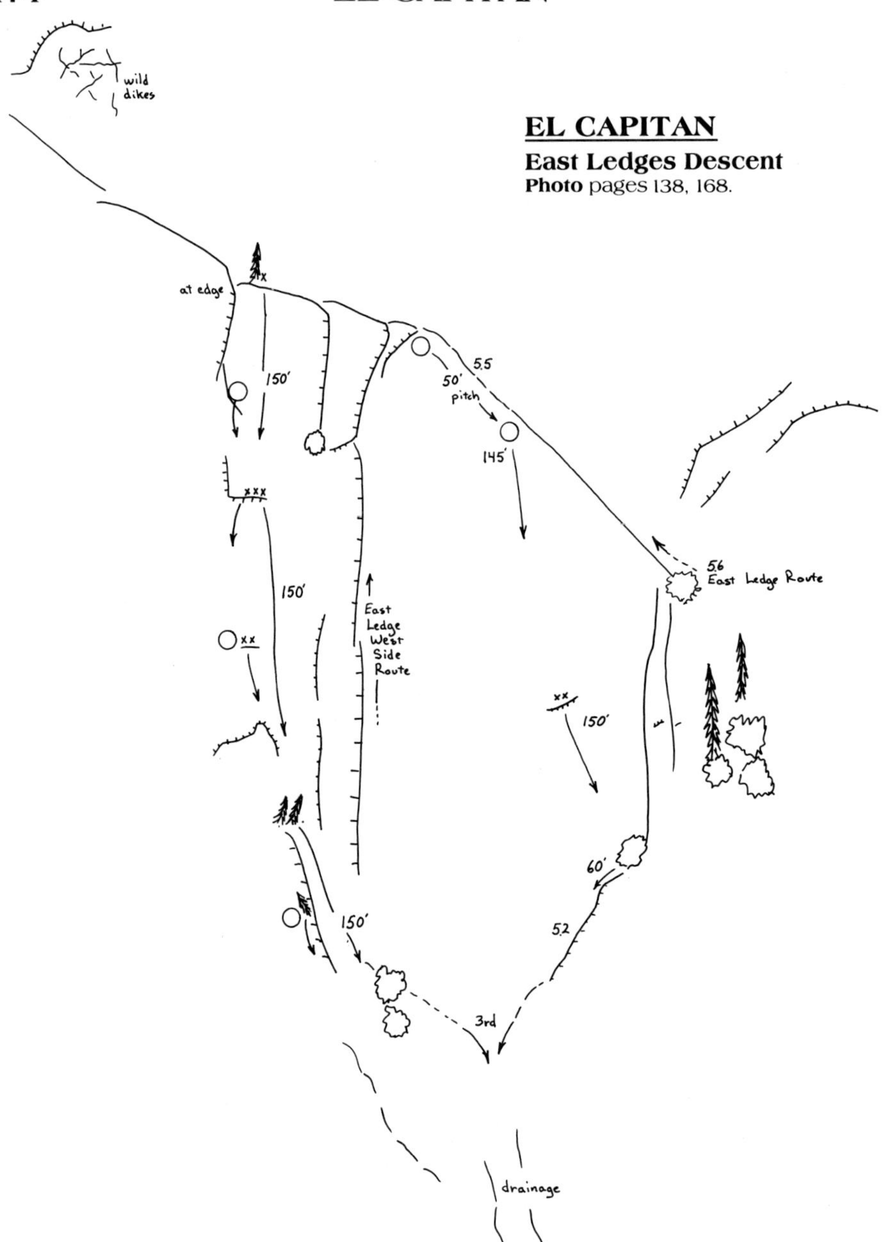
wild dikes
EL CAPITAN
East Ledges Descent
Photo pages 138, 168.
at edge
150'
5.5
50' pitch
145'
150'
East Ledge West Side Route
5.6 East Ledge Route
150'
60'
5.2
150'
3rd
drainage
to Manure Pile Buttress

MANURE PILE BUTTRESS

Approach Park at the El Cap Picnic Area, 1.6 miles west of the gas station. Walk the closed dirt road on the north side of the highway to the formation.
Descent Scramble off the top of the formation to the west to gain a steep and dirty descent gully.
Photo on page 168, 180.

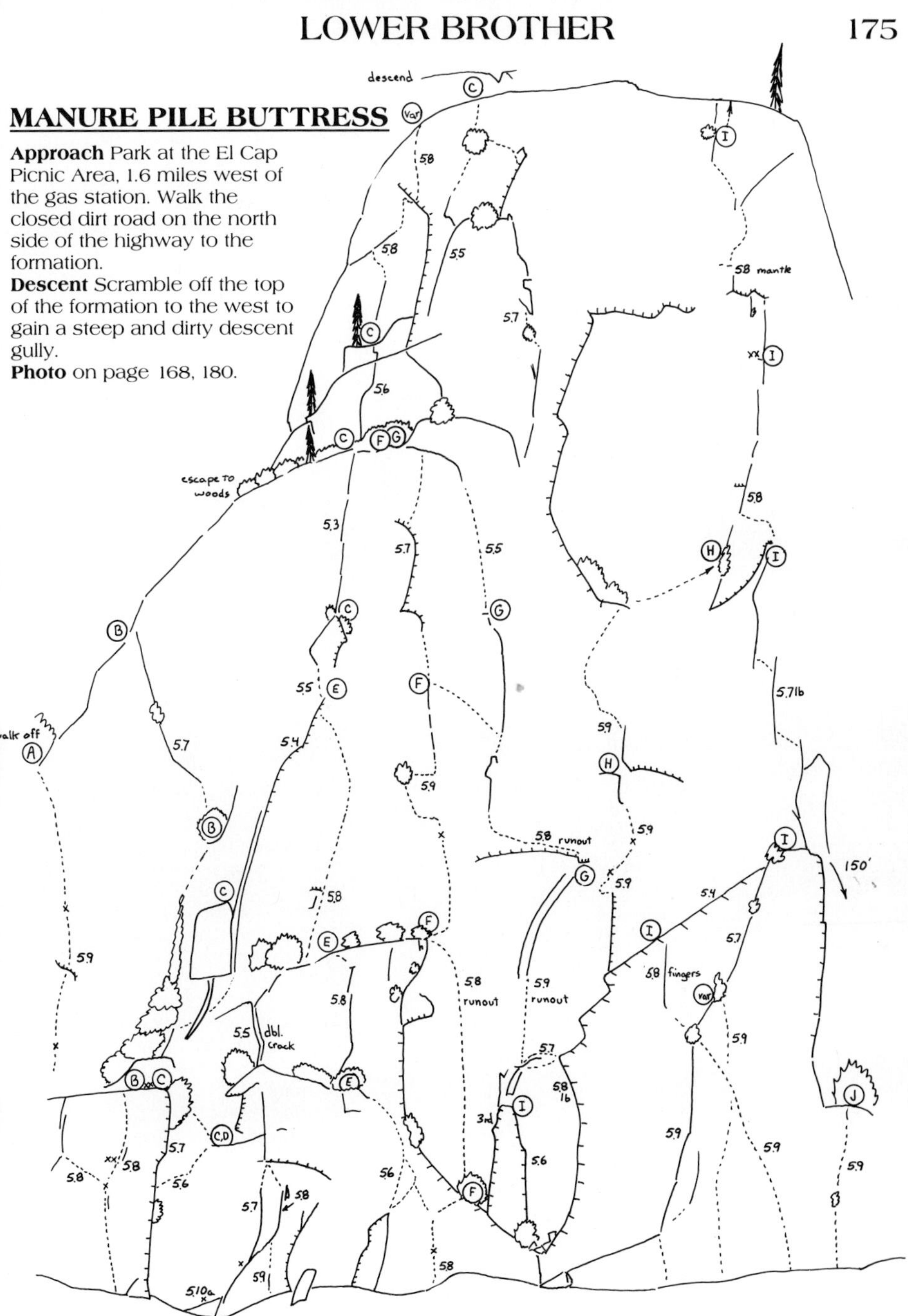

A **God's Creation** 5.9 pro: to 3"
B **Jump for Joy** 5.8
C **After Six** 5.6
D **After Seven** 5.7
E **C.S. Concerto** 5.8 pro: many small nuts
F **Fecophilia** 5.9
G **Easy Wind** 5.9 pro: many small nuts
H **The Mouse King** 5.9
I **Nutcracker** 5.8 pro: many small nuts
J **The Gardener Did It** 5.9

COMMISSIONER BUTTRESS

(B)
5.4
AB
slab
5.7
(B)
5.9
(A)
(B)
3rd and an 80' rappel
squeeze
5.8
5.10d
(A)
(B)
5.8
(A)
5.5
5.9

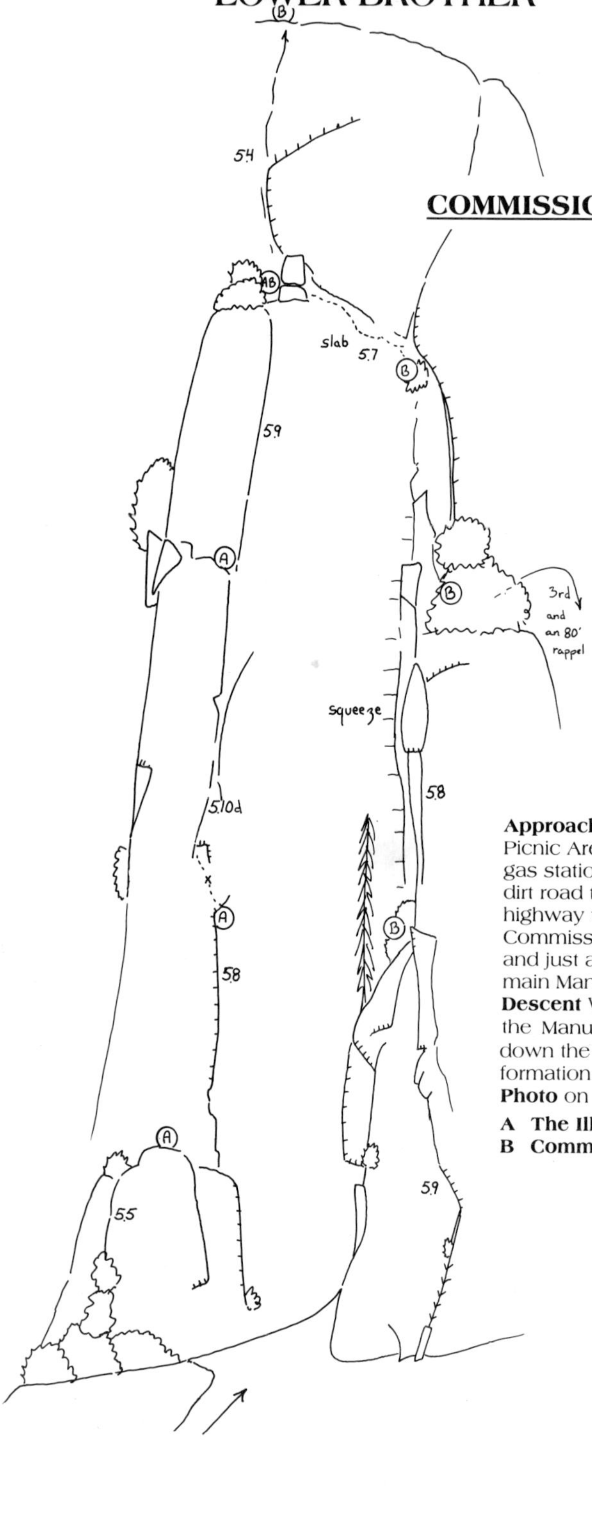

Approach Park at the El Cap Picnic Area, 1.6 miles west of the gas station and walk the closed dirt road to the north of the highway to Manure Pile. Commissioner's is connected to and just a little further east of the main Manure Pile formation.
Descent Work west to the top of the Manure Pile and the descent down the west side of that formation.
Photo on page 168.

A The Illusion 5.10d
B Commissioner Buttress 5.9

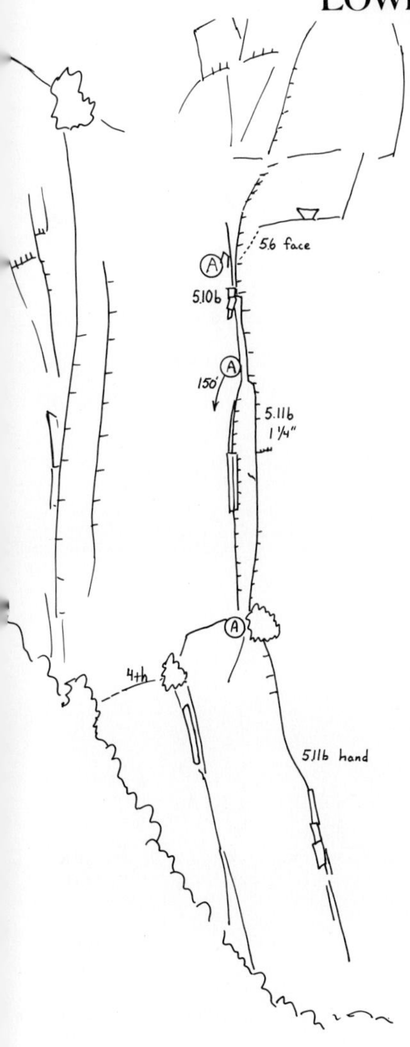

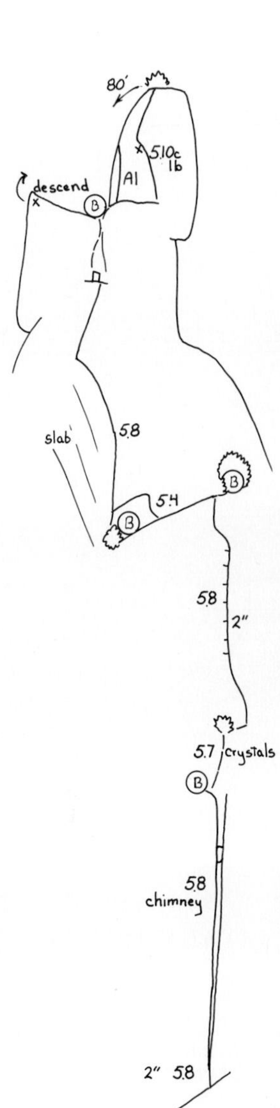

EAGLE CREEK AREA

Approach Park in a broad dirt pullout one mile west of the gas station and at the crossing of Eagle Creek. Split Pinnacle is the yellow spire on the west slopes of the creek. Essence is reached by continuing the hike up the gully immediately to the right of Split Pinnacle, trending back to the west, up and to the wall.

Photo on page 168.

A Essence 5.11b

B Split Pinnacle – East Arête 5.8 A1 or 5.10c

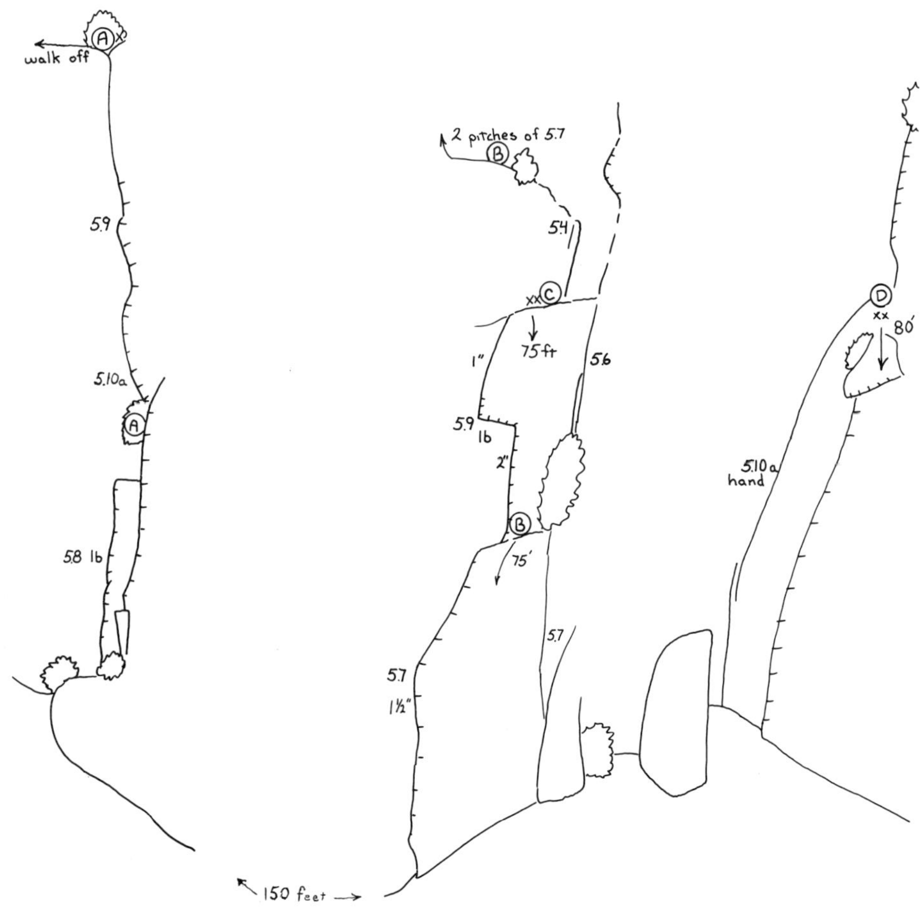

LOWER BROTHER – 4th Street Area

Approach Park in a dirt turnout on the river side of the road, just past the "S" curves 0.8 mile west of the gas station. The routes are located closest to the road.
Photo on page 180.

A **Maple Jam** 5.10a pro: to 3"
B **Nutty Buddy** 5.8 pro: to 2½"
C **Positively 4th Street** 5.9
D **Fuddy Duddy** 5.10a

ABSOLUTELY FREE

Approach Hike up from the "S" curves 0.8 mile west of the gas station, skirting the toe of Lower Brother to the right. 3rd and 4th class ledge systems diagonal up and left to the base of Absolutely Free.

Descent Michael's Ledge is the broad ledge system that diagonals across the face of Lower Brother. From the top of Absolutely Free this leads down west to Eagle Creek.

Photo on page 180.

A **Left Side** 5.9 pro: to 3"
B **Center Route** 5.9 pro: to 3"
C **Right Side** 5.10a pro: to 4"
D **Vantage Point** 5.11a pro: to 3½"

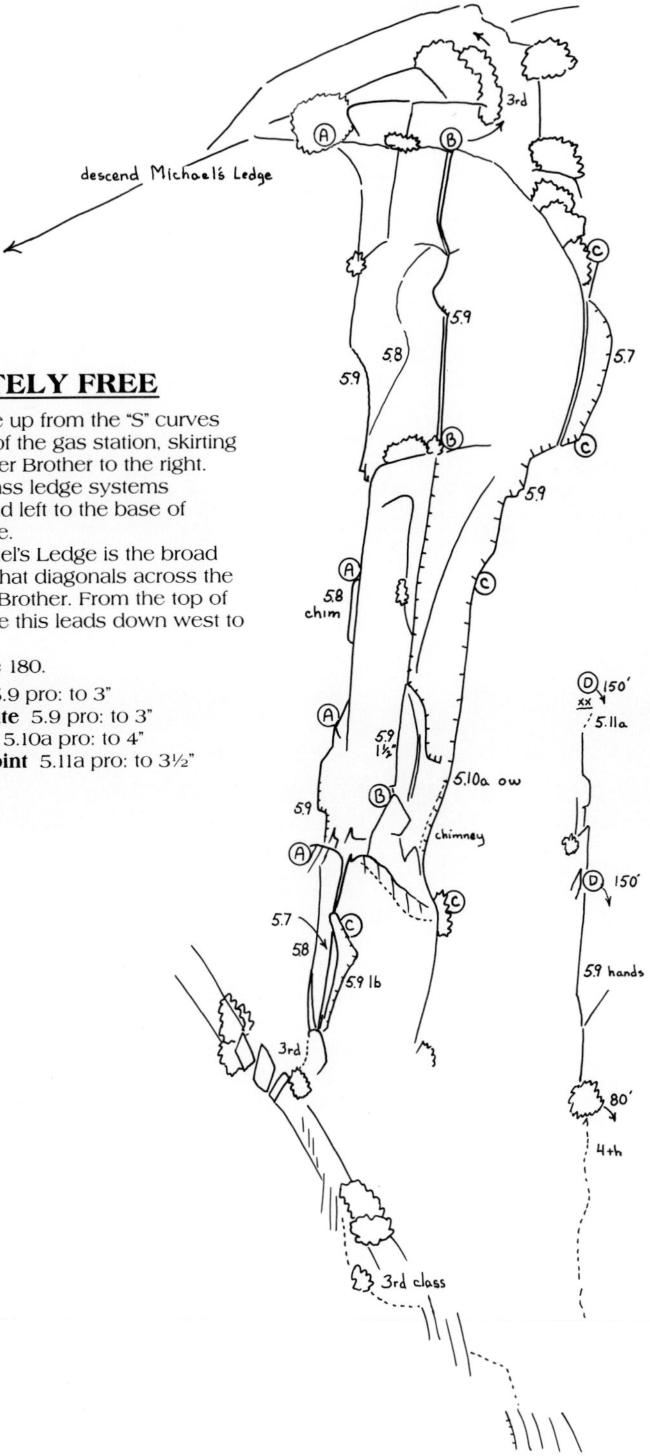

LOWER BROTHER

1 MANURE PILE BUTTRESS
2 Positively 4th Street
3 ABSOLUTELY FREE
4 Hawkman's Escape
5 KOKO LEDGE
6 RIXON'S PINNACLE
7 THE FOLLY
8 Cost of Living

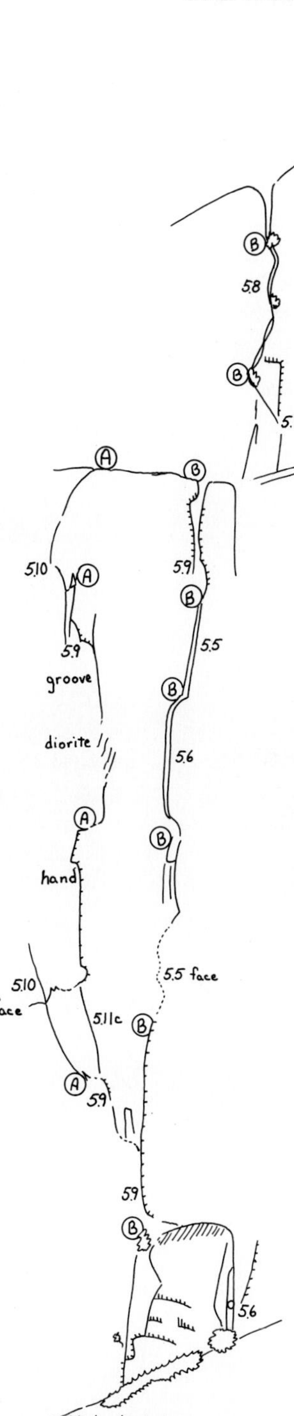

LOWER BROTHER

Hawkman's Area

Approach Most people climb one of the Absolutely Free routes to approach these climbs. Otherwise, walk up the long ledge system (Michael's Ledge) that slants up and east from Eagle Creek across the face of Lower Brother.

Descent Scramble up to where Middle Brother steepens above. There are two alternative descents from this point. The upper part of Michael's Ledge can be down climbed. The route is circuitous through the central section and a rappel may be handy. Alternatively, by keeping close to the junction of Middle Brother, the west slabs of Lower Brother can be descended with a minimum of rappels, oftentimes from trees. Two ropes are advisable.

Photo on page 180.

A Ramblin' Rose 5.10 pro: to 3"
B Hawkman's Escape 5.9 pro: to 3"

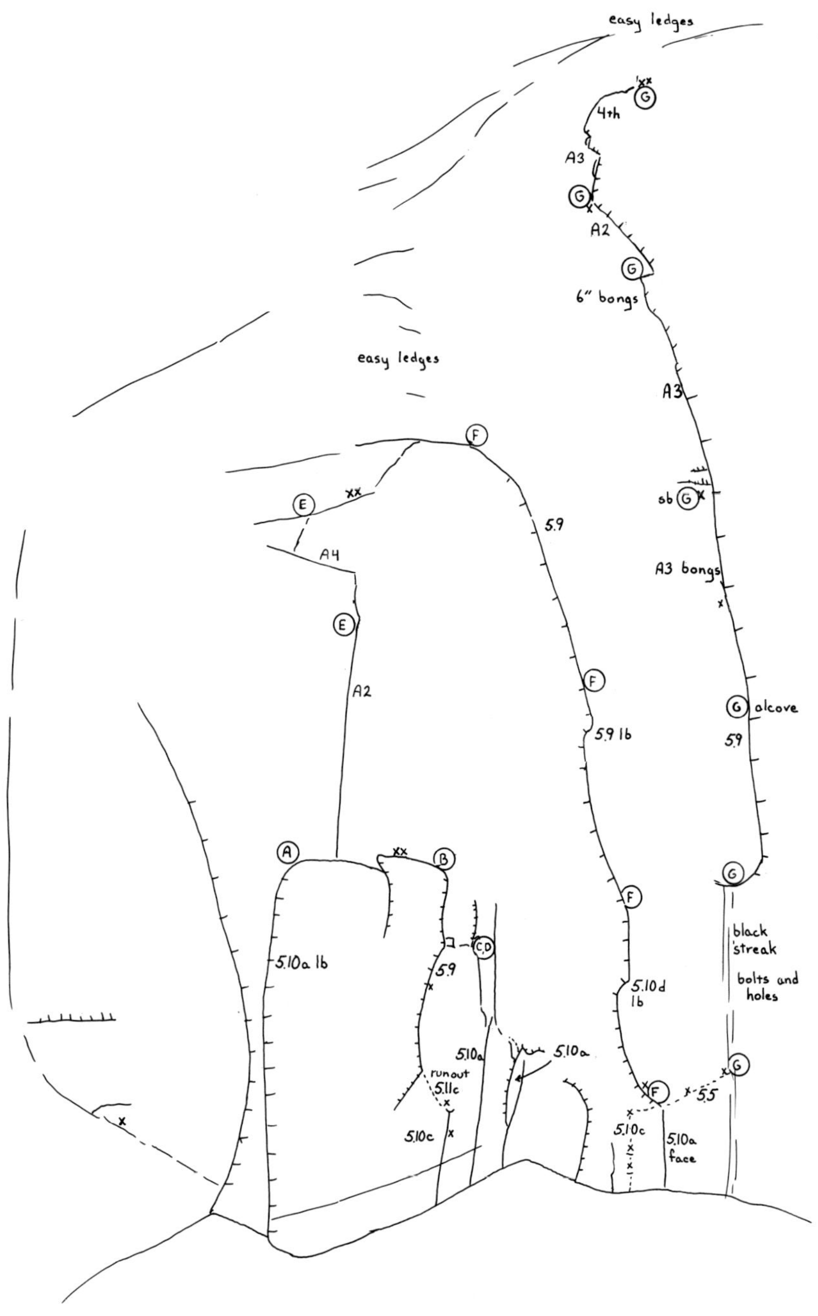
easy ledges
4th
A3
A2
6" bongs
easy ledges
A3
5.9
sb
A3 bongs
A4
A2
alcove
5.9 lb
5.9
5.10a lb
5.9
black streak
bolts and holes
5.10d lb
5.10a
5.10a
runout
5.11c
5.5
5.10c
5.10c
5.10a face

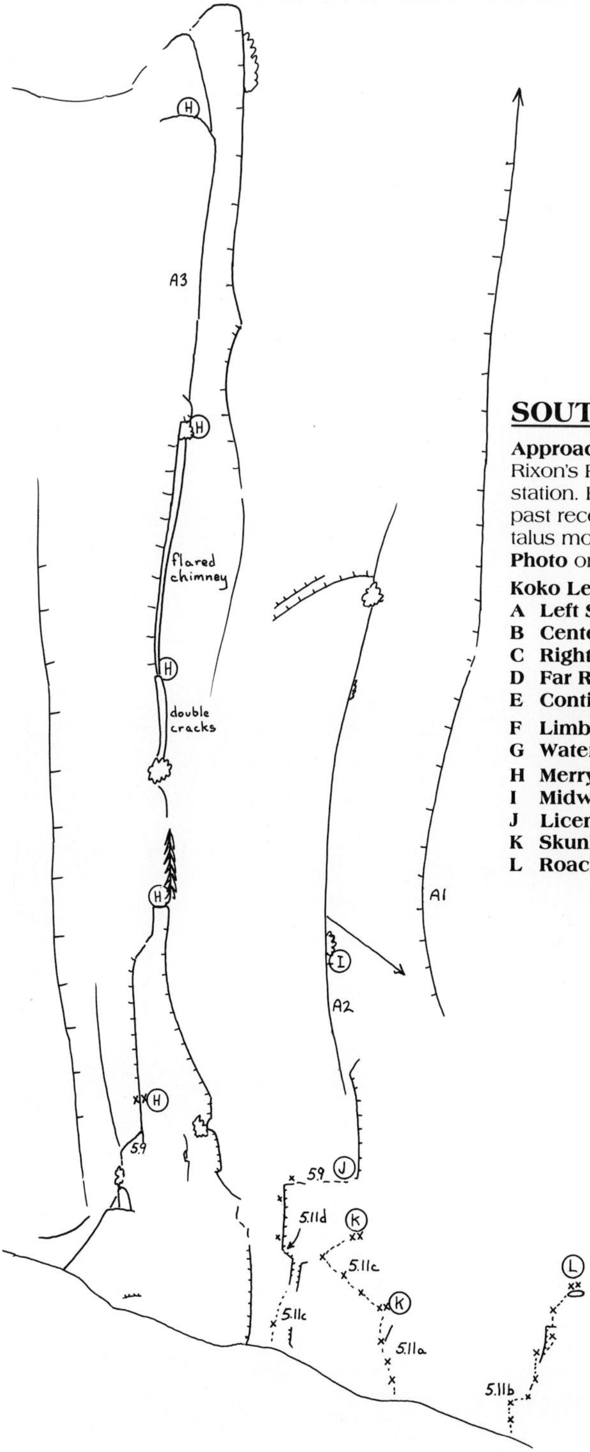

SOUTHEAST SLABS

Approach Park at the paved lot beneath Rixon's Pinnacle, 0.4 mile west of the gas station. Hike the short distance to Rixon's, past recent rockfall, then left up the huge talus mound.

Photo on page 180.

Koko Ledge

- **A Left Side** 5.10a
- **B Center Route** 5.11c
- **C Right Side** 5.10a
- **D Far Right** 5.10a
- **E Continuation** A4
- **F Limbo Ledge** 5.10b
- **G Watermelon Rind** 5.9 A4
- **H Merry Old Ledge** 5.9 A3
- **I Midwall** 5.9 A4 hardware: rurps to 4"
- **J Licensed to Fly** 5.11d
- **K Skunk Weed** 5.11c
- **L Roachweed** 5.11b

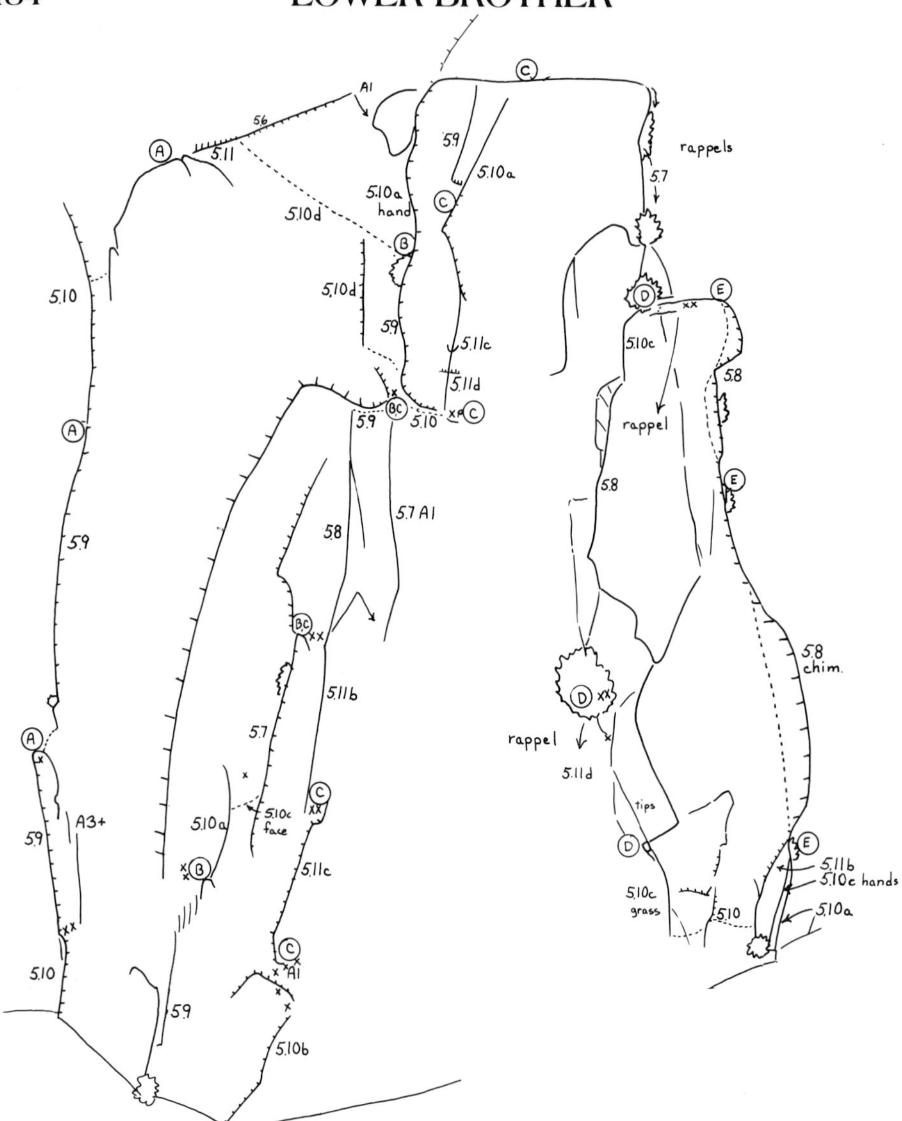

RIXON'S PINNACLE

Approach There is a parking lot directly beneath Rixon's, 0.4 mile west of the gas station.

Descent There are rappel anchors off the east side of the pinnacle. While two ropes are needed for most of the rappels, the first rappel is notorious for jamming and thus it is best to make it a short one.

Photo on page 180.

A **Far West** 5.11 A1 pro: to 3"
B **West Face** 5.10c pro: to 3"
C **Direct South Face** 5.11d A1 pro: to 3"
D **South Face** 5.11d A1
E **East Chimney** 5.10a
Klemens Variation 5.10c
Final Decision 5.11b

THE FOLLY

Approach Park at Rixon's, 0.4 mile west of the gas station, and from the wall hike up and right to the routes.
Descent Rappel the right side.
Photo on page 180.

- **A** **Left Side** 5.9 A3 hardware: 1 KB, 5 LA, 2 ea. ½"-⅝", 2 ea. nuts to 3"
- **B** **Disconnected** 5.11c
- **C** **Frosted Flakes** 5.10d
- **D** **Childhood's End** 5.10d pro: to 3"
- **E** **Follying** 5.11c
- **F** **Wild Thing** 5.10c pro: to 6", incl. several 2"-3½"
- **G** **Pink Torpedo** 5.11b
- **H** **Right Side** 5.10d pro: to 3"
- **I** **Preface** 5.11b

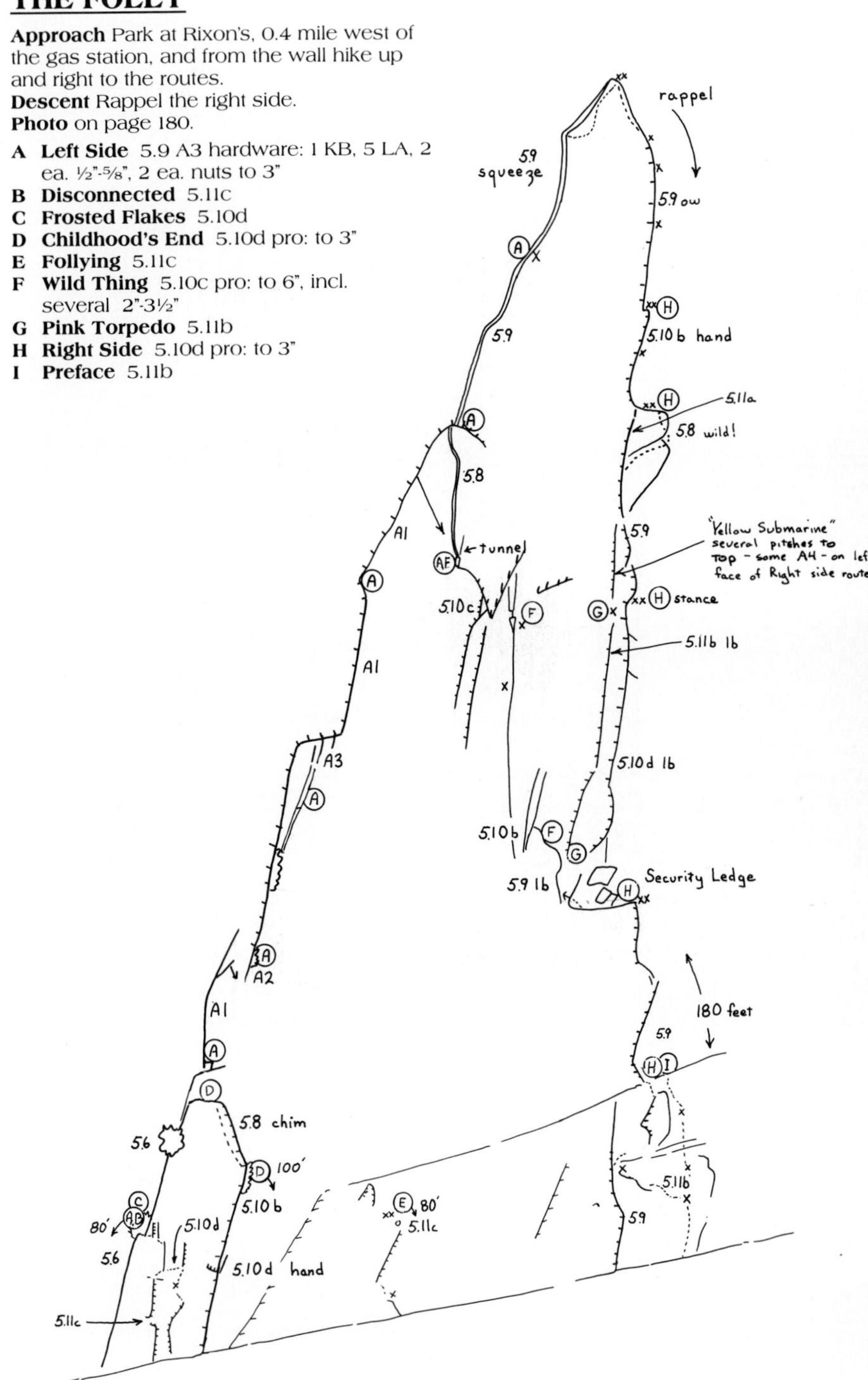

CAMP 4 WALL

Approach These routes lie along the wall to the right of the Folly. For Space Doubt and routes to the right, it is easiest to hike up the streambed that meets the west end of Camp 4. **Photo** on page 180.

A **Young and the Restless** 5.10c
B **Cost of Living** 5.10c
C **Space Doubt** 5.10c
D **General Hospital** 5.11c pro: tiny to 3"
E **Chopper** 5.10c pro: to 5"
F **One Life to Live** 5.11a
G **Edge of Night** 5.10c pro: to 4"
H **Secret Storm** 5.10a pro: to 3"
I **Tweedle Dee** 5.8

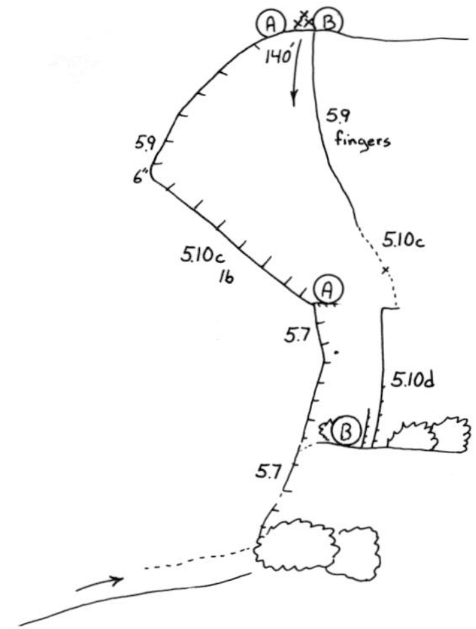

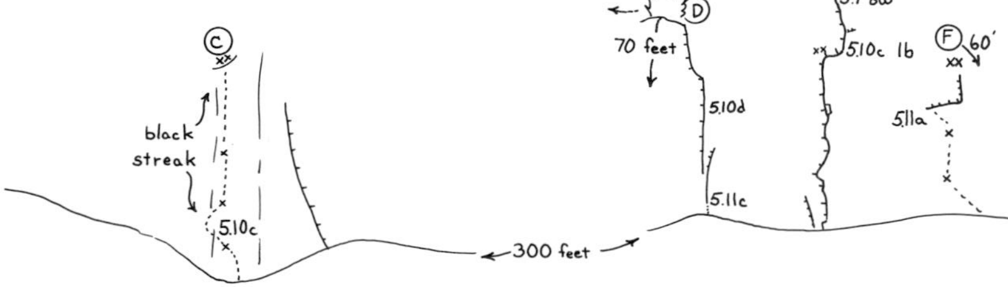

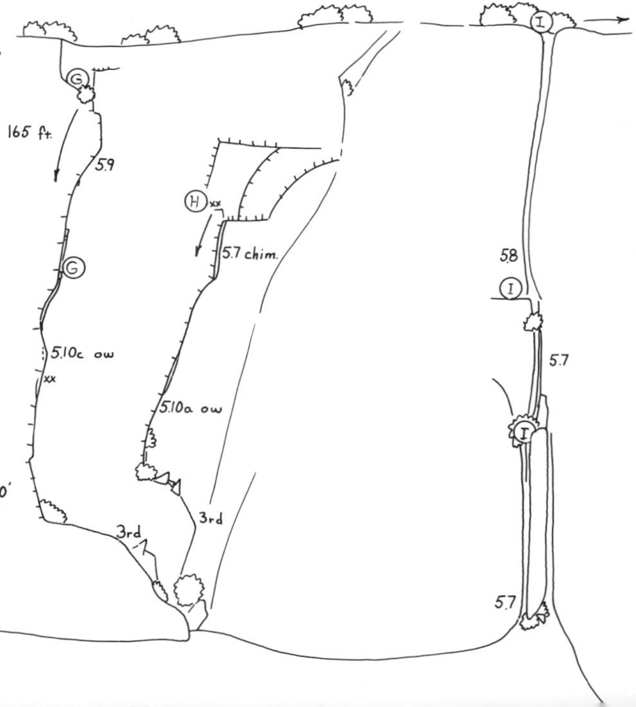

CAMP 4 WALL

Approach Hike up the streambed that meets the west end of Camp Four.
Photo on page 180.

- **A Doggie Do** 5.10a pro: to 3½"
- **B Doggie Diversions** 5.9 pro: to 3½", extra 2"-3½"
- **C Doggie Deviations** 5.9 pro: to 2½"
- **D Bottom Line** 5.11d
- **E Rock Bottom** 5.11d pro: to 2½"
- **F The Buttocks** 5.9 pro: to 3½"
- **G Cheek** 5.10d

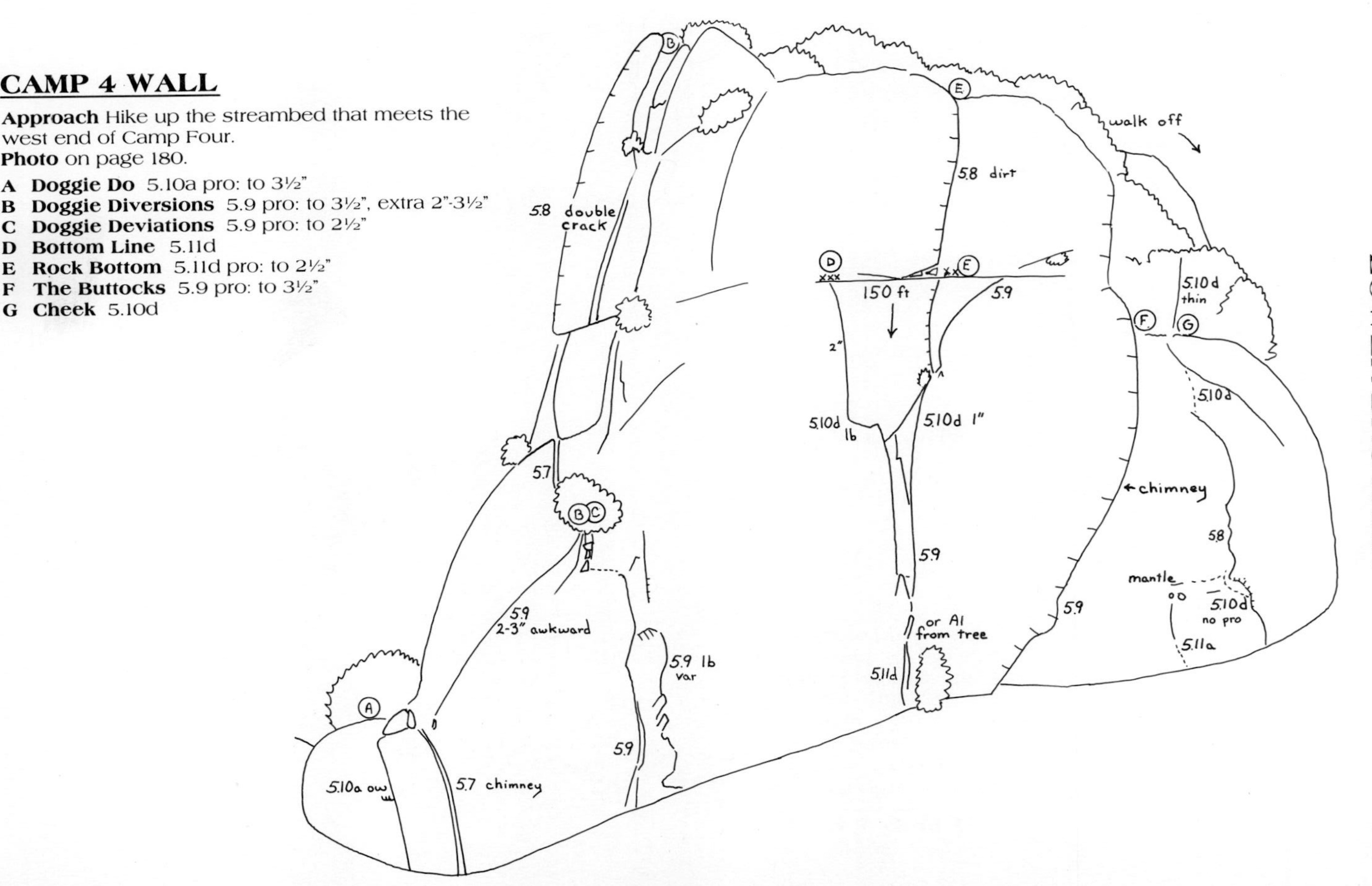

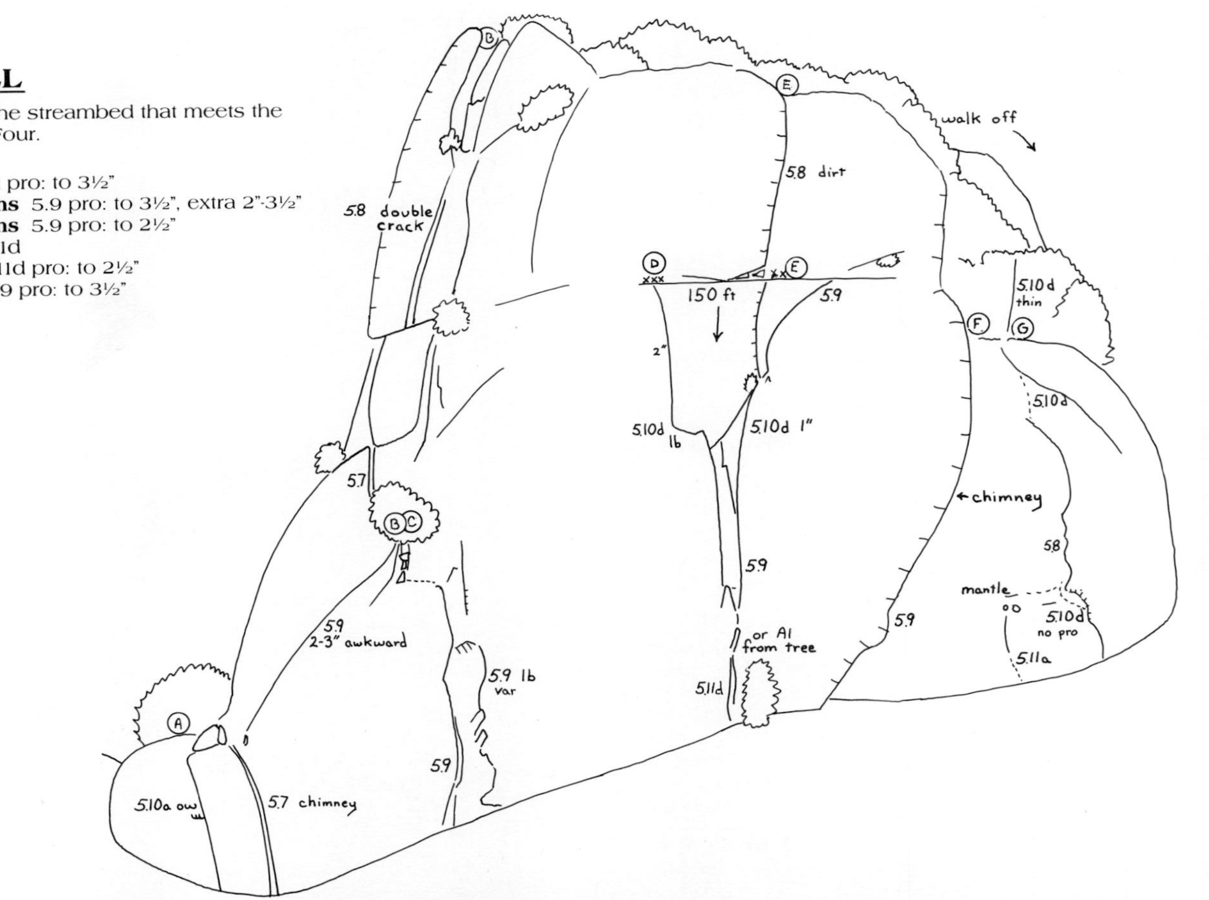

CAMP 4 WALL

Approach Hike up the streambed that meets the west end of Camp Four.
Photo on page 180.

A Cristina 5.11b pro: to 3½"
B Henley Quits 5.10a pro: to 3½"
C Cid's Embrace 5.8
D Lancelot 5.9 pro: to 3"
E Dynamo Hum 5.11d pro: many small to 1¾"

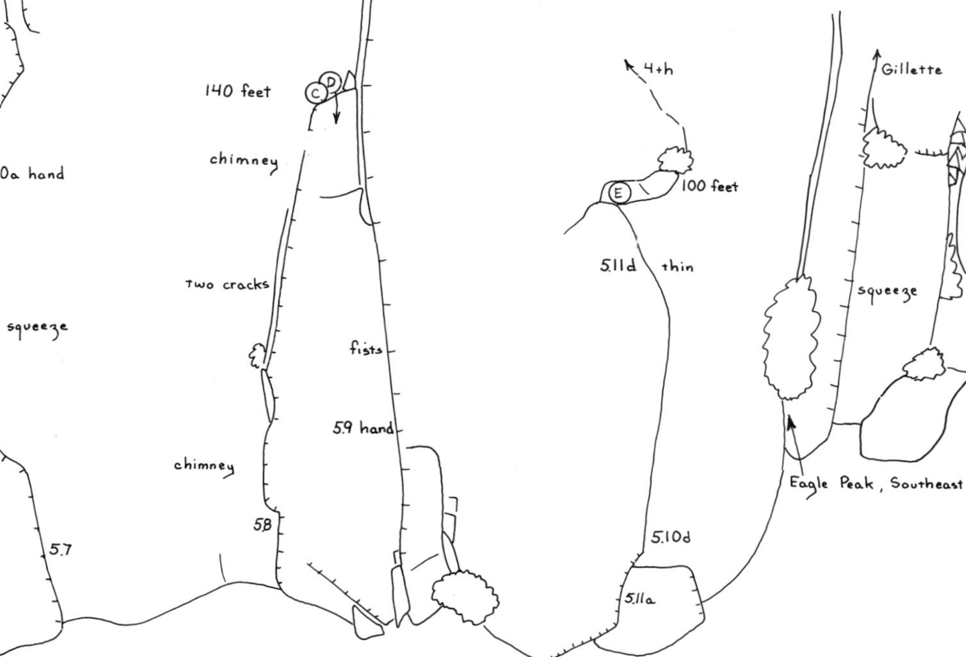

CAMP 4 WALL

Approach Hike the streambed that meets the west end of Camp 4. **Gillette** is passed enroute. At the top of the talus a 3rd class ledge system leads up and left, past **Apple Seeds**, up to the wooded terrace of Camp 4 Tree and the base of **Fallout**. **Photo** on pages 180 and 190.

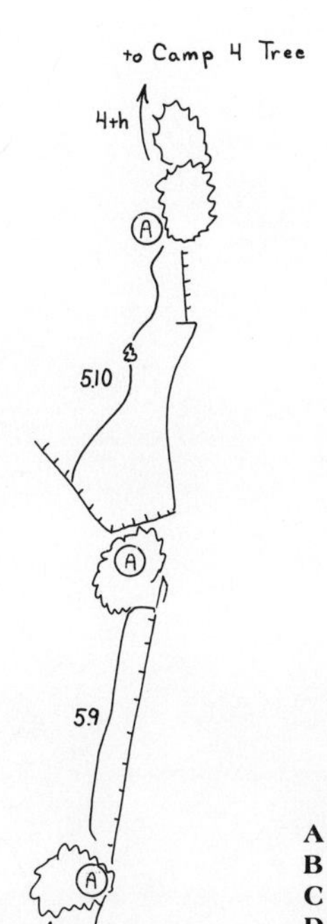

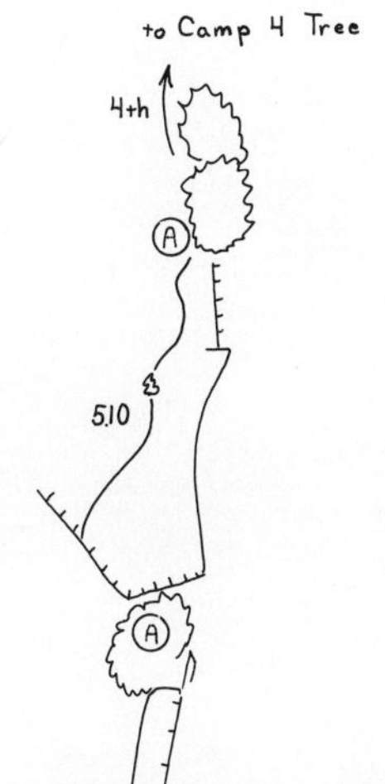

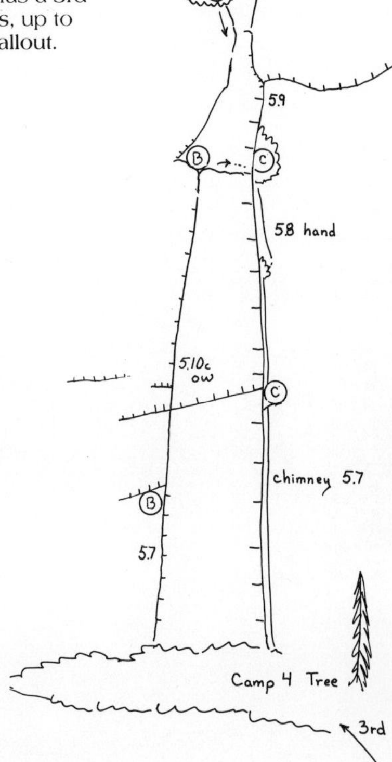

A Gillette 5.10 pro: to 3"
B Fallout 5.10c pro: 2 ea. 3"- 3½"
C Jolly Green Giant 5.9
D Apple Seeds 5.10a pro: to 3", incl. 5 pitons to ½"

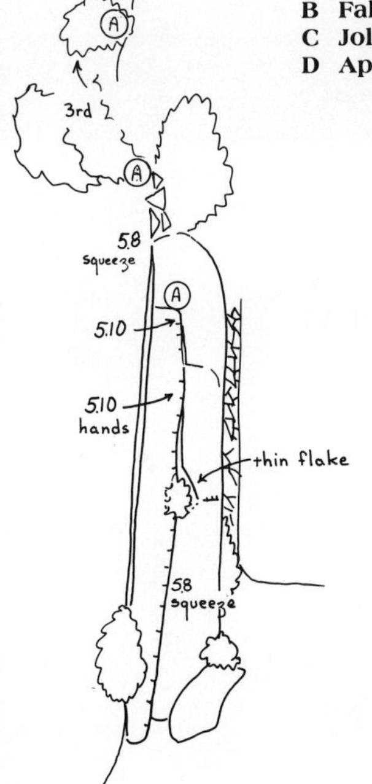

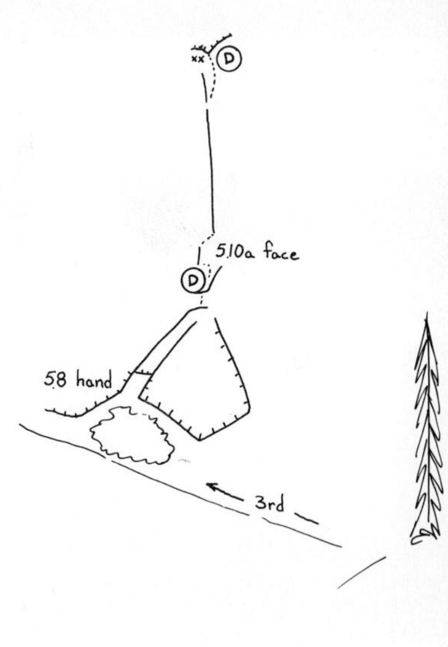

CAMP FOUR WALL

1 **Camp 4 Terror** V 5.8 A4
2 **Apple Seeds**
3 **Comedy of Folly** V 5.9 A4
4 **Sunday Tree** 5.6
5 **Stay Free**
6 **The Girl Next Door**
7 **Joe Palmer**
8 **Psychopath** 5.9

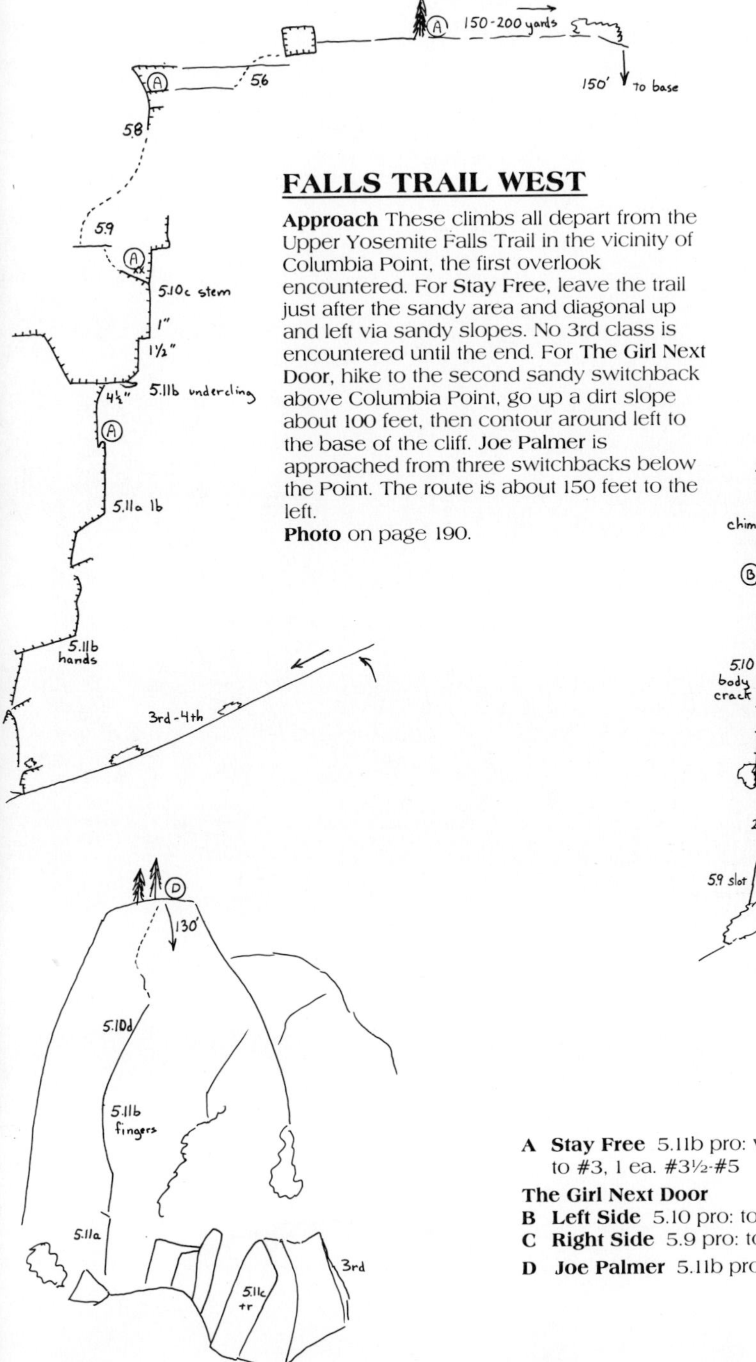

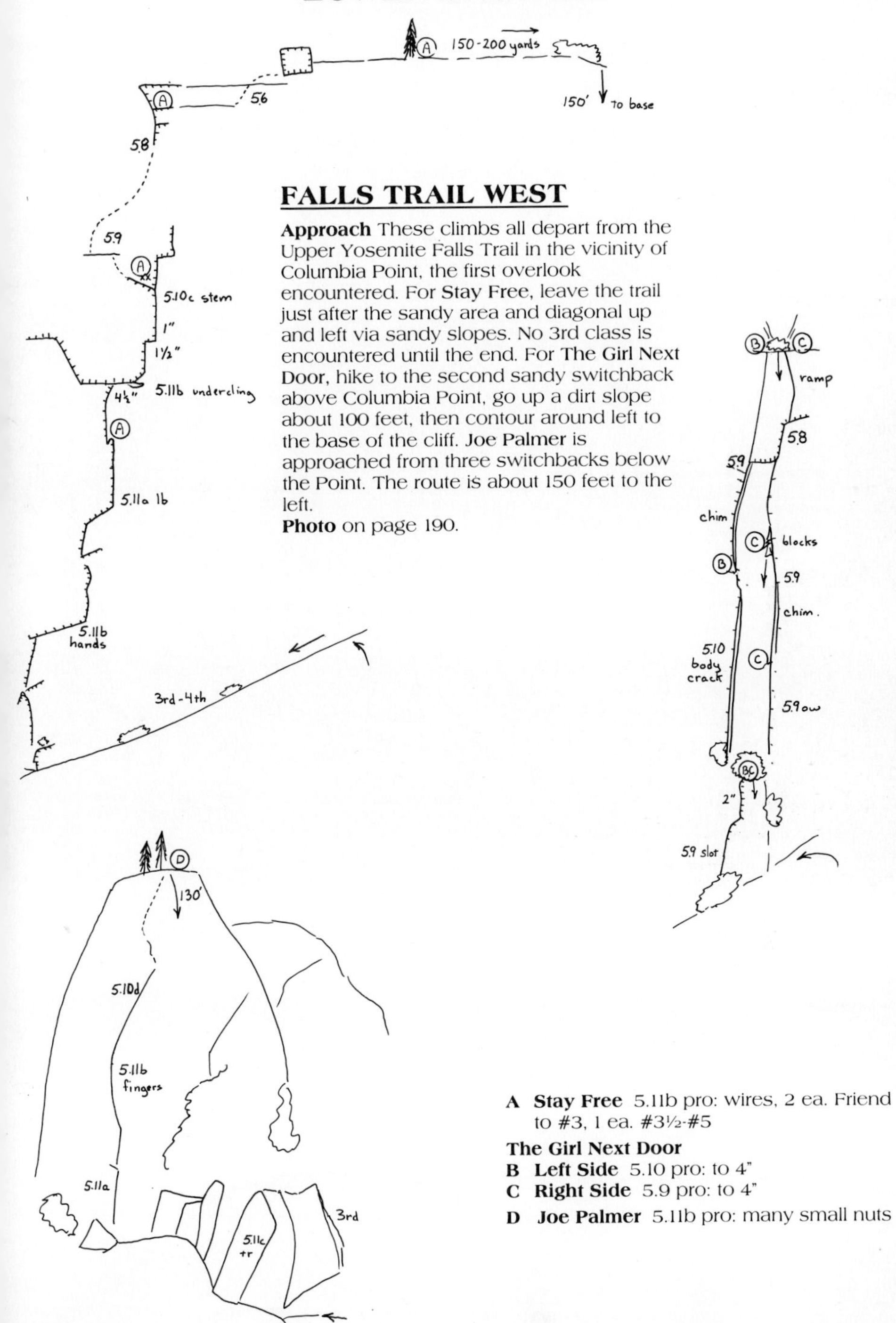

FALLS TRAIL WEST

Approach These climbs all depart from the Upper Yosemite Falls Trail in the vicinity of Columbia Point, the first overlook encountered. For Stay Free, leave the trail just after the sandy area and diagonal up and left via sandy slopes. No 3rd class is encountered until the end. For The Girl Next Door, hike to the second sandy switchback above Columbia Point, go up a dirt slope about 100 feet, then contour around left to the base of the cliff. Joe Palmer is approached from three switchbacks below the Point. The route is about 150 feet to the left.

Photo on page 190.

A Stay Free 5.11b pro: wires, 2 ea. Friend to #3, 1 ea. #3½-#5

The Girl Next Door

B Left Side 5.10 pro: to 4"

C Right Side 5.9 pro: to 4"

D Joe Palmer 5.11b pro: many small nuts

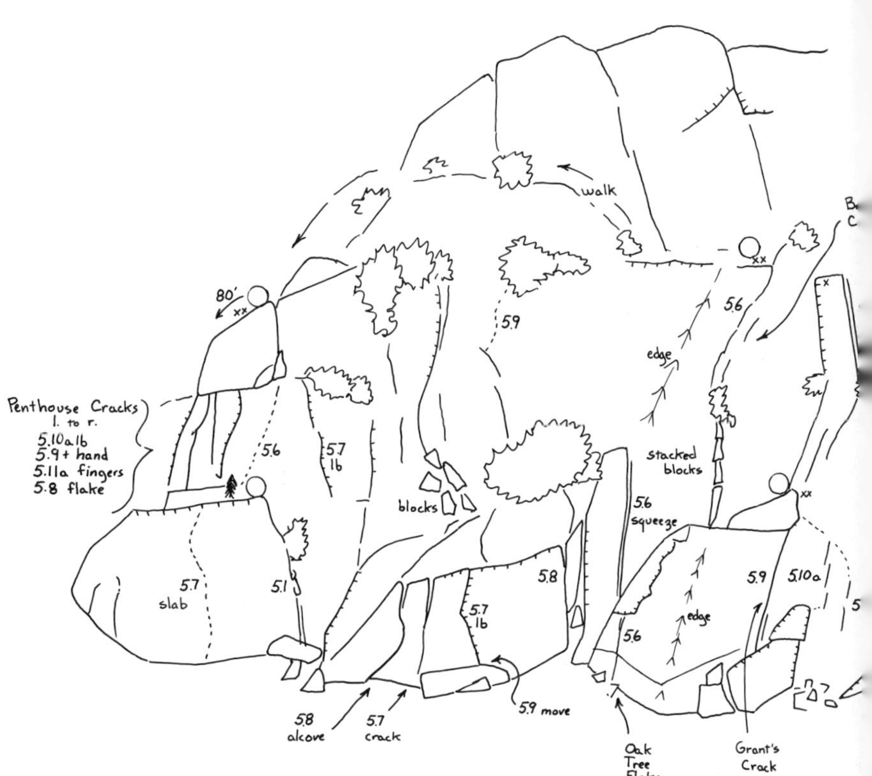

walk
80'
xx
5.9
5.6
edge
xx
Penthouse Cracks
l. to r.
5.10a lb
5.9+ hand
5.11a fingers
5.8 flake
5.6
5.7
lb
blocks
stacked
blocks
5.6
squeeze
xx
5.7
slab
5.1
5.8
5.7
lb
5.6
edge
5.9
5.10a
5.8
alcove
5.7
crack
5.9 move
Oak
Tree
Flake
Grant's
Crack

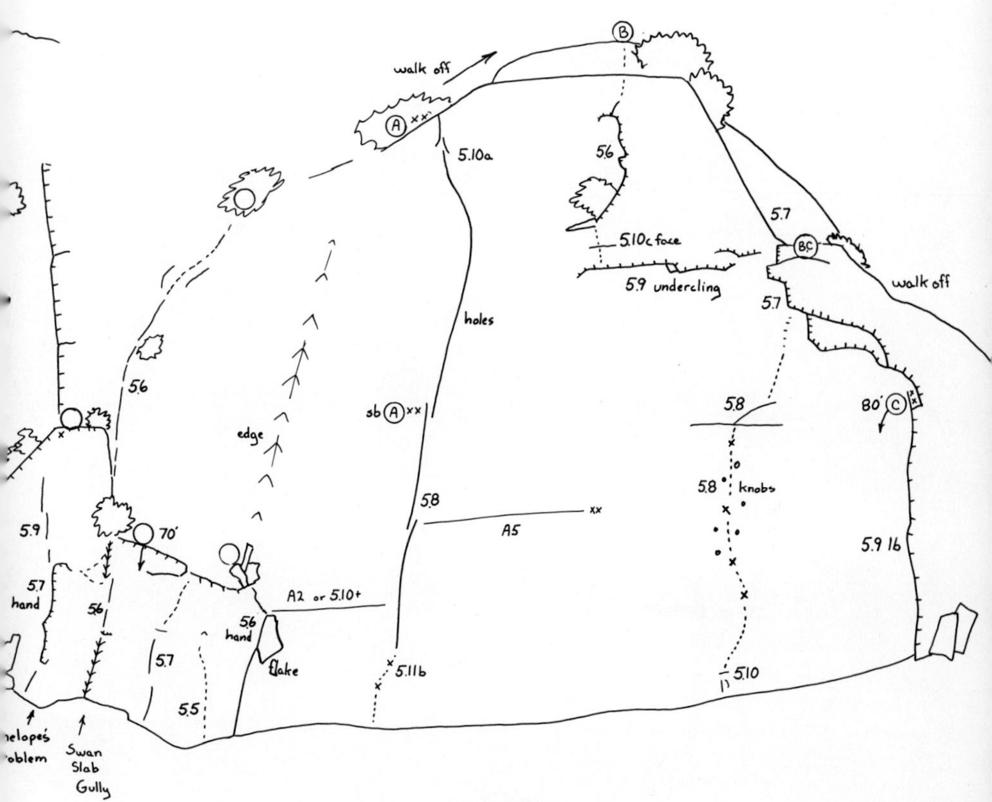

SWAN SLAB

Approach This cliff is located directly across the main road from Yosemite Lodge and offers bouldering and moderate free climbs on the complicated left side, with clean and more difficult routes on the main slab itself.

Descent Routes that lead to the top of the cliff can be walked off on either direction.

A Aid Route 5.11b
B Ugly Duckling 5.10c
C Lena's Lieback 5.9

YOSEMITE FALLS AREA

1 T.D.'s Dihedral
2 Galloping Consumption
3 Seaside
4 Diversions
5 Smoky Pillar
6 Chain Reaction
7 The Peanut
8 Selaginella
9 Observation Point
10 The Green Strip

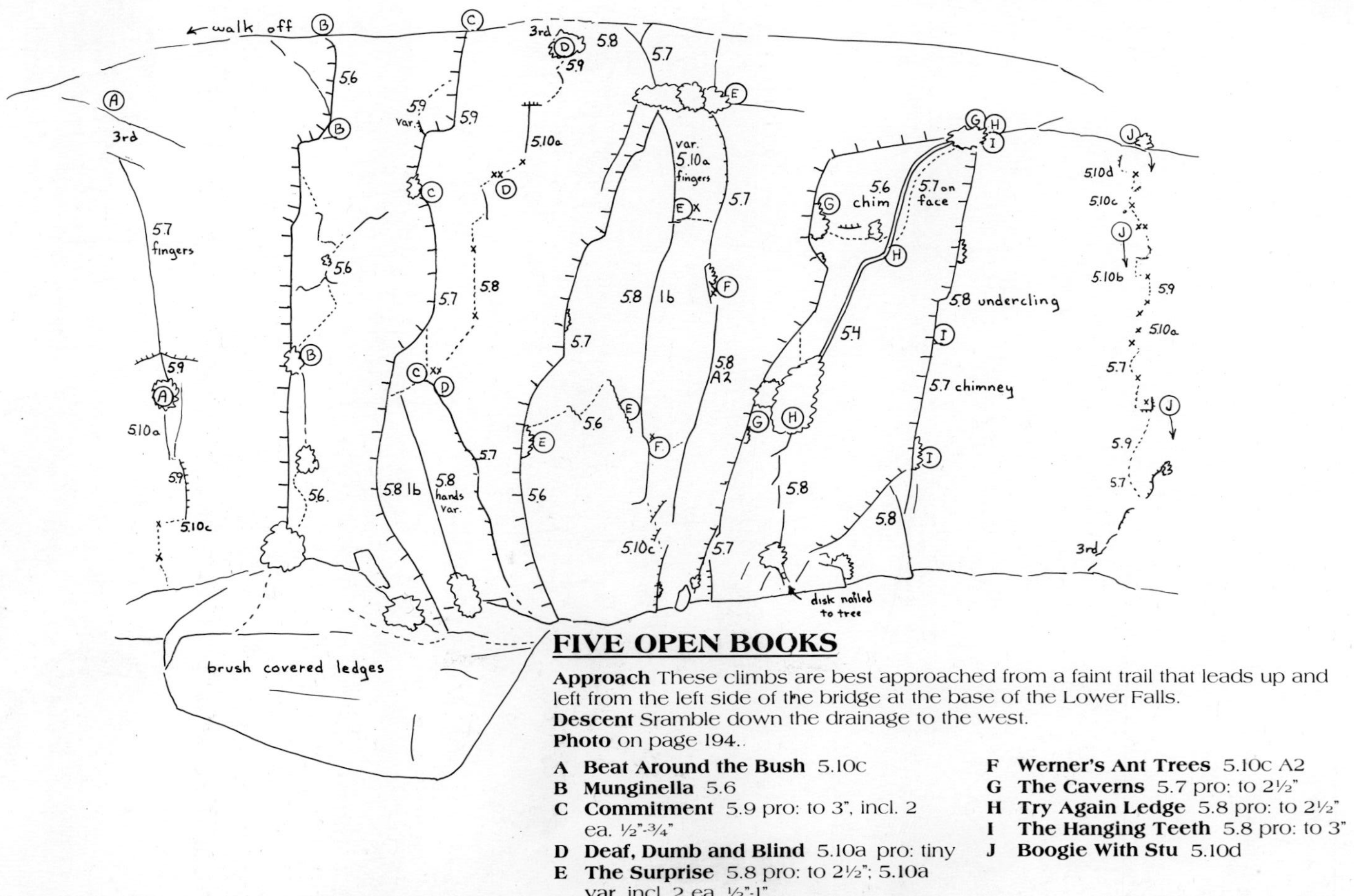

FIVE OPEN BOOKS

Approach These climbs are best approached from a faint trail that leads up and left from the left side of the bridge at the base of the Lower Falls.
Descent Sramble down the drainage to the west.
Photo on page 194..

- **A Beat Around the Bush** 5.10c
- **B Munginella** 5.6
- **C Commitment** 5.9 pro: to 3", incl. 2 ea. ½"-¾"
- **D Deaf, Dumb and Blind** 5.10a pro: tiny
- **E The Surprise** 5.8 pro: to 2½"; 5.10a var. incl. 2 ea. ½"-1"
- **F Werner's Ant Trees** 5.10c A2
- **G The Caverns** 5.7 pro: to 2½"
- **H Try Again Ledge** 5.8 pro: to 2½"
- **I The Hanging Teeth** 5.8 pro: to 3"
- **J Boogie With Stu** 5.10d

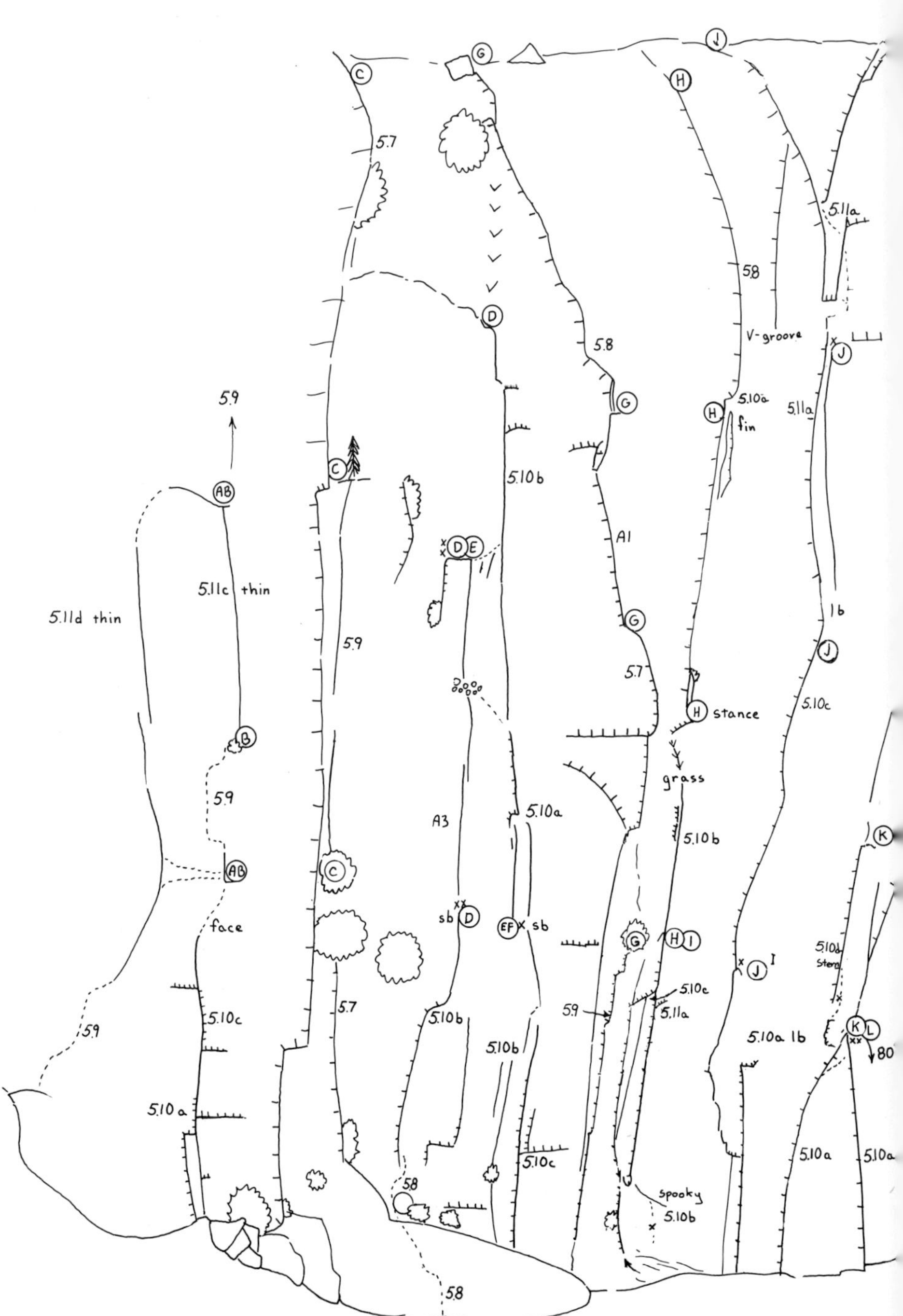
5.9
5.11d thin
5.11c thin
5.9
face
5.9
5.10c
5.10a
5.7
5.9
5.7
5.8
5.8
A3
sb
5.10b
5.10b
5.10b
5.10a
sb
5.10c
5.8
A1
5.7
5.9
5.10c
5.11a
spooky
5.10b
5.8
V-groove
5.10a
fin
stance
grass
5.10b
5.11a
5.11a
1b
5.10c
5.10a 1b
5.10d
5.10a
5.10a
80'

LOWER FALLS AREA – Left

Approach The cliff is the left side of the Lower Yosemite Falls ampitheatre.
Descent Walk off ledges to the left.
Photo on page 194.

A **Auntie Gravity** 5.11d
B **The Fin** 5.11c
C **The Green Strip** 5.9
D **Eggplant** 5.10b A3
E **Eclipse** 5.10b
F **Blackout** 5.10c
G **Black Wall** 5.9 A1
H **Fawlty Towers** 5.10c
I **Dagger** 5.11a
J **Shadow Wall** 5.11a
K **Guiding Light** 5.10d
L **Lightweight Guides** 5.10a
M **Full Stem Ahead** 5.11d pro: tiny to 3½" esp. small
N **The Podium** 5.10d
O **Public Opinion** 5.10c
P **Dark Star** 5.10b
Q **Nanbeeb** 5.10b
R **Isosceles Revisited** 5.10b

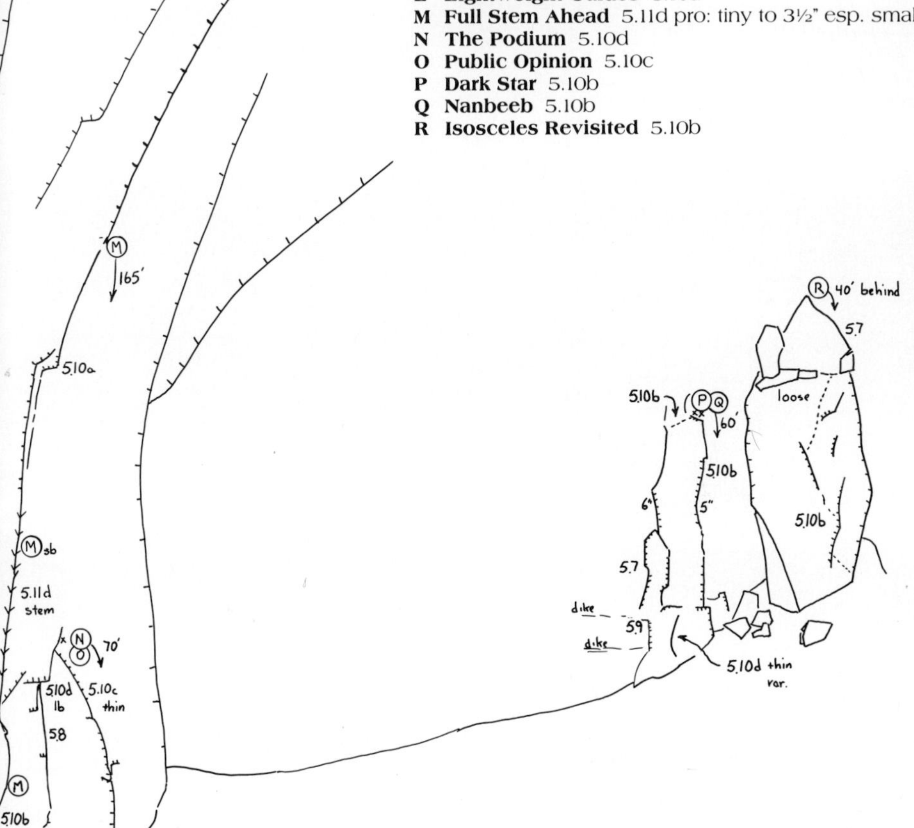

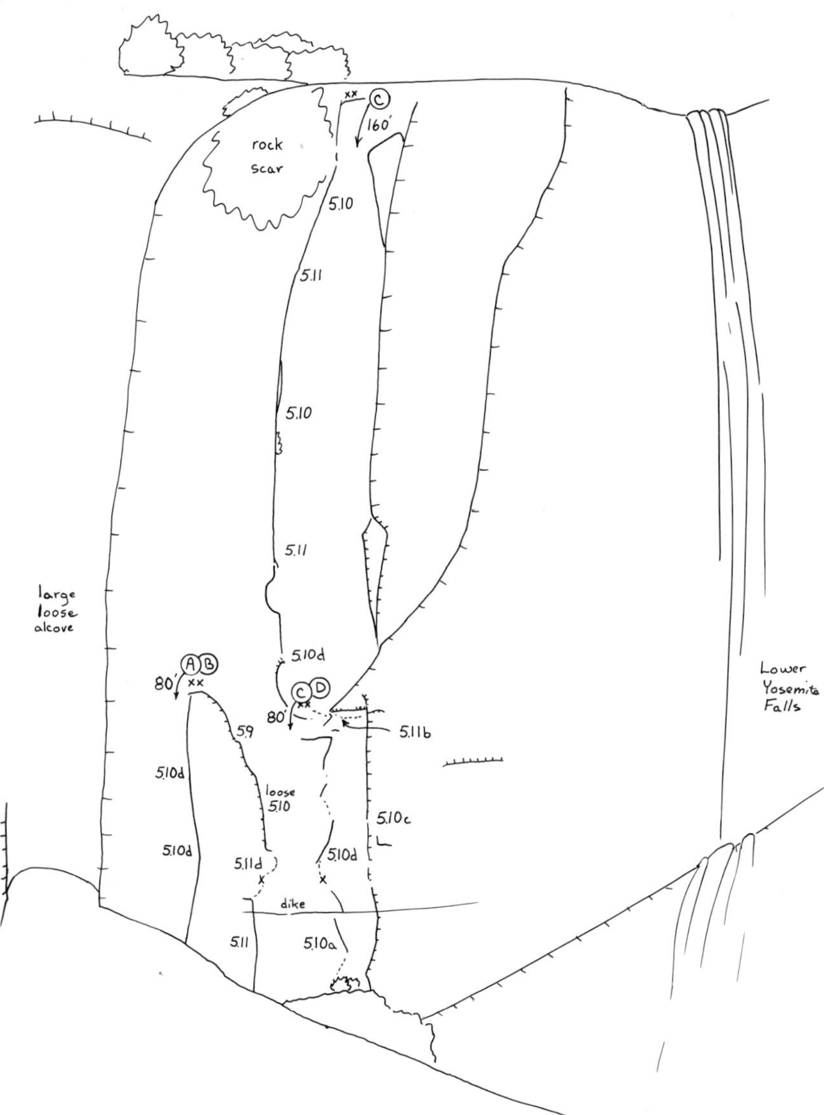

LOWER FALLS AREA – Right

Approach This is the right side of the Lower Yosemite Falls ampitheatre.
Descent Rappel the routes or scamble down the 5.2 Sunnyside Bench route.

A Ten Years After 5.10d
B Mistfitz 5.11d
C Play Misty for Me 5.11
D Powerslave 5.11b

Ten Years After and the 2nd pitch of Play Misty . . . were originally aided as Lower Yosemite Falls – West Side.

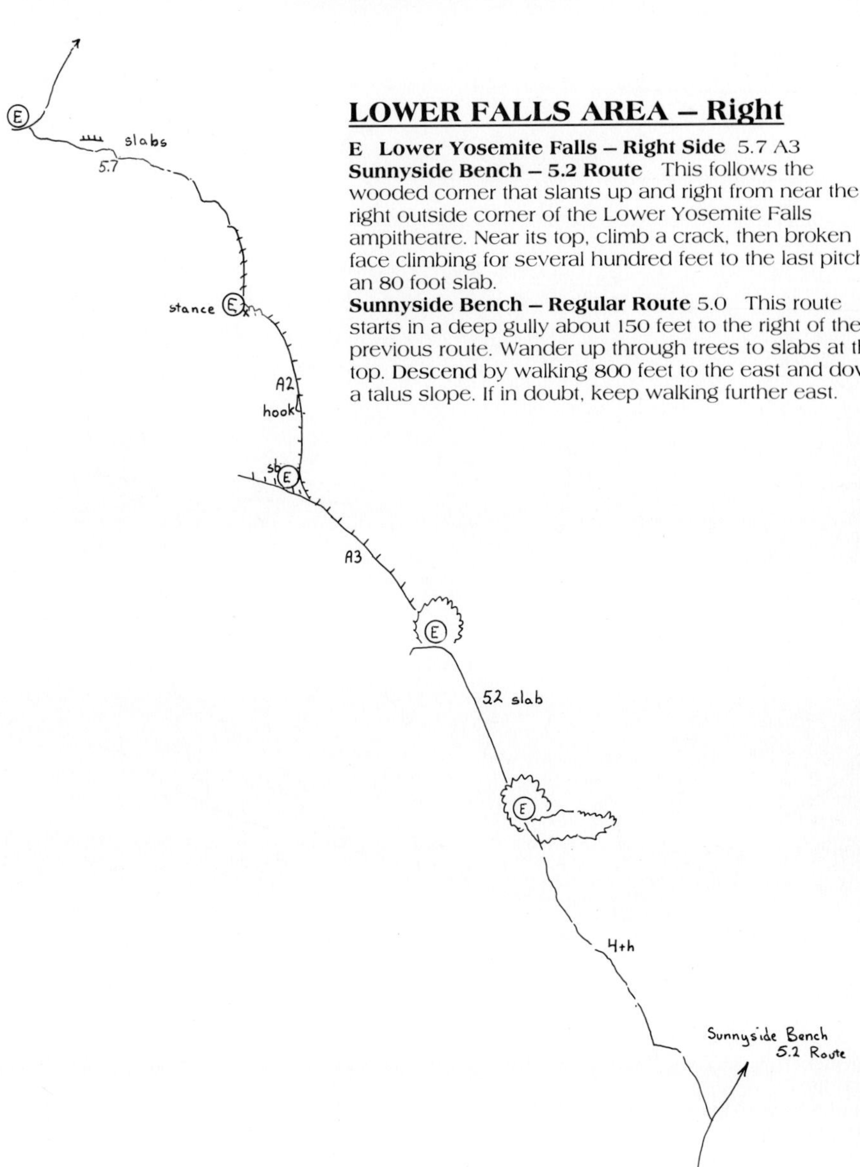

LOWER FALLS AREA – Right

E Lower Yosemite Falls – Right Side 5.7 A3

Sunnyside Bench – 5.2 Route This follows the wooded corner that slants up and right from near the right outside corner of the Lower Yosemite Falls ampitheatre. Near its top, climb a crack, then broken face climbing for several hundred feet to the last pitch, an 80 foot slab.

Sunnyside Bench – Regular Route 5.0 This route starts in a deep gully about 150 feet to the right of the previous route. Wander up through trees to slabs at the top. Descend by walking 800 feet to the east and down a talus slope. If in doubt, keep walking further east.

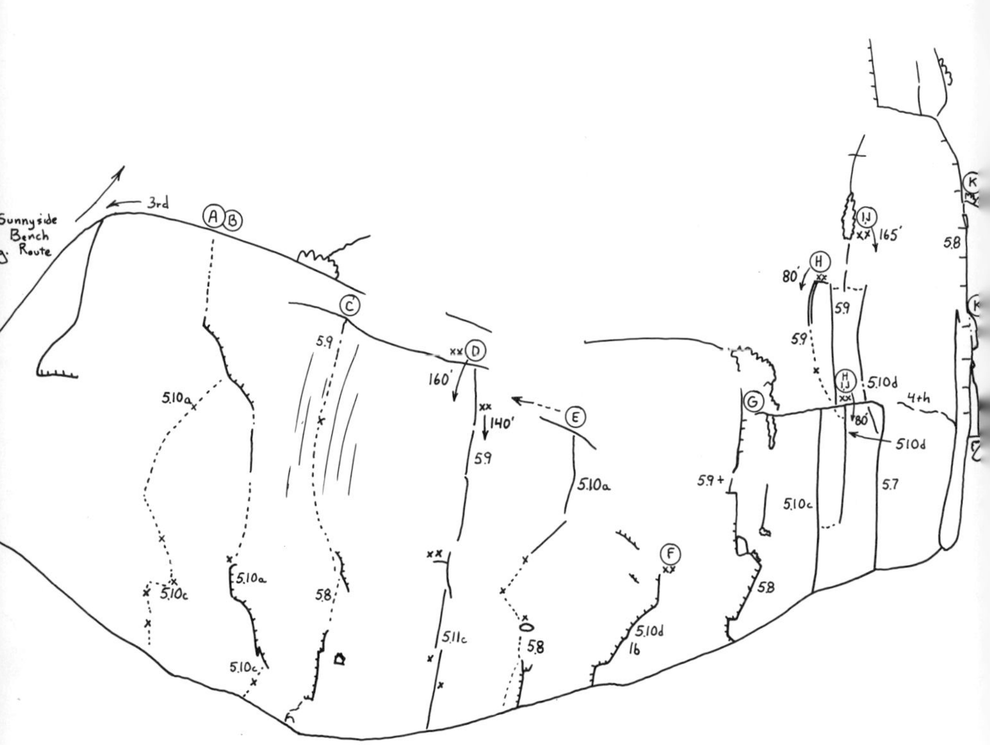

SUNNYSIDE BENCH

Approach This wall starts just above the trail and immediately east of the Lower Yosemite Falls footbridge.

Descent Those routes that lead to the top of the bench can be descended by down climbing the Regular Route.

Photo on page 194.

- **A Butthole Climbers** 5.10c
- **B Sultans of Sling** 5.10c
- **C Raisin** 5.9
- **D Mud Flats** 5.11c
- **E Prune** 5.10a
- **F Lingering Lie** 5.10d
- **G Lemon** 5.9+
- **H Bummer** 5.10c
- **I Lazy Bum** 5.10d
- **J Jamcrack Route** 5.9
- **K Lieback Route** 5.8

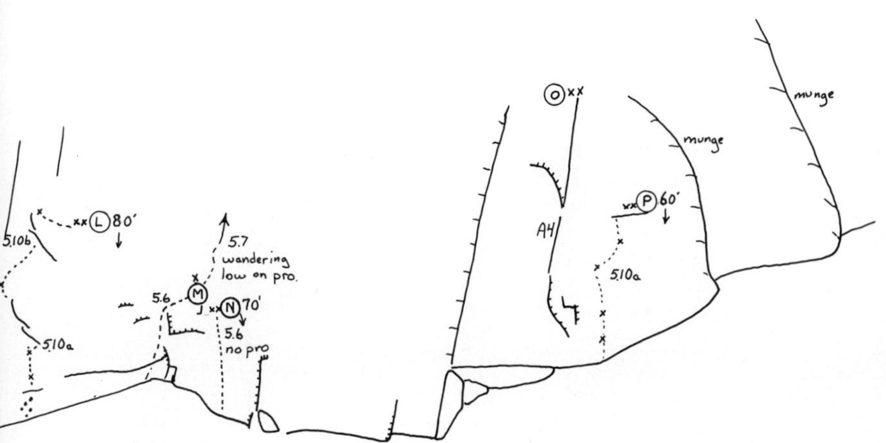

SUNNYSIDE BENCH

L **Blackballed** 5.10b pro: small stoppers to a #2 Friend
M **Tiny Tim** 5.7
N **Guide's Route** 5.6
O **Riptide** A4
P **Safe to Surf** 5.10a

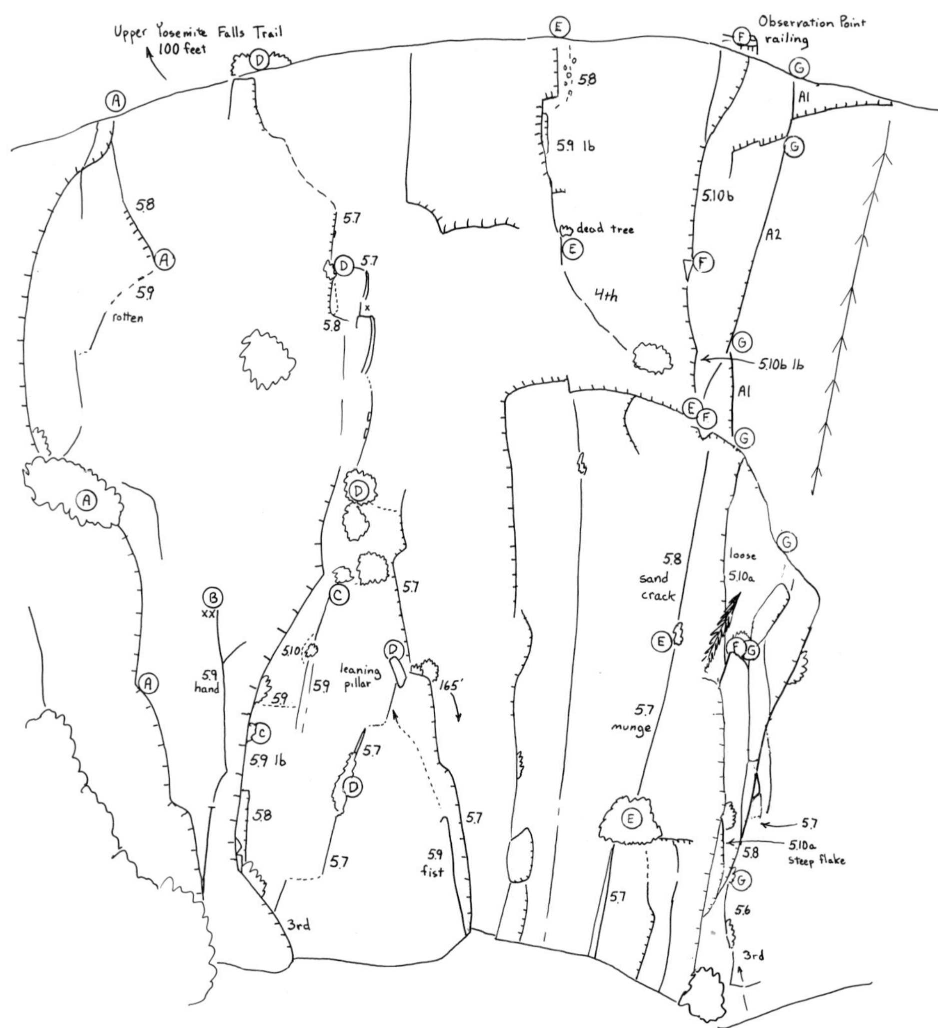

YOSEMITE FALLS – 2nd Tier

Approach Climb one of the Five Open Books or ascend the drainage gully just to the west.
Descent Walk down the Yosemite Falls Trail.
Photo on page 194.

A Bacchigaloupe Wall 5.9
B Handshake 5.9
C Marvin Gardens 5.10
D Selaginella 5.8
E Observation Point 5.9
F Indica Point 5.10b
G Mischief 5.8 A2

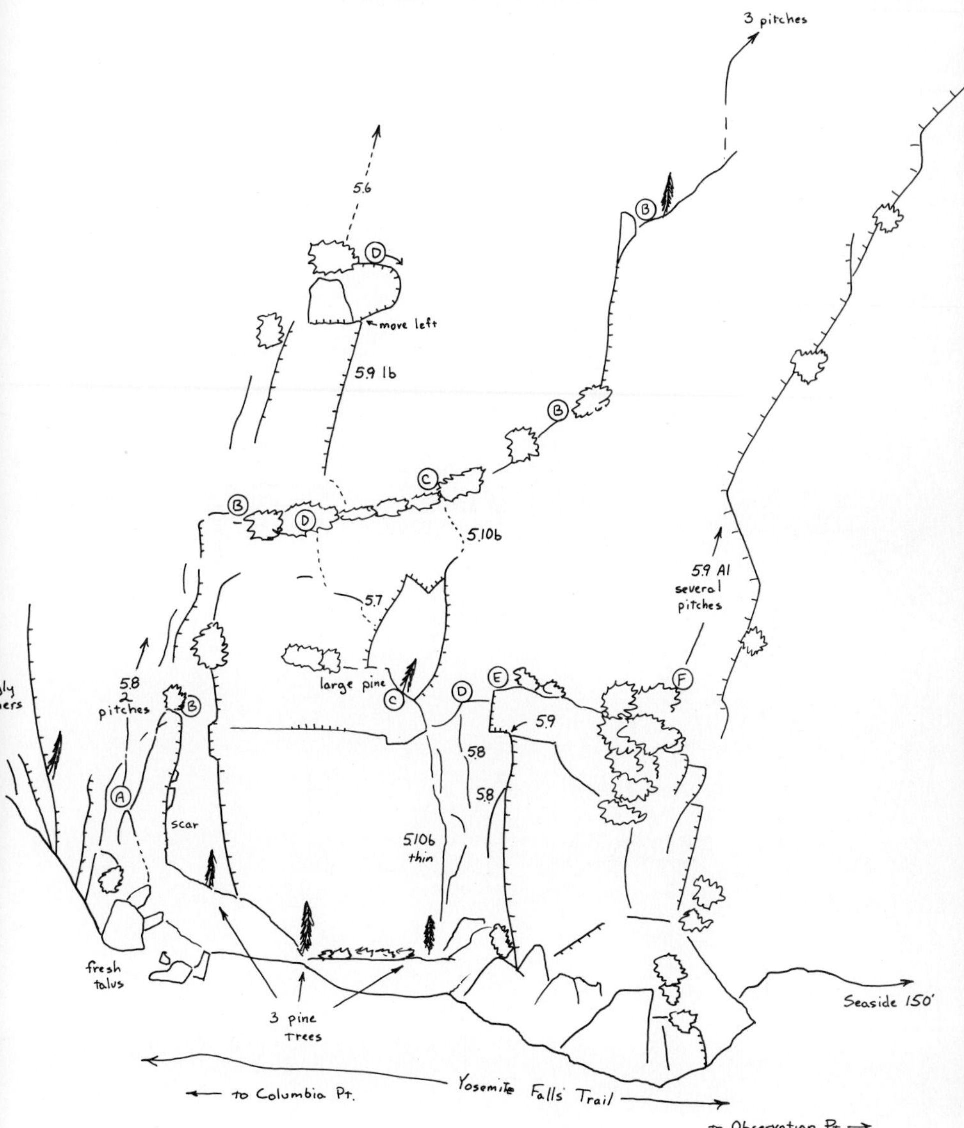

YOSEMITE FALLS – 3rd Tier

Approach Hike up the Yosemite Falls Trail.
Descent Rappel the route or scramble and rappel down to the west.
Photo on page 194.

A **Roger Stokes Route** 5.8
B **R.F.** 5.8
C **Avalon** 5.10b
D **T.D.'s Dihedral** 5.9
E **Wild Child** 5.9
F **Galloping Consumption** 5.9 A1

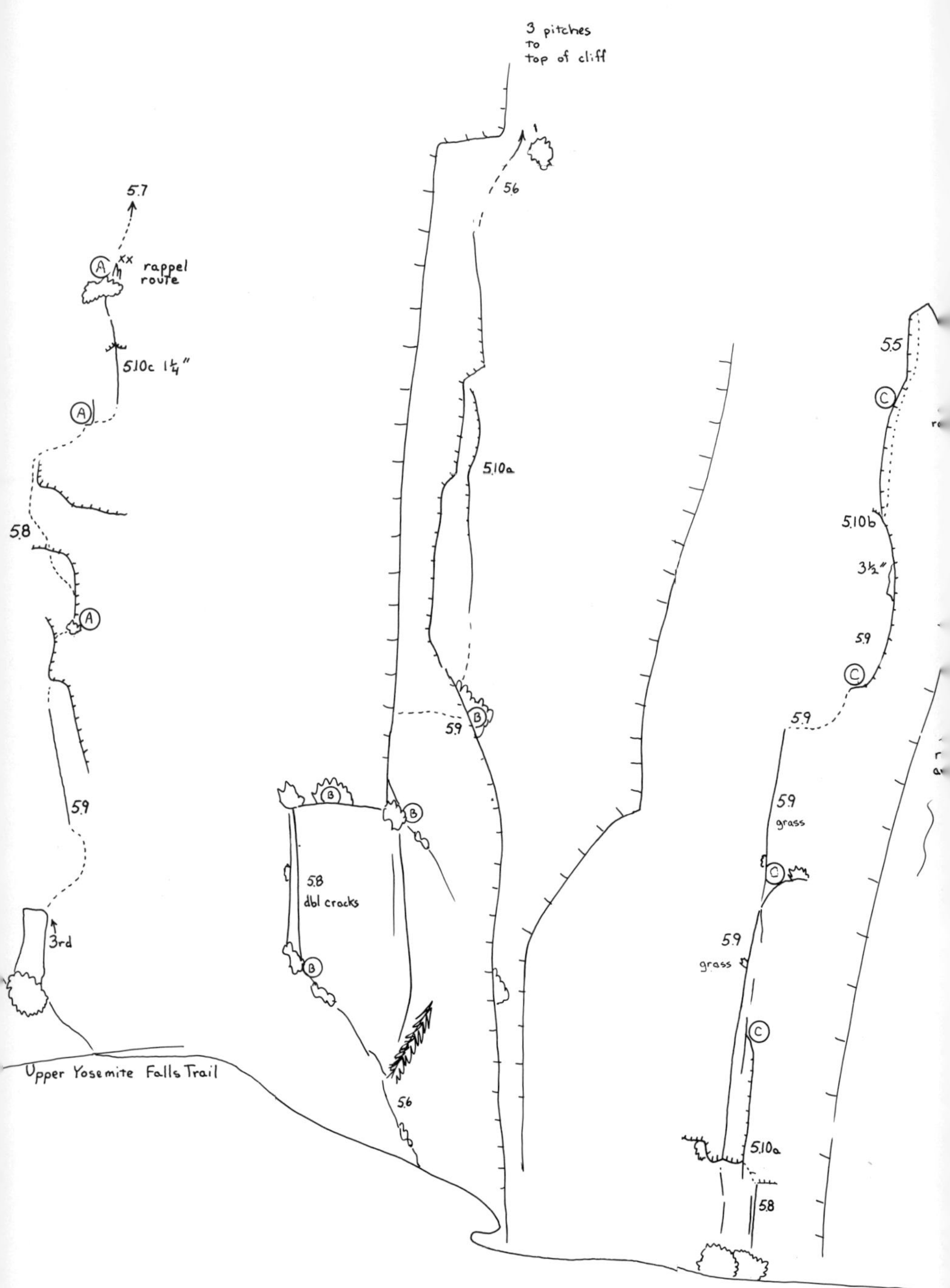
3 pitches
to
top of cliff
5.6
5.7
rappel
route
5.10c 1¼"
5.10a
5.8
5.5
5.10b
3½"
5.9
5.9
5.9
5.9
5.9
grass
5.8
dbl cracks
3rd
5.9
grass
Upper Yosemite Falls Trail
5.6
5.10a
5.8

CHARLIE BROWN APRON

Approach Walk up the Yosemite Falls Trail.
Photo on page 194.

- **A** **Seaside** 5.10c pro: incl. 2 ea. 1/8"-3/4"
- **B** **Diversions** 5.10a
- **C** **Smoky Pillar** 5.10b pro: to 3½"
- **D** **Dumbo Go Home** 5.9
- **E** **Chain Reaction** 5.10c pro: RP's and larger
- **F** **The Peanut** 5.10b pro: to 2½"
- **G** **No Teats** 5.10a

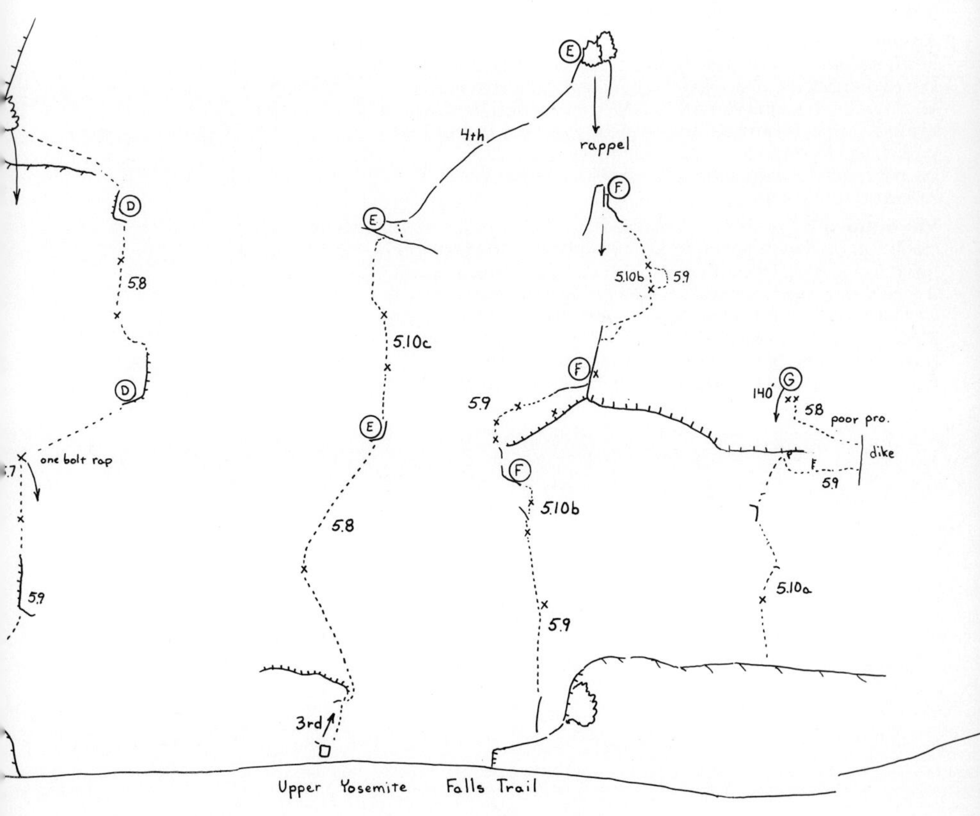

UPPER FALLS AREA

Photo on pages 194, 207.

Israeli Bomber 5.10c
200 feet left of the main cliff described on page 203 are two one pitch climbs, both beginning from the trail. **Israeli Bomber** starts on white rock, left of a thin roof, climbing up, then right to a manzanita. Another route, 5.9, climbs straight up to the manzanita, skirting a shallow roof/arch and following a thin crack.

A Forbidden Pinnacle 5.10a
Hike up the Falls Trail until about a mile beyond The Peanut. Under an orange spot where the trail cuts back and almost touches the wall is a slab, the left side of which forms the route. Two pitches.

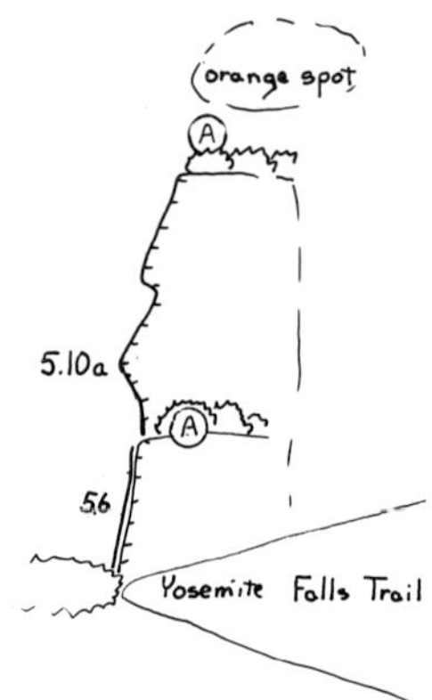

B Taboo Treat 5.9
After the spring on the upper switchback section the Falls Trail comes within a few feet of the main Forbidden Wall. A boulder move is followed by an easy ramp to a 110 foot open book.

C Brush Off 5.9
This is a slab route on the prominent apron at the lower left edge of the Upper Yosemite Falls wall. Hike up the switchbacks until reaching the left edge of the apron. The route starts at the apron's lowest point.

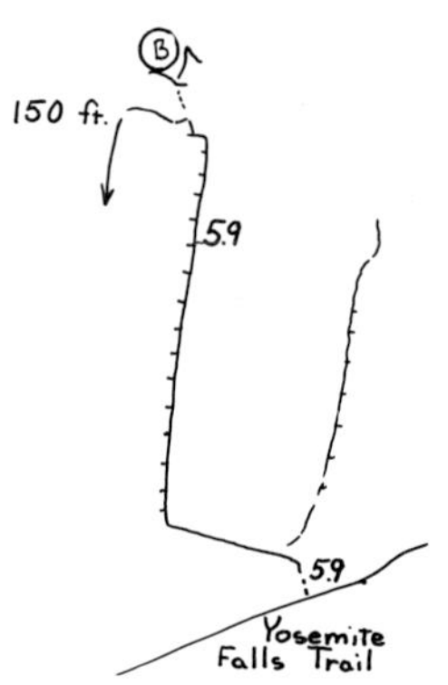

Aquamist 5.6
From a point approximately two-thirds of the way up the last switchbacks, a sloping, brush covered ledge leads south a few hundred feet to a large tree near a rock with a "window" in it. From this tree, walk toward the Upper Fall on an exposed ledge. Shortly after passing a giant boulder, a large right-facing open book/chimney is followed to the top.

Via Aqua 5.7
Continue on the exposed ledge described in the previous route to its end. Two moderate 5th class pitches lead up a series of broken corners. A bolt on the 3rd lead protects climbing over two flakes. Above, high angle face climbing leads to a large platform which is followed right to the base of the last pitch, a prominent chimney. A short 3rd class section leads to the railing overlooking the waterfall.

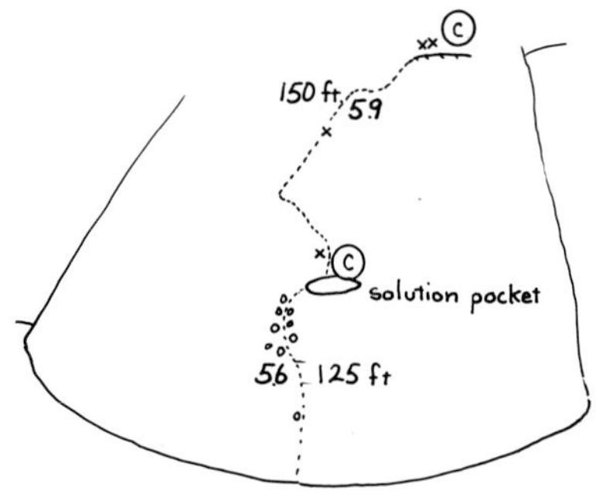

UPPER YOSEMITE FALLS

1 Brush Off
2 Aquamist
3 Via Aqua
4 Miscreant Wall
5 Misty Wall
6 GEEK TOWERS
7 Lost Arrow Chimney
8 Lost Arrow Spire Direct
9 ABC Route
10 Yosemite Pointless
11 Rainbow
12 Czech Route
13 Yosemite Point Buttress Direct
14 Arrowhead Arête

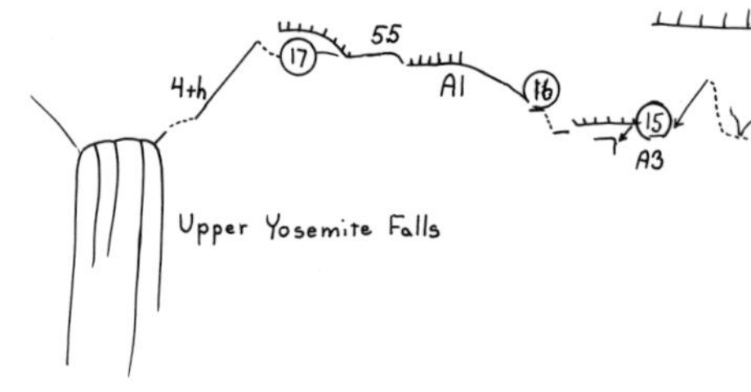

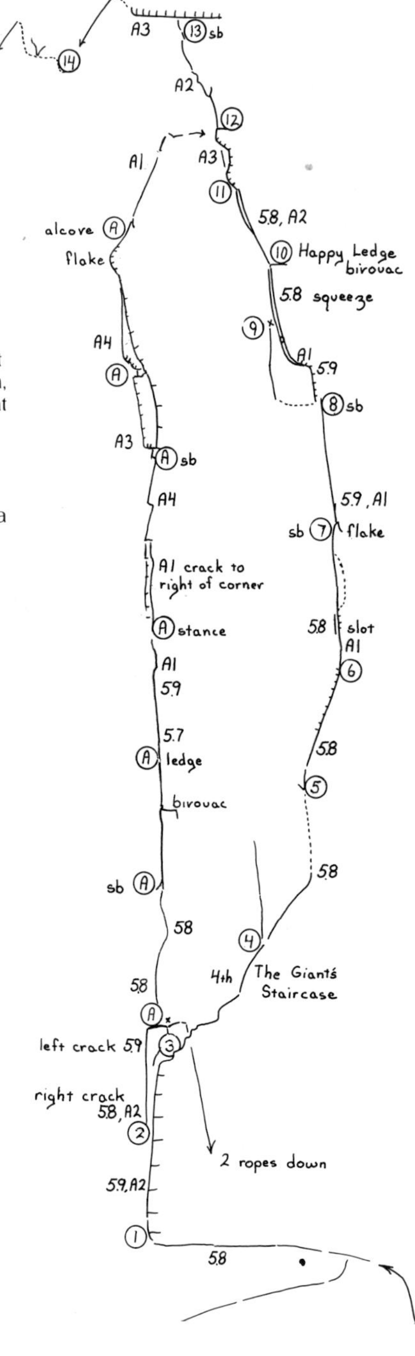

Misty Wall
VI 5.9 A3

Approach To get to the base of the upper wall it is necessary to gain the top of Sunnyside Bench, the lowest and most prominent wooded tier right of Yosemite Falls. Either climb the Sunnyside Bench 5.0 route or a talus field directly behind the Park Service maintainence yard and fire station. At a point overlooking the lip of Lower Yosemite Fall a tiny section of 3rd class begins a right diagonalling wooded ramp. Class 3 friction off the ramp leads to the 2nd tier. The final section involves a march through oaks and manzanita before sandy slopes lead to the base of the Lost Arrow.

Photo on page 207.

Hardware

3 KB
8 LA
2 ea. ½"-⅝"
5 ea. ¾"-1"
2 ea. 1¼"-3"
1 ea. 4"

A Miscreant Wall
V 5.9 A4

Hardware

4 LA
2 ea. ½"-1"
many nuts
hooks
Friends

GEEK TOWERS

Approach Hike up to the wall as described on page 208.
Photo on page 207.

A **Freestone** 5.11b pro: to 5", incl. extra ⅛"-¾"; 2 ea. 2"-4"
B **Center Route** 5.10a pro: to 3½"
C **Right Side** 5.10a A2 pro: to 3½" incl. dowel hangers

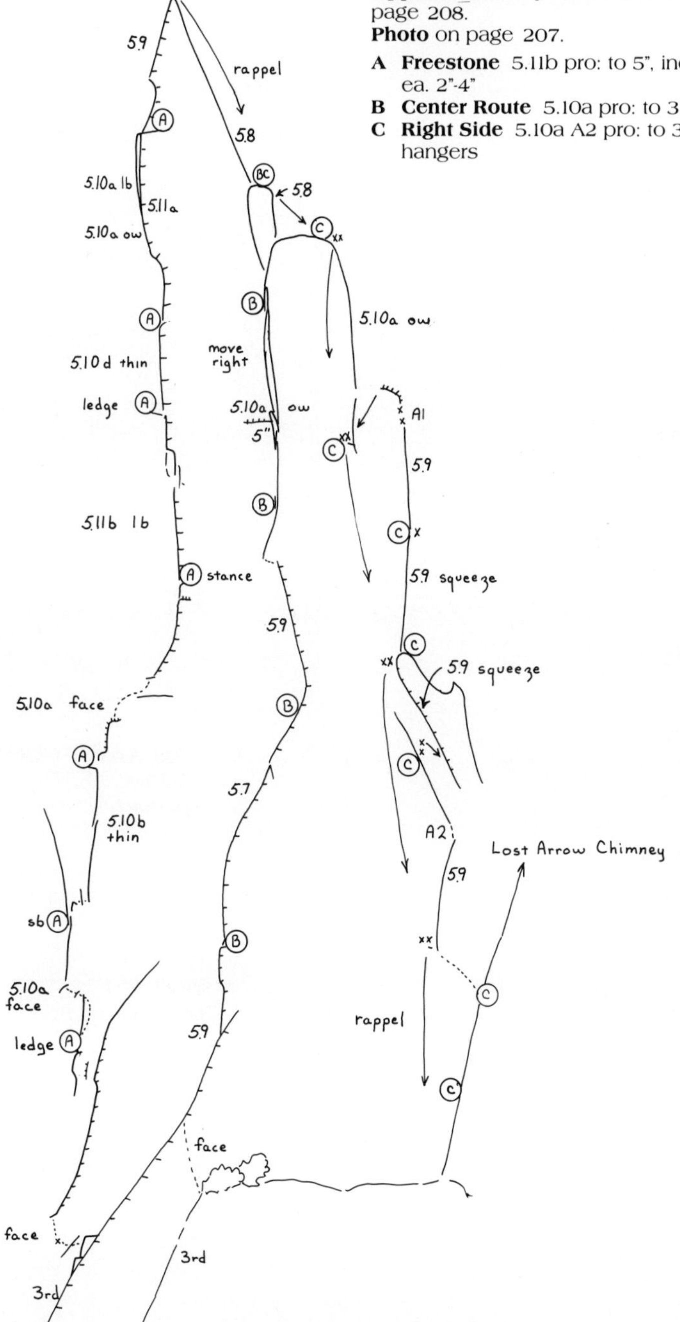

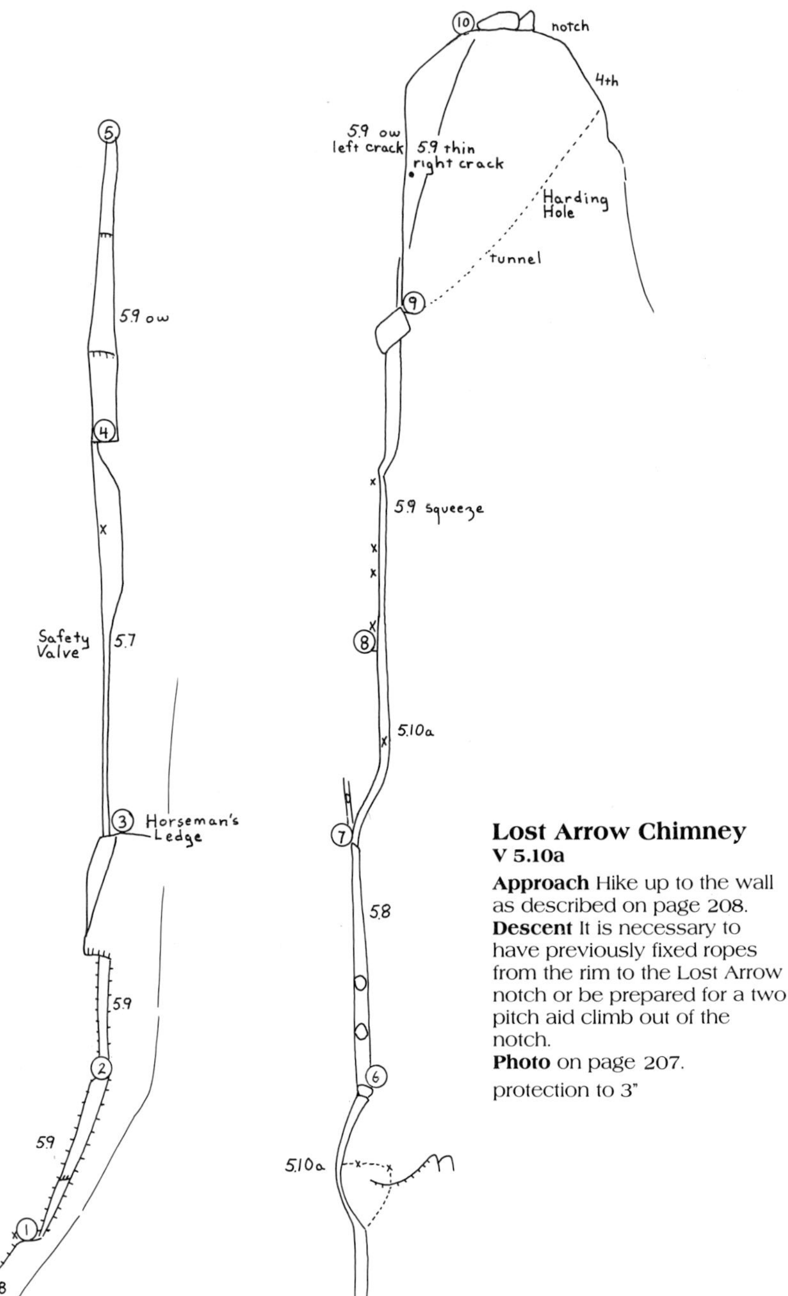

Lost Arrow Chimney
V 5.10a

Approach Hike up to the wall as described on page 208.
Descent It is necessary to have previously fixed ropes from the rim to the Lost Arrow notch or be prepared for a two pitch aid climb out of the notch.
Photo on page 207.
protection to 3"

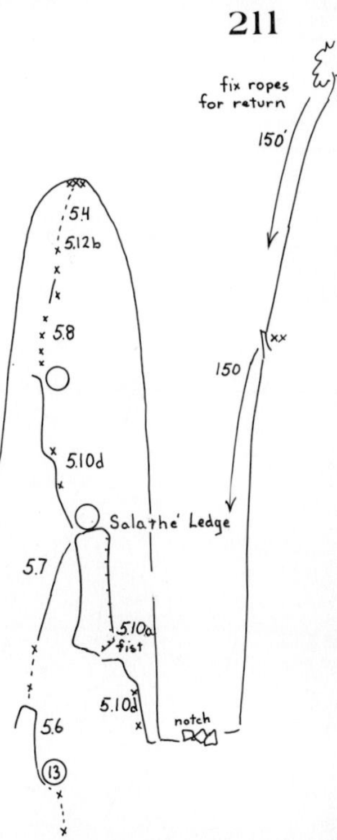

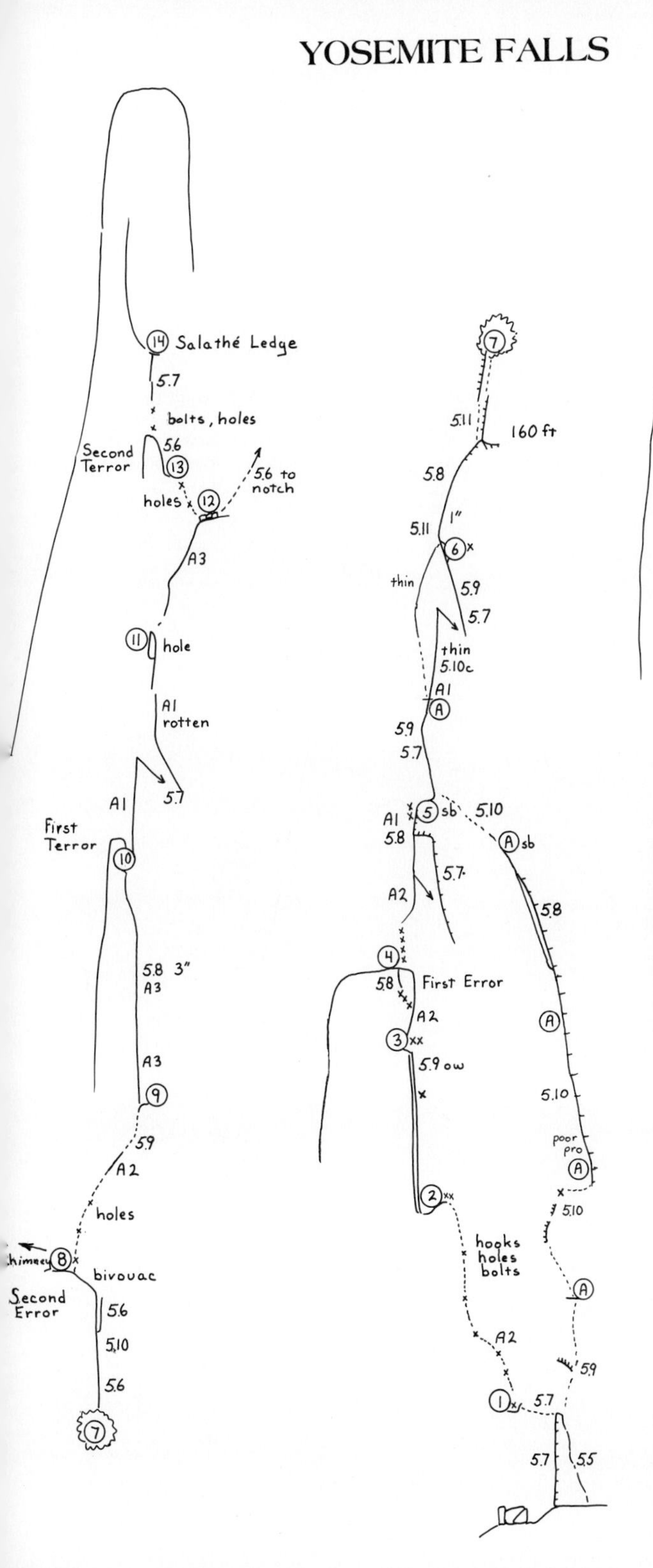

LOST ARROW SPIRE

Approach Hike up to the base of the wall as described on page 208.
Descent Ropes must be fixed from the rim for the escape out of the notch.
Photo on page 207.

Direct Route
V 5.11 A3

Hardware
- 1 rurp
- 3 KB
- 8 LA
- 2 ea. ½"-⅝"
- 3 ea. ¾"-1"
- 2 ea. 1¼"
- 4 ea. 1½"
- 1 ea. 2"-4"
- nuts to 3"
- Friends to #4
- Bat hooks

A ABC Route
V 5.11
protection to 4"

Lost Arrow Tip
5.12b or 5.8 A2
aid rack: nuts to 2½", incl. extra ¾-1¾"

Yosemite Pointless

V 5.9 A3

Approach Described on page 208.
Photo on page 207.
Hardware

1 rurp
3 KB
5 LA
2 ea. ½"-¾"
1 ea. 1"-1½"
bongs
many Friends, incl. several large
copperheads
all hooks
10 keyhole hangers
nuts

This route crosses the path of a Rohrer rappel route down from the right side of the notch.

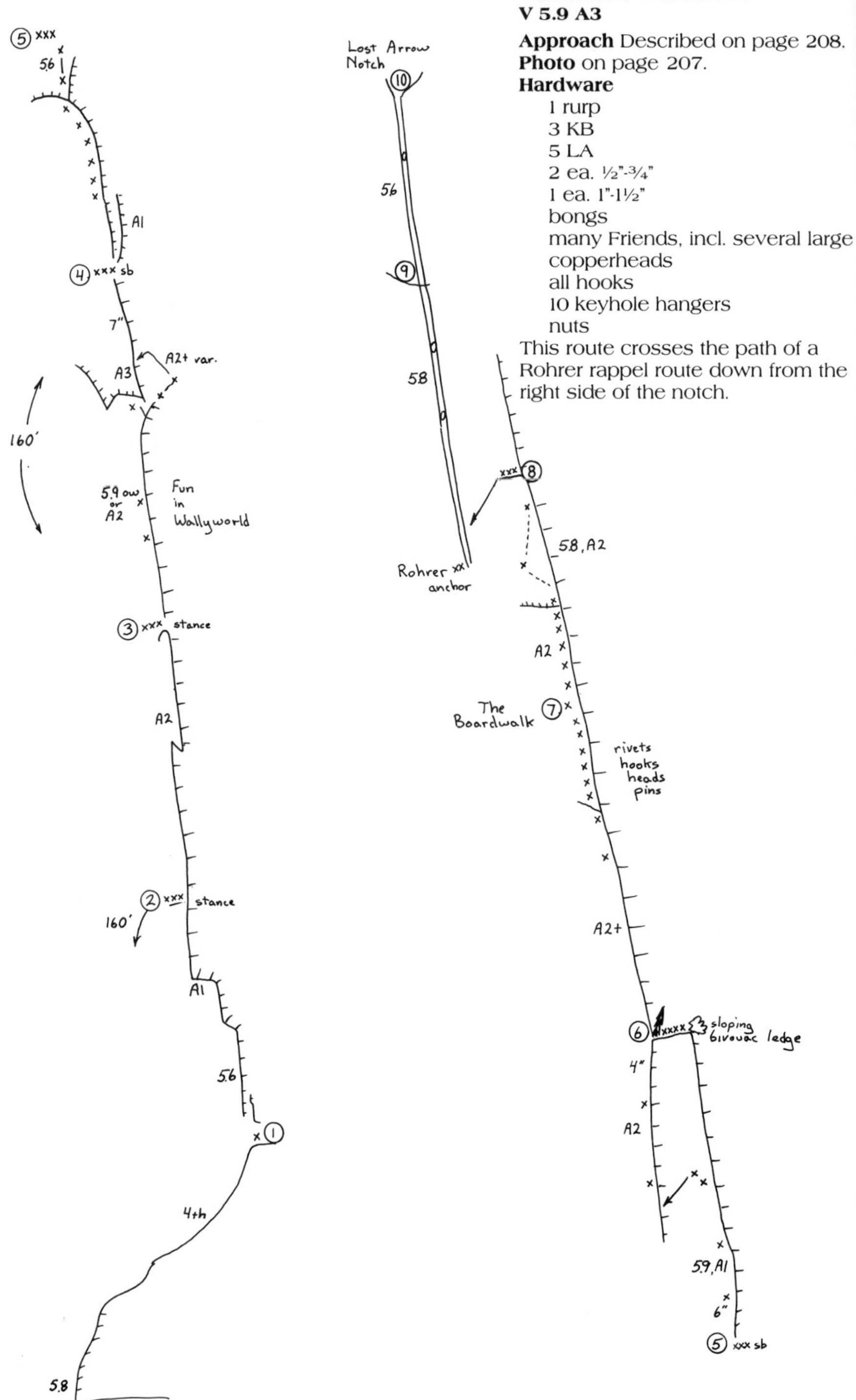

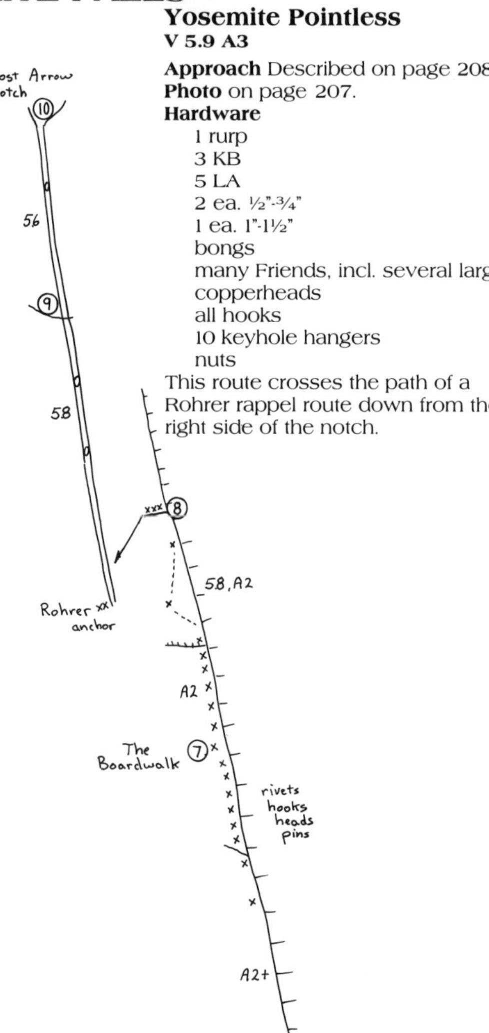

Rainbow

V 5.10 A3

Approach Hike up as described on page 208.

Photo on page 207.

Hardware

8 KB
16 LA
3 ea. ½"-¾"
2 ea. 1"-1½"
RP's
rivet hangers
Friends to #6
hooks

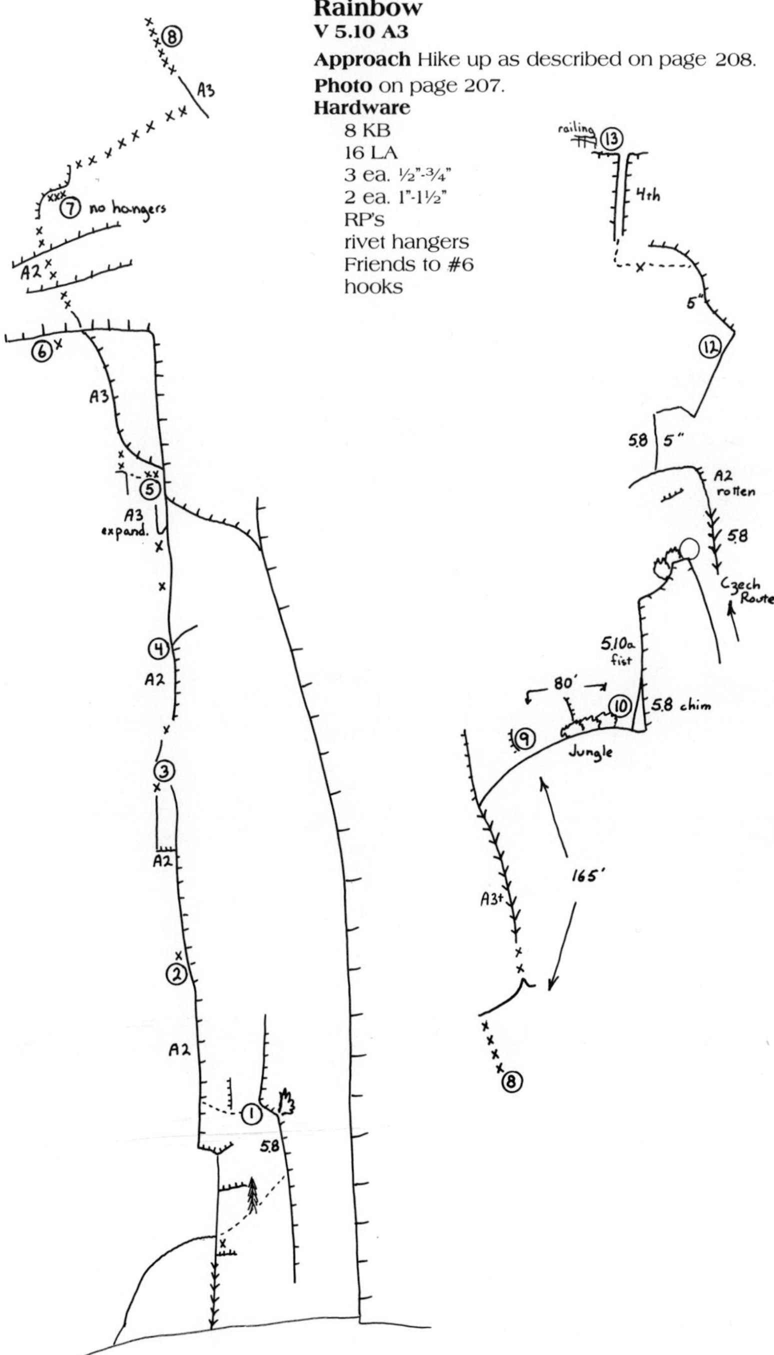

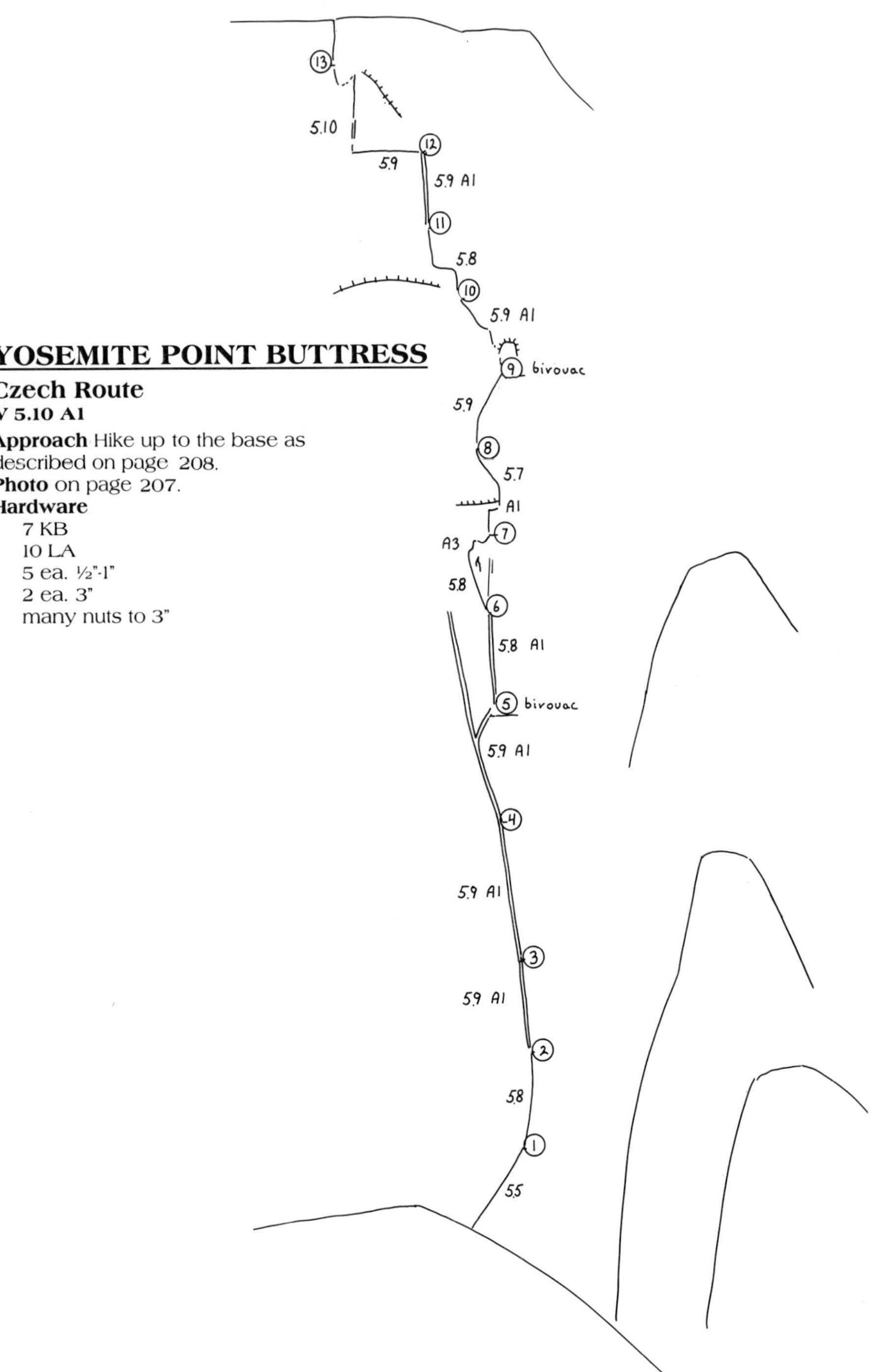

YOSEMITE POINT BUTTRESS

Czech Route

V 5.10 A1

Approach Hike up to the base as described on page 208.
Photo on page 207.
Hardware
- 7 KB
- 10 LA
- 5 ea. ½"-1"
- 2 ea. 3"
- many nuts to 3"

YOSEMITE POINT BUTTRESS

Direct Route

5.9

Approach After scrambling up Sunnyside Bench, as described on page 208, 3rd class up the lower of two prominent pedestals leaning against the wall.

Photo on page 207.

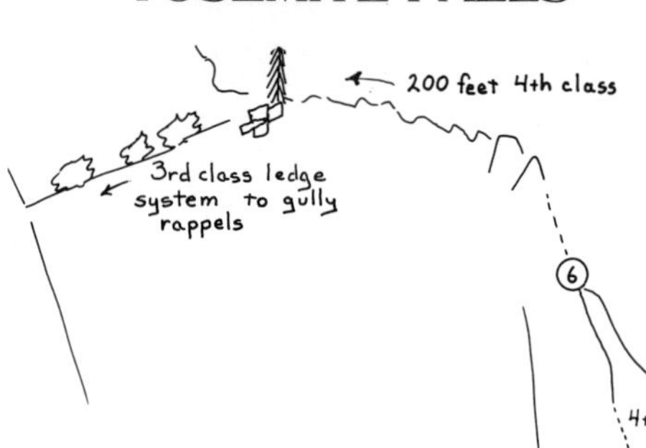

Arrowhead Arête
5.8

Approach The approach is best made in the following manner: Gain the trail that traverses the north side of the Valley at the Church Bowl and walk west. At a point above the government utility area the first open view of the Valley is obtained. On the slope above is a trail, faint at first, that leads upwards toward Indian Canyon. Above, where the first clear view of the arête is possible, a 100 foot dirty, low angle rock wall is scrambled to its top and a trail leads left, first up a little, then down 100 feet or so and around to the west into West Arrowhead Chimney. Wander up this until the arète base is reached.
Descent Work left along the crest of the arête to a major chimney system. Three 80 foot rappels pass several chockstones down this gully.
Photo on page 207.

A Arrowhead Spire – South Arête 5.5

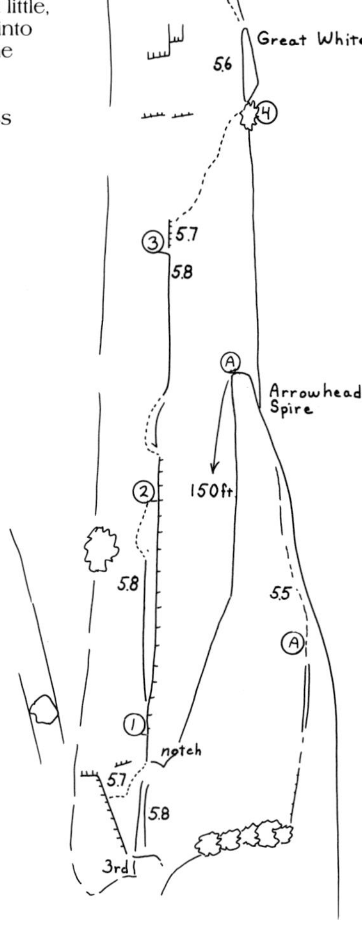

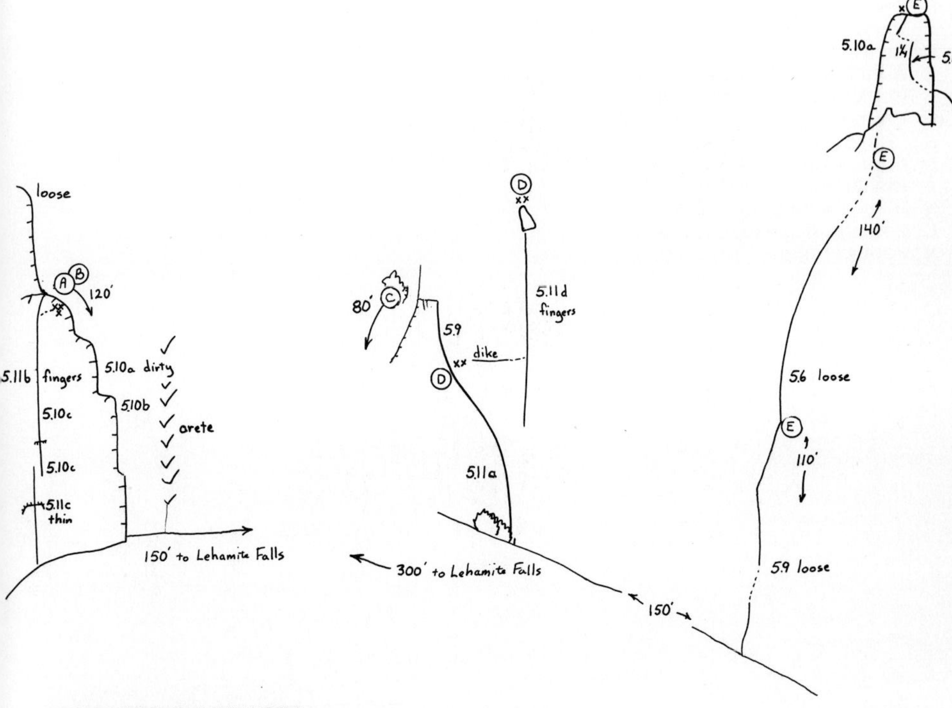

INDIAN CANYON

Approach Start up the canyon as described on the previous page. Ascend to the east (right side) of Indian Creek. Lehamite Creek (the subsidiary waterfall on the right side of the the canyon) may be difficult to cross in high water. The climbs are located on either side of Lehamite Falls.

A Maps and Legends 5.11b pro: to 2", esp. ½"-¾"
B Police State 5.10b pro: to 4"
C Knuckle Buster 5.11a
D The Wand 5.11d
E A-5 Pinnacle 5.10a

CHURCH BOWL

Approach Generous turnouts on the road just east of the village and medical clinic lie beneath the cliff.

A **Black is Brown** 5.8
B **Deja Thorus** 5.10a
C **Uncle Fanny** 5.7
D **Revival** 5.10a
E **Aunt Fanny's Pantry** 5.4
F **Book of Revelations** 5.11a
G **Church Bowl Tree** 5.10b
H **Church Bowl Chimney** 5.6
I **Church Bowl Terrace** 5.8
J **Bishop's Terrace** 5.8
K **Bishop's Balcony** 5.5 A3
L **Fire and Brimstone** 5.11d
M **Fool's Finger** 5.11c pro: to 3"

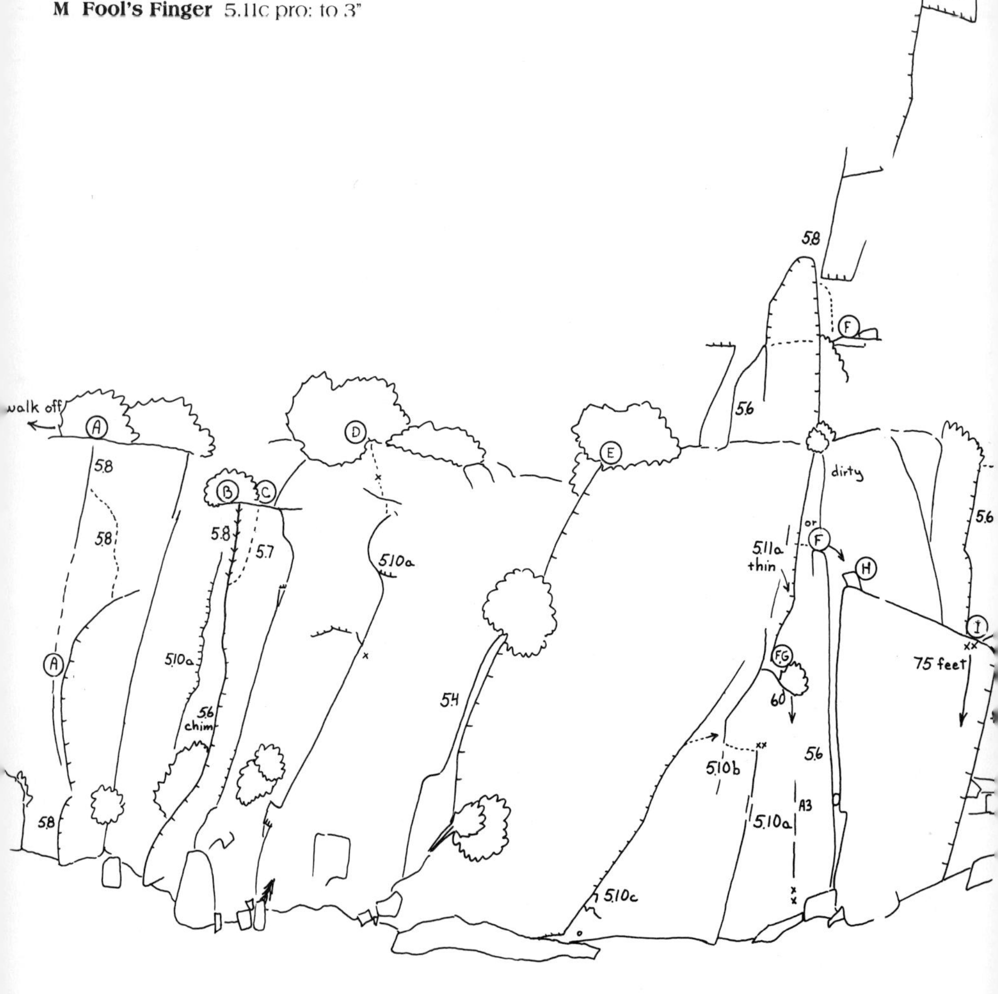

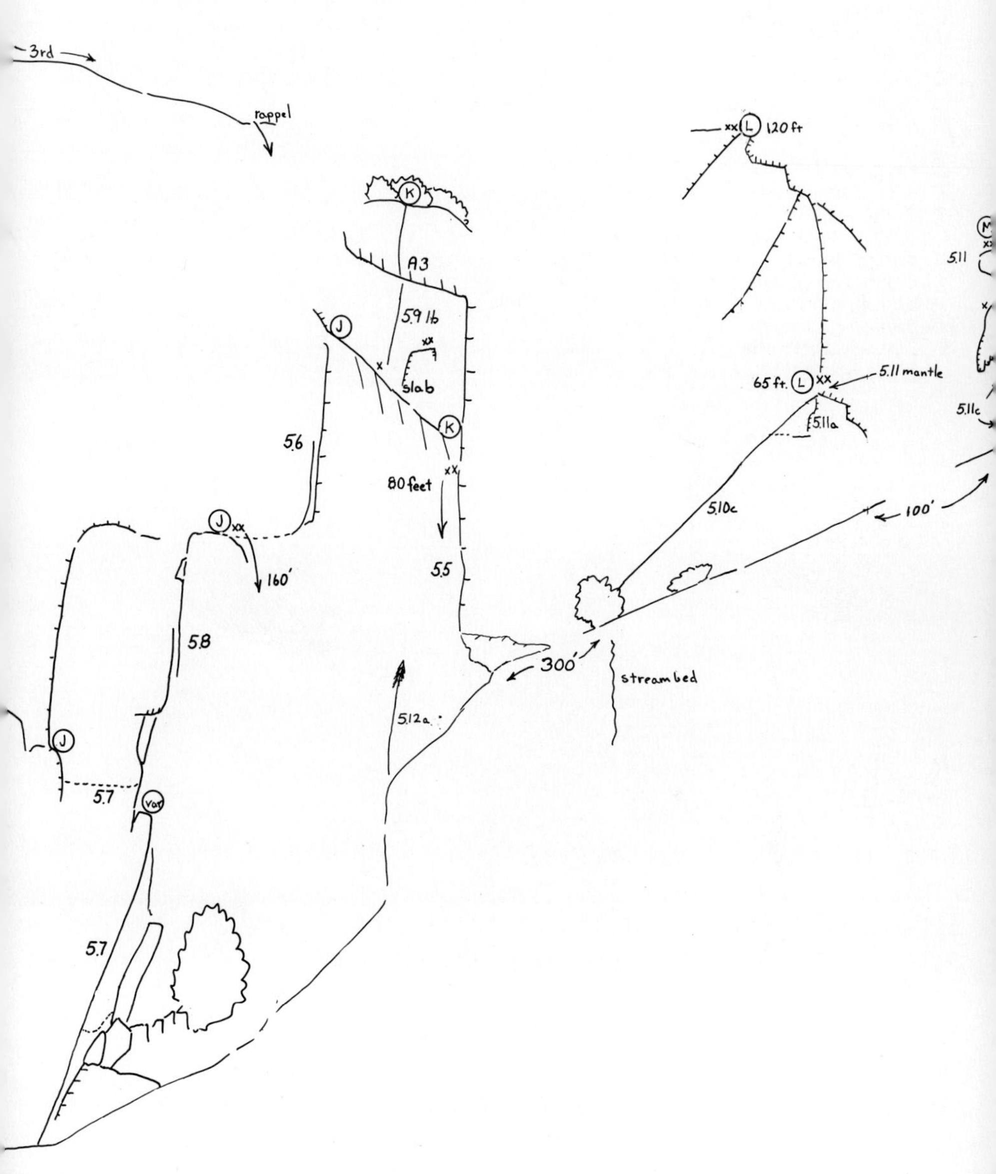
3rd
rappel
A3
5.9 1b
slab
5.6
80 feet
160'
5.5
5.8
300'
streambed
5.12a
5.7
var
5.7
120 ft
65 ft.
5.11 mantle
5.11a
5.10c
100'
5.11
5.11c

THE ROYAL ARCHES

1 Die Schweine Von Oben
2 Serenity Crack
3 Moan Fest
4 Devil's Bathtubs
5 Royal Arches Route
6 King Snake

THE ROYAL ARCHES

7 The Cobra
8 Shakey Flakes
9 Greasy but Groovy
10 Arches Terrace
11 Bulging Puke

Die Schweine Von Oben

VI 5.11 A3+

Photo on page 220.

Hardware

10 KB
15 LA
3 ea. ½"-¾"
2 ea. 1"-1¼"
1 ea. 1½"-3"
Friends to #4
all hooks
bolt hangers
keyhole hangers

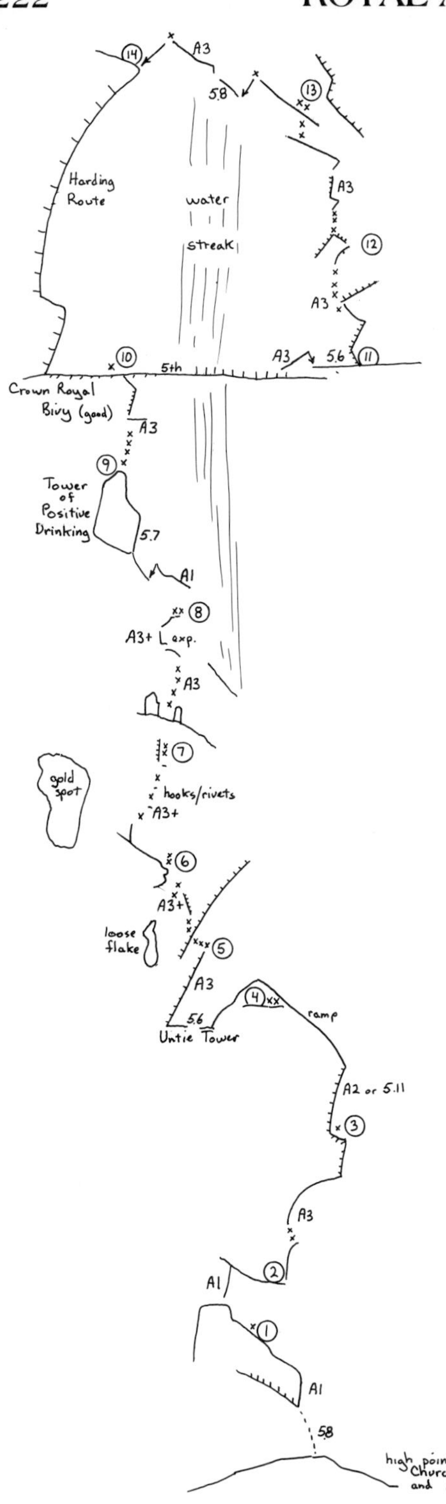

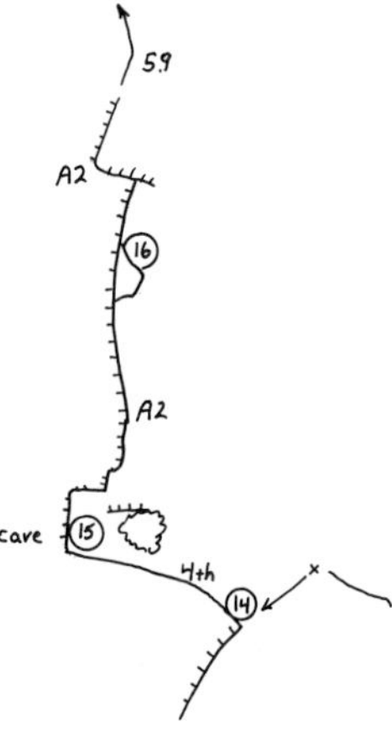

SERENITY CRACK AREA

Photo on page 220.

A East of Eden 5.10b pro: RP's
B Rupto Pac 5.11c
C Super Slide 5.10a
D Eagle Roof A1
E Peter's Out 5.12
F Trial by Fire 5.8
G Serenity Crack 5.10d
H Adrenaline 5.11b pro: small wires
I Maxine's Wall 5.10c pro: to 3"
J Firefingers 5.11b pro: incl. #3½ Friend
K Pigs in Space 5.12
L Permanent Waves 5.10b pro: incl. #½ Friend
M Deviltry 5.10d
N Hell's Hollow 5.10a
O Moan Fest 5.10c pro: incl. KB's

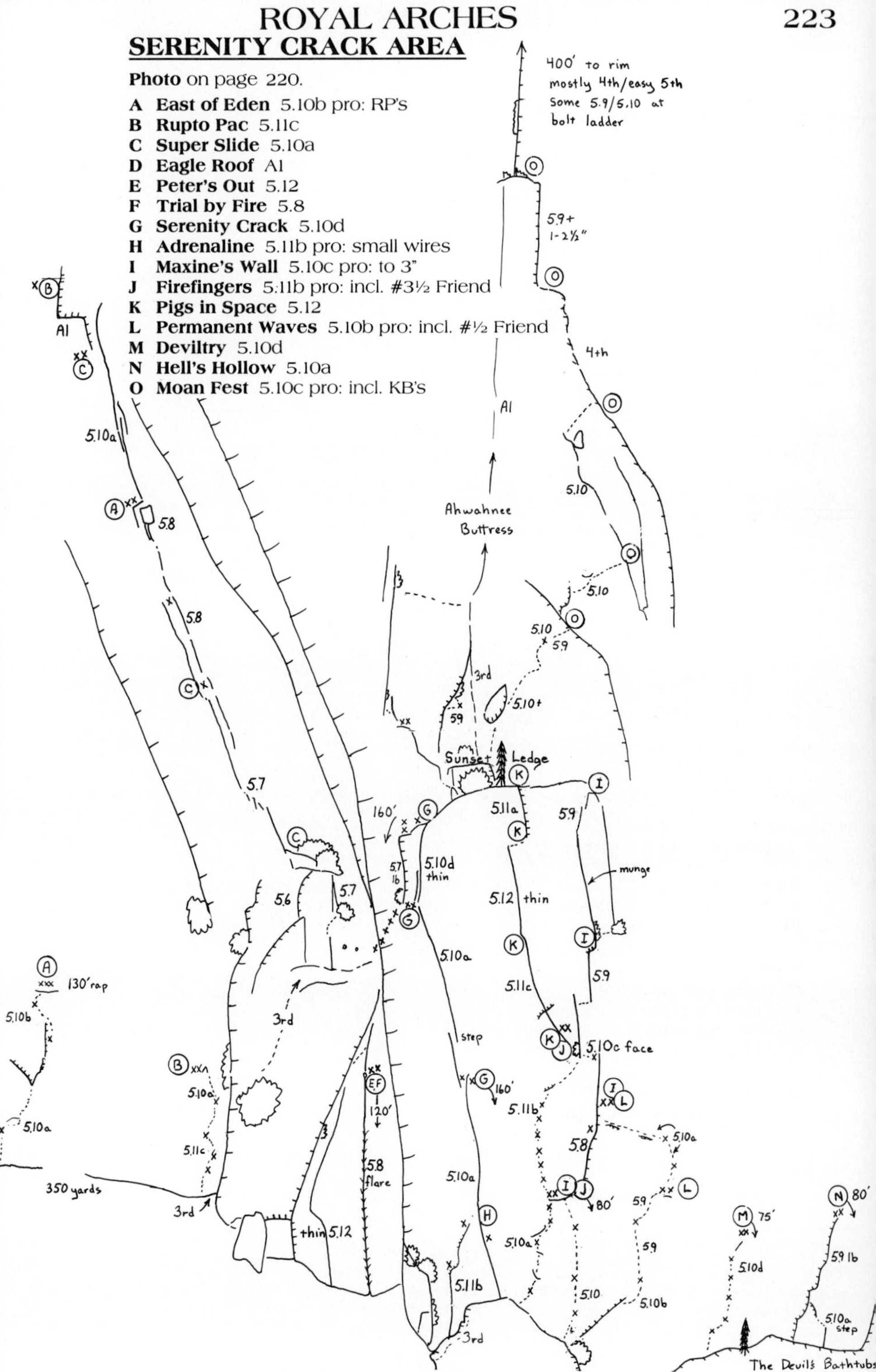

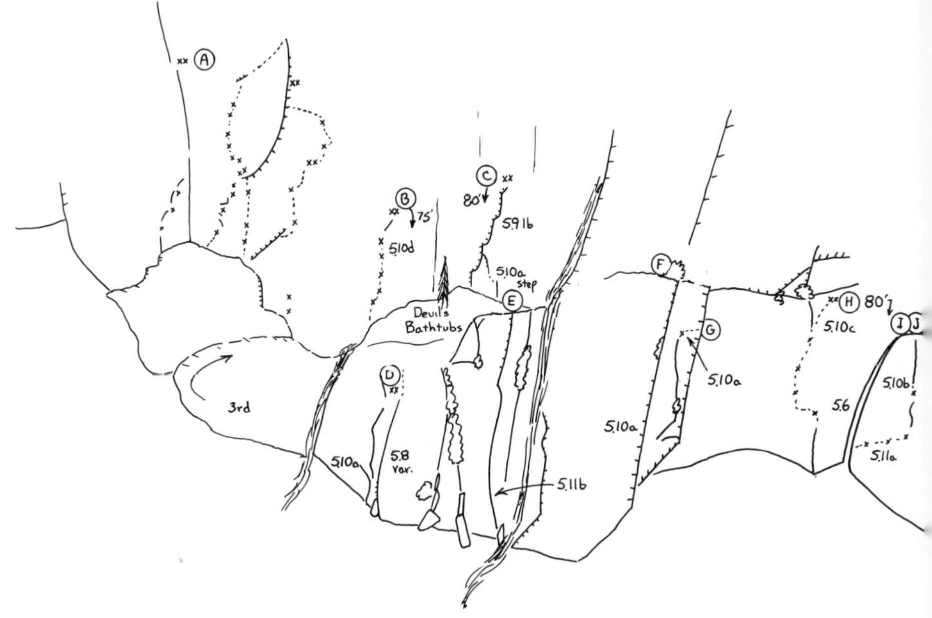

ARCHES BASE DETAIL

Approach This area is located a short distance east of the Ahwahnee Hotel along the horse trail. Follow the first creekbed up to the base of the wall.
Photo on page 220.

A **Serenity Crack** 5.10d (see previous page)
B **Deviltry** 5.10d
C **Hell's Hollow** 5.10a
D **Peruvian Flake** 5.10a
E **Draw the Line** 5.11b pro: thin
F **Fine Line** 5.10a
G **Peeping Tom** 5.10a
H **Surplus Cheaper Hands** 5.10c
I **Royal Arches Route** (first pitch) 5.6
J **Astro Spam** 5.11a

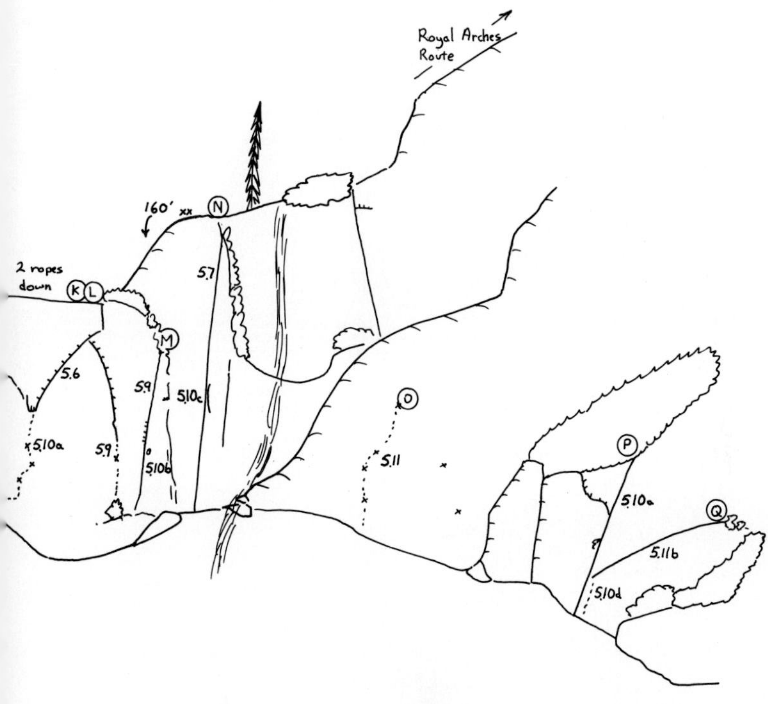

K Arète Butler 5.10a
L Royal Prerogative 5.9
M Krovy Rookers 5.10b
N Ilsa She Wolf of the S.S. 5.10c
O Facade 5.11
P Y Crack 5.10a
Q Fish Fingers 5.11b pro: many nuts to ½"

Royal Arches Route

5.7 A1 or 5.9

Approach Hike east from the Ahwahnee Hotel on the horse trail. 100 feet after crossing a small creek head up the hill to the first pitch chimney. The previous page may also help orientation.

Descent Scramble down North Dome Gully, described in detail on page 999.

Photo on page 221.

The Cobra

5.11a

ARCHES CENTRAL

Approach Hike east on the horse trail from the Ahwahnee Hotel. After several hundred yards, scramble up the hill toward the **Royal Arches Route** and follow the wall along to the routes. **Photo** on page 220.

A Royal Arches Route 5.7 A1 (see previous page)
B Royal Cornpad 5.10a
C Facade 5.11
D Y Crack 5.10a
E Fish Fingers 5.11b
F Wise Crack 5.10a
G Cornball 5.7
H Texas Chain Saw Massacre 5.11a
I King Snake 5.12 pro: many small nuts to 1"
J Poker Face 5.10b
K Face Card 5.10c
L King of Hearts 5.10d
M Sleight of Hand 5.10b

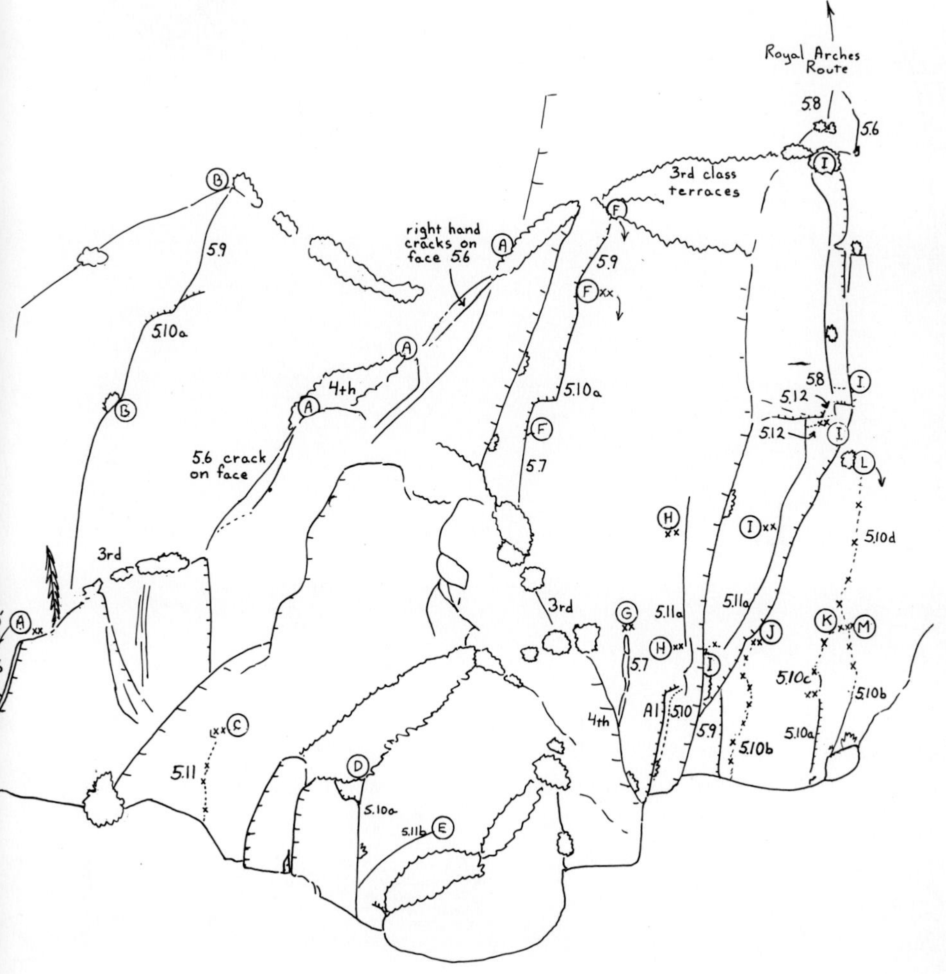

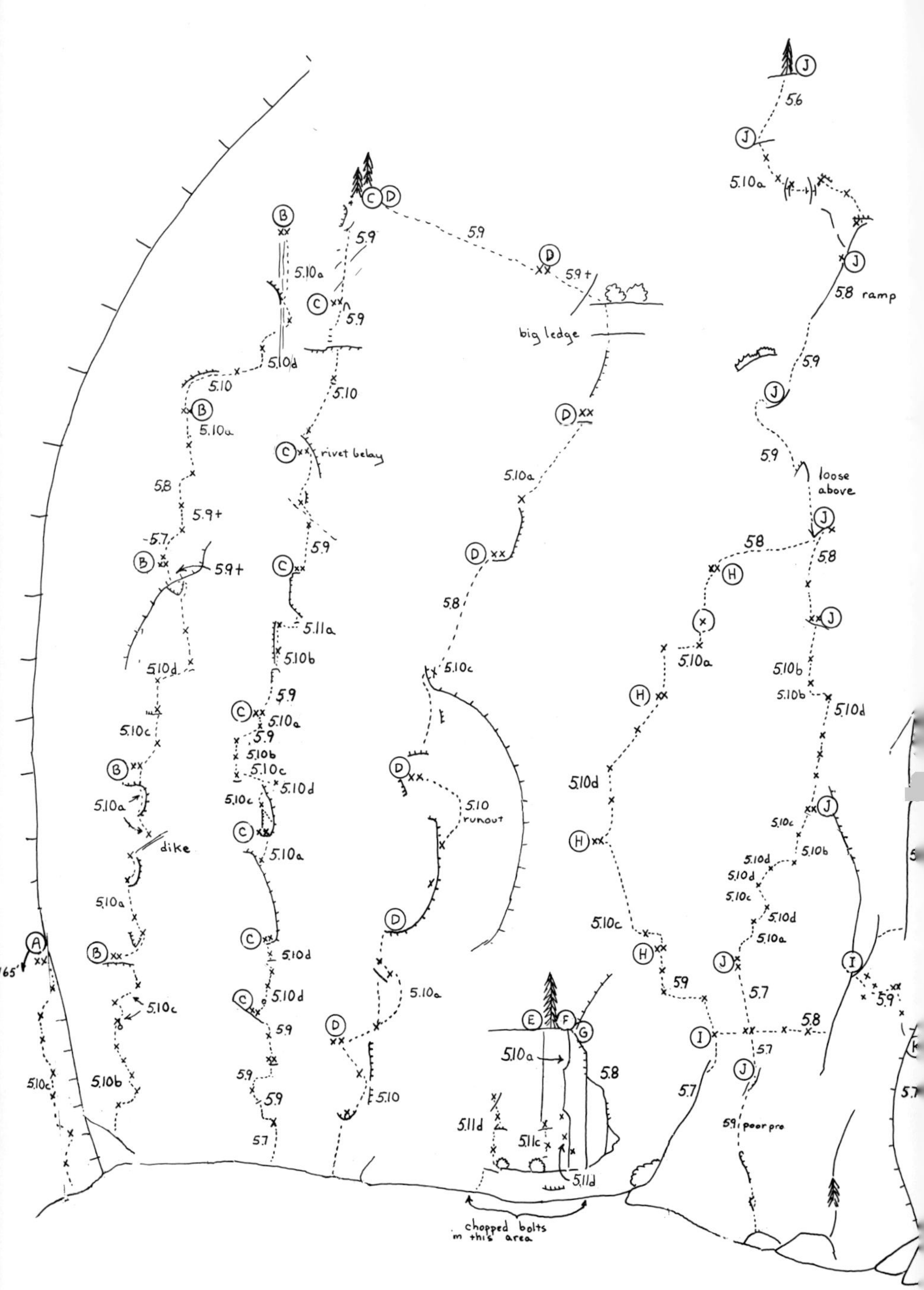

big ledge
rivet belay
dike
5.10 runout
loose above
5.8 ramp
5.9 poor pro
chopped bolts in this area
165'

ARCHES TERRACE AREA

Approach Walk several hundred yards east along the horse trail from the Ahwahnee Hotel before striking steeply up the hill.
Photo on page 221.

A **The Violent Bear it Away** 5.10c
B **The Rambler** 5.10d pro: small to 3/4" plus a #2½ Friend
C **Shakey Flakes** 5.11a
D **Friday the 13th** 5.10b pro: small plus #1-3½ Friend
E **Flakes Away** 5.11c
F **Samurai Crack** 5.11d
G **Hershey Highway** 5.8
H **Reefer Madness** 5.10d
I **Arches Terrace** 5.8 pro: to 3"
J **Greasy but Groovy** 5.10d
K **Fallen Arches** 5.9
L **Crying for Mama** 5.10a
M **Arches Terrace Direct** 5.11a
N **Hang Dog Flyer** 5.12
O **10.96** 5.10d
P **The Plank** 5.10b
Q **Movin' Like a Stud** 5.10d
R **Benzoin and Edges** 5.10c
S **The Kids are All Right** 5.7
T **Lynnea's Birthday Surprise** 5.10a

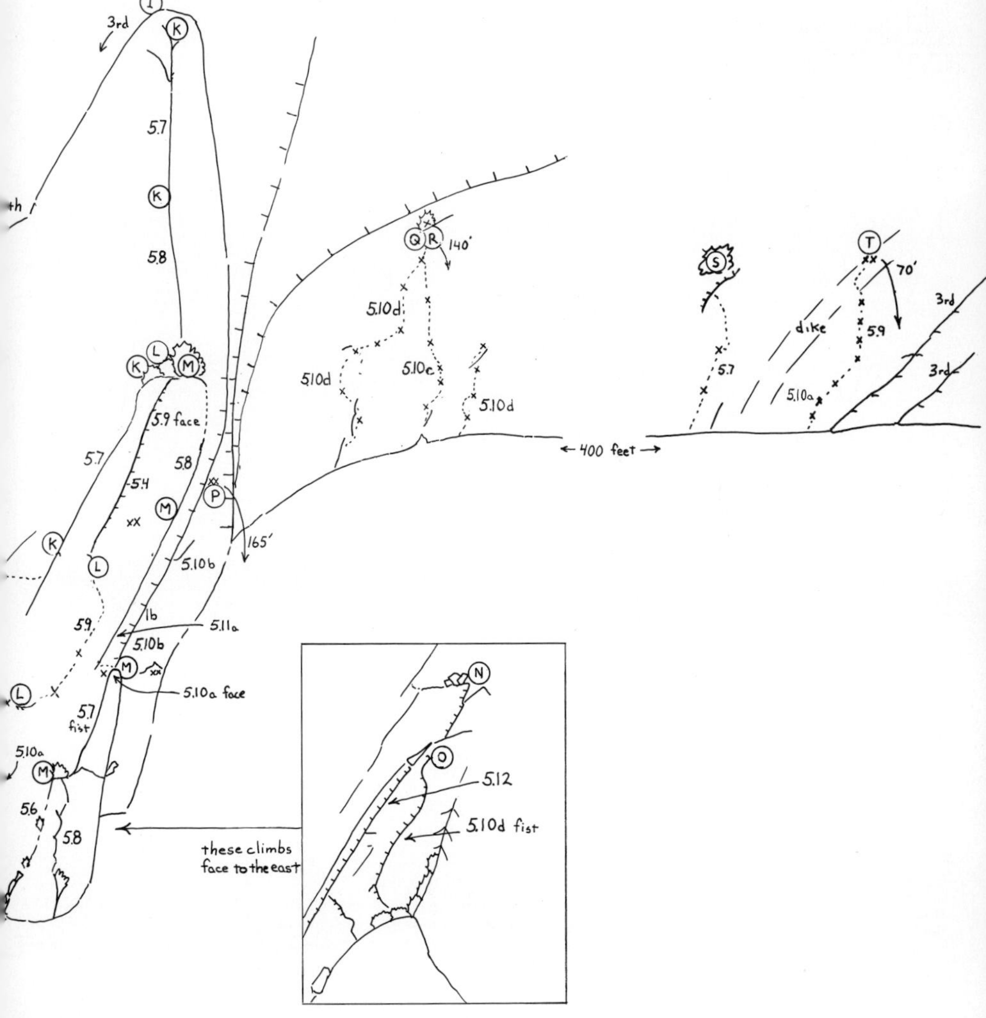

Bulging Puke
V 5.9 A4

Photo on page 221.
Hardware
- 1 rurp
- 5 KB
- 15 LA
- 3 ea. 5/8"-1 1/4"
- 2 ea. 1 1/2"-2"
- 1 ea. 2 1/2"-4"
- bat hooks
- copperheads

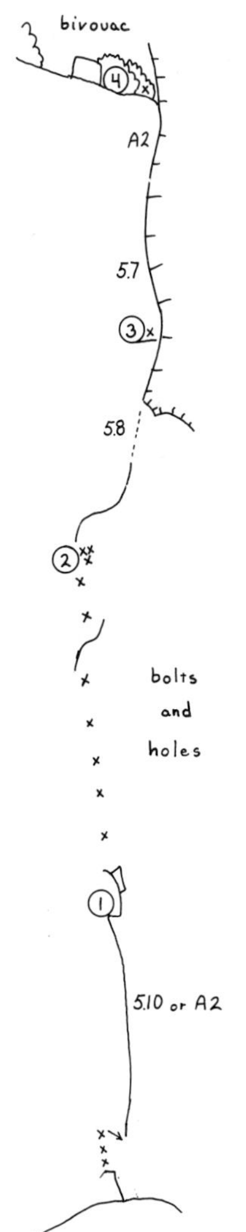

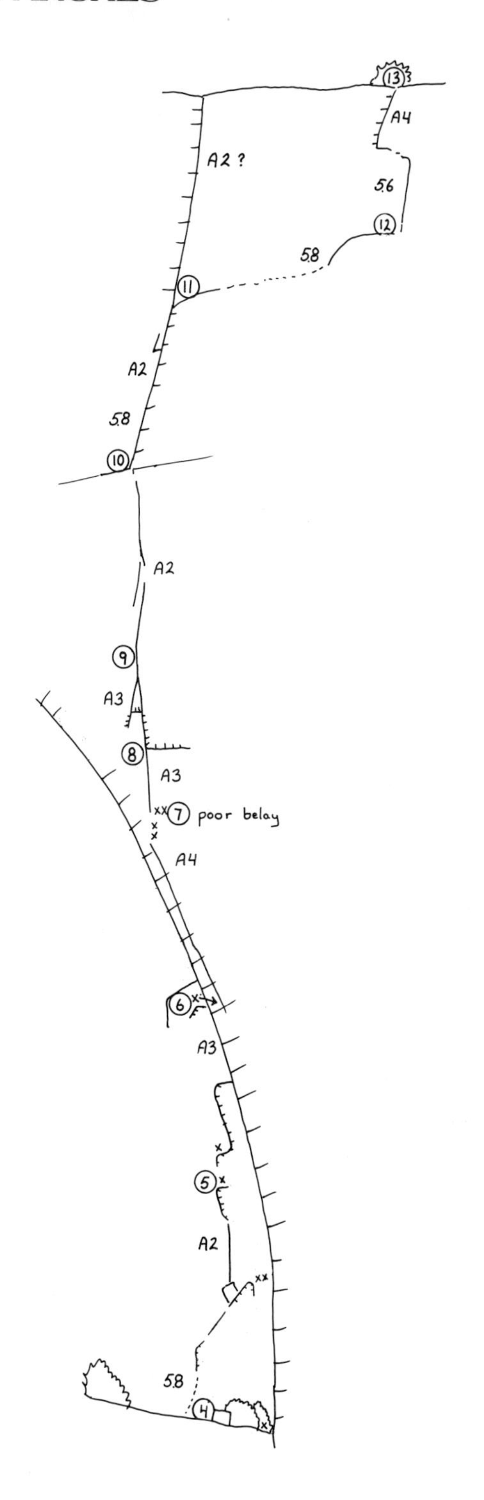

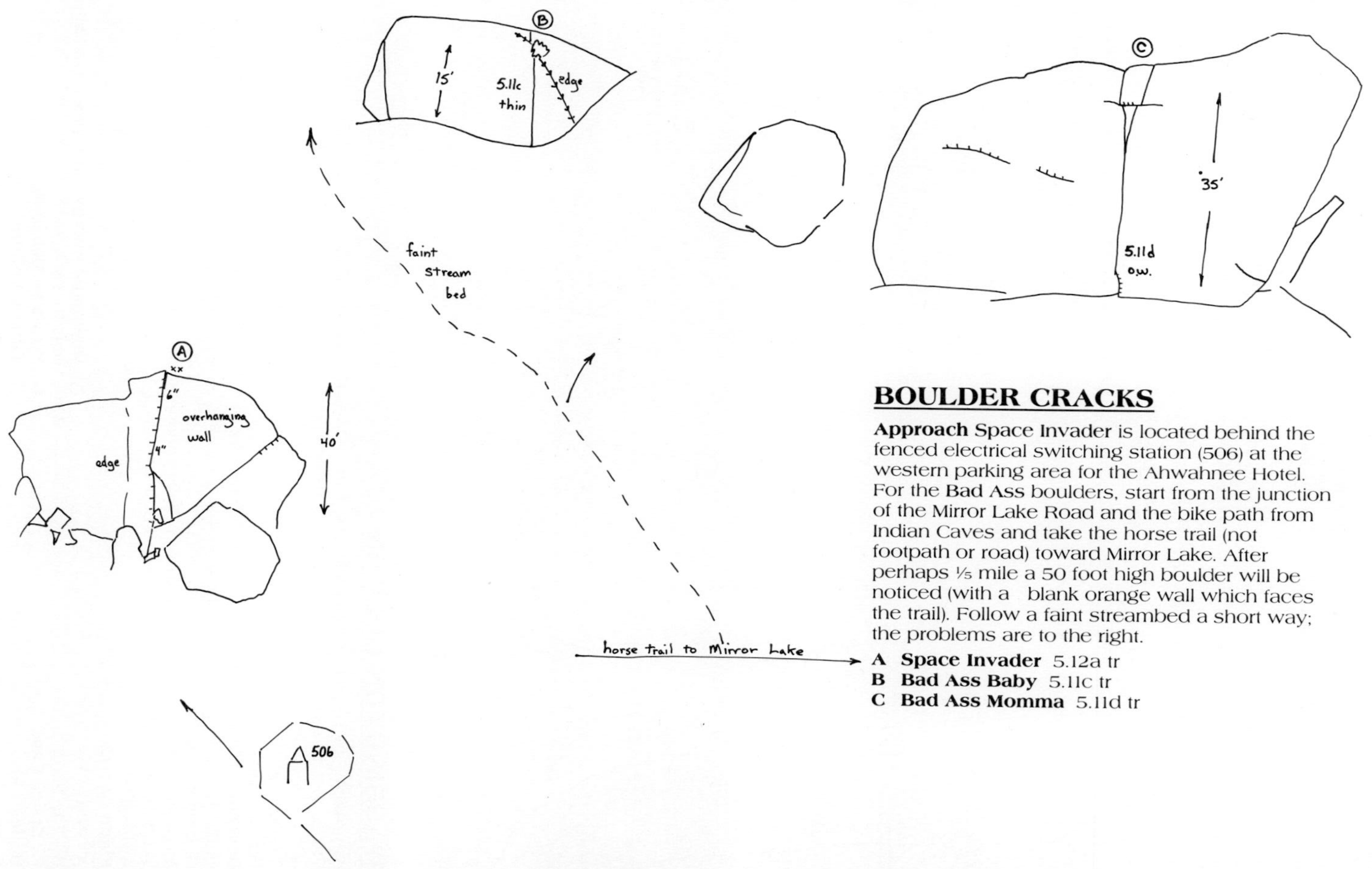

BOULDER CRACKS

Approach Space Invader is located behind the fenced electrical switching station (506) at the western parking area for the Ahwahnee Hotel. For the Bad Ass boulders, start from the junction of the Mirror Lake Road and the bike path from Indian Caves and take the horse trail (not footpath or road) toward Mirror Lake. After perhaps ⅕ mile a 50 foot high boulder will be noticed (with a blank orange wall which faces the trail). Follow a faint streambed a short way; the problems are to the right.

A Space Invader 5.12a tr
B Bad Ass Baby 5.11c tr
C Bad Ass Momma 5.11d tr

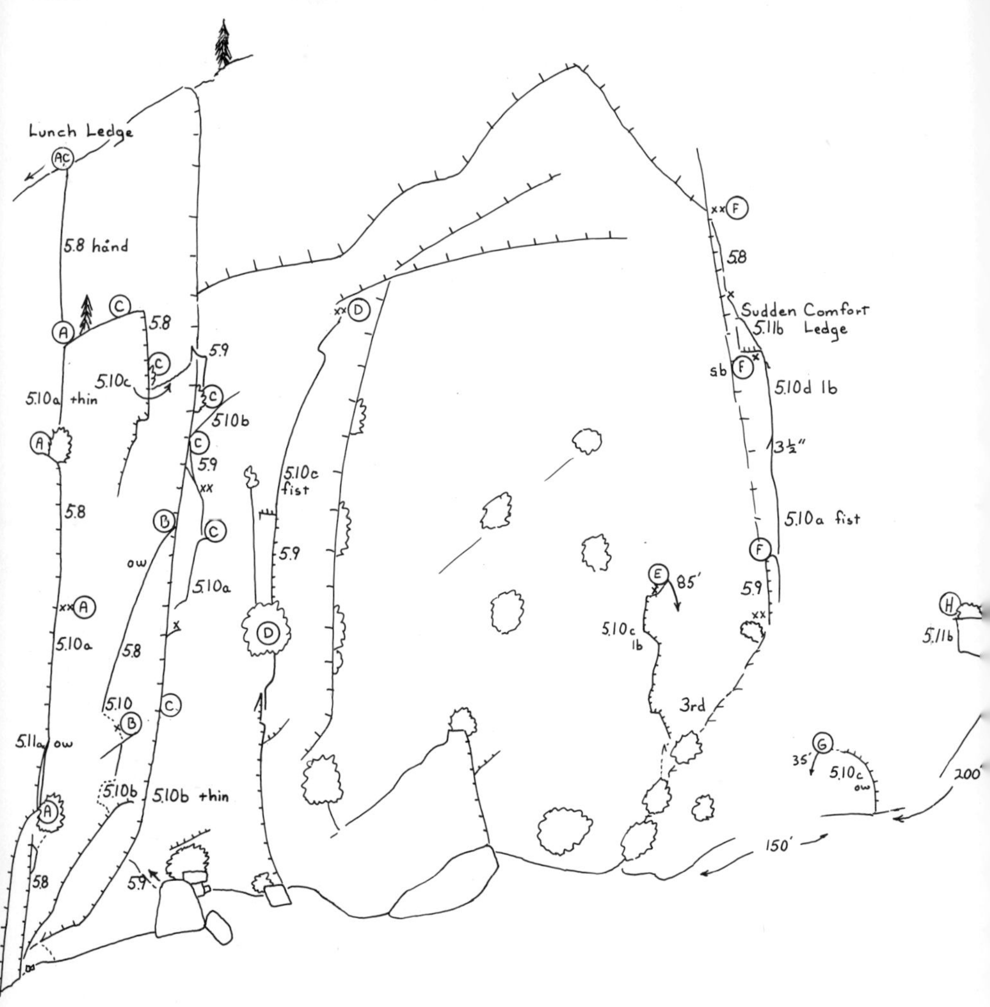

WASHINGTON COLUMN

Approach From the Ahwahnee Hotel or North Pines Campground take the trail toward Indian Caves. Before the caves are reached, however, head up north (near a point where the bike path and the horse trail almost touch), and follow the drainage that comes down fromthe left side of the Column. A climber's trail skirts the base of the cliff all the way east to the bottom of North Dome Gully.

Descent Routes that end atop Washington Column necessitate a familiarity with North Dome Gully, the easiest access to and from the rim in the vicinity. The descent down North Dome Gully is the scene of frequent accidents. The trail from the top of the Column traverses east all the way to the forested gully and completely above the death slabs. Don't descend too early; if in doubt and contemplating rappels, keep traversing. If unfamiliar with the descent, don't attempt it at night.

Photo on pages 233, 237.

- **A Power Failure** 5.11a pro: to 3½"
- **B The Fang** 5.10b
- **C Space Case** 5.10c
- **D Jesu Joy** 5.10c pro: to 3½"
- **E Wing of Bat** 5.10c pro: ¾"-3½"
- **F Dwindling Energy** 5.11b pro: extra large nuts to 3½"
- **G Nowhere Man** 5.10c
- **H Turkey Vulture** 5.11b

WASHINGTON COLUMN – South Face

1 Space Case
2 Direct Route 5.7
3 The Odyssey
4 South Central
5 South Face Route
6 Skull Queen

The Odyssey

V 5.11

Approach Described on the previous page.
Descent Descend North Dome Gully, as described on the previous page.
Photo on page 233.

This route is characterized by rotten rock, bolt hangers that require oval carabiners, and bolts that may not be sound.

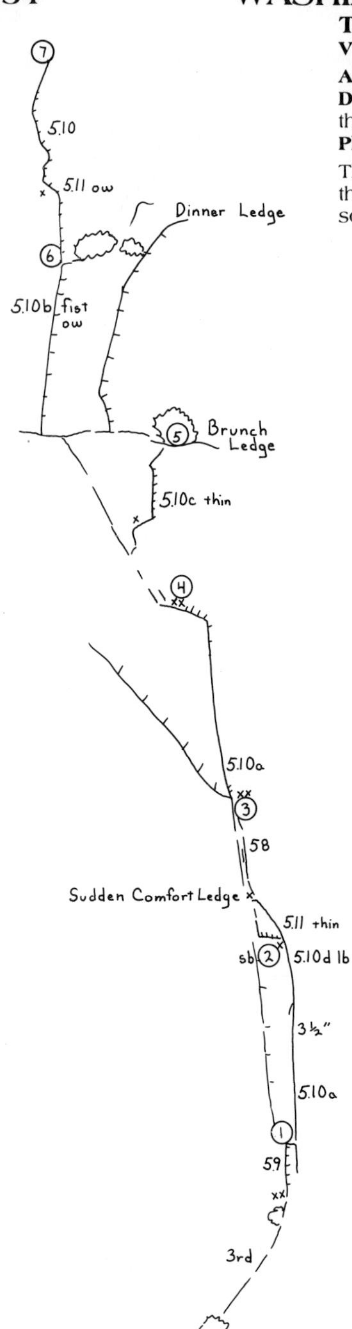

7
5.10
5.11 ow
Dinner Ledge
6
5.10b fist ow
Brunch Ledge
5
5.10c thin
4
5.10a
3
5.8
Sudden Comfort Ledge
5.11 thin
sb 2 5.10d lb
3½"
5.10a
1
5.9
3rd

200 feet
4th loose
13
rotten
5.9
tunnel 12
5.10b
11
5.6
5.10b undercling
10
loose
5.10d
loose 9
5.9
8
1"
5.10c
7

WASHINGTON COLUMN

South Central

V 5.10a A2

Approach, Descent described on page 232.
Photo on page 233.
Hardware

- 1 rurp
- 2 KB
- 5 LA
- 3 ea. ½"-1½"
- 2 ea. 2"
- 1 ea. 2½"-3"
- small hooks
- nuts, including several ⅛"-½"

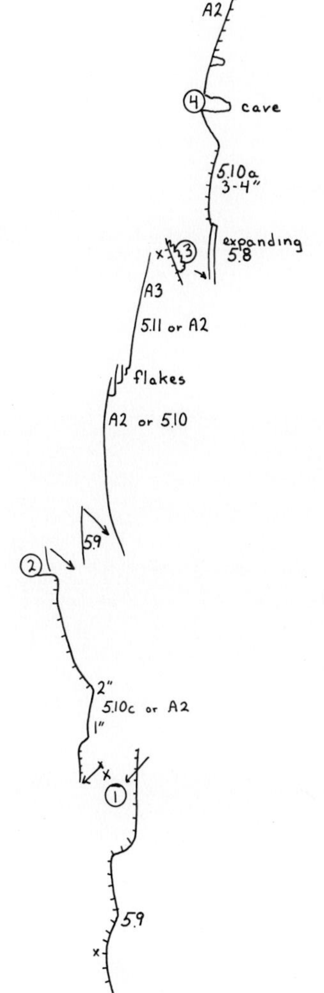

WASHINGTON COLUMN

South Face

V 5.9 A2

Approach, Descent described on page 232.
Photo on page 233.
Hardware
nuts to 3", incl. many 1/8"- 1½"

Skull Queen

V 5.8 A3

Hardware
40 pitons, incl. KB to 2"
rivet hangers
big copperheads

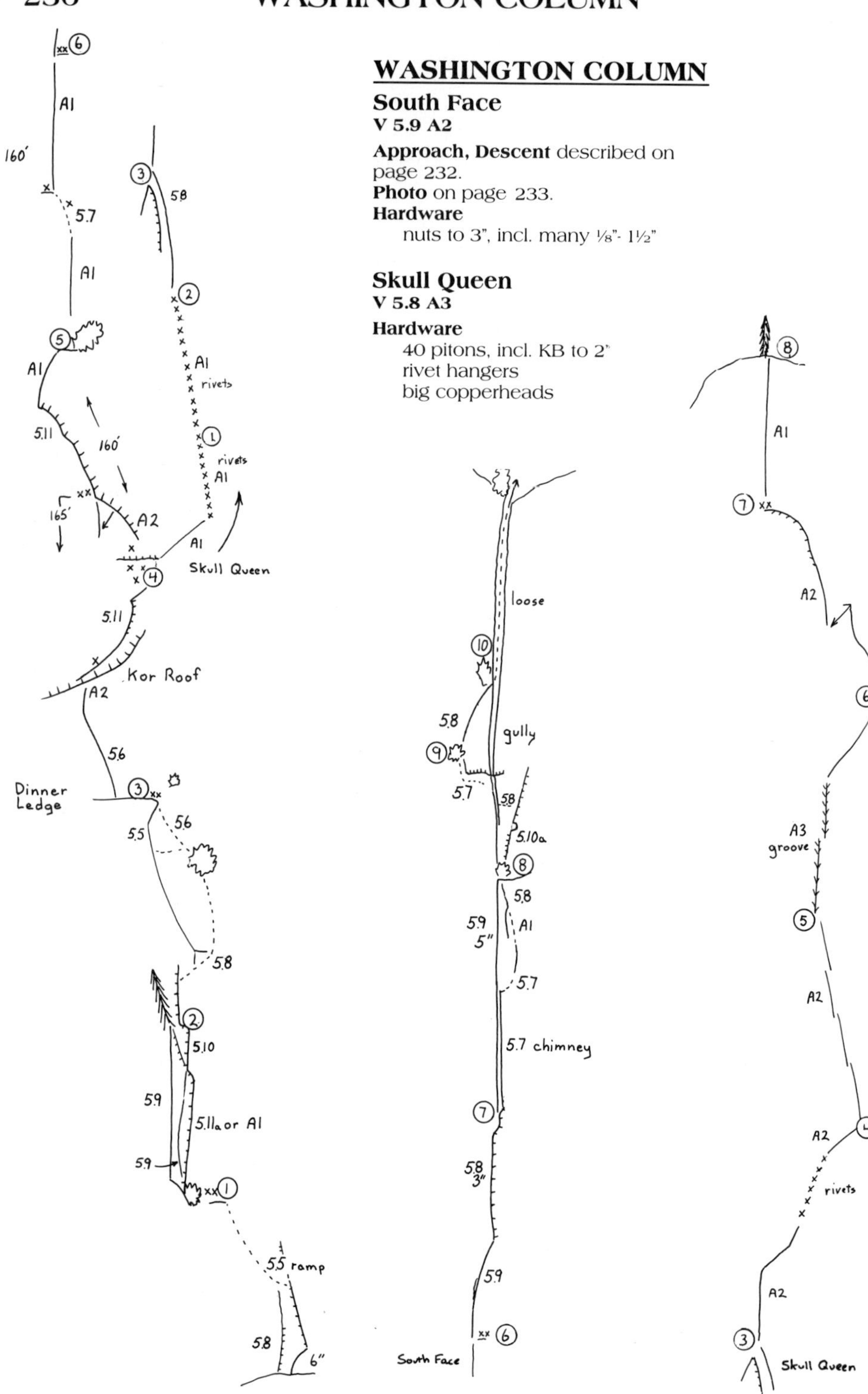

WASHINGTON COLUMN – East Face *N.P.S.*

1 **The Prow**
2 **Electric Ladyland**
3 **Astro Man**
4 **Mideast Crisis**
5 **Great Slab Route**
6 **Bad Wall** V 5.8 A4

WASHINGTON COLUMN

The Prow

V 5.10a A3

Approach, Descent described on page 232.

Photo on page 237.

Hardware

10 LA
3 ea. ½"-1½"
1 ea. 2"
2 ea. 2½"
3 ea. 3"
1 ea. 4"
several copperheads
hooks
tiny nuts to 3½"

A Jojo 5.10b pro: to 3½"
B Tom Cat 5.10b

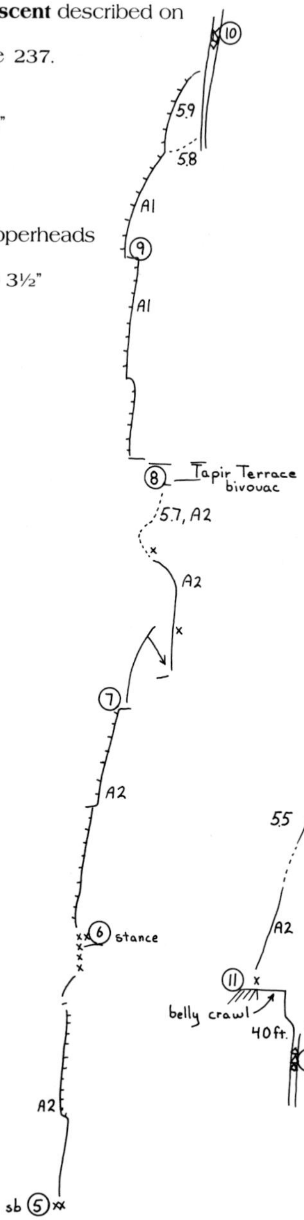

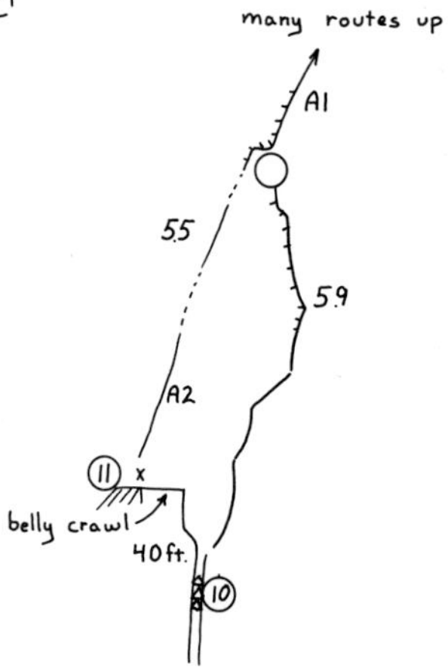

WASHINGTON COLUMN

Electric Ladyland

VI 5.10a A4

Approach This route starts down and right of **Jojo**, around the corner and right of the trees.
Descent described on page 232.
Photo on page 237.
Hardware

4 rurps
8 KB
15 LA
5 ea. ½"-⅝"
4 ea. ¾"-1½"
3 ea. 2"-4"
20 copperheads
tiny nuts to 5"

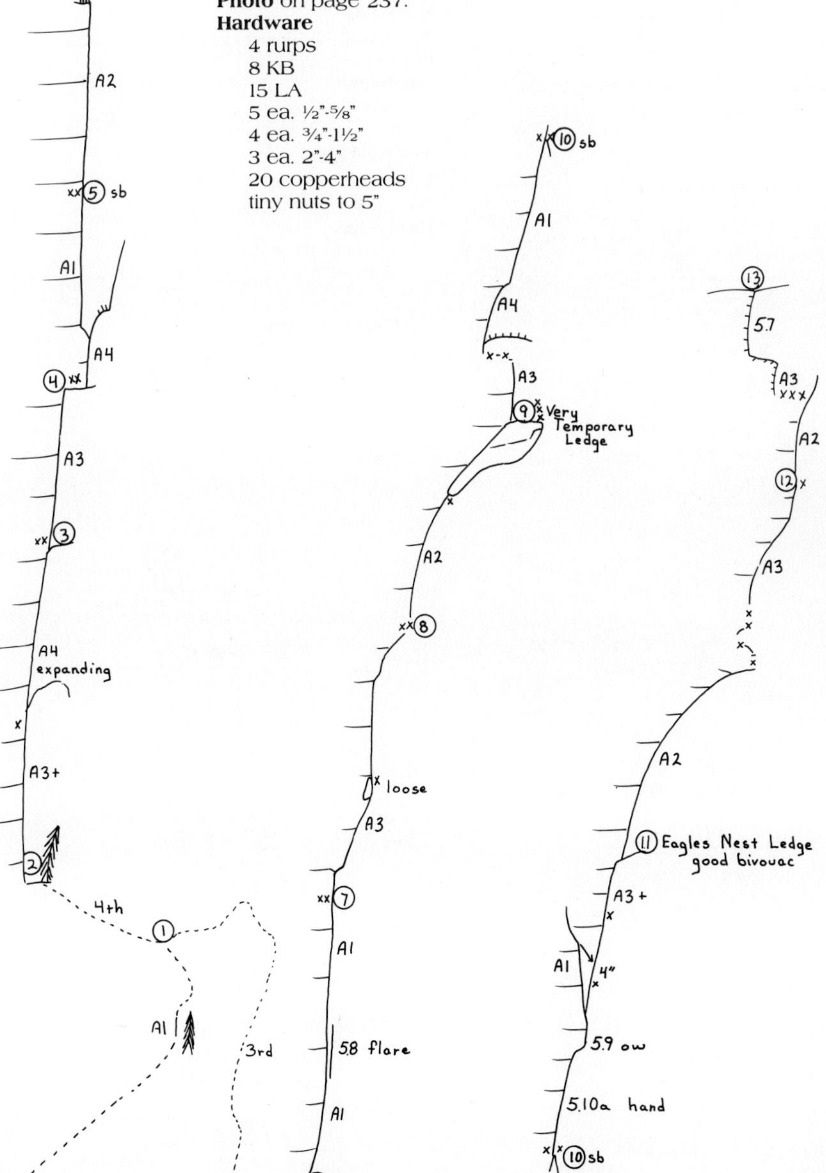

WASHINGTON COLUMN

East Face Route

V 5.10 A2

Approach, Descent described on page 232.
Photo on page 237.
Hardware
nuts to 3½"

Astro Man

V 5.11c

This is the free climb.
Hardware
tiny nuts to 3½",
extra ¼"-2½"

A Terminal Research 5.11c

Washington Column, East Face, 1960. *Tom Frost*

WASHINGTON COLUMN

Mideast Crisis

V 5.8 A4

Approach, Descent described on page 232.
Photo on page 237.
Hardware

7 KB
15 LA
4 ea. ½"-1"
3 ea. 1¼"-1½"
1 ea. 2"-4"
3 ea. Friends to #2½
2 ea. Friends #3-4
2 hooks
many nuts

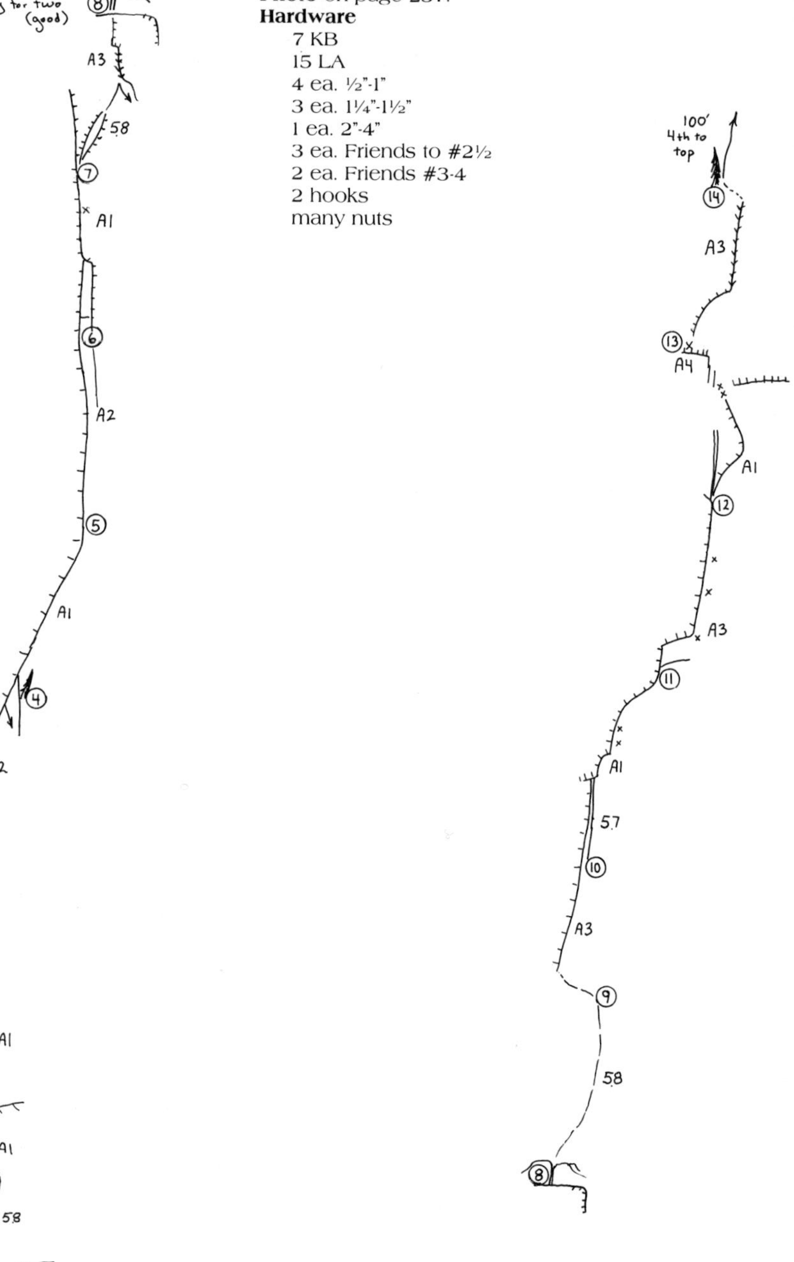

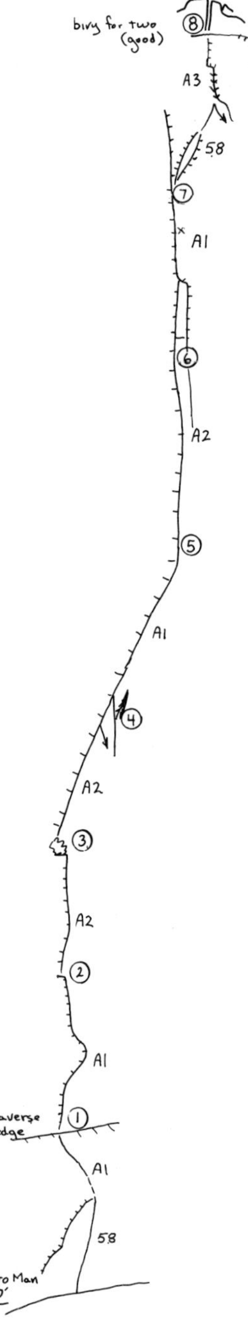

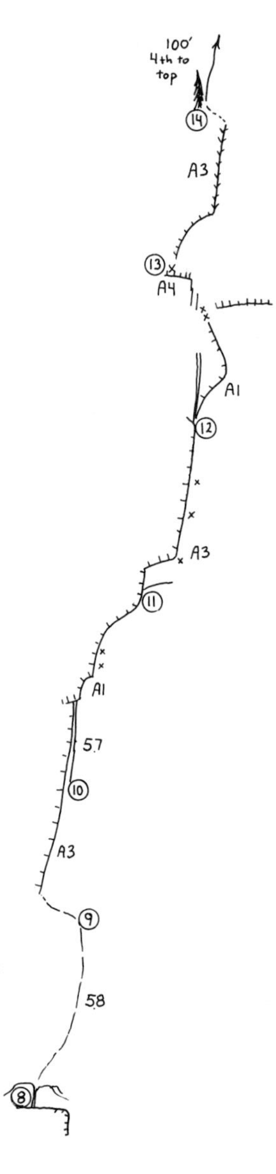

WASHINGTON COLUMN

Great Slab Route

V 5.8 A4

Approach, Descent described on page 232.
Photo on page 237.

Hardware

10 rurps
10 KB
20 LA
3 ea. ½"-1"
2 ea. 1¼"-2"
1 ea. 2½"-4"
nuts
copperheads
hooks

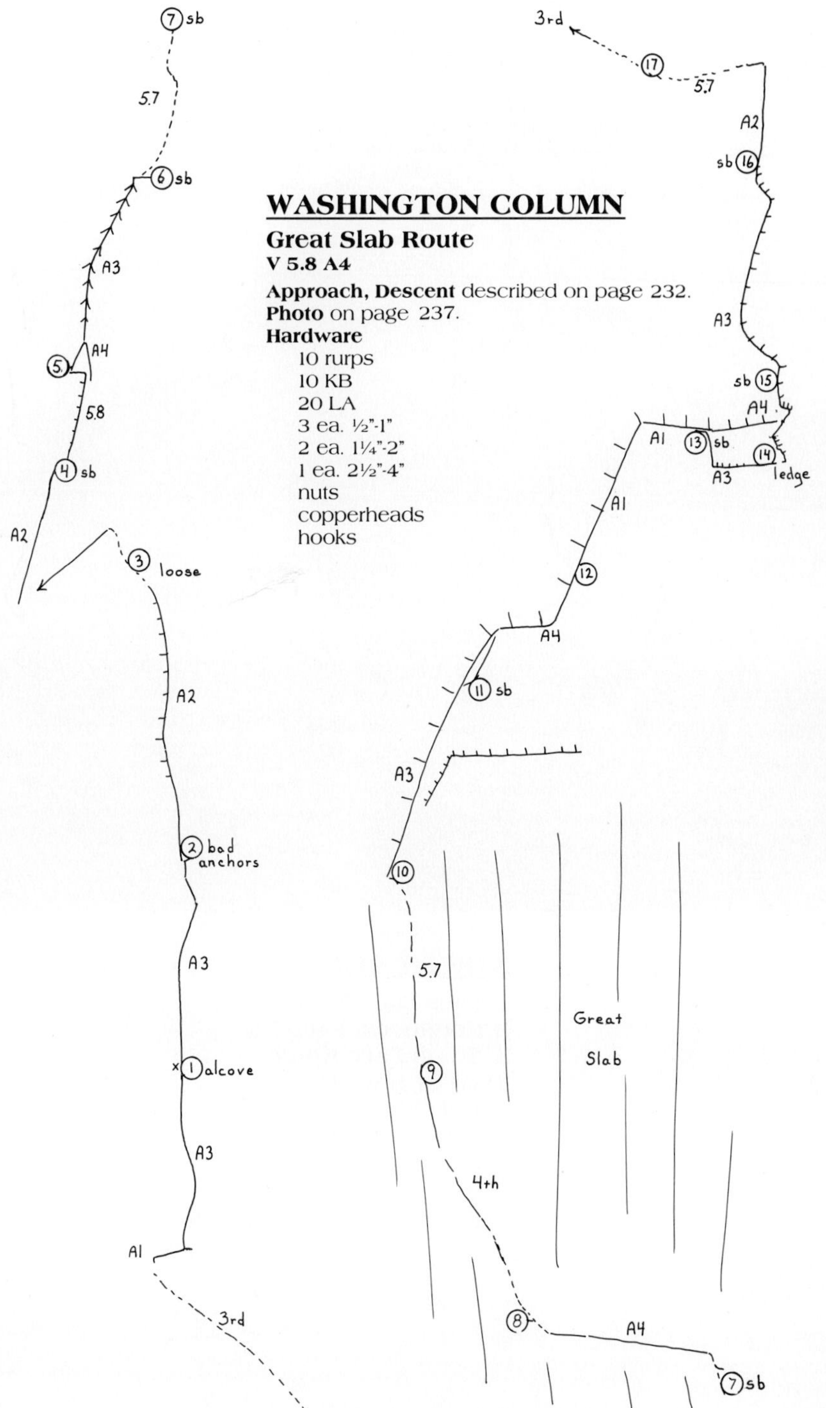

NORTH DOME

1 **West Face Route**
2 **Southwest Face** 5.9
3 **South Face Route**
4 **Crest Jewell**
5 **Dakshina**
6 **Masş Assault** 5.9

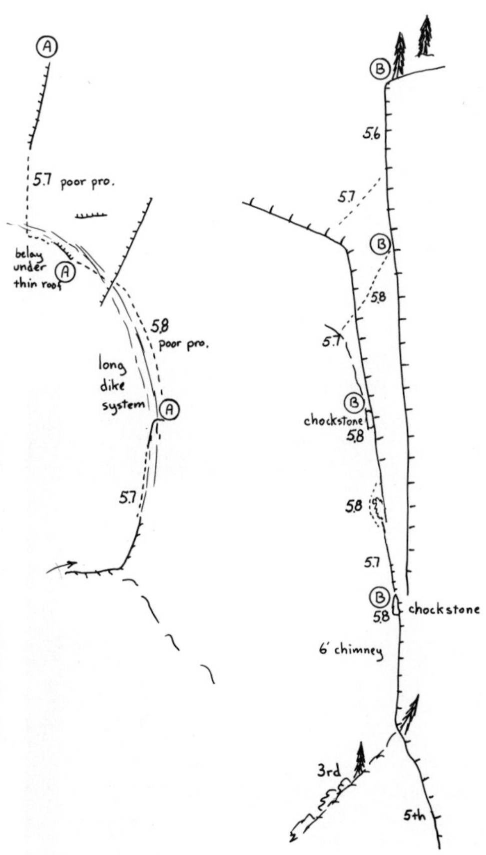

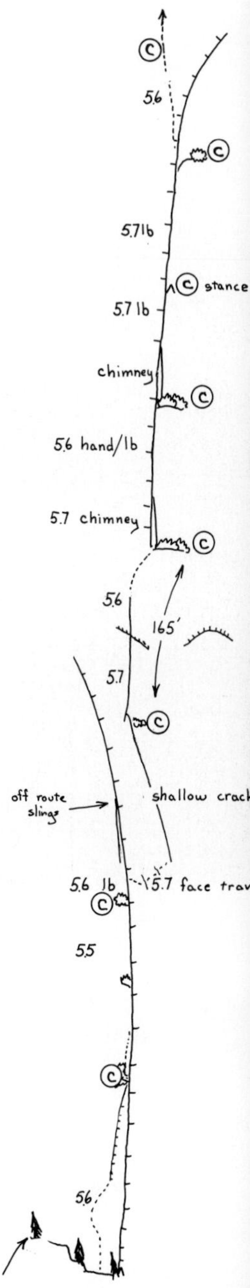

NORTH DOME

Approach The routes on North Dome are often approached by doing the **Royal Arches Route**. Otherwise, walk in from the Tioga Road on the North Dome Trail, or slog up North Dome Gully, described on page 232.
Descent Walk off the west side of the dome and hike down North Dome Gully, as described on page 232.
Photo on page 244.

A Skid Row 5.8 pro: to 2½"
B West Face Route 5.8 pro: to 3"
C South Face Route 5.7

Mass Assault 5.9
From a point near the highest trees, up and right of the huge overhangs on the southeast face, this five pitch route meanders up the slabs above.

NORTH DOME

Crest Jewel

5.10a

Approach described on page 245.
Descent as described on page 245.
Photo on page 244.
Protection
slings and biners

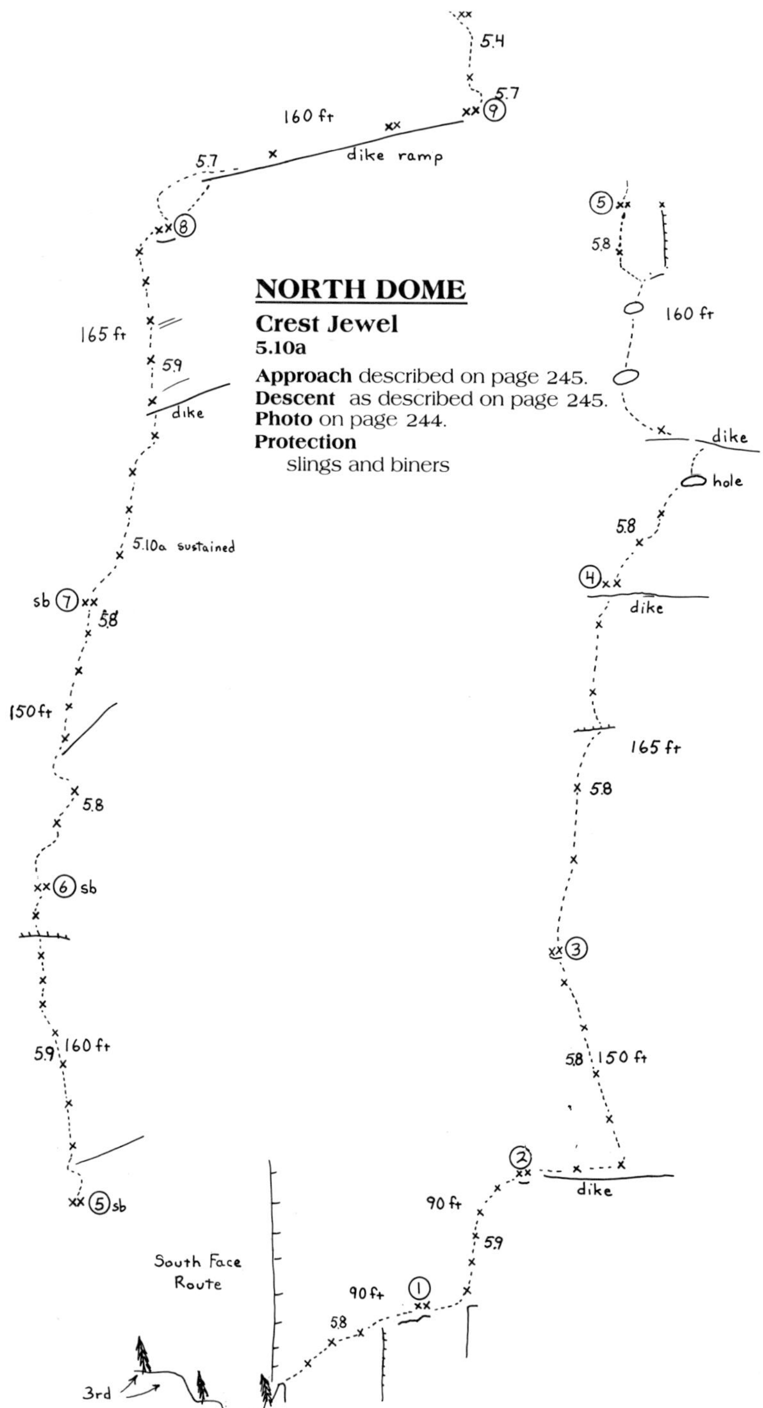

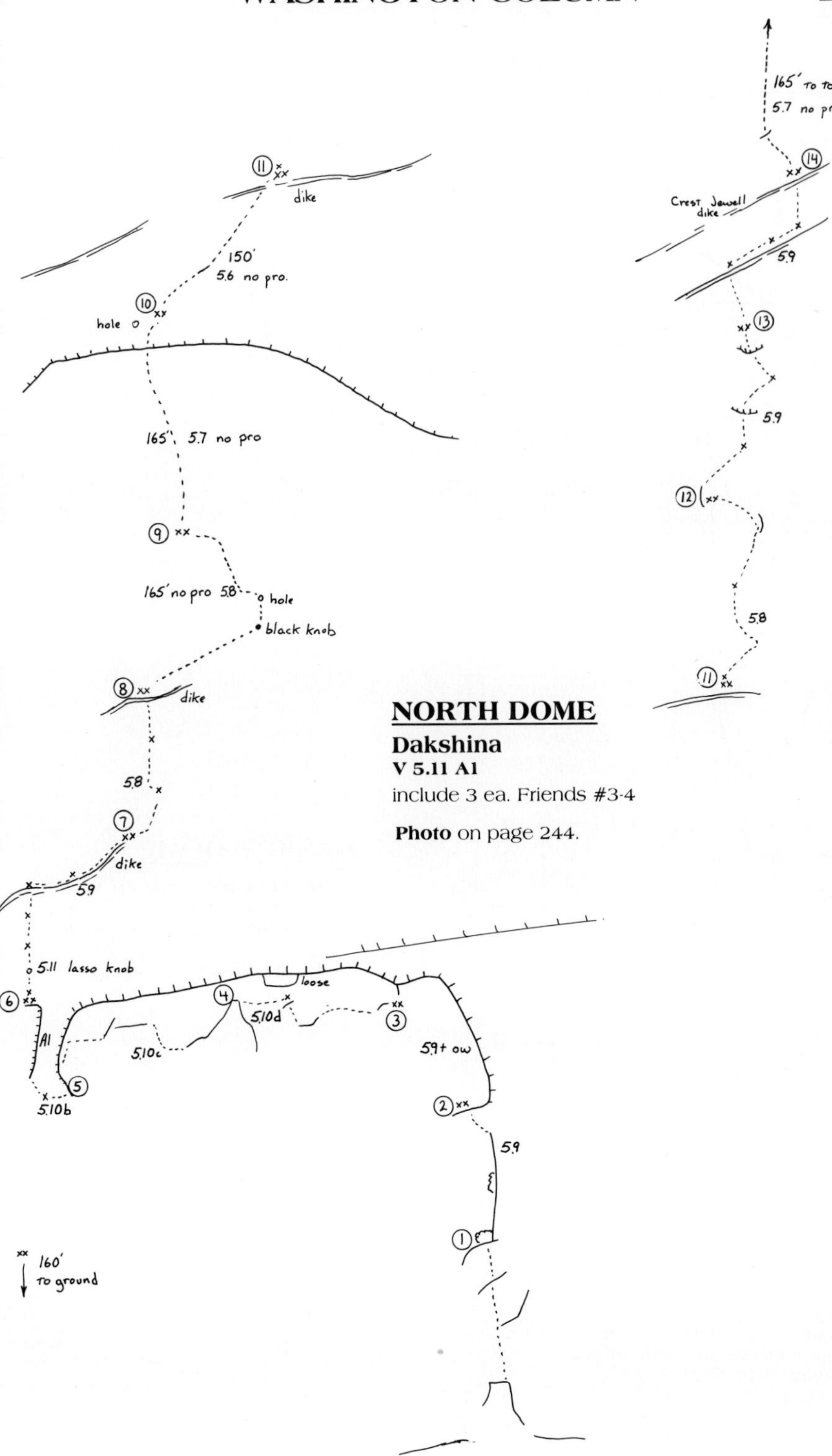

NORTH DOME

Dakshina

V 5.11 A1

include 3 ea. Friends #3-4

Photo on page 244.

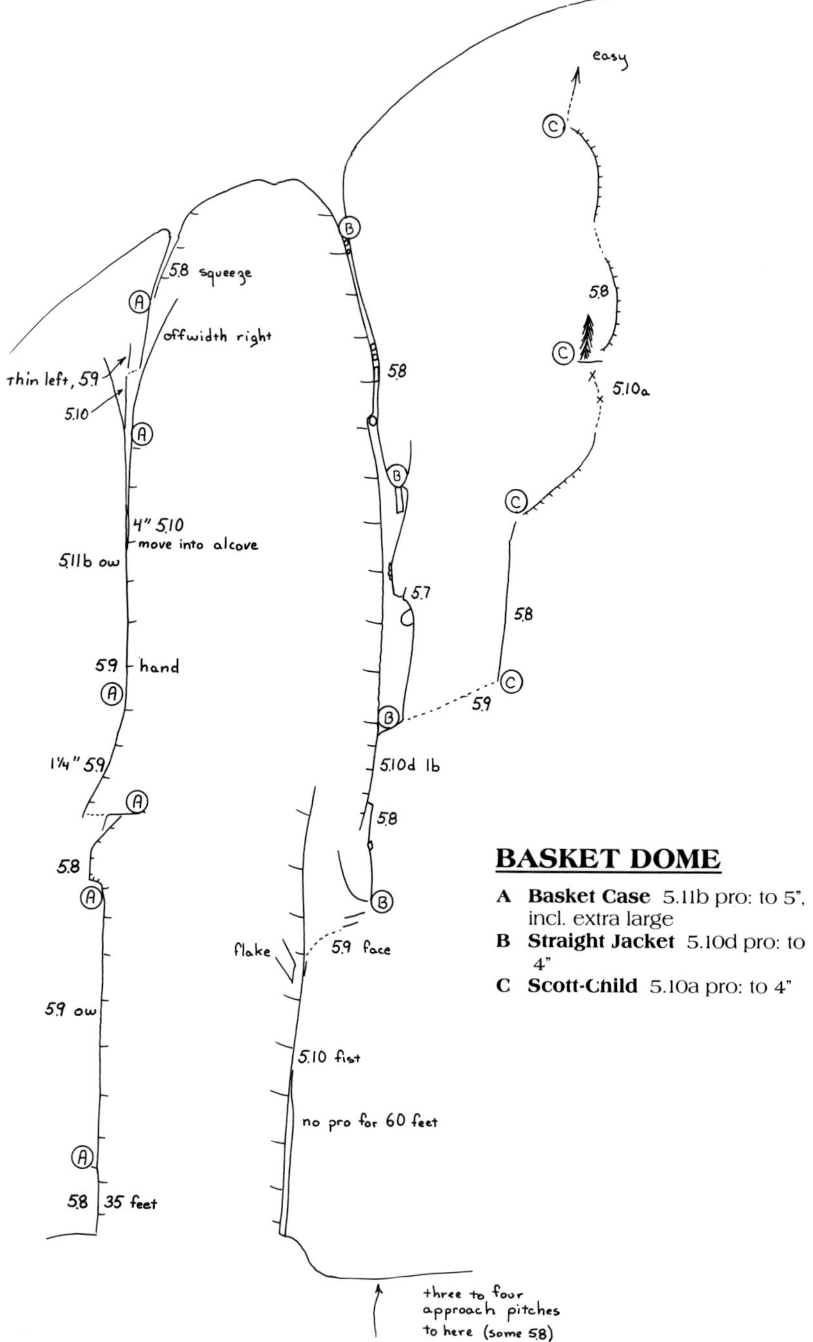

Approach Hike up the Snow Creek Trail almost to the rim, then contour through heavy brush – with some scrambling. Alternatively, try the gully to the right of Apathy Buttress before contouring right. Neither approach is a bargain and several other equally messy ways have been used.

Descent Walk off east to the Snow Creek Trail.

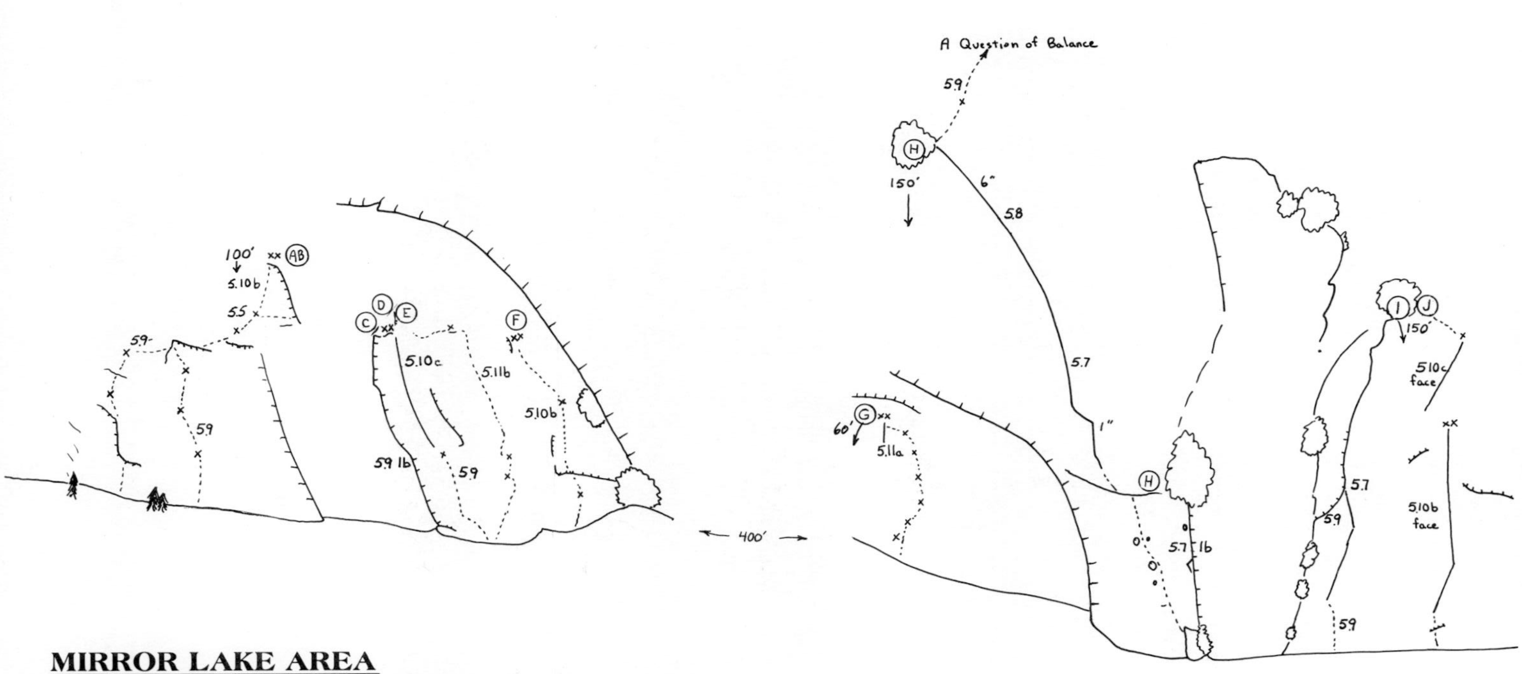

MIRROR LAKE AREA

Approach From the Mirror Lake trailhead, walk east along the north side of the lake for about 1000 feet until within easy reach of south facing slabs to the north.

Mirror Mirror

A Left 5.10b
B Right 5.9

C Eric's Book 5.9
D Thin Man 5.10c pro: to 1"
E Groundhog 5.11b
F Breathalizer 5.10b

G Precious Powder 5.11a
H Werner's Crack 5.8 pro: to 3½"
I The Prude 5.9 pro: to 3½"
J Rurp Rape 5.10c

A Question of Balance 5.9 This route continues for 4 more pitches.

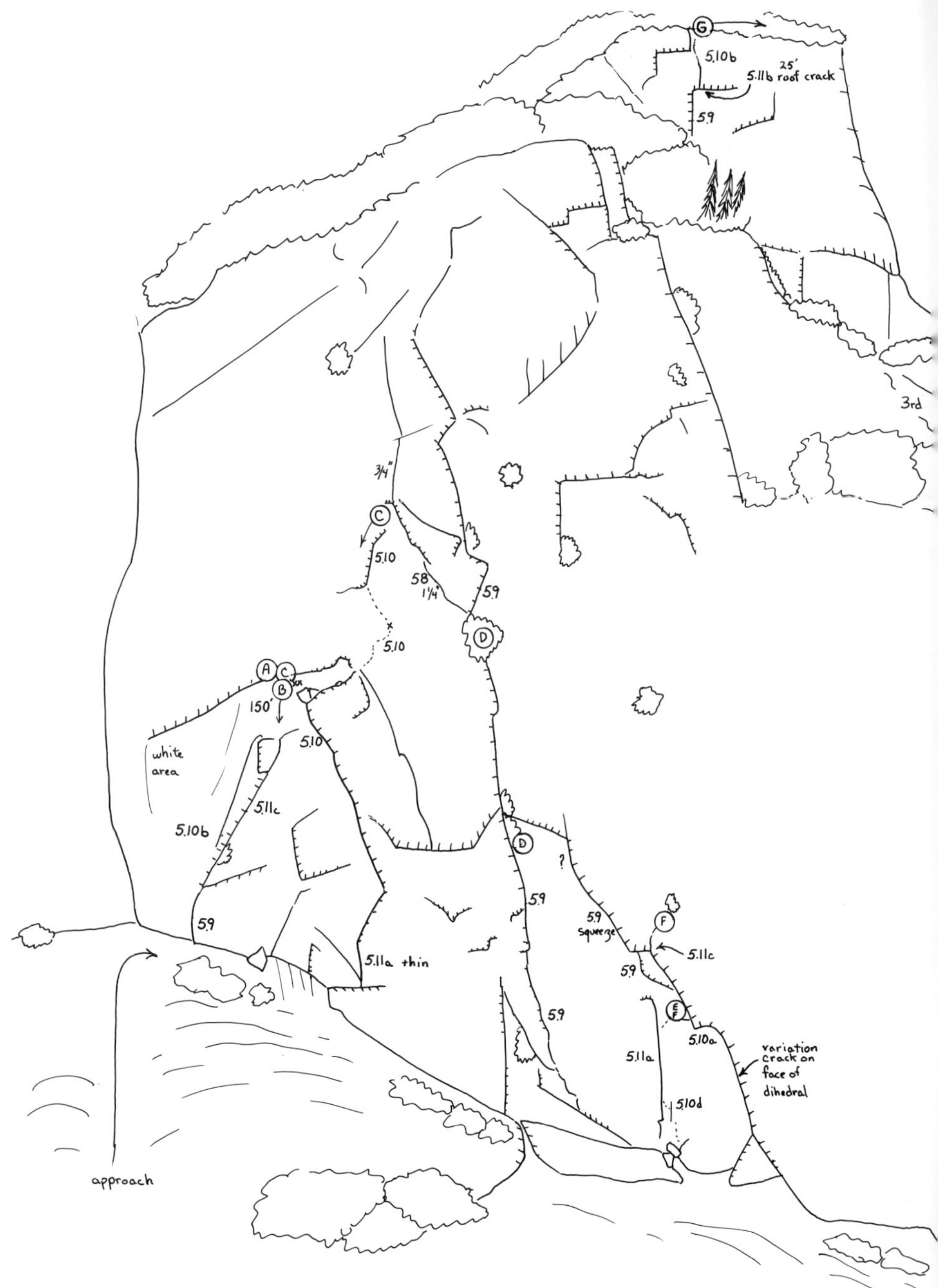

G
5.10b
25'
5.11b roof crack
5.9
3rd
3/4"
C
5.10
58
1 1/4"
5.9
D
5.10
A
C
B
150'
5.10
white area
5.11c
5.10b
D
?
5.9
5.9
5.9 squeeze
F
5.11c
5.9
5.11a thin
5.9
E F
5.10a
variation crack on face of dihedral
5.11a
5.10d
approach

APATHY BUTTRESS

Approach Hike east from the Mirror Lake trailhead for about a half mile, until crossing the first series of creek beds. These are followed straight up the hill until a traverse right leads to the base of the left side of the wall. Ken's Dream is best approached from directly beneath. Free Clinic is approached from a gully on the right side of the wall.

A **Creeping Lethargy** 5.10b
B **Neil Down** 5.11c
C **Water Babies** 5.11a
D **Apathy Buttress** 5.9
E **Destination Zero** 5.11a
F **Valley Syndrome** 5.11c
G **Free Clinic** 5.11b
H **Ken's Dream** 5.10a

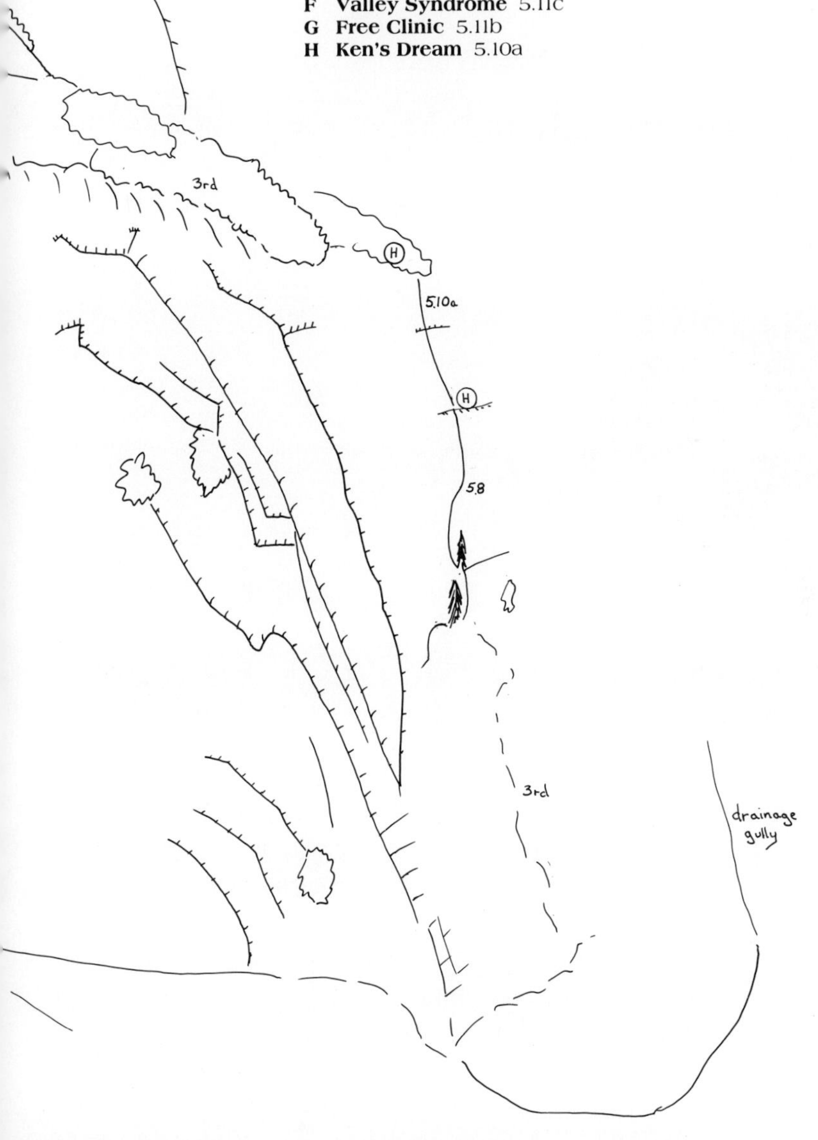

Mt. WATKINS

1 Hook, Line and Sinker
2 South Face Route
3 Tenaya's Terror
4 Bob Locke Memorial Buttress

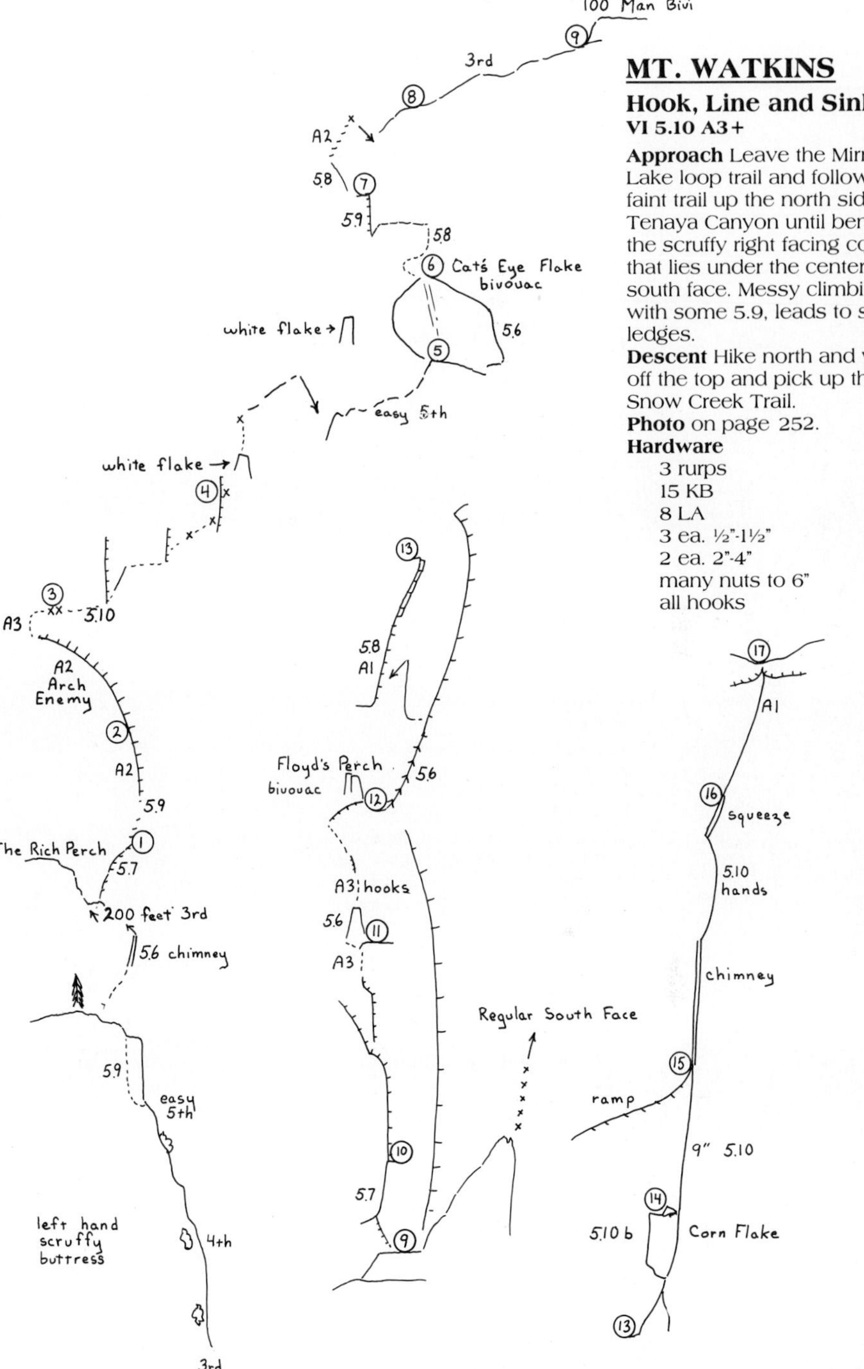

MT. WATKINS

Hook, Line and Sinker

VI 5.10 A3+

Approach Leave the Mirror Lake loop trail and follow a faint trail up the north side of Tenaya Canyon until beneath the scruffy right facing corner that lies under the center of the south face. Messy climbing, with some 5.9, leads to scree ledges.

Descent Hike north and west off the top and pick up the Snow Creek Trail.

Photo on page 252.

Hardware

3 rurps
15 KB
8 LA
3 ea. ½"-1½"
2 ea. 2"-4"
many nuts to 6"
all hooks

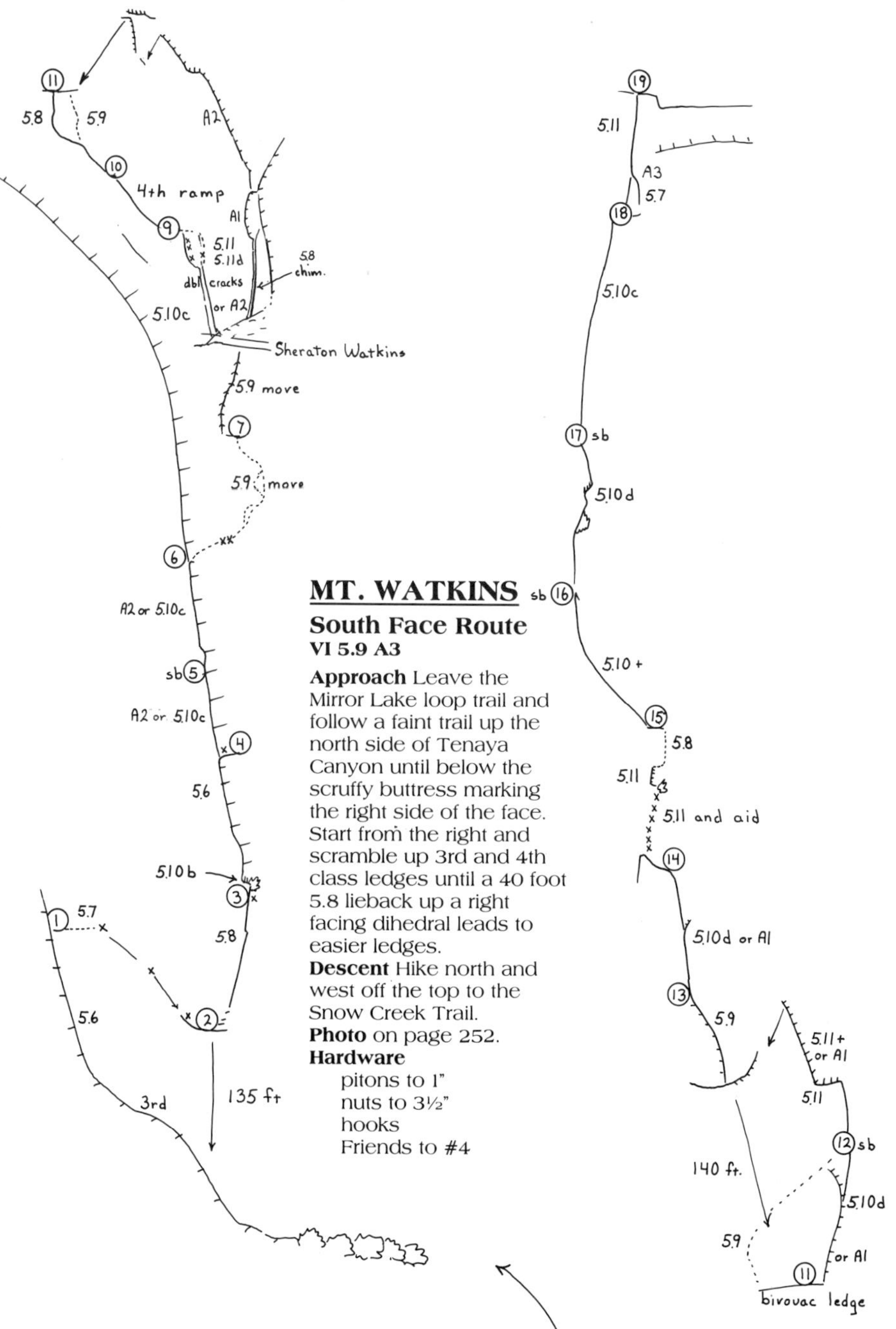

MT. WATKINS

South Face Route

VI 5.9 A3

Approach Leave the Mirror Lake loop trail and follow a faint trail up the north side of Tenaya Canyon until below the scruffy buttress marking the right side of the face. Start from the right and scramble up 3rd and 4th class ledges until a 40 foot 5.8 lieback up a right facing dihedral leads to easier ledges.

Descent Hike north and west off the top to the Snow Creek Trail.

Photo on page 252.

Hardware

pitons to 1"
nuts to 3½"
hooks
Friends to #4

MT. WATKINS

Tenaya's Terror

VI 5.9 A4

Approach Scramble up to the start of the route as for the South Face Route.

Descent Hike north and west off the top to the Snow Creek Trail.

Photo on page 252.

Hardware

- 2 rurps
- 10 KB
- 20 LA
- 3 ea. 5/8"-1"
- 2 ea. 1¼"-1½"
- 2 ea. Friend to #4
- 1 ea. #6 Friend
- hooks
- 10 copperheads
- rivet hangers

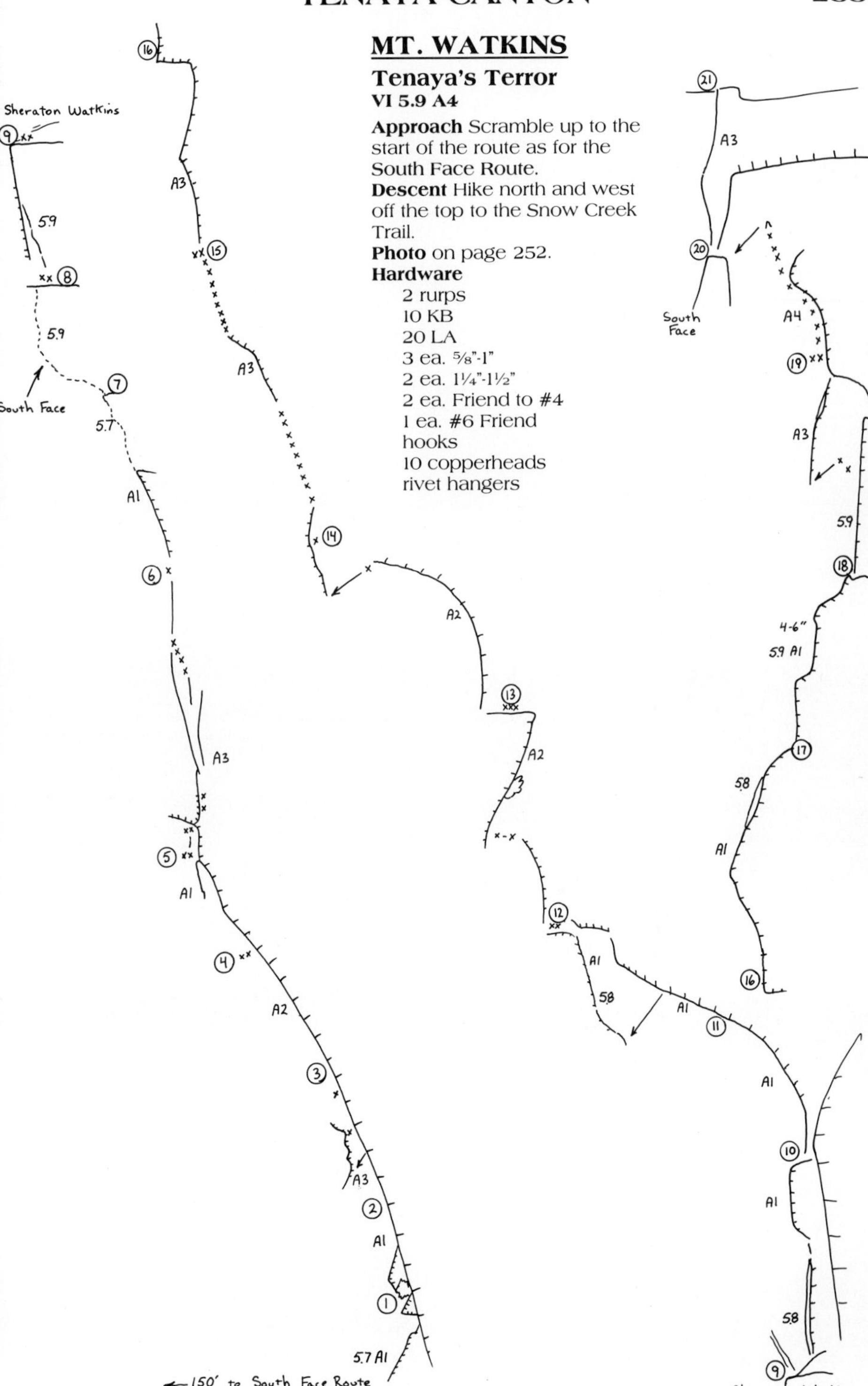

MT. WATKINS

Bob Locke Memorial Buttress

Approach, Descent
Described on page 254.
Photo on page 252.
Hardware

- 8 rurps
- 12 KB
- 12 LA
- 4 ea. 1/2"-5/8"
- 3 ea. 1"-1 1/4"
- 2 ea. 1 1/2"
- many Friends
- 6 copperheads
- dowel hangers
- hooks

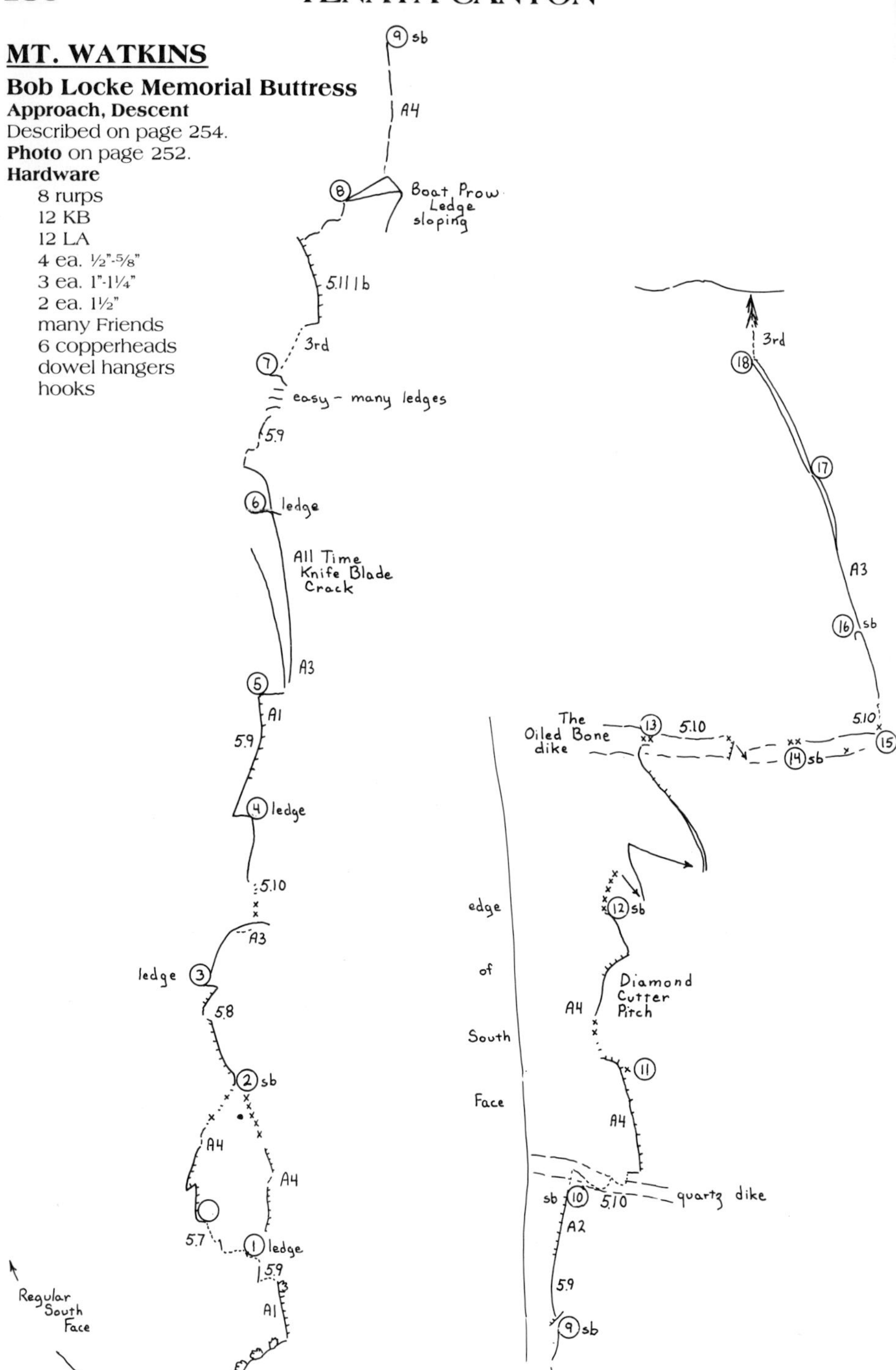

QUARTER DOMES *N.P.S.*

1 East Quarter Dome, North Face
2 East Quarter Dome, Route of All Evil
3 West Quarter Dome, North Face

EAST QUARTER DOME

North Face
V 5.9 A2

Approach Hike far enough up the north side of Tenaya Canyon and an open talus slope will be seen leading most of the way to the base of the rock.
Descent Hike south and west toward the Cloud's Rest trail.
Photo on page 257.
Hardware
light aid rack
nuts to 2½"

Pegasus
V 5.12

This is the free climb.
Protection
many small nuts to 1"
4 ea. #1 Friends
3 ea. #2 Friends
2 ea. #3 Friends

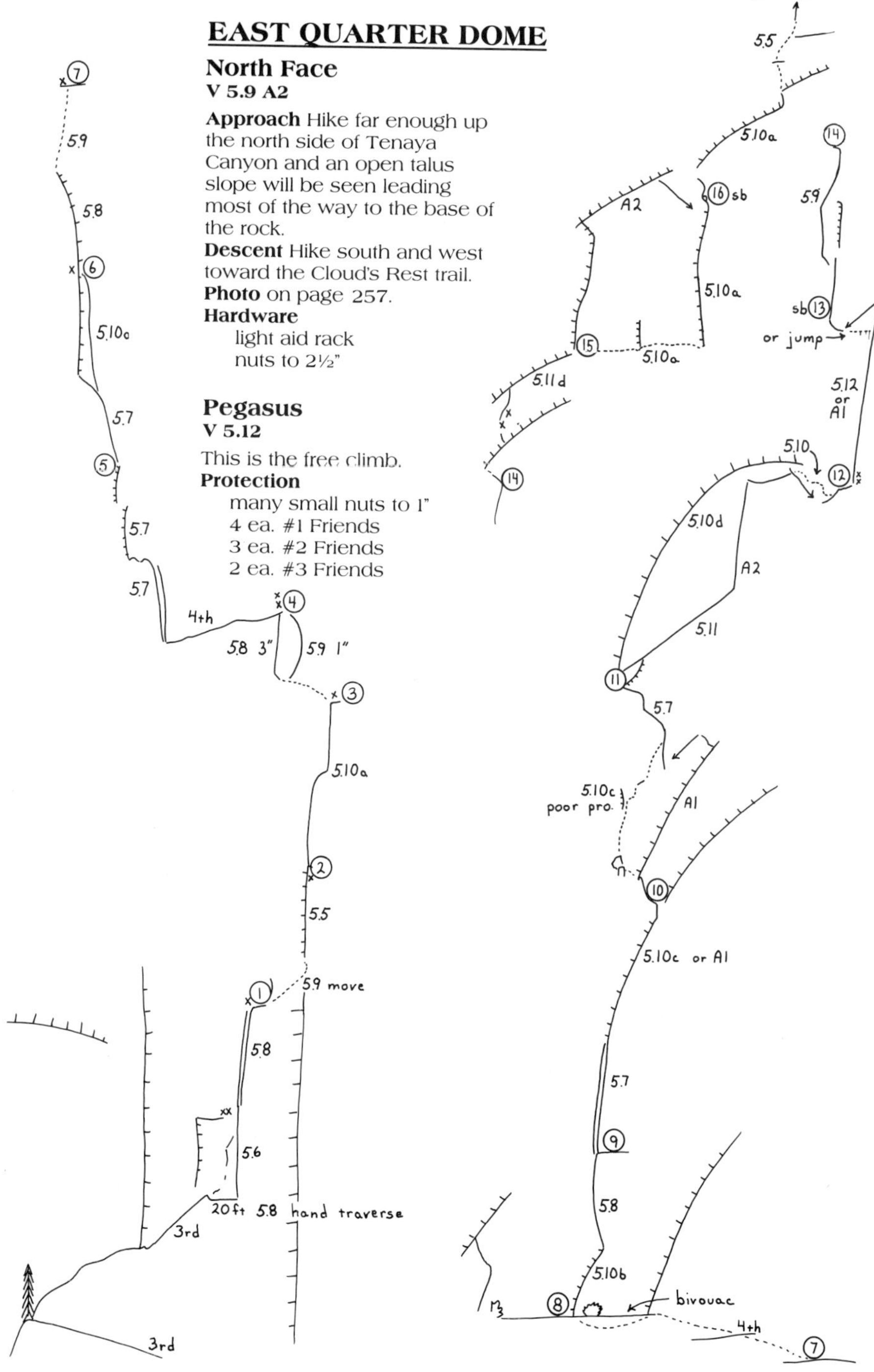

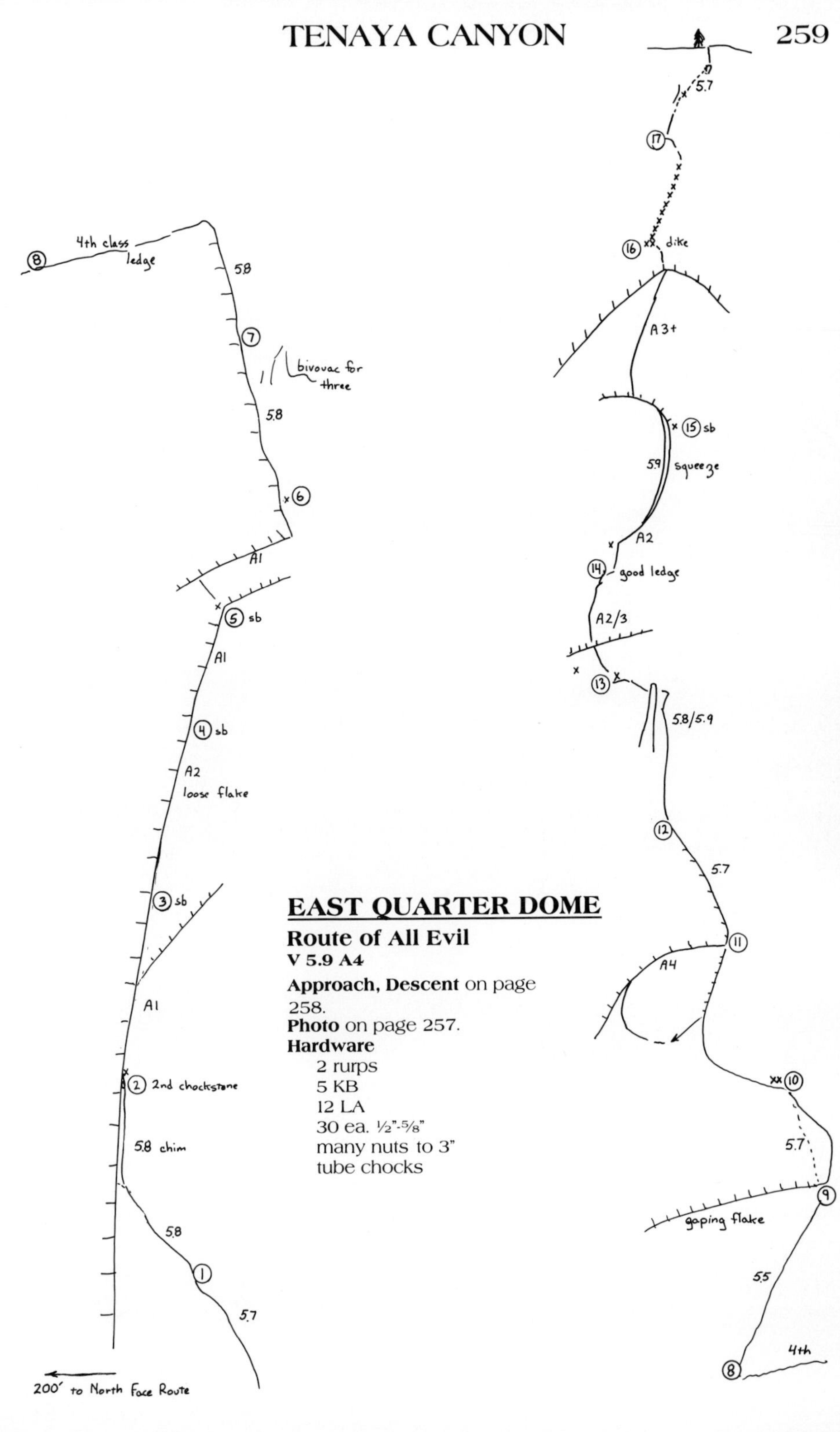

EAST QUARTER DOME

Route of All Evil

V 5.9 A4

Approach, Descent on page 258.

Photo on page 257.

Hardware

2 rurps
5 KB
12 LA
30 ea. ½"-⅝"
many nuts to 3"
tube chocks

WEST QUARTER DOME

North Face

V 5.8 A3

Hardware

2 rurps
5 KB
10 LA
many nuts to 2"

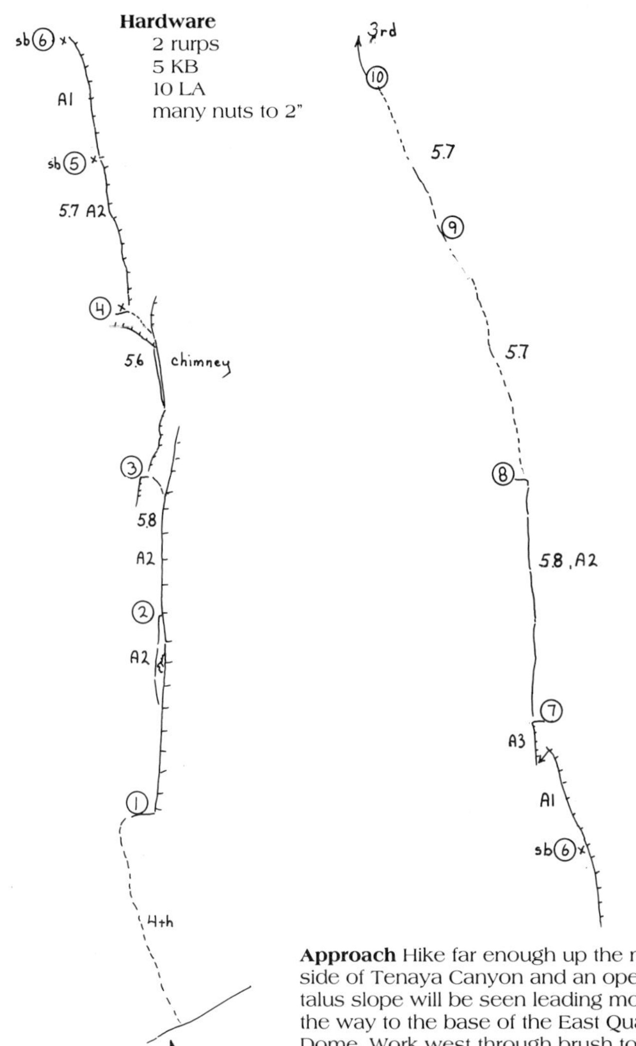

Approach Hike far enough up the north side of Tenaya Canyon and an open talus slope will be seen leading most of the way to the base of the East Quarter Dome. Work west through brush to the base of the rock.

Photo on page 257.

HALF DOME

Northwest Buttress

5.7 A3

Approach Hike up the trail from Happy Isles to the eastern shoulder of Half Dome (about 7.5 miles). From the broad wooded ridge before the cables and sandy switchbacks, drop down and around to the base of the northwest face via a climber's trail. A quicker, more direct, yet very devious approach can be made from the vicinity of Mirror Lake. In general, this begins somewhat upstream from Mirror Lake, trending up and right, with the final section ascending beneath Tis-sa-ack.

Photo on page 262.

Hardware

3 rurps
3 KB
12 LA
4 ea. 1/4"-1½"
1 ea. 2"-3"

A Final Exam 5.10d
pro: to 3½", incl. many 2½"-3"

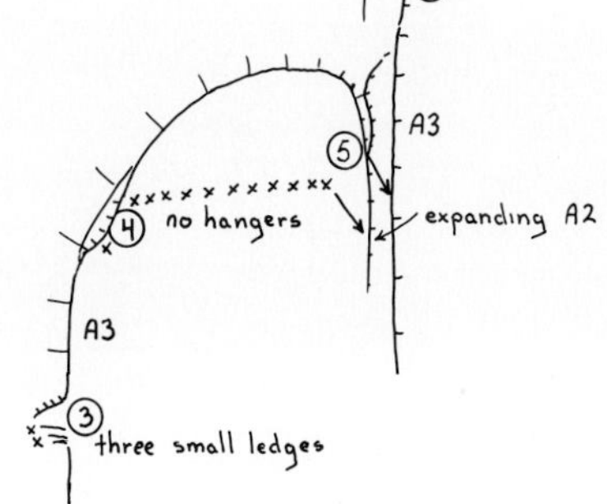

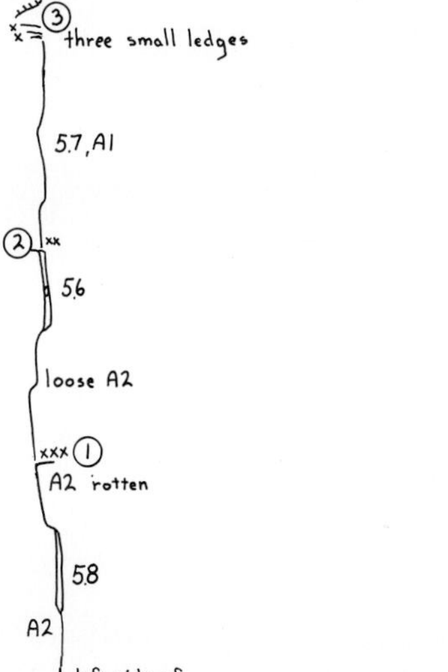

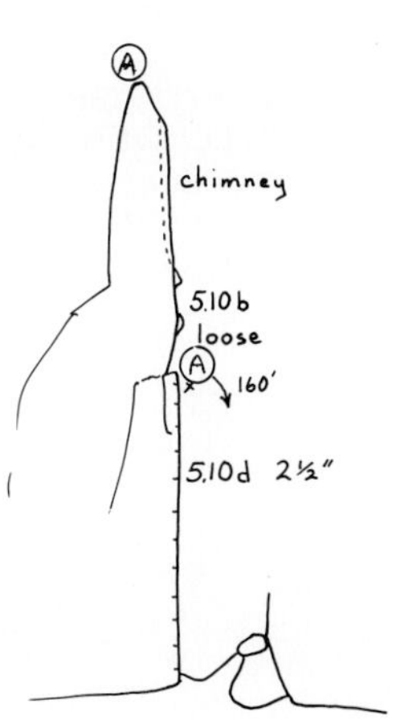

HALF DOME – Northwest Face

N.P.S.

1 Northwest Buttress
2 Final Exam
3 Regular Northwest Face Route
4 Arcturas
5 Direct Northwest Face
6 Tis-sa-ack
7 Zenith
8 Bushido

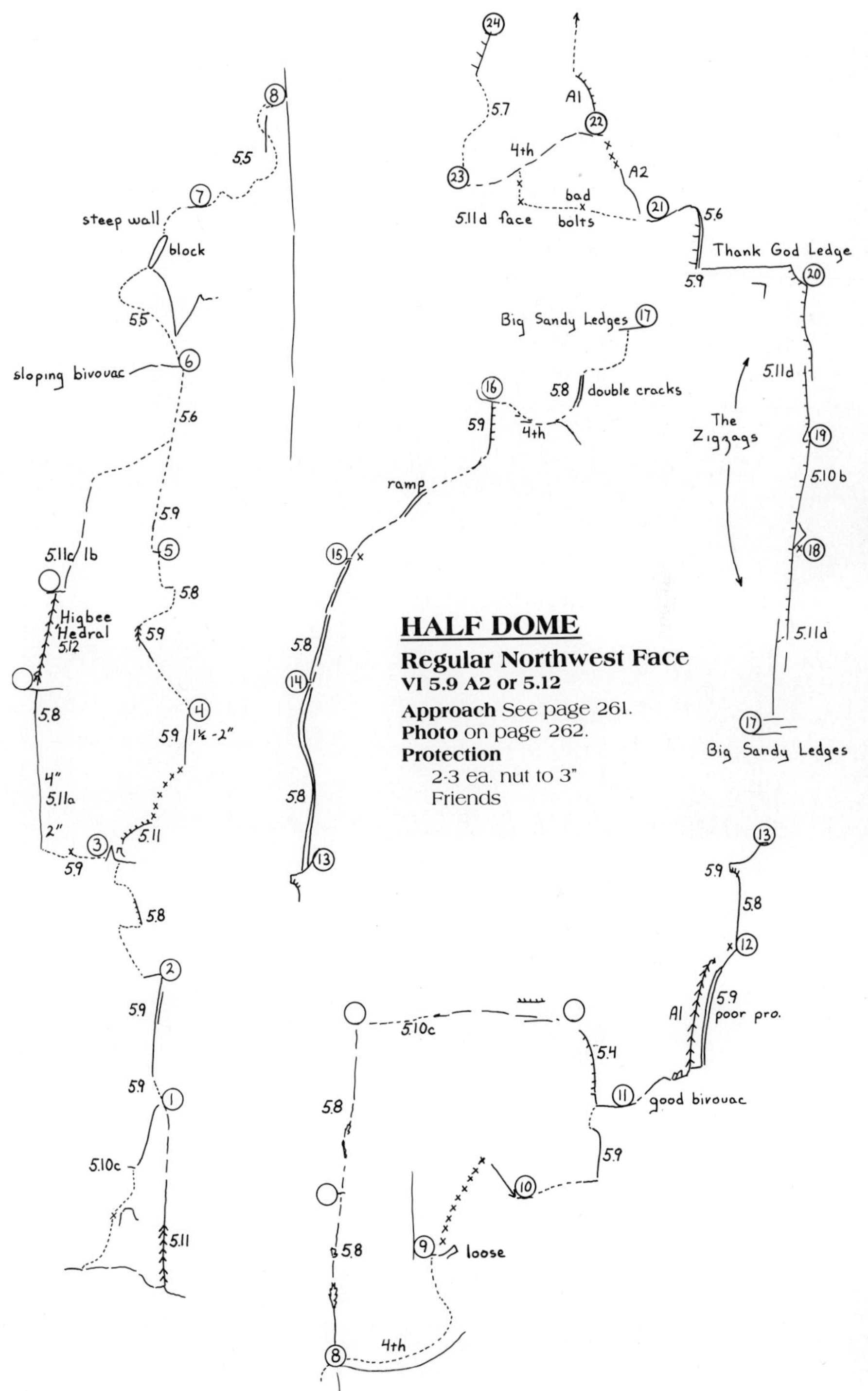

HALF DOME

Regular Northwest Face

VI 5.9 A2 or 5.12

Approach See page 261.
Photo on page 262.
Protection
2-3 ea. nut to 3"
Friends

HALF DOME

Arcturas

VI 5.7 A4

Approach as described on page 261.
Photo on page 262.

4 rurps
4 KB
12 LA
4 ea. ½"-1½"
3 ea. 2"
1 ea. 2½"-4"

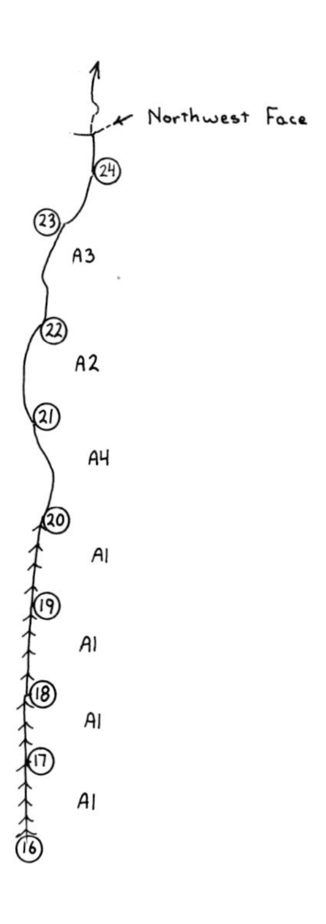

HALF DOME

Direct Northwest Face

VI 5.10 A3+

Approach as described on page 261.

Photo on page 262.

- 1 rurp
- 3 KB
- 8 LA
- 2 ea. ½"-1¼"
- 1 ea. 2½"
- large hooks
- nuts to 3½"

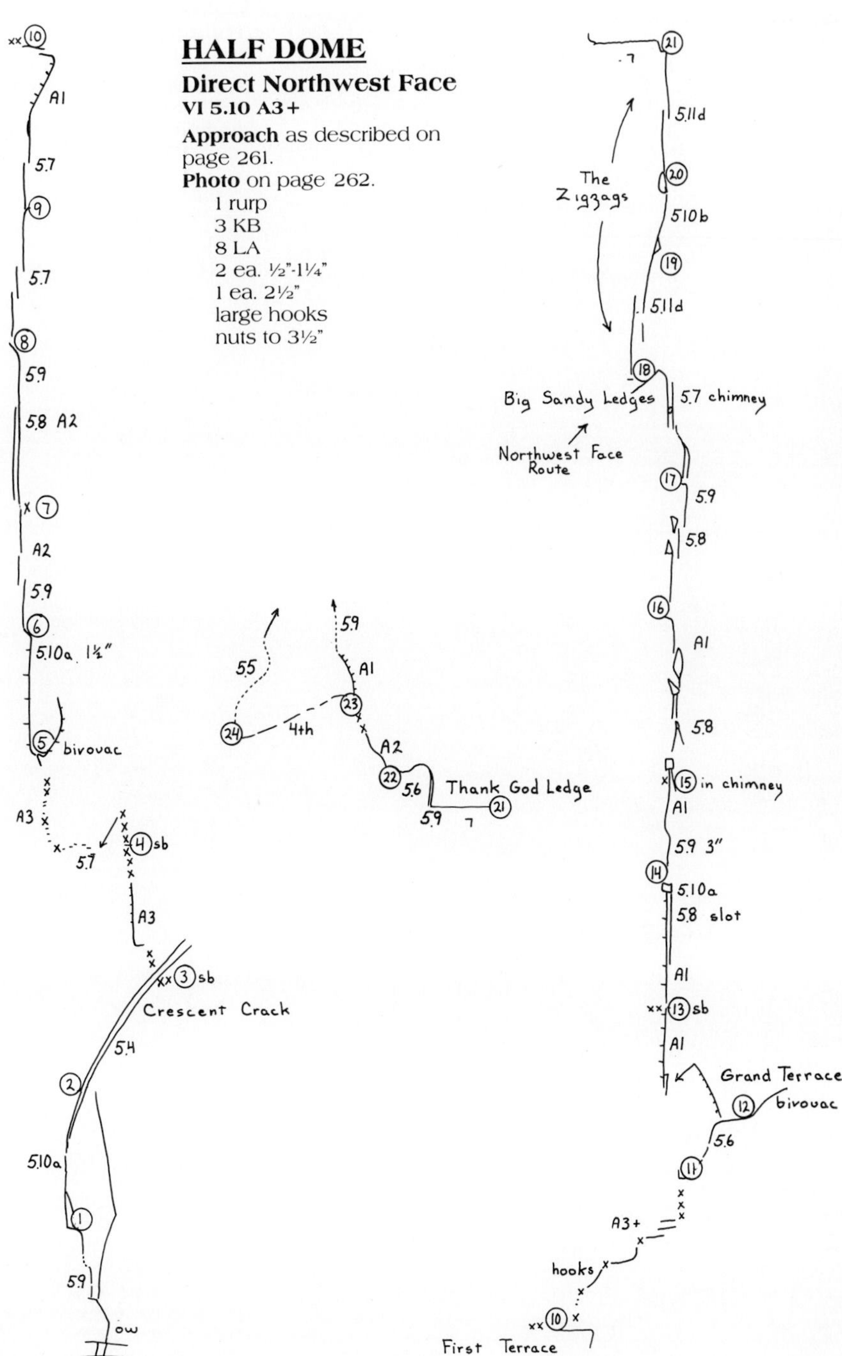

HALF DOME

Tis-sa-ack

VI 5.10 A4

Approach as described on page 261.
Photo on page 262.

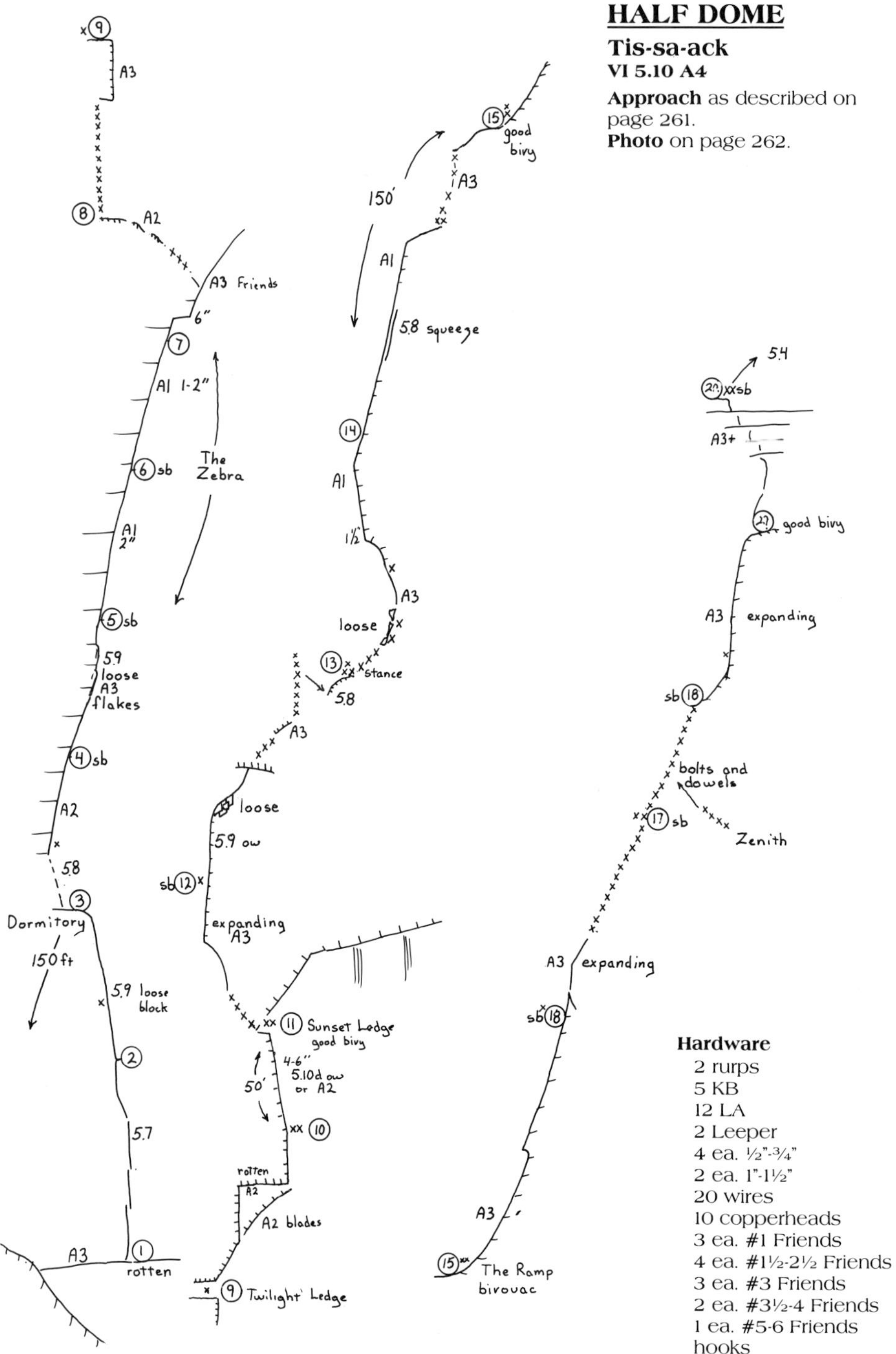

Hardware
- 2 rurps
- 5 KB
- 12 LA
- 2 Leeper
- 4 ea. ½"-¾"
- 2 ea. 1"-1½"
- 20 wires
- 10 copperheads
- 3 ea. #1 Friends
- 4 ea. #1½-2½ Friends
- 3 ea. #3 Friends
- 2 ea. #3½-4 Friends
- 1 ea. #5-6 Friends
- hooks

HALF DOME

Zenith

VI 5.9 A5

Approach as described on page 261.
Photo on page 262.
Hardware
- 8 rurps
- 25 KB
- 25 LA
- 6 ea. ½"-¾"
- 5 ea. 1"
- 2 ea. 1¼"-2"
- 1 ea. 2½"
- 1 ea. 4"
- many Friends
- nuts

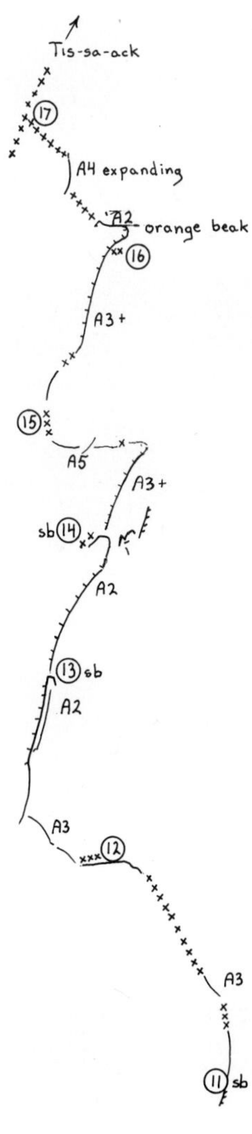

HALF DOME

Arctic Sea

VI 5.10 A4

Approach as described on page 261.

Hardware

10 rurps
15 KB
15 LA
3 ea. ½"-¾"
2 ea. 1"-1½"
4 ea. 3"-7" } for 2nd pitch
wood blocks } only
3 ea. Friend
wires
50 copperheads
all hooks

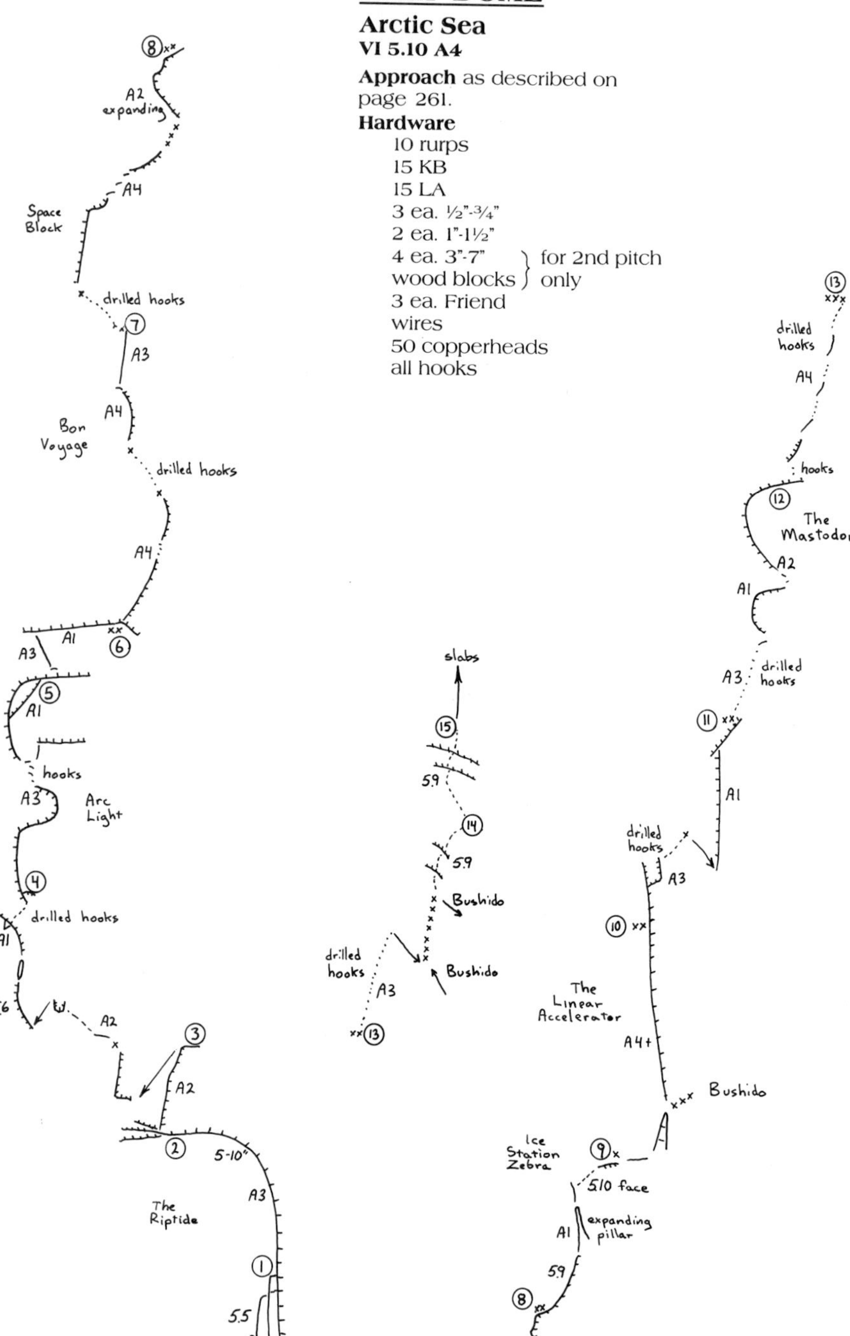

HALF DOME

Bushido

VI 5.10 A4

Approach as described on page 261.
Photo on page 262.
Hardware
60 pitons to 6"
many Friends and nuts

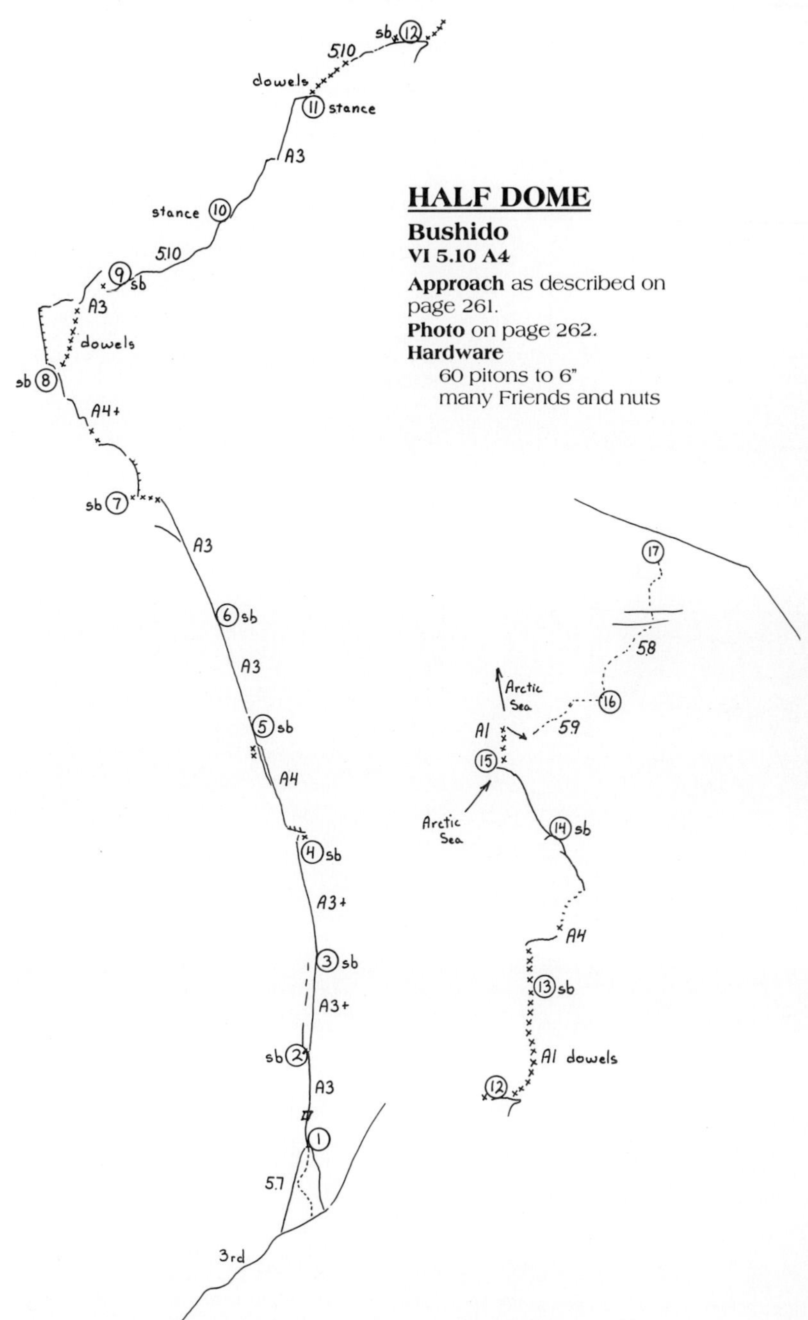

HALF DOME – Southwest Face

Approach Hike up from Happy Isles towards Little Yosemite. Once the trail levels out above Nevada Falls, walk up a short hillside and work to the north and west to Lost Lake. Lost Lake may also be reached from between Mt. Broderick and Liberty Cap. In this case, work up talus slopes under the northwest corner of Liberty Cap (site of recent rockfall activity) well before Nevada Falls is reached, and contour around into the chasm between the two formations. The other side of this canyon opens out directly at Lost Lake. A trail leading along its left side heads up towards slabs and the Dome. Slabs that lie under the brushy southwest shoulder of Half Dome are best skirted on the right. Traverse left on ledges above these slabs further than you think, and follow rough paths back right and up to the base of the southwest face in the vicinity of the Snake Dike. **Photo** on page 272.

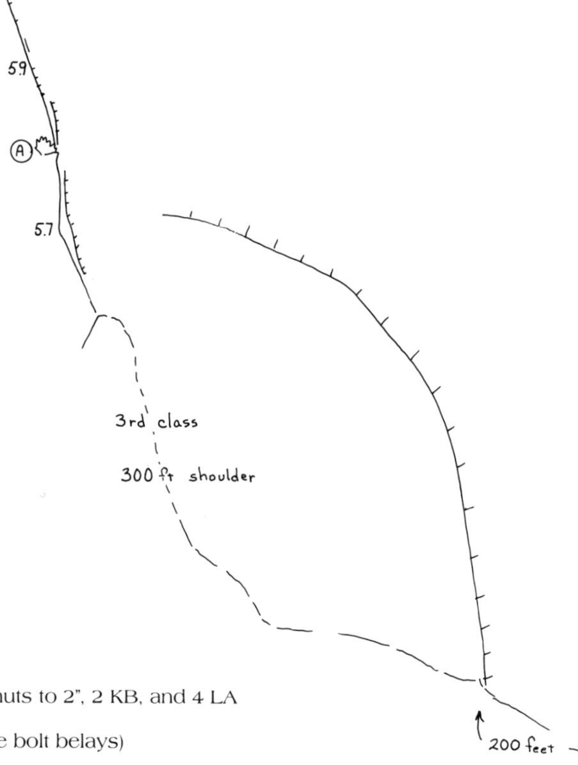

A **On the Edge** 5.11b pro: nuts to 2", 2 KB, and 4 LA
B **Salathé Route** 5.10b
C **The Deuceldike** 5.9 (one bolt belays)
D **Snake Dike** 5.7
E **Eye in the Sky** 5.10b
F **Snake Dance** 5.9+

D
5.2
D
5.5
165'+
2nd / 3rd class slabs
xx D
5.6
E
2nd / 3rd class slabs
5.3
5.7
F
xx D
165'
5.4
5.5
5.2
5.10b
C
5.3
xx E
5.2
dike
F
C
5.6
5.6
B
5.2
5.4
D xx
xx E
5.5
5.9
dike
F
5.4
5.3
B
5.9+
runout
5.9 face
C
5.2
xx
dike
5.10b
E
5.10a
5.8+
D xx
5.10a
F
sb xx
5.9
5.4
5.8+
B
xC
dike
dike
5.8
5.9
5.7
D xx
5.9 traverse
5.7
5.7
xx E F
D xx
B
5.9+
165'
5.5
5.7
friction
no pro.
5.8
E
5.6
400'
approach

HALF DOME – Southwest Face

1 Salathé Route
2 Snake Dike
3 Autobahn

HALF DOME

The Fast Lane

5.11+

Approach as described on page 270. Traverse around east on ledges below the start of Snake Dike.
Photo on page 272.
Protection
RP's
Rocks
1 ea. Friends to #3

Autobahn

5.11+

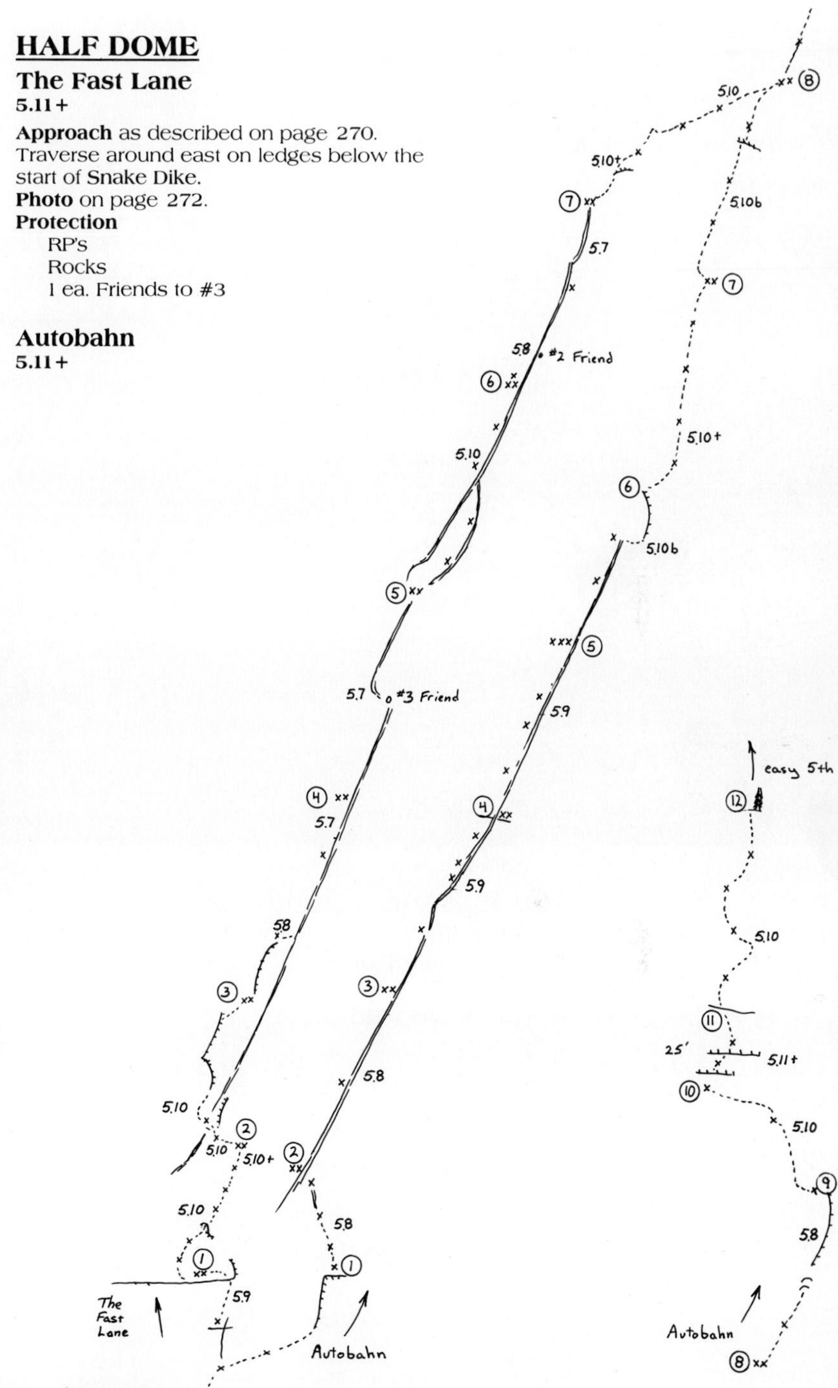

HALF DOME – South Face

1 **Autobahn**
2 **South Face Route**
3 **Karma**
4 **Call of the Wild** 5.10a

HALF DOME

South Face Route

VI 5.8 A4

Approach Hike up to the south face as for the southwest face, page 270.
Photo on page 274.
Hardware
3 KB
20 LA
7 Leepers
4 ea. ½"-¾"
6 ea. 1"-1½"
5 ea. 2"
3 ea. 2½"
2 ea. 3"-5"
rivet hangers
bat hooks
bolt hangers, nuts

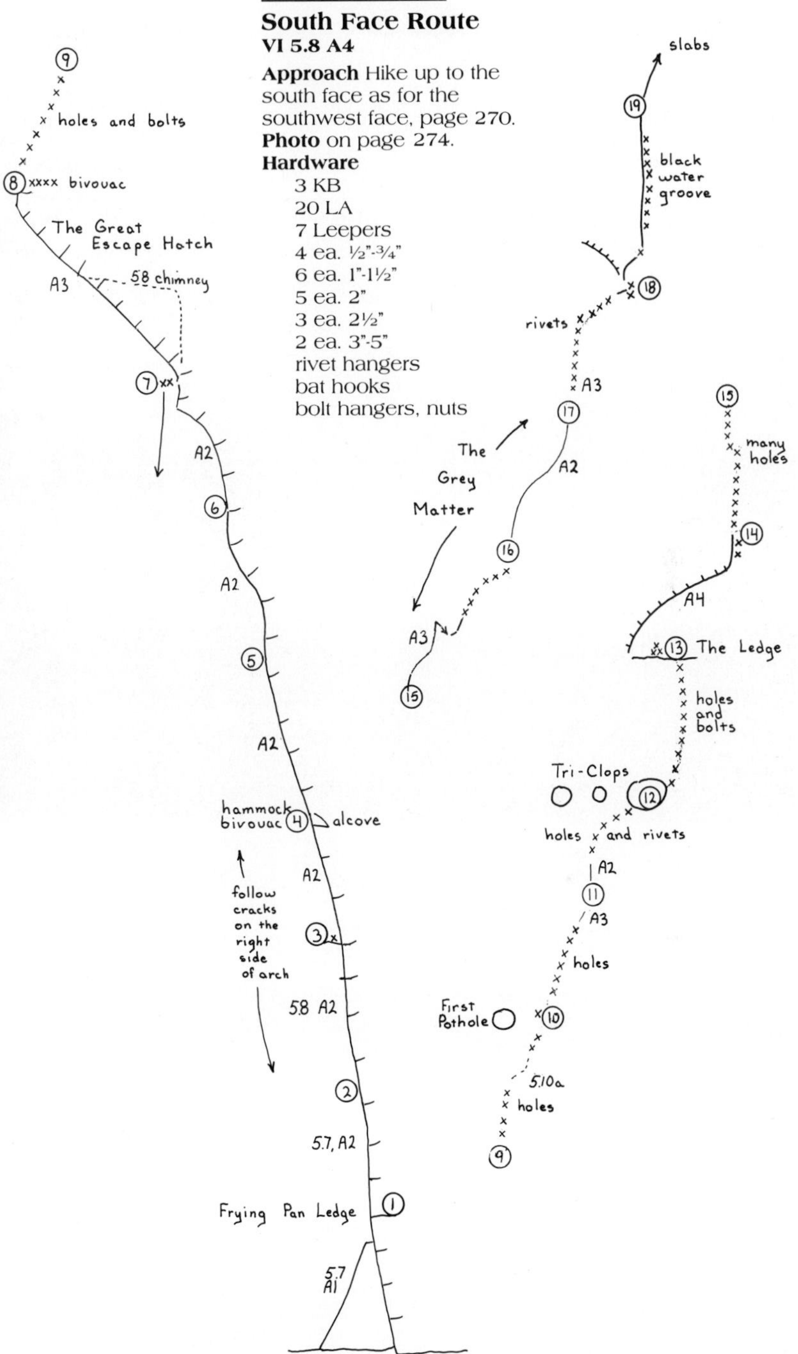

HALF DOME

Karma
V 5.11d A0

Approach Hike up to this part of the south face from the trail to the top of Half Dome, cutting left when the wall becomes close.
Photo on page 274.
Protection
- 1 ea. Friend to #4, incl. #½ and #¾
- nuts
- slings
- bolt kit
- bat hooks
- 2 ropes recommended

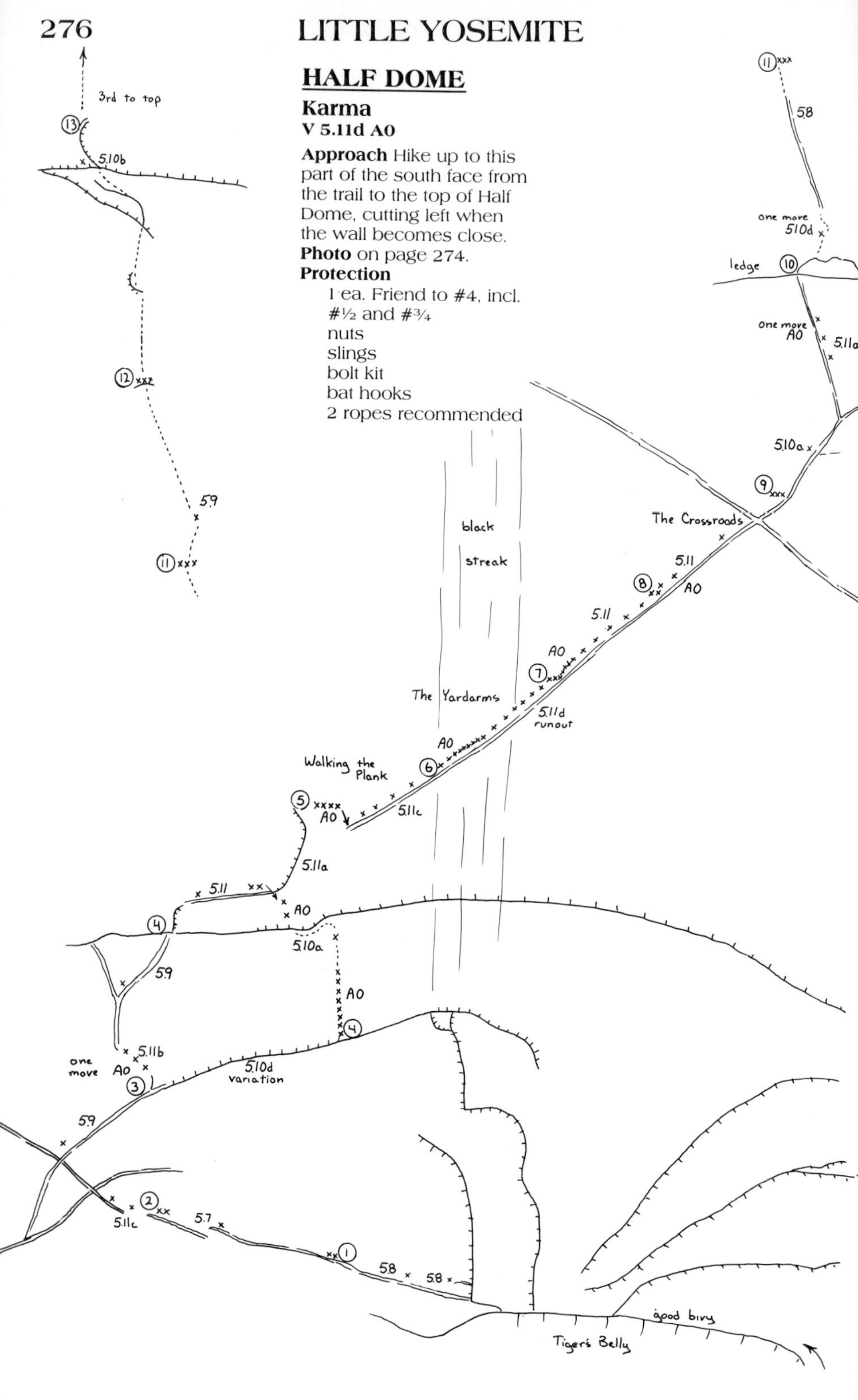

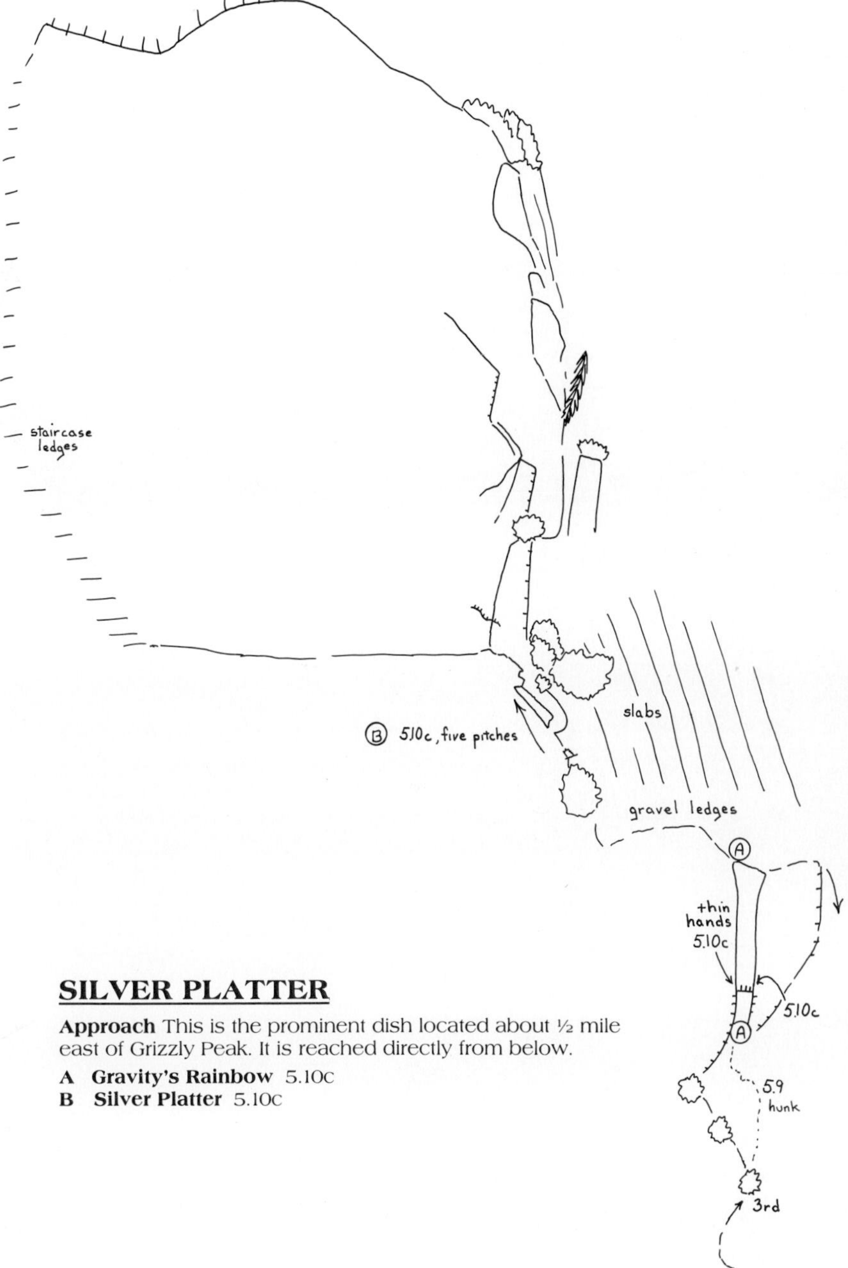

SILVER PLATTER

Approach This is the prominent dish located about ½ mile east of Grizzly Peak. It is reached directly from below.

A **Gravity's Rainbow** 5.10c
B **Silver Platter** 5.10c

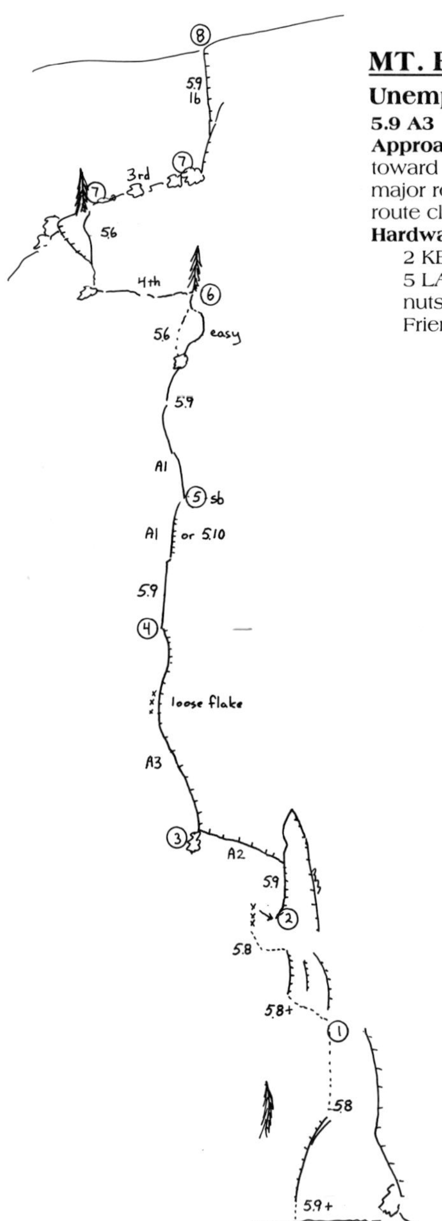

MT. BRODERICK

Unemployment Line

5.9 A3

Approach Hike up the trail from Happy Isles toward Little Yosemite. Mt. Broderick is the major rock to the west of Liberty Cap. This route climbs the center of the west face.

Hardware

2 KB
5 LA
nuts to 3½"
Friends

LIBERTY CAP

1 West Buttress
2 Regular Southwest Face
3 Direct Southwest Face

LIBERTY CAP

West Buttress

V 5.10 A3

Approach Hike up to all the Liberty Cap routes from Happy Isles.
Photo on page 279.
Hardware

15 KB
15 LA
3 ea. ½"-⅝"
5 ea. ¾"-1"
3 ea. 1¼"-1½"
2 ea. 2"
1 ea. 2½"-3"
2 ea. Friends to #4

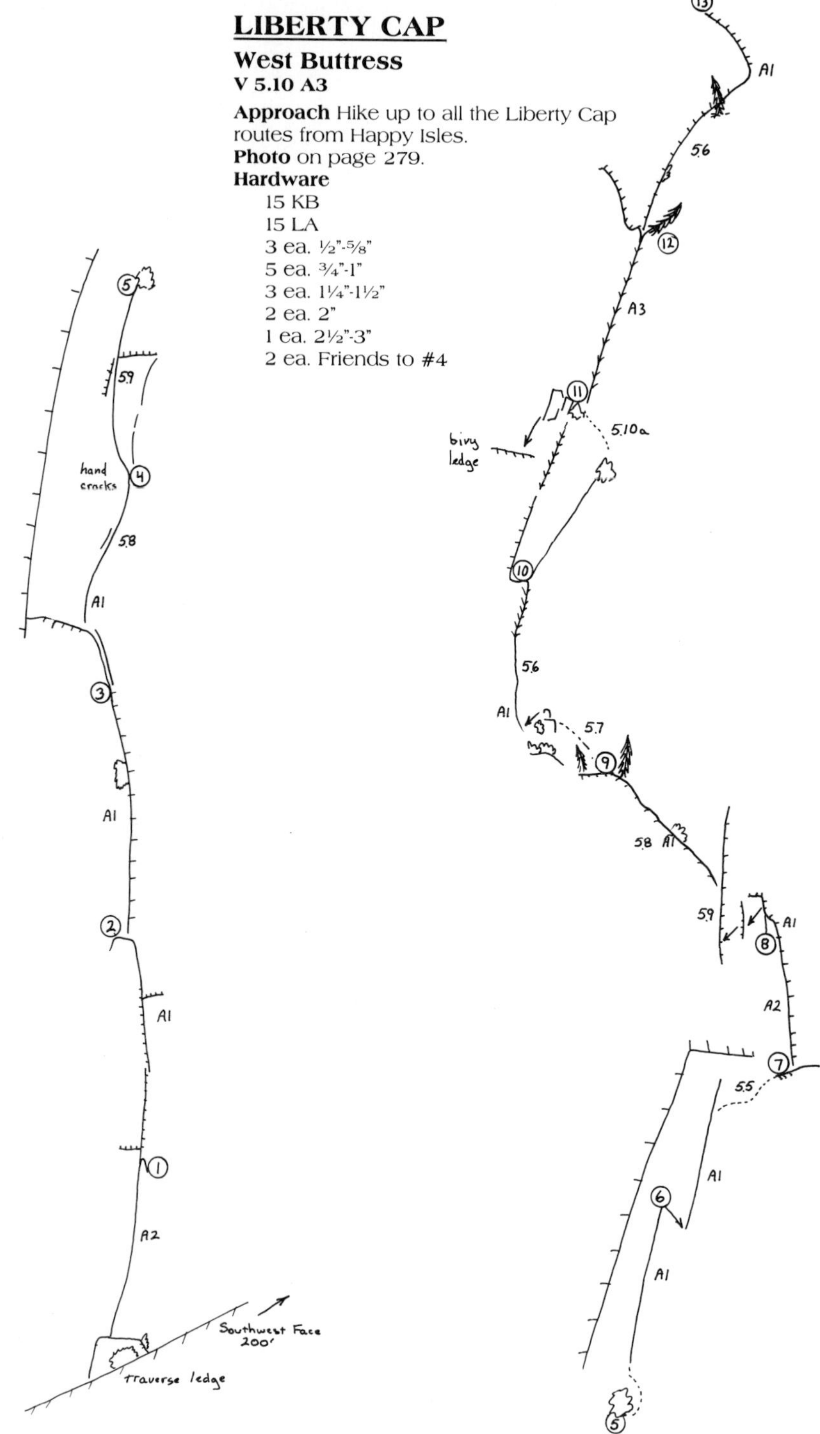

LIBERTY CAP

Southwest Face

VI 5.10 A3

Photo on page 279.

Hardware

5 KB
12 LA
3 ea. ½"-1½"
2 ea. 2"-3"
2 ea. Friends to #4
nuts to 3½"
hooks

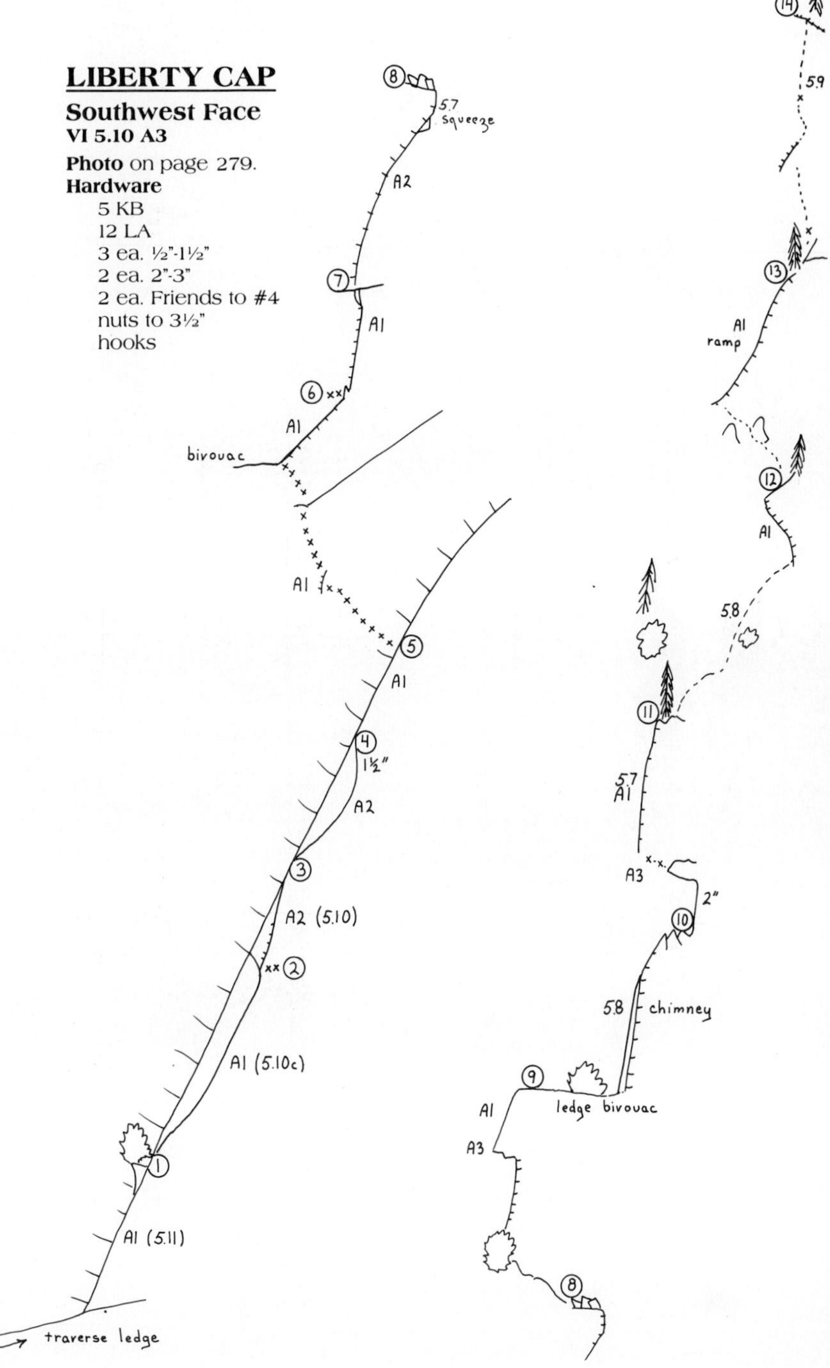

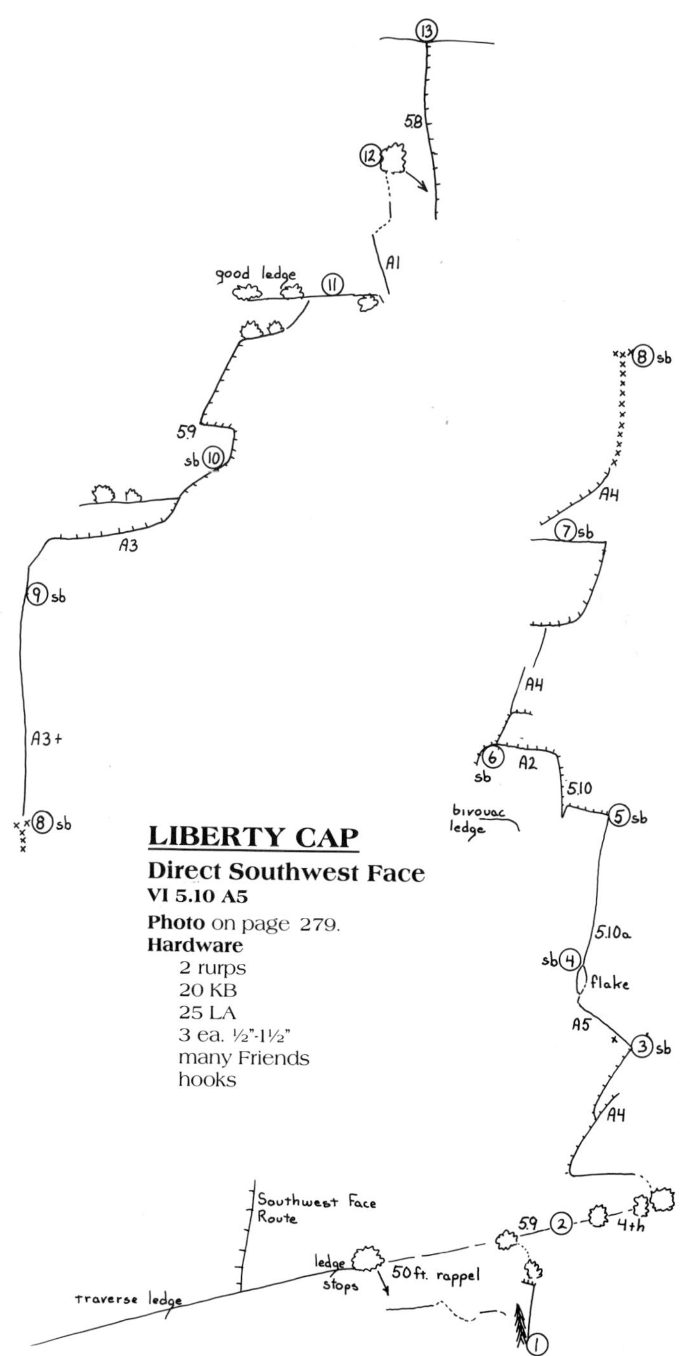

LIBERTY CAP

Direct Southwest Face

VI 5.10 A5

Photo on page 279.

Hardware

- 2 rurps
- 20 KB
- 25 LA
- 3 ea. ½"-1½"
- many Friends
- hooks

LIBERTY CAP

A Joint Adventure

5.9 A3+

Hardware

5 rurps
6 KB
6 LA
4 ea. ½"-⅝"
3 ea. ¾"-1½"
nuts to 3½"
small copperheads
hooks

Approach This is located on the south side of the rock.

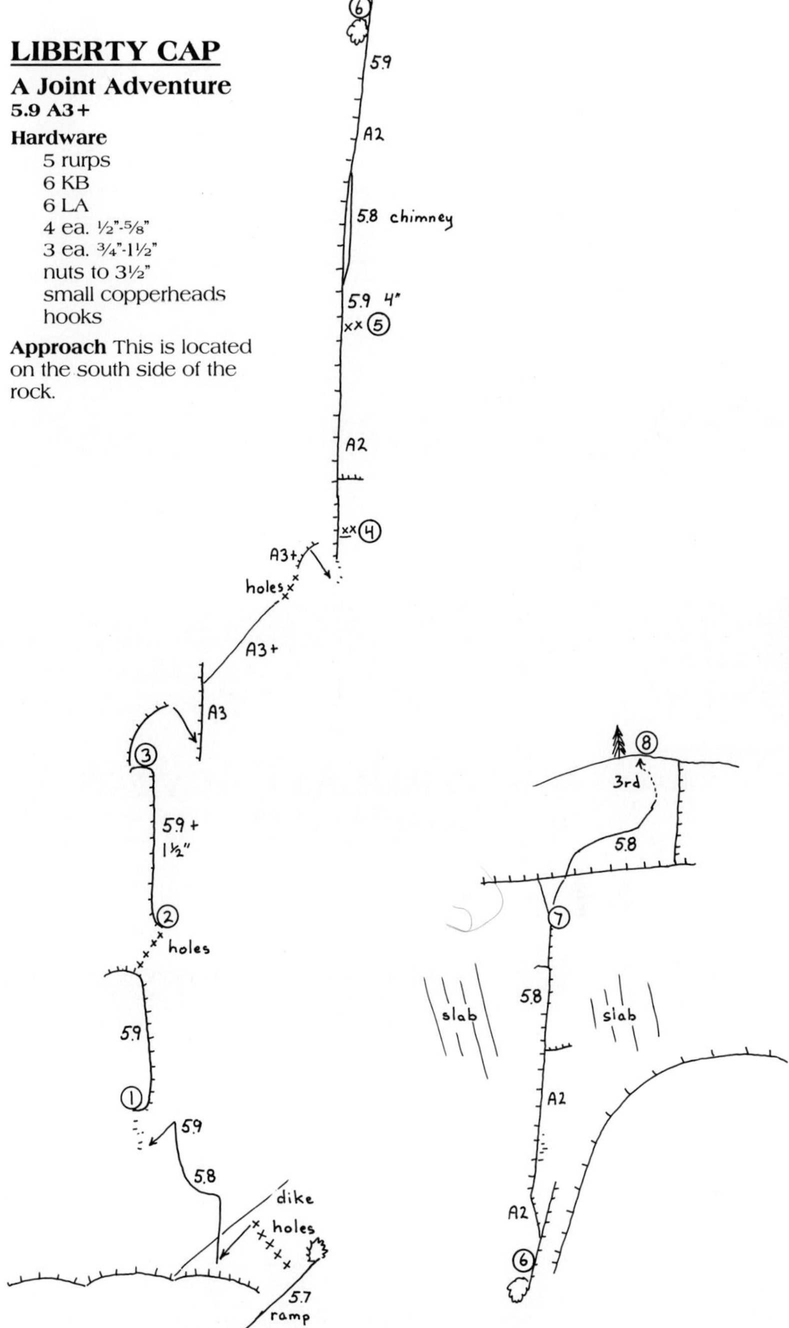

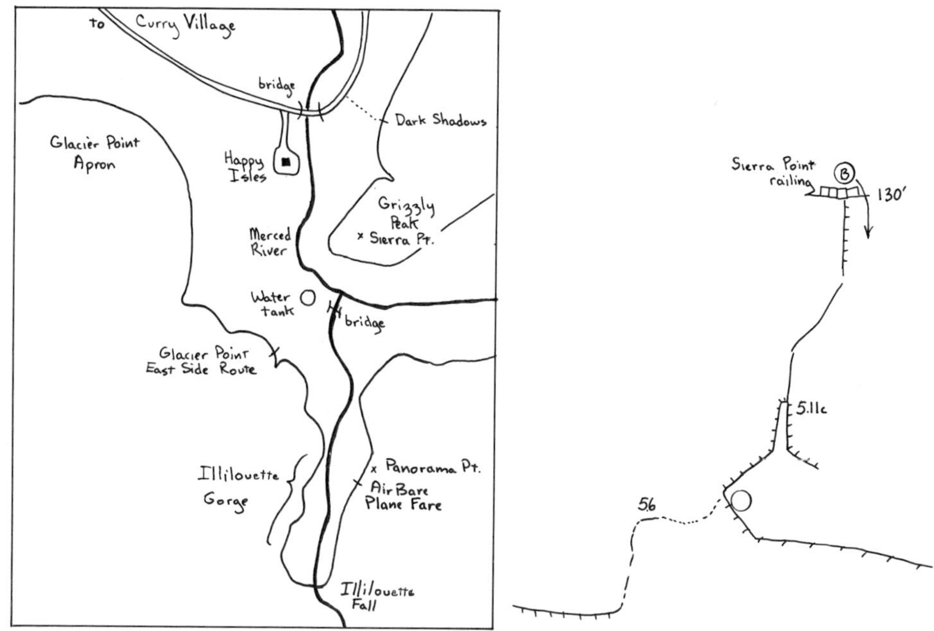

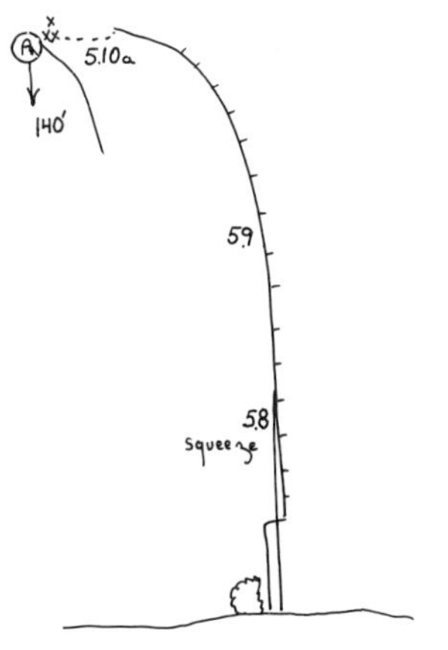

ILLILOUETTE CANYON

Approach Approach all these routes from the parking lot at Curry Village. For **Dark Shadows** cross the first bridge over the Merced and diagonal up and right about 200 yards to a small cliff band. The route is set against a low angle slab. **Fistibule** lies just below the railing at the top of Sierra Point. **Ape Index** is reached by using the utility road that leads from the Happy Isles Nature Center to the water tank. At the Illilouette bridge follow a vague trail along the west side of the creek for about 0.1 mile. Head straight up to the cliff. The climbs of the **Ape Index** area lie left of conspicuous yellow headwalls. **Plane Fare** lies next to the rockfall below Panorama Point.

A Dark Shadows 5.10a
B Fistibule 5.11c
C Air Bare 5.10c
D Plane Fare 5.10b
E Fresh Squeezed 5.10a
F Ape Index 5.11
G Cynical Pinnacle
Wrong 5.10b
Right 5.10c

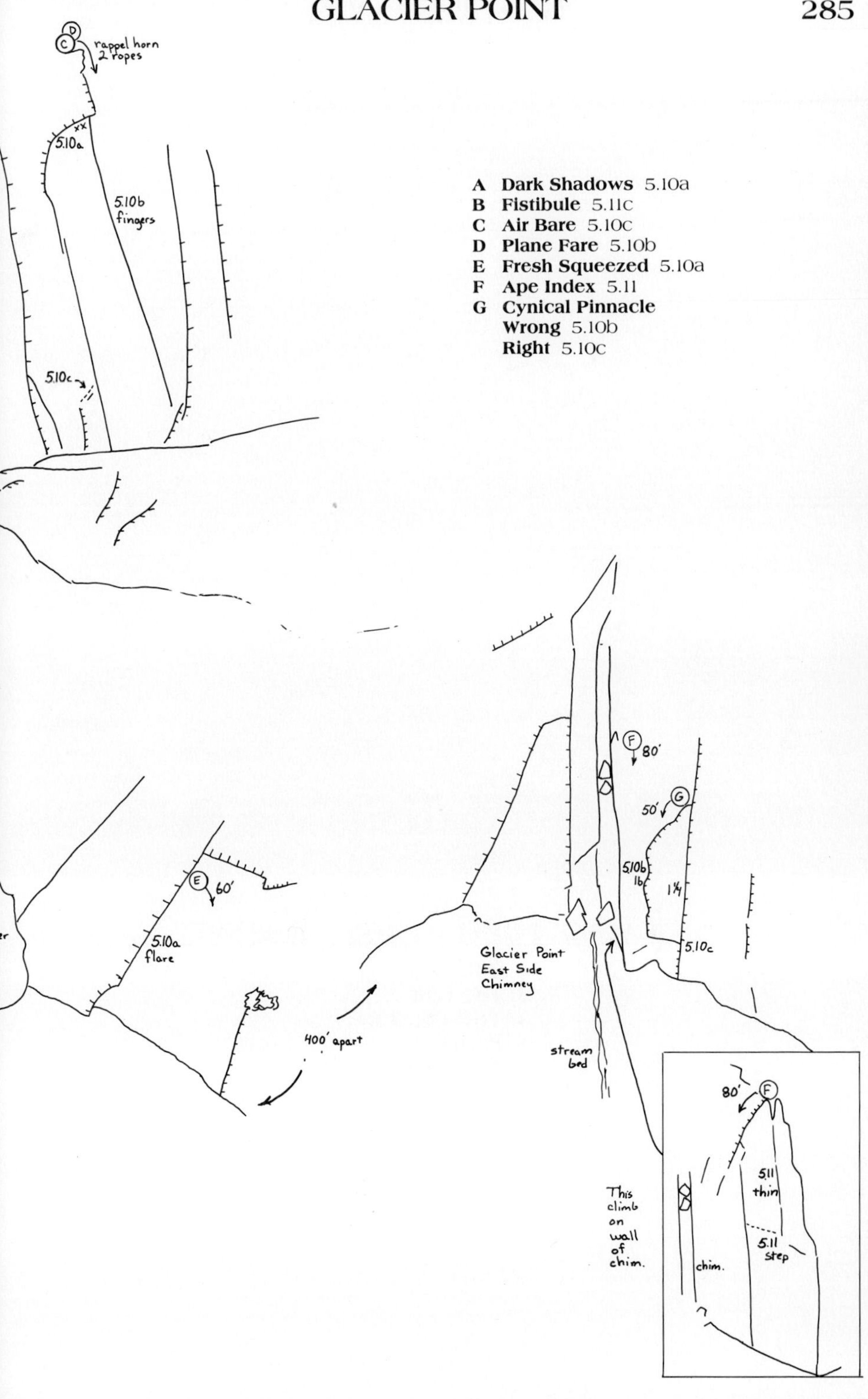

GLACIER POINT APRON – East Side

1 Milk Dud
2 The Calf
3 THE GRACK
4 Perhaps
5 The Mouth
6 GOODRICH PINNACLE

GLACIER POINT APRON – Northeast Side

1 Perhaps
2 The Mouth
3 GOODRICH PINNACLE
4 PATIO PINNACLE
5 COONYARD PINNACLE
6 MONDAY MORNING SLAB
7 POINT BEYOND
8 Lucifer's Ledge
9 The Punch Bowl

GLACIER POINT APRON – East

Approach Immediately west of Happy Isles is a small creek. An old wooden footbridge and a small A-frame structure are landmarks for the short hike up the horsetrail. Strike up the hill where a concrete slab with a pipe abuts the trail.
Photo on page 286.

A **Strange Energy** 5.11b pro: to 4"
B **Synapse Collapse** 5.10a pro: to 2½"
C **B.T. Connection** 5.10a
D **Shuttle Madness** 5.9
E **Milk Dud** 5.10a pro: to 3½"
F **Jack the Zipper** 5.12a
G **The Calf** 5.11c
H **Dead Baby** 5.11a
I **Psychic Energy** 5.11b
J **Transistor Sister** 5.10c
K **Calf Continuation** 5.10b
L **A Mother's Lament** 5.10c
M **Tightrope** 5.11b
N **The Cow**
Left 5.8
Center 5.5
Right 5.7
O **An Udder Way** 5.10a
P **Hoppy's Favorite** 5.10b
Q **Hoppy's Creed** 5.11

The Grack
R **Left Side** 5.7
S **Center Route** 5.6
T **Marginal** 5.9
U **Right Side** 5.8
V **Perhaps** 5.10d A4 pro: KB, RP's to tubes
W **Roller Coaster** 5.8
X **Hot Tin Roof** 5.9
Y **Ochre Fields** 5.11a pro: to 3"

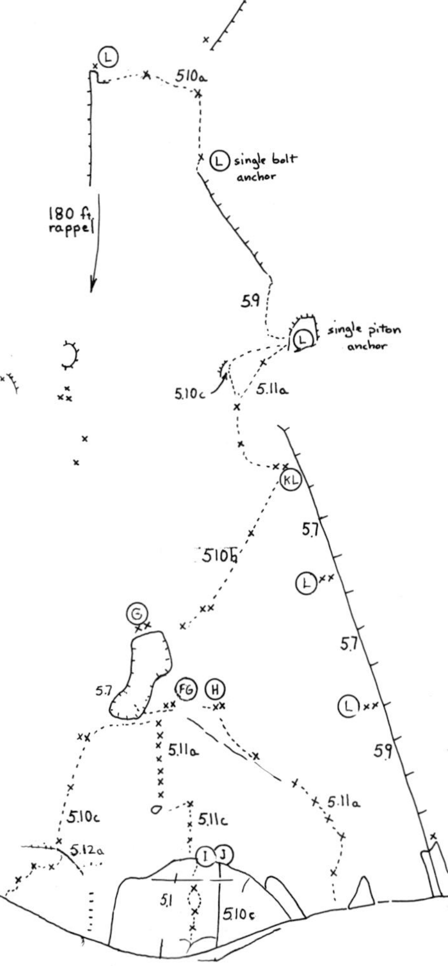

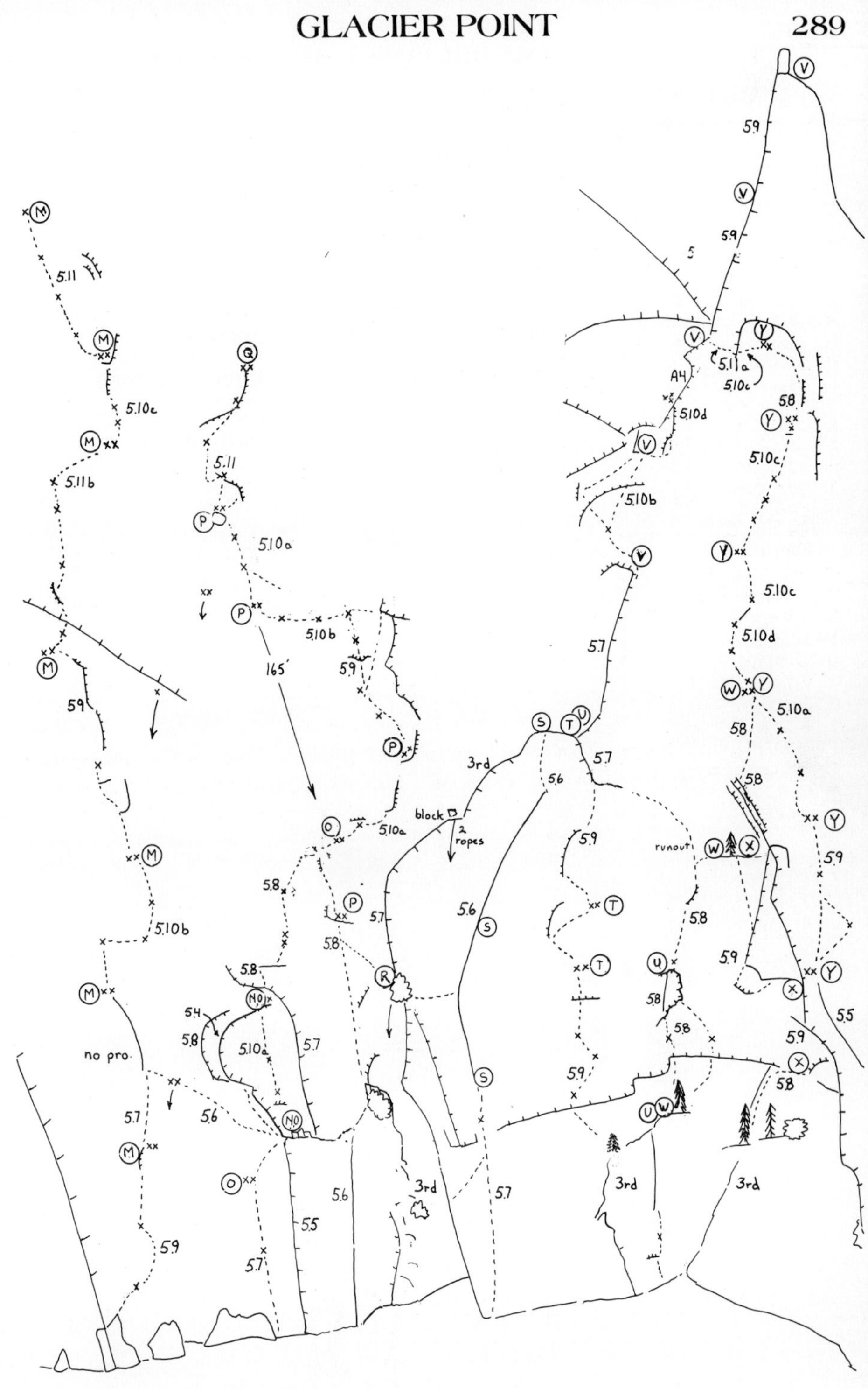

GLACIER POINT

GLACIER POINT APRON – Center

Approach as described on page 288.
Descent for routes ending at the Oasis, see page 296.
Photo on page 287.

A Ochre Fields 5.11a
B Deep Throat 5.10a

The Mouth

C Boche-Hennek Variation 5.9
D Regular Mouth 5.9
E Mouth to Perhaps 5.11b
F Flakey Foont 5.9
G Misty Beethoven 5.10d
H Hall of Mirrors 5.12?
continues on page 999.

Goodrich Pinnacle

I Left Side 5.9
J Right Side 5.9
K Hoosier's Highway 5.10c

Patio Pinnacle

L Left Side 5.9
M Regular Route 5.8
Monday Morning to Patio 5.9
N Angelica 5.9
O Coonyard Pinnacle 5.9
P Patio to Coonyard 5.10a or 5.8
Q Coonyard to the Oasis 5.9

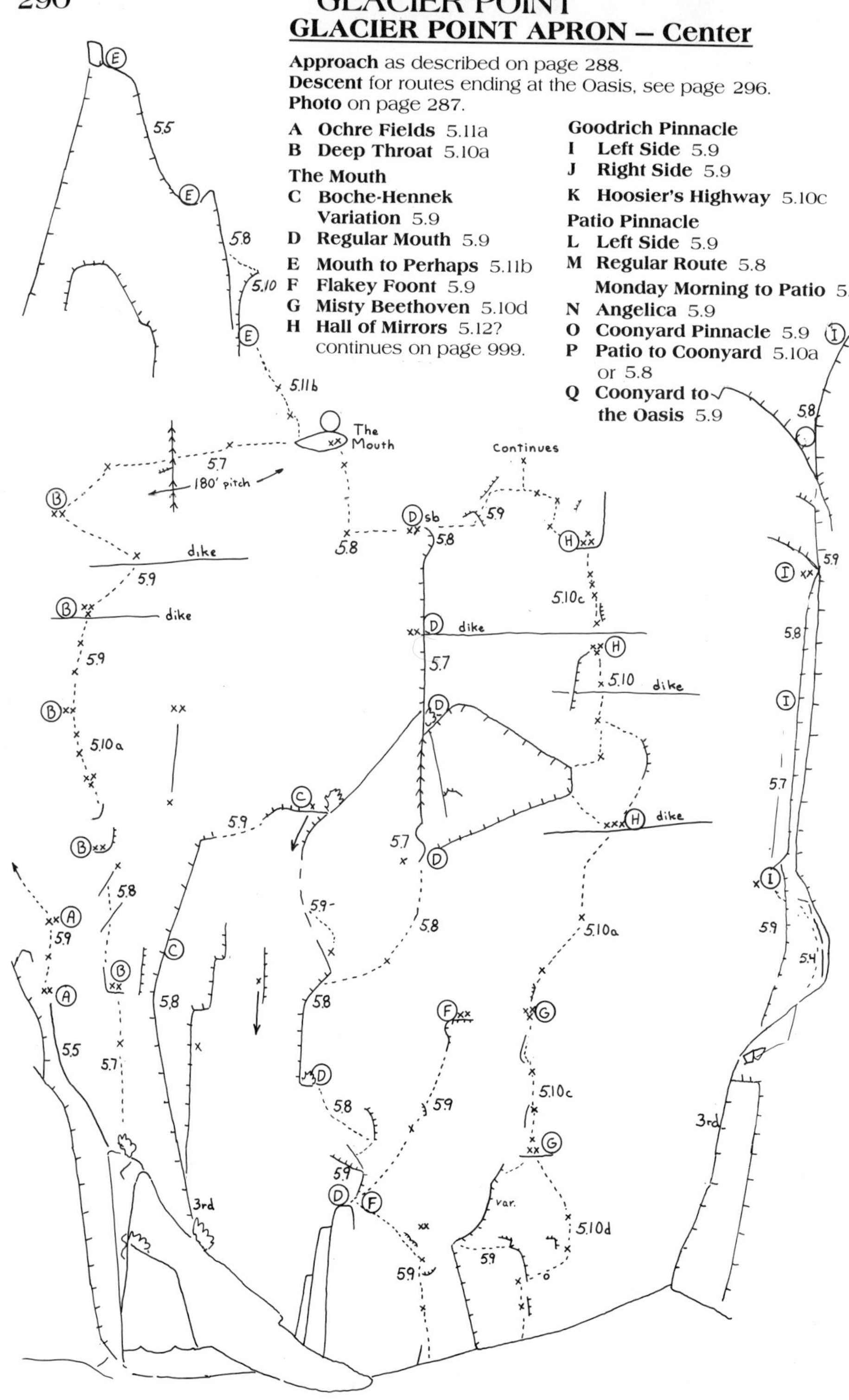

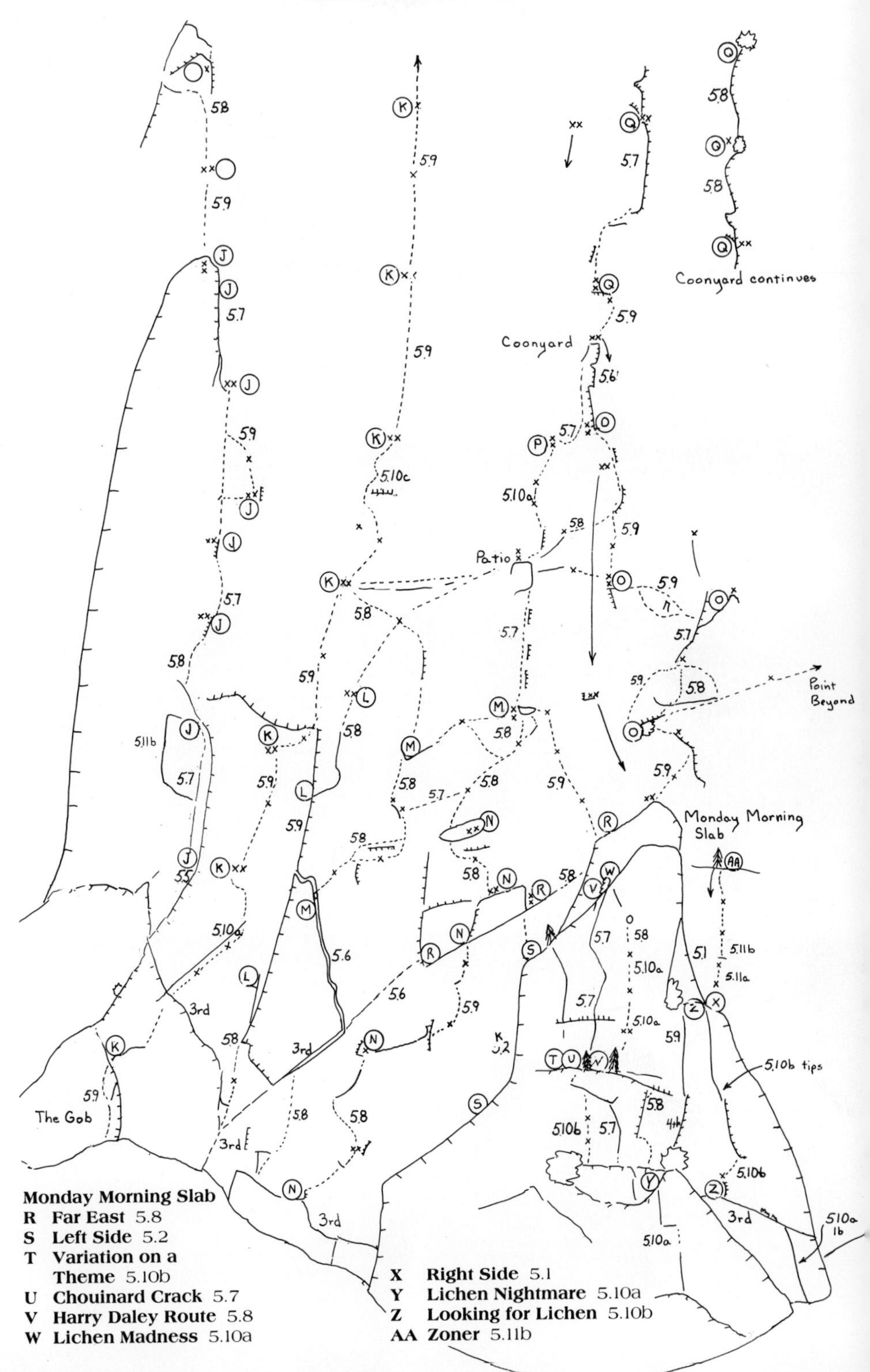
Coonyard continues
Coonyard
Patio
Point Beyond
Monday Morning Slab
The Gob
5.10b tips
Monday Morning Slab
R Far East 5.8
S Left Side 5.2
T Variation on a Theme 5.10b
U Chouinard Crack 5.7
V Harry Daley Route 5.8
W Lichen Madness 5.10a
X Right Side 5.1
Y Lichen Nightmare 5.10a
Z Looking for Lichen 5.10b
AA Zoner 5.11b

GLACIER POINT APRON – West

Approach Hike up from the abandoned dump site at the extreme eastern end of Curry Village.
Descent For routes that end at the Oasis, see page 296.
Photo on page 287.

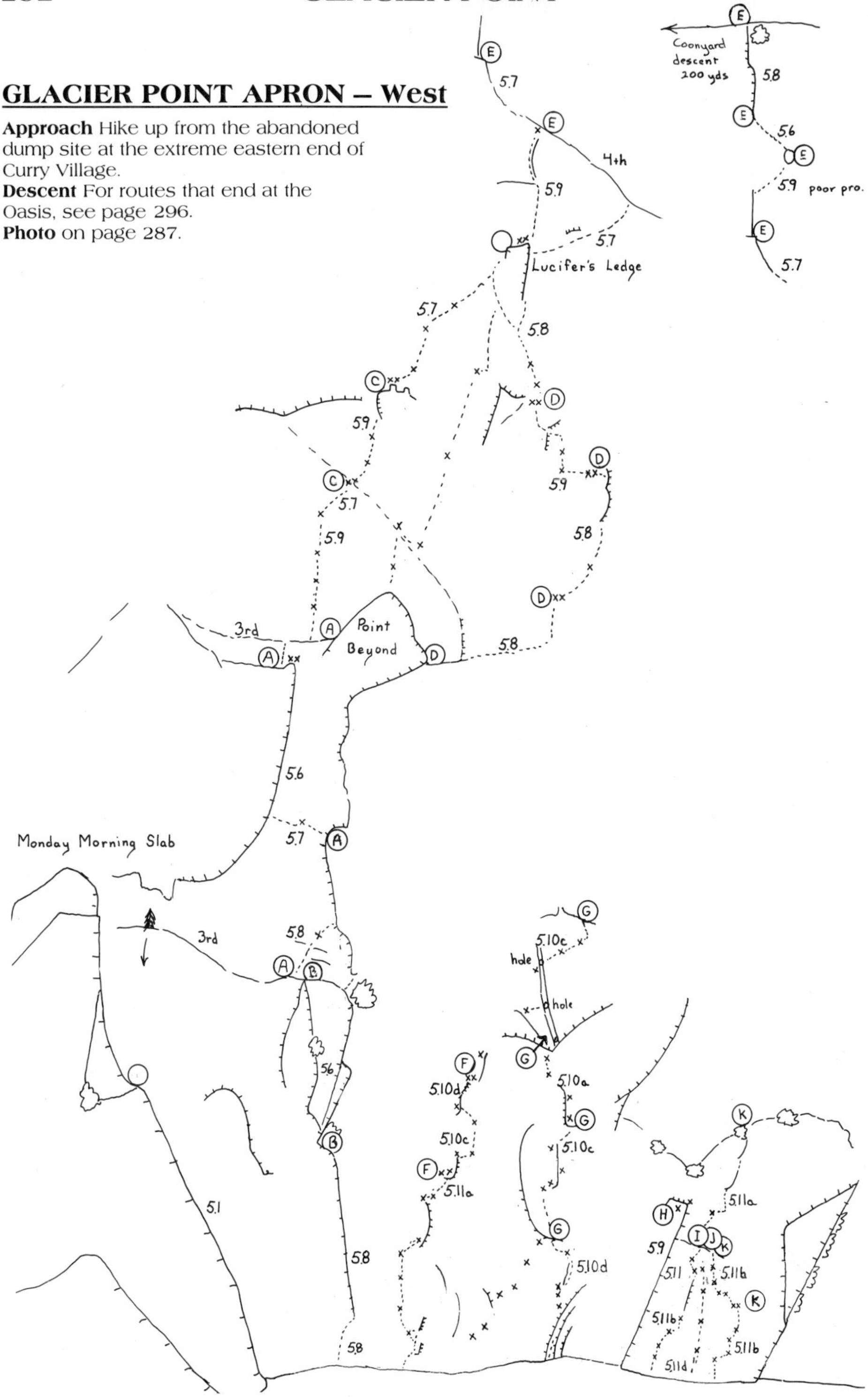

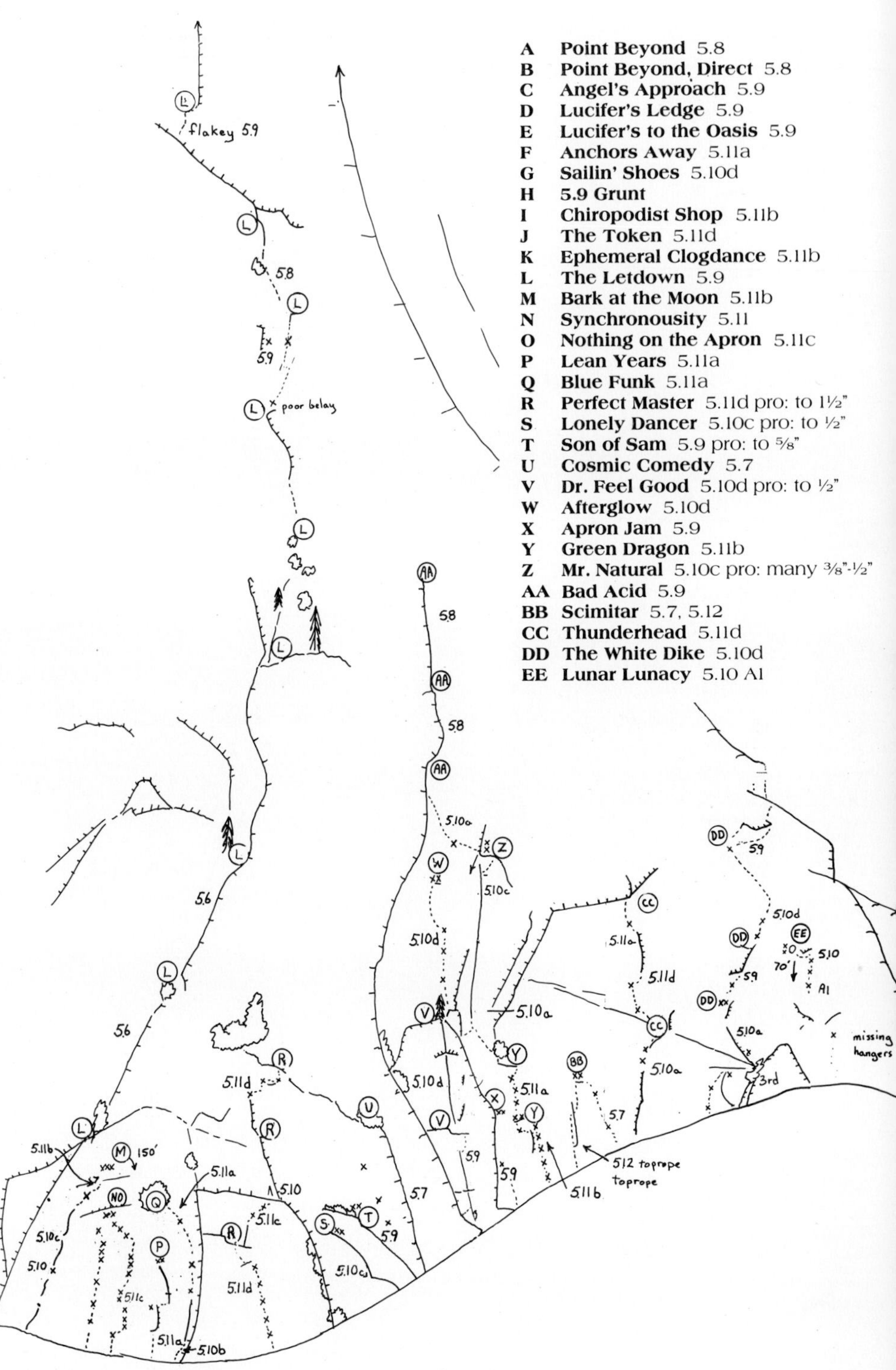
A Point Beyond 5.8
B Point Beyond, Direct 5.8
C Angel's Approach 5.9
D Lucifer's Ledge 5.9
E Lucifer's to the Oasis 5.9
F Anchors Away 5.11a
G Sailin' Shoes 5.10d
H 5.9 Grunt
I Chiropodist Shop 5.11b
J The Token 5.11d
K Ephemeral Clogdance 5.11b
L The Letdown 5.9
M Bark at the Moon 5.11b
N Synchronousity 5.11
O Nothing on the Apron 5.11c
P Lean Years 5.11a
Q Blue Funk 5.11a
R Perfect Master 5.11d pro: to 1½"
S Lonely Dancer 5.10c pro: to ½"
T Son of Sam 5.9 pro: to ⅝"
U Cosmic Comedy 5.7
V Dr. Feel Good 5.10d pro: to ½"
W Afterglow 5.10d
X Apron Jam 5.9
Y Green Dragon 5.11b
Z Mr. Natural 5.10c pro: many ⅜"-½"
AA Bad Acid 5.9
BB Scimitar 5.7, 5.12
CC Thunderhead 5.11d
DD The White Dike 5.10d
EE Lunar Lunacy 5.10 A1
flakey 5.9
poor belay
M 150'
70'
missing hangers
3rd
5.12 toprope
toprope

GLACIER POINT APRON

Hall of Mirrors

V 5.12

Approach This route starts above Misty Beethoven on page 290.
Photo on page 286.
Protection #1-2 Friends

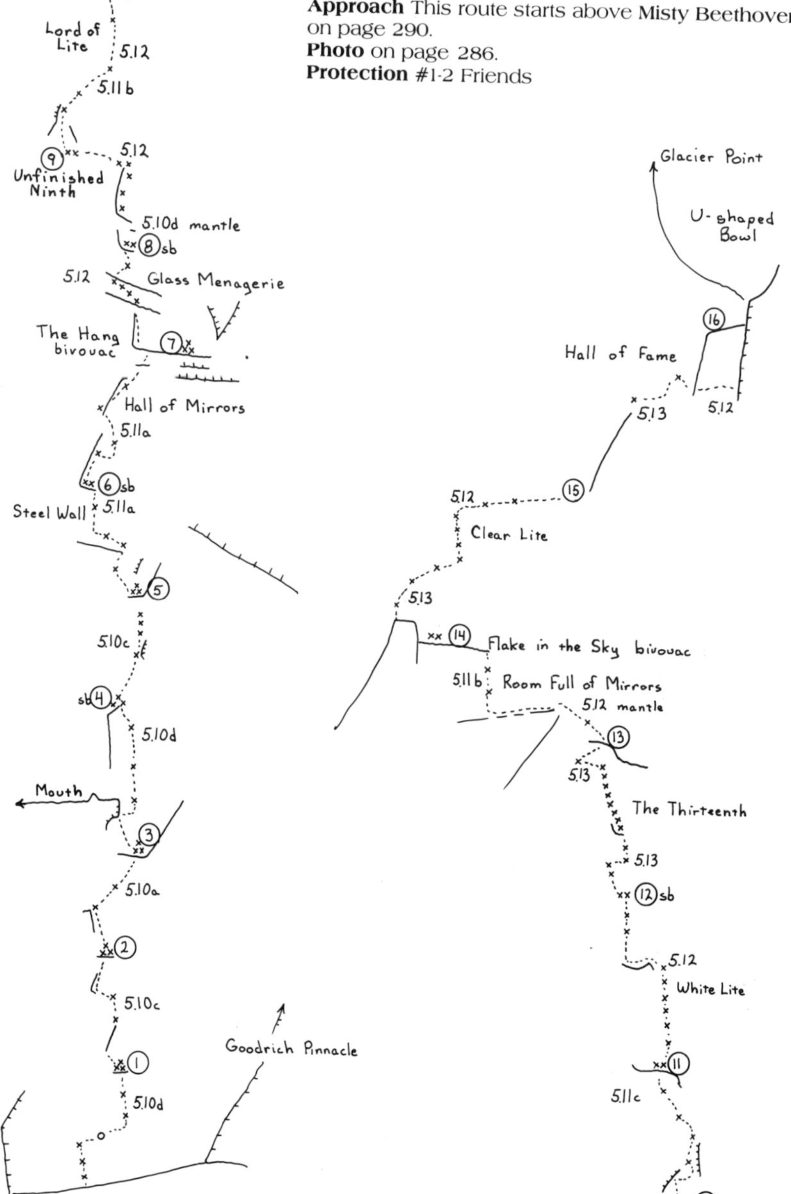

GLACIER POINT APRON

Approach This is the far west side of the Apron, and can be approached from directly below.
Descent See page 296 for descent from Glacier Point Terrace.
Photo on page 287.

- **A** **Thunderhead** 5.11d
- **B** **The White Dike** 5.10d
- **C** **Fire Drill** 5.9
- **D** **The Punch Line** 5.10d pro: small nuts
- **E** **Run With Me** 5.10a pro: RP's to #2½ Friend
- **F** **The Punch Bowl** 5.10a

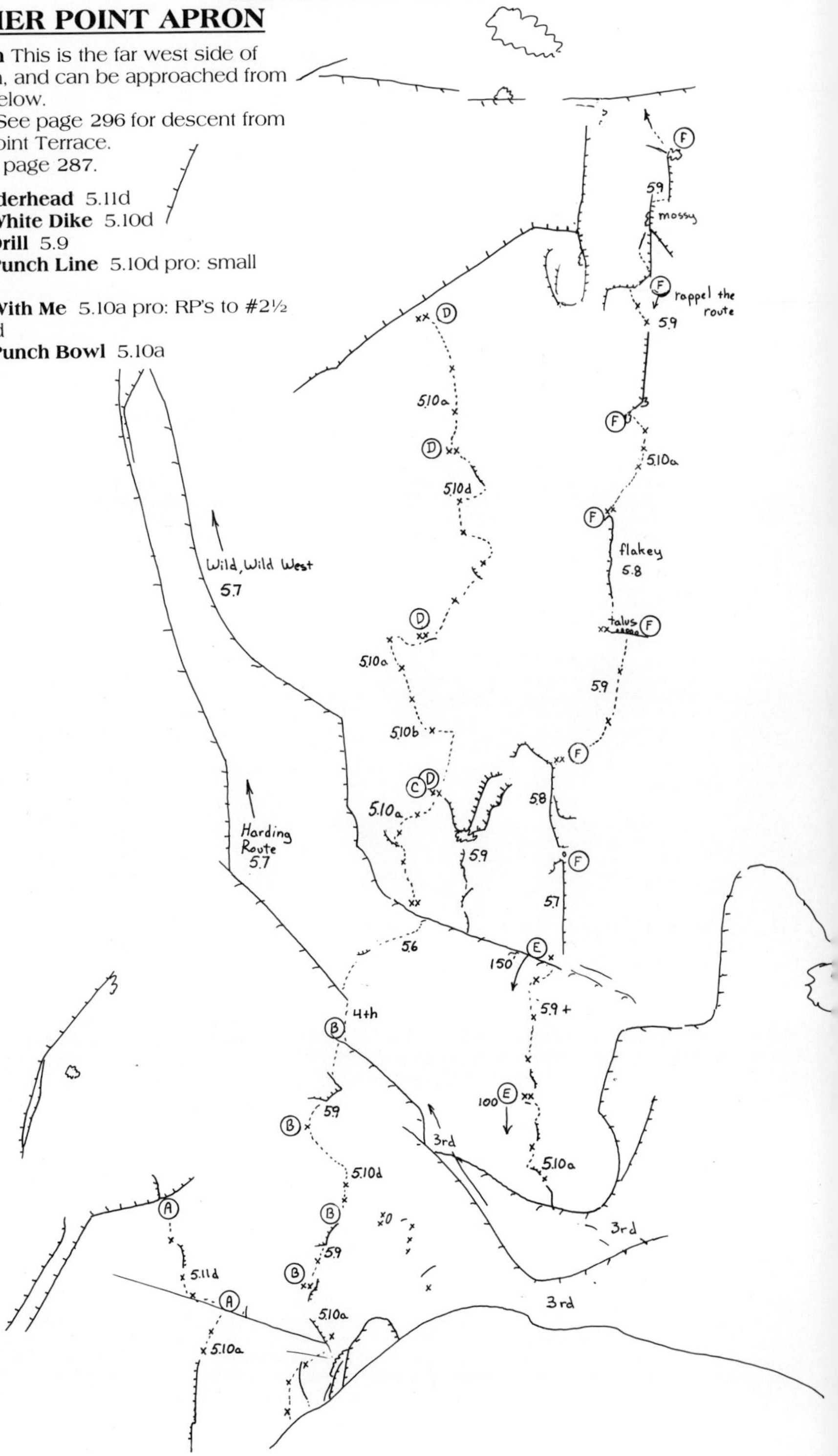

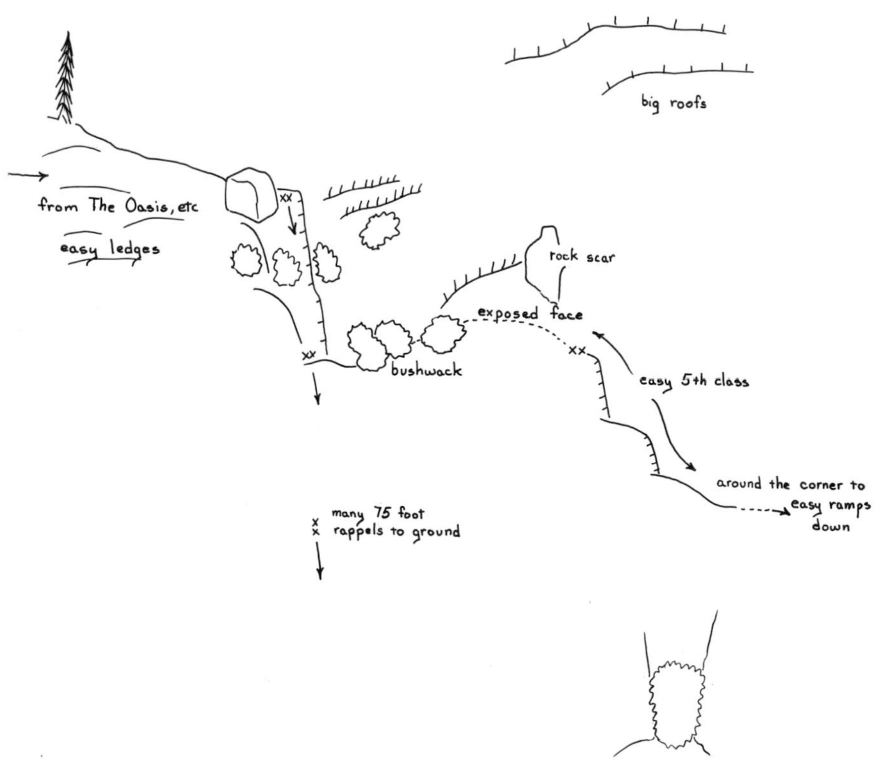

GLACIER POINT TERRACE DESCENT

Photo on page 287.

This is the descent for all routes that lead to the Oasis and Glacier Point Terrace. Walk as far west on the Terrace as you can without having to rope up. From bolt anchors next to a block, make one 70 foot rappel down a low angle corner. This leads to another ledge with bolts. To follow the Terrace descent, do not rappel again here, but climb up and right through bushes. Traverse across a steep, exposed but easy slab for almost a rope length to anchors on another ledge. Now rappel down and west for a pitch, following corners and easy ledges. You should see the final, elusive ramps just west of you.

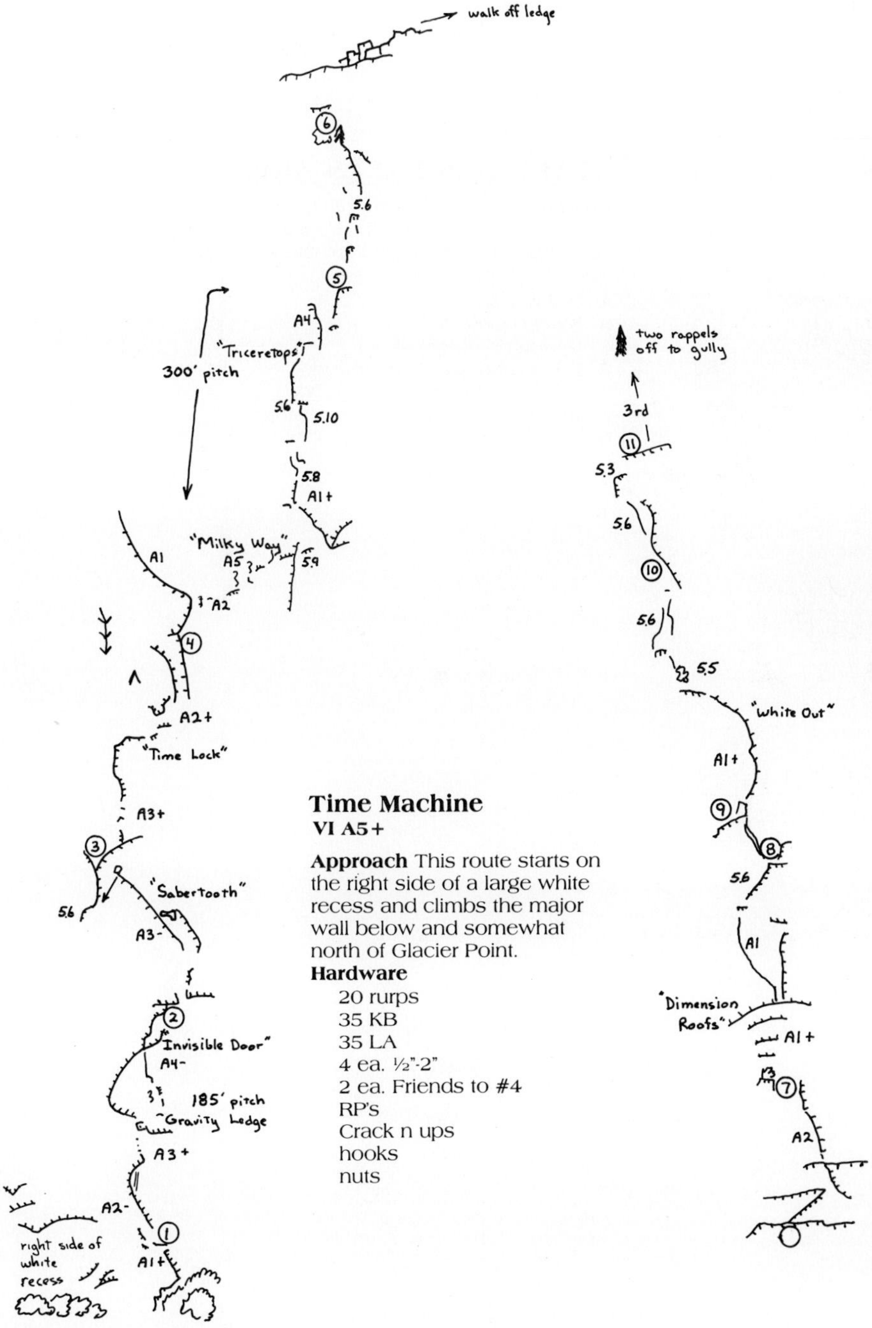

Time Machine

VI A5+

Approach This route starts on the right side of a large white recess and climbs the major wall below and somewhat north of Glacier Point.

Hardware

20 rurps
35 KB
35 LA
4 ea. ½"-2"
2 ea. Friends to #4
RP's
Crack n ups
hooks
nuts

STAIRCASE FALLS AREA

Approach This is the gray cliff to the right of the Glacier Point Apron and the Ledge Trail. Hike up from the cabins at Curry Village gaining vague trails adjacent to the watercourse.

A **Old A5** A3
B **Blockbuster** 5.11c A1 pro: hooks to a #3 Friend
C **Derelict's Diagonal** A4
D **Broken Circuit** 5.12 top rope
E **Circuit Breaker** 5.11b top rope
F **Derelict's Delight** 5.11c pro: small
G **Doggie Submission** 5.10b pro: extra small

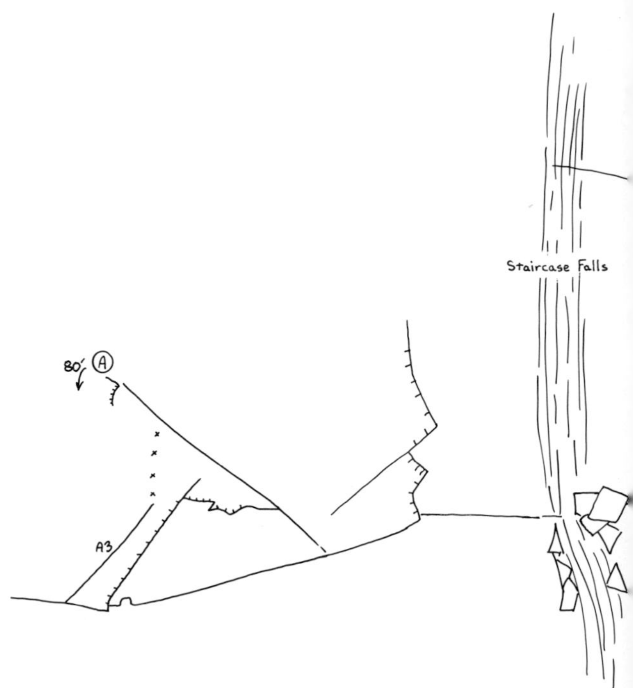

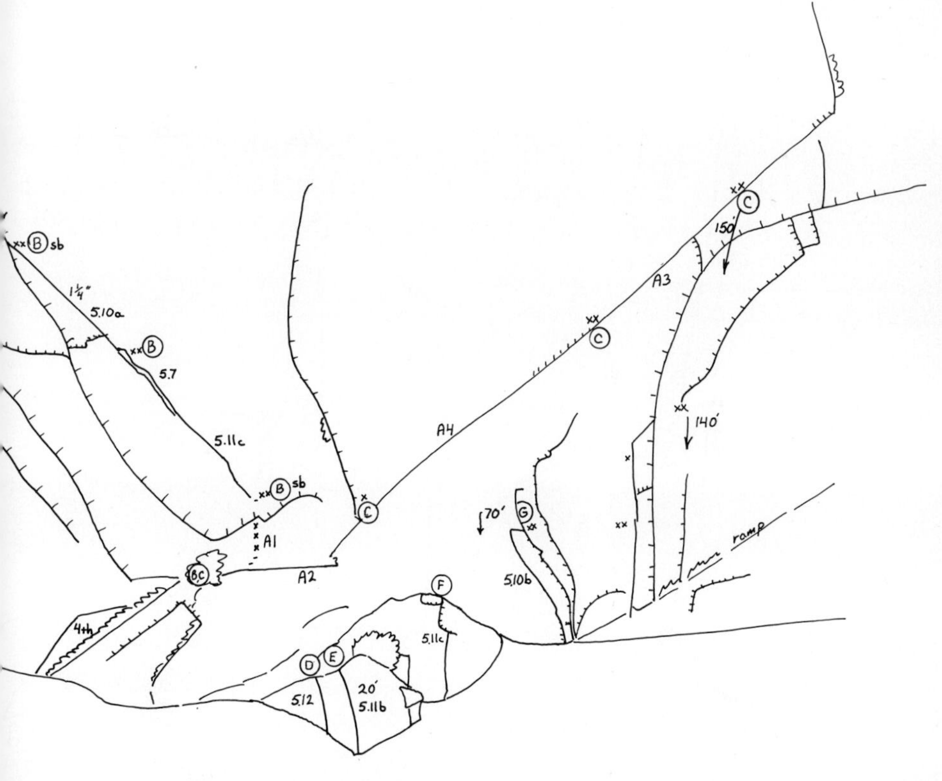
xx B sb
1¼"
5.10a
xx B
5.7
5.11c
xx B sb
A1
B,C
A2
4th
C
A4
xx C
A3
xx C
150'
xx
140'
70'
G
xx
5.10b
ramp
F
5.11c
D
E
5.12
20'
5.11b

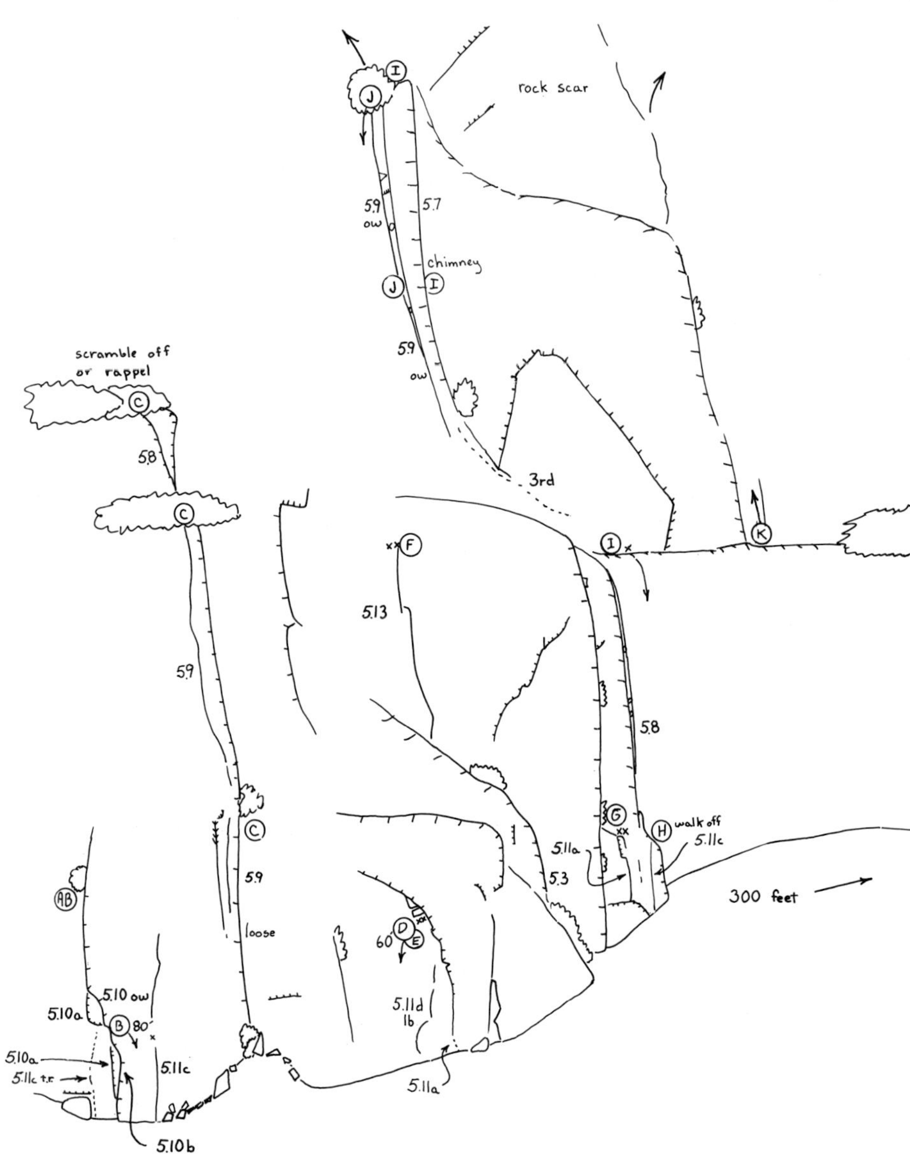
rock scar
I
J
5.9
ow
5.7
chimney
J
I
5.9
ow
3rd
scramble off
or rappel
C
5.8
C
F
5.13
I
K
5.9
5.8
G
H
walk off
5.11c
5.11a
5.3
300 feet
C
5.9
AB
loose
D
60'
E
5.10 ow
5.10a
B
80'
5.11d
lb
5.10a
5.11c t.r.
5.11c
5.11a
5.10b

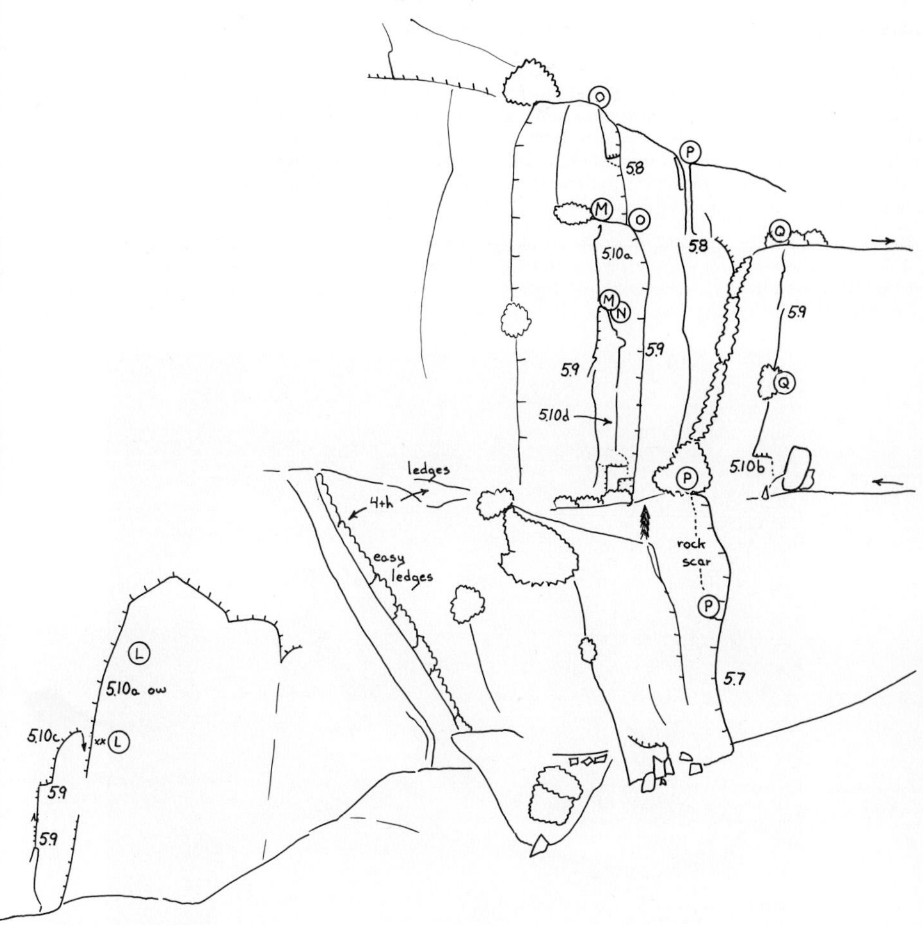

CHAPEL WALL

Approach A horse trail runs along the base of this cliff. Begin from the chapel for climbs on the left side of the cliff; Gold Dust is level within a stone's throw from the trail.

- **A Heathenistic Pursuit** 5.10a
- **B Gold Dust** 5.10b
- **C On The Loose** 5.9
- **D Scattered Youth** 5.11d
- **E Controlled Burn** 5.11a pro: to 3½"
- **F Cosmic Debris** 5.13
- **G Lay Lady Lieback** 5.11a
- **H Delicate Delineate** 5.11c
- **I Chockblock Chimney** 5.8
- **J Tithe** 5.9
- **K The Symphony** 5.9 A1?
- **L Dorn's Crack** 5.10c A0 pro: to 3", plus 5"-6"
- **M Resurrection** 5.10a
- **N New Testament** 5.10d
- **O Betrayal** 5.9
- **P Bryan's Crack** 5.8
- **Q Sixth Heaven** 5.10b

SENTINEL ROCK

Approach The routes on the north and west faces of Sentinel Rock are approached by 3rd class ledges that traverse up and right across the lower broken area of the formation. First, hike up the Four-Mile Trail for about a mile to the stream that comes down from the east side of the rock. Leave the trail and hike up the streambed several hundred feet and move over to the prominent ramp that starts the long scramble up and right. This leads to the base of the Flying Buttress, an 800 foot pillar that sits at the right side of the flat north face and is the start of the **Flying Buttress Direct** and **the Steck-Salathé**. The routes on the west face are around the corner. The routes on the north face require further scrambling up and left on ledges. Allow two hours approach time from Camp Four.

Descent From the summit, work south to the notch behind Sentinel Rock via manzanita tunnels that skirt small outcrops. From the notch, scramble down the loose, class 2 gully that leads east to a stream. Further down, descend improbable terrain in the middle of a scruffy buttress that separates two chasms. Eventually the Four-Mile Trail is reached.

Bill Long, Sentinel Rock, 1950. *Allen Steck*

SENTINEL ROCK – North Face

N.P.S.

1 **Kor-Denny** V 5.9 A3
2 **Psychedelic Wall** V 5.8 A4
3 **Direct North Face**
4 **Gobi Wall**
5 **Chouinard-Herbert**
6 **Flying Buttress Direct**
7 **Steck-Salathé**

SENTINEL ROCK

Direct North Face

V 5.9 A3

Approach Scramble up to the start of the route as described on page 302.
Descent described on page 302.
Photo on page 303.
Hardware

1 rurp
4 KB
13 LA
6 ea. ½"-1"
3 ea. 1½"-3"

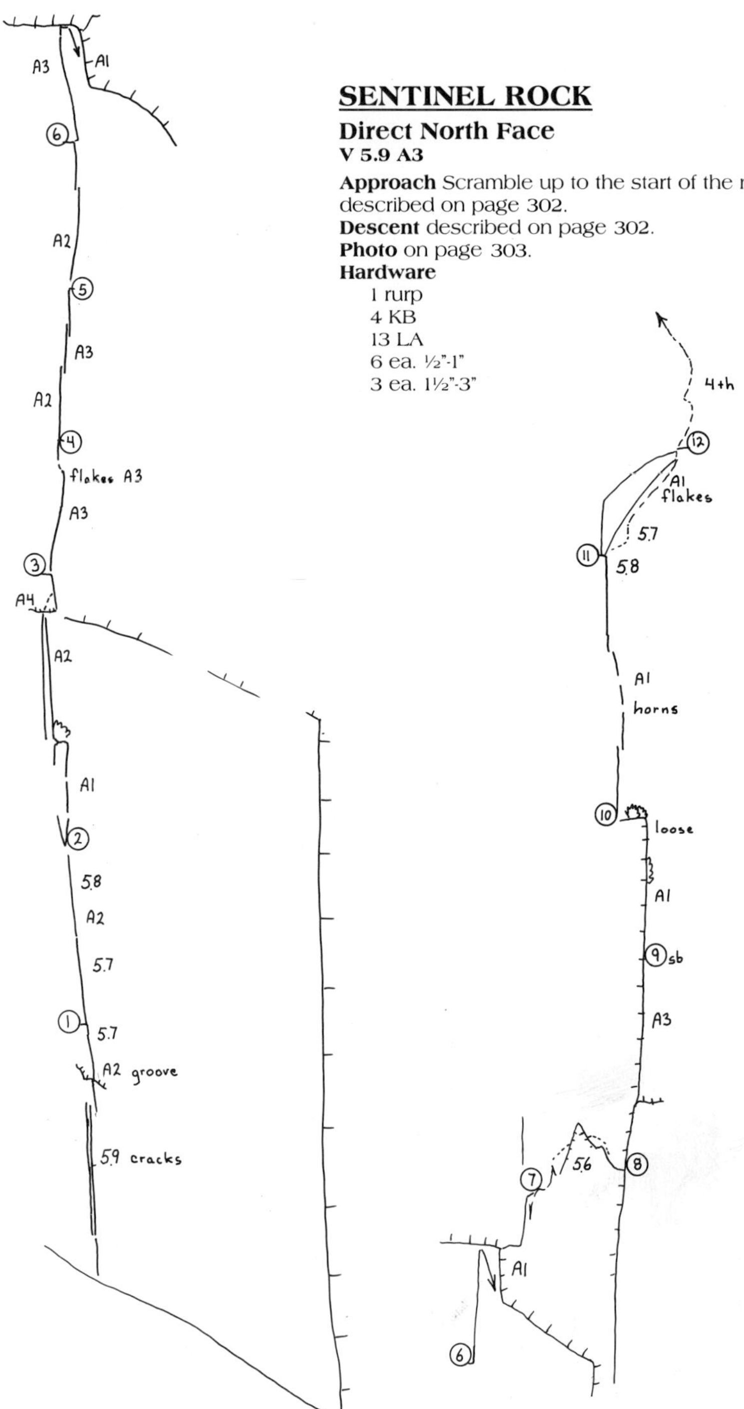

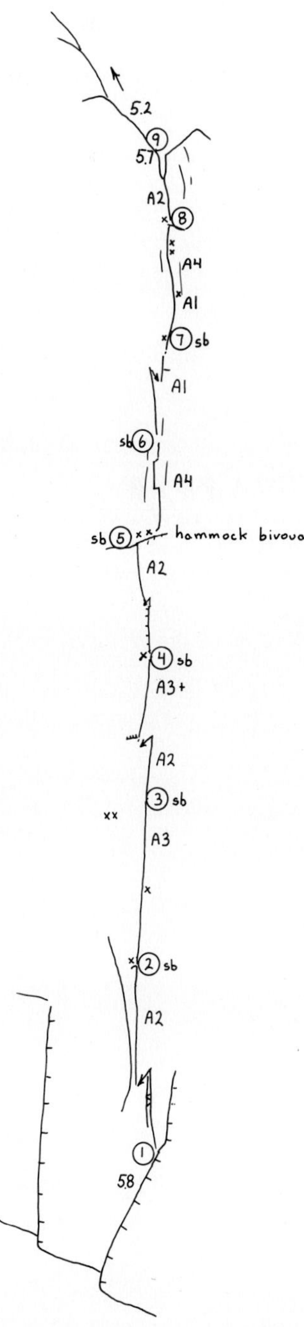

SENTINEL ROCK

Gobi Wall

V 5.8 A4

Approach described on page 302.
Photo on page 303.
Hardware

- 10 rurps
- 6 KB
- 15 LA
- 3 ea. ½"-⅝"
- 5 ea. ¾"
- 6 ea. 1"-1½"
- 2 ea. 2"-2½"
- 1 ea. 3"
- hooks

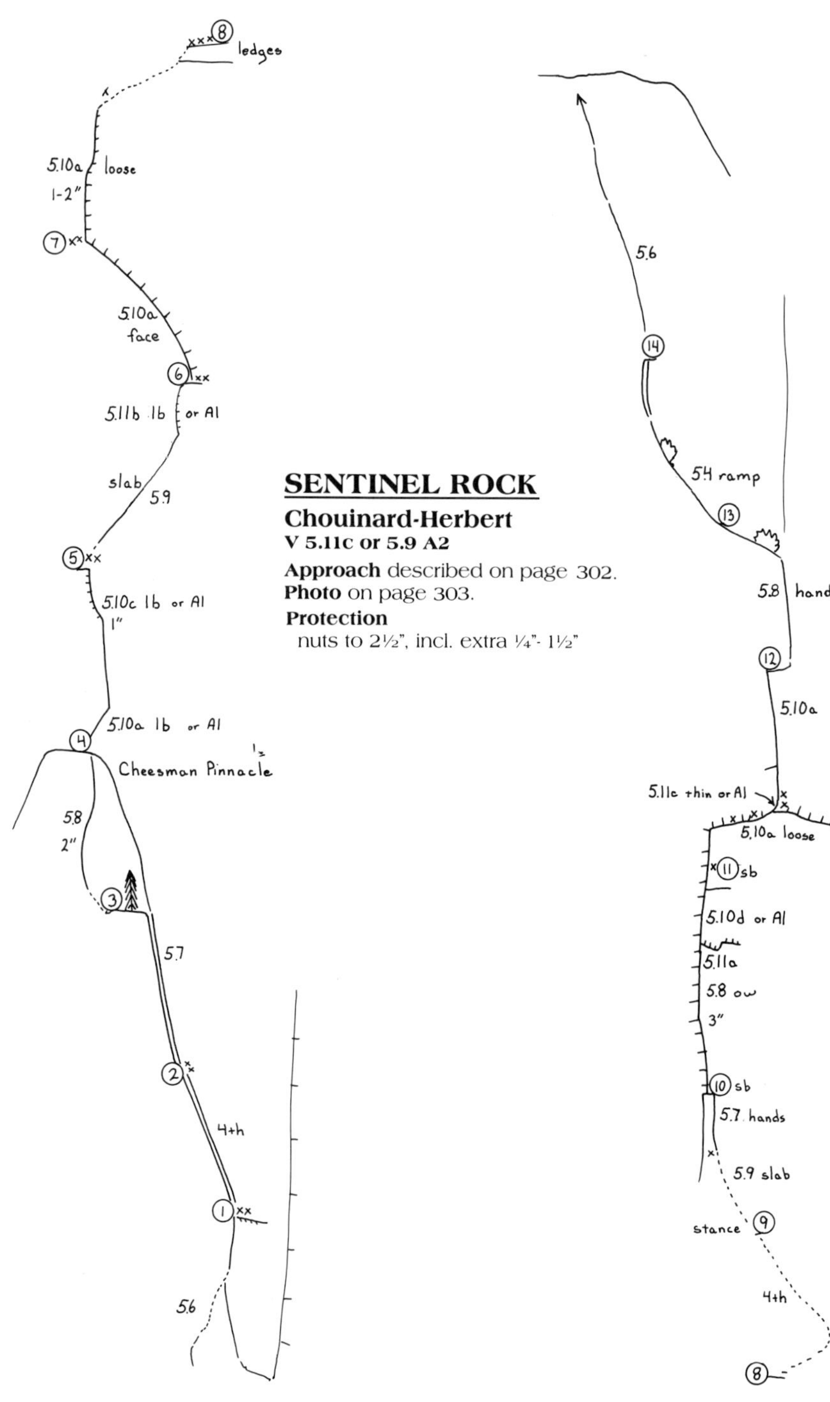

SENTINEL ROCK

Chouinard-Herbert

V 5.11c or 5.9 A2

Approach described on page 302.
Photo on page 303.

Protection
nuts to 2½", incl. extra ¼"- 1½"

SENTINEL ROCK

Flying Buttress Direct

V 5.9 A3

Approach described on page 302.
Photo on page 303.
Hardware

- 10 LA
- 3 ea. ½"-⅝"
- 5 ea. ¾"
- 6 ea. 1"
- 2 ea. 1½"-2"

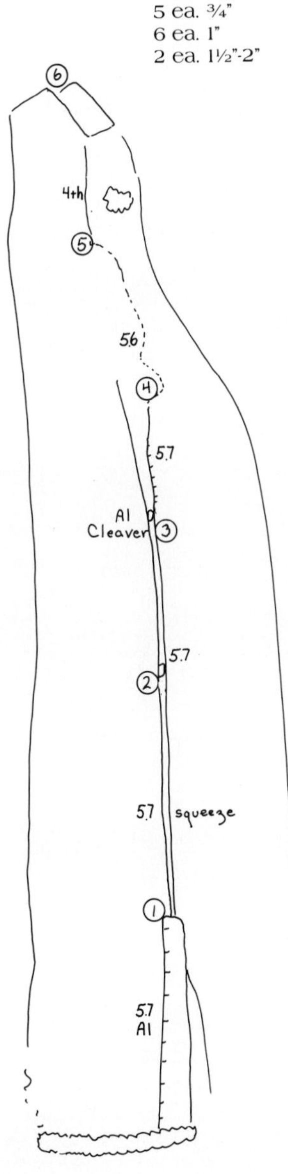

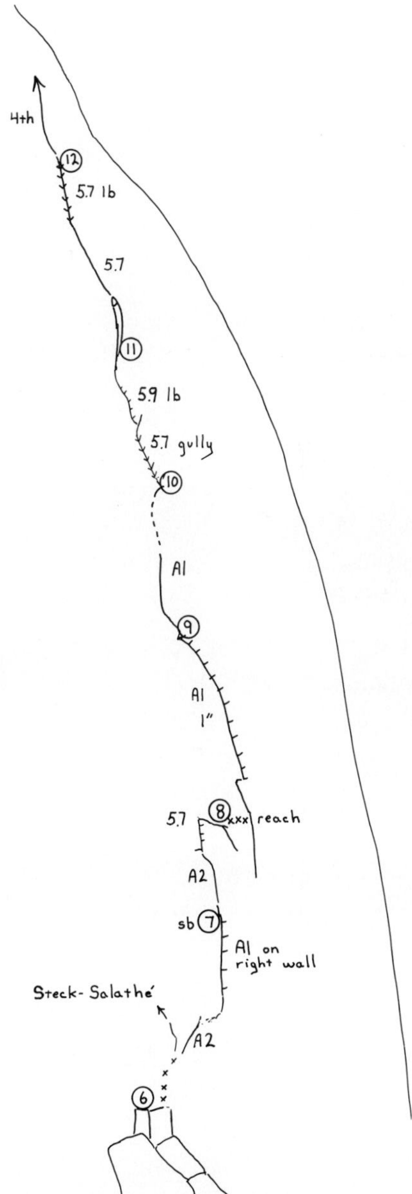

SENTINEL ROCK

Steck-Salathé

V 5.9

Approach described on page 302.
Photo on page 303.
Protection to 3"

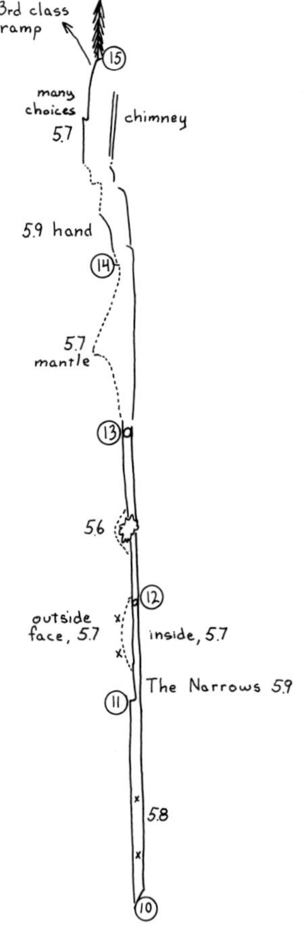

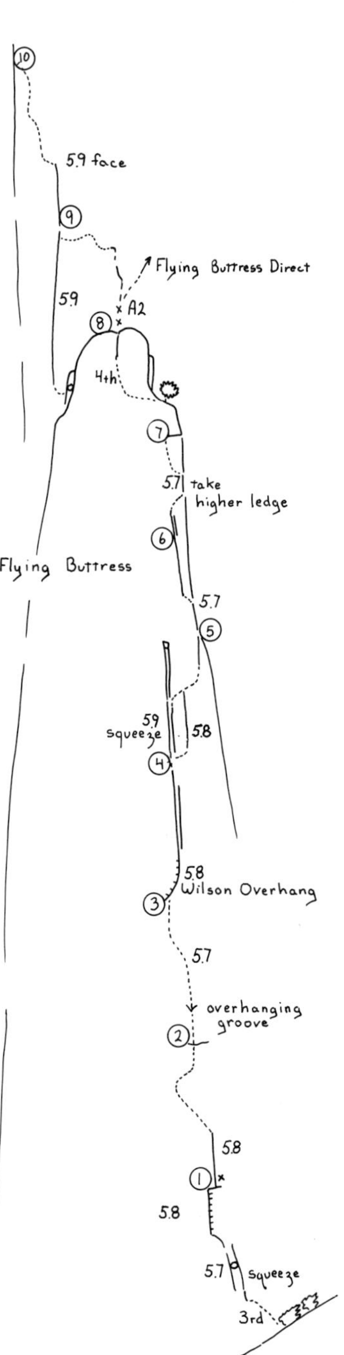

SENTINEL ROCK

West Face
V 5.11d A2
Protection many to 4"

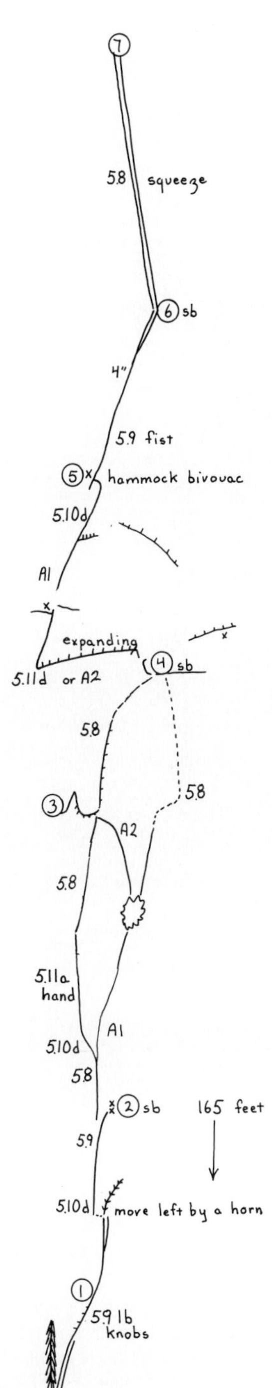

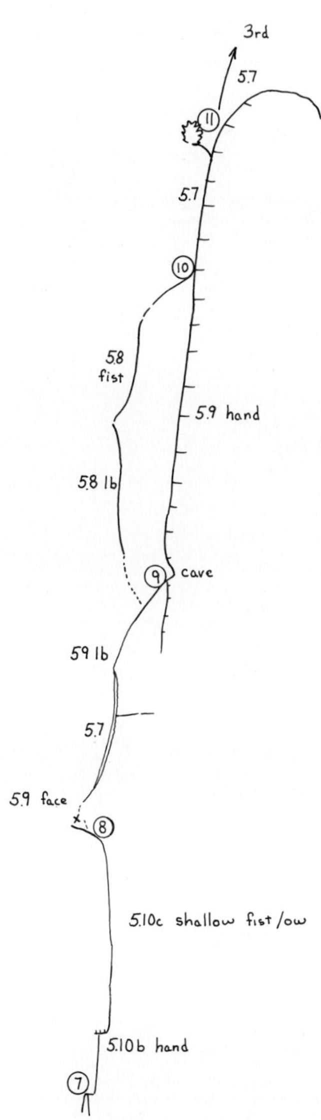

SENTINEL ROCK

In Cold Blood

V 5.11b A3

Approach described on page 302.
Photo on page 303.
Hardware

- 10 KB
- 12 LA
- 4 ea. ½"-⅝"
- 2 ea. ¾"-1"
- 1 ea. 1¼"

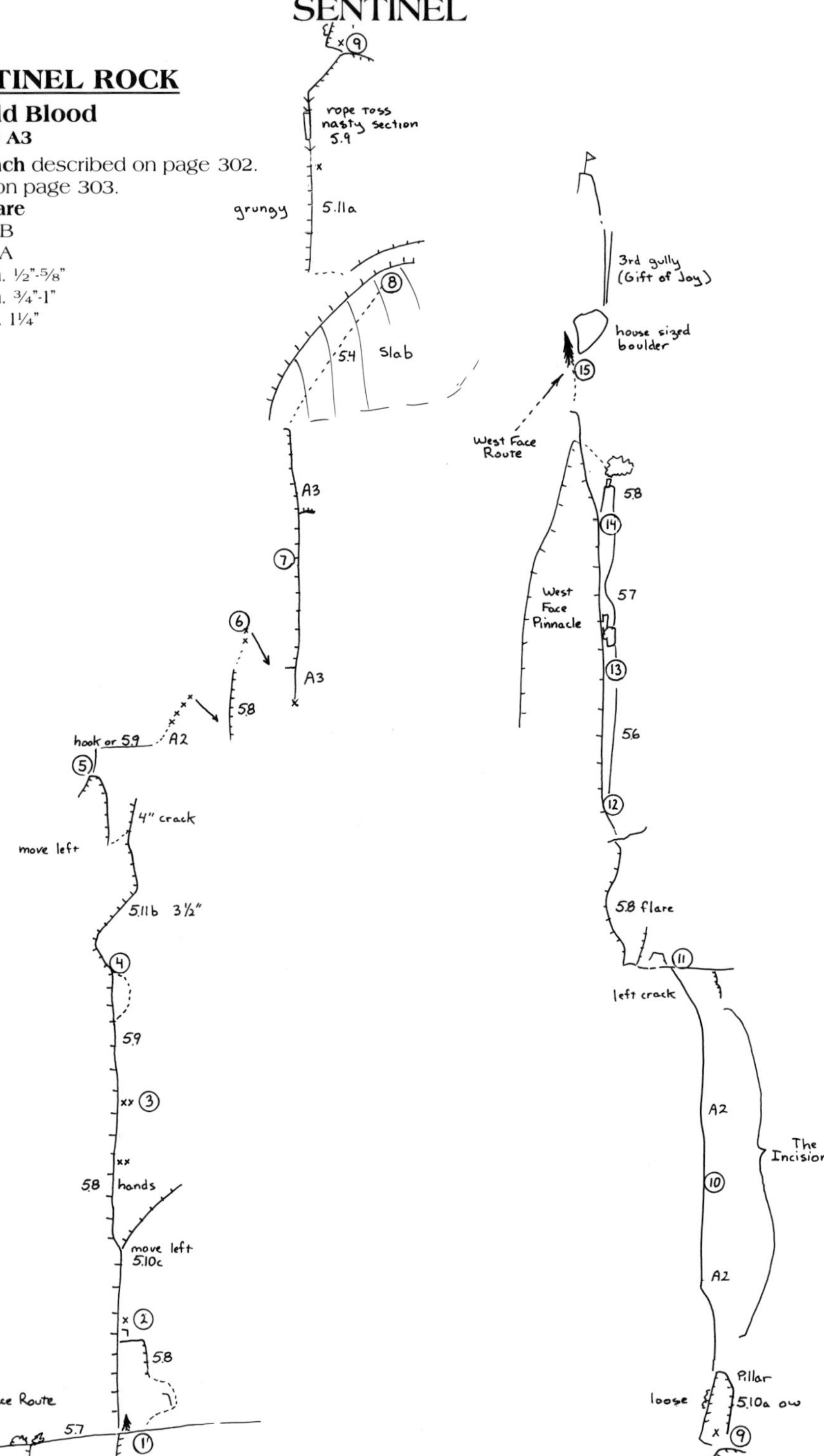

SENTINEL CREEK

1 Vanishing Point
2 Tilted Mitten
3 King Tut's Tomb
4 Pharaoh's Beard

SENTINEL CREEK AREA

Approach Park at turnouts (one on either side of the road) 1.3 miles east of the El Cap Bridge and hike up the hill.
Photo on page 311.

A **Spiderman** 5.11c
B **Vanishing Point** 5.10d

Tilted Mitten

C **Left Side** 5.9 pro: to 5"
D **Right Side** 5.8 pro: to 3"
E **The Hand Me Down** 5.10a pro: to 3", incl. extra 2"-3"
F **Mental Block** 5.10c pro: to 6", incl. extra 4"-6"

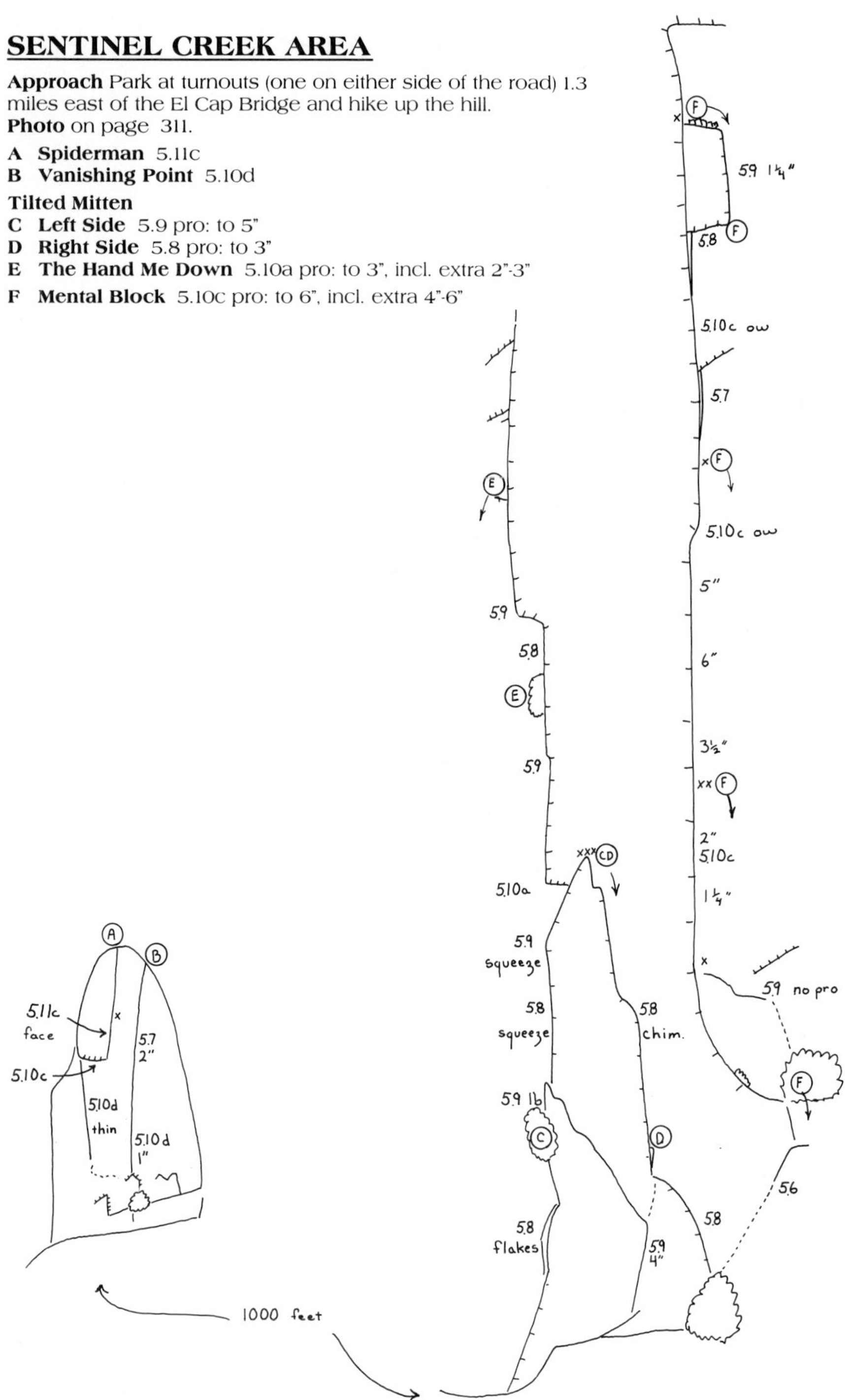

SENTINEL CREEK AREA

Approach Park at turnouts (one on either side of the road) 1.3 miles east of the El Cap Bridge and hike up the hill.

Photo on page 311.

- **A** **Hara-kiri** 5.10a
- **B** **Ying-Yang** 5.10d
- **C** **Manana** 5.10d
- **D** **King Tut's Tomb** 5.10b pro: to 6"
  Mummy's Revenge 5.9
- **E** **Into the Fire** 5.11b pro: to 3½", incl. 2 ea. #½ Friend
- **F** **Kung Pao Chicken** 5.10b pro: to 3"
  Boulderfield Gorge 5.9

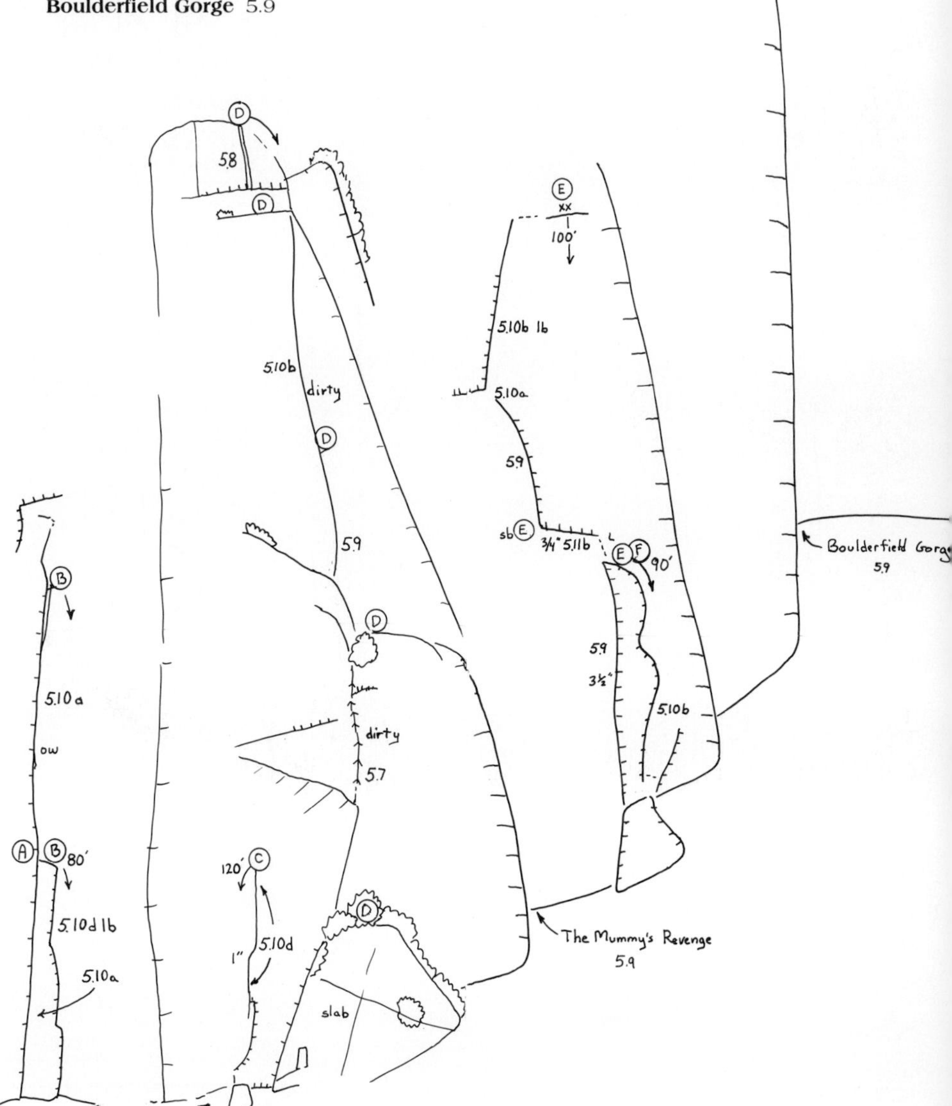

SENTINEL CREEK AREA

Approach Park at turnouts (one on either side of the road) 1.3 miles east of the El Cap Bridge and hike up the hill.

Photo on page 311.

Pharaoh's Beard

A Regular Route 5.8
B Whisker 5.11d pro: many to 1"
C Right Side 5.10d pro: to 3½"
D Look Before You Leap 5.11a
E Buried Treasure 5.11a A0 pro: incl. 3 ea. #4 Friends
F Sheba A4+

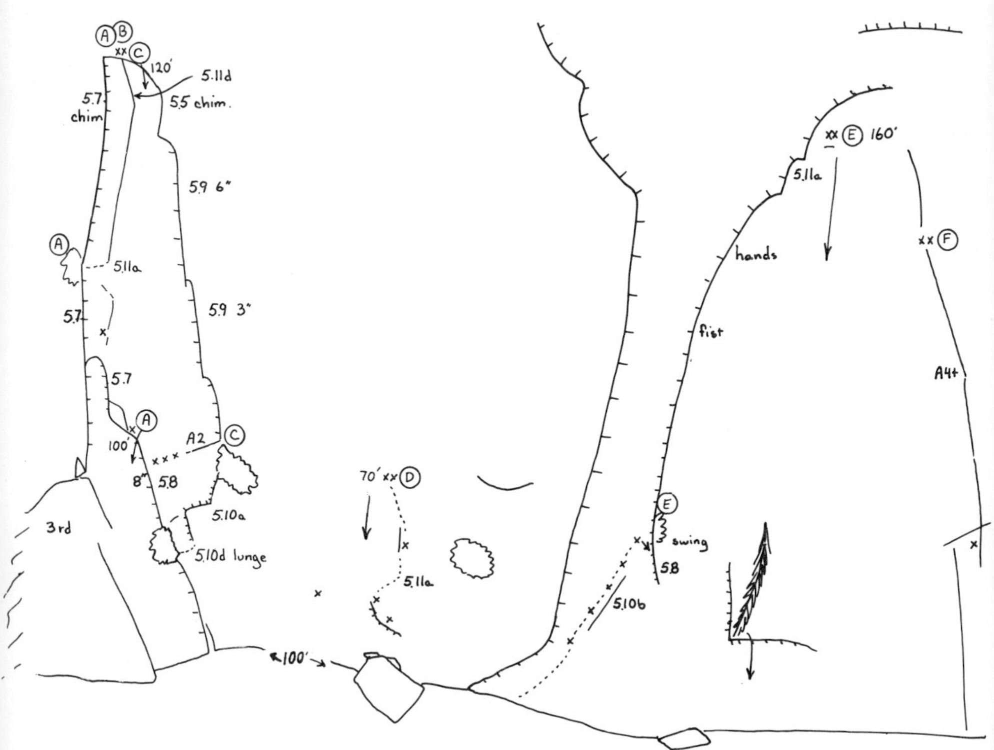

LOST BROTHER

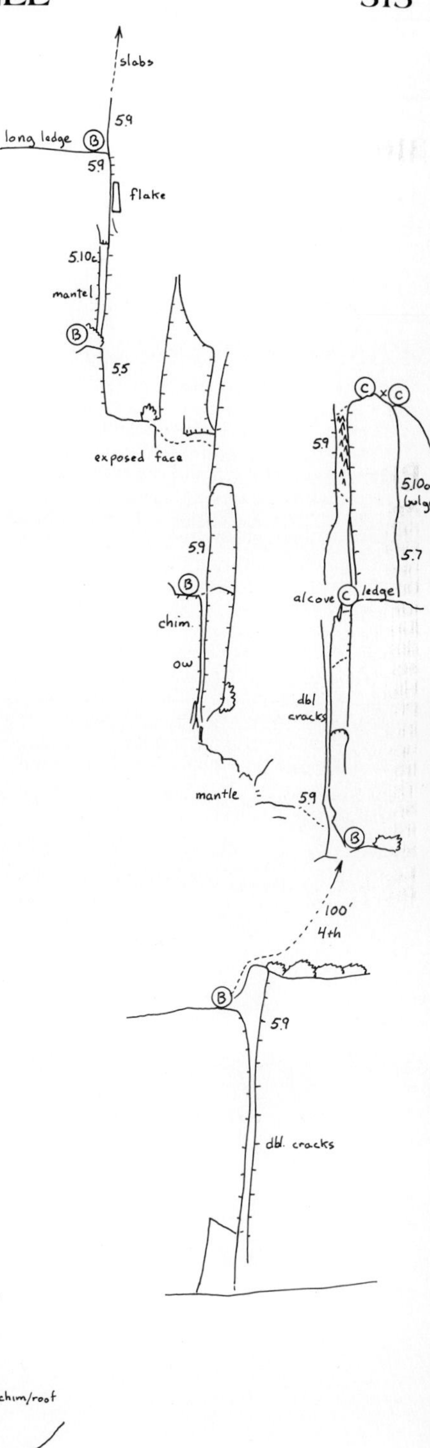

Approach Lost Brother is the large square-cut formation located directly across the Valley from Lower Brother. Park in a dirt turnout 1.1 miles east of El Cap Bridge and hike up. The Northwest Face Route follows, in general, the large corner system on that face. Brushy scrambling leads left across the lower angle north face. The route starts just before this sloping traverse leads to a huge drop-off Realm of the Lizard King lies just up from the toe of the Lower Brother buttress.

A **Realm of the Lizard King** 5.11c
B **Northwest Face Route** 5.10c
C **The Last Resort Pinnacle**
Left Side 5.9 pro: to 2½"
Center 5.10a pro: to 3"

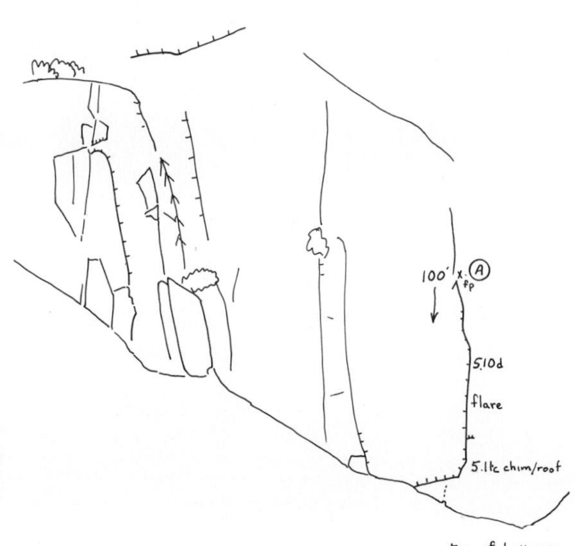

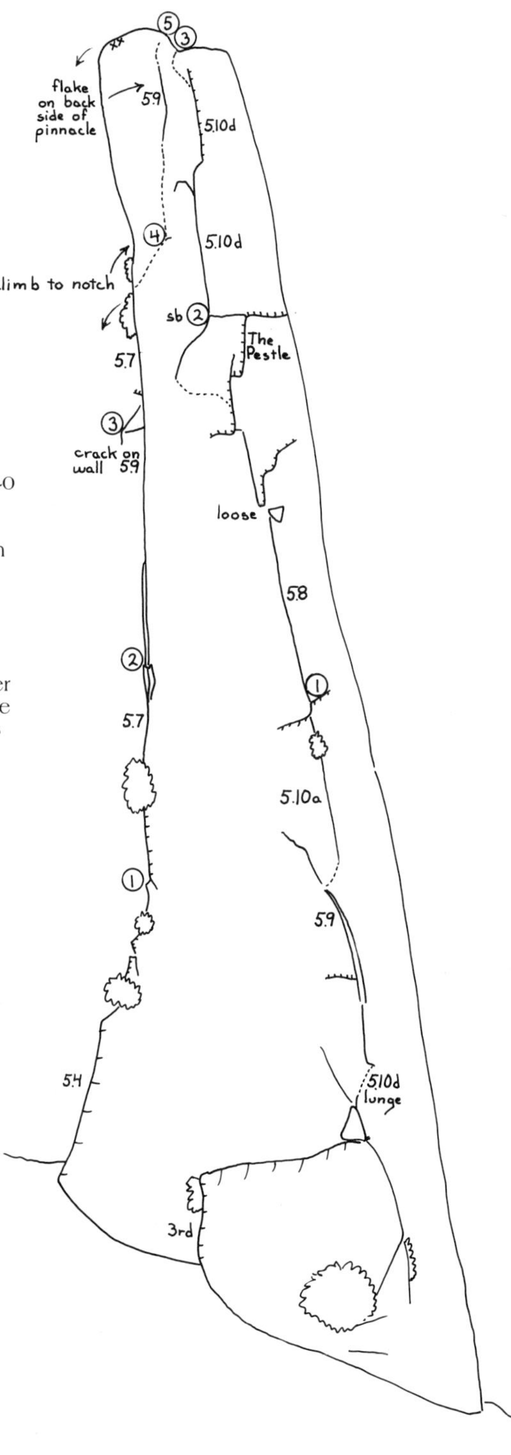

PHANTOM PINNACLE

Approach Phantom Pinnacle lies on the right side of the very broad gully east of Cathedral Spires and is seen in profile as a needle, slightly separated from the wall behind. Begin hiking at a double paved turnout 1.4 miles east of the Hwy 41/Hwy 140 junction. The rough Spires Gully trail heads directly back into the woods and up. It serves as the approach for all the routes on Higher Spire and Higher Cathedral Rock. Phantom Pinnacle is approached from an inobvious trail that branches off directly uphill from a point where the Spires Gully trail begins a definite diagonal up and right. This leads ultimately to the routes on Lower Spire, but for Phantom, a traverse left off the trail and up around the intervening buttress should be put off until the last opportunity.

Left Side 5.9
Outside Face 5.10d pro: to 3"

THE CATHEDRAL ROCKS

Approach The approach to the routes of the Higher Cathedral Spire and Higher Cathedral Rock is made from the climbers' trail up the Spires Gully. This leads ultimately to the notch between Higher Cathedral Rock and the wall that is up and behind. Start hiking at a road turnout 1.4 miles east of the Hwy 41/Hwy 140 junction at Bridalveil Falls. The trail heads directly back into the woods and up. Lower Cathedral Spire is reached from an inobvious trail that branches off directly uphill from a point where the Spires Gully Trail begins a definite diagonal up and right.

The **East Buttress** of Middle Cathedral Rock is hiked to from a turnout 1.3 miles from the Hwy 41/Hwy 140 junction. For all the routes that ascend the northeast face of Middle Rock, park in the same vicinity and hike back west to the rock along the horse trail that parallels the road in the woods to the south. The north face apron of Middle can be be reached either by hiking up along the wall from the **Direct North Buttress**, or from under Lower Rock, below the Gunsight. Park for the latter alternative 0.8 miles east of the Hwy 41/Hwy 140 junction.

The **East Buttress** of Lower Cathedral Rock and the routes on the east face are approached as above. **Beggar's Buttress** and the north buttress area is reached by walking east on the horse trail from the long parking turnout 0.3 miles from the Hwy 41/Hwy 140 junction.

Descent To descend from either Cathedral Spire it is necessary to rappel the regular routes of those rocks. From the summit of Higher Cathedral Rock walk south and around to the upper part of the Spires Gully.

The descent off Middle Cathedral Rock is a bit more complicated. While most of the routes of the northeast face do not lead to the summit, all that do eventually cross the Kat Walk, a fault line/ledge system that traverses the rock from the top of the **Direct North Buttress**, east to the **East Buttress** and on into the **Cathedral Chimney**, the great chasm that lies between Middle and Higher Cathedral Rocks. The goal of climbers ascending the **East Buttress** and routes that climb up in that vicinity is to scramble up from the top of the technical climbing to the Kat Walk, in this area more an area of sloping meadows and heavy brush. Work left toward the **Cathedral Chimney**, where some minor down climbing leads to talus and the Valley floor. A descent of the upper part of the **Cathedral Chimney** requires rappels, and the goal of the descending climber is to work left toward the chimney below this point.

Other routes on the northeast face of Middle (like **Stoner's Highway**) are best rappelled from their high points, but if the choice is to continue, they most often lead to the Powell- Reed Ledges, a sweeping and broad system that leads up and left into the U-shaped Bowl. With some careful routefinding a moderate 5th class scramble can be made up and out the left side of this feature to the Kat Walk. The **Direct North Buttress** and **North Buttress** lead to a spot behind Thirsty Spire, a lone pinnacle at the west end of the Kat Walk. Either work left along the ledge system to the **Cathedral Chimney** or continue on easy 5th class for 300 feet to brushy slopes that lead to the summit.

From the summit of Middle Cathedral there are several choices. One can walk down to the notch between Middle and Higher, scramble up to the top of Higher and then walk south to the top of the Spires Gully and the trail that leads down from there. Alternatively, steep slabs on the northeast side of the rock can be descended (with possible rappels) to the Kat Walk, where a scramble south leads to the **Cathedral Chimney** below the difficuties. Finally, it is possible to bushwack down the west side of Middle for a descent down the Gunsight, the notch between Middle and Lower Rocks. From the notch between Middle and Higher Rocks, walk down brush-covered slabs that lead west for about 400 feet or until very steep slabs are encountered. Traverse left into a thick brushfield, then head straight down toward Bridalveil Creek. When about 200 feet above the water, contour north and head uphill for the top of the Gunsight. Scrambling and short rappels lead to talus and the valley floor.

For the descent from all the routes that lead to the basin above Bridalveil Falls, including all Lower Rock routes, the Gunsight is about the only alternative.

Photo on page 331.

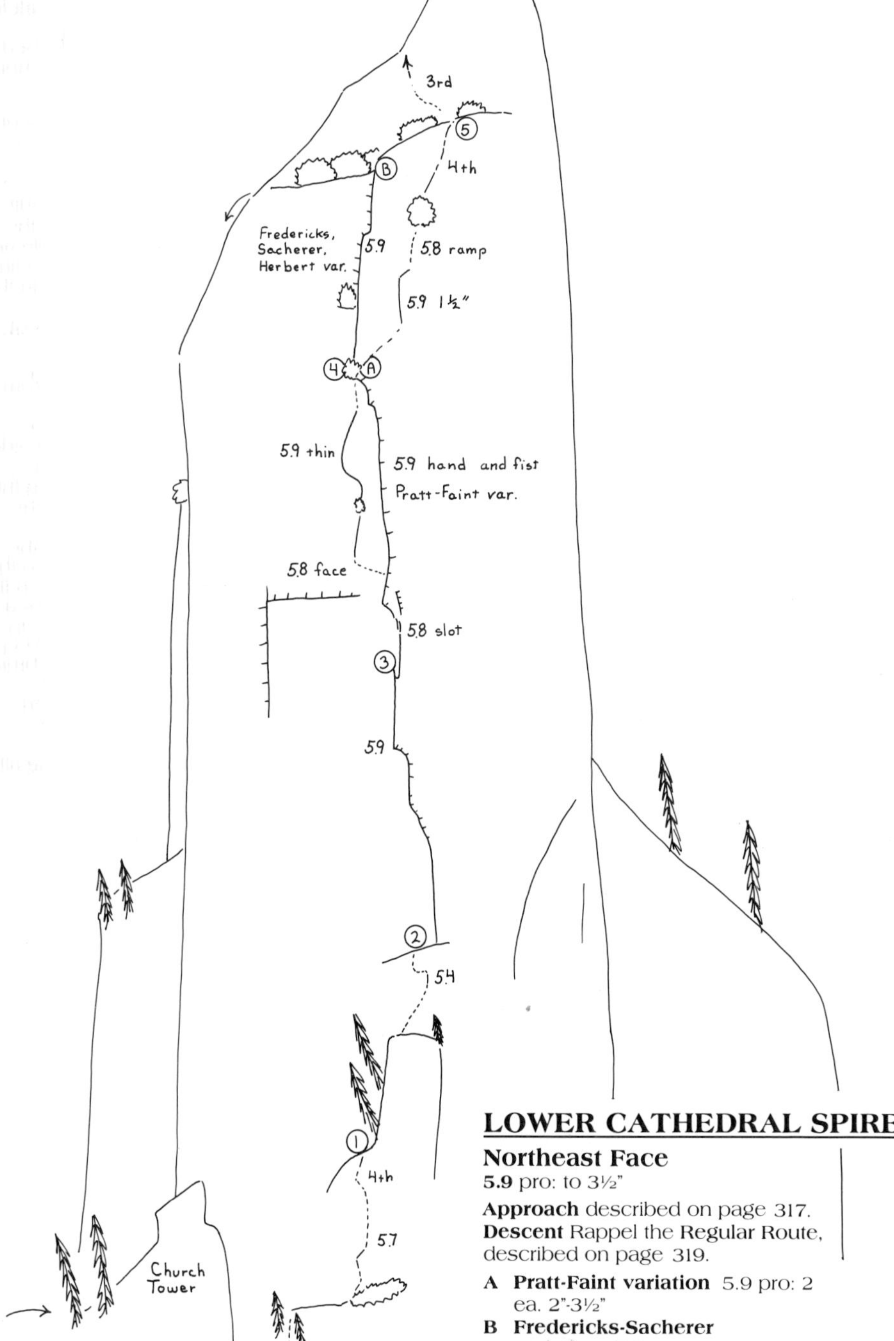

LOWER CATHEDRAL SPIRE

Northeast Face

5.9 pro: to 3½"

Approach described on page 317.
Descent Rappel the Regular Route, described on page 319.

A Pratt-Faint variation 5.9 pro: 2 ea. 2"-3½"

B Fredericks-Sacherer variation 5.9

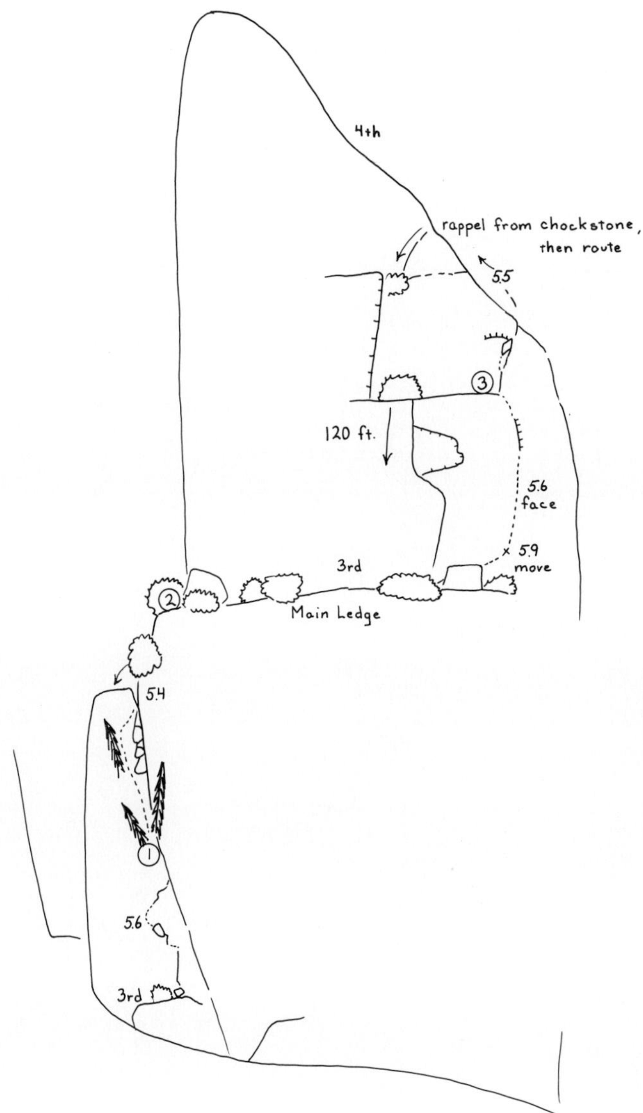

LOWER CATHEDRAL SPIRE

Regular Route

5.9 pro: to 2½"

Approach described on page 317.
Descent Rappel the route.

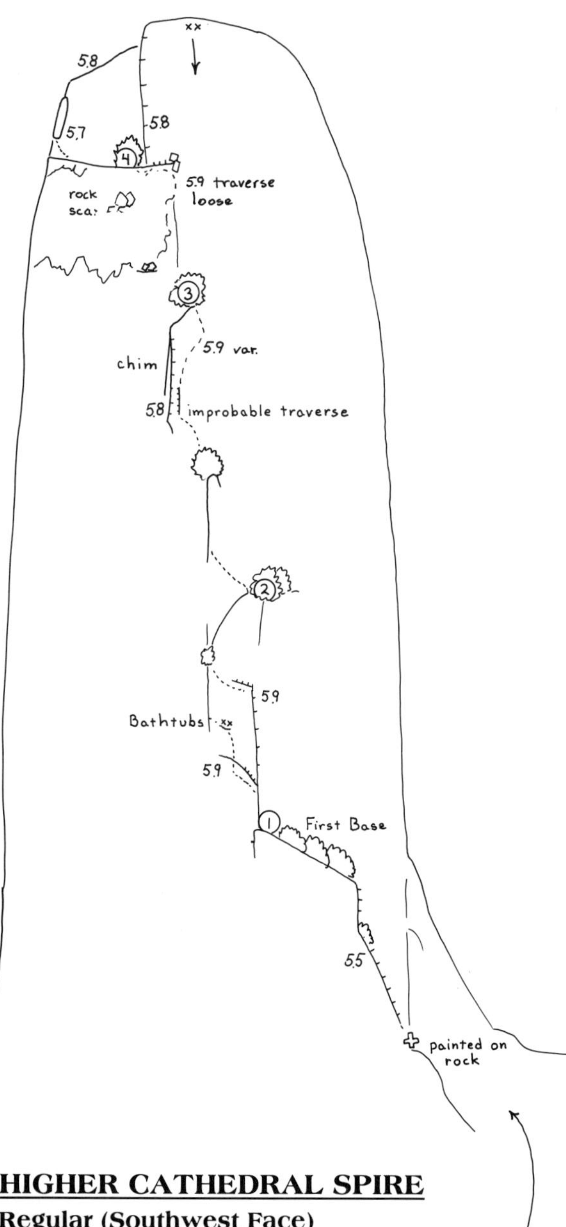

HIGHER CATHEDRAL SPIRE

Regular (Southwest Face) Route

5.9

Approach described on page 317.
Descent Rappel the route.

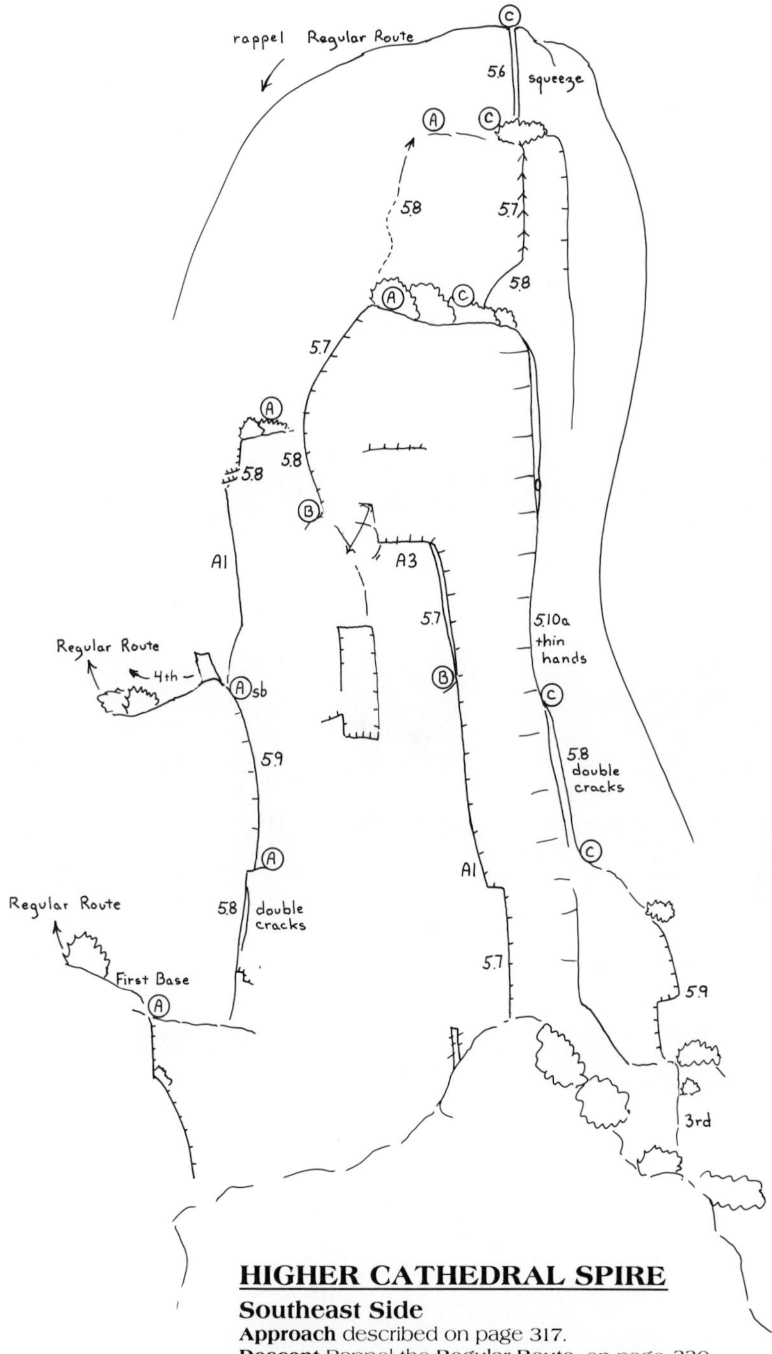

HIGHER CATHEDRAL SPIRE

Southeast Side

Approach described on page 317.
Descent Rappel the Regular Route, on page 320.

A **Steck Route** 5.9 A1 pitons: LA to ⅝"
B **Southeast Face** 5.8 A3 pitons: KB to 4"
C **East Corner** 5.10a

HIGHER CATHEDRAL SPIRE

Higher Aspirations

V 5.8 A3

Approach described on page 317.
Descent Rappel the Regular Route, page 320.
Hardware

35 pitons
10-15 rivet hangers
6 copperheads
hooks

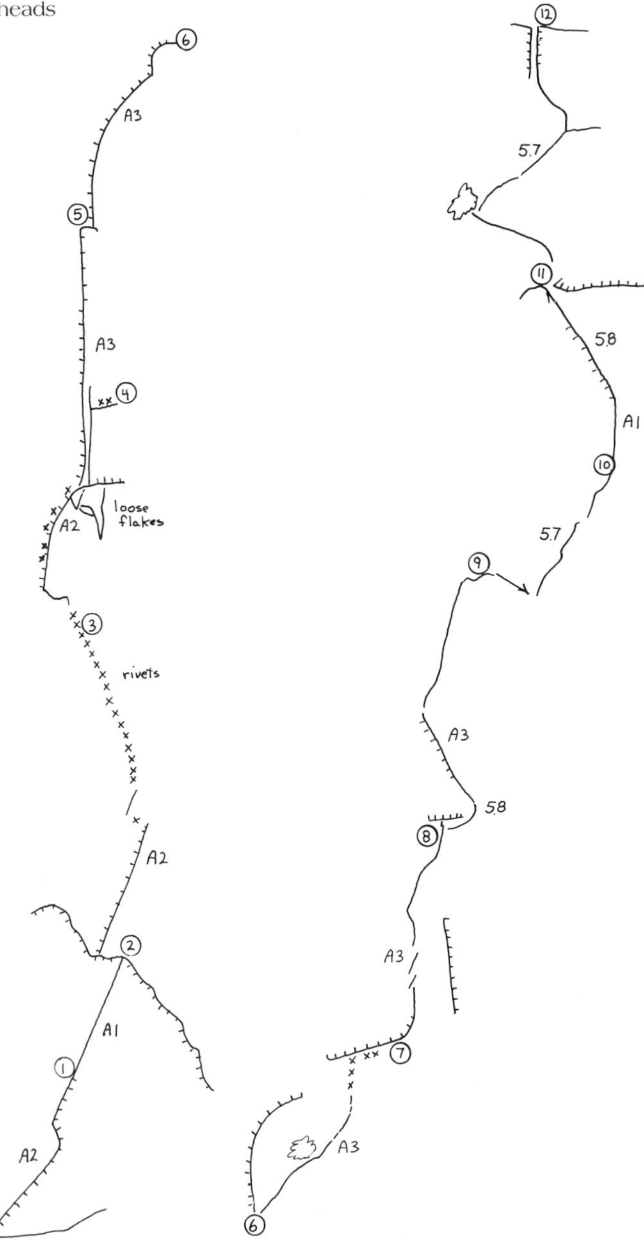

HIGHER CATHEDRAL SPIRE

Northwest Face

V 5.8 A3

Approach described on page 317.
Descent Rappel the Regular Route, page 320.
Hardware

2 KB
6 LA
3 ea. ½"-⅝"
6 ea. ¾"-1"
4 ea. 1¼"-2"
2 ea. 2½"-3"

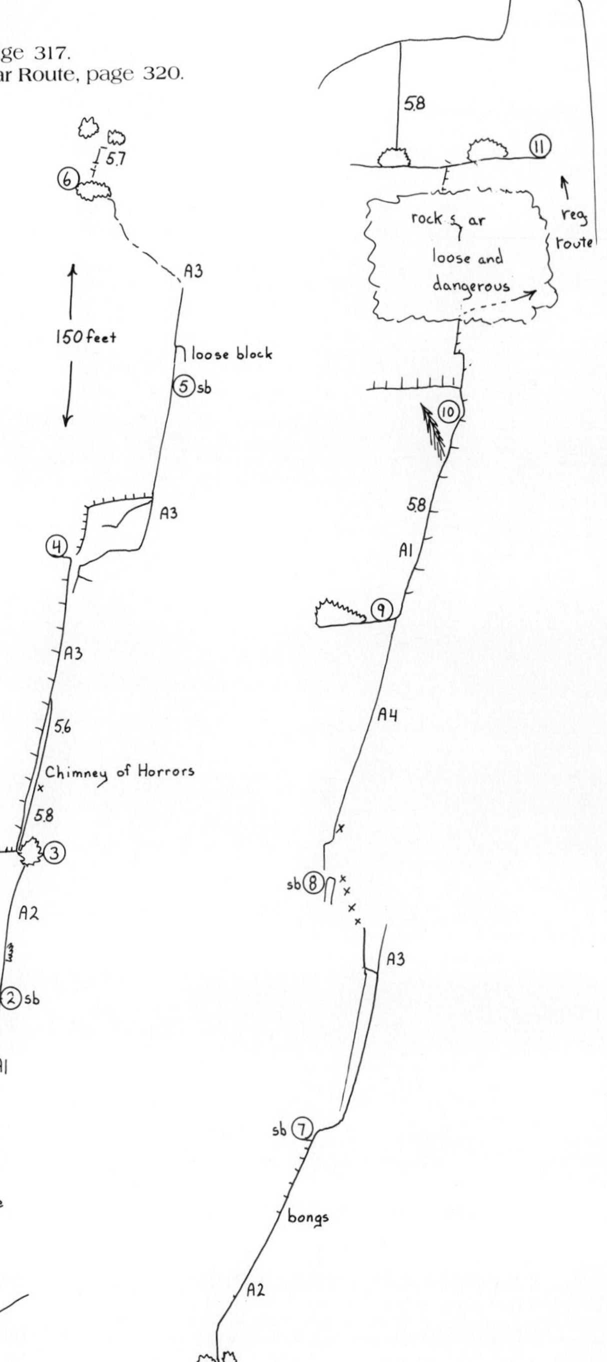

HIGHER CATHEDRAL ROCK – East Face

N.P.S.

1 LOWER CATHEDRAL SPIRE
2 HIGHER CATHEDRAL SPIRE
3 The Sequel
4 Braille Book
5 The Dictionary
6 East Face Route
7 Learning to Crawl
8 Mary's Tears
9 Northeast Buttress
10 Crucifix
11 Power Point

HIGHER CATHEDRAL ROCK – East Face

Approach, Descent See page 317.
Photo on page 324.

- **A** **The Syllable** 5.8
- **B** **The Sequel** 5.8
- **C** **Blind Man's Bluff** 5.9
- **D** **Braille Book** 5.8 pro: to 3"
- **E** **The Dictionary** 5.8
- **F** **Book of Job** 5.10b pro: to 4"

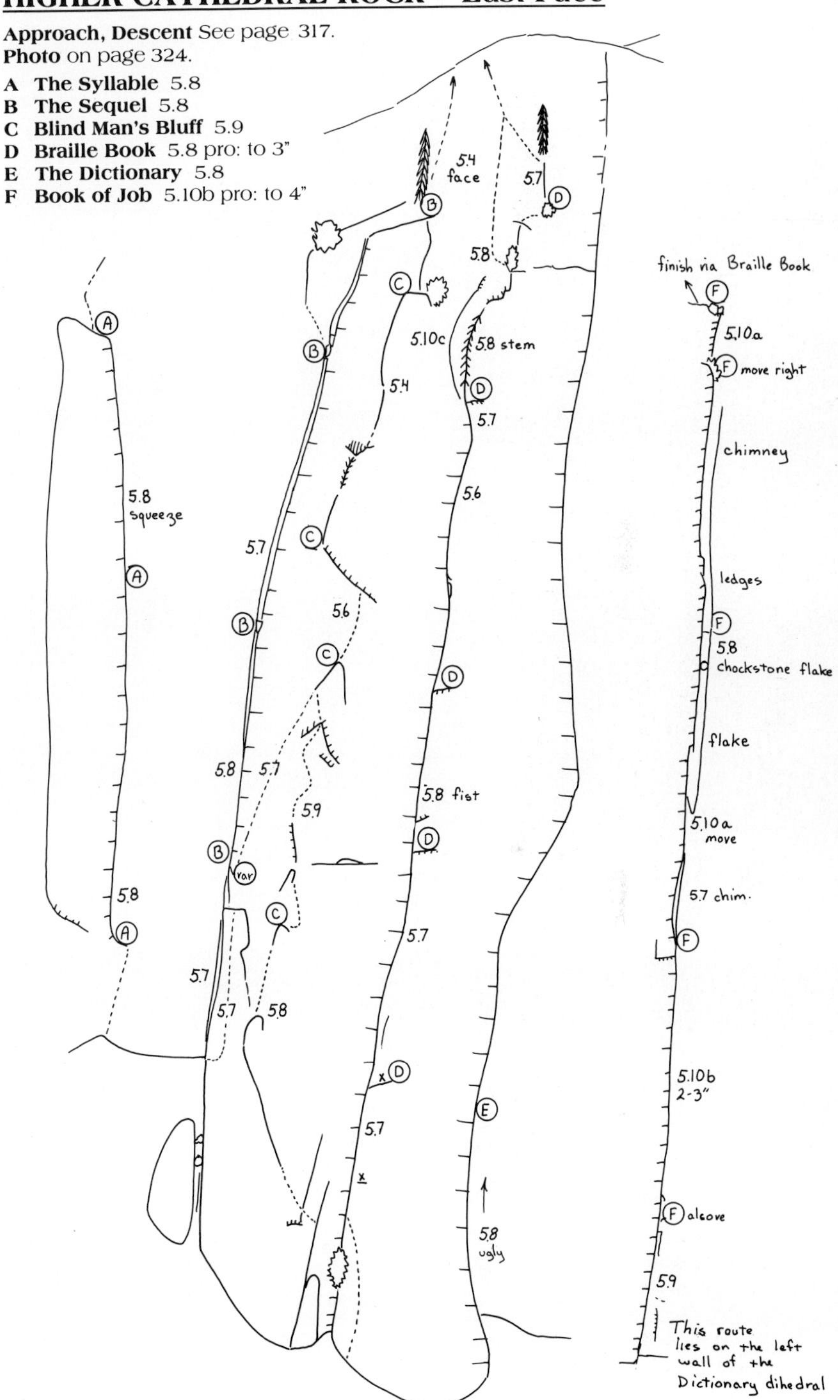

HIGHER CATHEDRAL ROCK

East Face Route

V 5.10 A4

Approach, Descent on page 317.
Photo on page 324.
Hardware

- 3 KB
- 10 LA
- 2 ea. ½"-⅝"
- 5 ea. ¾"-1"
- 4 ea. 1½"
- 3 ea. 2"
- 2 ea. 2½"
- 1 ea. 3"
- hooks
- copperheads
- nuts

10
50ft
9
A2
wide crack
8
stance
A1
stance 7
A2
5.7
6
chimney
bivouac
5.10
5
5.9
5"
4
5.8 step
5.7
3
expanding
A4
2
sb
A2
5.8 A4
F
1
slot
5.9 face

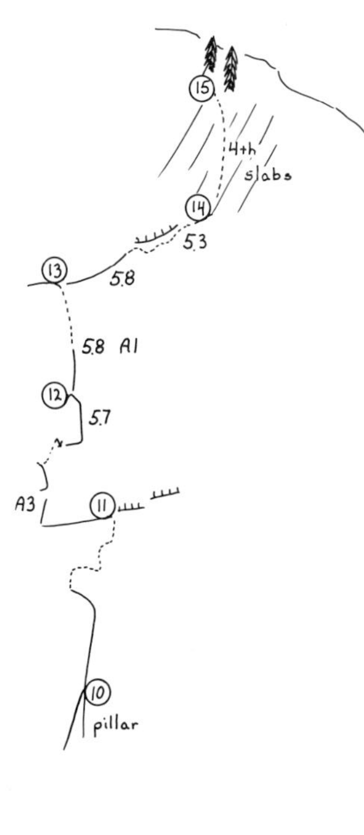

HIGHER CATHEDRAL ROCK

Learning to Crawl

V 5.9 A3+

Approach, Descent on page 317.
Photo on page 324.

Hardware

1 rurp
15 KB
15 LA
2 ea. ½"-⅝"
3 ea. ¾"-1"
2 ea. 1¼"
2 ea. Friends to #4

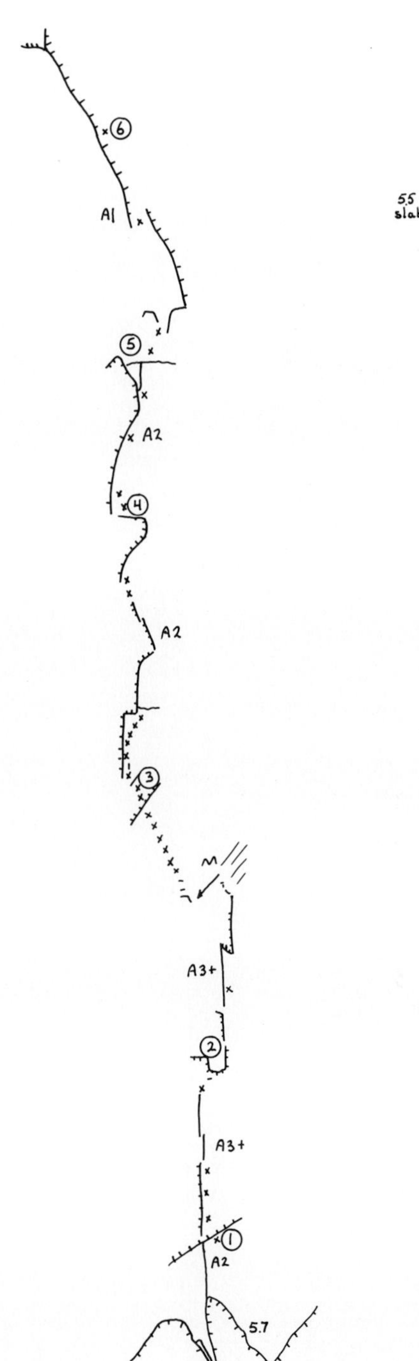

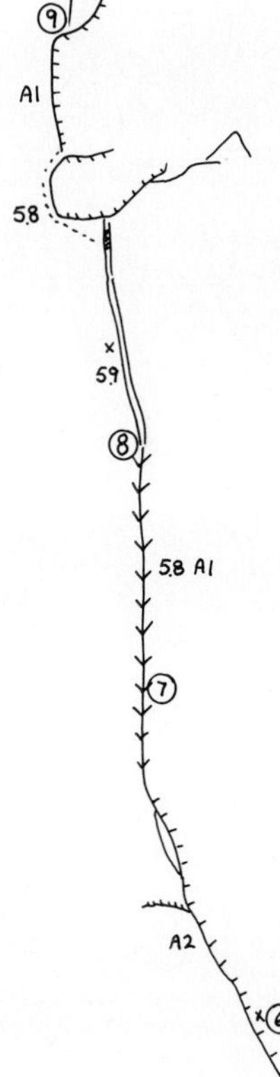

HIGHER CATHEDRAL ROCK

Approach, Descent on page 317.
Photo on page 324.

A Mary's Tears
5.11b
B Northeast Buttress
5.9 pro: to 3"

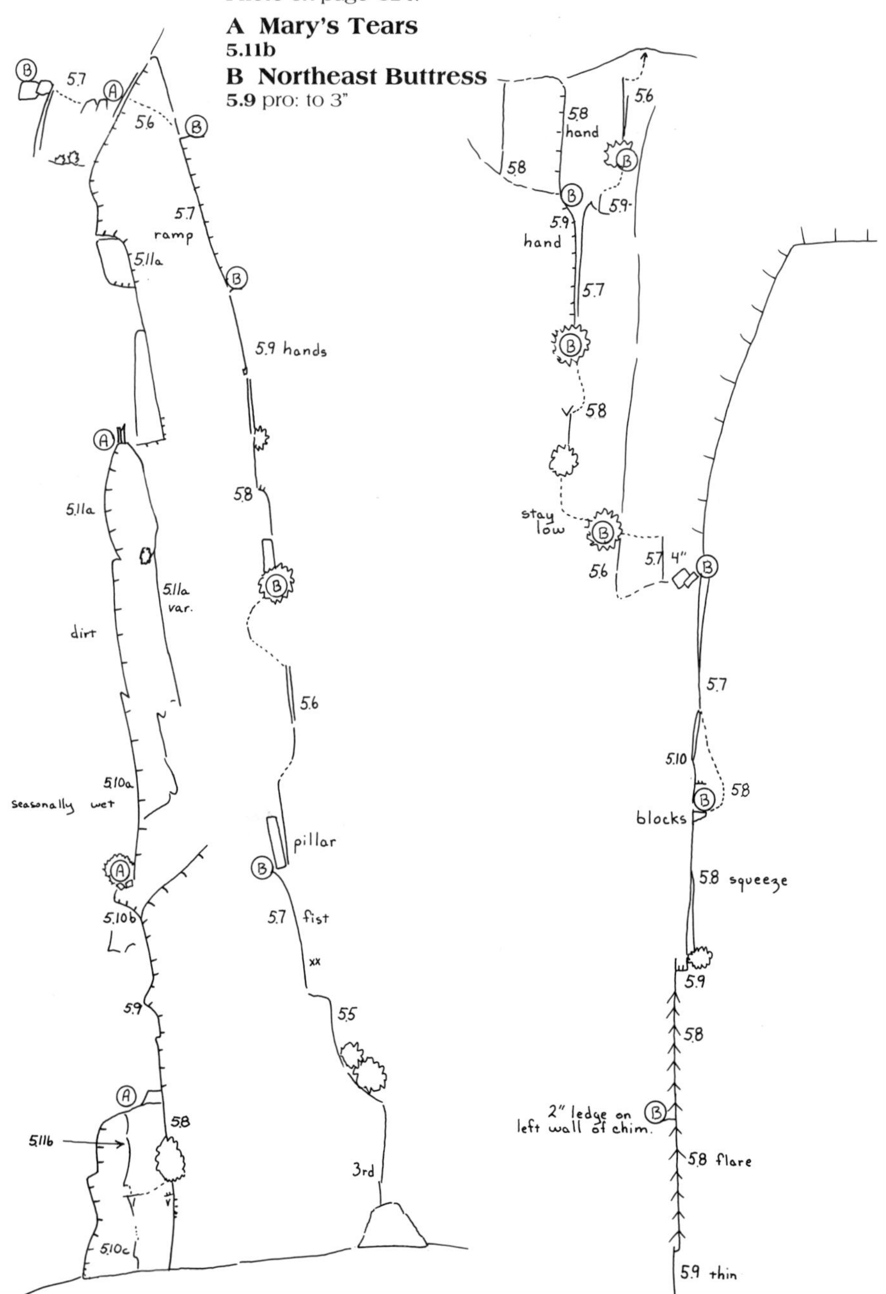

HIGHER CATHEDRAL ROCK

Approach, Descent on page 317.
Photo on pages 324, 331.

A Power Point
5.11c

Protection
2 ea. Friend to #4, incl. 3
ea. #3, #4
wires
RP's

B Crucifix
5.12a

Protection
wires to a #3½ Friend

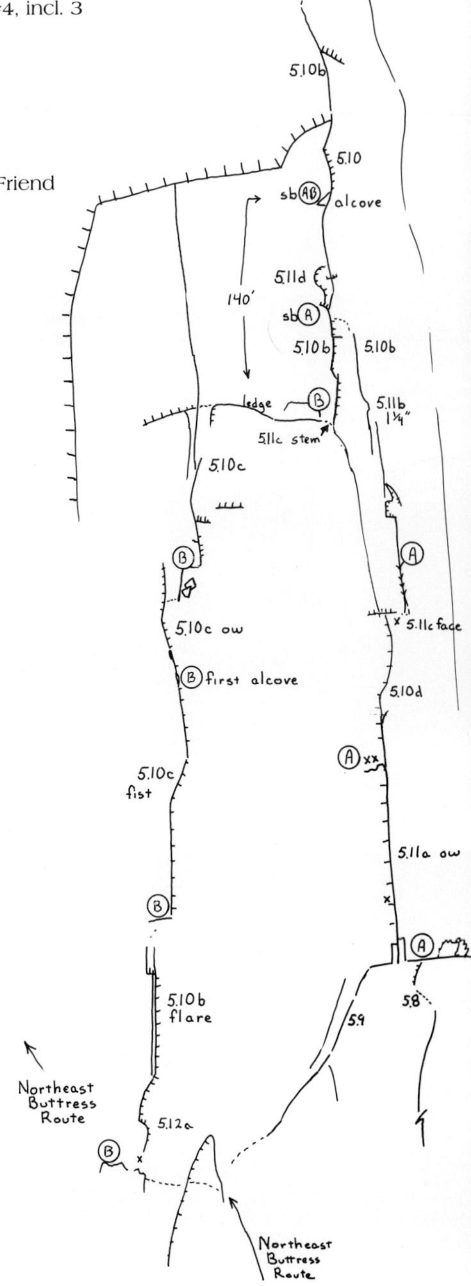

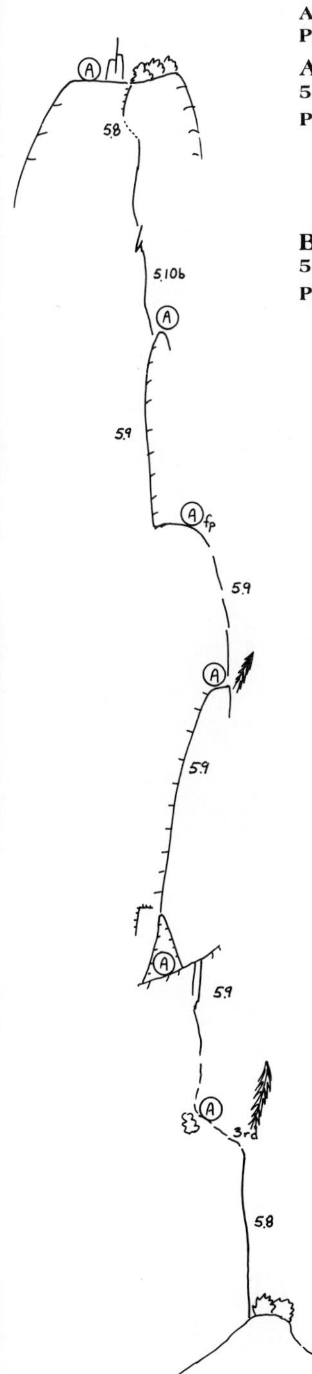

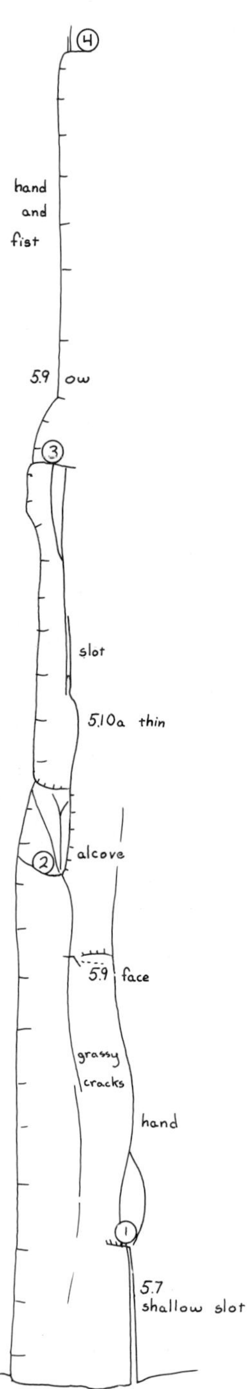

MIDDLE CATHEDRAL ROCK

Alley Cat

5.10a pro: to 6", incl. extra 2½"-3"

Approach This route is on the east face of Middle Cathedral Rock, just below the technical climbing in the Cathedral Chimney.

Descent Rappel and down climb the Cathedral Chimney.

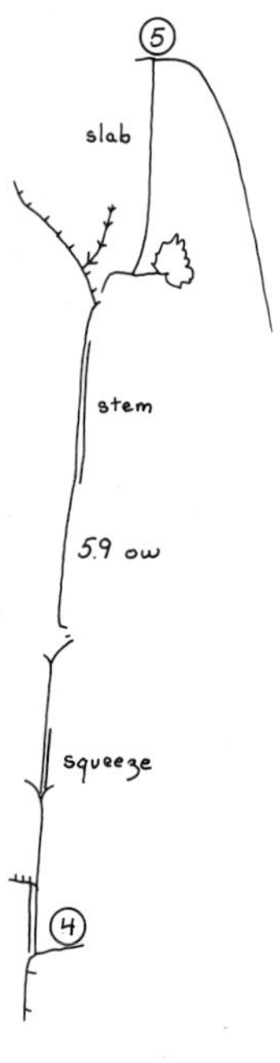

THE CATHEDRAL ROCKS *N.P.S.*

1 Braille Book
2 Power Point
3 East Buttress of Middle
4 Sacherer-Fredericks
5 Kor-Beck
6 Space Babble
7 Central Pillar of Frenzy
8 Stoner's Highway
9 Powell-Reed
10 Paradise Lost
11 Direct North Buttress
12 North Buttress
13 Mother Earth
14 East Buttress of Lower
15 North Face
16 Beggar's Buttress

MIDDLE CATHEDRAL ROCK

East Buttress

5.10c

Approach Take the gully left of Middle Cathedral Rock to gain the shoulder that begins the East Buttress.
Descent Work up to and then left on the Kat Walk, the ledge system that leads toward the Cathedral Chimney. Down climb and rappel.
Photo page 331.

A No Butts About It 5.10b

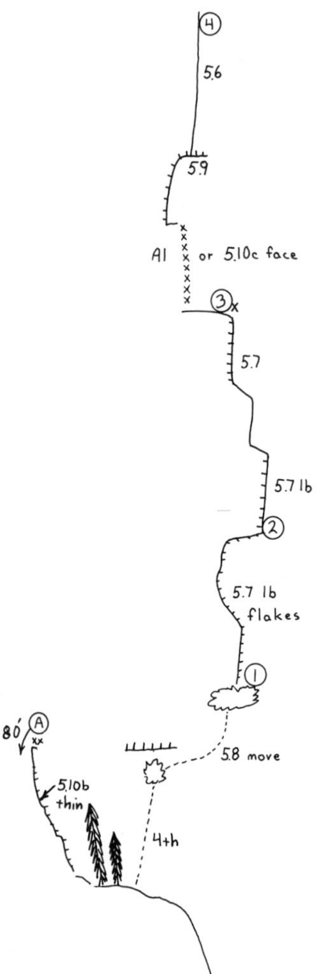

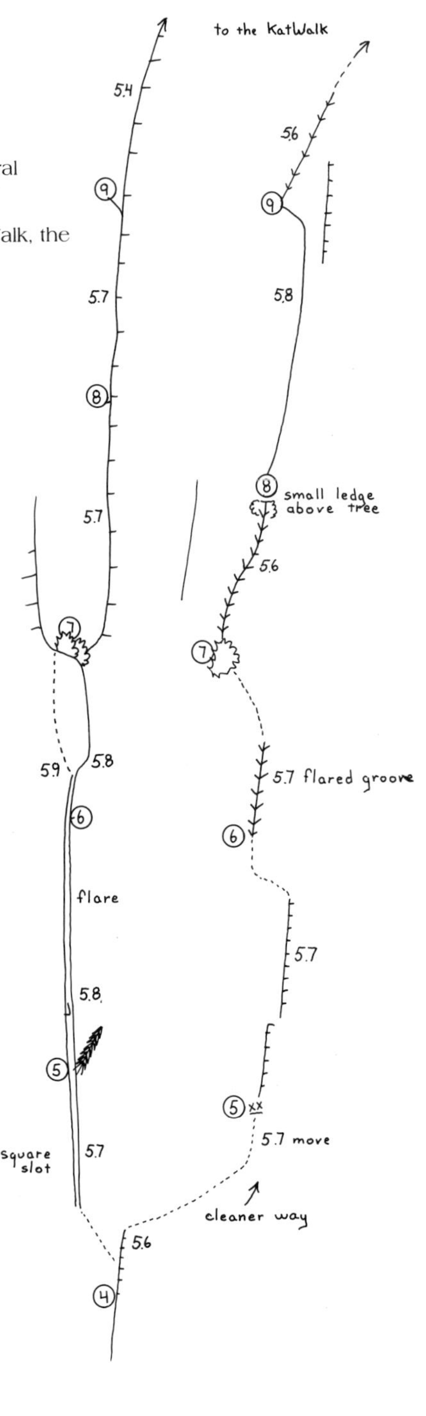

MIDDLE CATHEDRAL ROCK

Sacherer-Fredericks (with direct finish)

5.10c pro: to 3"

Descent Use the Kat Walk descent, page 317.

Photo page 331.

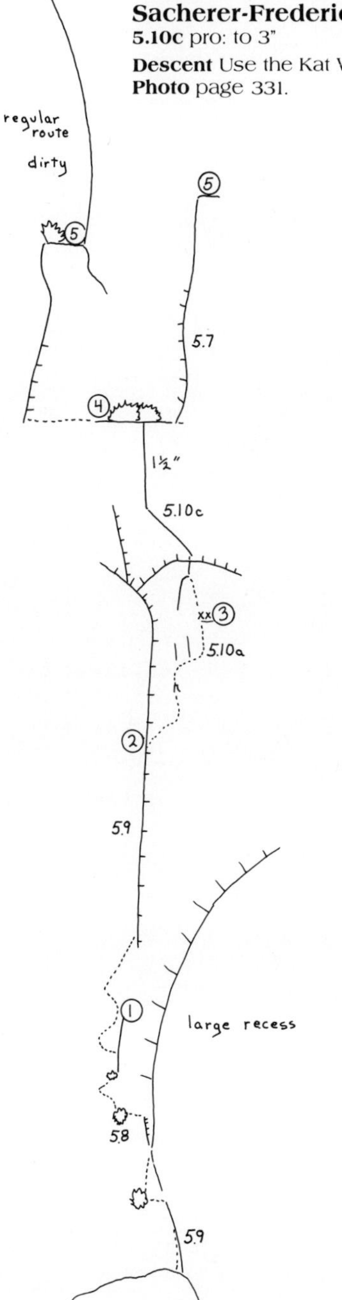

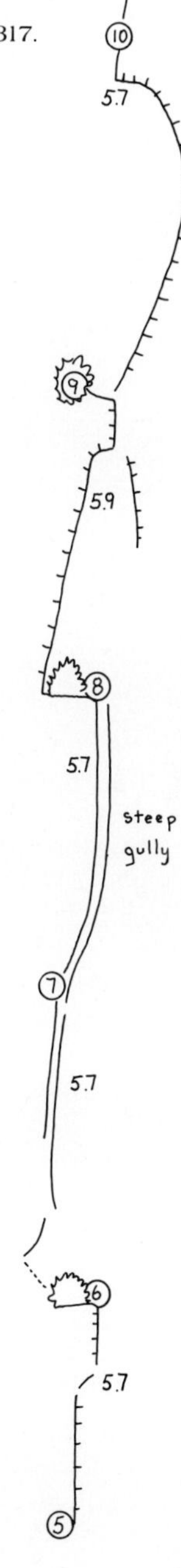

MIDDLE CATHEDRAL ROCK

Kor-Beck
5.9
Protection to 3"

Photo on page 331.

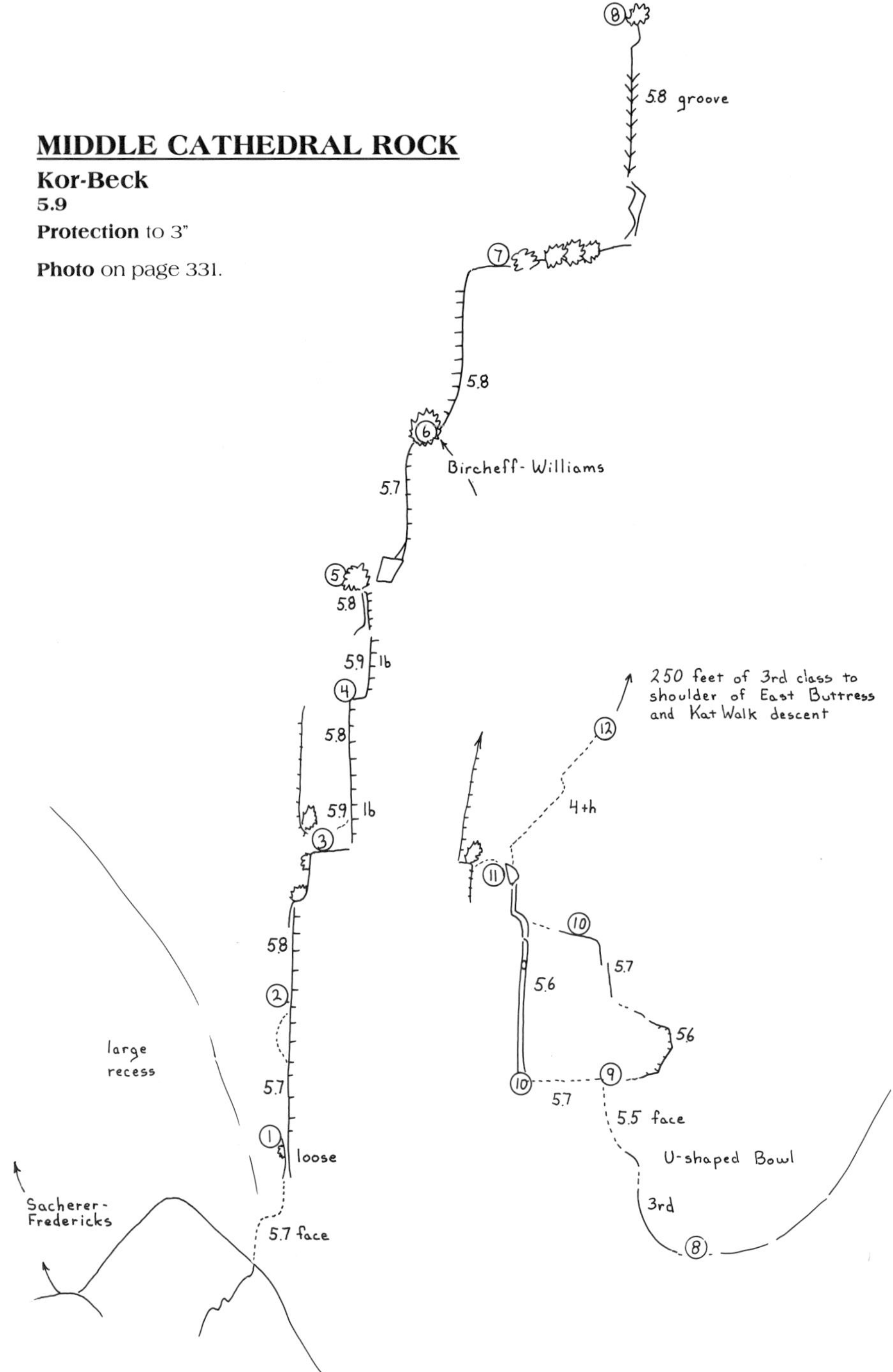

MIDDLE CATHEDRAL ROCK

Space Babble

5.11a

Descent Rappel the route.

Protection

RP's
nuts
2 ea. Friend to #2
1 ea. #4 Friend

Photo on page 331.

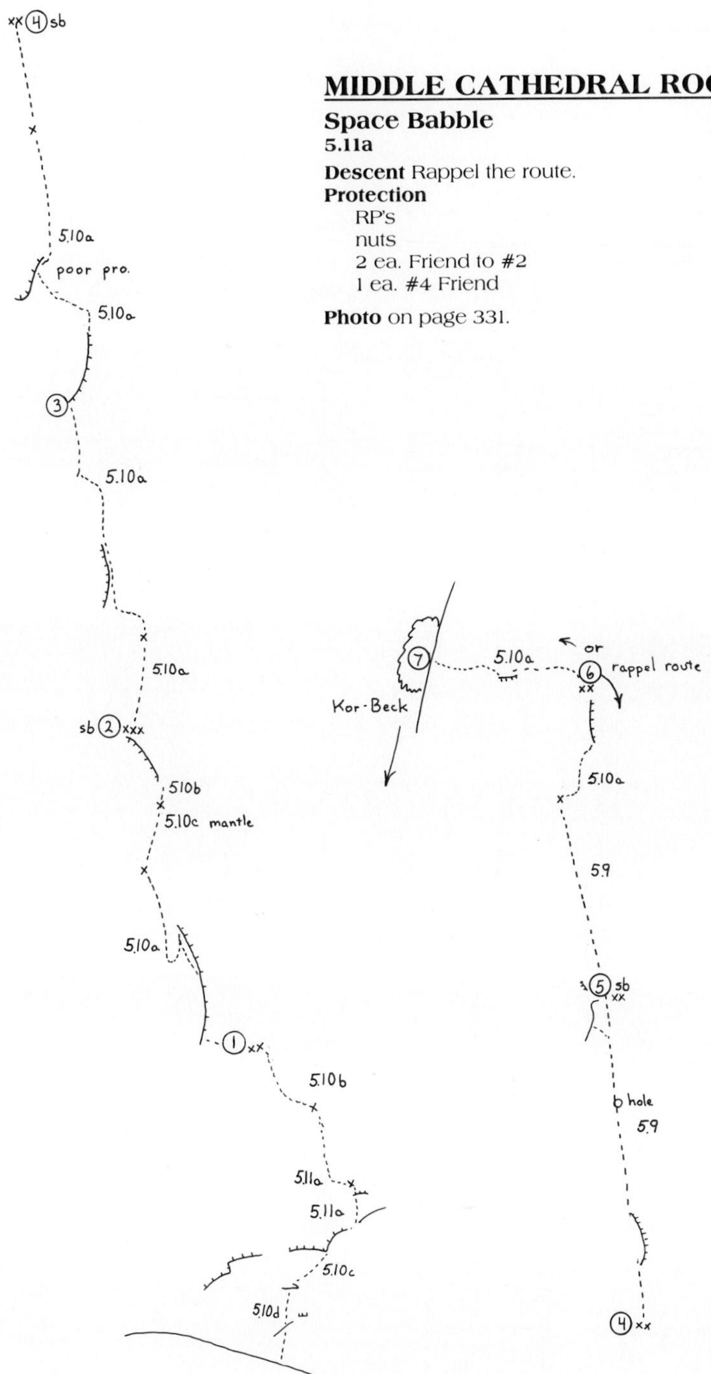

MIDDLE CATHEDRAL ROCK

Approach on page 317.
Descent The Bircheff-Williams and the escape off the Central Pillar are best descended by rappelling Space Babble, page 335, or the Kor-Beck.
Photo on page 331.

Bircheff-Williams
5.11b

Protection
to 3", incl. 2 ea. 1/8"- 3/4"

Central Pillar of Frenzy
V 5.10d

Protection to 3½"
This route is popularly done in one of three ways, by climbing the first five pitches and rappelling the route, by doing two more pitches and traversing to the Kor-Beck to rappel that route, or continuing to the Powell-Reed Ledges and off via the U-shaped Bowl. Extra thin protection is needed for the upper route.

Chouinard-Pratt
V 5.11

This route follows the right side of "The Pillar."

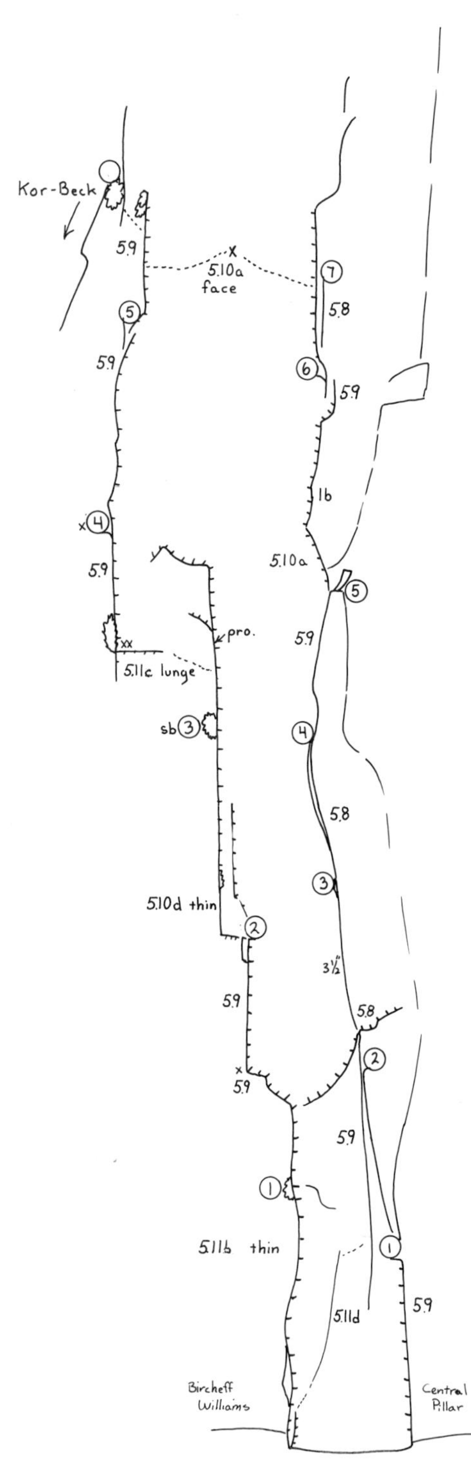

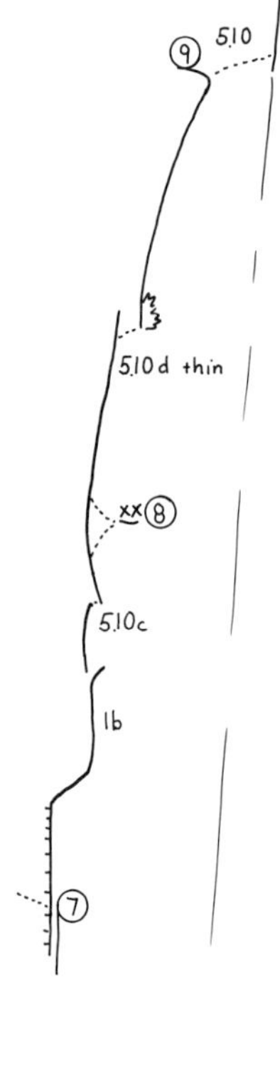

MIDDLE CATHEDRAL ROCK

Descent See page 317.
Photo on page 331.

A Rainbow Bridge 5.11d
B Stoner's Highway 5.10c pro: small Rocks, RP's
C Powell-Reed 5.10c

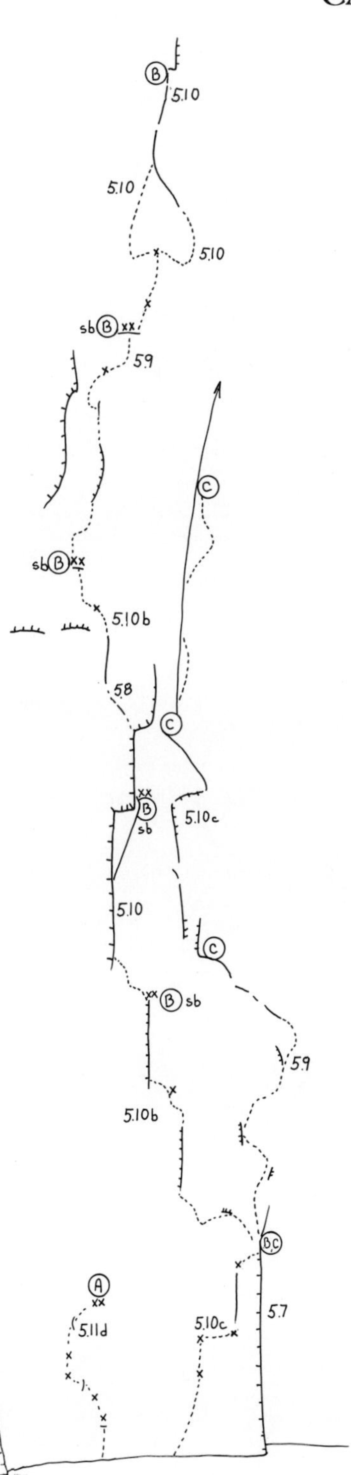

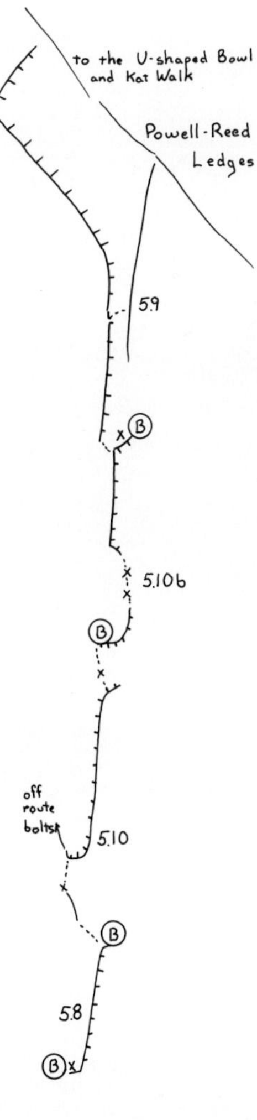

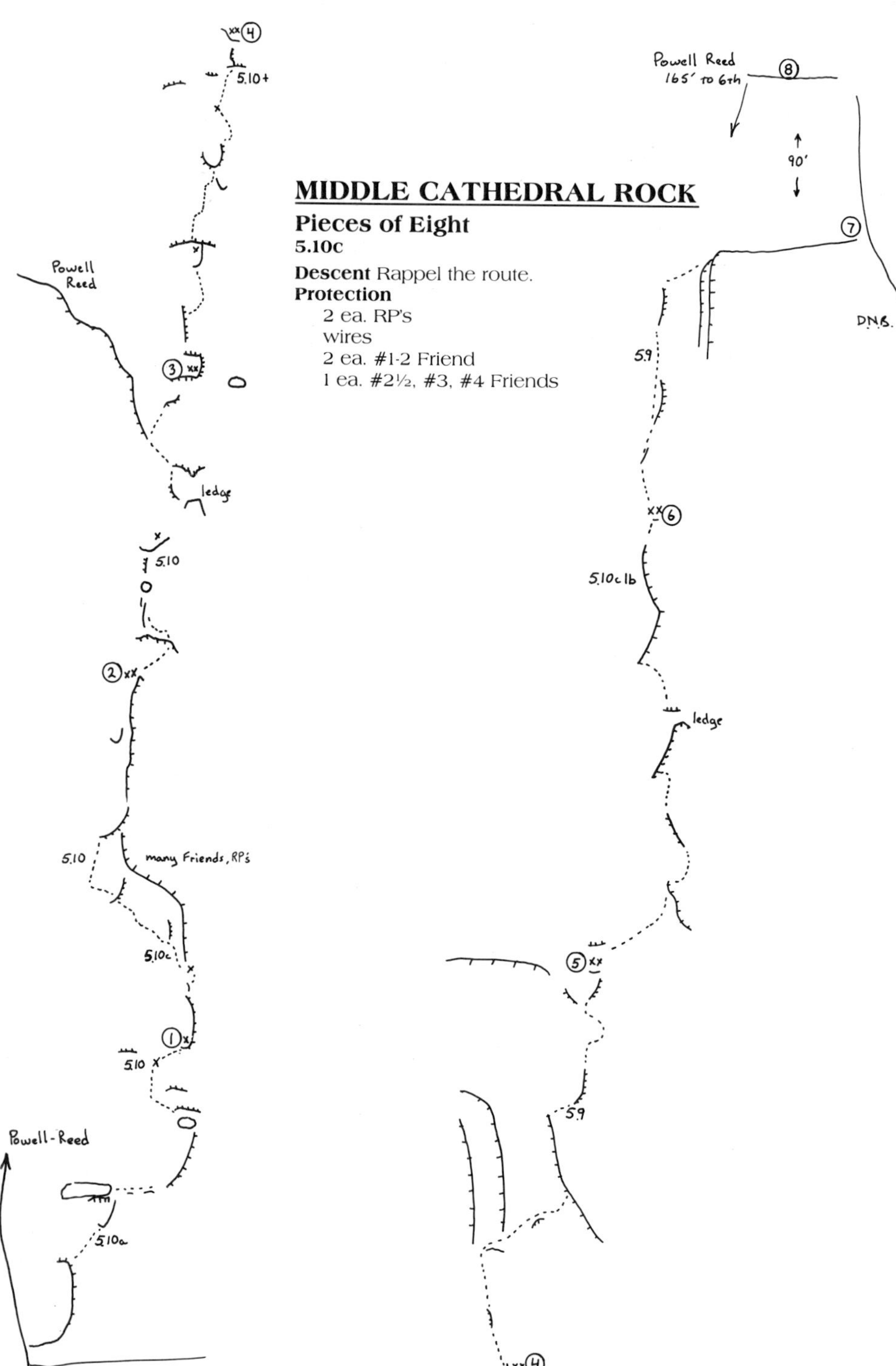

MIDDLE CATHEDRAL ROCK

Pieces of Eight

5.10c

Descent Rappel the route.

Protection

- 2 ea. RP's
- wires
- 2 ea. #1-2 Friend
- 1 ea. #2½, #3, #4 Friends

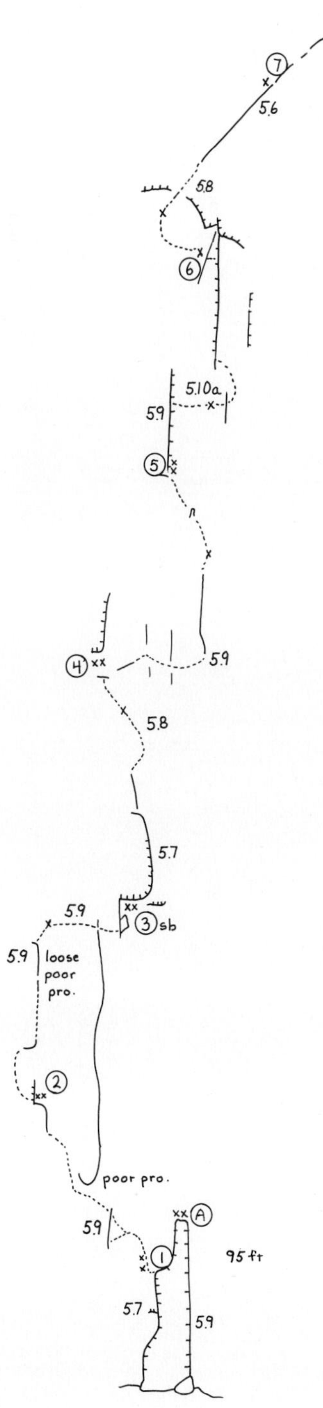

MIDDLE CATHEDRAL ROCK

Paradise Lost

5.10a

Protection small
Descent Rappel the route.
Photo on page 331.

A Pee Pee Pillar 5.9

Powell-Reed Ledges
11
5.7
10
D.N.B.
5.8 ow
flare
9
5.8
8
5.8
7
x
Direct North Buttress

MIDDLE CATHEDRAL ROCK

Direct North Buttress
V 5.10b

Protection to 3", incl. extra ⅛"-1"

Descent Work off the Kat Walk, page 317.

Photo on page 331.

A Picnic 5.10a

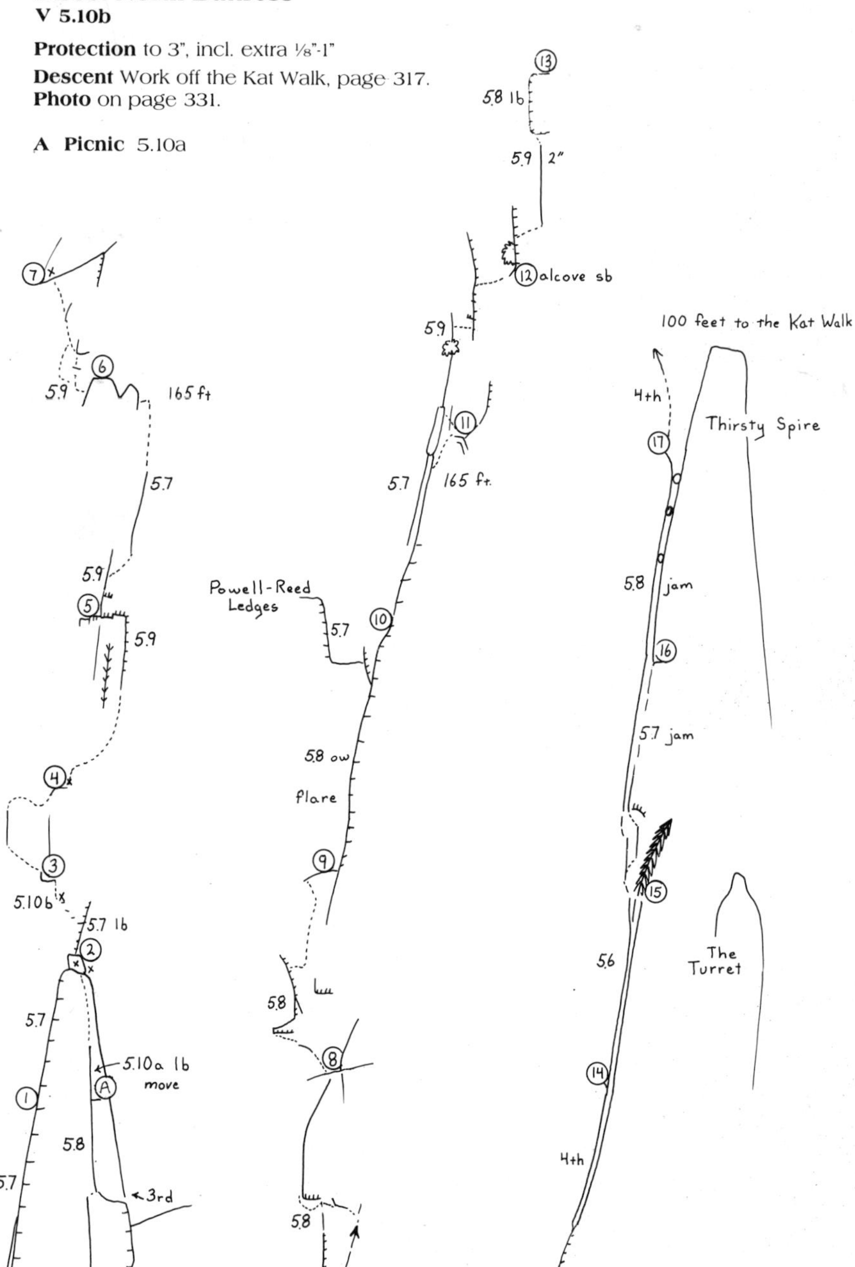

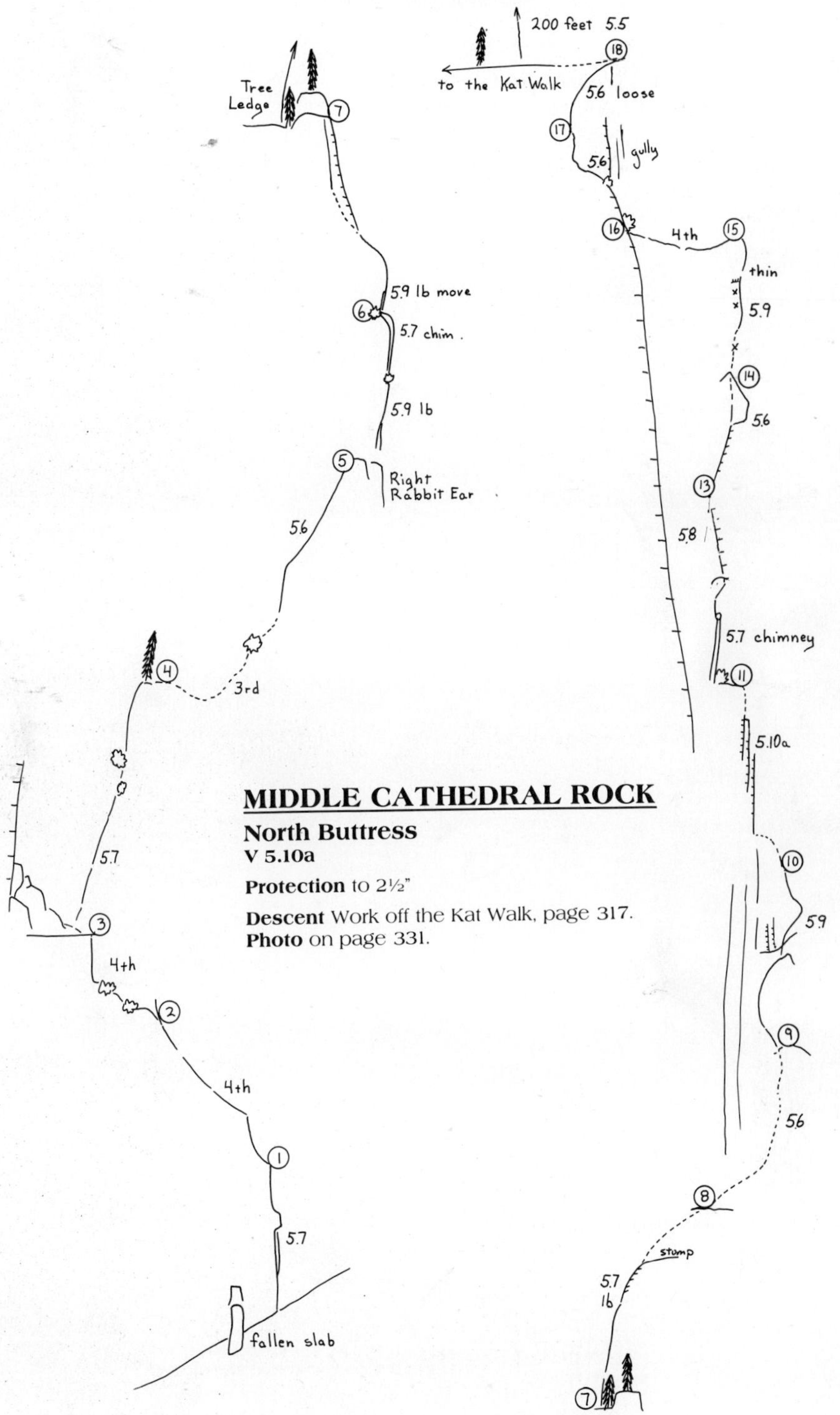

MIDDLE CATHEDRAL ROCK

North Buttress

V 5.10a

Protection to 2½"

Descent Work off the Kat Walk, page 317.
Photo on page 331.

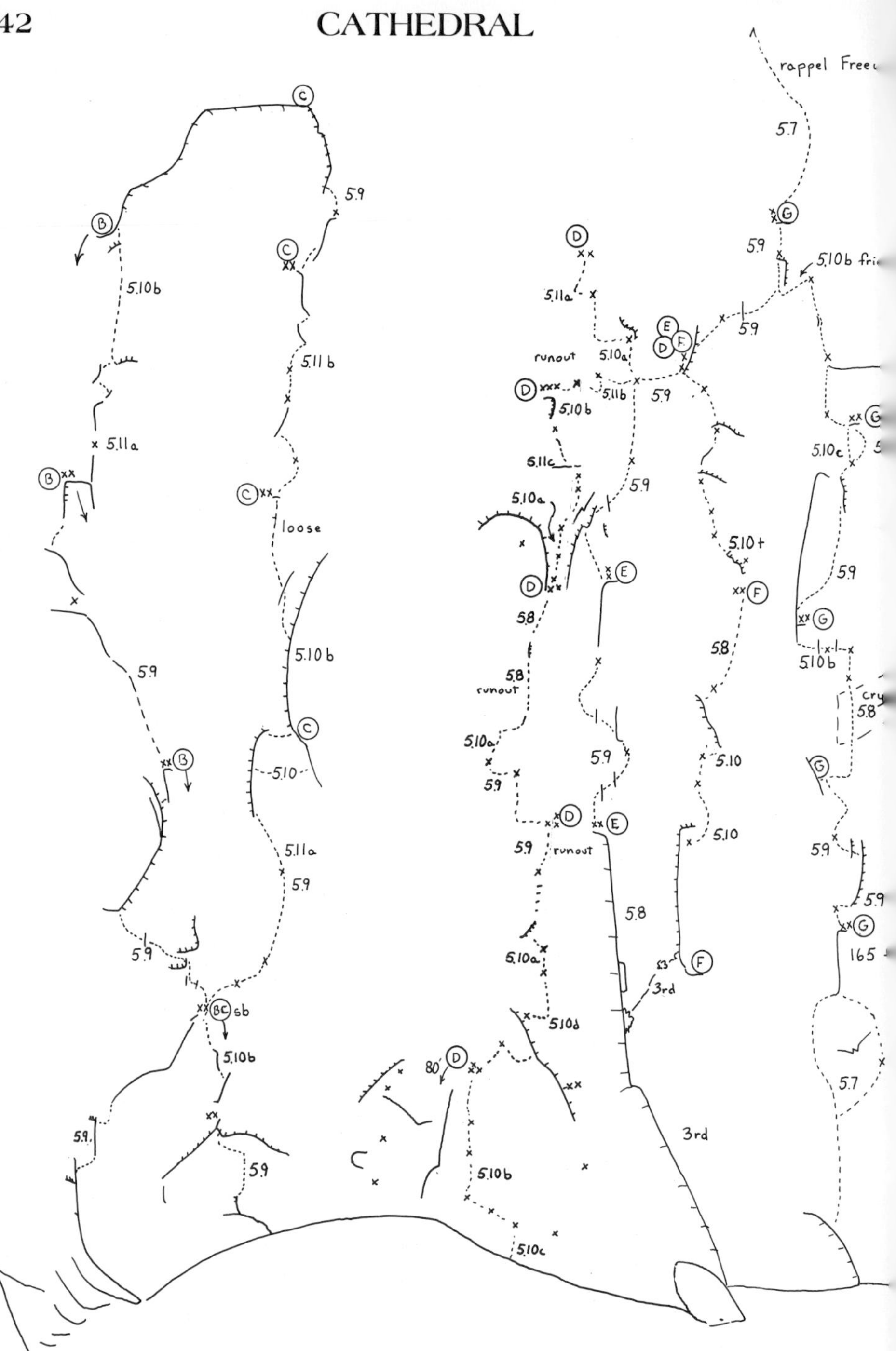

MIDDLE CATHEDRAL ROCK

North Face Apron

Approach Walk up along the wall past the North Buttress or more directly from below the Gunsight.

Photo on page 331.

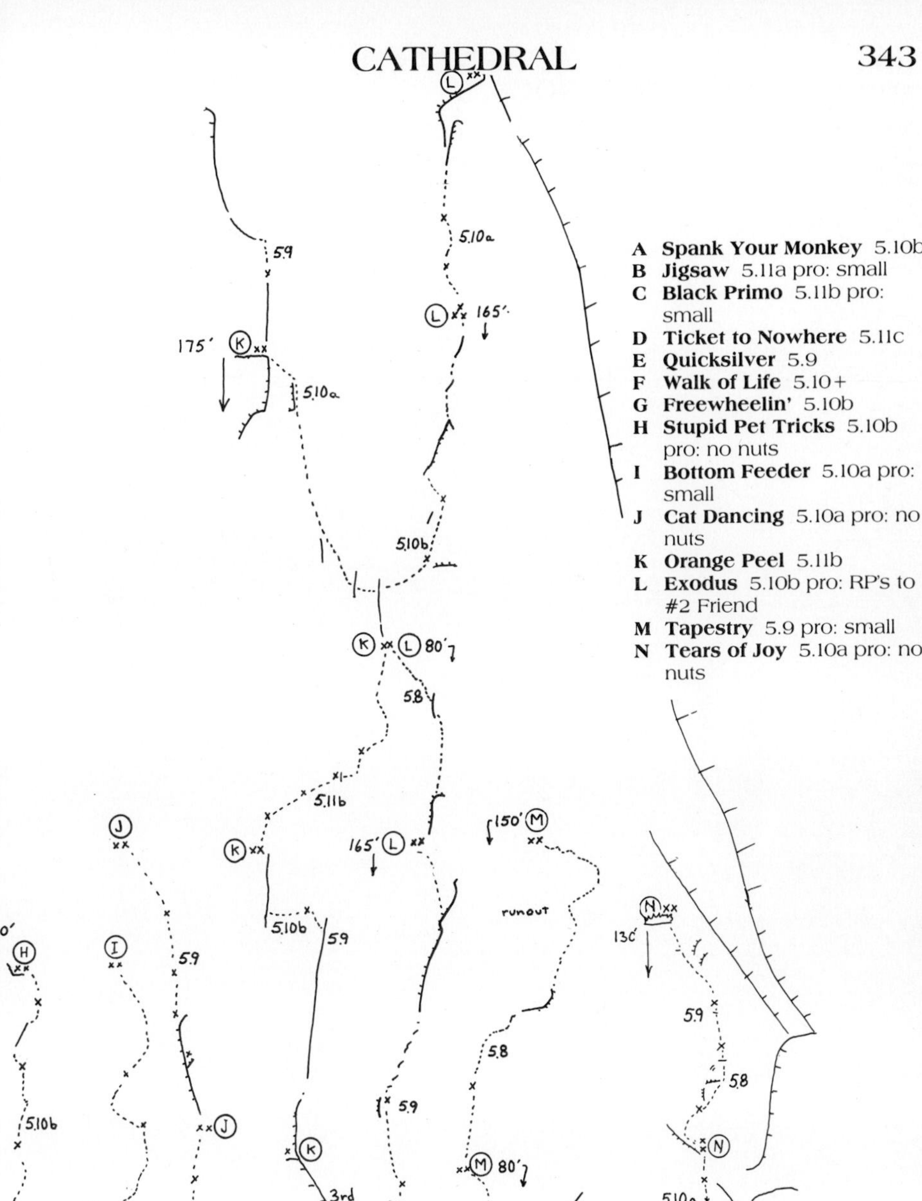

A **Spank Your Monkey** 5.10b
B **Jigsaw** 5.11a pro: small
C **Black Primo** 5.11b pro: small
D **Ticket to Nowhere** 5.11c
E **Quicksilver** 5.9
F **Walk of Life** 5.10+
G **Freewheelin'** 5.10b
H **Stupid Pet Tricks** 5.10b pro: no nuts
I **Bottom Feeder** 5.10a pro: small
J **Cat Dancing** 5.10a pro: no nuts
K **Orange Peel** 5.11b
L **Exodus** 5.10b pro: RP's to #2 Friend
M **Tapestry** 5.9 pro: small
N **Tears of Joy** 5.10a pro: no nuts

MIDDLE CATHEDRAL ROCK

Mother Earth

VI 5.11c A4

Photo on page 331.

Protection

For the route to the North Face Traverse, nuts to 3"; for the upper wall,

- 4 rurps
- 10 KB
- 10 LA
- 2 ea. ½"-1½"
- hooks

A Teaching Little Fingers
5.11a

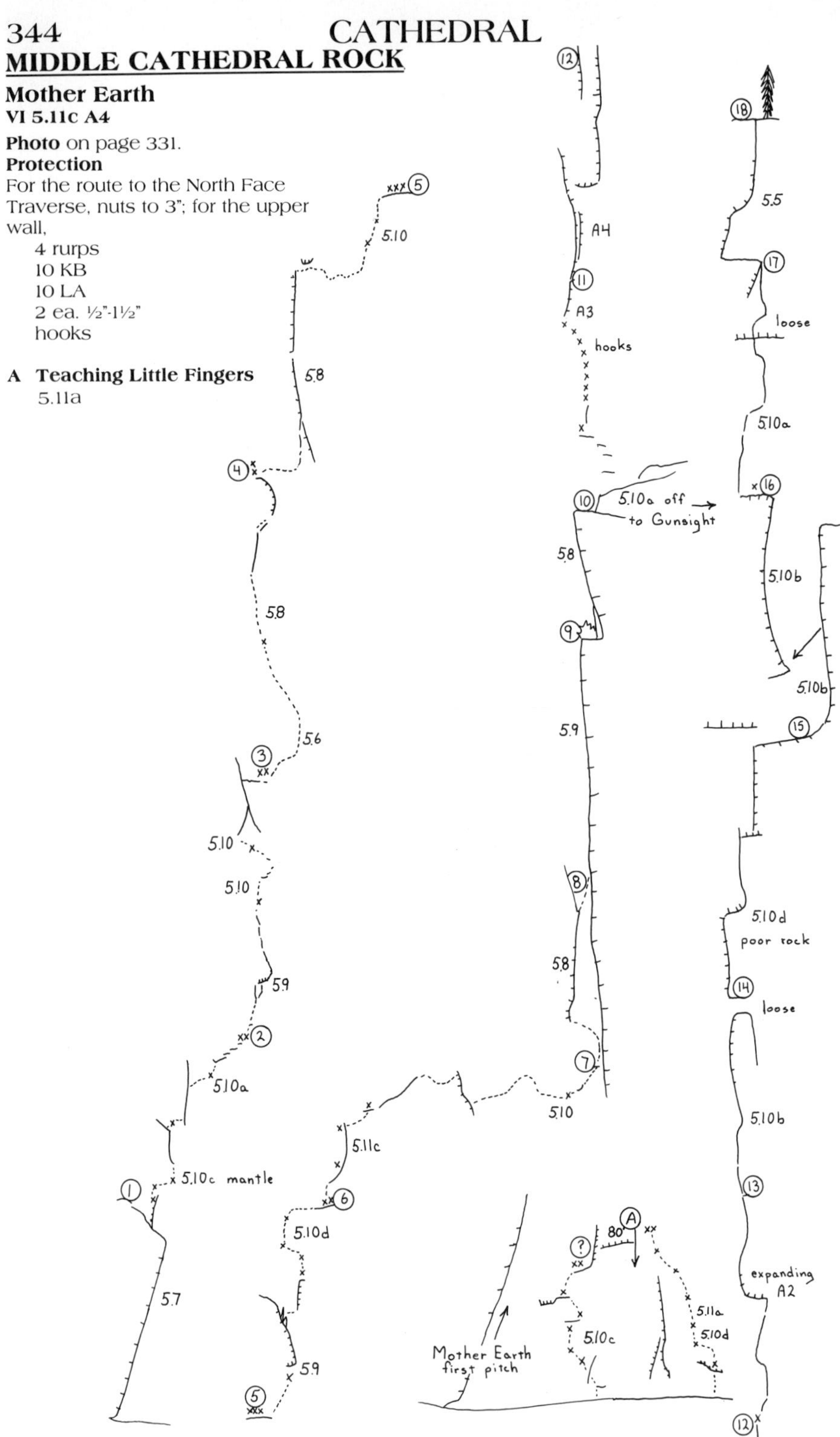

MIDDLE CATHEDRAL ROCK

Smith-Crawford

V 5.11d

Protection

RP's
wires
2 ea. Friends #½-#2
1 ea. #2½-#3 Friend

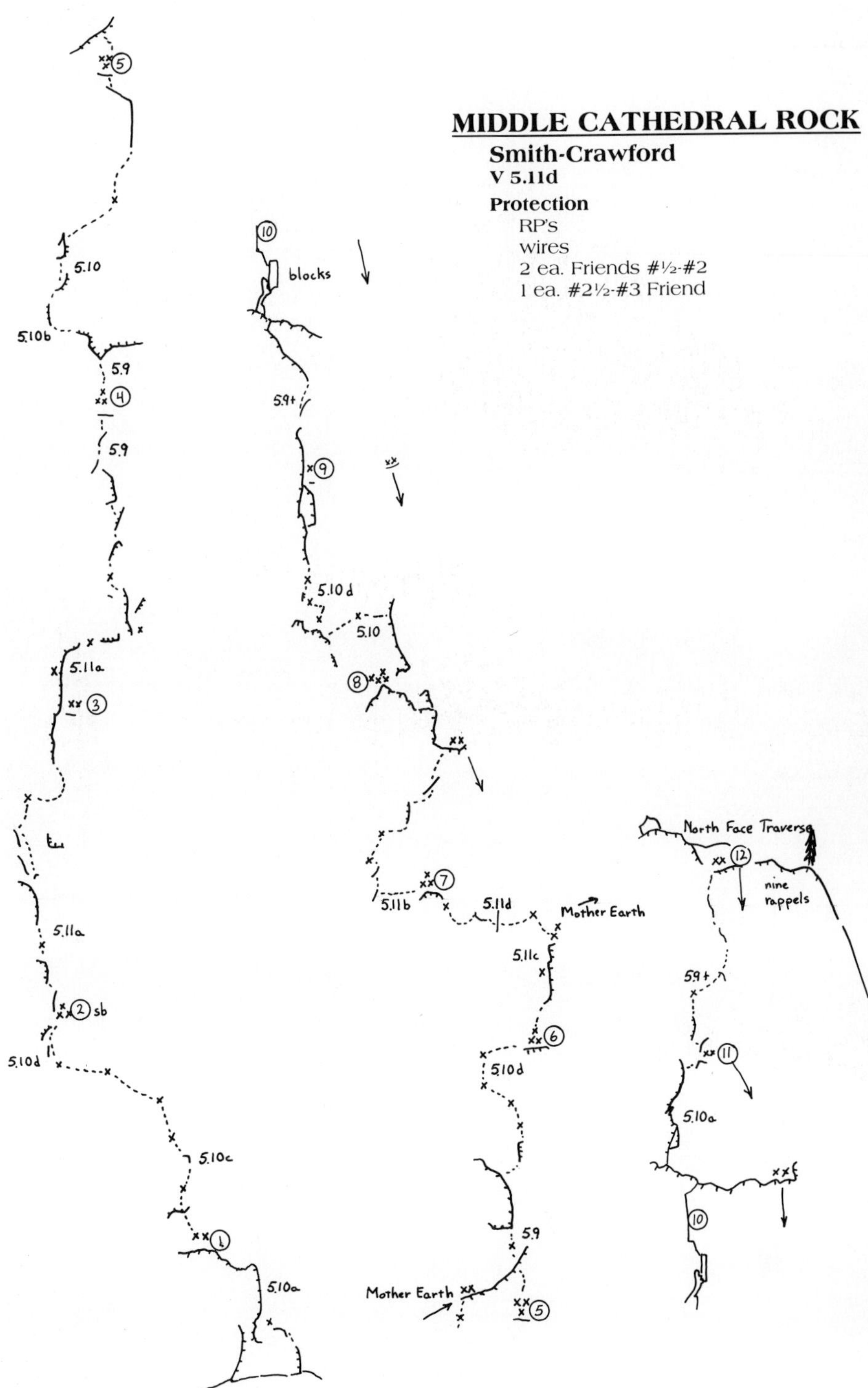

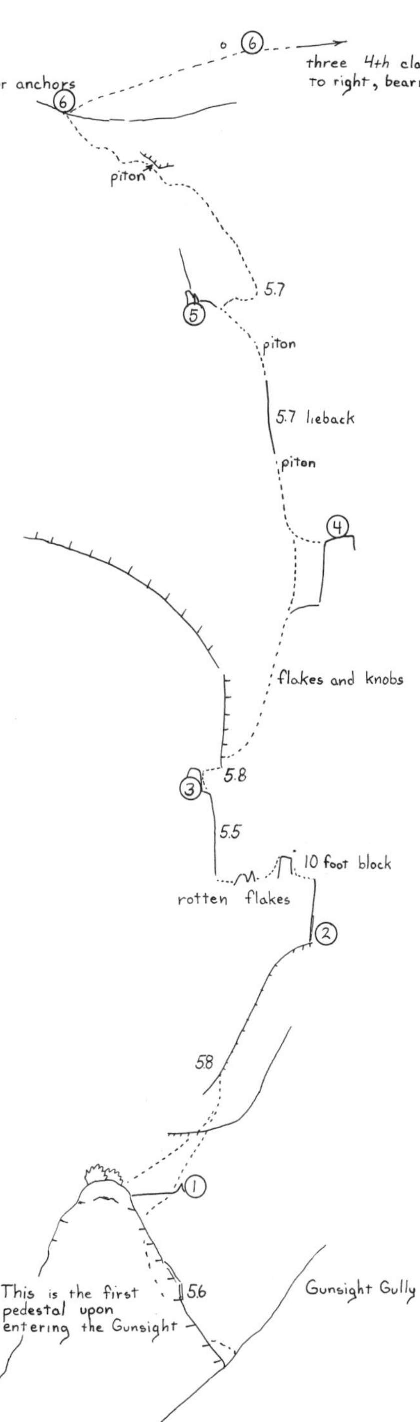

MIDDLE CATHEDRAL ROC

The Flakes

5.8

Note This route requires some route finding ability; by and large, there is no obvious line to follow.

Descent Down climb the Gunsight.

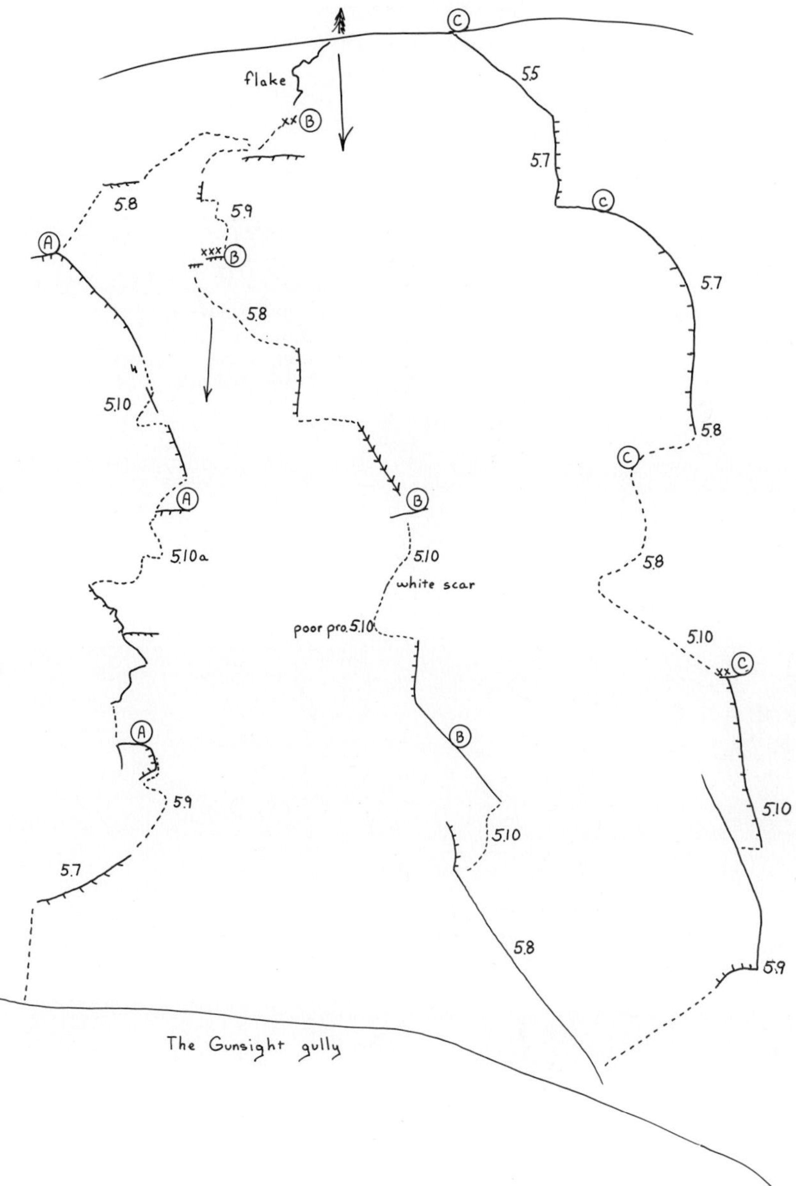

LOWER CATHEDRAL ROCK – East Face

A Spooky Tooth 5.10a pro: nuts and pitons: ¾"-1"
B Shake and Bake 5.10 pro: nuts and pitons: 4 KB, 4 LA, 2 ea. ½"-⅝"
C Starfire 5.10

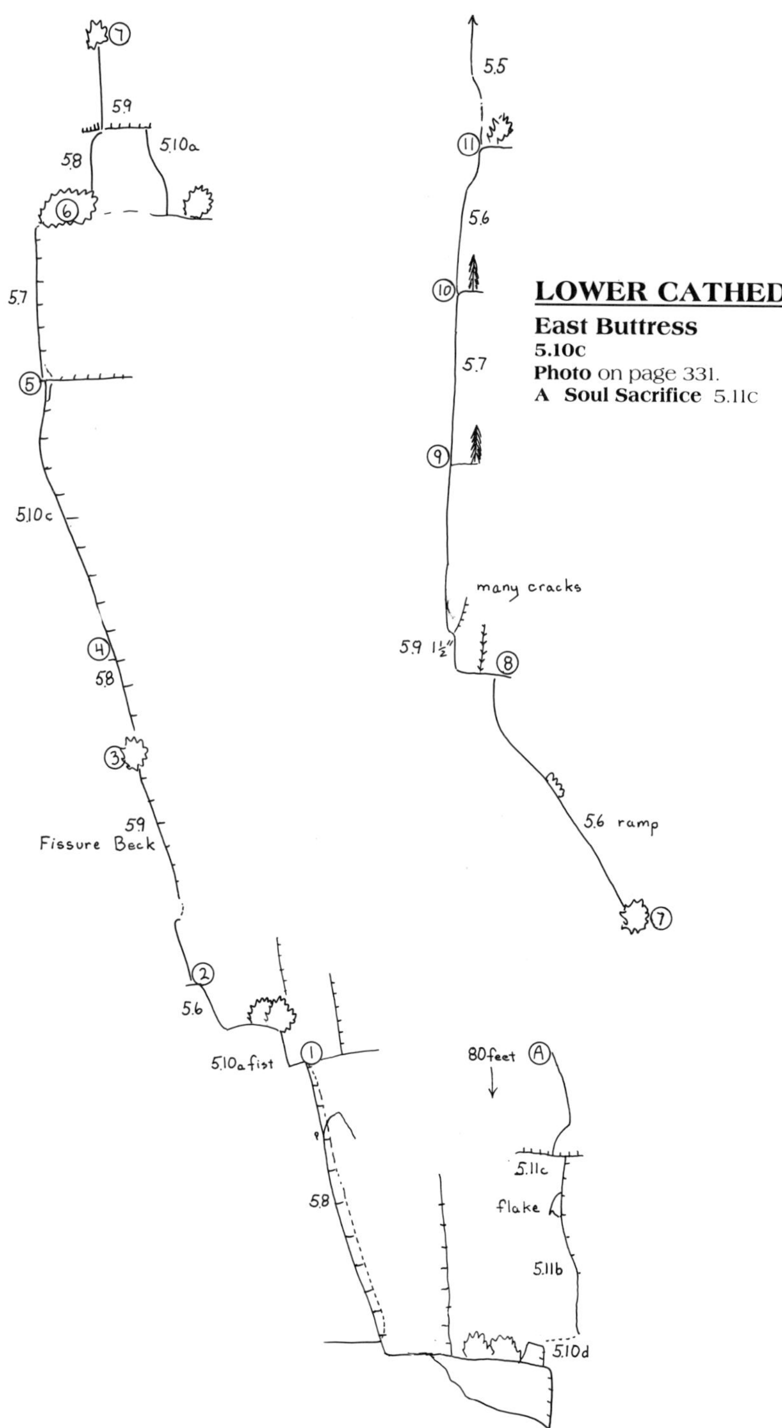

LOWER CATHEDRAL ROCK

East Buttress

5.10c

Photo on page 331.

A Soul Sacrifice 5.11c

LOWER CATHEDRAL ROCK

North Face

V 5.9 A3

Hardware

40 pitons, rurps to 4" bong

Photo on page 331.

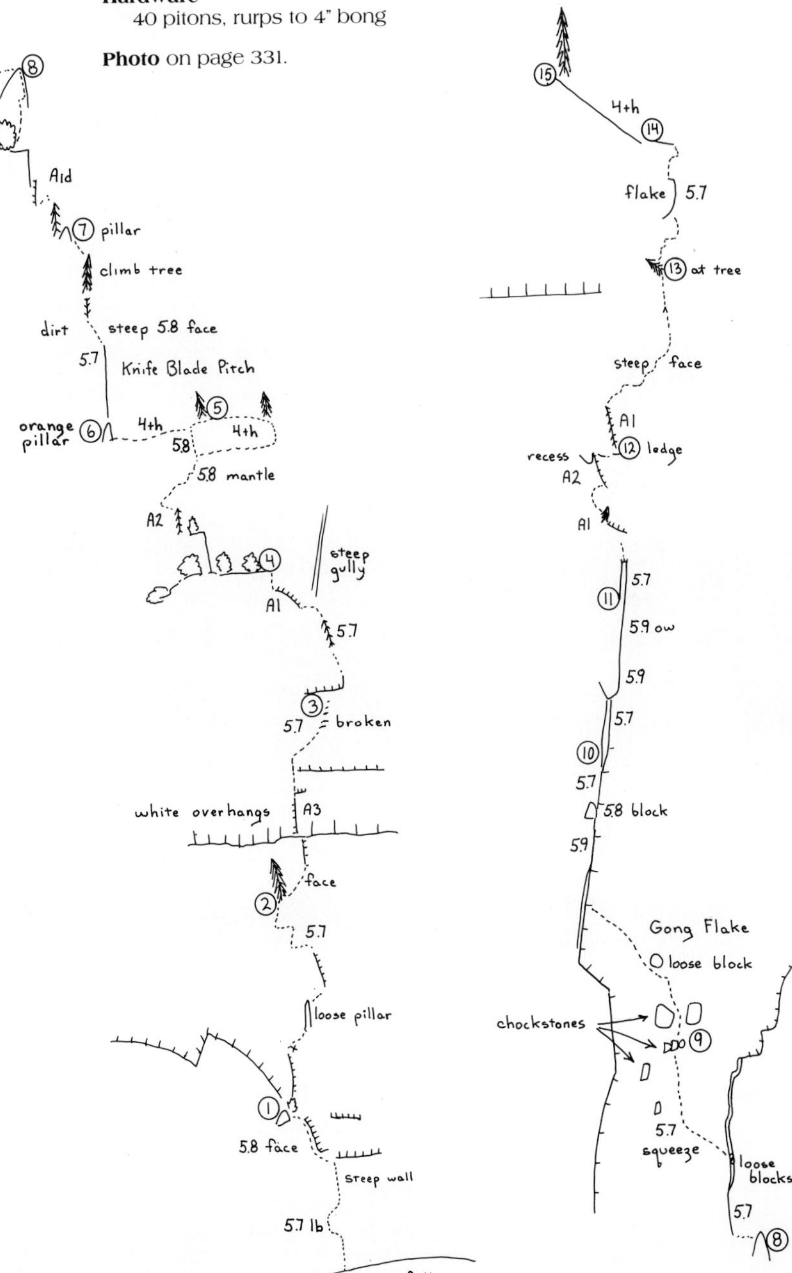

LOWER CATHEDRAL ROCK

Beggar's Buttress

5.11c

Approach Walk up and east from the toe of the north buttress to the first major crack system. See page 351.
Descent Scramble straight back 150 feet to a prominent tree. From here rappel 165 feet to 3rd class terrain near the beginning of **Overhang Bypass.** Now descend the wooded buttress (3rd class) used to approach that route.
Protection
to 3½", incl. extra ½"- 2"
Photo on page 331.

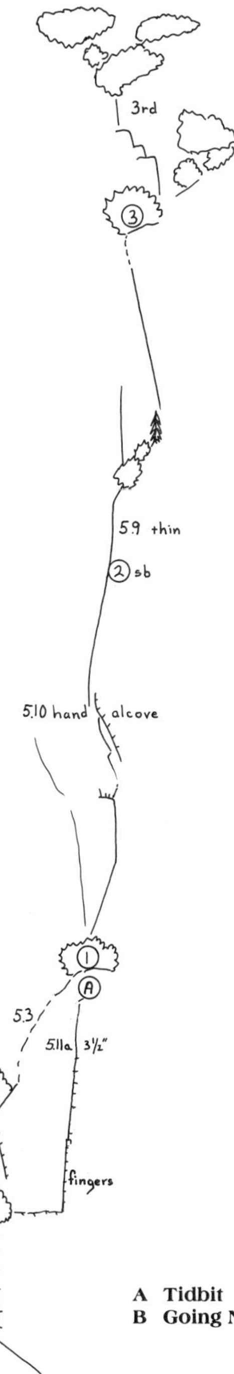

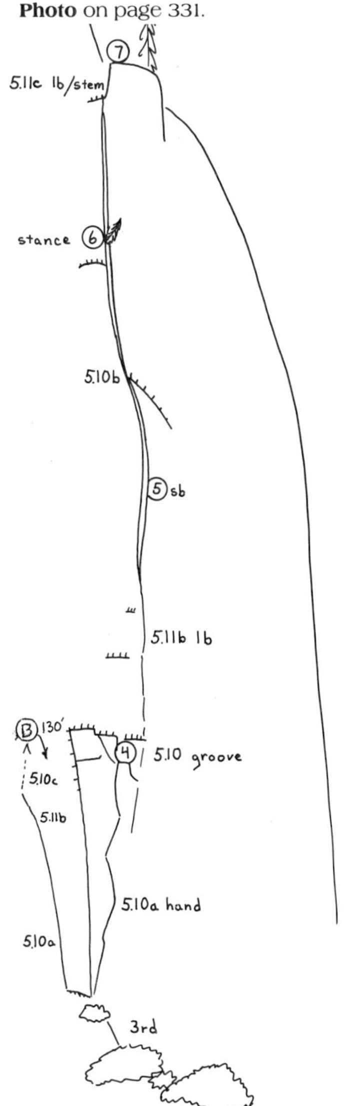

A Tidbit 5.11a
B Going Nowhere 5.11b

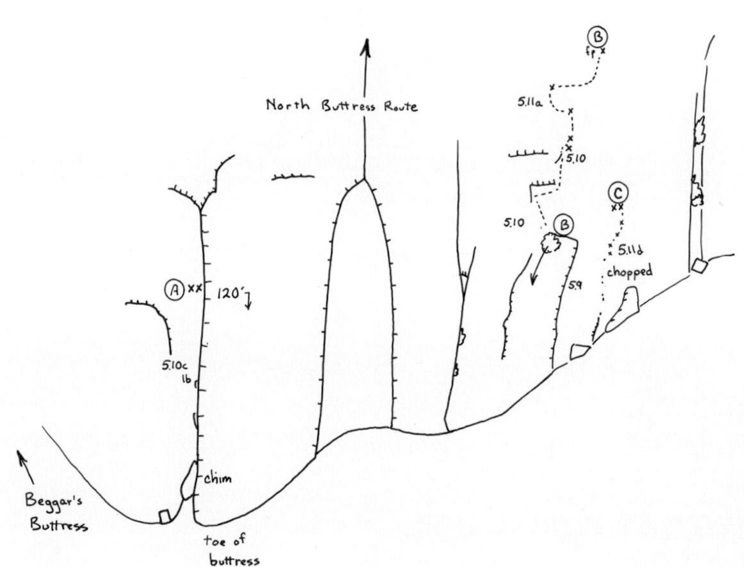

LOWER CATHEDRAL ROCK – North Buttress Area

Approach After driving east into Yosemite Valley, park at the long turnout below Bridalveil Falls, walk toward the rocks and gain the horse trail. Hike to the east and head up the hill from below the toe of the buttress.
Photo on page 354.

A **Sub-Mission** 5.10c pro: small to 3½"
B **North by Northwest** 5.11a
C **Brass Knuckles** 5.11d chopped

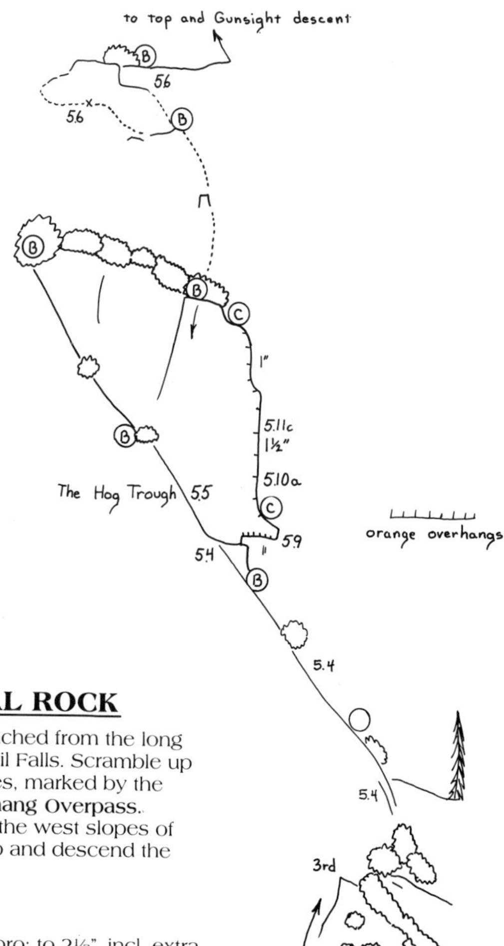

LOWER CATHEDRAL ROCK

Approach This route is approached from the long parking turnout below Bridalveil Falls. Scramble up talus and 3rd class to the routes, marked by the clean gray corner that is **Overhang Overpass**.
Descent These routes end on the west slopes of Lower Cathedral Rock. Hike up and descend the Gunsight, page 317.
Photo on page 354.

A **Overhang Bypass** 5.6
B **Overhang Overpass** 5.11c pro: to 2½", incl. extra ½"- 1¾"

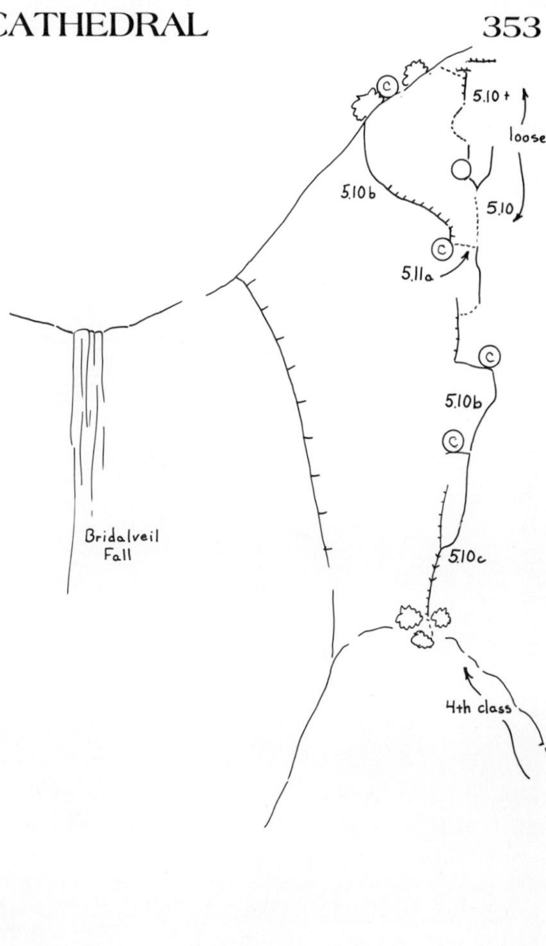

LOWER CATHEDRAL ROCK

Approach The footpath to the base of Bridalveil Falls forms a useful portion of the approach. These climbs are best done during times of low water.
Descent Hike up to and then down the Gunsight. Rattlesnake Buttress necessitates a crossing of Bridalveil Creek, only possible during low water.
Photo on page 354, 355.

A **Return to the Stone Age** 5.11a pro: 2 ea. RP's, 2 ea. Friend to #2, 1 ea. Friend #2½-3
B **Bridalveil East** 5.10c
C **Rattlesnake Buttress** 5.11a pro: RP's to #4 Friend

LOWER CATHEDRAL ROCK

1 NORTH BUTTRESS AREA
2 Overhang Bypass
3 Return to the Stone Age
4 Bridalveil East
5 Middle Cathedral Rock, Northwest Face 5.7
6 Middle Cathedral Rock, Northwest Buttress

LEANING TOWER

7 **Rattlesnake Buttress**
8 **The Yellow Corner** 5.7 A4
9 **Direct Assistance Route** 5.7 A4
10 **THE WATCHTOWER**
11 **THE CRACKER**
12 **Disco Strangler**
13 **West Face Route**
14 **Leaning Chimney**

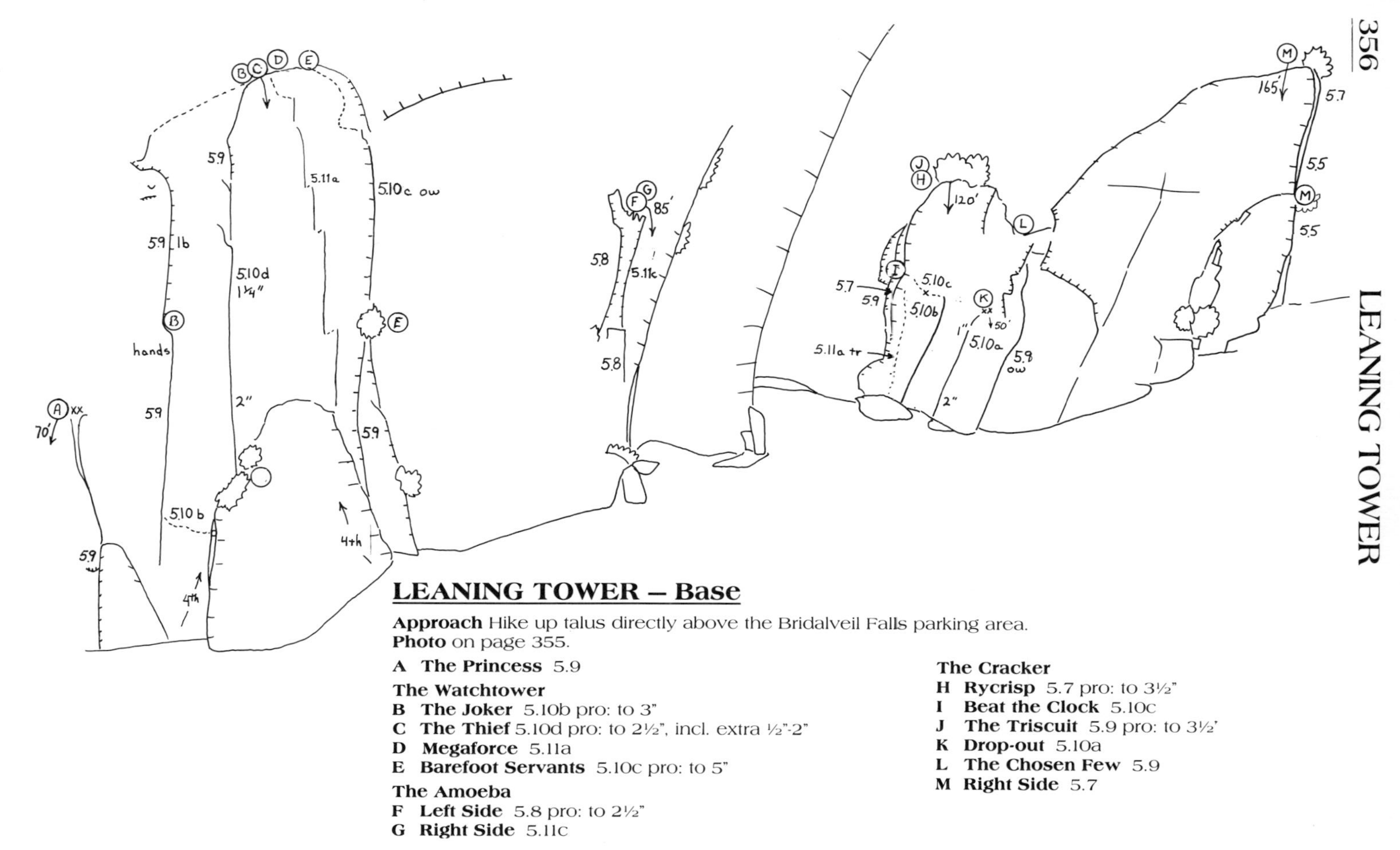

LEANING TOWER – Base

Approach Hike up talus directly above the Bridalveil Falls parking area.
Photo on page 355.

A The Princess 5.9

The Watchtower
B The Joker 5.10b pro: to 3"
C The Thief 5.10d pro: to 2½", incl. extra ½"-2"
D Megaforce 5.11a
E Barefoot Servants 5.10c pro: to 5"

The Amoeba
F Left Side 5.8 pro: to 2½"
G Right Side 5.11c

The Cracker
H Rycrisp 5.7 pro: to 3½"
I Beat the Clock 5.10c
J The Triscuit 5.9 pro: to 3½'
K Drop-out 5.10a
L The Chosen Few 5.9
M Right Side 5.7

LEANING TOWER

Disco Strangler

V 5.10 A4

Approach For this and all the routes on the west face of the Leaning Tower, hike up talus above the Bridalveil Falls parking area to gain the **Leaning Tower Traverse**, the obvious diagonal ledge.

Descent Two rappels or 4th class lead to scree on the south shoulder. In times of low water it is possible to cross Bridalveil Creek and to descend the Gunsight. Instead, it is common for parties to make a series of rappels down the major chimney system to the south of the Tower (the Leaning Tower Chimney).

Photo on page 355.

Hardware

10 rurps
15 KB
15 LA
5 ea. ½"-¾"
4 ea. 1"
2 ea. 1¼"-1½"
many RP's
many nuts to 1"
2 ea. Friends to #3
30 copperheads
rivet, bolt hangers
extra bolt nuts

Note no hangers at belays

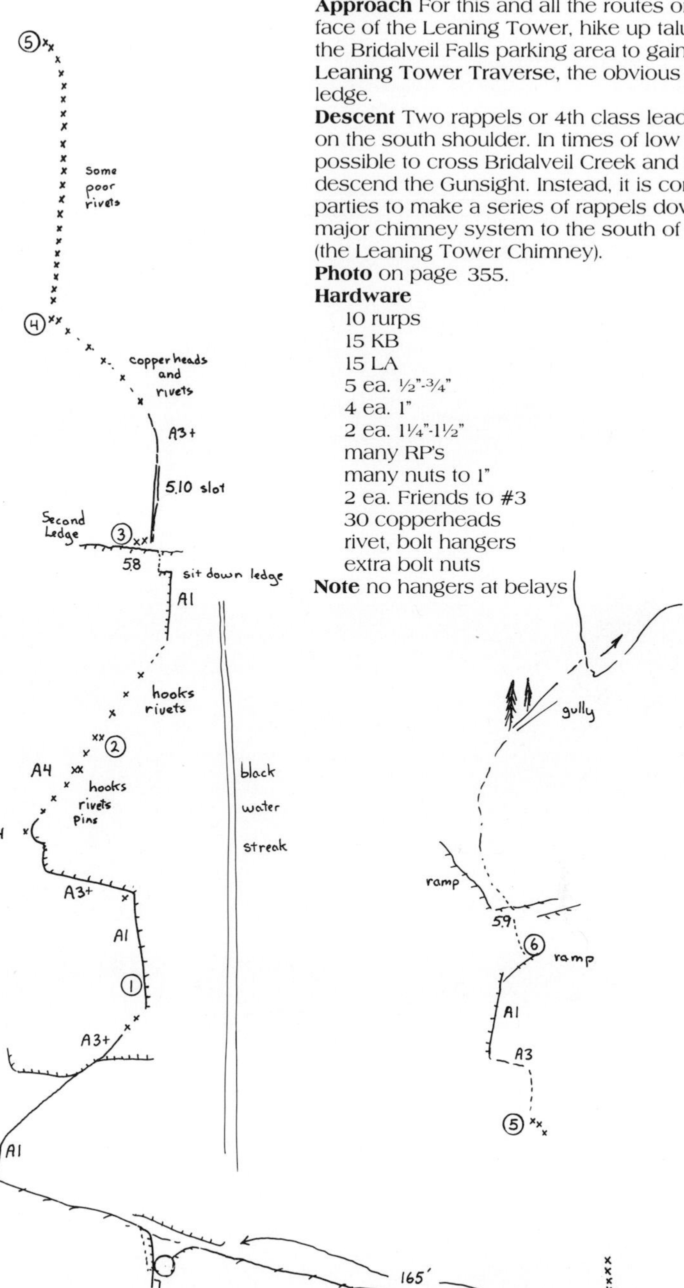

LEANING TOWER

West Face
V 5.7 A3

Approach, Descent on page 357.
Photo on page 355.
Hardware
- 4 LA
- 2 ea. ½"-¾"
- 2 ea. Friend to #2½
- 1 ea. #3, # 3½ Friend
- large hook
- many small nuts to 2"
- wires

A Wet Denim Daydream
V 5.7 A4

Hardware
- 6 rurps
- 12 KB
- 20 LA
- 4 ea. ½"-1½"
- 3 ea. 2"
- 2 ea. 2½"
- 1 ea. 3"
- Friends
- hooks
- copperheads

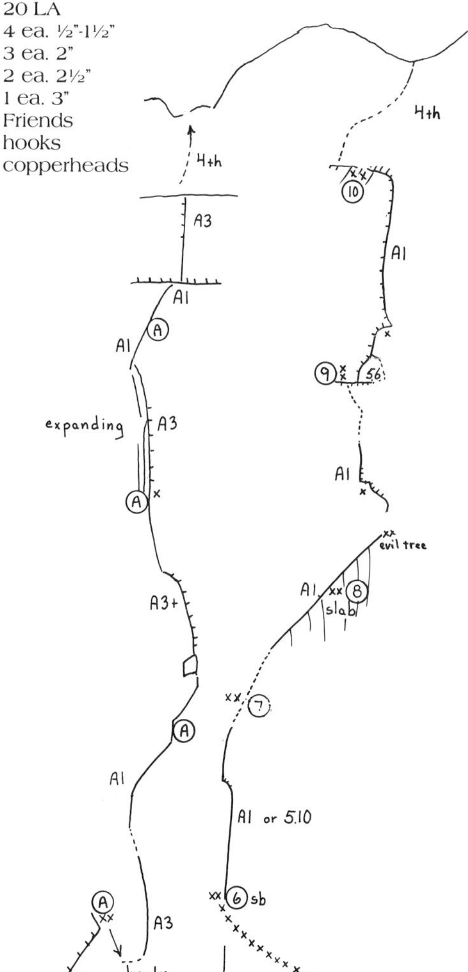

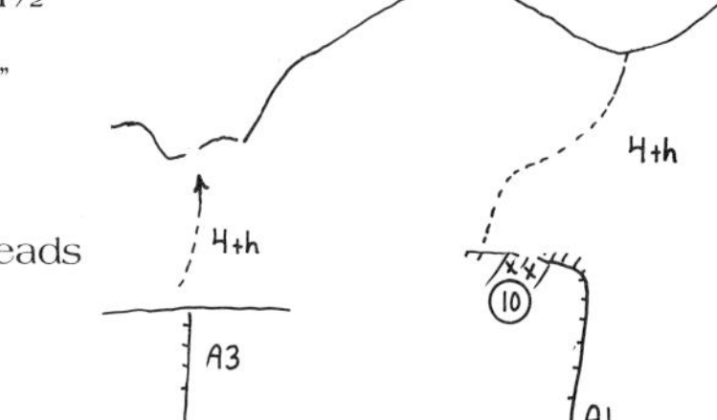

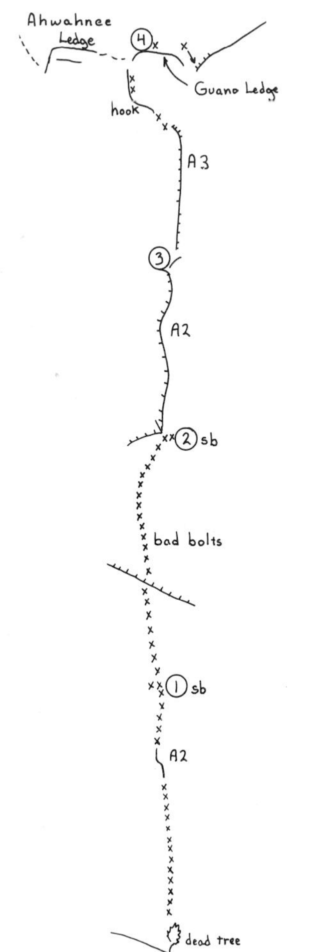

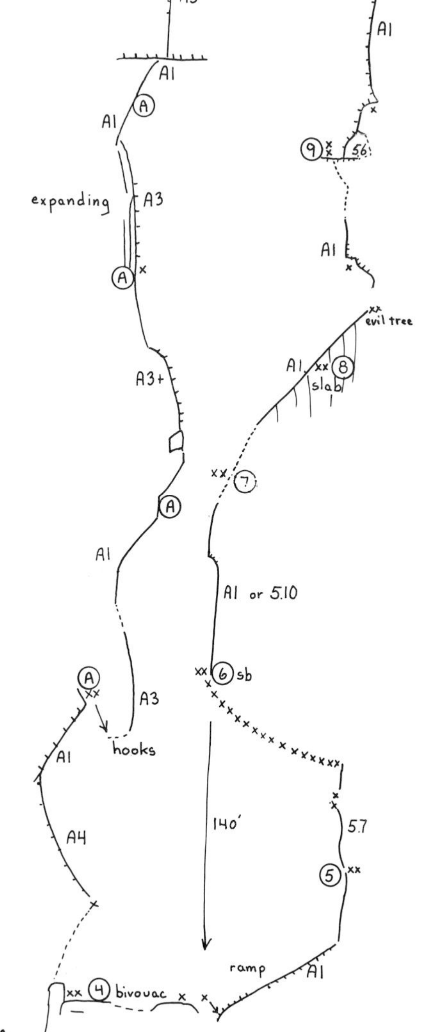

LEANING TOWER

Roulette

A5

Approach, Descent on page 357.
Photo on page 355.

Hardware

10 rurps
many KB, esp. short thin
many LA, esp. short thin
4 ea. ½"-⅝"
3 ea. ¾"
2 ea. 1"
2 ea. Friends
all hooks
100 copperheads, mostly tiny
crack n ups

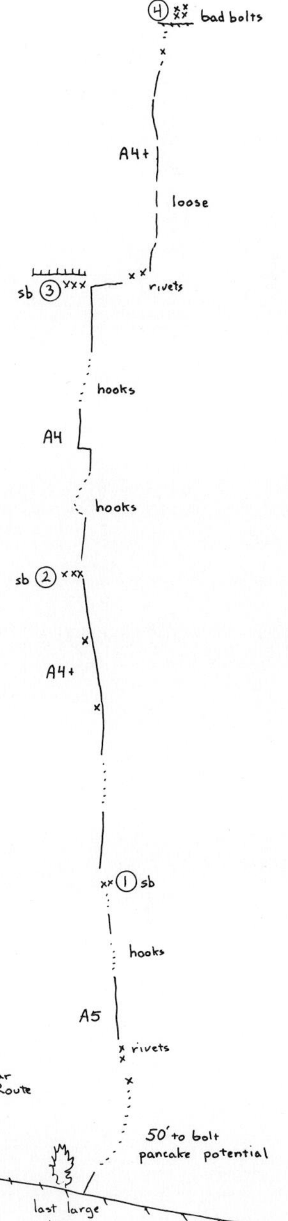

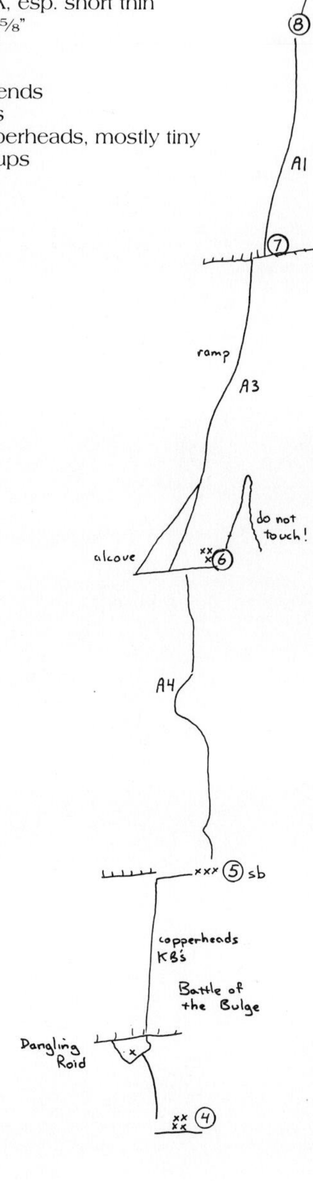

LEANING TOWER

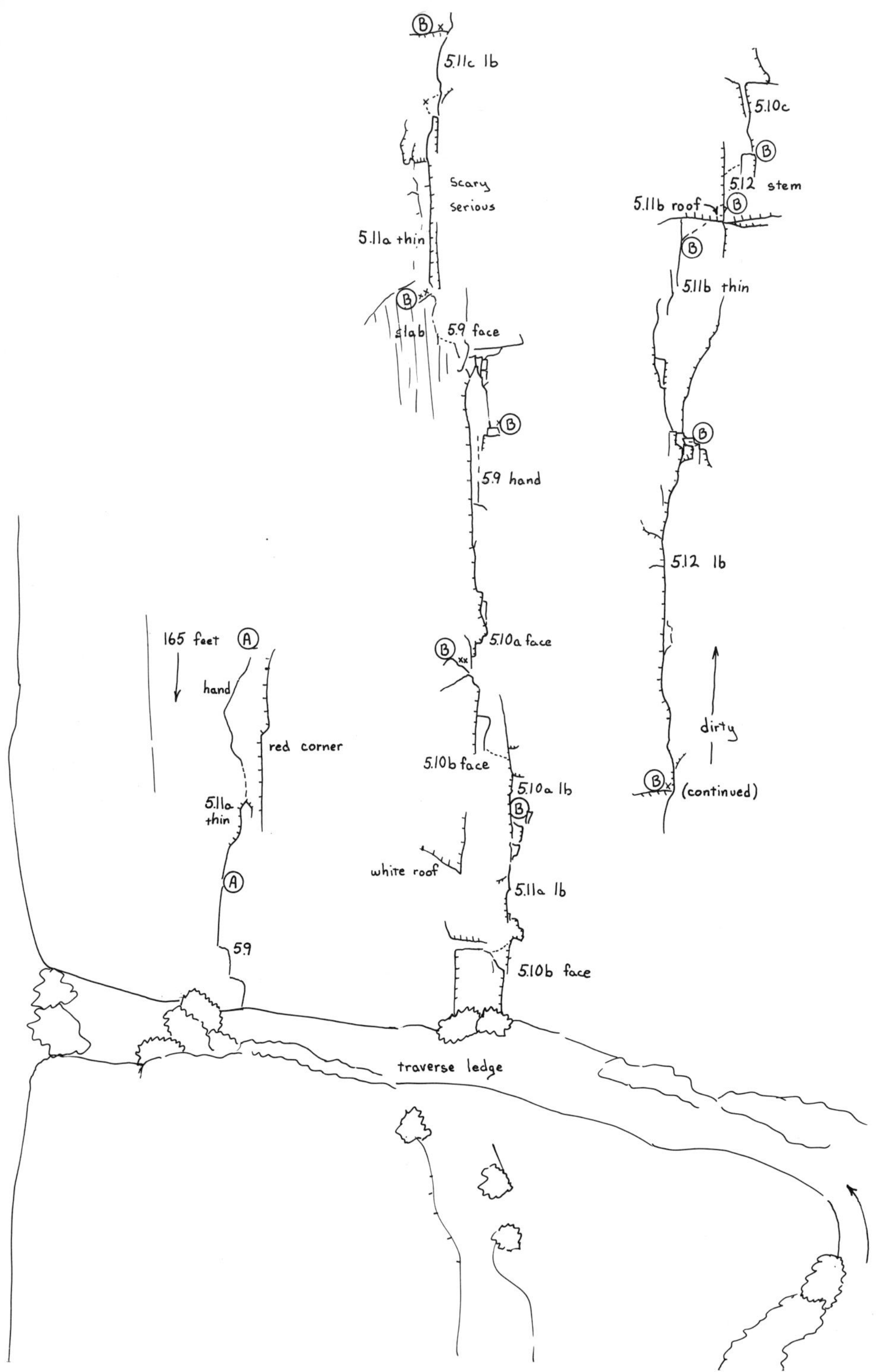

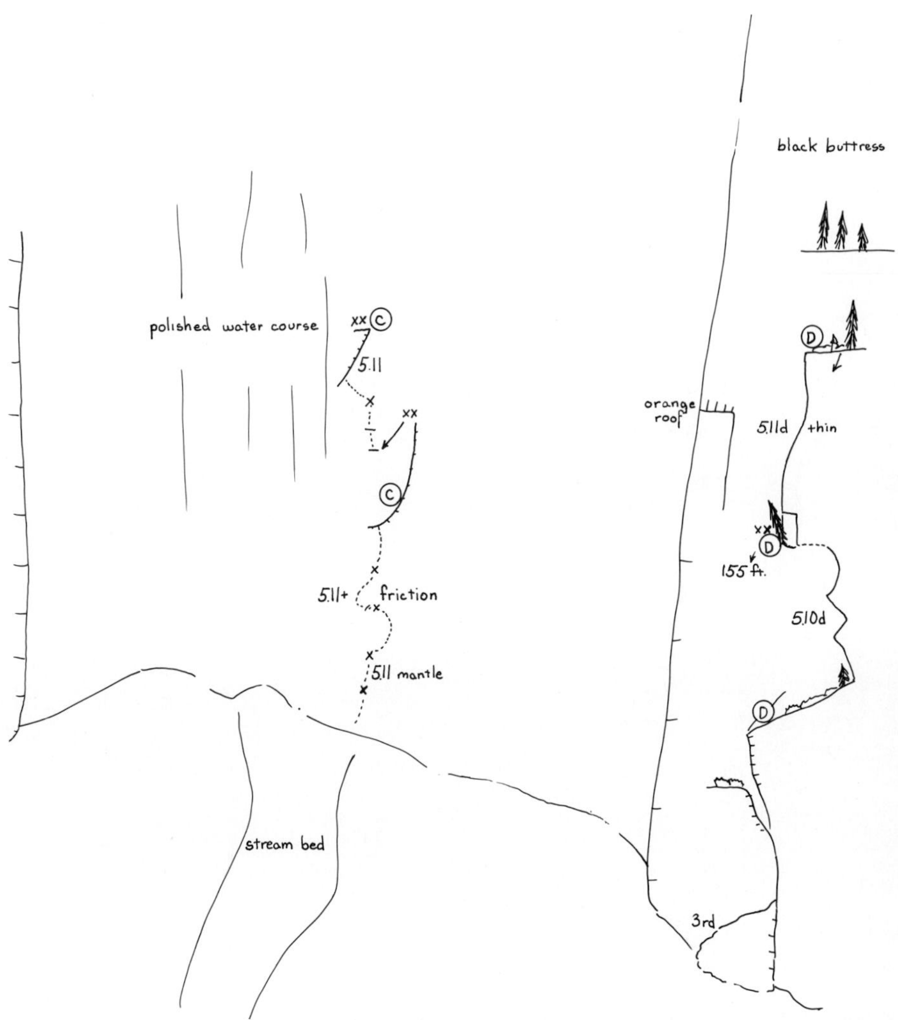

FIFI BUTTRESS

Approach This is the first buttress to the west of the Leaning Tower. From the Bridalveil parking lot walk southwest, avoiding the talus field, then follow a streambed that flows down immediately right of the buttress.

Descent Scramble down to the west via a long diagonal bushwhack ledge.

A Sunset Strip 5.11a
B Vortex 5.12 pro: 3-4 ea. Friends to #2, 2 ea. #3, plus a #4 Friend and a thin rack
C Colony of Slippermen 5.11+ A1
D The Warbler 5.11d

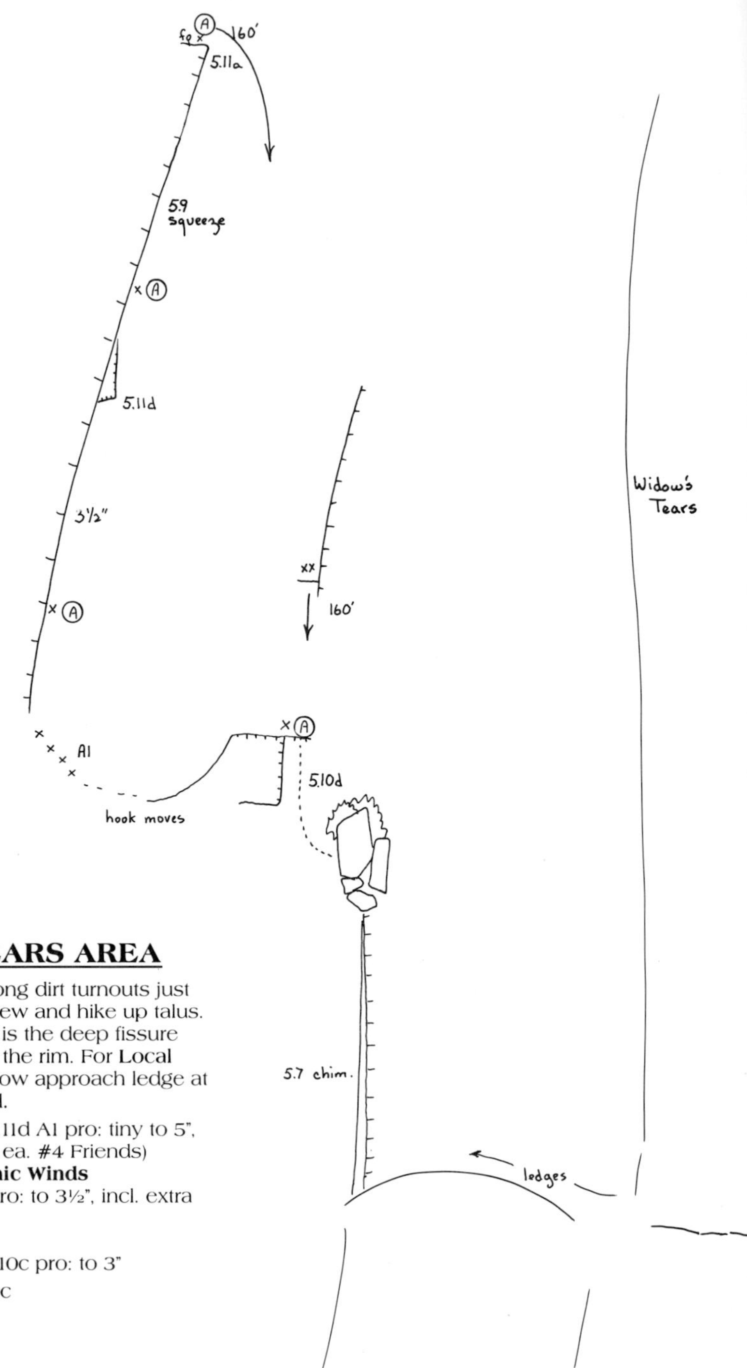

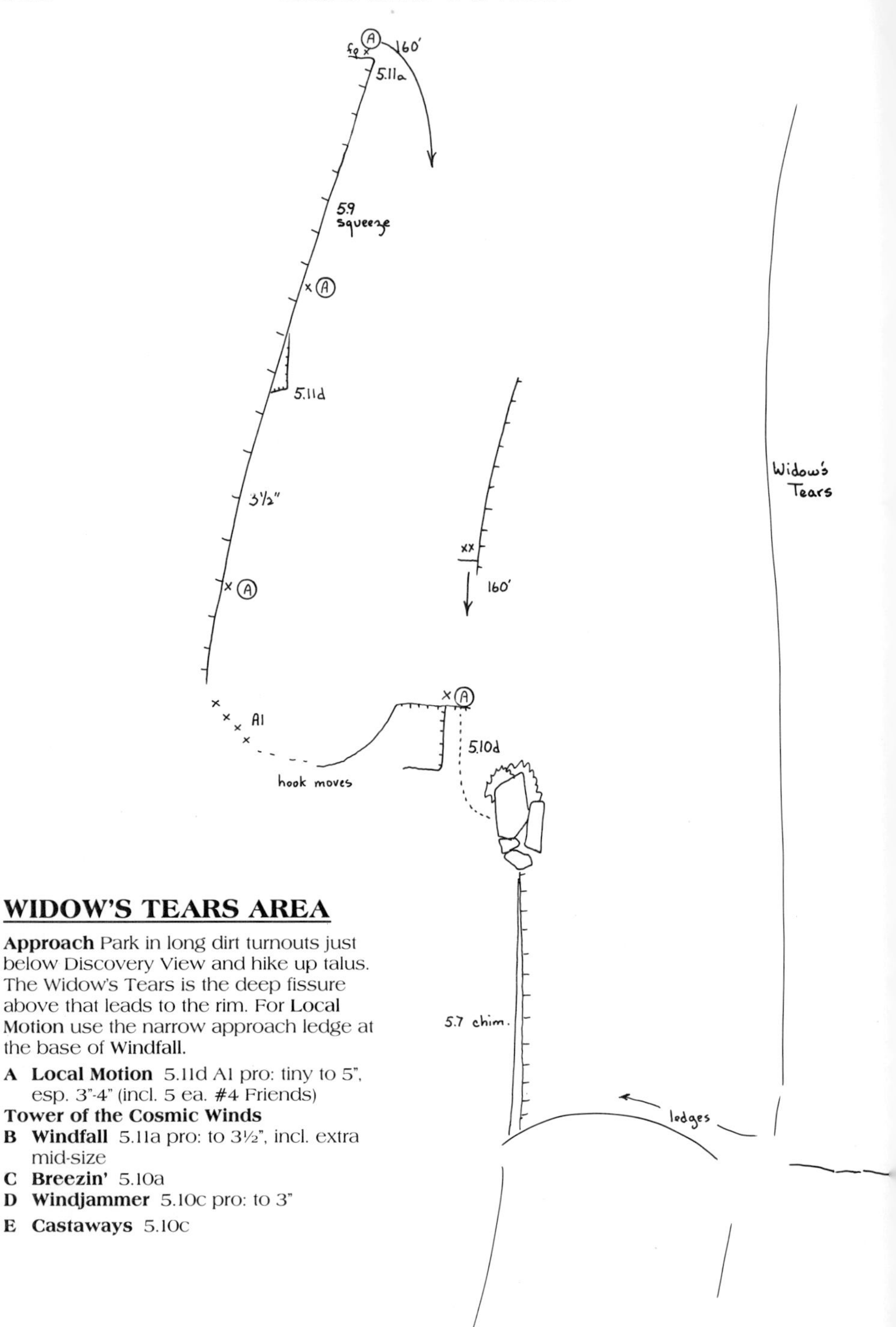

WIDOW'S TEARS AREA

Approach Park in long dirt turnouts just below Discovery View and hike up talus. The Widow's Tears is the deep fissure above that leads to the rim. For Local Motion use the narrow approach ledge at the base of Windfall.

A Local Motion 5.11d A1 pro: tiny to 5", esp. 3"-4" (incl. 5 ea. #4 Friends)

Tower of the Cosmic Winds

B Windfall 5.11a pro: to 3½", incl. extra mid-size

C Breezin' 5.10a

D Windjammer 5.10c pro: to 3"

E Castaways 5.10c

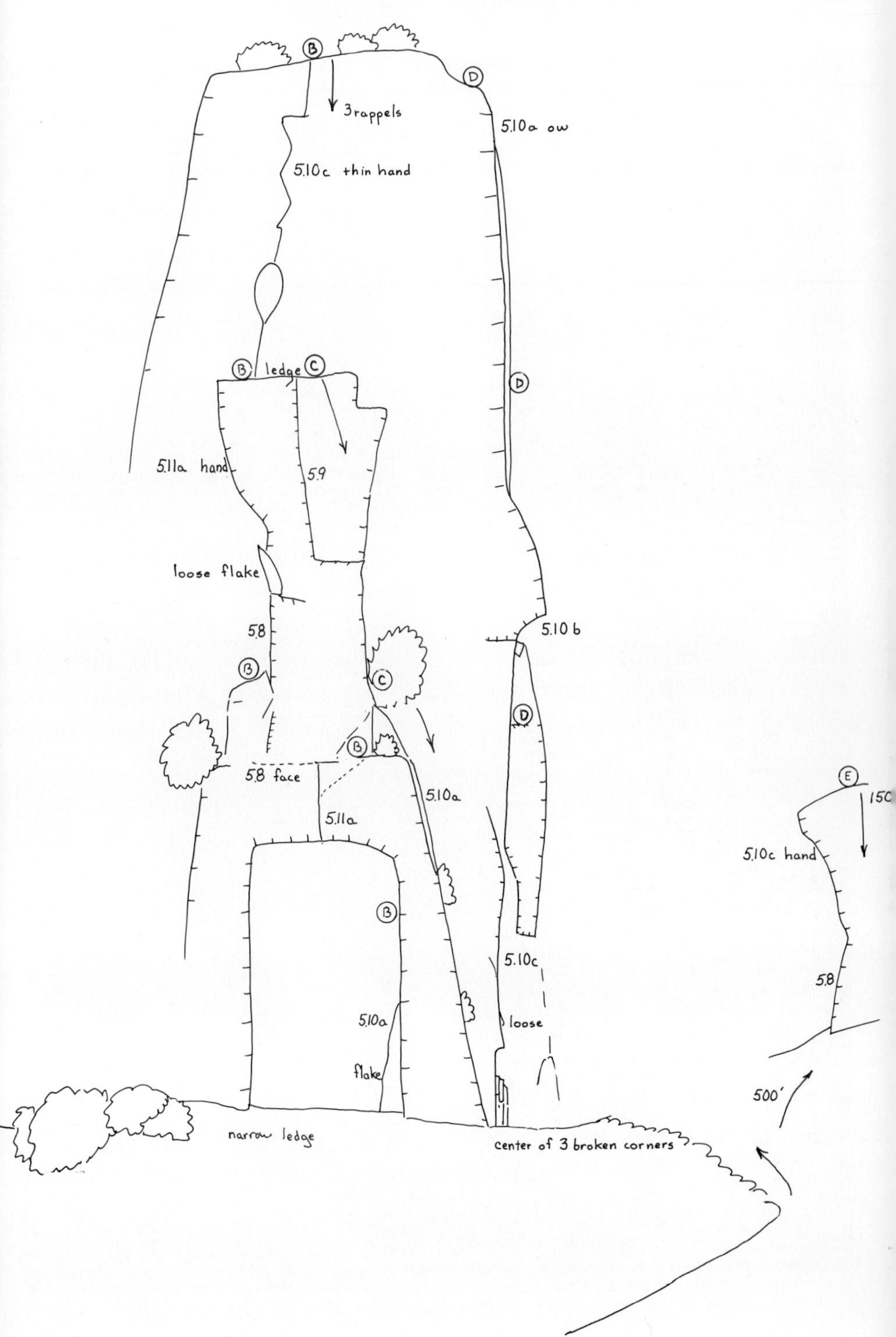

B
D
3 rappels
5.10a ow
5.10c thin hand
B
ledge
C
D
5.11a hand
5.9
loose flake
5.8
5.10 b
B
C
D
B
5.8 face
5.10a
E
150
5.11a
5.10c hand
B
5.10c
5.8
5.10a
loose
flake
500'
narrow ledge
center of 3 broken corners

Kevin Worrall on the **Widow's Tears**, 1975. *Mark Chapman*

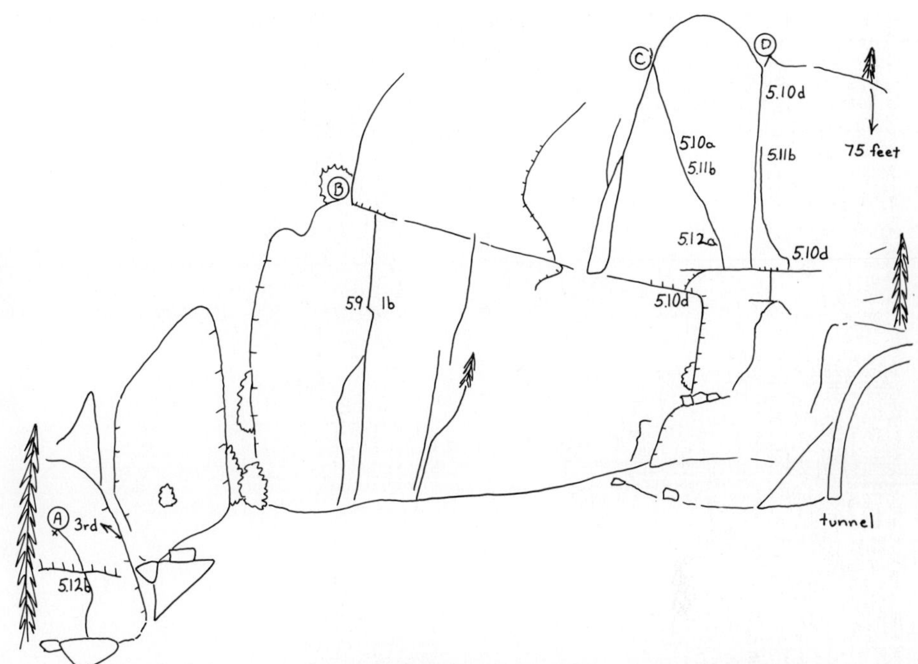

WAWONA TUNNEL – West End

A **A Dog's Roof** 5.12b
B **Eat at Degnan's** 5.9
C **Landshark** 5.12a
D **Dancin' Days** 5.11c

DISCOVERY VIEW

Approach These climbs are located below Discovery View. **Overdrive** is best approached from above. **High Pressure** is located downstream about ¼ mile from Pulpit Rock and may be reached from above or below. Beware poison oak that grows in abundance along the base of the valley in this area.

A Overdrive 5.11a

B High Pressure 5.11b pro: to 3½", incl. extra ⅛"- ½"

Open Trench 5.7 This is the next crack system to the right of **High Pressure**.

Lost on Venus 5.7 This is the flake system to the right of **Open Trench**.

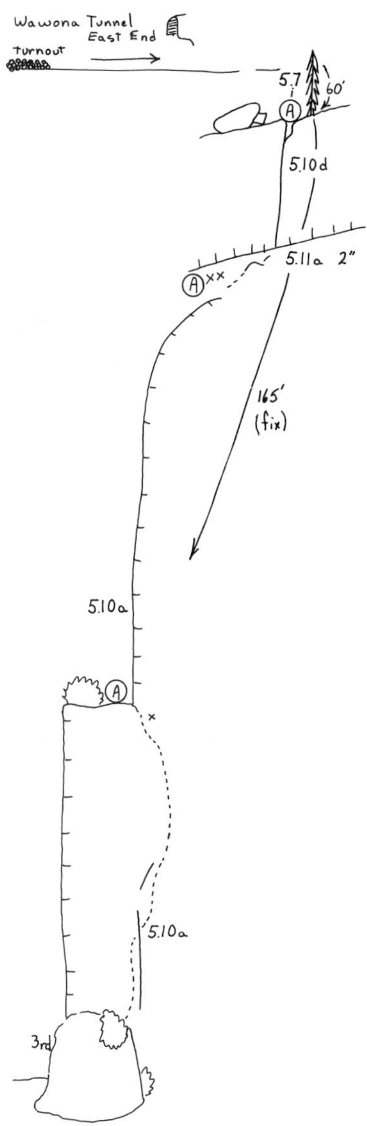

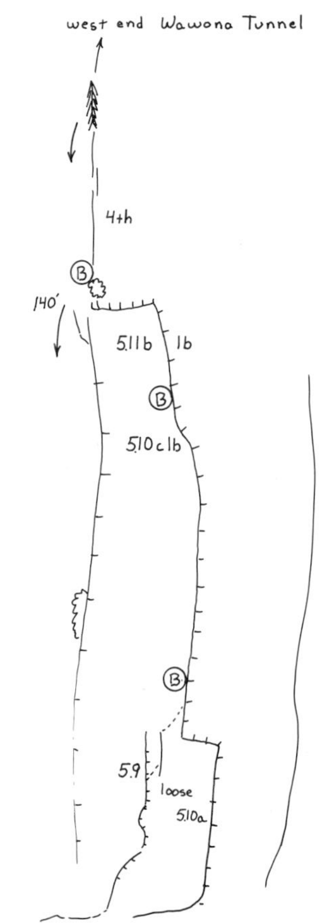

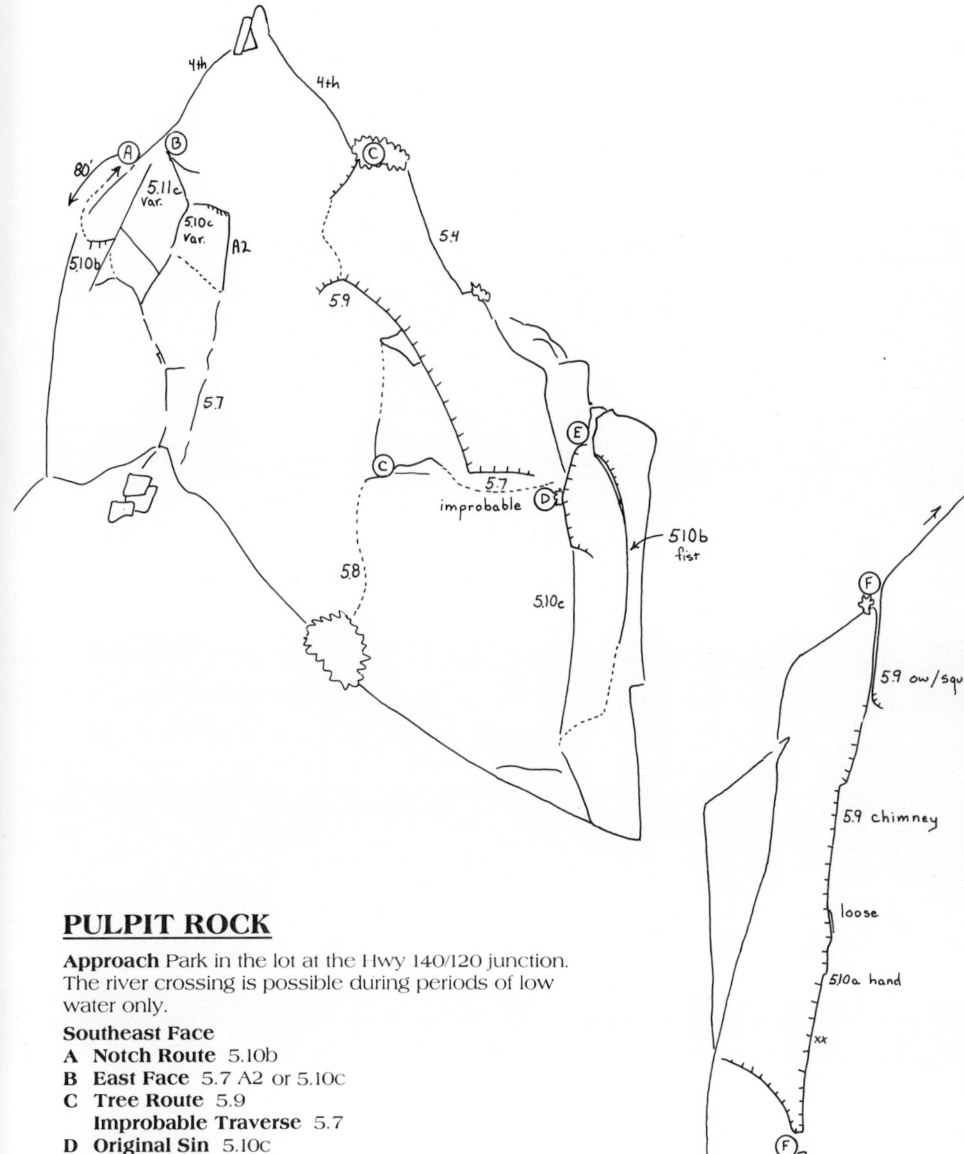

PULPIT ROCK

Approach Park in the lot at the Hwy 140/120 junction. The river crossing is possible during periods of low water only.

Southeast Face

A Notch Route 5.10b
B East Face 5.7 A2 or 5.10c
C Tree Route 5.9
Improbable Traverse 5.7
D Original Sin 5.10c
E Pulpit Pooper 5.10b pro: to 3½"

Northwest Face

F The Sermon 5.10b pro: to 3"

CREAM AREA

Approach These climbs are located on a faceted buttress below Hwy. 41. Park ½ mile past the west end of the Wawona Tunnel, just before the long stone wall.

A **Cream** 5.11a pro: to 6", incl. extra 4"-6"
B **Jam Session** 5.10b pro: to 5"
C **Cartwheel** 5.10a
D **Monkey Do** 5.10a pro: to 3", incl. extra 1"-2"
E **Energy Crisis** 5.11d
F **Shiver-Me-Timbers** 5.8

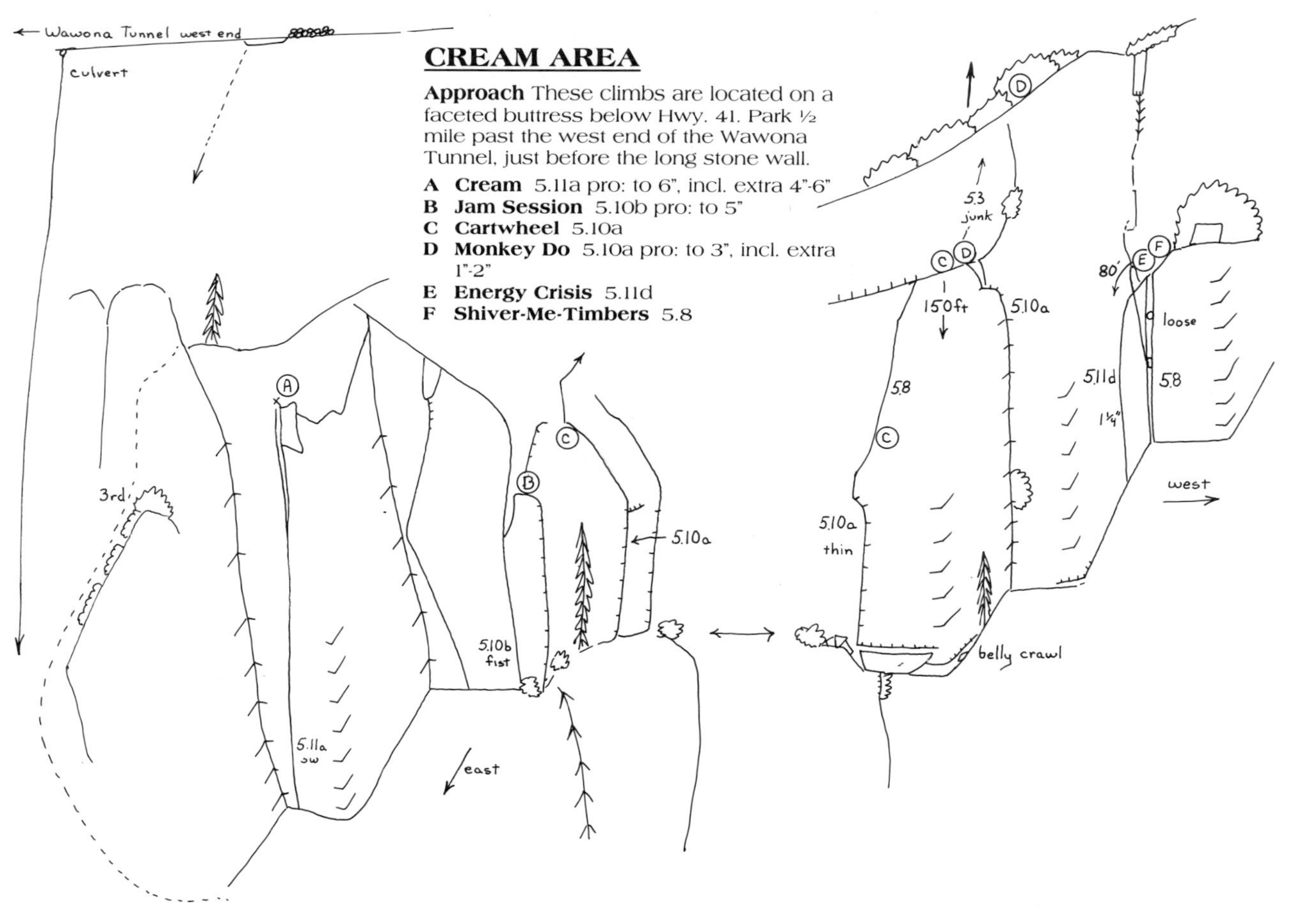

ROSTRUM AREA

N.P.S.

1 **Super Nova**
2 **Dime Bag**
3 **Crack the Whip**
4 **North Face Route**

SUPER NOVA AREA

Approach This is the silver/gray wall left (east) of the Rostrum. Wade across the river (low water only), then hike up talus.
Photo on page 369.

- **A** **Super Nova** 5.11a pro: to 4", incl. extra Friends #½-2
- **B** **Dime Bag** 5.10c
- **C** **Crack the Whip** 5.11b

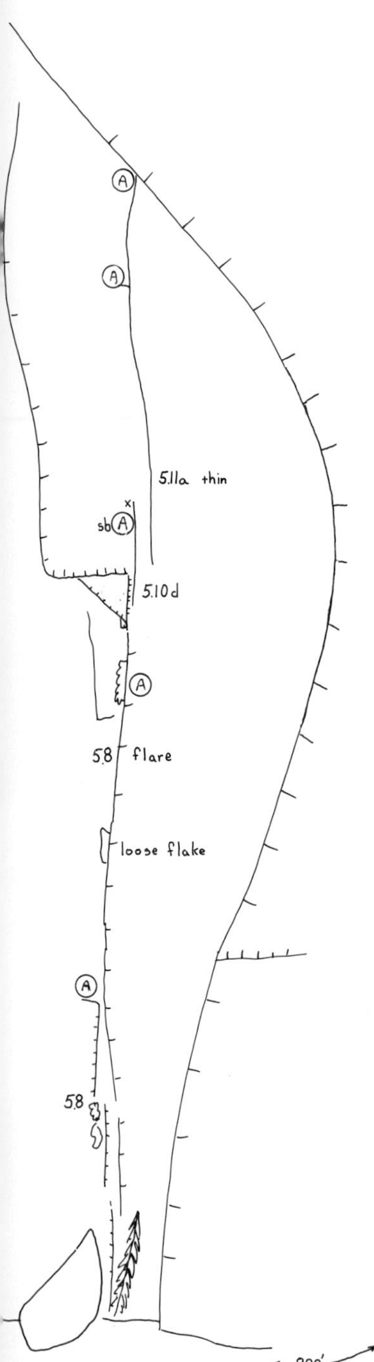

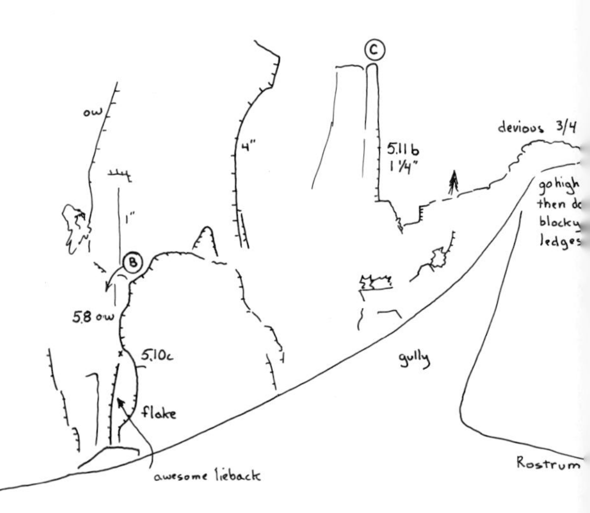

THE ROSTRUM

Approach These routes can be approached in times of low water by crossing the river and hiking up talus. They may also be reached from above. See the following page.

Photo on page 369.

A Regular North Face Route V 5.12b
B Mad Pilot 5.11b A1
C Alien 5.12a
D Blind Faith 5.11d

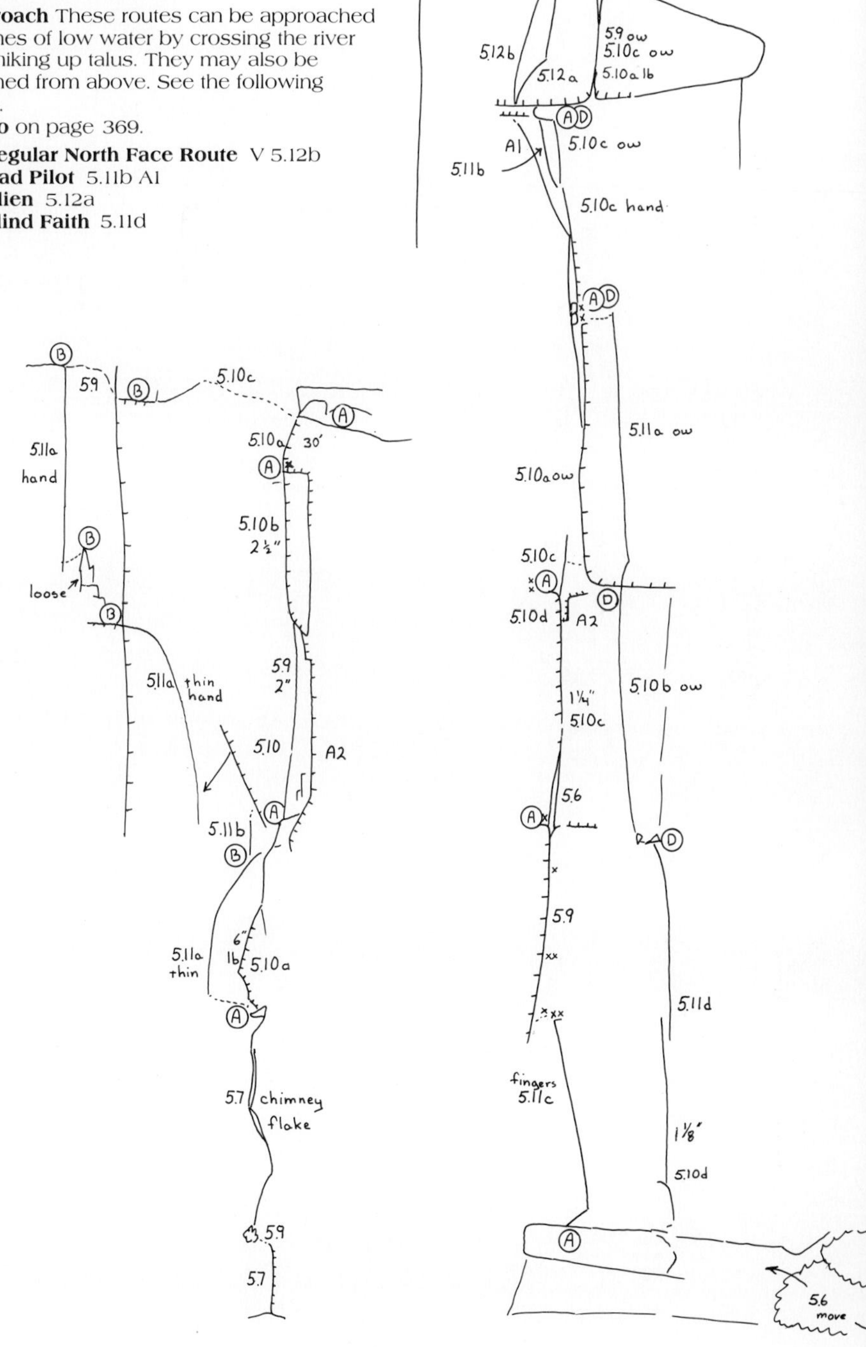

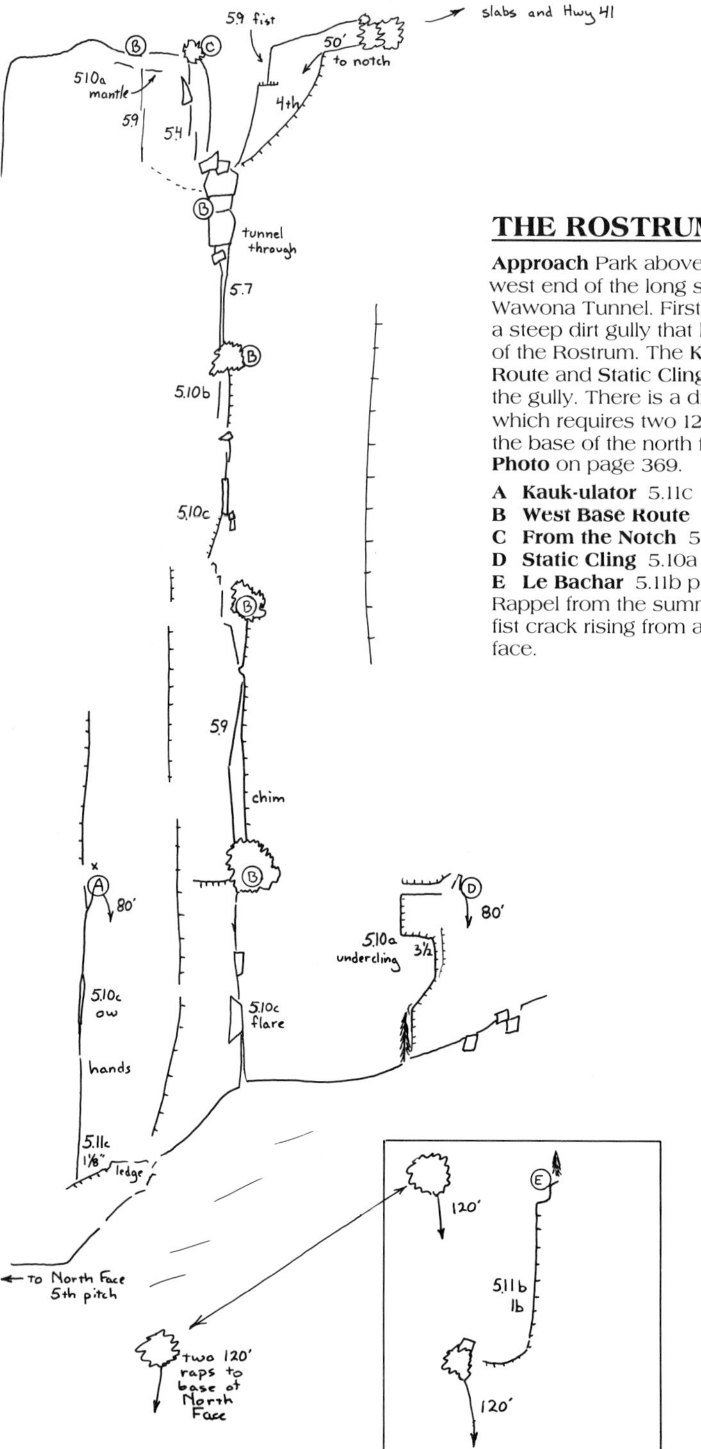

THE ROSTRUM

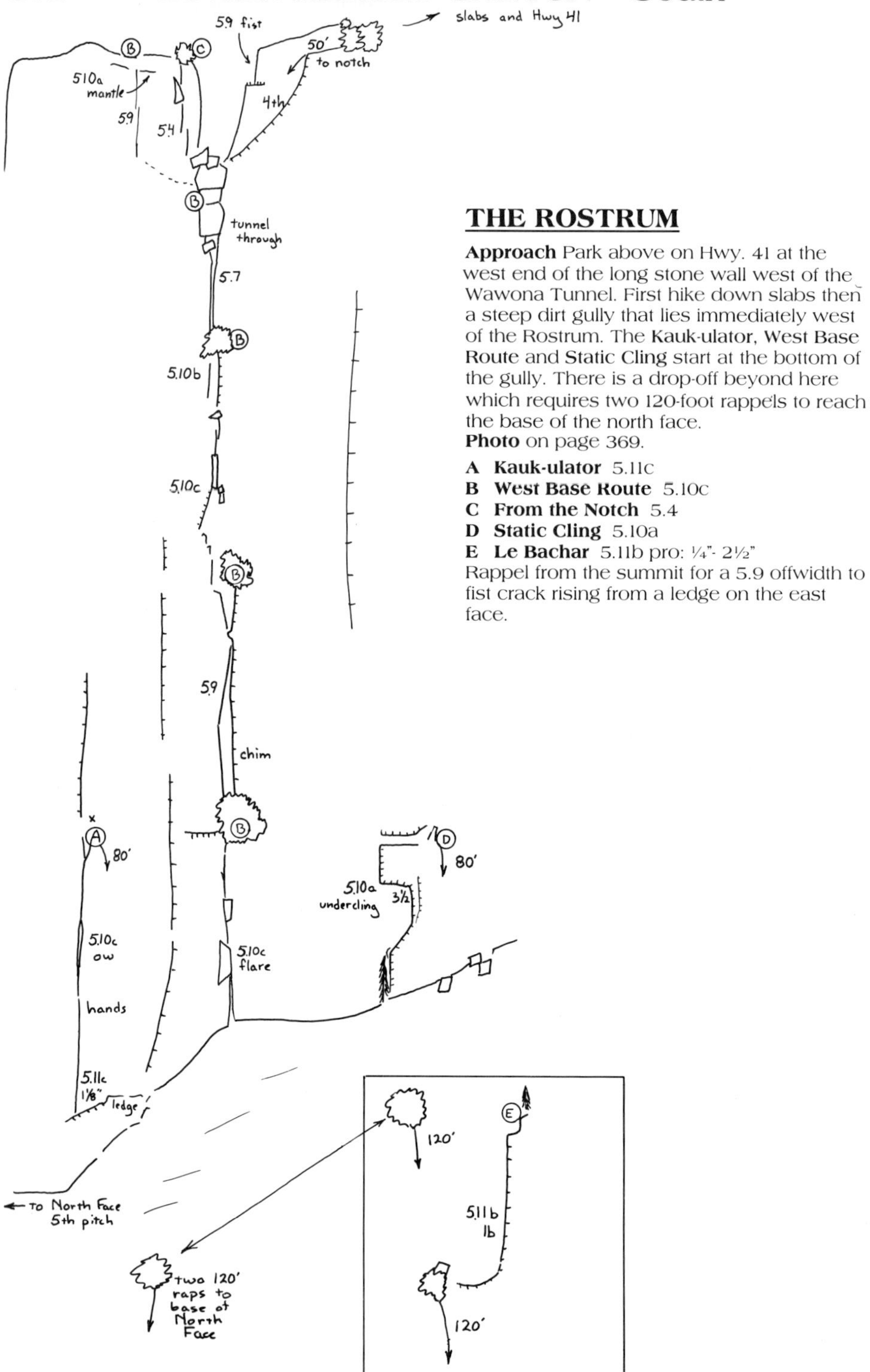

Approach Park above on Hwy. 41 at the west end of the long stone wall west of the Wawona Tunnel. First hike down slabs then a steep dirt gully that lies immediately west of the Rostrum. The **Kauk-ulator, West Base Route** and **Static Cling** start at the bottom of the gully. There is a drop-off beyond here which requires two 120-foot rappels to reach the base of the north face.

Photo on page 369.

A Kauk-ulator 5.11c
B West Base Route 5.10c
C From the Notch 5.4
D Static Cling 5.10a
E Le Bachar 5.11b pro: ¼"- 2½"
Rappel from the summit for a 5.9 offwidth to fist crack rising from a ledge on the east face.

JUNGLE GYM

Approach This area is the last part of the steep cliff that is part of the Rostrum wall. Park at the large parking area at Cascade Bridge on highway 140. Wade across the river (during low water only) and wander up the slope to the base of the wall.
Photo on page 369.

A Alamo 5.11a
Breast Feed 5.10c top rope
B Jungle Book 5.9
C Loyd's Lolly Pop 5.9
Poodle Bites 5.10c top rope
D Minor Kinda Unit 5.9
E Flight Attendant 5.10c pro: to 4"
F Dancing in the Dark 5.11b
G The Viper 5.11b pro: esp. ¾"-3½"

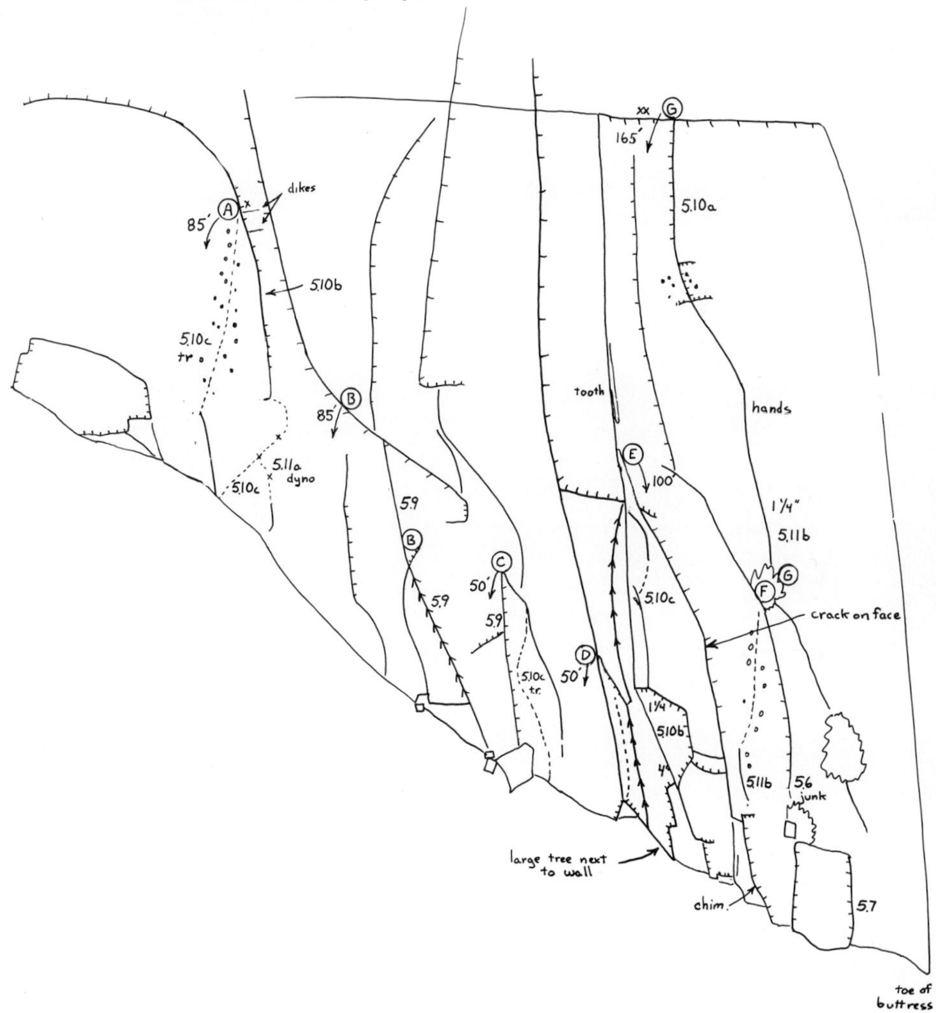

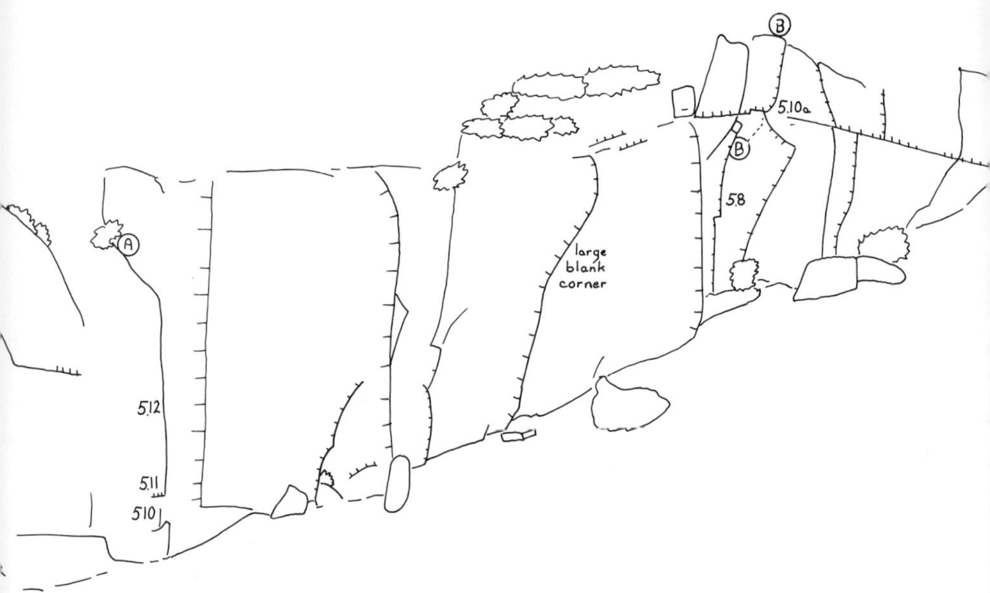

ELEPHANT'S GRAVEYARD

Approach This small cliff is located just to the east of Elephant Rock.

A Razor's Edge 5.12

B Eagle 5.10a

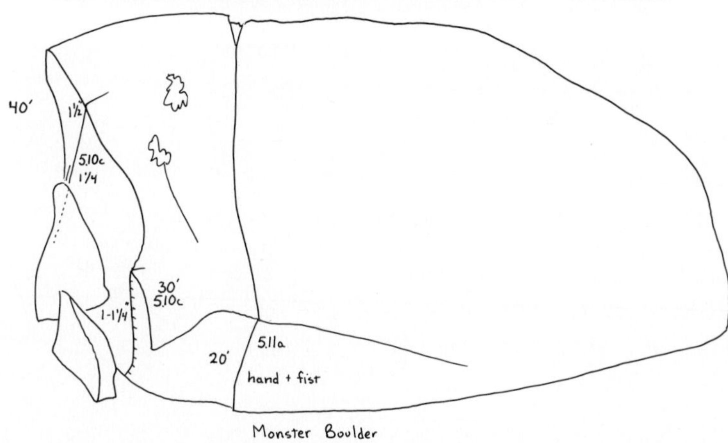

BOULDER CRACKS

Approach Park at the Cookie. The river crossing can be made even with the huge Monster Boulder only in times of low water.

Monster Boulder 5.11a tr
Jaws 5.12a tr

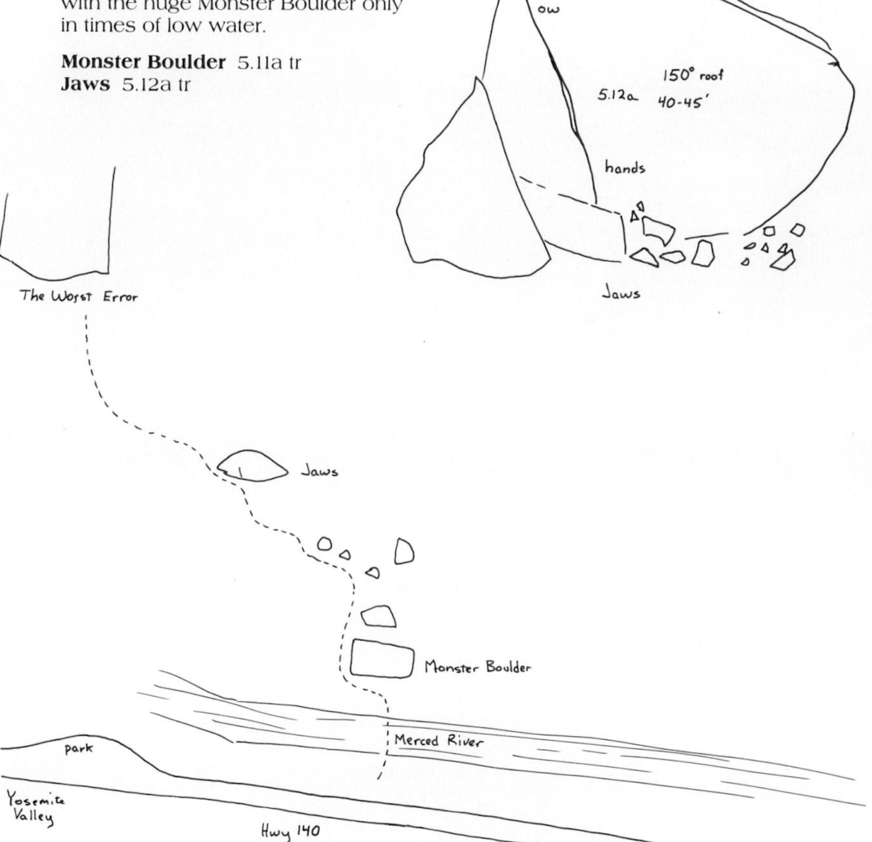

ow
150° roof
5.12a
40-45'
hands
Jaws

The Worst Error
Jaws
Monster Boulder
park
Merced River
Yosemite Valley
Hwy 140
Merced

ELEPHANT ROCK

1 Hotline
2 Crack of Doom
3 Crack of Despair
4 Hairline, Moongerms
5 Elephantiasis

ELEPHANT ROCK – East Side

Approach described on page 380.

A **Reality Check** 5.10c pro: to 4", incl. extra ½"-1½"

B **Plumb Line** 5.10d pro: to 6", incl. extra 2½"-3"

C **Trundling Juan** 5.10b pro: to 5"

D **Straight Error** 5.10c pro: to 3", incl. extra 2"-3"

E **Real Error** 5.7

F **Foaming at the Crotch** 5.10a pro: to 3½"

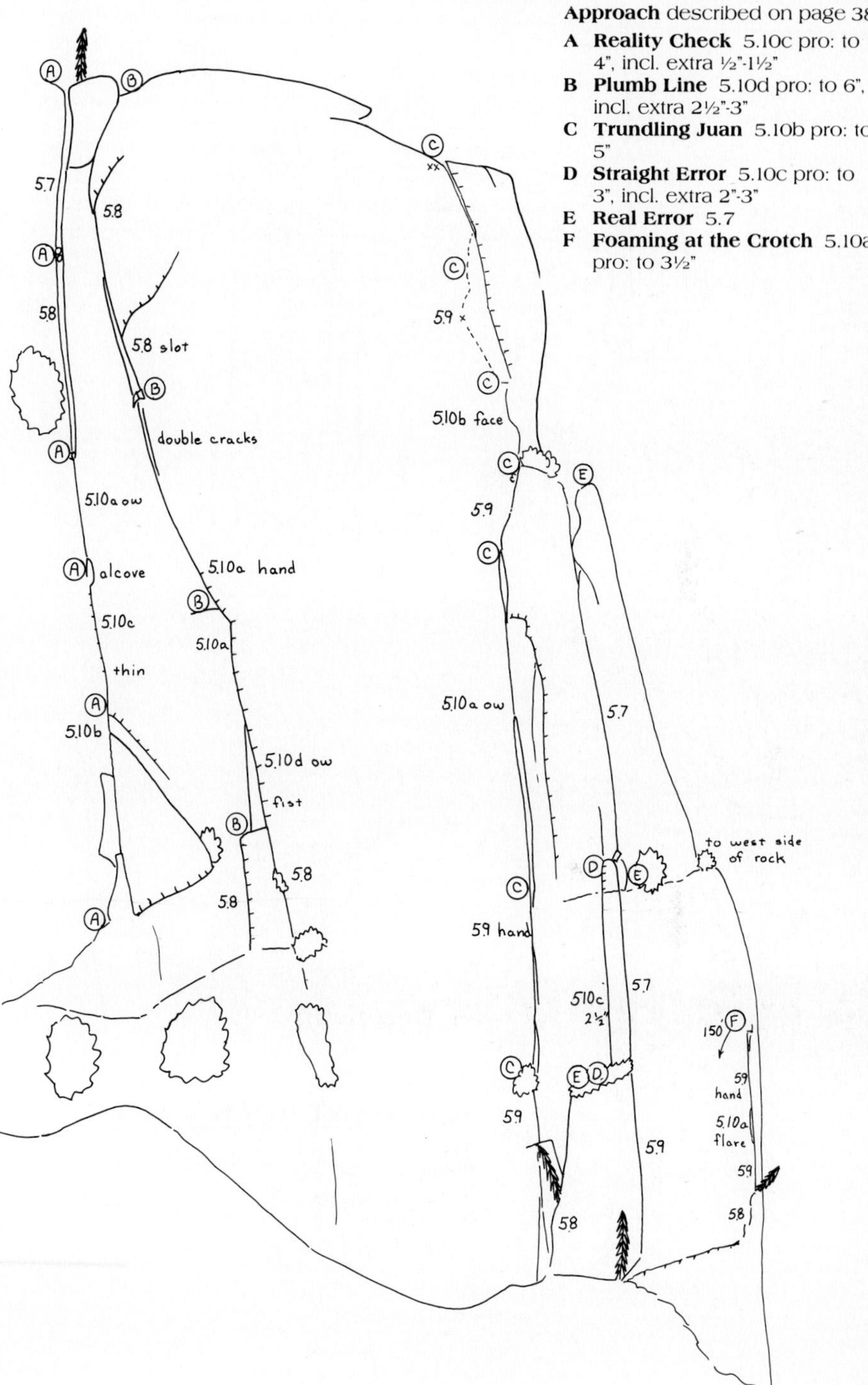

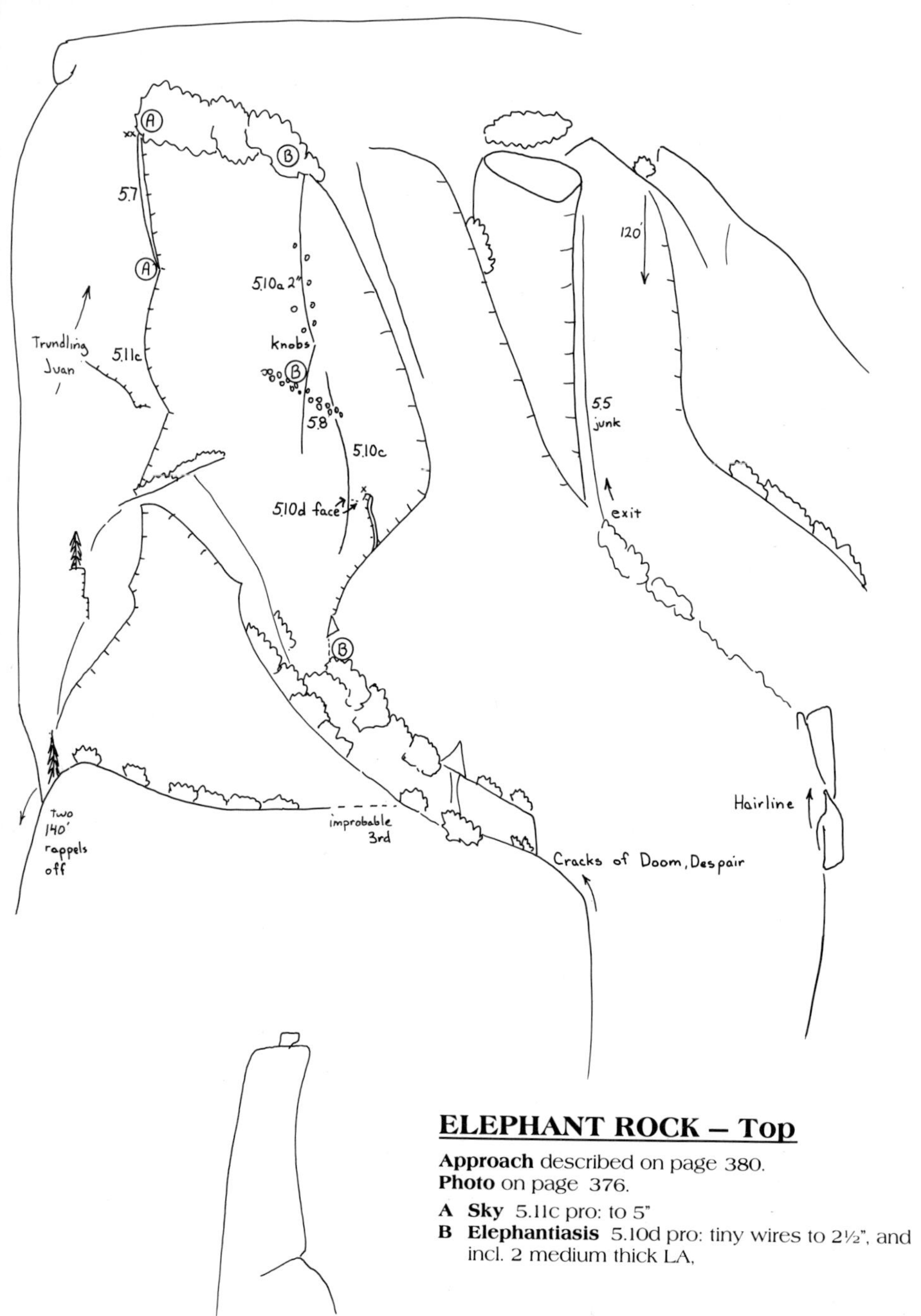

ELEPHANT ROCK – Top

Approach described on page 380.
Photo on page 376.

A **Sky** 5.11c pro: to 5"

B **Elephantiasis** 5.10d pro: tiny wires to 2½", and incl. 2 medium thick LA,

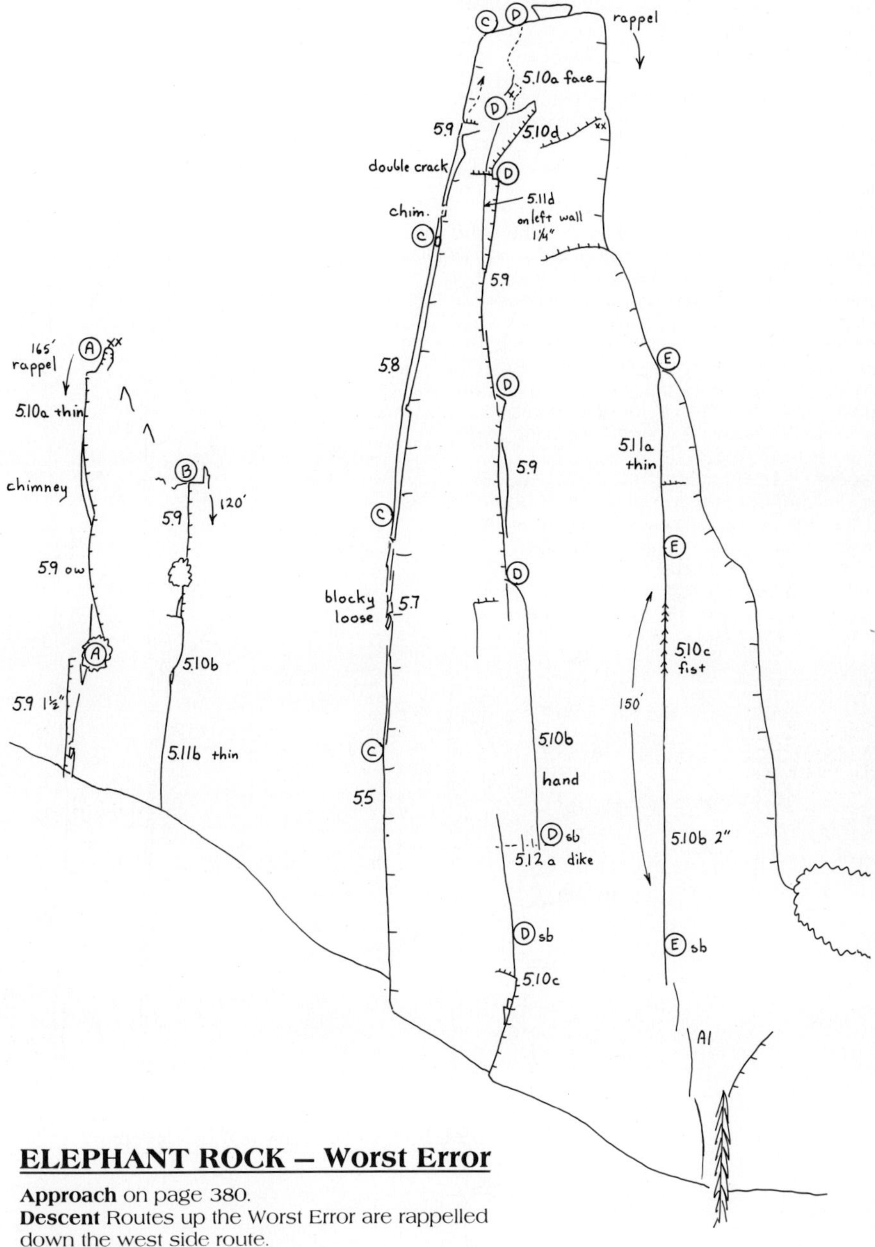

ELEPHANT ROCK – Worst Error

Approach on page 380.
Descent Routes up the Worst Error are rappelled down the west side route.
Photo on page 376.

A **Lost Error** 5.10a pro: small to 6"
B **Crashline** 5.11b pro: extra ½"-1¼"

Worst Error

C **Left Side** 5.9
D **Hotline** 5.12a pro: to 3", incl. extra 1½"-2½"
E **Fatal Mistake** 5.11a A1
It is possible to approach **Fatal Mistake** with a rappel from the top of **Pink Dream**.

ELEPHANT ROCK – West Side

Approach This cliff can be approached below from Hwy. 140 or from above off Hwy. 41. From below, park at the Cookie and walk down the road until even with the huge Monster Boulder that lies on the opposite side of the river. This is the best crossing but can only be done during periods of low water. Once across hike up the talus.

To approach Elephant Rock (as well as Elephant's Graveyard) from Hwy 41 park in the banked, gravelled turnout west of the stone wall that is the Rostrum parking. The rim is reached within minutes, though careful scouting is needed to find a class 2 descent that intrudes the short crown of cliffs between Elephant Rock and Elephant's Graveyard. This leads down the east side of Elephant Rock. Some of the short routes at the top of Elephant Rock can be reached from above by careful scouting and judicious rappelling.

Descent Descend most of the routes by rappel. The descent from the top of **Crack of Doom** and the like can be made by scrambling east on ledges to an improbable that leads to rappel anchors down **Real Error** (see page 377). Descend routes that lead to the top of the Worst Error by rappelling the **Right Side Route**.

Photo on page 376.

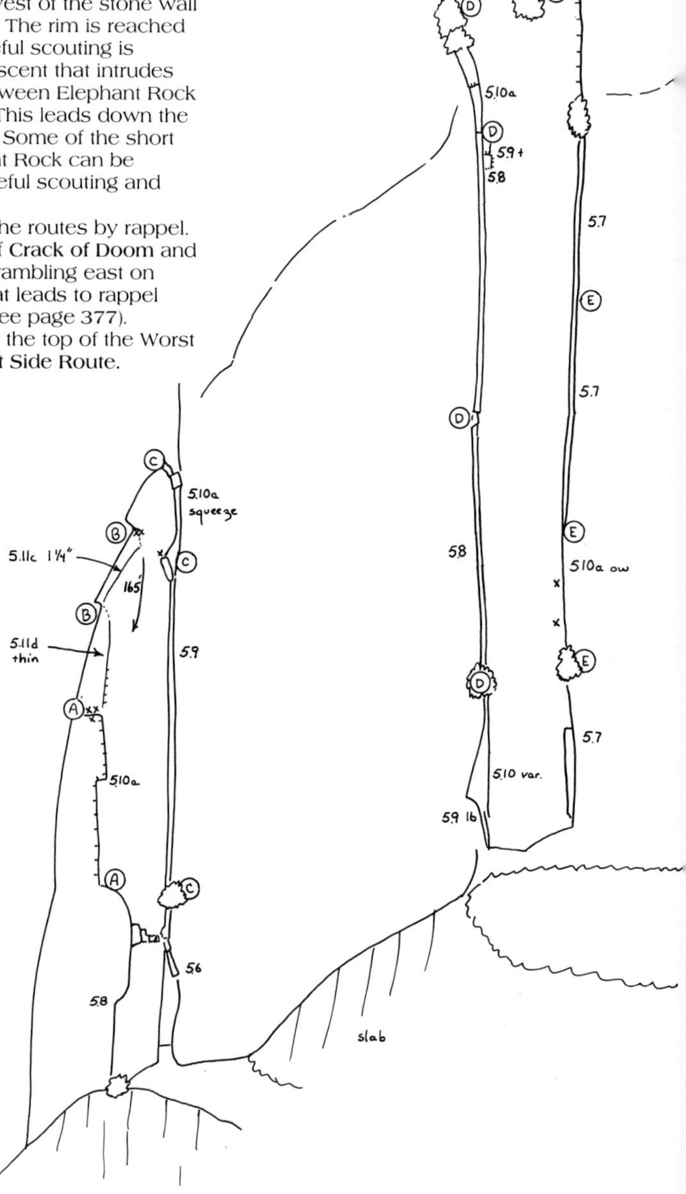

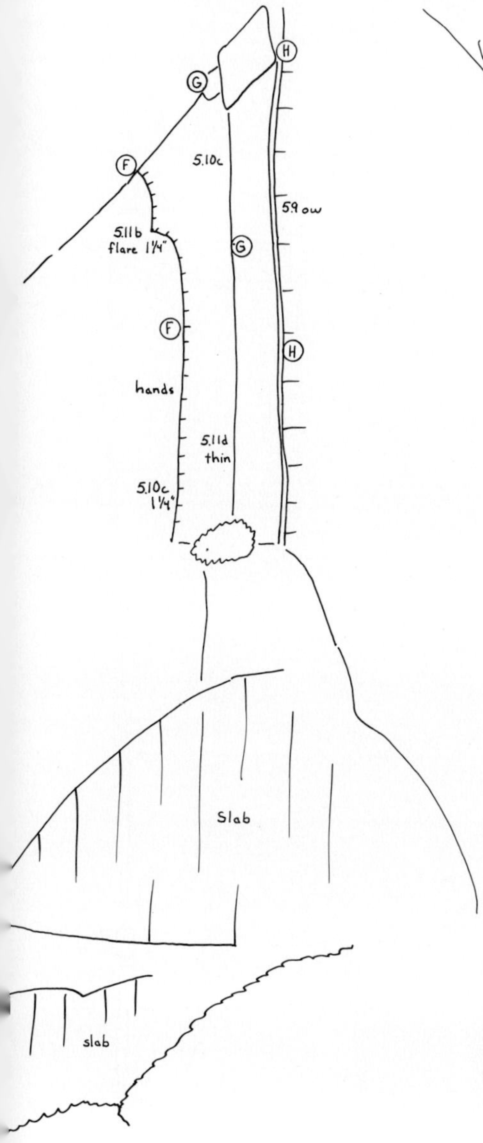

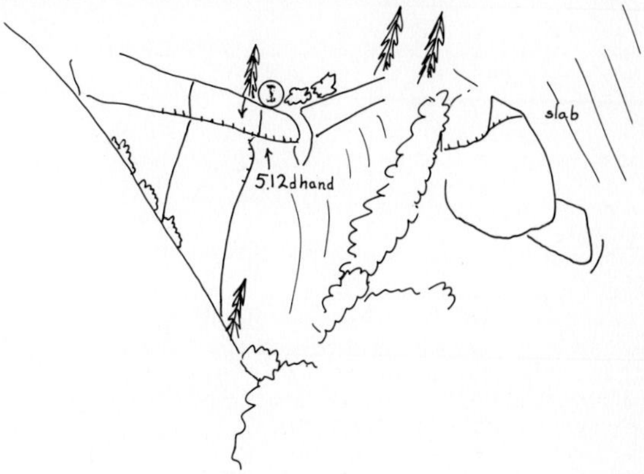

Worst Error

A **Pink Dream** 5.10a pro: to 3½", incl. extra 2"-3"
B **Nightmare Continuation** 5.11d
C **Right Side Route** 5.10a pro: to 3"
D **Crack of Doom** 5.10a pro: to 3"
E **Crack of Despair** 5.10a pro: to 5"
F **Hairline** 5.11b pro: to 3", incl. extra 1"-2½"
G **Moongerms** 5.11d
H **Crack of Deliverance** 5.9
I **Elephant's Eliminate** 5.12d

FREE CLIMBS COMPARED

The following list describes routes by the predominant character of the crux climbing. Grades 5.6 through 5.8 are described rather broadly, the harder routes more specifically.

5.6

Munginella
After Six
Aquamist
The Grack, Center Route
Overhang Bypass

5.7 Cracks

Pat Pinnacle
Jack Pinnacle
Gilligan's Chicken
Sloth Wall
Anti-Ego Crack
Chicken Pie
Inner Reaches
Delectable Pinnacle, Right Side
La Cosita, Left Side
Washington Column, Direct Route
North Dome, South Face Route
Monday Morning Slab, Chouinard Crack
The Cracker, Right Side

5.7 Face

After Seven
Via Aqua
The Kids are All Right
Snake Dike

5.8 Cracks

Cool Cliff 170
Elevator Shaft
The Remnant, Right Side
The Gray Bullet
Keystone Corner
Mojo Tooth
Little John, Left Side
Little John, Right Side
Gollum, Right Side
Cid's Embrace
The Surprise
Lieback Route
Selaginella
Arrowhead Arête
Bishop's Terrace
Church Bowl Terrace
North Dome, West Face Route
Monday Morning Slab, Harry Daley Route
Tilted Mitten, Right Side
Pharaoh's Beard, Regular Route

5.8 Face

Wart Hog
Golden Needles
Chicken Pox
Jugs
Holidays
Jump for Joy
C.S. Concerto
Nutcracker
Try Again Ledge
Black is Brown
Arches Terrace
The Grack, Right Side
Patio Pinnacle, Regular Route
Point Beyond
Point Beyond, Direct
Braille Book
Pulpit Rock, Improbable Traverse

FACE/SLAB CLIMBS

5.9

New Diversions
Fecophilia
Easy Wind
The Mouse King
The Prune
Tapestry
Color Me Gone
The Prude
Marginal
The Mouth
Flakey Foont
Goodrich Pinnacle, Right Side
Patio Pinnacle, Left Side
Patio Pinnacle, Regular Route
Coonyard Pinnacle
Angelica
Angel's Approach
Lucifer's Ledge
Higher Cathedral Spire, Regular Route
Lower Cathedral Spire, Regular Route
Quicksilver
Tapestry

5.10a

Punch Bowl
The Hawaiian
An Udder Way
Deaf, Dumb and Blind
Paradise Lost
Cat Dancing
Deep Throat
Patio to Coonyard
Tears of Joy
Spooky Tooth
Bottom Feeder

5.10b

Trough of Justice
New Traditionalists
Domehead
No Falls Wall
Slab Happy Pinnacle, Center Route
The Peanut
Dark Star
Church Bowl Tree
Hoppy's Favorite
Middle Cathedral, Direct North Buttress
Freewheelin'
Stupid Pet Tricks
Exodus
The Joker

5.10c

W'allnuts
Miramonte
Rixon's Pinnacle, West Face (2nd pitch)
Space Doubt
Cheek
Ugly Duckling
Beat Around the Bush
Butthole Climbers
Sultans of Sling
Chain Reaction
Maxine's Wall
Surplus Cheaper Hands
Benzoin and Edges
Rurp Rape
A Mother's Lament
Stoner's Highway
Shake and Bake

5.10d

Blotto
Old Five Ten
Cuthulu
Boogie With Stu
Movin' Like a Stud
Dead Baby
Misty Beethoven
Sailin' Shoes
Afterglow
Pharaoh's Beard, Right Side
Elephantiasis

5.11a

Black Heads
Moon Age Daydream
Pterodactyl Terrace, Right Side
Days of Our Lives
Greasy but Groovy
Precious Powder
Strange Energy
Ochre Fields
Anchors Away
Lean Years
Jigsaw
Teaching Little Fingers

5.11b

The Void
The Wedge
Nine Lives
The Promise
Catch-U
Preface
Christina
Swan Slab Aid Route
Adrenaline
Fire Fingers
The Calf
Tightrope
Mouth to Perhaps
Green Dragon
Chiropodist Shop
Ephemeral Clogdance
Orange Peel
Black Primo

5.11c

Gunks Revisited
Champagne on Ice
Koko Ledge, Center
Skunk Weed
Follying
General Hospital
Shakey Flakes
Flakes Away
Nothing on the Apron
Look Before You Leap
Spiderman
Power Point
Bircheff-Williams

5.11d

Abstract Corner
Rocket Man
The Remnant, Center Route
The Token
Thunderhead
White Zone
Annette Funicello
Rainbow Bridge

5.12a

The Believer
King Snake
Hotline

LIEBACK AND UNDERCLING

5.9

Enigma
Said and Done
Captain Hook, Right Side
La Cosita, Right Side
Positively 4th Street
Lenna's Lieback
Committment
Eric's Book
Tilted Mitten, Left Side
Pee Pee Pillar

5.10a

Babble On
Uncertain Ending
Nottingham
Koko Ledge, Left Side
Koko Ledge, Far Right
Lightweight Guides
Peruvian Flake
Wise Crack
The Hand Me Down
Static Cling

5.10b

Wheat Thin
The Remnant, Left Side
Nanbeeb
The Plank
Gold Dust
Sixth Heaven

5.10c

Supplication
Waverly Wafer
Hardly Pinnacle
Chow Chow Chow
Slab Happy Pinnacle, Dihardral
Split Pinnacle Lieback
Young and the Restless
Chopper
Wing of Bat
Dorn's Crack
Sub-Mission
Reality Check

5.10d

Scorpion Man
Shattered
Hourglass, Left Side
Mark of Art
The Folly, Right Side
The Podium
Lingering Lie

5.11a

Catchy Corner
The Tube
Eraser Flake
Trix
Duncan Imperial
Indubious Battle
Demon's Delight
Here on the Outside
Yin-Yang

5.11b

The Knife
Captain Crunch
La Escuela
End Game
Stay Free
High Pressure
Le Bachar

5.11c

Joe's Garage
Blankout
Sky

5.11d

Lycra Virgin
The High Arc

5.12

Hangdog Flyer

THIN CRACKS (to 1½")

5.9

Chicken Pie
Nutcracker (1st pitch variation)
Absolutely Free, Left Side
Doggie Deviations
Sunnyside Bench, Jamcrack Route
Phantom Pinnacle, Left Side
Shuttle Madness
Son of Sam
Eat at Degnan's

5.10a

Beverly's Tower
Try Again Ledge variation
Desperate Straights
Siberian Swarm Screw
Sex, Drugs and Violence
Sacherer Cracker
Moby Dick, Center Route
Koko Ledge, Right Side
Rixon's Pinnacle, East Chimney
Synapse Collapse
Super Slide
Heathenistic Pursuit
Lost Error
Drop-out

5.10b

Midterm
Gripper
Outer Limits
Knob Job
Sherrie's Crack
Gay Bob's
Leisure Time
Eclipse
Stone Groove
Avalon
Jojo
Half Dome, Salathé Route
Plane Fare
Krovy Rookers
No Butts About It
Doggie Submission

5.10c

English Breakfast
Snatch Power
Tricky Fingers
Through Bein' Cool
Lunatic Fringe
Honor Thy Father
The Slack, Center Route
Rixon's Pinnacle, Klemens Variation
Blackout
Seaside
Gravity's Rainbow
Lonely Dancer
Mr. Natural
Sacherer-Fredericks
Turning Point
Original Sin

5.10d

Finger Lickin'
Brain Bucket
Catchy
White Cloud
Cramming
Five and Dime
Olga's Trick
Independence Pinnacle, Center
Mighty Crunchy
Ten Years After
Lazy Bum
Serenity Crack
Dr. Feel Good
Vanishing Point
Manana
The Thief
Little Wing

5.11a

New Dimensions
Stealth Technology
Butterfingers
Ladyfinger
Terminator, Right
Obscure Destiny
Whack and Dangle
Cosmic Ray
Ready or Not
Knuckle Buster
Book of Revelations
Arches Terrace Direct
Texas Chainsaw Massacre
Water Babies
Controlled Burn
Tidbit
Megaforce
Sunset Strip

5.11b

Leanie Meanie
Gripped
Hardd
Anticipation
Spring Fever
Moratorium
Essence (2nd pitch)
Aftershock
Terminator, Left
Guardian Angel
Humdinger
Skunk Crack
Short but Thin
Final Decision
Turkey Vulture
Crack the Whip
The Viper
Crashline
Hairline

5.11c

Pinky Paralysis
Butterballs
Little Thing
Disconnected
The Fin
Maps and Legends
Fool's Finger
Terminal Research
Soul Sacrifice
Dancin' Days
Overhang Overpass
Kauk-ulator

5.11d

Isotope
Constipation
Torque Converter
Opposition
The Cleft (1st pitch variation)
Red Zinger
The Wand
Gotham City
Robin
Gait of Power
Something for Nothing
The Warbler
Whisker
Energy Crisis
Moongerm

5.12a

Tennessee Strings
Tips
Cat's Squirrel
Stubs
Mirage
Ain't That a Bitch
Peter's Out
Pigs in Space
Alien

5.12b

Omakara
Goldfingers
Back to the Future
America's Cup
Fish Crack
Tales of Power
Atomic Finger Crack
A Dog's Roof
Rostrum Roof
Razor's Edge

5.12c

Ray's Pin Job

5.12d

Tunnel Vision

5.13a

Phoenix
Cosmic Debris
Dale's Pin Job
Phantom

HAND AND FIST (1½" to 3")

5.9

Application
The Cookie, Right
Fluke
Infraction
Pot Belly
Arlington Heights
Reed's Direct
Flatus
Grape Nuts
Commissioner Buttress
Doggie Diversions
Lancelot

5.10a

Highway Star
Quickie Quizzes
Jawbone
Maple Jam
Resurrection
Euellogy
Tiger's Paw
Rixon's Pinnacle, West Face (5th pitch)
Henley Quits
A-5 Pinnacle
Cartwheel
Monkey Do
Eagle
Pink Dream

5.10b

Midterm
Anathema
Strangers in the Night
Shake, Rattle, and Drop
Independent Route
Cosmic Messenger
Book of Job
The Lionheart

5.10c

Meat Grinder
Dromedary Direct
Polymorphous Perverse
Eagle Feather
Jesu Joy
Straight Error

5.10d

Slab Happy Pinnacle, Left Side
Childhood's End
Final Exam

5.11a

Overdrive
ala Moana
Short but Thick
Windfall
Fist Puppet

5.11b

Orangutan Arch
Enema
My-Toe-Sis
Goldrush
Shortcake
Essence (1st pitch)

5.11c

Fistabule

5.11d

Separate Reality

5.12a

Crimson Cringe

5.12b

5.12c

The Owl

5.12d

Elephant's Eliminate

OFF WIDTH (3½" to 8")

5.9

The Cleft
Side Kick
La Cosita, left variation
Sawyer Crack
Peter Pan
Apron Jam

5.10a

Banana Dream
The Cookie, Left Side
This and That
Chingando
Reed's Pinnacle, Left Sode
Bong's Away, Center Route
Hourglass, Right Side
Gollum, Left Side
Orange Juice Avenue
Secret Storm
Doggie Do
Geek Towers, Center Route
Geek Towers, Right Side
Pink Dream
Crack of Doom
Crack of Despair

5.10b

Vendetta
The Slack, Left Side
Smoky Pillar
Pulpit Pooper
Jam Session

5.10c

Wild Turkey
Edge of Night
Fallout
Mental Block
Barefoot Servants

5.10d

Twilight Zone
The Shaft
Steppin' Out
Plumb Line

5.11a

Cream
A Desperate Kneed
Power Failure

5.11b

Basket Case

CHIMNEY/FLARES

5.9

Moby Dick, Left Side
The Cookie, Center Route
Entrance Exam

5.10a

Handjob
Free Press
Worst Error, Right Side
Fresh Squeezed
The Riddler
Ahab
Reed's Direct (3rd pitch)
Absolutely Free, Right Side
Milk Dud

5.10b

5.10c

Twinkie

5.10d

10.96

5.11a

5.11b

On the Edge

5.11c

Realm of the Lizard King

FIRST ASCENTS

PARKLINE/NARROW ESCAPE

Woody Woodpecker Don Reid and Ron Skelton, 1/85
Sawyer Crack Bruce Price, Jerry Anderson, 4/72
Color Me Gone Don Reid and Ron Skelton, 2/85
The Hawaiian Don Reid and Ron Skelton, 1/85
Cool Cliff 170 Jerry Anderson, Bruce Price and John Yates, 3/70 **FFA** John Dill and Phil Gleason, 1973
Parkline Pinnacle, Center Route Bill Price, John Yates and Jerry Anderson, 3/70 **FFA** Claude Fiddler, 1972
Parkline Pinnacle, Right Side Dave Huson and Clyde Deal, 3/63
Teeter Tower Jack Delk and Bill Sorenson, 2/70
A Desperate Kneed John Yablonski, Don Reid and Rick Cashner, 1981
Narrow Escape Peter Haan, Jim Bridwell and Mark Klemens, 4/71.
Remember Ribbon Falls Rick Cashner and Dale Bard, 1980.

ARCH ROCK

Constipation Bill Price and Kurt Rieder, 1979.
Anticipation Mark Chapman and Jim Donini, 1974
Supplication Barry Bates and Bev Johnson, 1971
Application Barry Bates and Peter Haan, 10/71
Entrance Exam Chuck Pratt, Chris Fredericks, Larry Marshik and Jim Bridwell, 8/65
Blotto Henry Barber and Ajax Greene, 5/75
English Breakfast Crack Chris Fredericks and Kim Schmitz, 7/66
Midterm Chuck Pratt and Tom Frost, 8/64
Sidetrack Jim Bridwell and Dale Bard, 1974
Leanie Meanie Jim Donini, Rab Carrington and Mark Chapman, 1972
Gripper Jim Bridwell, Bruce Kumph and Mark Klemens, 8/70
Gripped Bill Price et al, 1978
New Dimensions Mark Klemens and Jim Bridwell, 5/70 **FFA** Barry Bates and Steve Wunsch, 1972
The Voyage Vern Clevenger and Ray Jardine, 5/75
Klemens' Escape Mark Klemens and Jim Bridwell, 1970
Inchworm John Bachar and Rick Cashner, 1984
Grokin' Ed Barry and Chris Falkenstein, 9/86
Now Werner Braun, Rick Cashner and Don Reid, 2/83
Omakara John Bachar, et al, 6/83
Later Werner Braun and Doug McDonald, 2/83
Arch Rock Pinnacle Warren Harding and George Whitmore, 4/55
Per-Spire-ation Kevin Worrall, Mark Chapman, Matt Pollock and Bruce Pollock, 1974
Pass or Fail Rick Sylvester and Gib Lewis, 11/71
Cross Country Crack Chuck Pratt and Tim Kimbrough, 10/65
Kindergarten Crack John Evans and Chuck Pratt, 8/65
Quickie Quizzes Mark Klemens and Dave N. Gerughty, 1970
Nerf Test Phil Gleason and Rick Sylvester, 11/71
Extra Credit Walt Shipley and Werner Braun, 1986
Julliette's Flake, Left Chuck Pratt and Jim Bridwell, 8/65
Julliette's Flake, Right Warren Harding and Rich Calderwood, 1960

Cosmic Messenger Bob Williams et al, 1980
Goldfingers Chick Holtkamp and Eric Zschiesche, 5/80
Torque Converter Dave Anderson and Chick Holtkamp, 5/80
Stealth Technology Don Reid at al, 2/85

DOG DIK/FINGER LICKIN'

Short but Thick Kevin Worrall, John Bachar and Ed Barry, 1975
Opposition John Bachar and Werner Braun, 1985
Happy Days Werner Braun, Rick Cashner and Chris Belizzi, 4/82
Pink Pussycat Don Reid and Greg Sonagere, 11/82
Fist Puppet Walt Shipley and Bill Russell, 1986
Finger Lickin' Mark Chapman and Kevin Worrall, 1973
Fun Flake Mark Chapman and Kevin Worrall, 1973
Pandora's Box Mark Chapman and Kevin Worrall, 1973
Snatch Power Bob Ashworth, Bruce Pollock and Matt Pollock, 1973
Jawbone Mark Chapman and Kevin Worrall, 1973
Pinky Paralysis John Bachar and Jim Bridwell, 1975

KAT PINNACLE AREA

Outa Hand Dale Bard and Rick Cashner, 1982
Hand Out Rick Cashner and Don Reid, 1982
Roadside Attraction unknown
Roadside Infraction Scott Cosgrove
Dale's Pin Job John Bachar, 12/86
Back to the Future Ron Kauk, 5/86
Kat Pinnacle via Tyrolean Traverse Dewitt Allen, Torcom Bedayan and Robin Hansen, 11/40
Kat Pinnacle, Northwest Corner Mark Powell and Don Wilson, 12/56 **(5.10 last pitch variation)** Chuck Pratt and Tom Gerughty, 7/65
Kat Pinnacle, Katchup John Long and Tony Zeek
Kat Pinnacle, Southwest Corner Yvon Chouinard and Tom Frost, 4/60
Kat Pinnacle, Compass Rick Cashner
ala Moana John Yablonski and Werner Braun, 1981

THE COOKIE AREA

Twinkie Ray Jardine and Chris Nelson, 1973
Tennessee Strings Rob Robinson, Kade Lloyd, 12/86
Coffin Nail unknown
Hardd Henry Barber and Ron Kauk, 5/75
Banana Dreams Vern Clevenger et al, 5/74
Crack-A-Go-Go Harvey Carter and Pete Pederson, 5/67 **FFA** Pete Livesey and Ron Fawcett, 1974
Orangutan Arch Steve Wunsch and John Bragg, 1974
Outer Limits Jim Bridwell and Jim Orey, 1971
Elevator Shaft Jim Bridwell and Phil Bircheff, 6/65
Twilight Zone Chuck Pratt and Chris Fredericks, 9/65
America's Cup Kim Carrigan and Geoff Weigand, 1985
Red Zinger Ray Jardine and Dave Altman, 9/79
Meat Grinder Royal Robbins and TM Herbert, 3/68
Beverly's Tower Gerry Czamanske and Warren Harding, 1959 **FFA** Roger Breedlove and Alan Bard, 5/73
Aftershock Tony Yaniro and Max Jones, 1981
Waverly Wafer Jim Bridwell, Barry Bates and Beverly Johnson, 10/70
Butterballs Henry Barber et al, 5/73

Wheat Thin Peter Haan and Jim Bridwell, 8/71
Butterfingers Jim Bridwell and Charley Jones, 8/71
Ladyfingers John Long and Mike Graham, 5/74
The Cookie Chuck Pratt and Dick Sykes, 8/58
The Cookie, Left Royal Robbins and Loyd Price, 2/68
The Cookie, Center Tom Kimbrough, Tom Hargis and Roman Laba, 1965
The Cookie, Right Royal Robbins and Loyd Price, 2/68
Vendetta Loyd Price and Roger Gordon, 6/67 **FFA** Royal Robbins and Galen Rowell, 1968 **(last pitch variation)** Jim Donini and Mark Chapman, 1973 **(second pitch variation)** Bruce Morris
Infraction Don Reid et al, 1977
Anathema Barry Bates et al, 1972
Jardine's Hand Ray Jardine et al, 1979
The Cleft Chuck Pratt and Wally Reed, 1958 **FFA** Chuck Pratt and Chris Fredericks, 1965
Catchy Jim Pettigrew, Jim Bridwell and Mark Klemens, 10/71
Catchy Corner Jim Bridwell and Dale Bard, 1974
Void Continuation Dimitri Barton and Steve Gerberding, 1984
The Void Tom Higgins et al, 1971
The Stigma Dennis Miller and Brian Birmingham, 1970 **FFA (first pitch)** Alan Watts, 1986
The Enigma
via 5.8 finish Barry Miller and Ray Barlow, 9/64
via 5.9 finish TM Herbert et al
Ramp of Deception Jim Bridwell et al, 1971
Abstract Corner Jim Bridwell et al, 1971
Shortcake Jim Bridwell and Dale Bard, 1971
Enema Jim Donini and John Bragg, 1974
Ray's Pin Job Kurt Smith and Dave Hatchettt, 5/85
Something for Nothing Kurt Smith and Dave Hatchettt, 5/85
Terminator, Left Don Reid, 2/85
Terminator, Right Bruce Brossman and Mike Breidenbach
Capital Punishment Chuck Pratt, Bruce Price and Jerry Anderson, 1972
Hobknob George Meyers and Merrill Wilson, 10/86
Joe's Garage Rick Cashner and Ed Barry, 1979
Gait of Power Ron Kauk and John Bachar, 1976
Tunnel Vision John Bachar et al, 6/82
Romantic Tension Jonny Woodward and Dimitri Barton, 5/85
Klingon Jonny Woodward and Dimitri Barton, 5/85
Miramonte Steve Schneider and Dimitri Barton, 10/85
Uncertain Ending Ray Jardine and John Lakey, 10/78
Obscure Destiny Ray Jardine and John Lakey, 5/77
Skunk Crack Ray Jardine and John Lakey, 5/77
Tales of Power Ron Kauk et al, 9/77
Separate Reality Ron Kauk et al, 1978
Through Bein' Cool Rick Cashner, Dimitri Barton and Dave Neilson, 4/86
Prime Time Rick Cashner, Dimitri Barton, Dave Neilson and Grant Hiskes, 4/86

CASCADE AREA

Pat Pinnacle Wayne Merry and Mike Borghoff, 1958
Jack Pinnacle, Left Tom Gerughty and Dave Calfee, 6/64
Jack Pinnacle, Right Wayne Merry and Warren Harding, 1957
Domehead Bill Russell and Pat Ranstrum, 1983
Scorpion Man Bill Russell and Pat Ranstrum, 1983

The Knife Matt Stein and Chris Bellizzi, TR, 7/82
Flailing Dog Cliff Howard and Larry Zulim, 1979
Gillagan's Chicken Drone Stephens and Bob Ashworth, 1973
Chicken Fever unknown
Sherrie's Crack Kevin Worrall and George Meyers, 1976
Nurdle Bob Ashworth and George Meyers, 1973
Knob Job Kevin Worrall and George Meyers, 1973
Book 'em, Dano Dimitri Barton and Dave Neilson
Trough of Justice Chris Cantwell et al, 1980
People's Court Paul Crawford, Paul Teare and Scott Woolums, 4/84
Desperate Straights Rick Sylvester and Mike Farrell, 1973
Cat's Squirrel Bill Price and Augie Klein, 1980
Nine Lives Bruce Morris and Dave Sessions, 10/82
Black Heads Jim Beyer and Bob Sullivan, 9/78
The Tube Jim Bridwell, Kevin Worrall, Dale Bard and George Meyers, 1974
Guardian Angel Larry Zulim and Cliff Howard, 1979
Gay Bob's Mike Borris and Larry Zulim, 1979
Tricky Fingers Jim Beyer, 4/78
Brainbucket Dave Schultz, Kurt Smith, Mike Hatchettt and Joe Hedge, 4/86
Babble On Jim Beyer, Mike Sawyer and Bob Sullivan, 1978
Porker Party Dave Schultz, John Middendorff and Joe Hedge, 1984
Wart Hog Grant Hiskes et al, 1984
My-Toe-Sis Ray Jardine and Chris Ball, 5/78
Eraser Flake Walt Shipley and Tucker Tech, 1/86
Sunblast Don Reid and Grant Hiskes, 12/81
The Wedge Ray Jardine and John Lakey, 5/75
White Cloud Jim Beyer and Misa Giesey, 1979
Filthy Rich Alan Bartlett and Don Reid, 6/83
Golden Needles Jim Beyer and Janice Linhares, 1979
Scurv Jim Beyer and Bob Sullivan, 1979
Mud Shark Billy Sernick, Charleen Sernick and Jack Dodalou, 1980
Fish Crack Henry Barber et al, 1975
Free Press Galen Rowell and Sibylle Hechtel, 11/71
Crimson Cringe Ray Jardine and John Lakey, 4/76
Phoenix Ray Jardine and John Lakey, 5/77
Verde Bruce Pollock, Jim Bridwell and Jim Pettigrew, 1975
Flake Off Bruce Pollock, Jim Bridwell, Jim Pettigrew and Mark Klemens, 1975

THIS AND THAT CLIFF

Weird Scenes in the Gold Mine Ken Ariza and Dave Hatchett, 1986
King Cobra Grant Hiskes and Dave Schultz, 1984
Agent Orange Don Reid and Grant Hiskes, 10/84
Gotham City Bill Price and John Long, 1980
Robin Bill Price and Tony Yaniro, 1981
Stubs Werner Braun, Dale Bard and Ed Barry, 1980
Tips John Bachar and Ron Kauk, 1975 **FFA** Jonny Woodward and Ron Kauk, 1985
Back in the Saddle Dimitri Barton et al, 1984
Whim Matt Donohoe and Pat Stewart, 1970
Said and Done Bob Finn, John Yablonsky, Richard Harrison and Don Reid, 1977
This and That Jim Donini and Jim Bridwell, 1972
Humdinger John Long, Ron Fawcett and Eric Ericksson, 1979 **(second pitch)** Jonny Woodward et al
Pink Banana Chris Cantwell, Bruce Morris, Mike Hernandez and Donald Cantwell, 1981

Cramming Steve Wunsch, Matt Donohoe, George Meyers, Jim Donini and Rab Carrington, 1972

NEW DIVERSIONS CLIFF

Falcon Chris Cantwell, Larry Zulim, Becky Plourd and Sue Moore, 1981
Rocket Man Chris Cantwell et al, 1981 **FFA** Paul Crawford and Jay Smith, 9/82
Chicken Pox Steve Wunsch and Diana Hunter, 1972
New Diversions Rick Sylvester, Claude Wreford-Brown and Jerry Coe, 6/71
Wasp Steve Wunsch and Rab Carrington, 1972
Strangers in the Night Jim Donini, Rab Carrington, Bev Johnson and Steve Wunsch, 1972
Electric Gully Jerry Coe and Rick Sylvester, 4/71
Radical Chic Dimitri Barton and Joe Hedge, 5/85
Chicken Pie Jerry Coe and Rick Sylvester, 4/71
Catch a Wave Scott Cosgrove et al, 1986
Jugs Henry Barber et al, 1974
Spring Chicken Murray Judge and Roger Whitehead, 8/83
Shake, Rattle and Drop Rick Sylvester, Chris Hassig and Alex Behr, 11/74
Chimney for Two Steve Shea and Jerry Coe, 4/71
Holidays Scott Cosgrove and Jenny Naquin, 1/86
Tail End George Meyers, 1975

KNOB HILL/OWL

Pot Belly Bill Griffin and Bruce Price, 4/73
Sloth Wall Steve Miller, Jerry Anderson and Elsie Anderson, 10/72
Anti-Ego Crack Steve Miller and Jerry Anderson, 10/72
Sloppy Seconds Jerry and Elsie Anderson, 9/72
Chicken Pie Jerry Anderson, 3/73
Knob Hill Rapist Chuck Pratt, Tim Auger and Jerry Anderson, 4/73
Deception Gully Chuck Pratt, Tim Auger and Jerry Anderson, 4/73
Arlington Heights Charlie Porter et al, 1972

Hampton Estates Alan Bartlett, Alan Roberts and Bill Critchlow, 9/82
Trix Ray Jardine and Chris Ballinger, 5/78
Pimper's Paradise Scott Cosgrove ad Dave Griffith, 10/86
White Owl Dimitri Barton et al, 1984
Dromedary, The Hump Barry Bates and Bev Johnson, 1971
Dromedary Direct Barry Bates, Matt Donohoe and Herb Swedlund, 1971
Dromedary Frank Sacherer and Gordon Webster, 11/65
The Shaft Matt Donohoe and George Meyers, 1971
The Owl Bypass unknown
Stroke (My Erect Ear Tufts) Dave Altman and Rob Oraveitz, 10/86
The Owl Roof John Lakey and Ray Jardine, 5/77
Mirage Dale Bard and Rick Cashner, 1980
Wicked Jones Crusher Dimitri Barton and Roy McClanahan, 4/86
Walrus Don Reid and Rick Cashner, 1/77

GOLDRUSH AREA

5.8 Chimney Matt Donohoe, 1970
Mongolian Clusterfuck Jim Donini et al, 1972
Siberian Swarm Screw Jim Donini, Steve Wunsch, John Bragg, Kevin Bein and Bev Johnson, 1972
Gang Bang Paul Cowan and Ray Jardine, 1974
Handjob Jim Donini, Steve Wunsch et al, 1972

Fun 5.9 unknown
Polymorphous Perverse Bruce Morris and Dave Altman, 11/77
Shit on a Shingle Ken Ariza, Dave Hatchett and Kurt Smith
Mainliner Bruce Morris and Dave Altman, 11/77
Goldrush Jim Bridwell, Steve Wunsch and Jim Donini, 1972

REED'S PINNACLE AREA

Danger Will Robinson Brian Bennett and Bob Ost, 9/86
Anal Tongue Darts Brian Bennett and Bob Ost, 9/86
Olga's Trick Rik Rieder, Mike Breidenbach and Drone Stephens, 1972
Crazy Train Mike Hatchettt and Ken Ariza, 5/86
Isotope John Bachar, Dimitri Barton, Ron Kauk and Werner Braun, 1983
Chingango Chuck Pratt et al, 6/65
The Iota Wally Reed and Bill Henderson, 1956
Phantom John Bachar, 10/86
The Tooth Tom Higgins and Pat Ament
Micron Eric Zschiesche
The Remnant, Left Pat Ament and Larry Dalke, 10/67 **FFA** Royal Robbins and Loyd Price, 1968
The Remnant, Center John Bachar et al, 1986
The Remnant, Right Wally Reed and Herb Swedlund, 1960
Reed's Pinnacle, Left Frank Sacherer, Wally Reed and Gary Colliver, 11/62 **FFA** Frank Sacherer, Dick Erb and Larry Marshik, 1964
Reed's Pinnacle, Direct (last pitch) Frank Sacherer, Mark Powell, Wally Reed, Gary Colliver and Andy Lichtman, 5/64 **(2nd pitch)** Frank Sacherer, Wally Reed and Chris Fredericks, 6/64 **(all pitches)** Royal Robbins, Gordon Webster and Terry Burnell, 10/66
Reed's Pinnacle, Blazing Buckets John Middendorf
Reed's Pinnacle, Regular Route Wally Reed and Herb Swedlund, 1957
Survival Sampler Alfred Randall and Bryan Burdo
Bong's Away, Left Jim Bridwell, 1970
Bong's Away, Center Barry Bates and Mark Klemens, 1970
Magical Mystery Tour Charlie Porter and Dave Altman, 1975
Old Five Ten Pat Ament and Tom Higgins, 1975
Midnight Rampest John Middendorf and Tucker Tech
Lunatic Fringe Barry Bates and Bev Johnson, 1971
Flatus Chuck Pratt and Tom Bauman, 5/68
The Rorp Wally Reed and Frank Sacherer, 7/63
Tooth or Consequences Charles Cole, Lidija Painkiher, 5/86
Stone Groove Jim Bridwell and Galen Rowell, 5/71
Independence Pinnacle, Independent Route Jim Bridwell and Mark Klemens, 8/70
Independence Pinnacle, Center Dave Hampton, Barry Bates and Matt Donohoe, 7/ 70
Independence Pinnacle, Steppin' Out Mark Klemens and Jim Bridwell, 1971
The Gray Bullet Don Reid and Dennis Oakeshott, 10/82
Rocket in My Pocket Jim Elias, Bruce Morris and Kevin Lollard, 10/83
Cosmic Ray Ray Jardine and Rick Cashner, 5/79
Ejesta Charlie Porter, Bob Ashworth and Jeff Stubbs, 1/74
Porter's Pout Charlie Porter and Bruce Pollock, 1974
Sylvester's Meow Rick Sylvester and Sue Odom, 12/86
Fasten Your Seat Belts John Bachar and Rick Cashner
Free Ride John Bachar and Rick Cashner
Cro Magnon Capers Kevin Worrall, Werner Braun and Rick Cashner, 1979
Nothing Good Ever Lasts Joe Hedge, 1986

Spring Fever Don Reid and Rick Cashner, 4/83
Headhunter John Bachar and Rick Cashner
Fireside Chat Walt Shipley and John Middendorf, 12/85

FIVE AND DIME CLIFF

Chump Change Doug McDonald, 1985
Keystone Corner Don Reid and Jay Fiske, 10/75
Copper Penny Don Reid and Jay Fiske, 1975
Five and Dime Barry Bates et al, 1971
Whack and Dangle Ajax Greene and Don Peterson, 4/76
Penny Ante unknown
The Reception Mike Breidenbach and Mike Farrell, 1974
Inner Reaches Chuck Pratt, Tim Auger and Jerry Anderson, 4/73
Crack n' Face Ed Barry et al

MOJO TOOTH

Fluke unknown
Tongue and Groove Andreas Maurer, 1975
Mojo Tooth Peter Haan and Darwin Alonso, 10/70
New Traditionalist Rick Cashner and Werner Braun, 4/82
Figment Mike Breidenbach and Bruce Hawkins, 1975
Grape Nuts Mike Breidenbach and Bruce Hawkins, 1975
Euellogy Bruce Hawkins, Mike Breidenbach and Bruce Brossman, 1975
Mighty Crunchy Andreas Maurer, 1975
Bad News Bombers Steve Annecone and TomHayes, 4/85
Natural End Will Gilmer and Jay Anderson, 10/83
Hey Walt Walt Shipley, 1985
Highway Star Chris Falkenstein, Don Reid and Edd Kuropat, 1/75

LAST RESORT CLIFF

Turning Point Rick Cashner and Don Reid, 9/77
Side Kick Chris Falkenstein, Don Reid and TM Herbert, 11/75
Tiger's Paw Don Reid and Rick Cashner, 1978
Plumkin Rik Reider and Doug Scott, 1972
Moon Age Daydream Don Reid and Rick Cashner, 1978
The Steal Rick Cashner and Angie Morales, 1978
Sex, Drugs and Violence Don Reid and Rick Cashner, 11/77
P.M.S. Tucker Tech and Mike Sciacca, 1985
B and B Rick Cashner, Ray Jardine and Frank Brown, 10/78
No Falls Wall Chris Cantwell and Mike Borelli, 1980
Black Sunday Chris Cantwell and Bruce Morris, 1980
Shattered Rick Cashner, Ray Jardine and Frank Brown, 1979
Ready or Not Rick Cashner and Ray Jardine, 5/79
Slumgullion Jim Bridwell, Kevin Worrall and Marco Milano, 1978
Neutron Escape Ray Jardine and Rick Cashner, 1979
Radioactive Rick Cashner and Ray Jardine, 1979
Atomic Finger Crack Ray Jardine and Rick Cashner, 5/79

AUDUBON BUTTRESS TO LITTLE WING

Wild Turkey Dale Bard et al, 1974
The Dove Kevin Worrall and Jane Witucki, 1975
Birds of a Feather Kevin Worrall and Jane Witucki, 1975
Eagle Feather John Long, Jim Bridwell and Kevin Worrall, 1974

Duncan Imperial Kevin Worrall, Werner Braun and Ed Barry, 1977
Catch-U Steve Wunsch and John Bragg, 1974
W'allnuts Steve Wunsch and Jim Donini, 1973
Scuz Ball Don Reid, 2/85
Squeeze-n' Tease Rick Cashner and Angie Morales, 9/77
L.D. Getaway Rick Cashner and Angie Morales, 9/77
Andy DeVine Rick Cashner and Angie Morales, 9/77
He Can't Shout, Don't Hear You Bob Ashworth and Jeff Stubbs, 4/74
Gunks Revisited Ron Kauk and Kim Carrigan, 1980
Honor Thy Father Ajax Greene and Matt Cox, 4/76
Leisure Time George Meyers, Bob Ashworth and Mike Breidenbach, 4/76
The Riddler Bruce Pollock, Matt Pollock, Mark Chapman and Charlie Porter, 1/74
Little Wing Mark Chapman, Charlie Porter and Bruce Pollock, 1/74
Dolly Dagger Alan Bartlett, 1984
Building Blocks Alan Bartlett and Bill Frey, 1984
Crash Landing Dave Schultz et al
Angelina Rick Cashner and Angie Morales, 9/77
Little Thing Tony Yaniro and Alan Nelson, 1981
Red House unknown
Too Much Paranoia Rick Cashner and Don Reid, 3/82

RIBBON FALLS AREA

The Slabs Wolfgang Heinritz, Andrzej Ehrenfaucht and Les Wilson, 5/63
West Buttress Frank Sacherer and Bob Kamps, 6/62
Golden Bough Roger Breedlove and Ed Drummond, 6/79
Gold Wall Layton Kor and Tom Fender, 5/65
Silent Line Rick Cashner and Werner Braun, 4/82
Fool's Gold Don Reid and Rick Cashner, 8/83
Thin Line Werner Braun and Scott Cosgrove, 10/86
West Portal Chris Fredericks and Steve Roper, 9/63
Straight In Werner Braun and Rick Cashner, 9/81
Rainbows Ken Boche and Russ McLean, 6/71
Dyslexia Ellie Hawkins, 8/85
Keel Haul Charlie Porter and Walter Rosenthal, 1972
East Portal Al Steck, John Evans, Chuck Pratt and Dick Long, 6/64
Gold Ribbon Jim Bridwell and Mike Graham, 5/76
Vain Hope Royal Robbins, Kim Schmitz and Jim Bridwell, 5/70
Star Drive Mike Corbett and Steve Bosque, 1983
Crack Me Up Mike Corbett and Ernie Maylon, 1983
Chockstone Chimney Les Wilson, Wolfgang Heinritz, Andrzej Ehrenfeucht and Leif Patterson, 12/62 **FFA** Ray Jardine and Mark Moore, 5/76
The Lionheart Ray Jardine and Mark Moore, 5/76
Nottingham Ray Jardine and Mark Moore, 5/76
The Hourglass, Left Bob Kamps and Joe McKeown, 7/62 **FFA** Peter Haan, Rick Linkert and Mike Farrell, 9/71
The Hourglass, Right Bob Kamps and Frank Sacherer, 7/62 **FFA** Sacherer and Tom Gerughty, 8/64
The Rappel Chimney Wolfgang Heinritz, Les Wilson, Leif Patterson and Andrzej Ehrenfeucht, 4/63
Hidden Chimney Les Wilson, Wolfgang Heinritz and Andrzej Ehrenfeucht, 7/63

EL CAPITAN

El Capitan Gully J.L. Staats, 6/05 Staats' climbing partner, Charles Bailey, was killed in a fall near the top.

K-P Pinnacle Ted Knoll and Jack Piontaki, 5/41 **FFA** Mark Powell, Larry Hawley, Bryan Milton and Merle Alley, 1955

El Capitan, West Chimney Ethel Mae Hill, Owen Williams and Gordon Patten, 10/37 **FFA** Galen Rowell and Tom Fender, 1966

J.M. Barrie Dick Dorworth and Rick Sylvester, 5/68

West Buttress Variation Michael Forkash and Peter Lehrach, 6/81

Peter Pan Bob Kamps and Jim Sims, 7/62

Cuthulu Eric Weinstein and Dave Anderson, 10/75

Indubious Battle Ray Jardine and Kris Walker, 5/75

Peter Left Mead Hargis and Kim Schmitz, 1971

Tinkerbell, Left Bruce Kumph and Joe Cote, 10/69

Tinkerbell, Right Jim Bridwell and Kim Schmitz, 1971

Lost Boys Dave Bircheff and Roger Breedlove, 1975

Wendy Frank Sacherer and Bob Kamps, 7/62 **FFA** Kim Schmitz and Marty Martin, 6/70

Smee's Come-on Dave Bircheff and Roger Breedlove, 1976

Captain Hook, Left unknown

Captain Hook, Right Glen Denny, Eric Beck and Dave Cook, 3/63 **FFA** Tom Gerughty and Chris Fredericks, 1965

Captain Crunch Tony Yaniro and Paul Vance, 1977

Delectable Pinnacle, Left Jim Baldwin, 5/62

Delectable Pinnacle, Center Art Gran and Eric Beck, 5/62

Delectable Pinnacle, Right Warren Harding and Brian Small, 5/62

La Escuela Yvon Chouinard and TM Herbert, 5/62 **FFA** Steve Wunsch and Mark Chapman, 1973

La Escuela, Direct Eric Beck and Steve Williams, 10/69

The Slack, Left Chuck Pratt and Royal Robbins, 5/65

The Slack, Center Charlie Raymond and Wally Reed, 8/58 **FFA** Pat Ament and Larry Dalke, 1967

Sacherer Cracker Frank Sacherer and Mike Sherrick, 1964

The Mark of Art Mark Chapman and Art Higbee, 1974

Short but Thin Tobin Sorenson and John Bachar, 5/74

La Cosita, Left Bob Kamps, Galen Rowell, Dan Doody and Wally Upton, 6/62

La Cosita, Right TM Herbert and Steve Roper, 5/63

Little John, Left Dan Doody, Bob Kamps, Galen Rowell and Wally Upton, 8/62

Hardly Pinnacle Dale Bard et al, 1972 **FFA** Michael Forkash and John Tuttle, 9/85

Little John, Center Tom Frost and Harry Daley, 1961

Little John, Right Jack Turner and Royal Robbins, 4/62

Sunday Driver Ken Ariza, Mark Carpenter and Dimiti Barton

Moby Dick, Left Bob Kamps and Frank Sacherer, 10/63

Moby Dick, Center Herb Swedlund and Penny Carr, 5/63 **FFA** Frank Sacherer and Steve Roper, 5/63

Moby Dick, Ahab Frank Sacherer and Jim Bridwell, 9/64

Reed's Leads Wally Reed and Mike Borghoff, 1963

Seedy Leads Mark Chapman and Rick Sylvester, 8/71

Pterodactyl Terrace, Left Jim Sims and Steve Roper, 4/63

Pterodactyl Terrace, Right Glen Denny and Eric Beck, 4/63 **FFA** Vern Clevenger et al, 1975

Pine Line Jeff and Greg Schaffer, 7/66

Negative Pinnacle, Left Gary Colliver, 1964

Negative Pinnacle, Center Jim Beyer, 1978

Negative Pinnacle, The High Arc Tom Cochrane, 1964 **FFA** Peter Mayfield and Augie Klein, 1981

Rock Neurotic Dave Caunt, Rob Settlemeyer, and John Barbella, 3/86

Armageddon Dave Yerian, Greg Sonagere, Craig Connel, Dave Rubine and Ray Olson, 1978. **FFA** Dimitri Barton, 1978

Say Mama, Say Daddy John Middendorf and Scott Cosgrove, 5/84
Simulkrime John Middendorf and Tucker Tech
Gollum, Left Peter Haan, Rick Linkert and David Moss, 3/72
Gollum, Right Joe Kelsey, Roman Laba and John Hudson, 9/67
Dock of the Bay Bill Price and Larry Zulim, 1981
The Footstool, Left Clyde Deal and Steve Roper, 1/63
The Promise John Bachar and Dimitri Barton, 1983
The Believer John Bachar et al, 1984
The Footstool, Right Mark Powell, Beverly Powell and Bill Feuerer, 1959
Life Worth Living Scott Cosgrove and Ken Ariza, 1985
El Cap Tree Direct Glen Denny and Frank Sacherer, 12/61
El Cap Tree, Regular Route Al Steck, Will Siri, Bill Dunmire and Bob Swift, 3/52
Blank Out Eric Zschiesche and Peter Croft, 1984
Champagne on Ice Steve Schneider, Dave Caunt, 1982. **(second pitch)** Steve Schneider and Rob Oraveitz, 10/85
Submen Steve Schneider, Rob Oraveitz and John Middendorf, 10/85
El Matador Dimitri Bevc and Steve Schneider, 10/85

Salami Ledge Route Les Wilson and Wolfgang Heinritz, 1965
West Face TM Herbert and Royal Robbins, 6/67 **FFA** Ray Jardine and Bill Price, 5/79
Mr. Midwest Bill Russell and Doug McDonald, 8/85
Realm of the Flying Monkeys Steve Bosque and Dan McDevitt, 9/85
Mirage Jim Bridwell, Kim Schmitz and Jim Pettigrew, 5/76
Lurking Fear Dave Bircheff and Jim Pettigrew, 5/76
Squeeze Play Mike Corbett, Gary Edmondson and Rich Albuschkat, 4/82
Lost World Cal Folsom, Dave Anderson and Mike Warburton, 4/75
West Buttress Layton Kor and Steve Roper, 1963
Never Never Land Bruce Hawkins and Mark Chapman, 1978
Aquarian Wall Jim Bridwell and Kim Schmitz, 6/71
Wings of Steel Richard Jensen and Mark Smith, 7/81
Horse Chute Charlie Porter and Hugh Burton, 10/74
Horse Play Steve Grossman and Sue Harrington, 1984
Dihedral Wall Ed Cooper, Jim Baldwin and Glen Denny, 11/62
Cosmos Jim Dunn, 1972
Excalibur Charlie Porter and Hugh Burton, 1975
Heart Route Chuck Kroger and Scott Davis, 4/70
Bermuda Dunes Steve Schneider and John Barbella, 1984
Pacemaker Steve Bosque, Mike Corbett, Murray Barnett and Jim Siler, 6/82
Verano Magico José Luis Gallego and Javier Gallego, 1985
Heart Woute (Son of Heart) Rick Sylvester and Claude Wreford-Brown, 1971
Sunkist Bill Price and Dale Bard, 10/78
Jolly Rodger Charles Cole and Steve Grossman, 1979
Magic Mushroom Hugh Burton and Steve Sutton, 5/72
Shield Route Charlie Porter and Gary Bocarde, 1972
Dorn Direct Tony Yaniro and Ron Olevsky, 6/77
False Shield Charles Cole, 5/84
Turning Point Steve Grossman, 5/84
Muir Wall Yvon Chouinard and TM Herbert, 6/65
Triple Direct (connection to the Nose) Jim Bridwell and Kim Schmitz, 1969
Meditterraneo Miguel Angel Gallego, José Luis Gallego, Javier Gallego and Carlos Gallego, 1981
Salathé Wall Royal Robbins, Chuck Pratt and Tom Frost, 9/61 **Free Blast** (free to Mammoth Ledges) Jim Bridwell, John Long, Kevin Worrall, Mike Graham, John Bachar and Ron Kauk, 5/75
Grape Race Charlie Porter and Bev Johnson, 5/74

Nose Route Warren Harding, Wayne Merry and George Whitmore, 11/58 **(free variations to Camp IV)** Ray Jardine et al, 1980
The Real Nose Charles Cole and Steve Grossman, 1984
Tribal Rite Walter Rosenthal, Tom Carter and Alan Bard, 10/78
New Dawn (right side of El Cap Towers) Yvon Chouinard, Chuck Pratt, Dennis Hennek and Chris Jones **(complete route)** Charlie Porter, 1972
Mescalito Charlie Porter, Hugh Burton, Steve Sutton and Chris Nelson, 10/73
Hockey Night in Canada Darrell Hatton and Bill Stern, 5/77
Wall of the Early Morning Light Warren Harding and Dean Caldwell, 11/70
Space Charles Cole, 7/85
South Seas Bill Price, Charlie Row and Guy Thompson, 9/79
Pacific Ocean Wall Jim Bridwell, Bill Westbay, Jay Fiske and Fred East, 5/75
Sea of Dreams Jim Bridwell, Dale Bard and Dave Diegelman, 10/78
North America Wall Tom Frost, Yvon Chouinard, Chuck Pratt and Royal Robbins, 10/64
Wyoming Sheep Ranch Rob Slater and John Barbella, 8/84
New Jersey Turnpike Bruce Hawkins, Ron Kauk, Dale Bard and Hugh Burton, 4/77
Atlantic Ocean Wall John Middendorf and John Barbella, 9/85
Iron Hawk Dale Bard and Ron Kauk, 9/78
Aurora Peter Mayfield and Greg Child, 9/81
Tangerine Trip Charlie Porter and John-Paul de St. Croix, 1973
Lost in America Randy Leavitt and Greg Child, 1985
Zenyatta Mondatta Jim Bridwell, Peter Mayfield and Charlie Row, 9/81
Zodiac Wall Charlie Porter, 11/72
Lunar Eclipse John Barbella and Steve Schneider, 7/82
Born Under a Bad Sign Bill Price and Tim Washick, 1979
Bad to the Bone Jay Smith Lidija Painkiher, 8/84
Eagle's Way Mark Chapman, Mike Graham and Jim Orey, 1976
On the Waterfront Steve Bosque, Mike Corbett and Gwen Schneider, 8/86
Waterfall Route Darryl Teske and T. Polk, 10/75
Chinese Water Torture Karl McConachie and Jay Smith, 7/81
Snake Knez Franček and Walace, 5/83
East Buttress Allen Steck, Will Siri, Willi Unsoeld and Bill Long, 6/53 **FFA** Frank Sacherer and Wally Reed, 8/64
End of the World Werner Braun and Don Reid, 1/83
Eura Mura Knez Franček, Lidija Painkiher and Igor Skamprle, 5/83

El Capitan, East Ledge Traverse Allen Steck, Bill Dunmire and Jim Wilson, 9/54
El Capitan, East Ledges, West Side Henry Kendall and Bill Pope, 3/61
El Capitan, East Ledges, East Side Henry Kendall and Gerry Czamanske, 12/58
Schultz's Ridge John Shonle and Steve Roper, 10/59
The White Zone Chris Cantwell and Mark Grant, 1980
Annette Funicello Chris Cantwell and Mark Grant, 1980
Bikini Beach Party Chris Cantwell and Mark Grant, 1980
Demon's Delight Ed Barry and Dave Hitchcock, 9/78
Supertoe Chris Cantwell and Larry Zulim, 5/82
Brown Sugar John Bragg and Peter Barton, 10/72
Free Bong Larry Zulim and Chris Cantwell, 5/82
Ain't That a Bitch Dale Bard and Ed Barry, 1976
Abazaba Charlie Porter and Walter Rosenthal, 1972 **(FFA first pitches)** Scott Cosgrove and Walt Shipley, 4/86
End Game Walt Shipley, Tucker Tech and Scott Cosgrove
Moratorium Bruce Price, Bill Griffin and Bob Edwards, 11/69 **FFA** Pete Livesey and Trevor Jones, 8/75
Orange Juice Avenue Chris Falkenstein and Don Reid, 12/75
Lycra Virgin Ron Kauk, 5/86

Le Nocturne Brian Bennett and Michael Forkash, 1985
Here on the Outside Urmas Franosch and Bruce Morris, 1982
Chow Chow Chow Dave Yerian and Bruce Morris, 1982
Slab Happy Pinnacle, Left Royal Robbins and Jack Turner, 5/62 **FFA** Mark Chapman and Art Higbee, 2/74
Slab Happy Pinnacle, Center Royal Robbins, Tom Frost and Harry Daley, 5/61 **FFA** Vern Clevenger, George Meyers and Tom Carter, 1974
Slab Happy Pinnacle, The Dihardral Tom Frost and Royal Robbins, 5/61 **FFA** Frank Sacherer and Tom Gerughty, 8/64

MANURE PILE AREA

God's Creation Chris Cantwell and Eric Zichi, 4/81
Jump for Joy Yvon Chouinard and Joy Herron, 1967
After Six Yvon Chouinard and Ruth Schnieder, 6/65
After Seven unknown
C.S. Concerto Yvon Chouinard, Chuck Pratt and Mort Hempel, 1967
Fecophilia Yvon Chouinard et al, 1972
Easy Wind Kevin Worrall and Bill Westbay, 1975
The Mouse King George Meyers et al, 1976
Nutcracker Royal and Liz Robbins, 5/67
The Gardener Did It Chris Cantwell and Mike Borelli, 4/81
After Five TM Herbert et al, 1968
The Illusion Tom Higgins, Galen Rowell, Loyd Price and John Kanepej, 11/71
Commissioner Buttress Galen Rowell and Joe Faint, 3/69
True Grit Dave Altman and Will Crljenko, 5/74
Essence Werner Braun and Don Reid, 1/83
Split Pinnacle, Regular Jack Reigelhuth, Raffi Bedayn, Dick Leonard and Muir Dawson, 5/38
Split Pinnacle, East Arête Chuck Pratt and Krehe Ritter, 9/58

LOWER BROTHER

Lower Brother, West Face, North Corner H.B. Blanks, Boynton Kaiser and Elliot Sawyer, 10/34
Lower Brother, West Face, Middle Don Goodrich and Gary Lundberg, 4/52
Lower Brother, Southwest Arête David Brower and Morgan Harris, 6/37
Maple Jam Chris Falkenstein and Dennis Miller, 1973
Nutty Buddy Brian Birmingham and Dave Bircheff, 3/72
Positively 4th Street Dennis Miller, Jeff Mathis and Chris Falkenstein, 3/73
Fuddy Duddy Bruce Brossman and Gene Foley, 5/75
Absolutely Free, Left Jim Bridwell, Bev Johnson and Mark Klemens, 9/70
Absolutely Free, Center Sheldon Smith, Mark Klemens and Rick Sylvester, 8/70
Absolutely Free, Right Mark Klemens and Jim Bridwell, 5/70
Vantage Point Don Reid and Werner Braun, 1/84
Lower Brother, Michael's Ledge Charles Michael, in the 1920's
Ramblin' Rose Kevin Worrall and Mark Chapman, 1975
Hawkman's Escape John Dill and Phil Gleason, 1972 (last pitch variation) Peter Haan and Ed Drummond
Middle Brother, Southwest Arête, Left Nick Clinch, Dave Harrah, Sherman Lehman and John Mowat, 5/50
Middle Brother, Southwest Arête, Right David Brower and Morgan Harris, 5/41
Middle Brother, from Michael's Ledge John Salathé, Anton Nelson, Dave Hammack and Rob Hahn, 6/51
Betsy Pinnacle Betsy Nelson and Rick Sylvester, 8/70
Lower Brother, Southeast Face Wally Reed and Charlie Raymond, 8/58

Koko Ledge, Left Bill Amborn and Bob Klose, 1961 **FFA** Kevin Bein, 1968
Koko Ledge, Center unknown **FFA** Pete Livesey et al, 1975
Koko Ledge, Right Glen Denny and Jim Posten, 7/61 **FFA** unknown
Koko Ledge, Far Right Barry Bates and Sergio Roch, 1970
Koko Continuation Glen Denny and Frank Sacherer, 8/62
Limbo Ledge Jim Baldwin and Steve Roper, 10/62 **FFA** Pete Livesey et al, 1975
Watermelon Rind John Svenson, Sharon Young, Kent Stokes and Bob Schneider, 9/71
Merry Old Ledge Warren Harding and Gerry Czamanske, 4/59
Midwall Tom Fender and Kim Schmitz, 4/66
Licensed to Fly Jim Elias and Bruce Morris, 11/84
Skunk Weed Scott Burke and Dave Caunt, 1981
Roachweed Bruce Morris and Jim Elias, 10/83
Rixon's Pinnacle, Far West Royal Robbins and Dick McCracken, 6/63
Rixon's Pinnacle, West Face Tom Frost Bill Feuerer, 1959 **FFA** Pat Ament et al, 1971
Rixon's Pinnacle, Direct South Face Glen Denny and Gary Colliver, 3/63
Rixon's Pinnacle, South Face Chuck and Ellen Wilts, 1948 **FFA** Tobin Sorenson and John Bachar, 1974
Rixon's Pinnacle, East Chimney Don Goodrich and Dick McCracken, 1956 **FFA** Royal Robbins and Dave Rearick, 1960 **Final Decision** Anders Lundahl and Eva Selim, 1981 **Klemens Variation** Mark Klemens, 1970
The Plume Don Reid and Chuck Goldmann, 1/79
The Folly, Left Layton Kor and Jim Bridwell, 9/64
Disconnected Chris Cantwell and Eric Zichi, 5/81
Frosted Flakes Eric Kohl, 1986
Childhood's End Ray Jardine and John Lakey, 4/76
Follying Walt Shipley, 5/86
The Folly, Wild Thing Ray Jardine and Ian Wade, 4/73 **FFA** Lou Dawson and Don Peterson, 1973
Pink Torpedo John Sherman and Todd Skinner, 1985
Yellow Submarine unknown
The Folly, Right Side Warren Harding and Tom Fender, 1965 **FFA** Dale Bard, Jim Bridwell, Kevin Worrall and Ron Kauk, 1973
Preface John Bachar and Tobin Sorenson, 1975

CAMP 4 AREA

Chicken's Choice Sigrid and Jerry Anderson, 1/86
Young and the Restless Werner Braun, Rick Cashner, Grant Hiskes, Scott Cole and Dimitri Barton, 4/82
Cost of Living Rick Cashner and Don Reid, 4/79
Space Doubt Alan Nelson and Y. Matsumoto, 1980
General Hospital Rik Rieder, Phil Gleason and Chris Wegener, 1972
Chopper Mead Hargis and Rick Sylvester, 1971
One Life to Live Walt Shipley et al
Edge of Night Chris Fredericks, Rich Doleman and Jim Bridwell, 10/67
Secret Storm Peter Haan and Roger Breedlove, 1971
Tweedle Dee Frank Sacherer and Jim Baldwin, 6/63
Doggie Do Chris Fredericks
Doggie Diversions Joe Faint and Yvon Chouinard, 6/67
Doggie Deviations Kim Schmitz and Jim Bridwell, 1968
Bottom Line Bill Price and Dimitri Barton, 1983
Rock Bottom Kevin Worrall and George Meyers, 5/74 **FFA** John Long et al, 1980
The Buttocks Kim Schmitz and Don Peterson, 1969
Cheek Jim Bridwell et al, 1972
Christina Mead Hargis and Dave Davis, 1971 **FFA** John Long et al

Henley Quits Mark Klemens and Rick Sylvester, 7/70
Cid's Embrace Rick Sylvester and Mark Klemens, 7/70
Lancelot Rick Sylvester and Mark Klemens, 1970
Camp 4 Tree Mort Hempel and Bob Kamps, 1960 **FFA (Dynamo Hum)** Tobin Sorenson and John Long, 8/75
Eagle Peak, Southeast Face Jon Linberg and Ron Hayes, 6/52
Gillette Pete Livesey and Ron Fawcett, 8/74
Fallout Jim Donini and Steve Wunsch, 10/72
Jolly Green Giant John Bragg and Rab Carrington, 10/72
Apple Seeds Bob Sullivan and Jim Beyer, 10/78
Camp 4 Terror Bob Kamps and Dave Rearick, 7/60
Comedy of Folly Rik Rieder, 1973
Sunday Tree Leigh Ortenburger and Bill Briggs, 10/58
Stay Free Dave Schultz and Walt Shipley, 6/86
The Girl Next Door, Left John Bragg and Bev Johnson, 6/72
The Girl Next Door, Right John Bragg, Bob Harding and Al Rubin, 6/72
Joe Palmer Michael Forkash and Andy Burnham, 10/86
Psychopath Charlie Porter, 1972
Penelope's Problem John Long and Tony Zeek
Swan Slab Aid Route Joe Oliger and Steve Roper, 4/61 **FFA** Loyd Price et al, 1967
Ugly Duckling Kevin Worrall and George Meyers, 1974
Lena's Lieback Kim Schmitz and Jim Madsen
Derelichs Delight Claude Fiddler and Peter Olander, 8/72
Werner's Oversight Mark Moore and Dave Hitchcock, 1972

YOSEMITE FALLS AREA – Lower Tiers

Beat Around the Bush Jeff Hornerbrook, Mark Carpenter and Ken Ariza, 6/86
Munginella Tom Fender and Vic Tishous, 1966
Commitment Jim Bridwell, Dave Bircheff and Phil Bircheff, 6/66
Deaf, Dumb and Blind Jeff Hornerbrook and Mark Carpenter, 1986
The Surprise Pete Spoecker and Steve Herrero, 4/65
Werner's Ant Trees Werner Braun, Jerry Coe and Jerry Anderson, 8/70
The Caverns Jim Pettigrew and Jerry Anderson, 1/70
Try Again Ledge Ed Leeper, Dave Trantor and Steve Herrero, 6/64
The Hanging Teeth Jim Bridwell and Vic Tishous, 1968
Boogie With Stu Tracy Dortn, Walt Shipley, Steve Gerberding and Stu Richie, 1986
Auntie Gravity Steve Monks and L. Broomhead, 9/80
The Fin Les Wilson and Glen Denny, 10/61 **FFA** John Long and Jay Wilson, 6/74
The Green Strip Al Macdonald and Les Wilson, 2/62 **FFA** Tom Higgins and Mike Dent, 1965
The Eggplant Kent Stokes and John Svenson, 10/71
Eclipse Don Reid and Rick Cashner, 1978
Blackout Don Reid and Rick Cashner, 1978
Black Wall Glen Denny and Al Macdonald, 10/61
Fawlty Towers Alec Sharp and Arni Strapcans, 8/77
Dagger Walt Shipley and Russ Walling, 10/85
Black Wall Glen Denny and Roger Derryberry, 9/63 **FFA (Shadow Wall)** Pete Livesey, Ron Fawcett and Geoff Birtles, 10/77
Guiding Light Rick Cashner and Don Reid, 1978
Lightweight Guides Grant Hiskes et al
Full Stem Ahead Rob Robinson and Chris Synder, 12/86
The Podium Grant Hiskes and Ken Yager, 10/86
Public Opinion Grant Hiskes and Ken Yager, 10/86
Dark Star Andy Burnham and Michael Forkash, 10/86

Nanbeeb Michael Forkash and Andy Burnham, 10/86
Isosceles Revisited Urmas Franosch, Steve Plunkett and Michael Forkash, 11/86
Lower Yosemite Fall, West Corner Alan M. Hedden and L. Bruce Meyer, 9/42
Lower Yosemite Fall, West Side Herb Swedlund and Errol Bohannon, 1959
Ten Years After Ken Ariza and Kurt Smith, 8/85
Mistfitz Kurt Smith and Chris Beigh, 8/85
Play Misty for Me Kurt Smith, Dave Hatchettt, Ken Ariza and Dave Griffith, 9/85
Powerslave Kurt Smith, Dave Hatchettt and Ken Ariza, 9/85
Lower Yosemite Fall, Right Side John Svenson and Kent Stokes, 10/71
Sunnyside Bench, 5.2 Route David Brower and William Van Voorhis, 7/35
Sunnyside Bench, MW Route Art Gran and Jack Hansen, 9/60
Sunnyside Bench, Regular Route unknown
Butthole Climbers Brian Bennett and John Tuttle, 1986
Sultans of Sling Brian Bennett, George Watson and Norman Boles, 1985
Raisin unknown
Mud Flats Kim Schmitz and Don Peterson, 10/69 **FFA** Roger Greatrick and Carl Jonasson, 4/84
Prune Mike Caldwell and Eric Craig, 1974
Lingering Lie unknown
Lemon Dave Sessions and Scott Burke, 8/79
Bummer Bruce Morris, Scott Cole and Peter Thurston, 10/77
Lazy Bum Eric Beck and Steve Williams, 1971 **FFA** Chris Falkenstein et al, 1972
Jamcrack Route Loyd Price and Kim Schmitz, 1967 **FFA** Kim Schmitz and Jim Madsen
Lieback Route unknown
Blackballed Dan McDevitt and Sue Bonovich
Combustable Knowledge Mark Carpenter and Dave Bengston, 11/86
Tiny Tim Tim Fitzgerald and Bob Korte, 6/66
Guide's Route Roy McClanahan, 1986
The Easter Egg Rob Foster and Greg Schaffer, 3/67
Riptide unknown
Safe to Surf Bob Ost and Matt Hilden, 10/85
Pygmy Pillar Mike White and Ron Cagle, 1970

YOSEMITE FALLS – Upper Tiers

Bacchiagaloupe Wall Pete Spoecker and Steve Herrero, 4/65
Handshake Mark Ingdal et al
Marvin Gardens Bill Matthies, Tom Tumiano and Brent Reynolds, 9/86
Selaginella Wally Reed and Jim Posten, 9/63
Observation Point Les Wilson, Wolfgang Heinritz and Andrzej Ehrenfeucht, 11/62 **FFA** Frank Sacherer and Wally Reed, 1964
Indica Point Walt Shipley and Dimitri Barton, 1985
Mischief Marshall Ravenscroft and Tim Kemple, 4/82
Gorge Traverse Dave Hammack and George Larrimore, 1950
Roger Stokes Route Marshall Ravenscroft and Tim Kemple, 8/82
RF Greg Schaffer and Rob Foster, 8/66
Avalon John Tuttle, Brian Bennet and Michael Forkash, 1986
T.D.'s Dihedral Tim Kemple and Marshall Ravenscroft, 2/82
Wild Child Tim Kemple and Marshall Ravenscroft, 8/82
Galloping Consumption Chuck Pratt anf Steve Roper, 10/70
Seaside Kevin Worrall and Mike Breidenbach, 1973
Diversions Marshall Ravenscroft and Tim Kemple, 4/82
Smoky Pillar Jim Bridwell, George Meyers, Vern Clevenger and Larry Bruce, 1973
Colonel unknown

Dumbo Go Home John Middendorf and Tucker Tech, 1985
Chain Reaction Rik Rieder, Mark Chapman, Ed Barry and Rab Carrington, 9/72
The Peanut Tom Higgins and Gary Colliver, 6/67
No Teats Susan Lilly and Tucker Tech, 10/86
Israeli Bomber Walt Shipley and Howard Chapman, 5/86
Forbidden Pinnacle Mark Klemens and Bruce Pollock, 5/72
Taboo Treat Don Reid and Bob Bartlett, 7/76

UPPER FALLS WALL

Brush Off Ed Barry and Mark Chapman, 1972
Aquamist Nathan King, 1965
Via Aqua Dave Rearick, Herb Swedlund and Glen Denny, 4/60 **FFA** Dick McCracken and Steve Roper, 1960
Via Sin Aqua Rick Sylvester and Bugs McKeith, 9/70
Misty Wall Dick McCracken and Royal Robbins, 6/63
Miscreant Wall Bruce Hawkins and Keith Nannery, 1973
Geek Towers, Left (Freestone) Jim Bridwell, Ron Kauk and Dale Bard, 10/74
Geek Towers, Center Jim Bridwell and John Syrett, 6/74
Geek Towers, Right Mark Klemens and Jim Bridwell, 7/71
Lost Arrrow Chimney John Salathé and Anton Nelson, 9/47 **FFA** Chuck Pratt and Frank Sacherer, 1964
Lost Arrow Spire, Direct Warren Harding and Pat Callis, 6/68
ABC Route Ron Kauk and Jerry Moffat, 6/85
Lost Arrow Tip Fritz Lippmann, Jack Arnold, Anton Nelson and Robin Hansen, 9/46 **FFA** Dave Schultz et al
Yosemite Pointless Bob Ost and Norman Boles, 5/86
Rainbow Paul Fida and Chris Freel, 1983
Seand Paradise Knez Frančeк and Frešer Marjan, 4/82
Yosemite Point, Czech Route Jan Porvazik and A. Behia, 10/78
Est of Paradise Knez Franček and Freser Marjan, 4/83
Yosemite Point Buttress Allen Steck and Bob Swift, 1952 **(free variations)** Yvon Chouinard and Tom Frost, 1960; Frank Sacherer and Don Telshaw, 8/64 **(direct outside face)** Galen Rowell and Scott Walker, 1963
Yosemite Point, Southeast Face Gordon Webster and TM Herbert, 6/65
Yosemite Point Couloir Dave Brower, Morgan Harris and Torcom Bedayan, 6/38

INDIAN CANYON

Castle Cliffs Dave Brower and Morgan Harris, 5/40
West Arrowhead Chimney Torcom Bedayan and Fritz Lippmann, 12/41
Arrowhead Spire, South Arête Dave Brower and Richard Leonard, 9/37
Arrowhead Spire, East Face Fritz Lippmann and Anton Nelson, 12/46
Arrowhead Spire, Northeast Side John Fiske and Dick Scheible, 8/58
Arrowhead Arête Mark Powell and Bill Feuerer, 10/56
East Arrowhead Chimney Mark Powell and Warren Harding, 12/56
East Arrowhead Buttress, Overhang Route Mark Powell and Wayne Merry, 8/57
East Arrowhead Buttress, Overhang Bypass Mark Powell, Wally Reed and Warren Harding, 3/57
Maps and Legends Drew Davol and John Tuttle **FFA** Joe Hedge and Drew Davol, 1986
Police State Urmas Franosch, John Tuttle and Bill Rose
Knuckle Buster Chris Falkenstein and Dennis Oakeshott, 1975
The Wand Dimitri Barton, 1982
A-5 Pinnacle Larry Zulim, Bob Jasperson and Scott Cole, 1981
Lehamite Buttress Les Wilson and Wolfgang Heinritz, 1965

Yoghurt Rick Sylvester and Barry Bates, 8/70
Chocolate Dihedral Rick Sylvester, Matt Donohoe and Barry Bates, 8/70

CHURCH BOWL

Black is Brown Kim Schmitz and Frank Trummel, 1966
Deja Thorus Jim Beyer and Misa Giesey, 1978
Uncle Fanny Bruce Price and Michael McLean, 1/70
Aunt Fanny's Pantry Sheridan Anderson and Leo Le Bon, 1965
Book of Revelations Gordon Webster and Chuck Ostin, 10/65 **FFA** Bob Finn and Chris Falkenstein, 1974
Church Bowl Tree Mike Jefferson and Dave Collins, 8/70
Church Bowl Chimney unknown
Church Bowl Terrace Jim Bridwell and Hamish Mutch, 12/65
Bishop's Terrace Russ Warne, Dave McFadden and Steve Roper, 12/59 **FFA** Chuck Pratt and Herb Swedlund, 1960
Bishop's Balcony Frank Sacherer and Gary Colliver, 11/62
Fire and Brimstone Chick Holtkamp and Chris Ballinger, 9/81
Fool's Finger Bill Price

ROYAL ARCHES

Rhombus Wall Warren Harding et al, 1975
Die Schweine Von Oben Bill Russel and Paul Fida, 1983
East of Eden Bob Gaines and Jay Smith, 9/85
Rupto Pac Eric Mayo and Brian Bennett, 1984
Super Slide Gene Drake and Rex Spaith, 1971
Eagle Roof Dave Diegleman, Bill Price and Augie Klein, 1974
Peter's Out Peter Croft and Tami Knight, 1978
Trial by Fire Chris Falkenstein and Don Reid, 3/74
Serenity Crack Glen Denny and Les Wilson, 10/61 **FFA** Tom Higgins and Chris Jones, 1967
Adrenaline Mark Hudon et al, 1976
Maxine's Wall Les Wilson and Al Macdonald, 3/62 **FFA** Pete Livesey and Andreas Maurer, 1973
Firefingers Charles Cole et al
Pigs in Space Peter Croft, Tami Knight and Larry Zulim, 10/78
Permanent Waves Chris Hash, Gene Hash and Scott Burke, 11/86
Deviltry John Tuttle and Michael Forkash
Hell's Hollow Ken Ariza, Doe DeRoss, Nick Arms and Mark Carpenter
Sons of Yesterday John Tuttle, Drew Davol and Vince Depasque, 1986
Moan Fest Dimitri Barton and Steve Gerberding, 4/84
Ahwahnee Buttress George Sessions, George Whitmore, Jerry Dixon and Merle Alley, 5/59
Peruvian Flake Bruce Morris, Kevin Leary and Bill Taylor
Draw the Line Mark Carpenter and Nick Arms, 1986
Fine Line Grant Hiskes and Doe DeRoss, 1985
Peeping Tom Grant Hiskes, Neal Newcomb and Tim Noonan, 1985
Surplus Cheaper Hands John Tuttle, Norman Boles and George Watson
The Trowel Eric Beck and Jim Harper, 5/62
The Hanging Boulders Les Wilson, Wolfgang Heinritz and Andrzej Ehrenfeucht, 10/62
The Crack of Dawn Royal Robbins, Chuck Pratt and Tom Frost, 9/59
Royal Arches Route Ken Adam, Morgan Harris and W. Kenneth Davis, 10/36
Astro Spam Norman Boles and Brian Bennett, 1986
Arête Butler Norman Boles, George Watson and Brian Bennett, 1986
Royal Prerogative Don Reid and Rick Cashner, 2/78

Krovy Rookers Norman Boles and Brian Bennett, 1986
Ilsa She Wolf of the S.S. George Watson, Norman Boles and Brian Bennett, 1986
Facade unknown
Y Crack Gene Drake et al, 1975
Fish Fingers Jonny Woodward and Maria Cranor, 5/85
The Cobra Mark Powell and Bob Kamps, 6/66 **FFA** Tobin Sorenson and Tim Sorenson, 1975
Royal Cornpad Ray Jardine and Linda McGinnis, 4/76
Wise Crack Chris Falkenstein, Chuck Cochrane and Dennis Oakeshott, 1979
Cornball unknown
Texas Chain Saw Massacre Chris Cantwell and Augie Klein, 1980
King Snake Chris Cantwell and Mark Grant, 1980
Poker Face Dan McDivett and Sue Bonavich, 3/86
Face Card unknown
King of Hearts unknown
Sleight of Hand Bob Ost and Norman Boles, 1/85
Arches Direct Royal Robbins and Joe Fitschen, 6/60
The Violent Bear it Away John Tuttle and Vince Depasque, 1986
The Rambler Steve Gerberding, Scott Burke, Chris Hash, and Gene Hash, 6/86
Shakey Flakes Chris Flakenstein, Ken Bishop, Edd Kuropat, Tom Carter and Mike McPheron, 1973
Friday the 13th Dimitri Barton and Scott Burke, 9/85
Flakes Away Chris Cantwell, 9/78
Samurai Crack Bill Price and Chris Cantwell, 9/78
Hershey Highway Lance Lynch and Malcolm Jolly, 1978
Reefer Madness Pat Timson and Don Harter, 1976
Arches Terrace Rich Calderwood and Merle Alley, 12/57 **FFA** Merle Alley, Rich Calderwood, John Ohrenschall and George Sessions, 1958
Greasy but Groovy John Long, Rick Accomazzo and Richard Harrison, 5/74
Fallen Arches Yvon Chouinard and Dave Bathgate, 10/66 **FFA** Yvon Chouinard and Tom Frost, 10/66
Crying for Mama Charles Cole and John Middendorf, 1986
Arches Terrace Direct Bob Grow, Rick Sylvester and Kelly Minnick, 10/70
Hangdog Flyer Ray Jardine and John Lakey, 9/76
10.96 Jim Bridwell, John Long and Mark Klemens, 1972
The Plank Don Reid and Alan Roberts, 10/85
Movin' Like a Stud Pat Timpson, Julie Brugger, Bob Crawford and Dave Anderson, 1978
Benzoin and Edges Pat Timpson, Jeff Vance, Don Harter, Rick LeDuc and Bruce Hildenbrand, 4/78
The Kids are All Right Jerry, Sigrid, Lynnea, and William Anderson, 5/86
Lynnea's Birthday Surprise Jerry, Sigrid and Lynnea Anderson, 5/86
Lower Arch Traverse Krehe Ritter, Mara Unterman and Judy Beyers, 8/57
Bulging Puke Bill Russell and Chris Friel, 11/81

WASHINGTON COLUMN

Lunch Ledge Hervey Voge, Richard Leonard, Jules Eichorn and Bester Robinson
Direct Route John Dyer, Robin Hansen and DeWitt Allen, 8/40
Piton Traverse Morgan Harris, Jack Reigelhuth and Richard Leonard, 5/35
Power Failure Ray Jardine, Linda McGinnis and Mark Vallance, 10/75
The Fang Ray Jardine et al, 1975
Lunch Ledge Direct Yvon Chouinard and Wally Reed, 7/61 (free variation; **Space Case**) Ray Jardine and Linda McGinnis, 10/76
Direct Direct Route Bill Bostick, Jack Delk, and Bill Sorenson, 3/71

Jesu Joy Ray Jardine and Rick Sylvester, 10/75
Wing of Bat Don Reid and Mike Corbett, 1/84
Dwindling Energy Ray Jardine and Mark Vallance, 10/75
Nowhere Mandon Reid and Dave Yerian, 1984
Turkey Vulture Jeff Smith and Kevin Lathrop, 1981
The Odyssey Ray Jardine and John Lakey, 5/76
Dinner Ledge Direct Jim Madsen and Kim Schmitz, 1967
Dinner Ledge Don Goodrich and Dave Dows, 4/52 **FFA** John Hudson and Chris Fredericks, 1966
Obscurity Traverse Bill Loughman and Don Goodrich, 10/55
South Central Jim Bridwell and Joe Faint, 10/67
South Face Layton Kor and Chris Fredericks, 6/64
Skull Queen Dave Altenburg, Chuck Clance and Steve Bosque, 6/84
The Prow Royal Robbins and Glen Denny, 5/69
Jojo Bruce Pollock, Matt Pollock and Luke Freeman, 1972
Tom Cat Ken Ariza and Tommy Thompson
Electric Ladyland Gib Lewis, Rick Accomazzo and Richard Harrison, 5/75
East Face Warren Harding, Glen Denny and Chuck Pratt, 7/59 **FFA (Astroman)** John Bachar, John Long and Ron Kauk, 5/75
Terminal Research Randy Leavitt, Gary Zaccor and Tony Yaniro, 1980
Mideast Crisis Steve Bosque and Mike Corbett, 4/83
Great Slab Route Layton Kor, Jim Madsen and Kim Schmitz, 5/67
Bad Wall Jim Madsen and Kim Schmitz, 1967

TENAYA CANYON

Skid Row Alan Bartlett and Dimitri Barton, 5/82
North Dome, West Face Art Gran and Steve Roper, 4/62 **FFA** Peter Barton and Mark Chapman, 1972
North Dome, Southwest Face Bev Clark and Chuck Pratt, 4/68
North Dome, South Face Mark Powell and Wally Reed, 8/57 **FFA** Mort Hempel, Irene Ortenburger and Steve Roper, 1960
Crest Jewell Dan Dingle and Michael Lucero, 9/81
Dakshina Dan Dingle and Ken Black, 8/83
Mass Assault Ken Boche, Dennis Hennek, Judy Sterner, Russ McLean, Sibylle Hechtel, Tim Auger and Mike Farrell, 3/72
Basket Dome, Basket Case Jim Donini and TM Herbert, 6/72 **FFA** Mark Klemens and Jim Bridwell, 7/72
Basket Dome, Straight Jacket Dale Bard, Jim Bridwell and Ron Kauk, 1977
Basket Dome, Scott-Child Doug Scott and Greg Child, 1982
Mirror Mirror, Left Eric Brand and Jonell Geller, 8/85
Mirror Mirror, Right Eric Brand and tom Shores, 8/86
Eric's Book Eric Barrett et al, 1979
Thin Man Eric Barrett et al, 1979
Groundhog Eric Kohl and Eric Brand, 11/86
Breathalizer Eric Kohl and Eric Brand, 11/86
Precious Powder Bruce Morris and Jim Elias, 10/83
Werner's Crack Werner Braun and Bruce Steakly, 6/71
The Prude David and Alan Bard, 3/72
Rurp Rape Bruce Steakly, 1971
A Question of Balance Paul Fortpates and Scott Shristie, 10/74
Creeping Lethargy Dimitri Barton et al, 1986
Neil Down Dimitri Barton, Ken Ariza and Tracy Dorton, 5/86
Water Babies Dimitri Barton, Ken Ariza and Tracy Dorton, 2/86
Apathy Buttress Dimitri Barton , Ken Ariza and Tracy Dorton, 2/86

Destination Zero Bruce Morris and Ken Ariza, 1986
Valley Syndrome Dimitri Barton, Ken Ariza and tracy Dorton, 1986
Free Clinic Dimitri Barton and Ken Ariza, 1986
Ken's Dream Dimitri Barton and Ken Ariza, 1986
Snow Creek Slabs Bob Summers and Ken Boche, 6/69
BHOS Dome Doug Scott, TM Herbert, Don Lauria and Dennis Hennek, 4/70
Watkins Gully Robin Hansen, Fritz Lippmann and Rolf Pundt, 9/46
Upper Watkins Pinnacle Al Baxter, Ulf Ramm-Ericson and Rupert Gates, 5/47 **FFA** Joe Oliger, Wayne Hildebrand and Steve Roper, 1961
Middle Watkins Pinnacle Al Baxter and Rupert Gates, 12/46
Lower Watkins Pinnacle Mark Powell, Herb Swedlund, Wally Reed, George Sessions and Merle Alley, 7/57
Watkins Pinnacles (from Tenaya Canyon) Gary Hemming, Dick Long, Jim Wilson and Larry Lackey, 5/58
Mt. Watkins, Hook, Line and Sinker Mike Munger, Angus Thuermer and Steve Larson, 5/78
Mt. Watkins, South Face Warren Harding, Yvon Chouinard and Chuck Pratt, 7/64
Mt. Watkins, Tenaya's Terror Mike Corbett and Steve Bosque
Mt. Watkins, Bob Locke Memorial Buttress Jim Bridwell, Ron Kauk, John Long and Kim Schmitz, 10/78
Yasoo Dome Jim Baldwin and Kit Carr, 7/63
Clouds Rest, Northwest Face Bob Kamps and Bud Couch, 7/63
Clouds Rest, Northwest Ledges Dick Long and Jack Davis, 8/52
Quarter Dome, North Face Yvon Chouinard and Tom Frost, 9/62 **FFA (Pegasus)** Max Jones and Mark Hudon, 1980
Quarter Dome, Route of All Evil Matt Donohoe and Cliff Jennings, 1971
West Quarter Dome, North Face Phil Koch and Dave Goeddel, 9/69
Ahwiyah Point, Northeast Gully Dave Brower and Morgan Harris, 8/37
Ahwiyah Point, Northwest Buttress Wayne Merry and Warren Harding, 1957

HALF DOME

Northwest Buttress Andy Embick and Bob Jensen, 9/69
Final Exam Mark Klemens and Jim Bridwell, 1971
North Ridge Chuck Wilts and Royal Robbins, 6/61
Regular Northwest Face Route Royal Robbins, Jerry Gallwas and Mike Sherrick, 7/57 **FFA** Jim Erickson and Art Higbee, 1976
Arcturas Royal Robbins and Dick Dorworth, 7/70
Same As it Never Was Karl McConachie, Jay Smith and Randy Grandstaff, 7/86
Direct Northwest Face Royal Robbins and Dick McCracken, 6/63
Queen of Spades Charles Cole, 7/84
Tis-sa-ack Royal Robbins and Don Peterson, 10/69
Zenith Jim Bridwell and Kim Schmitz, 1978
Arctic Sea Tom Cosgrove and Duane Raleigh, 1983
Bushido Jim Bridwell and Dale Bard, 10/77
On the Edge Dale Bard and George Meyers, 1975
West Corner Bob Kamps and Dave Rearick, 6/61
Salathé Route (Southwest Face Route) John Salathé and Anton Nelson, 10/46 FFA Frank Sacherer, Bob Kamps and Andy Lichtman, 1964
The Deuceldike Charles Cole, Rusty Reno and John Middendorf, 4/85
Snake Dike Eric Beck, Jim Bridwell and Chris Fredericks, 7/65
Eye in the Sky Mark Spencer, Shirley Spencer, Dan Abbot and David Abbot, 4/85
Snake Dance Claude Fiddler and Bob Jones, 1973
The Fast Lane Dimitri Barton, Scott Burke and Chris Hash, 6/86
Autobahn Charles Cole, Rusty Reno and John Middendorf, 4/85
South Face Route Warren Harding and Galen Rowell, 7/70

Karma Dave Schultz, Ken Yager and Jim Campbell, 7/86
Call of the Wild Peter Haan and Roger Briggs, 7/75
Happy Gully Joe Faint, Warren Harding and Chris Fredericks, 5/66
Diving Board, from Mirror Lake Charles Michael, prior to 1927
Diving Board, Porcelain Wall Warren Harding, Dave Lomba and Steve Bosque, 1975
Diving Board, Sunshine Buttress Dick Long, Al Macdonald and Jim Wilson, 8/62
Diving Board, West Side Ken Adam and W. Kenneth Davis, 1938
The Silver Platter Ray Jardine and John Lakey, 4/76
Gravity's Rainbow Ray Jardine and John Lakey, 4/76
Grizzly Peak, West Face Dick Houston and Ralph McColm, 6/42
Bare Necessities Mark Chapman and Rik Rieder, 7/72
Grizzly Peak, South Gully David Brower and Moragan Harris, 6/38
Sierra Point, Southeast Farce Greg Shaffer, Roger Evje and Rob Foster, 6/66

LITTLE YOSEMITE

Mt. Broderick, Unemployment Line Alan Bartlett, Jim May and Steve Gerberding, 11/82
South Face Bob Kamps, Joe Fitschen and Chuck Pratt, 6/60
Liberty Cap, West Corner Dick McCracken and Steve Roper, 6/60
Liberty Cap, West Buttress Mike Corbett, Steve Bosque, 12/85
Liberty Cap, Southwest Face Galen Rowell, Joe Faint and Warren Harding, 5/69
Liberty Cap, Direct Southwest Face Werner Braun and Rick Cashner, 5/82
Liberty Cap, A Joint Adventure Paul Gagner, Karl McConachie and John Barbella, 7/79
Liberty Cap, South Face Mark Powell, Royal Robbins and Joe Fitschen, 9/56
Liberty Cap, Southern Buttress Mike Loughman and Dick Armstrong, 6/57
Leverage Joe Faint and Chris Fredericks, 5/66
Base Pinnacle Mark Klemens and Bruce Pollock, 5/72
Sugarloaf Dome, South Face John Salathé and Cliff Hopson, 11/51 **FFA** Yvon Chouinard and Tom Frost, 1960
Nevada Fall, Left Side Royal Robbins and Lin ephraim, 7/60
Nevada Flake, The Slot Machine unknown **FFA** Bruce Morris and Paul Cowen, 10/77
Nevada Flake, Center Route Bill Amborn, Tom Naylor and Steve Roper, 1/61
Nevada Flake, Right Side Glen Denny and Charles Fisher, 4/61
Vernal Fall, Right Side Allen Steck, Jim Wilson and Dick Long, 10/66
Mt. Starr King, Northeast Slopes George Bayley and E.S. Schuyler, 1876
Mt. Starr King, East Face John Roebig, Ron Schroder and Tom Distler, 7/69
Mt. Starr King, West Face Ken Boche and Lee Panza, 5/70
Mt. Starr King, Nuts and Bolts Tim Harrison and Ken Boche, 1971
Mt. Starr King, Northwest Face Ken Boche and Mary Bomba, 9/70
Panorama Cliff Dave Brower and Morgan Harris, 10/36
Dark Shadows Dave Yerian, Bruce Morris and Malcolm Jolley, 10/78
Fistibule Werner Braun and Walt Shipley, 4/86
Air Bare Eric Mayo et al, 1982
Plane Fare Eric Mayo et al, 1982
Fresh Squeezed Grant Hiskes and Sean Plunkett
Ape Index Werner Braun et al, 1981
Cynical Pinnacle Chris Cantwell et al, 1981

GLACIER POINT APRON

Mud, Sweat and Beers Tony Dailley and Bob Madison, 8/73
Strange Energy Dean Miller, Bruce Morris and Chris Cantwell
Synapse Collapse Bruce Morris and Steve Cerrada, 1979
Shuttle Madness unknown

Milk Dud Jack Roberts et al, 9/71
Jack the Zipper Tony Yaniro, Nick Turvey and Scott Cole, 1978. **FFA** Scott Cosgrove, 10/85
The Calf Joe McKeown and Jim Harper, 7/63 **FFA** John Long et al, 1974
Dead Baby Dave Austin and Dimitri Barton, 11/78
Psychic Energy John Pruett et al, 10/86
Transistor Sister unknown
Calf Continuation Dennis Oakeshott and Vern Clevenger, 1975
A Mother's Lament Rab Carrington and Rik Rieder, 9/72
Tightrope Vern Clevenger, Tom Carter et al, 1975
The Cow, Left Ken Boche and Mary Bomba, 3/70
The Cow, Center Jeff and Greg Schaffer, 7/66
The Cow, Right Ken Boche, 5/70
An Udder Way Bill Zauman and Dave Jensen, 1977
Hoppy's Favorite Dennis Oakeshott and Vern Clevenger, 1974
Hoppy's Creed Dave Diegleman et al, 1978
The Grack, Left Side Bob Kamps and Andy Lichtman, 8/63
The Grack, Center Route Bill Sorenson and Jack Delk, 1967
The Grack, Marginal Ken Boche, Mary Bomba and Joe McKeown, 5/70
The Grack, Right Side TM Herbert and Ken Boche, 3/70
Perhaps Bob Kamps and Andy Lichtman, 8/63
Roller Coaster Ken Ariza, Mike Hatchett and Mark Carpenter, 1986
Hot Tin Roof Ed Barry, Matt Pollock and Bruce Pollock, 1973
Ochre Fields Carl Austrom and Darryl Jones, 4/78
Deep Throat unknown
The Mouth Variation Ken Boche and Dennis Hennek, 1966
Regular Mouth Bob Kamps and Tom Cochrane, 1964
Mouth to Perhaps Rick Accomazzo and Mike Breidenbach, 1974
Flakey Foont Vince Goetz, Rick Lee and Al Hu, 8/72
Misty Beethoven Mark Wilford et al, 1975
Hall of Mirrors Chris Cantwell, Bruce Morris, Scott Burke, Dave Austin and others, 1978-80
Goodrich Pinnacle, Left Side Don Goodrich and Krehe Ritter, 5/59 **FFA** Bob Kamps and Andy Lichtman, 1962
Goodrich Pinnacle, Right Side Royal Robbins, Liz Robbins and TM Herbert, 5/64
Goodrich to the Oasis Eric Beck, Mike Cohen and Tom Gerughty, 1966
Goodrich-Coonyard Traverse Jeff Dozier and Loyd Price, 7/66
Hoosier's Highway Steve Shea, Molly Higgins, Larry Bruce and Lou Dawson, 1974
Patio Pinnacle, Left Side Gordon Webster and Joh Morton, 1965
Patio Pinnacle, Regular Jeff Foott, 8/63
Monday Morning to Patio Mark Chapman and Ed Barry, 1973
Angelica Fremont Bainbridge, Conrad Van Bruggen, Simon King, Gordon Rhodes and Jeff Panetta, 1978
Coonyard Pinnacle Bill Amborn, Joe McKeown and Rich Calderwood, 9/60 **FFA** Chuck Ostin and Frank Sacherer, 1961
Patio to Coonyard Russ McLean and Ken Boche, 4/65
Coonyard to the Oasis Layton Kor and Yvon Chouinard, 9/60
The Hinterland (Oaisis to the rim) Bob Kamps and Joe McKeown, 1962
Monday Morning Slab, Far East Dennis Hennek and Ken Boche, 5/65
Monday Morning Slab, Left Side unknown
Monday Morning Slab, Variation on a Theme unknown
Monday Morning Slab, Chouinard Crack Yvon Chouinard et al
Monday Morning Slab, Harry Daley Route Ken Weeks and Harry Daley, 1960
Monday Morning Slab, Lichen Madness unknown

Monday Morning Slab, Right Side Don Goodrich and Mac Fraser, 1958
Monday Morning Slab, Lichen Nightmare Rik Rieder and John Long, 1972
Monday Morning Slab, Looking for Lichen Brian Knight, Linus Plalt and Michael Harris, 5/86
Zoner Mark Spencer, Shirley Spencer and Floyd Hayes, 7/85
Point Beyond Don Goodrich and Bill Loughman, 1955 **FFA** Howard Sturgis and Ron Harrison, 1959
Point Beyond Direct Yvon Chouinard and Ken Weeks, 1965
Angel's Approach Tom Higgins et al
Lucifer's Ledge Ken Boche and Dave Bircheff, 9/65
Lucifer's to the Oasis Ken Boche and Russ McLean, 9/65
Anchors Away Tim Harrison and Mike Breidenbach, 1972
Sailin' Shoes Bruce Morris, Dave Austin, Chuck Neifield, Gary Robbe, Peter Thurston and Val Lecont, 5/78
5.9 Grunt unknown
Chiropodist Shop Rick McGregor, 10/81
The Token Scott Burke et al
Ephemeral Clogdance Rick McGregor and Robert Parker, 1981
The Letdown Bob Kamps and Tom Higgins, 9/67
Bark at the Moon Ken Ariza, Mark Carpenter and Dave Walters, 1986
Synchronousity Drew Bedford and Mike Ortz
Nothing on the Apron Bruce Morris, Ken Ariza, Gary Rabbe and Stu Ritchie, 5/86
Lean Years Chris Cantwell and Bruce Morris, 6/79
Blue Funk Mike Artz and Drew Bedford
Perfect Master Bruce Morris and Chris Cantwell, 12/79
Lonely Dancer Dave Yerian, Shary McVoy and Bruce Morris, 1979
Son of Sam Dave Austin and Bruce Morris, 4/78
Cosmic Comedy Leon Borowski, Kevin Minto and Claude Fiddler, 11/72
Dr. Feel Good Bruce Morris, Mike Herandez and Scott Cole, 5/81
Afterglow Chris Cantwell and Scott Burke, 9/81
Apron Jam Galen Rowell and Gordon Webster, 10/65
Green Dragon Chris Cantwell and Dean Young, 9/79
Mr. Natural Chris Cantwell and Bruce Morris, 9/79
Bad Acid Al Swanson and Norman Boles
Scimitar unknown
Thunderhead Jim Beyer and Janice Linhares **FFA** Jonny Woodward and Maria Cranor, 5/85
The White Dike Brian Bennett, George Watson and Eric Mayo, 1986
Lunar Lunacy Gene Drake and Bob Bartlett, 6/77
Fire Drill Brian Bennett and John Tuttle, 1986
The Punch Line Al Swanson, Brian Bennett and Brian Bailey, 1986
Run With Me Brian Bennett and John Tuttle, 1986
The Punch Bowl Bob Kamps and Tom Higgins, 9/66
Harding Route Warren Harding and Bea Vogel, 6/57
Wild, Wild, West Greg Shaffer, Jeff Shaffer, Rob Foster and Roger Evje, 6/66
Glacier Point Terrace Dave Brower and Morgan Harris, 6/37
Flake Route Jerry Gray et al, 6/62
Firefall Face Galen Rowell and Warren Harding, 9/69
Time Machine Bob Shonerd, 10/84
Old A5 Peter Chesko et al, 1982
Blockbuster Don Reid, Grant Hiskes and Dimitri Barton, 5/83
Derelict's Diagonal Chuck Goldman and Mathew Moore, 1979
Broken Circuit unknown
Circuit Breaker unknown

Derelict's Delight Mike Corbett, 1976 **FFA** Dan Phillips and John Ockerman, 10/85
Doggie Submission John Tuttle and Brian Bennett, 1986
Once is Enough Bill Price, Larry Zulim and Jim Hevner, 1980
Public Sanitation Rick Sylvester and Roy Kligfield, 9/71

CHAPEL WALL

Heathenistic Pursuit Jim Beyer and Bob Sullivan, 1978
Gold Dust Jim Beyer and Bob Sullivan, 1978
On the Loose Kim Schmitz, Jim Bridwell and Rick Christiani, 9/70
Scattered Youth unknown
Controlled Burn Don Reid and Grant Hiskes, 10/80
Cosmic Debris Bill Price et al, 5/80
Lay Lady Lieback Jerry and Sigrid Anderson, 10/86
Delicate Delineate Jerry and Sigrid Anderson, 10/86
Chockblock Chimney Greg Schaffer and Rob Foster, 9/68
Tithe Don Reid et al
The Symphony Chuck Ostin and Tim Fitzgerald, 7/69
First Movement Variation Dan Gates and Tim Fitzgerald, 1969
Dorn's Crack Jack Dorn, Jim Beyer and Bob Sullivan, 1978
The Den Tim Fitzgerald and Dave Ralston, 8/67
Resurrection Rick Cashner and Angie Morales, 1978
New Testament Don Reid and Rick Cashner, 9/82
Betrayal Rick Cashner and Angie Morales, 1978
Bryan's Crack Frank Brown and Dave Bryan, 1973
Sixth Heaven Ray Jardine and Frank Brown
Fusilade John Bragg and Kevin Bein, 10/72
Wrinkle John Bragg and Rab Carrington, 10/72

SENTINEL ROCK

Potato Masher J. George Maring, Don Curry, Don Sorensen and John Marten, 7/51
The Block Mark Powell, 6/57
Sentinel Spire Warren Harding and George Whitmore, 6/54
The Nail Wayne Merry and Warren Harding, 1957
Sentinel Rock, East Arête Allen Steck, Les Wilson and Al Macdonald, 7/62
The Flue Warren Harding and Bob Kamps, 8/62
Northeast Bowl John Salathé and Anton Nelson, 6/48
Kor-Denny Route Layton Kor and Glen Denny, 6/63
Psychedelic Wall Ken Boche and Dennis Hennek, 9/66
Direct North Face Royal Robbins and Tom Frost, 5/62
Gobi Wall Chuck Pratt and Ken Boche, 7/69
Chouinard-Herbert Route Yvon Chouinard and TM Herbert, 8/62 **FFA** John Long, Pete Minks and Eric Ericksson, 1976
Flying Buttress Direct Chris Fredericks and Layton Kor, 6/65
Steck-Salathé Allen Steck and John Salathé, 7/50 **FFA** various parties
West Face Yvon Chouinard and Tom Frost, 6/60
In Cold Blood Royal Robbins, 5/70
Circular Staircase Dave Brower and Morgan Harris, 5/40 **FFA** Krehe Ritter and Steve Roper, 1959
The Bannister Dick Long, Danny Tavistock, Hans Vander Laan and John Morton, 11/62

SENTINEL CREEK

Spiderman Bill Price and Craig Hanna, 1978
Vanishing Point Barry Bates and Loyd Price, 1971
The Bay Bush Chris Fredericks and Steve Miller, 5/65

The Tilted Mitten, Left Side Galen Rowell and Gary Colliver, 8/62
The Tilted Mitten, Right Side Galen Rowell and Jim Harper, 7/62
The Tilted Mitten, The Hand Me Down Mark Chapman and Jim Donini, 1974
Mental Block Dale Bard and Jim Bridwell, 5/73
The Sphinxter Galen Rowell and Ben Borson, 9/68
Hara-kiri Tom Gilje et al, 1981
Ying-Yang Werner Braun, Ron Kauk and Nic Taylor, 1978
Manana Werner Braun and Jim Pettigrew, 1977
King Tut's Tomb Galen Rowell and Mike Covington, 5/68
Mummy's Revenge Tom Kimbrough and Chuck Pratt, 8/67
Into the Fire Dan Hare and Mike O'Donnell, 6/83
Kung Pao Chicken Dan Hare and Kathy Cassidy, 5/82
Boulderfield Gorge Royal Robbins, Liz Robbins, Mike Dent and Victor Cowley, 10/66
Pharaoh's Beard, Regular Route Tom Frost, Yvon Chouinard and Ken Weeks, 1959
Pharaoh's Beard, Whisker Bill Price et al, 1979
Pharaoh's Beard, Right Side Chuck Ostin and Tim Fitzgerald, 9/65 **FFA** Loyd Price et al
Look Before You Leap Steve Schneider and Rob Oraveitz, 1983
Buried Treasure Steve Schneider and John Barbella, 1983
Sheba Charlie Porter et al, 1972

Pohono Pinnacle, North Face George Sessions and Felix Knauth, 8/58
Pohono Pinnacle, Northwest Corner Bill Amborn and Harry Daley, 1960
Realm of the Lizard King Kevin Worrall and John Yablonski, 1975
Lost Brother, Regular Route Dave Brower and L. Bruce Meyer, 7/41
Lost Brother, Northwest Face Al Macdonald, Jeff Dozier, Dave French and Gary Westernof, 6/63 **FFA** Barry Bates and Rik Rieder, 1972
The Last Resort Pinnacle, Left Side Rik Rieder and Dale Bard, 1972
The Last Resort Pinnacle, Center Barry Bates and Rik Rieder, 1972
Lost Brother, Southwest Side George Whitmore and Merle Alley, 1958
Promulgated Pinnacle Warren Harding and Bob Swift, 1956
Taft Point Arête Al Macdonald and Galen Rowell, 5/64
Will-O'-The Wisp (first known ascent) Jim Chamberlain and Bob Grow, 5/67

CATHEDRAL SPIRES AREA

Phantom Pinnacle, Left Side Bill Dunmire and Bob Swift, 9/50 **FFA** Rich Calderwood and Mike Borghoff, 1957
Phantom Pinnacle, Outside Face Chris Fredericks and Joe Faint, 6/65 **FFA** Mike Graham, Roger Breedlove and Jim Bridwell, 4/76
Hangover Buttress Rich Calderwood and Jerry Dixon, 6/60
Harris's Hangover Oscar Cook, Bill Dunmire and Bob Swift, 8/49
The Ski Jump Chuck Pratt and Bob Kamps, 7/59
Spireview Point George Sessions and dick Irvin, 4/54
Church Tower, East Arête Ken Adam, Olive Dyer and Morgan Harris, 10/35 **variation** Dick Houston, Ed Koskinen, Bill Horsfall and Newton McCready, 5/41
Church Tower, Soutwest Notch unknown
Church Tower, North Face John Salathé, Anton Nelson, DeWitt Allen and Fritz Lippmann, 6/46
Lower Cathedral Spire, Regular Route (via Flake) Richard Leonard, Jules Eichorn and Bestor Robinson, 8/34 **(current route)** Roy Gorin, Paul Estes, Jerry Ganapole and Raffi Bedayn, 5/48
Lower Cathedral Spire, Northeast Chimney Chuck Pratt and Steve Roper, 6/58 **FFA** Tom Kimbrough and Roman Laba, 1966
Lower Cathedral Spire, Northeast Face Mark Powell, Frank Sacherer and Bob Kamps, 9/63 **variations** Chuck Pratt and Joe Faint, 1965; Chris Fredericks, Frank Sacherer and TM Herbert, 1965

Lower Cathedral Spire, Lower North Face Les Wilson and Wolfgang Heinritz, 7/62
Lower Cathedral Spire, Upper North Face Galen Rowell and Al Macdonald, 6/62
Higher Cathedral Spire, Regular Route Jules Eichorn, Bestor Robinson and Dick Leonard, 4/34 **FFA** Chuck Wilts and Spencer Austin, 1944
Higher Cathedral Spire, Steck Route Allen Steck, Fletcher Hoyt and William Hoyt, 8/48
Higher Cathedral Spire, Southeast Route Keith Edwards and Fred Cady, 6/70
Higher Cathedral Spire, East Corner Tom Gerughty and Chuck Pratt, 7/65
Higher Cathedral Spire, North Couloir, Upper Part Dick Long and Jim Wilson, 4/54 **complete route** Dick Long, Ray D'Arcy and Wally Reed, 6/61
Higher Cathedral Spire, Higher Aspirations Rik Derrick and Steve Bosque, 11/82
Higher Cathedral Spire, Northwest Face Tom Frost and Royal Robbins, 6/61

HIGHER CATHEDRAL ROCK

The Syllable Rick Sylvester and Sibylle Hechtel, 11/71
The Sequel Joe Faint and Chuck Pratt, 10/66
Blind Man's Bluff Roger Breedlove and Bill St. Jean, 1976
Braille Book Jim Bridwell, Chris Fredericks and Brian Berry, 6/66
Book of Job Rick Sylvester and Ben Read, 11/71 **FFA** Jim Donini and Rik Rieder, 6/72
The Dictionary Ken Jern, J. McMillan and J. Catland, 1970
Higher Cathedral Rock, East Face Route Jim Bridwell and Chris Fredericks, 6/67
Higher Cathedral Rock, Learning to Crawl Mike Corbett, Steve Bosque and Fritz Fox, 1985
Mary's Tears Bill Price and Mike Borris, 5/80
Higher Cathedral Rock, Northeast Buttress Dick Long, Ray D'Arcy and Terry Tarver, 6/59 **FFA** Frank Sacherer and Jeff Dozier, 1964
Higher Cathedral Rock, Northeast Corner Chuck Pratt and Joe Kelsey, 10/70 **Free variation (Powerpoint)** Werner Braun and Scott Cosgrove, 4/86
Crucifix Jim Bridwell and Kevin Worrall, 1973 **FFA** Peter Croft et al, 1985
Higher Cathedral Rock, North Face Yvon Chouinard, Chuck Pratt and Bob Kamps, 7/60
Cathedral Chimney Dave Brower and Morgan Harris, 10/36

Penny Pinnacle, South Face Torcom Bedayan and Fritz Lippmann, 4/46
Penny Pinnacle, West Face unknown, 1950's
Penny Pinnacle, North Face unknown
Penny Pinnacle, East Arête Mark Powell and Bill Feuerer, 5/59
Nickel Pinnacle, from the notch Mark Powell and George Whitmore, 11/54 **FFA** Mort Hempel and Steve Roper, 1960
Nickel Pinnacle, East Face Chuck Kroger and Kep Stone, 4/68
Penny-Nickel Arête Chuck Pratt, George Sessions and Krehe Ritter, 9/58
John's Other Chimney John Ohrenschall and Mary Ann Corthell, 6/53

MIDDLE CATHEDRAL ROCK

Alley Cat Dave Anderson, Mark Moore and K. Eastman, 5/75
Kat Walk Ralph Griswold, 9/29
Cork Screw Peter Markle and Jim Pettigrew, 1974
No Butts About It Phil Bard et al, 1983
East Buttress Warren Harding, Jack Davis and Bob Swift, 1954. **FFA** Frank Sacherer and Ed Leeper, 1965 **right variation** Yvon Chouinard and Mort Hempel, 1961
Sacherer-Fredericks Frank Sacherer and Chris Fredericks, 7/64
Kor-Beck Layton Kor and Eric Beck, 4/63 **FFA** Eric Beck and Mark Klemens, 1966
Space Babble Ron Kauk and Kevin Worrall, 1976
Bircheff-Williams Phil Bircheff and Steve Williams, 6/69 **FFA** Kevin Worrall and George Meyers, 1973
Central Pillar of Frenzy (first eight) Jim Bridwell, Roger Breedlove and Ed Barry, 5/73 **finish** Jim Bridwell, John Long and Billy Westbay, 5/75 **direct start** John Long and Ron Fawcett, 1979

Chouinard-Pratt Chuck Pratt and Yvon Chouinard, 10/60 **direct finish** Chuck Pratt and Bob Kamps, 6/64

Rainbow Bridge Chris Cantwell, Scott Burke and Bruce Morris, 1980

Stoner's Highway Kevin Worrall, John Long, Ed Barry, Peter Barton and Vern Clevenger, 1973

Powell-Reed Mark Powell and Wally Reed, 7/57 **FFA** Bob Kamps and Tom Higgins, 1964

Pieces of Eight Scott Burke, Steve Schneider et al

Paradise Lost Ray Jardine and Rik Rieder, 6/72

Pee Pee Pillar Peter Barton, Eric Schoen, George Meyers and Bob Ashworth, 1974

Direct North Buttress Yvon Chouinard and Steve Roper, 6/62 **FFA** Frank Sacherer and Eric Beck, 1965

Picnic Peter Barton, Eric Schoen and George Meyers, 1974

North Buttress Warren Harding, Frank Tarver, Craig Holden and John Whitmer, 5/54 **FFA** Frank Sacherer and Jim Bridwell, 1964

The Turret Bob Kamps and Mark Powell, 7/62 **FFA** Jim Donini and John Bragg, 1973

North Face Route Chuck Pratt, Bob Kamps and Steve Roper, 6/59

Spank Your Monkey Brian Bennett, Stu Ritchie and Norman Boles, 1984

Jigsaw Kevin Worrall, George Meyers and Mark Chapman, 1976

Black Primo Kevin Worrall, John Long and George Meyers, 5/74

Ticket to Nowhere Bob Gaines, John Mallery, Tom Callahan, Mike Paul and Franciso Blanco, 1983-1986

Quicksilver Kevin Worrall, George Meyers and Vern Clevenger, 1973

Walk of Life Ron Kauk, Kevin Worrall and Mark Chapman, 6/86

Freewheelin' Kevin Worrall, George Meyers and Roger Breedlove, 1973

Stupid Pet Tricks Brian Bennett, Vince Deposque and Jack Wenzel, 1985

Bottom Feeder Norman Boles, Brian Bennett and Stu Ritchie, 1984

Cat Dancing P. Landrum, John Haek and Bruce Casey, 9/79

Orange Peel George Meyers and Bruce Hawkins, 1975

Exodus Jay Smith and Gary Anderson, 8/83

Tapestry Heidi Pesterfield and Brian Bennett, 1986

Tears of Joy Gene Drake, Rick Stockwell and Bob Bartlett, 6/77

Mother Earth (to traverse ledges) George Meyers, John Long, Kevin Worrall and Mark Chapman, 1975 **complete route** John Long, Mark Chapman and Ron Kauk, 1978

Teaching Little Fingers Eric Gompper, Dan Parks and Ralph Shaffer, 8/85

Smith-Crawford Jay Smith and Paul Crawford, 9/84

The Flakes Frank Sacherer and Mark Powell, 6/64

North Face Traverse Dick Long, George Mandatory, Jack Davis and Bob Skinner, 7/54

Thirsty Spire Dick Long and Bob Skinner, 7/54

Northwest Face Les Overstreet, Jerry Gray and George Ewing, 9/57 **FFA** Margaret Young and Steve Roper, 1959

Northwest Buttress Bill Dunmire, Marj Dunmire, Jack Davis, Dale Webster, Dick Long and Dick Houston, 4/53

Gunsight unknown

LOWER CATHEDRAL ROCK

Spooky Tooth John Yablonski, Fred East and Richard Harrison, 1976

Shake and Bake Rick Accomazzo and Richard Harrison, 1976

Starfire Rick Accomazzo and Richard Harrison, 1976

East Buttress Mark Powell, Jerry Gallwas and Don Wilson, 6/56 **FFA** Steve Thompson and Chris Fredericks, 1965

Soul Sacrifice Werner Braun et al, 1981

North Face Joe Fitschen, Chuck Pratt and Royal Robbins, 6/60

Beggar's Buttress Kevin Worrall and Mark Chapman, 5/76
Tidbit Don Ried and Grant Hiskes, 1978
Going Nowhere Werner Braun and Scott Cosgrove, 9/86
Sub-Mission Don Reid and Grant Hiskes, 8/84
North by Northwest Dimitri Barton et al, 1986
Brass Knuckles Chris Cantwell and Bruce Morris, 1981
The Roof Tom Frost and Henry Kendall, 4/58
Overhang Route Dick Leonard, Doris Leonard and Bestor Robinson, 9/35 **FFA** Mark Powell and Bill Feuerer, 1956
Overhang Bypass Bill Dunmire, Ed Robbins, Bill Long and Dick Long, 6/52
Overhang Overpass Jim Donini et al, 1974
West Face Frank Sacherer and Wally Reed, 8/63
Return to the Stone Age Ed Barry and Scott Cosgrove, 10/85
Bridalveil Fall, East Buttress Royal Robbins and TM Herbert, 9/63
Bridalveil East Mark Powell and Warren Harding, 8/57 **FFA via Midget Chimney** Frank Sacherer and John Morton, 1964 **free var. from pitch 3** Royal Robbins and Rich Calderwood, 1961

LEANING TOWER

Rattlesnake Buttress Layton Kor and Fred Beckey, 6/65 **FFA** Werner Braun and Rick Cashner, 5/82
The Yellow Corner Layton Kor and Tom Fender, 6/65
Direct Assistance Route Layton Kor, John Hudson and Dick Williams, 6/66
The Princess Brian Bennett, Brian Hoffmann and Michael Forkash, 1986
The Watchtower, The Joker Mark Chapman and Kevin Worrall, 1975
The Watchtower, The Thief Mark Chapman and Kevin Worrall, 1975
The Watchtower, Megaforce Doug and Maurice Reed, 1983
The Watchtower, Barefoot Servants Don Reid, Alan Bartlett and Alan Roberts, 6/80
The Amoeba, Left Side Rick Sylvester and Larry Young, 8/71
The Amoeba, Right Side Michael Forkash and Andy Burnham, 10/85
Rycrisp Rick Sylvester and Jim Downs, 8/71
Beat the Clock Michael Forkash and Norman Boles, 1986
The Triscuit Alan Bartlett et al, 1982
Drop-out Rick Sylvester and Larry Young, 8/71
The Chosen Few Jim Bridwell and Mark Klemens, 1971
The Cracker, Southwest Corner Bill Sorenson and Ann Rehder, 6/69
Cracker, Right Side Mike Loughman and others of the U.C. Hiking Club, 1959
Northeast Slopes Charles Michael, in the 1920's
East Face Russ McLean and Ken Boche, 5/70
Disco Strangler Earl Redfern, Tom Bepler and Eric Brand, 3/85
West Face Warren Harding primarily, with Glen Denny and Al Macdonald, 1961
Wet Denim Daydream Darrell Hatton and Angus Thuermer, 1977
Roulette Earl Redfern and Tom Bepler, 3/84
Leaning Tower Traverse Chuck Wilts, Ellen Wilts and G.B. Harr, 9/57
Leaning Chimney Dave Brower, Ken Adam, Morgan Harris, Richard Leonard and Carl Rosberg, 10/40
Fifi Buttress Dick McCracken and Steve Roper, 5/60
Sunset Strip Chick Holtkamp and Eric Zschiesche, 4/82
The Vortex Chick Holtkamp and Randy Russell, 10/80 **FFA** Chick Holtkamp and Eric Zschiesche, 5/82
Colony of Slippermen Chris Cantwell and Mark Grant, 1981
The Warbler Werner Braun and Ed Barry **FFA** Chris Bellizzi et al, 5/82
Stanford Point, North Face Dave Brower, L. Bruce Meyer, Morgan Harris and Alan Hedden, 9/42

Local Motion Doug McDonald and Werner Braun, 5/86
Tower of the Cosmic Winds, Windfall Mark Chapman and Kevin Worrall, 5/76
Tower of the Cosmic Winds, Breezin' Mark Chapman and Kevin Worrall, 5/76
Tower of the Cosmic Winds, Windjammer Mark Chapman and Kevin Worrall, 1975
Castaways Mark Chapman and Kevin Worrall, 1976
Inspiration Buttress Joe Faint and Mike Borghoff, 6/65
Green Carpet Treatment Rick Sylvester and Jerry Coe, 10/70
Deadline Dihedral Rick Sylvester and Jerry Coe, 10/70
You Asked For It Rick Sylvester and Jerry Coe, 10/70
Autumn Crescent Rick Sylvester and Jerry Coe, 10/70
Jungle Train Rick Sylvester and Matt Donohoe, 8/70
A Dog's Roof Ray Jardine, 5/77
Eat at Degnan's Royal Robbins, 1965
Landshark Jonny Woodward and Chris Peisker, 5/85
Dancin' Days Bob Williams et al, 1980

LOWER MERCED CANYON – SOUTH

Overdrive Dale Bard, Ron Kauk, Nic Taylor and George Meyers, 1976
Shadyside Bench Alan Gillespie and Bill Nelson, 11/68
High Pressure Jim Bridwell and John Bragg, 1972
Open Trench Ed Barry et al, 1972
Lost on Venus Ed Barry and Mark Chapman, 1972
Pulpit Rock, from the Notch unknown, 1950's? **FFA** Royal Robbins, 1966
Pulpit Rock, East Face Dave Rearick and Tom Frost, 1960 **FFA var.** Don Reid and Ken Yager, 11/86
Pulpit Rock, Tree Route Raffi Bedayn, Carl Jensen and Randolph May, 5/39 **FFA** Tom Frost, 1960
Pulpit Rock, Improbable Traverse Wally Reed and Mark Powell, 7/57 **variation** Frank Sacherer and Jim Yensen, 1962 **Original Sin variation** Rick Cashner and Don Reid, 1980
Pulpit Rock, Pulpit Pooper Jim Orey and Jack Roberts, 6/72
Pulpit Rock, The Serman Ron Kauk and Jim Orey, 1974
The Mosstrum Bob Bauman, Chuck Pratt and Bruce Kumph, 9/68
Cream Mark Klemens et al, 8/71
Jam Session Mark Klemens and Jim Bridwell, 1971
Cartwheel Mark Klemens and Jim Bridwell, 1971
Monkey Do Don Reid and Rick Cashner, 10/77
Energy Crisis Bill Price et al, 1980
Shiver-Me-Timbers Mike Borris, 1979
Super Nova Ray Jardine and John Lakey, 9/76
Dime Bag Dale Bard and Werner Braun, 1975
Crack the Whip Don Reid and Grant Hiskes, 9/84
The Rostrum, Regular North Face Route Glen Denny and Warren Harding, 7/62 **FFA (to last pitch)** Ron Kauk and John Yablonski, 1977 **FFA (entire route)** Kim Carrigan et al, 1985
The Rostrum, Mad Pilot Rob Rohn and Peter Croft, 5/81
Alien Tony Yaniro, 1980
The Rostrum, Blind Faith Dale Bard and Ron Kauk, 10/75
Kauk-ulator Ron Kauk et al, 1975
The Rostrum, West Base Route (from the bench) Gerry Czamanske and Larry Wood, 9/59 **FFA** Don Reid and Rick Cashner, 6/82 (route to the bench) Chuck Pratt and John Fiske, 9/60
The Rostrum, from the notch Dave Brower, Ken Adam, Richard Leonard and Rolf Pundt, 10/41

Static Cling Don Reid and Rick Cashner, 1984
Le Bachar John Bachar, Mike Lechlinski and Mari Gingery, 1982
Easy Street Jim Bridwell and Jim Pettigrew, 1972
Alamo Al Swanson, Ken Yager, Dave Schultz and Grant Hiskes, 10/86
Jungle Book Ron Kauk and Jim Pettigrew, 1974
Loyd's Lolly Pop Dave Schultz, Ken Yager and Grant Hiskes, 10/86
Minor Kinda Unit Dave Schultz, Ken Yager and Grant Hiskes, 10/86
Flight Attendant Ken Yager, Dave Schultz and Grant Hiskes, 10/86
Dancing in the Dark Scott Cosgrove and Al Swanson, 11/86
The Viper Werner Braun and John Middendorf, 10/85
Razor's Edge Mark Hudon and Max Jones, 1979
Eagle Ron Kauk and George Meyers, 1973

ELEPHANT ROCK

Crack of Redemption Chuck Pratt and Chris Fredericks, 7/65
Reality Check Ray Jardine and Linda McGinnis, 10/76
Plumb Line Dale Bard, Jim Bridwell and Kevin Worrall, 5/74
Trundling Juan Ray Jardine and John Lakey, 10/76
Straight Error Mark Chapman and Jim Bridwell, 1973
Real Error Galen Rowell, Joe McKeown and Scott Walker, 6/62
Foaming at the Crotch Lance Rowlands and Tucker Tech, 10/85
Sky Dale Bard and Ron Kauk, 1976
Elephantiaisis John Yablonski and Richard Harrison, 1977
Lost Error Don Reid, Rick Cashner and Ken Yager, 7/77
Crashline John Yablonski, Rick Cashner and Don Reid, 8/77
Worst Error, Left Side Warren Harding and Wayne Merry, 9/57
Worst Error, Hotline Jim Bridwell and Mark Chapman, 1973. **FFA** Ron Kauk and John Bachar, 1975
Worst Error, Fatal Mistake Charlie Porter and Walter Rosenthal, 1972 **FFA (above 1st pitch)** Dale Bard and Werner Braun, 1975
Pink Dream Barry Bates and Steve Wunsch, 1971
Nightmare Continuation John Bachar and Rick Cashner, 1984
Worst Error, Right Side Frank Sacherer and Galen Rowell, 11/62
A Shot in the Dark Rob Ramey and Nick Badyrka, 9/78
Crack of Doom Chuck Pratt and Mort Hempel, 10/61
Crack of Despair Frank Sacherer and Galen Rowell, 10/62 **FFA** Frank Sacherer, Chuck Pratt and Tom Gerughty, 1964
Crack of Deliverance Galen Rowell and Al Macdonald, 9/64
Hairline Jim Bridwell, Kevin Worrall, Dale Bard and George Meyers, 1974
Moongerms John Bachar and Werner Braun, 5/82
Crack of Destiny Galen Rowell and Joe Faint, 3/70
Elephant's Eliminate Ray Jardine and John Lakey, 5/78
October Country Darwin Alonso and Jack Roberts, 9/71

ROUTE INDEX

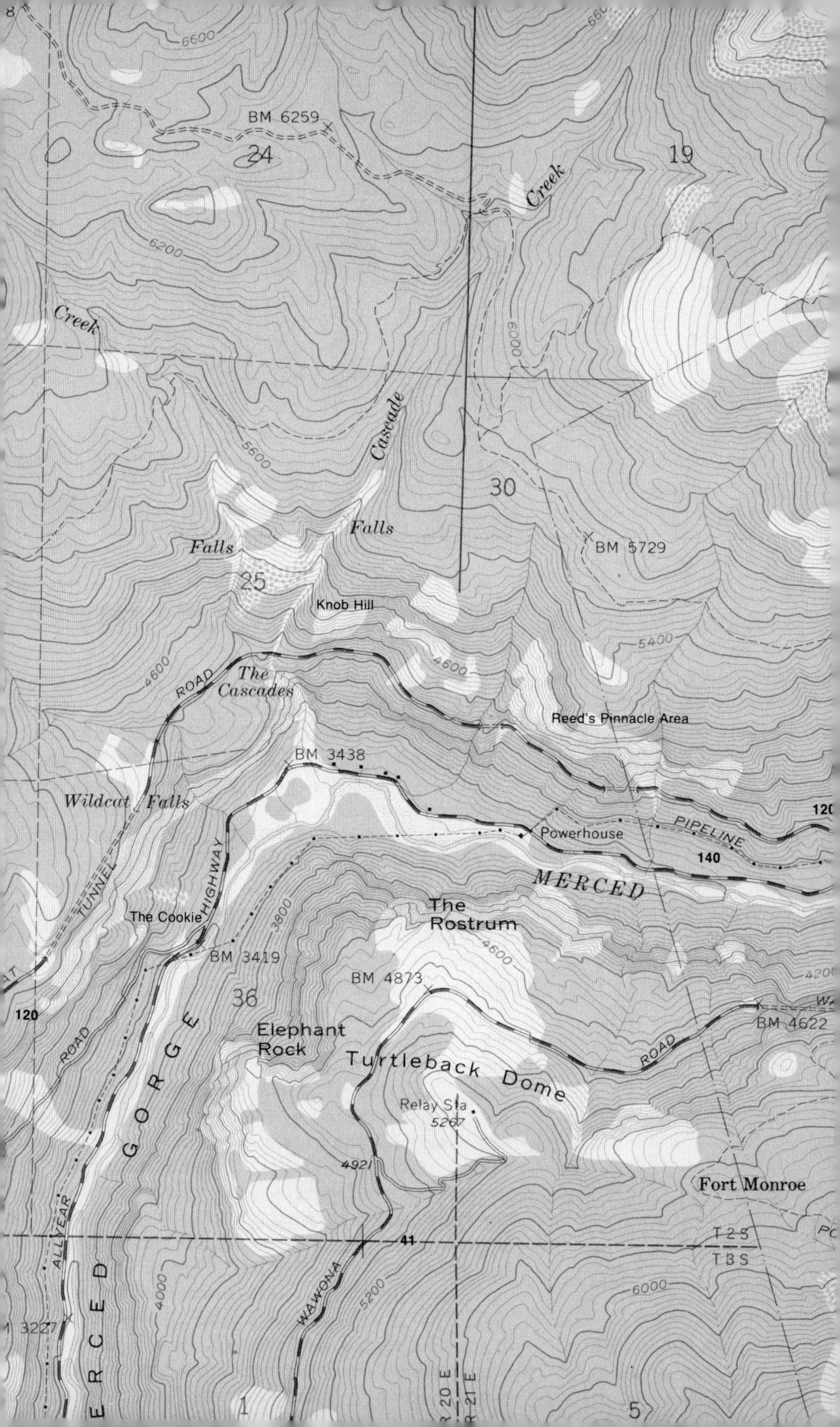

6600
BM 6259
24
19
Creek
6200
Creek
6000
Cascade
5600
30
Falls
Falls
BM 5729
25
Knob Hill
5400
4600
ROAD
The Cascades
4600
Reed's Pinnacle Area
BM 3438
Wildcat Falls
120
Powerhouse
PIPELINE
140
MERCED
TUNNEL
HIGHWAY
The Cookie
3800
The Rostrum
BM 3419
4600
BM 4873
4200
36
120
Elephant Rock
BM 4622
ROAD
ROAD
Turtleback Dome
GORGE
Relay Sta
5267
4921
Fort Monroe
ALL-YEAR
41
T 2 S
T 3 S
6000
ERCED
4000
5200
WAWONA
3227
R 20 E
R 21 E
1
5

7600
EL CAPITAN TRAIL
Ribbon Meadow
7600
Creek
7200
7400
Ribbon Fa
6600
Bluffs
5200
6000
5323
ROCK SLIDE
Nuts Only
Audubon
Old Big Oak Flat Road
4800
Little Wing
BM 4953
Rainbow View
4200
ONE WAY
Last Resort Cliff
Black Spring
BM Mojo Tooth 3817
140
BM 3908
Sewa Dispos
Diversion Dam
RIVER
Valley View
Bridalveil Meadow
13
TUNNEL
BM 4410
Pohono Bridge
Gaging Sta
Brida
4
Discovery View
Fern Spr
Moss Spr
41
Cr
Artist Pt
BM 4127
4200
5000
Washburn Slide
4600
Artist
5600
Widow's Tears
Stanford Pt
Old Inspiration Point
TRAIL
Crocker Pt
VABM 7385
Dewey
Silver Strand Falls

Ribbon
Meadow
Creek
7925
7600
7600
Ribbon
TRAIL
El Capitan Gully
7200
7400
Ribbon Fall
7400
K P Pinnacle
7569
5200
El Capitan
7042
ROCK SLIDES
4144
6000
4200
Nuts Only
12
BM 3955
BM
3976
El Ca
Br
Little Wing
El Capitan
Meadow
BM 3954
4200
Sewage
Disposal
Bridalveil
Moraine
ONE WAY
Black Spring
ONE WAY
BM
3908
Cathedral Rocks
Lower
Gunsight
y View
Bridalveil
Meadow
140
13
Gaging
Sta
Bridalveil
Fall
5000
Middle
6545
Moss Spr
5907
BM
4127
4200
Higher
Cathe
Leaning
Tower
6118
41
5600
Bridalveil
Fifi Buttress
6400
tanford
Pt
Crocker Pt
VABM
7385
Dewey Pt
6000
Creek

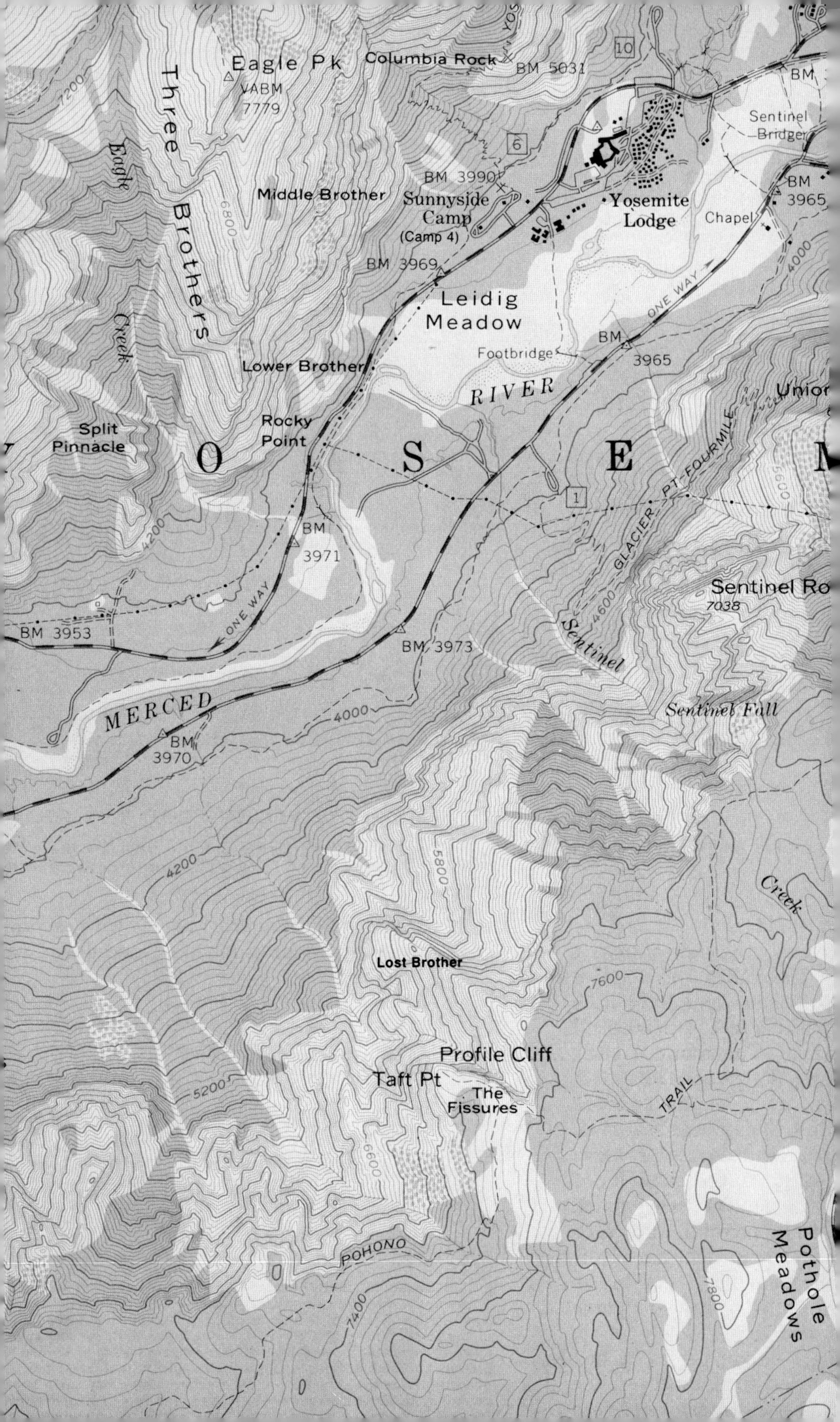
Eagle Pk
VABM
7779
Columbia Rock
BM 5031
Three Brothers
Eagle Creek
Middle Brother
BM 3990
Sunnyside
Camp
(Camp 4)
Yosemite
Lodge
Sentinel
Bridge
BM 3965
Chapel
BM 3969
Leidig
Meadow
ONE WAY
Footbridge
BM
3965
Lower Brother
RIVER
Split
Pinnacle
Rocky
Point
O
S
E
GLACIER PT-FOURMILE
BM
3971
Sentinel Ro
7038
BM 3953
ONE WAY
BM 3973
Sentinel
Sentinel Fall
MERCED
BM
3970
Creek
Lost Brother
Profile Cliff
Taft Pt
The
Fissures
TRAIL
POHONO
Pothole
Meadows

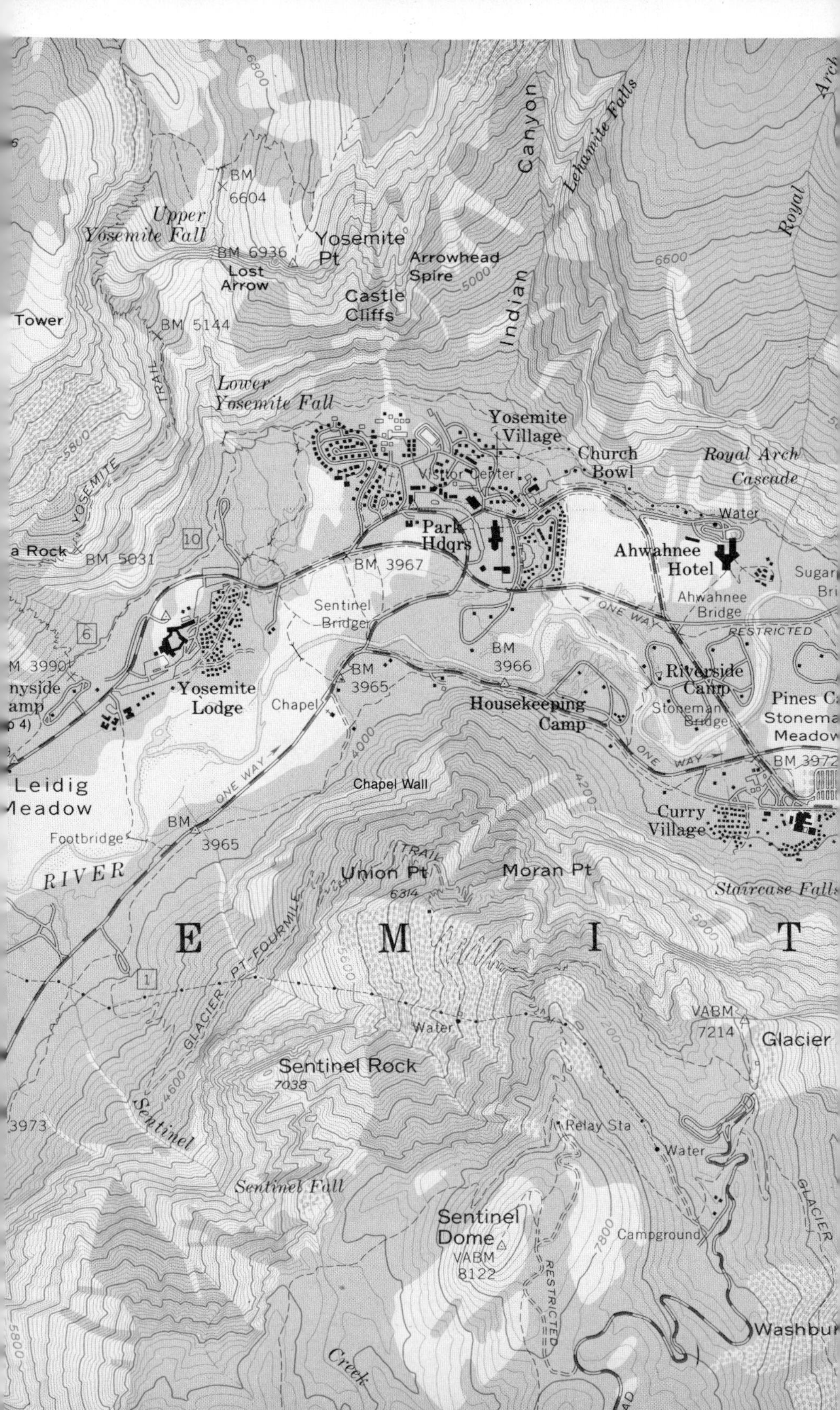

Upper Yosemite Fall
BM 6604
BM 6936
Lost Arrow
Yosemite Pt
Arrowhead Spire
Castle Cliffs
Canyon
Indian
Lehamite Falls
Royal Arch
Tower
BM 5144
TRAIL
Lower Yosemite Fall
YOSEMITE
Yosemite Village
Church Bowl
Royal Arch Cascade
Visitor Center
Water
Park Hdqrs
Ahwahnee Hotel
Sugar
Ahwahnee Bridge
a Rock
BM 5031
BM 3967
Sentinel Bridge
ONE WAY
RESTRICTED
BM 3990
BM 3966
Riverside Camp
Yosemite Lodge
BM 3965
Chapel
Housekeeping Camp
Stoneman Bridge
Pines
Stoneman Meadow
BM 3972
Chapel Wall
Leidig Meadow
Curry Village
BM 3965
Footbridge
RIVER
Union Pt
6314
Moran Pt
Staircase Falls
E M I T
GLACIER PT-FOURMILE
Water
VABM 7214
Glacier
Sentinel Rock
7038
3973
Sentinel
Relay Sta
Water
Sentinel Fall
Sentinel Dome
VABM 8122
Campground
RESTRICTED
GLACIER
Washbur
Creek

Falls
Basket Dome
7612
6200
4600
Tenaya
4400
Tenaya
TENAYA
North Dome
6400
Apathy Buttress
5000
4200
Ahwiyah Point
5200
Mirror Lake
BM 4094
Washington Column
6800
Footbridge
8842
Half Dome
Indian Cave
RESTRICTED
5400
BM 4002
Iron Spring
Diving Board
Tenaya Bridge
Stables
RESTRICTED
4400
Clarks Bridge
Silver Platter
Medial Moraine
Pines Camp
ONE WAY
4400
5800
6400
Lost La
RESTRICTED
E
Mt Broderick
6706
Happy Isles Bridge
Gaging Sta
BM 4035
Trail Center
6200
Happy Isles
Grizzly Peak
5400
Emerald Pool
7076
Liberty Cap
Vernal Fall
Sierra Pt
MERCED LAKE
MIST TR
Silver Apron
5305
TRAIL
Water
Clark Pt
5481
5910
Nevada Fall
MERC
JOHN MUIR TR
5800
4400
Illiouette Gorge
6200
Panorama Cliff
GLACIER PT PANORAMA TRAIL